Mind Design III

Mind Design III

Philosophy, Psychology, and Artificial Intelligence

Edited by John Haugeland, Carl F. Craver, and Colin Klein

The MIT Press
Cambridge, Massachusetts
London, England

The MIT Press would like to thank the anonymous peer reviewers who provided comments on drafts of this book. The generous work of academic experts is essential for establishing the authority and quality of our publications. We acknowledge with gratitude the contributions of these otherwise uncredited readers.

This book was set in LaTeXby the editors. Printed and bound in the United States of America.

Library of Congress Cataloging-in-Publication Data

Names: Haugeland, John, 1945-2010, editor. | Craver, Carl F., editor. | Klein, Colin, 1979- editor.
Title: Mind design III : philosophy, psychology, and artificial intelligence / edited by John Haugeland, Carl F. Craver, and Colin Klein.
Other titles: Mind design 3
Description: Cambridge, Massachusetts : The MIT Press, [2023] | Includes bibliographical references.
Identifiers: LCCN 2023007001 (print) | LCCN 2023007002 (ebook) | ISBN 9780262546577 (paperback) | ISBN 9780262376570 (epub) | ISBN 9780262376563 (pdf)
Subjects: LCSH: Artificial intelligence. | Cognitive psychology.
Classification: LCC Q335.5 .M492 2023 (print) | LCC Q335.5 (ebook) | DDC 006.3–dc23/eng20230715
LC record available at https://lccn.loc.gov/2023007001
LC ebook record available at https://lccn.loc.gov/2023007002

10 9 8 7 6 5 4 3 2 1

Contents

Introduction to Mind Design III

1

Carl F. Craver and Colin Klein
2023

Mind Design II was published in 1997. In the quarter century since, computer scientists have hit many of the old target objectives for successful artificial intelligence (AI). Computers have beaten chess grandmasters and 9-*dan* Go professionals. Face and voice recognition skills once beyond the capacity of supercomputers can now be found on commodity smartphones. The first driverless cars have appeared on the streets of major cities. An autonomous robot is currently vacuuming the kitchen.

Do these achievements indicate that artificial intelligence is or will soon achieve its aim? Have we made machines that think? Some of these successes, and many more besides, are due to massive theoretical advances in computer science. They rely on techniques and algorithms that were barely in their infancy twenty-five years ago. Yet a more skeptical person might retort that these tools have simply made it easier to pull off mindless tricks. The same period of success, after all, has also witnessed geometric growth in processor speeds, huge strides in miniaturization, standardization of platforms for machine learning, and the ability to handle previously unimaginably large training data sets. Perhaps the best explanation for the success of AI has more to do with these instrumental developments than with theoretical insight into how minds can be implemented in machines. Engineering has made incredible strides. But have we made progress in understanding and building minds? What really has changed?

The present volume is an invitation to reflect upon this question. As in previous editions of John Haugeland's *Mind Design*, we have collected here a mix of classic and contemporary articles that address the nature of computation, the nature of thought, and the question of whether (and, if so, how) computers can be made to think. As with the second edition of *Mind Design*, ours carries over some pieces and introduces new ones. We wanted to make a book with a readable font that could still be carried in a backpack. We also aimed for a more inclusive reading list. This led to some difficult decisions about what had to be cut or abridged.

For example, we have removed Timothy van Gelder's insightful defense of a dynamical approach to cognition and Paul Churchland's argument that connectionist architectures ought to supplant propositional theories of mind and epistemology. We have also removed the vigorous debates about whether connectionist architectures can do the kind of symbolic processing that propositional thought required. We have cut Hubert Dreyfus's classic discussion of what computers can't do, which itself was based on extrapolations from then-current pain points in AI research.

We have not cut this material because we take the issues to be settled. Rather, we did so because the hard contrasts between dynamic and representational, or between connectionist and symbolic architectures, have blurred with time. The key debates no longer seem to us to travel along those lines. Further, good philosophy should always keep an eye on the actual as it thinks about what is possible. Many of the old arguments seemed to us to turn on particular architectures and programming styles that have since been supplanted by more powerful techniques. It remains of historical interest that PDP networks struggled with certain kinds of syntactic transformations, but a quick peek on Google Translate will show that these particular issues have been solved. As Melanie Mitchell notes in her contribution to this volume, new problems have cropped up in the meantime; they deserve our attention.

In return for these cuts, we hope that the additions will represent a broader range of contemporary, philosophically relevant thinking about AI. Some of the additions—like the excerpt from David Marr's *Vision*—are from older works, but they have become entrenched classics, cited across a range of disciplines. Similarly so with Margaret Boden's response to John Searle, which is often mentioned but has become difficult to find. Others are newer commentaries on older issues: Stuart Russell on the nature of rationality, for example, or Barbara Webb's update on neurally inspired robotics.

The bulk of the additions, however, come from adding material that reflects the explosive growth and diversification of AI approaches. We have added new chapters that discuss advances in deep neural networks, reinforcement learning, and causal learning. Indeed, if one of the overarching themes of *Mind Design II* was the fight between old-fashioned symbolic AI and simple neural networks, then the main lesson of *Mind Design III* might be how much the field has settled into a kind of pragmatic pluralism—a willingness to mix and match techniques according to domains and aims. Whether this pluralism will continue to make progress remains to be seen.

Alongside the advancement of AI, the explosive growth of the cognitive neurosciences in the 1990s and 2000s also changed the way that we think about cognitive machinery. *Mind Design II* was assembled in the heyday of nonreductive physicalism. It was a time when most philosophers of mind agreed that learning about the brain would give little insight into the mind; indeed, part of the attraction of computationalism was that it allowed you to abstract away from implementational details. Nonreductive physicalism, at least of that particularly austere sort, is no longer the dominant position. We are firmly on the side of an integrative approach. Outside of philosophy, the hard boundaries between cognition and implementation have fallen: computational neuroscience now coexists alongside neurally inspired AI. As such, we've also added several chapters that reflect how neuroscience and AI have come to complement one another.

Rather than the broadly chronological ordering of previous editions, this third edition is divided into six thematic parts. Each part begins with a stand-alone introduction designed to place these essays in philosophical and scientific context. We wrote these both for instructors, who might use the discussions to flesh out syllabi around the various areas of interest, and for general readers, who might want to dive deeper into one or more of these topics. The selections in the main text were chosen to give a mix of historical and contemporary relevance, with a focus on building syllabi. On its own, this reader should provide the basis for a solid mid- or upper-level undergraduate course on the challenges and limits of computational approaches to the mind. The introduction to each part has an annotated bibliography, which we hope readers can use as a starting point when going further than the included essays. Those bibliographies still include only a fragment of what is available—we intend them as starting points, not as comprehensive lists.

The choice of six topical areas also required leaving out whole domains of interesting work, including some that we had initially hoped to cover. We have not discussed the likelihood of superhuman intelligence or the arrival of the "singularity." Nor do we discuss AI ethics. That field is growing so rapidly that it merits a collection of its own, and changing so rapidly that any collection would be outdated before it arrived at the printer. We have kept the focus on intelligence, so we do not consider whether machines can also be conscious. The hard problem of consciousness seems to us a very difficult one—one made neither more nor less tractable by the construction of good computational models of mind. It is also a problem about which there are other very good volumes. Finally, AI is a field that moves quickly. Transformer architectures (such as those that power ChatGPT) became widespread while the volume was in preparation. Rather than delay it further by chasing new developments, we can only hope that the chapters included have hit the right balance between contemporary relevance and philosophical timelessness.

Assembling a reader has been an unexpectedly complicated task. We appreciate the help that we received along the way. From the start, we thank Joan Wellman for permitting us the honor of continuing John Haugeland's edited collection into a new century. Phil Laughlin at the MIT Press was enthusiastic about our pitch and helped to shepherd the volume through the COVID-19 pandemic. Peter Clutton did the detective work on copyright permissions. Ge Feng helped with converting the chapters from previous editions. Pamela Speh assisted with duplicating figures. Andre Santana assisted with the formatting of texts and figures, as well as with preparing the bibliography. Jeremy Strasser assisted with proofreading and typesetting. Nicholas Carroll assisted with final copyedits. Many thanks to the students in an intermural course (WUSTL and UMSL), co-taught with Gualtiero Piccinini, on "Computation and Cognition"; they helped to determine what was working and what was not.

Finally, we owe a tremendous debt to the late John Haugeland. Earlier editions of *Mind Design* didn't just collect existing work—they defined a whole subfield, and established philosophy of AI as a respectable topic in its own right. Both of us had our intellectual trajectories shaped by earlier editions of this volume. Updating it has been a labor of love, and we hope above all that this new edition will introduce Haugeland's achievement, as well as his inimitable philosophical style and voice, to a new generation.

COMPUTERS, COMPUTING, AND COMPUTATION

Part I: Computers, Computing, and Computation

The core conviction motivating artificial intelligence (AI) is that computers have all the raw ingredients they need to make minds. This is one reason why one might hope to study what minds are—and how biological systems make minds possible—by attempting to build intelligent systems out of computing systems. This motivating conviction depends, in the first instance, on an understanding of what computers are.

Haugeland's original introduction to *Mind Design II*, given in chapter 2, lays out a theory of what computers are (automatic formal systems) and articulates the central challenges for AI. His essay provides an excellent introduction to the topics of this volume and to the key concepts one should master: What is a computer? What is a formal system? What is the difference between digital and analog? What is intentionality? This essay also contains, in primitive form, Haugeland's pithy challenge: "The problem with computers is that they don't give a damn." What, we can ask, would it take to build a system that actually gives a damn?

In chapter 3, Newell and Simon, pioneers of computer science and AI, advance a key empirical hypothesis at the heart of AI and, as a consequence, of computational theories of mind more generally: the Physical Symbol System Hypothesis. According to them, physical symbol systems are necessary to produce intelligent action. Given resources and appropriate programming, they are also sufficient to produce intelligent action. These two claims are foundational for much of cognitive science. They raise the questions: What kinds of physical system do interesting things without manipulating symbols? What might cognition be if it is not, at base, symbol manipulation?

David Marr is well known for his classic articulation of the links between computational explanation, cognitive science, and neuroscience. The essay in chapter 4, extracted from his book, *Vision* (1982), introduces his now-classic tripartite division of levels of analysis: the computational level (describing what the system does and why), the algorithmic level (describing the representational system and rules for processing) and the implementational level (describing the hardware that instantiates the algorithm). He explains how this division of labor applies to his own work on a core task of vision: that of extracting shapes of objects from patterns of shading on the retina. Marr famously argues that computational-level understanding of a system is autonomous from the algorithm in which that computation is instantiated and the (biological or artificial) mechanism by which it is implemented. Marr's essay is important not only because it has become stock in trade among computational cognitive scientists, but because it has been used to frame debates about the relative import of these different levels of explanation for cognitive science.

In the final essay of this part, Corey Maley takes up the important and often-neglected topic of analog computation. As he notes, discussions of computation often focus narrowly on digital computers, neglecting a large portion of the space of computational possibilities.

The contrast between digital and analog, as well as the distinctive features of analog computation, make them especially important for understanding connectionist, dynamic, and embodied theses that are explored in later parts of the book.

Combinations and Additions
The articles in this part can usefully be combined with those in part II, especially Turing's "Computing Machinery and Intelligence" (chapter 6), which articulates his own account of computing while providing a very clear introduction to the Turing Machine, his exemplar of a computer. Readers might also benefit from exploring, in combination with part V, how this core idea of computation can or cannot be stretched to apply to biological/neural computing systems (Churchland and Sejnowski, in chapter 20) and to the kinds of computers that are, at least on their surface, very unlike Turing Machines (e.g., Rummelhart, in chapter 19, and Clark, in chapter 17). Readers might also consider how the notion of computation can or cannot be combined with embodied and embedded approaches to cognition (e.g., Haugeland, in chapter 22, and Brooks, in chapter 23) in part VI.

We chose the essays in this part largely for their foundational import. Yet the topic of computation and its contrasts has developed extensively and seen considerable nuanced refinement over the past two decades. A fundamental assumption of at least many contributors to this discussion is that there is an objective distinction between systems that *really* compute and systems that do not, and hence that computers form a natural kind. The effort to provide a satisfactory definition of computers and computation faces the twin obstacles of triviality (i.e., that everything counts as a computer) and rigidity (i.e., the exclusion by definition of systems like brains that are widely accepted as computing).

The Triviality Challenge.   The triviality challenge (sometimes referred to as the "spectre of pancomputationalism") initially arose as a problem for simple mapping theories of computation. This was raised by Putnam (1991) and Searle (1992) as part of more general criticisms of the computational theory of mind. The starkest forms of the triviality challenge claims that any physical system implements every computable function, so long as you look at it in the right way. The more things that count as computing, the less interesting it is to call anything in particular a "computer." If a pail of water or a solid wall computes, then the fact that the brain *also* computes doesn't tell us much.

- Searle (1992) takes a simple mapping account as his target and uses this to argue that the mind cannot be the software running on the hardware of the brain.
- Putnam (1991) provides arguably the first rigorous argument from the simple mapping view to a trivializing form of pancomputationalism.
- Sprevak (2018) reviews different forms of the triviality argument, evaluating their strengths and weaknesses.

• Maudlin (1989) uses a limited form of a triviality claim to argue that computation cannot explain consciousness.

What Is Computation?   Piccinini and Maley (2021) provide a succinct overview of different views of computation, the desiderata for selecting among them, and their relative strengths and weaknesses. They group these into several different camps:

• According to *simple mapping accounts*, a physical system computes if there is a mapping between the actual state transitions in the physical system and the abstract states individuative of the computation in question. Godfrey-Smith (2009) is a clear recent discussion of a simple mapping account as part of an argument that it confronts the triviality problem.

• *Counterfactual/causal accounts* supplement simple mapping accounts by requiring that the physical state transitions in the computational system support counterfactuals of roughly the following form: if the prior physical state had been different, then the subsequent state would be different. Arguably, this constraint removes much of the space of possible counterexamples to the simple mapping view (e.g., the states of the pail of water do not support the relevant counterfactuals). According to causal/dispositional theories, the matching of physical states to computational states must follow change-relating counterfactual rules: antecedent states must cause subsequent states (e.g., Chalmers, 1994; Scheutz, 2001), subsequent states must depend counterfactually on antecedent states (Block, 1978; Copeland, 1996; Rescorla, 2014), or the subsequent states must be produced through the manifestation of a disposition triggered by the appearance of the antecedent states (Klein, 2008).

• *Semantic accounts.* Newell and Simon hold that the physical states among which the putative computer transitions must also have representational content. This view is embraced by, for example, Churchland and Sejnowski (chapter 20) and Shagrir (2006). It is also possible to restrict a semantic thesis further by limiting it to mathematical contents, for instance, as per Egan's contribution to this volume (chapter 14).

• *Mechanistic accounts.* One might also define computation in terms of the distinctive functional components of computing machines. On this view, computation is the processing of vehicles (regardless of their semantic interpretation) according to rules that are sensitive to properties of vehicles and the differences among them. Computation is functional in the sense that the system is teleologically understood as having the job or goal of computing, thus making "miscomputation" a live possibility. A computer is a system that has the function of computing in this sense. Recent books by Milkowski (2013) and Piccinini (2015) both develop the mechanistic theory in detail.

Marr's Levels of Analysis.   Those looking for a reflective treatment of Marr's levels and their continued significance for computer science and computational biology, cognitive science, and neuroscience might consider Bechtel and Shagrir (2015), who provide their own interpretation of Marr's levels of analysis and argue that each provides a nonredundant perspective required to explain information processing mechanisms. Churchland and Sejnowski (chapter 20) offer their own take on the nature and significance of Marr's levels for our understanding of the relationship between minds and computers and between computers and other physical systems.

Analog Computation.   Many foundational disputes about the nature of computation turn on a difference between digital and analog computers. Those interested in reading more about this distinction might consult the following:

- Haugeland (1981) raises the conceptual question of the distinction between digital and analog computers with an eye to assessing whether all analog computers can be simulated by an appropriately programmed digital computer. Haugeland locates the distinction not in the form of the representation itself, but rather (perhaps paradoxically) in what it represents.
- Kulvicki (2015) distinguishes an engineering sense of the analog/digital distinction that, he thinks, more perspicuously captures the distinctive feature of analog computations: their utility in open-ended search across levels of abstraction. Their ability to perform this function relies on their satisfying what Kulvicki calls the "parts principle."
- MacLennan (2003) compares the computational power of analog computers with Turing machines, arguing that there are limits on the latter that the former do not face.

What Is Mind Design?

2

John Haugeland
1996

MIND DESIGN is the endeavor to understand *mind* (thinking, intellect) in terms of its *design* (how it is built, how it works). It amounts, therefore, to a kind of cognitive psychology. But it is oriented more toward structure and mechanism than toward correlation or law, more toward the "how" than the "what", than is traditional empirical psychology. An "experiment" in mind design is more often an effort to *build* something and make it work, than to observe or analyze what already exists. Thus, the field of artificial intelligence (AI), the attempt to construct intelligent artifacts, systems with minds of their own, lies at the heart of mind design. Of course, natural intelligence, especially human intelligence, remains the final object of investigation, the phenomenon eventually to be understood. What is distinctive is not the goal but rather the means to it. Mind design is *psychology by reverse engineering*.

Though the idea of intelligent artifacts is as old as Greek mythology, and a familiar staple of fantasy fiction, it has been taken seriously as science for scarcely two generations. And the reason is not far to seek: pending several conceptual and technical breakthroughs, no one had a clue how to proceed. Even as the pioneers were striking boldly into the unknown, much of what they were really up to remained unclear, both to themselves and to others; and some still does. Accordingly, mind design has always been an area of *philosophical* interest, an area in which the conceptual foundations—the very questions to ask, and what would count as an answer—have remained unusually fluid and controversial.

The essays collected here span the history of the field since its inception (though with emphasis on more recent developments). The authors are about evenly divided between philosophers and scientists. Yet, all of the essays are "philosophical", in that they address fundamental issues and basic concepts; at the same time, nearly all are also "scientific" in that they are technically sophisticated and concerned with the achievements and challenges of concrete empirical research. Several major trends and schools of thought are represented, often explicitly disputing with one another. In their juxtaposition, therefore, not only the lay of the land, its principal peaks and valleys, but also its current movement, its still active fault lines, can come into view.

By way of introduction, I shall try in what follows to articulate a handful of the fundamental ideas that have made all this possible.

2.1 Perspectives and things

None of the present authors believes that intelligence depends on anything immaterial or
supernatural, such as a vital spirit or an immortal soul. Thus, they are all *materialists* in at
least the minimal sense of supposing that matter, suitably selected and arranged, suffices
for intelligence. The question is: How?

It can seem incredible to suggest that mind is "nothing but" matter in motion. Are we
to imagine all those little atoms thinking deep thoughts as they careen past one another in
the thermal chaos? Or, if not one by one, then maybe collectively, by the zillions? The
answer to this puzzle is to realize that things can be viewed from different *perspectives*
(or described in different terms)—and, when we look differently, what we are able to see
is also different. For instance, what is a coarse weave of frayed strands when viewed
under a microscope is a shiny silk scarf seen in a store window. What is a marvellous old
clockwork in the eyes of an antique restorer is a few cents' worth of brass, seen as scrap
metal. Likewise, so the idea goes, what is mere atoms in the void from one point of view
can be an intelligent system from another.

Of course, you can't look at anything in just any way you please—at least, not and be
right about it. A scrap dealer couldn't see a wooden stool as a few cents' worth of brass,
since it isn't brass; the antiquarian couldn't see a brass monkey as a clockwork, since it
doesn't work like a clock. Awkwardly, however, these two points taken together seem to
create a dilemma. According to the first, what something is—coarse or fine, clockwork or
scrap metal—depends on how you look at it. But, according to the second, how you can
rightly look at something (or describe it) depends on what it is. Which comes first, one
wants to ask, seeing or being?

Clearly, there's something wrong with that question. What something is and how it can
rightly be regarded are not essentially distinct; neither comes before the other, because
they are the same. The advantage of emphasizing perspective, nevertheless, is that it highlights the following question: What *constrains* how something can rightly be regarded or
described (and thus determines what it is)? This is important, because the answer will be
different for different kinds of perspective or description—as our examples already illustrate. Sometimes, what something is is determined by its shape or form (at the relevant
level of detail); sometimes it is determined by what it's made of; and sometimes by how
it works or even just what it does. Which—if any—of these could determine whether
something is (rightly regarded or described as) *intelligent*?

2.1.1 The Turing test

In 1950, the pioneering computer scientist A. M. Turing suggested that intelligence is a matter of behavior or behavioral capacity: whether a system has a mind, or how intelligent it is, is determined by what it can and cannot do. Most materialist philosophers and cognitive scientists now accept this general idea (though John Searle is an exception). Turing also proposed a pragmatic criterion or test of what a system can do that would be sufficient to show that it is intelligent. (He did not claim that a system would not be intelligent if it could not pass his test; only that it would be if it could.) This test, now called the *Turing test*, is controversial in various ways, but remains widely respected in spirit.

Turing cast his test in terms of simulation or imitation: a nonhuman system will be deemed intelligent if it acts so like an ordinary person *in certain respects* that other ordinary people can't tell (from these actions alone) that it isn't one. But the imitation idea itself isn't the important part of Turing's proposal. What's important is rather the specific sort of behavior that Turing chose for his test: he specified *verbal* behavior. A system is surely intelligent, he said, if it can carry on an ordinary conversation like an ordinary person (via electronic means, to avoid any influence due to appearance, tone of voice, and so on).

This is a daring and radical simplification. There are many ways in which intelligence is manifested. Why single out *talking* for special emphasis? Remember: Turing didn't suggest that talking in this way is required to demonstrate intelligence, only that it's sufficient. So there's no worry about the test being too hard; the only question is whether it might be too lenient. We know, for instance, that there are systems that can regulate temperatures, generate intricate rhythms, or even fly airplanes without being, in any serious sense, intelligent. Why couldn't the ability to carry on ordinary conversations be like that?

Turing's answer is elegant and deep: talking is unique among intelligent abilities because it gathers within itself, at one remove, all others. One cannot generate rhythms or fly airplanes "about" talking, but one certainly can *talk about* rhythms and flying—not to mention poetry, sports, science, cooking, love, politics, and so on—*and*, if one doesn't know what one is talking about, it will soon become painfully obvious. Talking is not merely one intelligent ability among others, but also, and essentially, the ability to *express* intelligently a great many (maybe all) other intelligent abilities. And, without *having* those abilities in fact, at least to some degree, one cannot talk intelligently about them. That's why Turing's test is so compelling and powerful.

On the other hand, even if not too easy, there is nevertheless a sense in which the test does obscure certain real difficulties. By concentrating on conversational ability, which can be exhibited entirely in writing (say, via computer terminals), the Turing test completely ignores any issues of real-world perception and action. Yet these turn out to be extraordinarily difficult to achieve artificially at any plausible level of sophistication. And, what may be worse, ignoring real-time environmental interaction distorts a system designer's assumptions about how intelligent systems are related to the world more generally. For instance, if a system has to deal or cope with things around it, but is not continually tracking them externally, then it will need somehow to "keep track of" or *represent* them internally. Thus, neglect of perception and action can lead to an overemphasis on representation and internal modeling.

2.1.2 Intentionality

"Intentionality", said Brentano (1874/1973), "is the mark of the mental." By this he meant that everything mental has intentionality, and nothing else does (except in a derivative or second-hand way), and, finally, that this fact is the *definition of the mental* 'Intentional' is used here in a medieval sense that harks back to the original Latin meaning of "stretching toward" something; it is not limited to things like plans and purposes, but applies to all kinds of mental acts. More specifically, intentionality is the character of one thing being "of" or "about" something else, for instance by representing it, describing it, referring to it, aiming at it, and so on. Thus, intending in the narrower modern sense (planning) is also intentional in Brentano's broader and older sense, but much else is as well, such as believing, wanting, remembering, imagining, fearing, and the like.

Intentionality is peculiar and perplexing. It looks on the face of it to be a relation between two things. My belief that Cairo is hot is intentional because it is *about* Cairo (and/or its being hot). That which an intentional act or state is about (Cairo or its being hot, say) is called its *intentional object*. (It is this intentional object that the intentional state "stretches toward".) Likewise, my desire for a certain shirt, my imagining a party on a certain date, my fear of dogs in general, would be "about"—that is, have as their intentional objects— that shirt, a party on that date, and dogs in general. Indeed, *having* an object in this way is another way of explaining intentionality; and such "having" seems to be a relation, namely between the state and its object.

But, if it's a relation, it's a relation like no other. Being-inside-of is a typical relation. Now notice this: if it is a fact about one thing that it is inside of another, then not only that first thing, but also the second has to *exist*; X cannot be inside of Y, or indeed be related to Y in any other way, if Y does not exist. This is true of relations quite generally; but it is *not* true of intentionality. I can perfectly well imagine a party on a certain date, and also have beliefs, desires, and fears about it, even though there is (was, will be) no such party. Of course, those beliefs would be false, and those hopes and fears unfulfilled; but they would be intentional—be about, or "have", those objects—all the same.

It is this puzzling ability to have something as an object, whether or not that something actually exists, that caught Brentano's attention. Brentano was no materialist: he thought that mental phenomena were one kind of entity, and material or physical phenomena were a completely different kind. And he could not see how *any* merely material or physical thing could be *in fact* related to another, if the latter didn't exist; yet *every* mental state (belief, desire, and so on) has this possibility. So intentionality is the definitive mark of the mental.

Daniel C. Dennett accepts Brentano's definition of the mental, but proposes a materialist way to view intentionality. Dennett, like Turing, thinks intelligence is a matter of how a system behaves; but, unlike Turing, he also has a worked-out account of what it is about (some) behavior that makes it intelligent—or, in Brentano's terms, makes it the behavior of a system with intentional (that is, *mental*) states. The idea has two parts: (i) behavior should be understood not in isolation but in *context* and as part of a consistent *pattern* of behavior (this is often called "holism"); and (ii) for some systems, a consistent pattern of behavior in context can be construed as *rational* (such construing is often called "interpretation").[1]

Rationality here means: acting so as best to satisfy your goals overall, given what you know and can tell about your situation. Subject to this constraint, we can surmise what a system wants and believes by watching what it does—but, of course, not in isolation. From all you can tell in isolation, a single bit of behavior might be manifesting any number of different beliefs and/or desires, or none at all. Only when you see a *consistent pattern of rational behavior*, manifesting the *same* cognitive states and capacities repeatedly, in various combinations, are you justified in saying that *those* are the states and capacities that this system has-or even that it has *any* cognitive states or capacities at all. "Rationality", Dennett says (1971, p. 19), "is the mother of intention."

This is a prime example of the above point about *perspective*. The constraint on whether something can rightly be regarded as having intentional states is, according to Dennett, not its shape or what it is made of, but rather what it does—more specifically, a consistently rational pattern in what it does. We infer that a rabbit can tell a fox from another rabbit, always wanting to get away from the one but not the other, from having observed it behave accordingly time and again, under various conditions. Thus, on a given occasion, we impute to the rabbit *intentional* states (beliefs and desires) *about* a particular fox, on the basis not only of its current behavior but also of the pattern in its behavior over time. The consistent pattern lends both specificity and credibility to the respective individual attributions.

Dennett calls this perspective the *intentional stance* and the entities so regarded *intentional systems*. If the stance is to have any conviction in any particular case, the pattern on which it depends had better be broad and reliable; but it needn't be perfect. Compare a crystal: the pattern in the atomic lattice had better be broad and reliable, if the sample is to be a crystal at all; but it needn't be perfect. Indeed, the very idea of a *flaw* in a crystal is made intelligible by the regularity of the pattern around it; only insofar as *most* of the lattice is regular, can particular parts be deemed flawed in determinate ways. Likewise for the intentional stance: only because the rabbit behaves rationally almost always, could we ever say on a particular occasion that it happened to be *wrong*—had *mistaken* another rabbit (or a bush, or a shadow) for a fox, say. False beliefs and unfulfilled hopes are intelligible as isolated lapses in an overall consistent pattern, like flaws in a crystal. This is how a specific intentional state can rightly be attributed, even though its supposed intentional object doesn't exist—and thus is Dennett's answer to Brentano's puzzle.

2.1.3   Original intentionality

Many material things that aren't intentional systems are nevertheless "about" other things—including, sometimes, things that don't exist. Written sentences and stories, for instance, are in some sense material; yet they are often about fictional characters and events. Even pictures and maps can represent nonexistent scenes and places. Of course, Brentano knew this, and so does Dennett. But they can say that this sort of intentionality is only *derivative*. Here's the idea: sentence inscriptions—ink marks on a page, say—are only "about" anything because we (or other intelligent users) *mean* them that way. Their intentionality is second-hand, borrowed or derived from the intentionality that those users already have.

So, a sentence like "Santa lives at the North Pole", or a picture of him or a map of his travels, can be "about" Santa (who, alas, doesn't exist), but *only because* we can *think* that he lives there, and *imagine* what he looks like and where he goes. It's really *our* intentionality that these artifacts have, second-hand, because we use them to *express* it. Our intentionality itself, on the other hand, cannot be likewise derivative: it must be *original* ('Original', here, just means *not* derivative, not borrowed from somewhere else. If there is any intentionality at all, at least some of it must be original; it can't all be derivative.)

The problem for mind design is that artificial intelligence systems, like sentences and pictures, are also artifacts. So it can seem that their intentionality too must always be derivative—borrowed from their designers or users, presumably—and never original. Yet, if the project of designing and building a system with a mind of its own is ever really to succeed, then it must be possible for an artificial system to have genuine *original* intentionality, just as we do. Is that possible?

Think again about people and sentences, with their original and derivative intentionality, respectively. What's the reason for that difference? Is it really that sentences are artifacts, whereas people are not, or might it be something else? Here's another candidate. Sentences don't *do* anything with what they mean: they never pursue goals, draw conclusions, make plans, answer questions, let alone *care* whether they are right or wrong about the world—they just sit there, utterly inert and heedless. A person, by contrast, relies on what he or she believes and wants in order to make sensible choices and act efficiently; and this entails, in turn, an ongoing concern about whether those beliefs are really true, those goals really beneficial, and so on. In other words, real beliefs and desires are integrally involved in a rational, active existence, intelligently engaged with its environment. Maybe this active, rational engagement is more pertinent to whether the intentionality is original or not than is any question of natural or artificial origin.

Clearly, this is what Dennett's approach implies. An intentional system, by his lights, is just one that exhibits an appropriate pattern of consistently rational *behavior*—that is, active engagement with the world. If an artificial system can be produced that behaves on its own in a rational manner, consistently enough and in a suitable variety of circumstances (remember, it doesn't have to be flawless), then it has *original* intentionality—it has a mind of its own, just as we do.

On the other hand, Dennett's account is completely silent about how, or even whether, such a system could actually be designed and built. Intentionality, according to Dennett, depends entirely and exclusively on a certain sort of pattern in a system's behavior; internal structure and mechanism (if any) are quite beside the point. For scientific mind design, however, the question of how it actually works (and so, how it could be built) is absolutely central—and that brings us to computers.

2.2 Computers

Computers are important to scientific mind design in two fundamentally different ways. The first is what inspired Turing long ago, and a number of other scientists much more recently. But the second is what really launched AI and gave it its first serious hope of success. In order to understand these respective roles, and how they differ, it will first be necessary to grasp the notion of 'computer' at an essential level.

2.2.1 Formal systems

A formal system is like a game in which tokens are manipulated according to definite rules, in order to see what configurations can be obtained. In fact, many familiar games—among them chess, checkers, tic-tac-toe, and go—simply *are* formal systems. But there are also many games that are not formal systems, and many formal systems that are not games. Among the former are games like marbles, tiddlywinks, billiards, and baseball; and among the latter are a number of systems studied by logicians, computer scientists, and linguists.

This is not the place to attempt a full definition of formal systems; but three essential features can capture the basic idea: (i) they are (as indicated above) token-manipulation systems; (ii) they are digital; and (iii) they are medium independent. It will be worth a moment to spell out what each of these means.

TOKEN-MANIPULATION SYSTEMS. To say that a formal system is a token-manipulation system is to say that you can define it *completely* by specifying three things:

(1) a set of types of formal tokens or pieces;
(2) one or more allowable starting positions—that is, initial formal arrangements of tokens of these types; and
(3) a set of formal rules specifying how such formal arrangements may or must be changed into others.

This definition is meant to imply that token-manipulation systems are entirely *self-contained*. In particular, the formality of the rules is twofold: (i) they specify *only* the allowable next formal arrangements of tokens, and (ii) they specify these in terms *only* of the current formal arrangement—nothing else is *formally* relevant at all.

So take chess, for example. There are twelve types of piece, six of each color. There is only one allowable starting position, namely one in which thirty-two pieces of those twelve types are placed in a certain way on an eight-by-eight array of squares. The rules specifying how the positions change are simply the rules specifying how the pieces move, disappear (get captured), or change type (get promoted). (In chess, new pieces are never added to the position; but that's a further kind of move in other formal games—such as go.) Finally, notice that chess is entirely self-contained: nothing is ever relevant to what moves would be legal other than the current chess position itself.[2]

And every student of formal logic is familiar with at least one logical system as a token-manipulation game. Here's one obvious way it can go (there are many others): the kinds of logical symbol are the types, and the marks that you actually make on paper are the tokens of those types; the allowable starting positions are sets of well-formed formulae (taken as premises); and the formal rules are the inference rules specifying steps—that is, further formulae that you write down and add to the current position—in formally valid inferences. The fact that this is called *formal* logic is, of course, no accident.

DIGITAL SYSTEMS. Digitalness is a characteristic of certain techniques (methods, devices) for *making* things, and then (later) *identifying* what was made. A familiar example of such a technique is writing something down and later reading it. The thing written or made is supposed to be of a specified type (from some set of possible types), and identifying it later is telling what type that was. So maybe you're supposed to write down specified letters of the alphabet; and then my job is to tell, on the basis of what you produce, which letters you were supposed to write. Then the question is: how well can I do that? How good are the later identifications at recovering the prior specifications?

Such a technique is *digital* if it is positive and reliable. It is *positive* if the reidentification can be *absolutely perfect*. A positive technique is *reliable* if it not only can be perfect, but almost always is. This bears some thought. We're accustomed to the idea that nothing— at least, nothing mundane and real-worldly—is ever quite *perfect*. Perfection is an ideal, never fully attainable in practice. Yet the definition of 'digital' requires that perfection be not only possible, but reliably achievable.

Everything turns on what counts as success. Compare two tasks, each involving a penny and an eight-inch checkerboard. The first asks you to place the penny *exactly* 0.43747 inches in from the nearest edge of the board, and 0.18761 inches from the left; the second asks you to put it *somewhere* in the fourth rank (row) and the second file (column from the left). Of course, achieving the first would also achieve the second. But the first task is strictly impossible—that is, it can never actually be achieved, but at best approximated.

The second task, on the other hand, can in fact be carried out *absolutely perfectly*—it's not even hard. And the reason is easy to see: any number of slightly different actual positions would equally well count as *complete* success—because the penny only has to be *somewhere* within the specified square.

Chess is digital: if one player produces a chess position (or move), then the other player can reliably identify it *perfectly*. Chess positions and moves are like the second task with the penny: slight differences in the physical locations of the figurines aren't differences at all from the chess point of view—that is, in the positions of the chess pieces. Checkers, go, and tic-tac-toe are like chess in this way, but baseball and billiards are not. In the latter, unlike the former, arbitrarily small differences in the exact position, velocity, smoothness, elasticity, or whatever, of some physical object can make a significant difference to the game. Digital systems, though concrete and material, are insulated from such physical vicissitudes.

MEDIUM INDEPENDENCE. A concrete system is medium independent if what it is does not depend on what physical "medium" it is made of or implemented in. Of course, it has to be implemented in *something*; and, moreover, that something has to support whatever structure or form is necessary for the kind of system in question. But, apart from this generic prerequisite, nothing specific about the medium matters (except, perhaps, for extraneous reasons of convenience). In this sense, only the *form* of a formal system is significant, not its matter.

Chess, for instance, is medium independent. Chess pieces can be made of wood, plastic, ivory, onyx, or whatever you want, just as long as they are sufficiently stable (they don't melt or crawl around) and are movable by the players. You can play chess with patterns of light on a video screen, with symbols drawn in the sand, or even—if you're rich and eccentric enough—with fleets of helicopters operated by radio control. But you can't play chess with live frogs (they won't sit still), shapes traced in the water (they won't last), or mountain tops (nobody can move them). Essentially similar points can be made about logical symbolism and all other formal systems.

By contrast, what you can light a fire, feed a family, or wire a circuit with is not medium independent, because whether something is flammable, edible, or electrically conductive depends not just on its form but also on what it's made of. Nor are billiards or baseball independent of their media: what the balls (and bats and playing surfaces) are made of is quite important and carefully regulated. Billiard balls can indeed be made either of ivory or of (certain special) plastics, but hardly of wood or onyx. And you couldn't play billiards or baseball with helicopters or shapes in the sand to save your life. The reason is that, unlike chess and other formal systems, in these games the details of the physical interactions of the balls and other equipment make an important difference: how they bounce, how much friction there is, how much energy it takes to make them go a certain distance, and so on.

2.2.2   Automatic formal systems

An *automatic* formal system is a formal system that "moves" by itself. More precisely, it is a physical device or machine such that:

(1) some configurations of its parts or states can be regarded as the tokens and positions of some formal system; and

(2) in its normal operation, it automatically manipulates these tokens in accord with the rules of that system.

So it's like a set of chess pieces that hop around the board, abiding by the rules, all by themselves, or like a magical pencil that writes out formally correct logical derivations, without the guidance of any logician.

Of course, this is exactly what computers are, seen from a formal perspective. But, if we are to appreciate properly their importance for mind design, several fundamental facts and features will need further elaboration—among them the notions of implementation and universality, algorithmic and heuristic procedures, and digital simulation.

IMPLEMENTATION AND UNIVERSALITY. Perhaps the most basic idea of computer science is that you can use one automatic formal system to *implement* another. This is what *programming* is. Instead of building some special computer out of hard are, you build it out of software; that is, you write a program for a "general purpose" computer (which you already have) that will make it act exactly as if it were the special computer that you need. One computer so implements another when:

(1) some configurations of tokens and positions of the former can be regarded as the tokens and positions of the latter; and

(2) as the former follows its own rules, it automatically manipulates those tokens of the latter in accord with the latter's rules.

In general, those configurations that are being regarded as tokens and positions of the special computer are themselves only a fraction of the tokens and positions of the general computer. The remainder (which may be the majority) are the program. The general computer follows its own rules with regard to *all* of its tokens; but the program tokens are so arranged that the net effect is to manipulate the configurations implementing the tokens of the special computer in exactly the way required by its rules.

This is complicated to describe, never mind actually to achieve; and the question arises how often such implementation is possible in principle. The answer is as surprising as it is consequential. In 1937, A. M. Turing—the same Turing we met earlier in our discussion of intelligence—showed, in effect, that it is *always* possible. Put somewhat more carefully, he showed that there are some computing machines—which he called *universal* machines—that can implement *any* welldefined automatic formal system whatsoever, provided only that they have enough storage capacity and time. Not only that, he showed also that universal machines can be amazingly simple; and he gave a complete design specification for one.

Every ordinary (programmable) computer is a universal machine in Turing's sense. In other words, the computer on your desk, given the right program and enough memory, could be made equivalent to any computer that is possible at all, in every respect except speed. Anything any computer can do, yours can too, in principle. Indeed, the machine on your desk can be (and usually is) lots of computers at once. From one point of view, it is a "hardware" computer modifying, according to strict formal rules, complex patterns of tiny voltage tokens often called "bits". Viewed another way, it is simultaneously a completely different system that shuffles machine-language words called "op-codes", "data" and "addresses". And, depending on what you're up to, it may also *be* a word processor, a spell checker, a macro interpreter, and/or whatever.

ALGORITHMS AND HEURISTICS. Often a specific computer is designed and built (or programed) for a particular purpose: there will be some complicated rearrangement of tokens that it would be valuable to bring about automatically. Typically, a designer works with facilities that can carry out simple rearrangements easily, and the job is to find a combination of them (usually a sequence of steps) that will collectively achieve the desired result. Now there are two basic kinds of case, depending mainly on the character of the assigned task.

In many cases, the designer is able to implement a procedure that is guaranteed always to work—that is, to effect the desired rearrangement, regardless of the input, in a finite amount of time. Suppose, for instance, that the input is always a list of English words, and the desired rearrangement is to put them in alphabetical order. There are known procedures that are guaranteed to alphabetize any given list in finite time. Such procedures, ones that are sure to succeed in finite time, are called *algorithms*. Many important computational problems can be solved algorithmically.

But many others cannot, for theoretical or practical reasons. The task, for instance, might be to find the optimal move in any given chess position. Technically, chess is finite; so, theoretically, it would be possible to check every possible outcome of every possible move, and thus choose flawlessly, on the basis of complete information. But, in fact, even if the entire planet Earth were one huge computer built with the best current technology, it could not solve this problem even once in the life of the Solar System. So chess by brute force is impractical. But that, obviously, does not mean that machines can't come up with good chess moves. How do they do that?

They rely on general estimates and rules of thumb: procedures that, while not guaranteed to give the right answer every time, are fairly reliable most of the time. Such procedures are called *heuristics*. In the case of chess, sensible heuristics involve looking ahead a few moves in various directions and then evaluating factors like number and kind of pieces, mobility, control of the center, pawn coordination, and so on. These are not infallible measures of the strength of chess positions; but, in combination, they can be pretty good. This is how chess-playing computers work—and likewise many other machines that deal with problems for which there are no known algorithmic solutions.

The possibility of heuristic procedures on computers is sometimes confusing. In one sense, every digital computation (that does not consult a randomizer) is algorithmic; so how can any of them be heuristic? The answer is again a matter of perspective. Whether any given procedure is algorithmic or heuristic depends on how you describe the task. One and the same procedure can be an algorithm, when described as counting up the number and kinds of pieces, but a mere heuristic rule of thumb, when described as estimating the strength of a position.

This is the resolution of another common confusion as well. It is often said that computers never make mistakes (unless there is a bug in some program or a hardware malfunction). Yet anybody who has ever played chess against a small chess computer knows that it makes plenty of mistakes. But this is just that same issue about how you describe the task. Even that cheap toy is executing the algorithms that implement its heuristics flawlessly every time; seen that way, it never makes a mistake. It's just that those heuristics aren't very sophisticated; so, seen as a chess player, the same system makes lots of mistakes.

DIGITAL SIMULATION. One important practical application of computers isn't really token manipulation at all, except as a means to an end. You see this in your own computer all the time. Word processors and spreadsheets literally work with digital tokens: letters and numerals. But image processors do not: pictures are *not* digital. Rather, as everybody knows, they are "digitized". That is, they are divided up into fine enough dots and gradations that the increments are barely perceptible, and the result looks smooth and continuous. Nevertheless, the computer can store and modify them because—*redescribed*—those pixels are all just digital numerals.

The same thing can be done with dynamic systems: systems whose states interact and change in regular ways over time. If the relevant variables and relationships are known, then time can be divided into small intervals too, and the progress of the system computed, step by tiny step. This is called *digital simulation*. The most famous real-world example of it is the massive effort to predict the weather by simulating the Earth's atmosphere. But engineers and scientists—including, as we shall see, many cognitive scientists—rely on digital simulation of nondigital systems all the time.

2.2.3 Computers and intelligence

Turing (1950 [chapter 6 in this volume], 442 [109]) predicted—falsely, as we now know, but not foolishly—that by the year 2000 there would be computers that could pass his test for intelligence. This was before any serious work, theoretical or practical, had begun on artificial intelligence at all. On what, then, did he base his prediction? He doesn't really say (apart from an estimate—quite low—of how much storage computers would then have). But I think we can see what moved him.

In Turing's test, the only relevant inputs and outputs are *words*—all of which are (among other things) formal tokens. So the capacity of human beings that is to be matched is effectively a formal input/output function. But Turing himself had shown, thirteen years earlier, that *any* formal input/output function from a certain very broad category could be implemented in a routine universal machine, provided only that it had enough memory and time (or speed)—and those, he thought, would be available by century's end.

Now, this isn't really a proof, even setting aside the assumptions about size and speed, because Turing did not (and could not) show that the human verbal input/output function fell into that broad category of functions to which his theorem applied. But he had excellent reason to believe that any function computable by any *digital* mechanism would fall into that category; and he was convinced that there is nothing immaterial or supernatural in human beings. The only alternative remaining would seem to be *non*digital mechanisms; and those he believed could be digitally simulated.

Notice that there is *nothing* in this argument about how the mind might actually work— nothing about actual *mind design*. There's just an assumption that there must be *some* (nonmagical) way that it works, and that, whatever that way is, a computer can either implement it or simulate it. In the subsequent history of artificial intelligence, on the other hand, a number of very concrete proposals have been made about the actual design of human (and/or other) minds. Almost all of these fall into one or the other of two broad groups: those that take seriously the idea that the mind itself is essentially a digital computer (of a particular sort), and those that reject that idea.

2.3   GOFAI

The first approach is what I call "good old-fashioned AI", or *GOFAI*. (It is also sometimes called "classical" or "symbol-manipulation" or even "language-of-thought" AI.) Research in the GOFAI tradition dominated the field from the mid-fifties through at least the mid-eighties, and for a very good reason: it was (and still is) a well-articulated view of the mechanisms of intelligence that is both intuitively plausible and eminently realizable. According to this view, the mind just *is* a computer with certain special characteristics— namely, one with internal states and processes that can be regarded as explicit *thinking* or *reasoning*. In order to understand the immense plausibility and power of this GOFAI idea, we will need to see how a computer could properly be regarded in this way.

2.3.1   Interpreted formal systems

The idea of a formal system emerged first in mathematics, and was inspired by arithmetic and algebra. When people solve arithmetic or algebraic problems, they manipulate tokens according to definite rules, sort of like a game. But there is a profound difference between these tokens and, say, the pieces on a chess board: they *mean* something. Numerals, for instance, represent numbers (either of specified items or in the abstract), while arithmetic signs represent operations on or relationships among those numbers. (Tokens that mean something in this way are often called *symbols*.) Chess pieces, checkers, and go stones, by contrast, represent nothing: they are not symbols at all, but *merely* formal game tokens.

The rules according to which the tokens in a mathematical system may be manipulated and what those tokens mean are closely related. A simple example will bring this out. Suppose someone is playing a formal game with the first fifteen letters of the alphabet. The rules of this game are very restrictive: every starting position consists of a string of letters ending in 'A' (though not every such string is legal); and, for each starting position, there is one and only one legal move—which is to append a *particular* string of letters after the 'A' (and then the game is over). The question is: What (if anything) is going on here?

Suppose it occurs to you that the letters might be just an oddball notation for the familiar digits and signs of ordinary arithmetic. There are, however, over a trillion possible ways to translate fifteen letters into fifteen digits and signs. How could you decide which—*if any*—is the "right" way? The problem is illustrated in table 2.1. The first row gives eight sample games, each legal according to the rules. The next three rows each give a possible translation scheme, and show how the eight samples would come out according to that scheme.

The differences are conspicuous. The sample games as rendered by the first scheme, though consisting of digits and arithmetic signs, look no more like real arithmetic than the letters did—they're "arithmetic salad" at best. The second scheme, at first glance, looks better: at least the strings have the shape of equations. But, on closer examination, construed as equations, they would all be *false*—*wildly* false. In fact, though the signs are plausibly placed, the digits are just as randomly "tossed" as the first case. The third scheme, by contrast, yields strings that not only look like equations, they *are* equations—they're all *true*. And this makes that third scheme seem much more acceptable. Why?

Consider a related problem: translating some ancient documents in a hitherto unknown script. Clearly, if some crank translator proposed a scheme according to which the texts came out gibberish (like the first one in the table) we would be unimpressed. Almost as obviously, we would be unimpressed if they came out *looking like* sentences, but *loony* ones: not just false, but scattered, silly falsehoods, unrelated to one another or to anything else. On the other hand, if some careful, systematic scheme finds in them detailed, sensible accounts of battles, technologies, facts of nature, or whatever, that we know about from other sources, then we will be convinced.[3] But again: why?

Translation is a species of interpretation (see p. 15 above). Instead of saying what some system thinks or is up to, a translator says what some strings of tokens (symbols) mean. To keep the two species distinct, we can call the former *intentional* interpretation, since

Eight sample games (before translation):			
Starting position	*Legal move*	*Starting position*	*Legal move*
OEO A	N	MMCN A	JJ
NIBM A	G	OODF A	OO
HCHCH A	KON	IDL A	M
KEKDOF A	F	NBN A	O

First translation scheme:			Sample games, by first translation:			
A⇒1	F⇒6	K⇒+	$=5=1$	$\div$	$\times\times3\div1$	00
B⇒2	G⇒7	L⇒−	$\div92\times1$	7	$==46\ 1$	$==$
C⇒3	H⇒8	M⇒×	83838 1	$+=+$	94− 1	$\times$
D⇒4	I⇒9	N⇒÷	$+5+4=6\ 1$	6	$\div2\div1$	$=$
E⇒5	J⇒0	O⇒=				

Second translation scheme:			Sample games, by second translation:			
A⇒=	F⇒0	K⇒5	$9\div9=$	8	$77-8=$	44
B⇒+	G⇒1	L⇒6	$83+7=$	1	$99\times0=$	99
C⇒−	H⇒2	M⇒7	$2-2-2=$	598	$3\times6=$	2
D⇒×	I⇒3	N⇒8	$5\div5\times90=$	0	$8+8=$	9
E⇒÷	J⇒4	O⇒9				

Third translation scheme:			Sample games, by third translation:			
A⇒=	F⇒0	K⇒5	$1+1=$	2	$33\times2=$	66
B⇒÷	G⇒9	L⇒4	$27\div3=$	9	$11-0=$	11
C⇒×	H⇒8	M⇒3	$8\times8\times8=$	512	$7-4=$	3
D⇒−	I⇒7	N⇒2	$5+5-10=$	0	$2\div2=$	1
E⇒+	J⇒6	O⇒1				

Table 2.1
Letter game and three different translation schemes.

it attributes intentional states, and the latter (translation) *semantic* interpretation, since it attributes meanings (= semantics).

Like all interpretation, translation is holistic: it is impossible to interpret a brief string completely out of context. For instance, the legal game 'HDJAN' happens to come out looking just as true on the second as on the third scheme in our arithmetic example ('$2 \times 4 = 8$' and '$8 - 6 = 2$', respectively). But, in the case of the second scheme, this is obviously just an isolated coincidence, whereas, in the case of the third, it is part of a consistent pattern. Finding meaning in a body of symbols, like finding rationality in a body of behavior, is finding a certain kind of consistent, reliable *pattern*.

Well, what *kind* of pattern? Intentional interpretation seeks to construe a system or creature so that what it thinks and does turns out to be consistently reasonable and sensible, given its situation. Semantic interpretation seeks to construe a body of symbols so that what they mean ("say") turns out to be consistently reasonable and sensible, given the situation. This is *why* the third schemes in both the arithmetic and ancient-script examples are the acceptable ones: they're the ones that "make sense" of the texts, and *that's* the kind of pattern that translation seeks. I don't think we will ever have a precise, explicit definition of any phrase like "consistently reasonable and sensible, given the situation". But surely it captures much of what we mean (and Turing meant) by *intelligence*, whether in action or in expression.

2.3.2   Intelligence by explicit reasoning

Needless to say, interpretation and automation can be combined. A simple calculator, for instance, is essentially an automated version of the letter-game example, with the third interpretation. And the system that Turing envisioned—a computer with inputs and outputs that could be understood as coherent conversation in English—would be an interpreted automatic formal system. But it's *not* GOFAI.

So far, we have considered systems the inputs and outputs of which can be interpreted. But we have paid no attention to what goes on *inside* of those systems—*how* they get from an input to an appropriate output. In the case of a simple calculator, there's not much to it. But imagine a system that tackles harder problems—like "word problems" in an algebra or physics text, for instance. Here the challenge is not doing the calculations, but figuring out what calculations to do. There are many possible things to try, only one or a few of which will work.

A skilled problem solver, of course, will not try things at random, but will rely on experience and rules of thumb for guidance about what to try next, and about how things are going so far (whether it would be best to continue, to back-track, to start over, or even to give up). We can imagine someone muttering: "If only I could get that, then I could nail this down; but, in order to get that, I would need such and such. Now, let me see . . . well, what if . . . " (and so on). Such canny, methodical exploration—neither algorithmic nor random—is a familiar sort of articulate *reasoning* or *thinking* a problem out.

But each of those steps (conjectures, partial results, subgoals, blind alleys, and so on) is—from a formal point of view—just another token string. As such, they could easily be intermediate states in an interpreted automatic formal system that took a statement of the problem as input and gave a statement of the solution as output. Should these intermediate strings themselves then be *interpreted as* steps in thinking or reasoning the problem through? If two conditions are met, then the case becomes quite compelling. First, the system had better be able to handle with comparable facility an open-ended and varied range of problems, not just a few (the solutions to which might have been "precanned"). And, it had better be arriving at its solutions actually via these steps. (It would be a kind of fraud if it were really solving the problem in some other way, and then tacking on the "steps" for show afterwards.)

GOFAI is predicated on the idea that systems can be built to solve problems by reasoning or thinking them through in this way, and, moreover, that this is how people solve problems. Of course, we aren't always consciously aware of such reasoning, especially for the countless routine problems—like those involved in talking, doing chores, and generally getting along—that we "solve" all the time. But the fact that we are not aware of it doesn't mean that it's not going on, subconsciously or somehow "behind the scenes".

The earliest GOFAI efforts emphasized problem-solving methods, especially the design of efficient heuristics and search procedures, for various specific classes of problems. (The article by Newell and Simon reviews this approach.) These early systems, however, tended to be quite "narrow-minded" and embarrassingly vulnerable to unexpected variations and oddities in the problems and information they were given. Though they could generate quite clever solutions to complicated problems that were carefully posed, they conspicuously lacked "common sense"—they were hopelessly *ignorant*—so they were prone to amusing blunders that no ordinary person would ever make.

Later designs have therefore emphasized broad, common-sense knowledge. Of course, problem-solving heuristics and search techniques are still essential; but, as research problems, these were overshadowed by the difficulties of large-scale "knowledge representation". The biggest problem turned out to be organization. Common-sense knowledge is vast; and, it seems, almost any odd bit of it can be just what is needed to avoid some dumb mistake at any particular moment. So all of it has to be at the system's "cognitive fingertips" all the time. Since repeated exhaustive search of the entire knowledge base would be quite impractical, some shortcuts had to be devised that would work most of the time. This is what efficient organizing or structuring of the knowledge is supposed to provide.

Knowledge-representation research, in contrast to heuristic problem solving, has tended to concentrate on natural language ability, since this is where the difficulties it addresses are most obvious. The principal challenge of ordinary conversation, from a designer's point of view, is that it is so often ambiguous and incomplete—mainly because speakers take so much for granted. That means that the system must be able to fill in all sorts of "trivial" gaps, in order to follow what's being said. But this is still GOFAI, because the filling in is being done rationally. Behind the scenes, the system is explicitly "figuring out" what the speaker must have meant, on the basis of what it knows about the world and the context. (The articles by Minsky and Dreyfus survey some of this work, and Dreyfus and Searle also criticize it.)

Despite its initial plausibility and promise, however, GOFAI has been in some ways disappointing. Expanding and organizing a system's store of explicit knowledge seems at best partially to solve the problem of common sense. This is why the Turing test will not soon be passed. Further, it is surprisingly difficult to design systems that can adjust their own knowledge in the light of experience. The problem is not that they can't modify themselves, but that it's hard to figure out just which modifications to make, while keeping everything else coherent. Finally, GOFAI systems tend to be rather poor at noticing unexpected similarities or adapting to unexpected peculiarities. Indeed, they are poor at recognizing patterns more generally—such as perceived faces, sounds, or kinds of objects—let alone *learning* to recognize them.

None of this means, of course, that the program is bankrupt. Rome was not built in a day. There is a great deal of active research, and new developments occur all the time. It *has* meant, however, that *some* cognitive scientists have begun to explore various alternative approaches.

2.4   New-fangled AI

By far the most prominent of these new-fangled ideas—we could call them collectively *NFAI (en-*fai)—falls under the general rubric of *connectionism*. This is a diverse and still rapidly evolving bundle of systems and proposals that seem, on the face of it, to address some of GOFAI's most glaring weaknesses. On the other hand, connectionist systems are not so good—at least not yet—at matching GOFAI's most obvious strengths. (This suggests, of course, a possibility of joining forces; but, at this point, it's too soon to tell whether any such thing could work, never mind how it might be done.) And, in the meantime, there are other NFAI ideas afloat, that are neither GOFAI nor connectionist. The field as a whole is in more ferment now than it has been since the earliest days, in the fifties.

2.4.1   Connectionist networks

Connectionist systems are networks of lots of simple active units that have lots of connections among them, by which they can interact. There is no central processor or controller, and also no separate memory or storage mechanism. The only activity in the system is these little units changing state, in response to signals coming in along those connections, and then sending out signals of their own. There are two ways in which such a network can achieve a kind of memory. First, in the short term, information can be retained in the system over time insofar as the units tend to change state only slowly (and, perhaps, regularly). Second, and in the longer term, there is a kind of memory in the connections themselves. For, each connection always connects the same two units (they don't move around); and, more significant, each connection has a property, called its "weight" or "strength", which is preserved over time.

Obviously, connectionist networks are inspired to some extent by brains and neural networks. The active units are like individual neurons, and the connections among them are like the axons and dendrites along which electro-chemical "pulses" are sent from neuron to neuron. But, while this analogy is important, it should not be overstressed. What makes connectionist systems interesting as an approach to AI is not the fact that their structure mimics biology at a certain level of description, but rather what they can do. After all, there are countless other levels of description at which connectionist nets are utterly *un*biological; and, if some GOFAI account turns out to be right about human intelligence, then there will be *some* level of description at which it too accurately models the brain. Connectionist and allied research may someday show that neural networks are the level at which the brain implements psychological structures; but this certainly cannot be assumed at the outset.

In order to appreciate what is distinctive about network models, it is important to keep in mind how simple and relatively isolated the active units are. The "state" of such a unit is typically just a single quantitative magnitude—specifiable with a single number—called its *activation level*. This activation level changes in response to signals arriving from other units, but only in a very crude way. In the first place, it pays no attention to which signals came from which other units, or how any of those signals might be related to others: it simply adds them indiscriminately together and responds only to the total. Moreover, that response, the change in activation, is a simple function of that total; and the signal it then sends to other units is just a simple function of that resulting activation.

Now there is one small complication, which is the root of everything interesting about these models. The signal that a unit receives from another is not the same as the signal that the other unit sent: it is multiplied—increased or decreased—by the weight or strength of the connection between them. And there are always many more connections in a network than there are units, simply because each unit is connected to many others. That means that the *overall* state of the network—that is, the *pattern* of activations of all its units—can change in very subtle and sophisticated ways, as a function of its initial state. The overall pattern of connection weights is what determines these complicated changes, and thus the basic character of the network.

Accordingly, connectionist networks are essentially *pattern processors*. And, it turns out, they can be quite good at certain psychologically important kinds of pattern processing. In particular, they are adept at finding various sorts of similarities among patterns, at recognizing repeated (or almost repeated) patterns, at filling in the missing parts of incomplete patterns, and at transforming patterns into others with which they have been associated. People are good at these kinds of pattern processing too; but GOFAI systems tend not to be, except in special cases. Needless to say, this is what gets cognitive scientists excited about connectionist models.

Two more points. First, when I say that networks are good at such pattern processing, I mean not only that they can do it well, but also that they can do it quickly. This is a consequence of the fact that, although each unit is very simple, there are a great many of them working at once—in *parallel*, so to speak—so the cumulative effect in each time increment can be quite substantial. Second, techniques have been discovered by means of which networks can be *trained* through exposure to examples. That is, the connection weights required for some desired pattern-processing ability can be induced ("taught") by giving the network a number of sample instances, and allowing it slowly to adjust itself. (It should be added, however, that the training techniques so far discovered are not psychologically realistic: people learn from examples too, but, for various reasons, we know it can't be in quite these ways.)

I mentioned a moment ago that GOFAI systems are not so good at pattern processing, except in special cases. In comparing approaches to mind design, however, it is crucial to recognize that some of these "special cases" are extremely important. In particular, GOFAI systems are remarkably *good* at processing (recognizing, transforming, producing) *syntactical* (grammatical) patterns of the sort that are characteristic of logical formulae, ordinary sentences, and many inferences. What's more, connectionist networks are *not* (so far?) particularly good at processing *these* patterns. Yet language is surely a central manifestation of (human) intelligence. No approach to mind design that cannot accommodate language ability can possibly be adequate.

Connectionist researchers use computers in their work just as much as GOFAI researchers do; but they use them differently. Pattern-processing networks are not themselves automatic formal systems: they do not manipulate formal tokens, and they are not essentially digital. To be sure, the individual units and connections are sharply distinct from one another; and, for convenience, their activations and weights are sometimes limited to a handful of discrete values. But these are more akin to the "digitization" of images in computer image processing than to the essential digitalness of chess pieces, logical symbols, and words. Thus, connectionist mind design relies on computers more in the way the weather service does, to simulate digitally systems that are not in themselves digital.

It has been shown, however, that some connectionist networks can, in effect, *implement* symbol manipulation systems. Although these implementations tend not to be very efficient, they are nevertheless interesting. For one thing, they may show how symbol manipulation could be implemented in the brain. For another, they might yield ways to build and understand genuine *hybrid* systems—that is, systems with the advantages of both approaches. Such possibilities aside, however, symbolic implementation would seem at best Pyrrhic victory: the network would be relegated to the role of "hardware", while the psychological relevance, the actual *mind design*, would still be GOFAI.

GOFAI is inspired by the idea that intelligence as such is made possible by explicit thinking or reasoning—that is, by the rational manipulation of internal symbol structures (interpreted formal tokens). Thus, GOFAI intentionality is grounded in the possibility of translation—*semantic* interpretation. Connectionist NFAI, by contrast, is inspired initially by the structure of the brain, but, more deeply, by the importance and ubiquity of non-formal pattern processing. Since there are no formal tokens (unless implemented at a higher level), there can be no semantically interpreted symbols. Thus, to regard these systems as having intentional states would be to adopt Dennett's intentional stance—that is, *intentional* interpretation.

2.4.2 Embodied and embedded AI

GOFAI is a fairly coherent research tradition, based on a single basic idea: thinking as internal symbol manipulation. 'NFAI', by contrast, is more a grab-bag term: it means, roughly, scientific mind design that is not GOFAI. Connectionism falls under this umbrella, but several other possibilities do as well, of which I will mention just one.

Connectionist and GOFAI systems, for all their differences, tend to have one feature in common: they accept an input from somewhere, they work on it for a while, and then they deliver an output. All the "action" is *within* the system, rather than being an integral part of a larger *interaction* with an active body and an active environment. The alternative, to put it radically (and perhaps a bit contentiously), would be to have the intelligent system *be* the larger interactive *whole*, including the body and environment as essential components. Now, of course, this whole couldn't be intelligent if it weren't for a special "subsystem" such as might be implemented in a computer or a brain; but, equally, perhaps, that subsystem couldn't be intelligent either except as part of a whole comprising the other components as well.

Why would anyone think this? It goes without saying that, in general, intelligent systems ought to be able to *act* intelligently "in" the world. That's what intelligence is for, ultimately. Yet, achieving even basic competence in real robots turns out to be surprisingly hard. A simple example can illustrate the point and also the change in perspective that motivates some recent research. Consider a system that must be able, among other things, to approach and unlock a door. How will it get the key in the lock? One approach would equip the robot with:

(1) precise sensors to identify and locate the lock, and monitor the angles of the joints in its own arm and hand;

(2) enough modelling power to convert joint information into a representation of the location and orientation of the key (in the coordinate system of the lock), compute the exact key motion required, and then convert that back into joint motions; and

(3) motors accurate enough to effect the computed motions, and thereby to slide the key in, smooth and straight, the first time.

Remarkably, such a system is utterly impractical, perhaps literally impossible, even with state-of-the-art technology. Yet insects, with far less compute power on board, routinely perform much harder tasks.

How would insectile "intelligence" approach the key-lock problem? First, the system would have a crude detector to notice and aim at locks, more or less. But, it would generate no central representation of the lock's position, for other subsystems to use in computing arm movements. Rather, the arm itself would have its own ad hoc, but more local, detectors that enable it likewise to home in on a lock, more or less (and also, perhaps, to adjust its aim from one try to the next). And, in the meantime, the arm and its grip on the key would both be quite flexible, and the lock would have a kind of funnel around its opening, so any stab that's at all close would be guided physically right into the lock. Now *that's* engineering—elegant, cheap, reliable.

But is it *intelligence*? Well surely not much; but that may not be the right question to ask. Instead, we should wonder whether some similar essential involvement of the body (physical flexibility and special purpose subsystems, for instance) and the world (conveniences like the funnel) might be integral to capacities that are more plausibly intelligent. If so, it could greatly decrease the load on central knowledge, problem solving, and even pattern processing, thereby circumventing (perhaps) some of the bottlenecks that frustrate current designs.

To get a feel for the possibilities, move for a moment to the other end of the spectrum. Human intelligence is surely manifested in the ability to design and make things—using, as the case may be, boards and nails. Now, for such a design to work, it must be possible to drive nails into pieces of wood in a way that will hold them together. But neither a designer nor a carpenter ever needs to think about that—it need never even *occur* to them. (They take it for granted, as a fish does water.) The suitability of these materials and techniques is embedded in the structure of their culture: the logging industry, the manufacture of wire, the existence of lumber yards—and, of course, countless bodily skills and habits passed down from generation to generation.

Think how much "knowledge" is contained in the traditional shape and heft of a hammer, as well as in the muscles and reflexes acquired in learning to use it—though, again, no one need *ever* have thought of it. Multiply that by our food and hygiene practices, our manner of dress, the layout of buildings, cities, and farms. To be sure, some of this was explicitly figured out, at least once upon a time; but a lot of it wasn't—it just evolved that way (because it worked). Yet a great deal, perhaps even the bulk, of the basic expertise that makes human intelligence what it is, is maintained and brought to bear in these "physical" structures. It is neither stored nor used inside the head of *anyone*—it's in their bodies and, even more, out there in the world.

Scientific research into the kinds of systems that might achieve intelligence in this way—embodied and embedded mind design—is still in an early phase.

2.5 What's missing from mind design?

A common complaint about artificial intelligence, of whatever stripe, is that it pays scant attention to feelings, emotions, ego, imagination, moods, consciousness—the whole "phenomenology" of an inner life. No matter how smart the machines become, so the worry goes, there's still "nobody home". I think there is considerable merit in these misgivings, though, of course, more in some forms than in others. Here, however, I would like briefly to discuss only one form of the worry, one that strikes me as more basic than the others, and also more intimately connected with cognition narrowly conceived.

No current approach to artificial intelligence takes *understanding* seriously—where understanding itself is understood as distinct from knowledge (in whole or in part) and prerequisite thereto. It seems to me that, taken in this sense, *only people* ever understand anything—no animals and no artifacts (yet). It follows that, in a strict and proper sense, no animal or machine genuinely believes or desires anything either—How could it believe something it doesn't understand?—though, obviously, in some other, weaker sense, animals (at least) have plenty of beliefs and desires. This conviction, I should add, is not based on any in-principle barrier; it's just an empirical observation about what happens to be the case at the moment, so far as we can tell.

So, what is it for a system to understand something? Imagine a system that makes or marks a battery of related distinctions in the course of coping with some range of objects. These distinctions can show up in the form of differing skillful responses, different symbol structures, or whatever. Let's say that, for each such distinction, the system has a *proto-concept*. Now I suggest that a system *understands* the objects to which it applies its proto-concepts insofar as:

(1) it takes responsibility for applying the proto-concepts correctly;

(2) it takes responsibility for the empirical adequacy of the proto-concepts themselves; and

(3) it takes a firm stand on what can and cannot happen in the world, when grasped in terms of these proto-concepts.

When these conditions are met, moreover, the proto-concepts are not merely *proto-*concepts, but *concepts* in the full and proper sense.

The three conditions are not unrelated. For, it is precisely in the face of something *impossible* seeming to have happened, that the question of *correct* application becomes urgent. We can imagine the system responding in some way that we would express by saying:

"This *can't* be right!" and then trying to figure out what went wrong. The responsibility for the concepts themselves emerges when, too often, it can't find any mistake. In that event, the conceptual structure itself must be revised, either by modifying the discriminative abilities that embody the concepts, or by modifying the stand it takes on what is and isn't possible, or both. Afterward, it will have (more or less) new concepts.

A system that appropriates and takes charge of its own conceptual resources in this way is not merely going through the motions of intelligence, whether evolved, learned, or programmed-in, but rather grasps the point of them for itself. It does not merely make discriminations or produce outputs that, when best interpreted by us, come out true. Rather, such a system appreciates for itself the difference between truth and falsity, appreciates that, in these, it must accede to the world, that the world determines which is which—and it *cares*. That, I think, is *understanding*.[4]

Notes for Chapter 2

1. Both parts of this idea have their roots in W.V.O. Quine's pioneering (1960) investigations of meaning. (Meaning is the linguistic or symbolic counterpart of intentionality.)

2. Chess players will know that the rules for castling, stalemate, and capturing *en passent* depend also on *previous* events; so, to make chess strictly formal, these conditions would have to be encoded in further tokens (markers, say) that count as part of the current position.

3. A similar point can be made about code-cracking (which is basically translating texts that are contrived to make that especially difficult). A cryptographer knows she has succeeded when and only when the decoded messages come out consistently sensible, relevant, and true.

4. These ideas are explored further in the last four chapters of Haugeland (1997a).

Computer Science as Empirical Inquiry: Symbols and Search 3

Allen Newell and Herbert A. Simon
1976

Computer science is the study of the phenomena surrounding computers. The founders of this society understood this very well when they called themselves the Association for Computing Machinery. The machine—not just the hardware, but the programmed living machine—is the organism we study.

This is the tenth Turing Lecture. The nine persons who preceded us on this platform have presented nine different views of computer science. For our organism, the machine, can be studied at many levels and from many sides. We are deeply honored to appear here today and to present yet another view, the one that has permeated the scientific work for which we have been cited. We wish to speak of computer science as an empirical inquiry.

Our view is only one of many; the previous lectures make that clear. However, even taken together the lectures fail to cover the whole scope of our science. Many fundamental aspects of it have not been represented in these ten awards. And if the time ever arrives, surely not soon, when the compass has been boxed, when computer science has been discussed from every side, it will be time to start the cycle again. For the hare as lecturer will have to make an annual sprint to overtake the cumulation of small, incremental gains that the tortoise of scientific and technical development has achieved in his steady march. Each year will create a new gap and call for a new sprint, for in science there is no final word.

Computer science is an empirical discipline. We would have called it an experimental science, but like astronomy, economics, and geology, some of its unique forms of observation and experience do not fit a narrow stereotype of the experimental method. Nonetheless, they are experiments. Each new machine that is built is an experiment. Actually constructing the machine poses a question to nature; and we listen for the answer by observing the machine in operation and analyzing it by all analytical and measurement means available. Each new program that is built is an experiment. It poses a question to nature, and its behavior offers clues to a new answer. Neither machines nor programs are black boxes; they are artifacts that have been designed, both hardware and software, and we can open them up and look inside. We can relate their structure to their behavior and draw many lessons from a single experiment. We don't have to build 100 copies of, say, a theorem prover, to demonstrate statistically that it has not overcome the combinatorial explosion of search in the way hoped for. Inspection of the program in the light of a few runs reveals the flaw and lets us proceed to the next attempt.

We build computers and programs for many reasons. We build them to serve society and as tools for carrying out the economic tasks of society. But as basic scientists we build machines and programs as a way of discovering new phenomena and analyzing phenomena we already know about. Society often becomes confused about this, believing that computers and programs are to be constructed only for the economic use that can be made of them (or as intermediate items in a developmental sequence leading to such use). It needs to understand that the phenomena surrounding computers are deep and obscure, requiring much experimentation to assess their nature. It needs to understand that, as in any science, the gains that accrue from such experimentation and understanding pay off in the permanent acquisition of new techniques; and that it is these techniques that will create the instruments to help society in achieving its goals.

Our purpose here, however, is not to plead for understanding from an outside world. It is to examine one aspect of our science, the development of new basic understanding by empirical inquiry. This is best done by illustrations. We will be pardoned if, presuming upon the occasion, we choose our examples from the area of our own research. As will become apparent, these examples involve the whole development of artificial intelligence, especially in its early years. They rest on much more than our own personal contributions. And even where we have made direct contributions, this has been done in cooperation with others. Our collaborators have included especially Cliff Shaw, with whom we formed a team of three through the exciting period of the late fifties. But we have also worked with a great many colleagues and students at Carnegie Mellon University.

Time permits taking up just two examples. The first is the development of the notion of a symbolic system. The second is the development of the notion of heuristic search. Both conceptions have deep significance for understanding how information is processed and how intelligence is achieved. However, they do not come close to exhausting the full scope of artificial intelligence, though they seem to us to be useful for exhibiting the nature of fundamental knowledge in this part of computer science.

3.1   Symbols and physical symbol systems

One of the fundamental contributions to knowledge of computer science has been to explain, at a rather basic level, what symbols are. This explanation is a scientific proposition about nature. It is empirically derived, with a long and gradual development.

Symbols lie at the root of intelligent action, which is, of course, the primary topic of artificial intelligence. For that matter, it is a primary question for all of computer science. For all information is processed by computers in the service of ends, and we measure the intelligence of a system by its ability to achieve stated ends in the face of variations, difficulties, and complexities posed by the task environment. This general investment of computer science in attaining intelligence is obscured when the tasks being accomplished are limited in scope, for then the full variations in the environment can be accurately foreseen. It becomes more obvious as we extend computers to more global, complex, and knowledge-intensive tasks—as we attempt to make them our agents, capable of handling on their own the full contingencies of the natural world.

Our understanding of the system's requirements for intelligent action emerges slowly. It is composite, for no single elementary thing accounts for intelligence in all its manifestations. There is no "intelligence principle", just as there is no "vital principle" that conveys by its very nature the essence of life. But the lack of a simple *deus ex machina* does not imply that there are no structural requirements for intelligence. One such requirement is the ability to store and manipulate symbols. To put the scientific question, we may paraphrase the title of a famous paper by Warren McCulloch (1961): What is a symbol, that intelligence may use it, and intelligence, that it may use a symbol?

3.1.1   Laws of qualitative structure

All sciences characterize the essential nature of the systems they study. These characterizations are invariably qualitative in nature, for they set the terms within which more detailed knowledge can be developed. Their essence can often be captured in very short, very general statements. One might judge these general laws, because of their limited specificity, as making relatively little contribution to the sum of a science, were it not for the historical evidence that shows them to be results of the greatest importance.

THE CELL DOCTRINE IN BIOLOGY. A good example of a law of qualitative structure is the cell doctrine in biology, which states that the basic building block of all living organisms is the cell. Cells come in a large variety of forms, though they all have a nucleus surrounded by protoplasm, the whole encased by a membrane. But this internal structure was not, historically, part of the specification of the cell doctrine; it was subsequent specificity developed by intensive investigation. The cell doctrine can be conveyed almost entirely by the statement we gave above, along with some vague notions about what size a cell can be. The impact of this law on biology, however, has been tremendous, and the lost motion in the field prior to its gradual acceptance was considerable.

PLATE TECTONICS IN GEOLOGY. Geology provides an interesting example of a qualitative structure law, interesting because it has gained acceptance in the last decade and so its rise in status is still fresh in our memory. The theory of plate tectonics asserts that the surface of the globe is a collection of huge plates—a few dozen in all—which move (at geological speeds) against, over, and under each other into the center of the earth, where they lose their identity. The movements of the plates account for the shapes and relative locations of the continents and oceans, for the areas of volcanic and earthquake activity, for the deep sea ridges, and so on. With a few additional particulars as to speed and size, the essential theory has been specified. It was of course not accepted until it succeeded in explaining a number of details, all of which hung together (for instance, accounting for flora, fauna, and stratification agreements between West Africa and Northeast South America). The plate-tectonics theory is highly qualitative. Now that it is accepted, the whole earth seems to offer evidence for it everywhere, for we see the world in its terms.

THE GERM THEORY OF DISEASE. It is little more than a century since Pasteur enunciated the germ theory of disease, a law of qualitative structure that produced a revolution in medicine. The theory proposes that most diseases are caused by the presence and multiplication in the body of tiny single-celled living organisms, and that contagion consists in the transmission of these organisms from one host to another. A large part of the elaboration of the theory consisted in identifying the organisms associated with specific diseases, describing them, and tracing their life histories. The fact that this law has many exceptions—that many diseases are not produced by germs—does not detract from its importance. The law tells us to look for a particular kind of cause; it does not insist that we will always find it.

THE DOCTRINE OF ATOMISM. The doctrine of atomism offers an interesting contrast to the three laws of qualitative structure we have just described. As it emerged from the work of Dalton and his demonstrations that the chemicals combined in fixed proportions, the law provided a typical example of qualitative structure: the elements are composed of small, uniform particles, differing from one element to another. But because the underlying species of atoms are so simple and limited in their variety, quantitative theories were soon formulated which assimilated all the general structure in the original qualitative hypothesis. With cells, tectonic plates, and germs, the variety of structure is so great that the underlying qualitative principle remains distinct, and its contribution to the total theory clearly discernible.

CONCLUSION. Laws of qualitative structure are seen everywhere in science. Some of our greatest scientific discoveries are to be found among them. As the examples illustrate, they often set the terms on which a whole science operates.

3.1.2 Physical symbol systems

Let us return to the topic of symbols, and define a *physical symbol system*. The adjective "physical" denotes two important features: (1) such systems clearly obey the laws of physics—they are realizable by engineered systems made of engineered components; and (2) although our use of the term "symbol" prefigures our intended interpretation, it is not restricted to human symbol systems.

A physical symbol system consists of a set of entities, called symbols, which are physical patterns that can occur as components of another type of entity called an expression (or symbol structure). Thus a symbol structure is composed of a number of instances (or tokens) of symbols related in some physical way (such as one token being next to another).

At any instant of time the system will contain a collection of these symbol structures. Besides these structures, the system also contains a collection of processes that operate on expressions to produce other expressions: processes of creation, modification, reproduction, and destruction. A physical symbol system is a machine that produces through time an evolving collection of symbol structures. Such a system exists in a world of objects wider than just these symbolic expressions themselves.

Two notions are central to this structure of expressions, symbols, and objects: designation and interpretation.

DESIGNATION. An expression designates an object if, given the expression, the system can either affect the object itself or behave in ways depending on the object.

In either case, access to the object via the expression has been obtained, which is the essence of designation.

INTERPRETATION. The system can interpret an expression if the expression designates a process and if, given the expression, the system can carry out the process.[1]

Interpretation implies a special form of dependent action: given an expression, the system can perform the indicated process, which is to say, it can evoke and execute its own processes from expressions that designate them.

A system capable of designation and interpretation, in the sense just indicated, must also meet a number of additional requirements, of completeness and closure. We will have space only to mention these briefly; all of them are important and have far-reaching consequences.

(1) A symbol may be used to designate any expression whatsoever. That is, given a symbol, it is not prescribed a priori what expressions it can designate. This arbitrariness pertains only to symbols: the symbol tokens and their mutual relations determine what object is designated by a complex expression. (2) There exist expressions that designate every process of which the machine is capable. (3) There exist processes for creating any expression and for modifying any expression in arbitrary ways. (4) Expressions are stable; once created, they will continue to exist until explicitly modified or deleted. (5) The number of expressions that the system can hold is essentially unbounded.

The type of system we have just defined is not unfamiliar to computer scientists. It bears a strong family resemblance to all general purpose computers. If a symbol-manipulation language, such as LISP, is taken as defining a machine, then the kinship becomes truly brotherly. Our intent in laying out such a system is not to propose something new. Just the opposite: it is to show what is now known and hypothesized about systems that satisfy such a characterization.

We can now state a general scientific hypothesis—a law of qualitative structure for symbol systems:

THE PHYSICAL SYMBOL SYSTEM HYPOTHESIS. A physical symbol system has the necessary and sufficient means for general intelligent action.

By "necessary" we mean that any system that exhibits general intelligence will prove upon analysis to be a physical symbol system. By "sufficient" we mean that any physical symbol system of sufficient size can be organized further to exhibit general intelligence. By "general intelligent action" we wish to indicate the same scope of intelligence as we see in human action: that in any real situation, behavior appropriate to the ends of the system and adaptive to the demands of the environment can occur, within some limits of speed and complexity.

The Physical Symbol System Hypothesis clearly is a law of qualitative structure. It specifies a general class of systems within which one will find those capable of intelligent action.

This is an empirical hypothesis. We have defined a class of systems; we wish to ask whether that class accounts for a set of phenomena we find in the real world. Intelligent action is everywhere around us in the biological world, mostly in human behavior. It is a form of behavior we can recognize by its effects whether it is performed by humans or not. The hypothesis could indeed be false. Intelligent behavior is not so easy to produce that any system will exhibit it willy-nilly. Indeed, there are people whose analyses lead them to conclude, either on philosophical or on scientific grounds, that the hypothesis is false. Scientifically, one can attack or defend it only by bringing forth empirical evidence about the natural world.

We now need to trace the development of this hypothesis and look at the evidence for it.

3.1.3 Development of the symbol-system hypothesis

A physical symbol system is an instance of a universal machine. Thus the symbol system hypothesis implies that intelligence will be realized by a universal computer. However, the hypothesis goes far beyond the argument, often made on general grounds of physical determinism, that any computation that is realizable can be realized by a universal machine, provided that it is specified. For it asserts specifically that the intelligent machine is a symbol system, thus making a specific architectural assertion about the nature of intelligent systems. It is important to understand how this additional specificity arose.

FORMAL LOGIC. The roots of the hypothesis go back to the program of Frege and of Whitehead and Russell for formalizing logic: capturing the basic conceptual notions of mathematics in logic and putting the notions of proof and deduction on a secure footing. This effort culminated in mathematical logic—our familiar propositional, first-order, and higher-order logics. It developed a characteristic view, often referred to as the "symbol game". Logic, and by incorporation all of mathematics, was a game played with meaningless tokens according to certain purely syntactic rules. All meaning had been purged. One had a mechanical, though permissive (we would now say nondeterministic), system about which various things could be proved. Thus progress was first made by walking away from all that seemed relevant to meaning and human symbols. We could call this the stage of formal symbol manipulation.

This general attitude is well reflected in the development of information theory. It was pointed out time and again that Shannon had defined a system that was useful only for communication and selection, and which had nothing to do with meaning. Regrets were expressed that such a general name as "information theory" had been given to the field, and attempts were made to rechristen it as "the theory of selective information"—to no avail, of course.

TURING MACHINES AND THE DIGITAL COMPUTER. The development of the first digital computers and of automata theory, starting with Turing's own work in the 1930s, can be treated together. They agree in their view of what is essential. Let us use Turing's own model, for it shows the features well.

A Turing machine consists of two memories: an unbounded tape and a finite-state control. The tape holds data, that is, the famous zeros and ones. The machine has a very small set of proper operations—read, write, and scan operations—on the tape. The read operation is not a data operation, but provides conditional branching to a control state as a function of the data under the read head. As we all know, this model contains the essentials of all computers, in terms of what they can do, though other computers with different memories and operations might carry out the same computations with different requirements of space and time. In particular, the model of a Turing machine contains within it the notions both of what cannot be computed and of universal machines—computers that can do anything that can be done by any machine.

We should marvel that two of our deepest insights into information processing were achieved in the thirties, before modern computers came into being. It is a tribute to the genius of Alan Turing. It is also a tribute to the development of mathematical logic at the time, and testimony to the depth of computer science's obligation to it. Concurrently with Turing's work appeared the work of the logicians Emil Post and (independently) Alonzo Church. Starting from independent notions of logistic systems (Post productions and recursive functions, respectively), they arrived at analogous results on undecidability and universality—results that were soon shown to imply that all three systems were equivalent. Indeed, the convergence of all these attempts to define the most general class of information-processing systems provides some of the force of our conviction that we have captured the essentials of information processing in these models.

In none of these systems is there, on the surface, a concept of the symbol as something that *designates*. The data are regarded as just strings of zeroes and ones—indeed, that data be inert is essential to the reduction of computation to physical process. The finite-state control system was always viewed as a small controller, and logical games were played to see how small a state system could be used without destroying the universality of the machine. No games, as far as we can tell, were ever played to add new states dynamically to the finite control—to think of the control memory as holding the bulk of the system's knowledge. What was accomplished at this stage was half of the principle of interpretation—showing that a machine could be run from a description. Thus, this is the stage of automatic formal symbol manipulation.

THE STORED-PROGRAM CONCEPT. With the development of the second generation of electronic machines in the mid-forties (after the Eniac) came the stored-program concept. This was rightfully hailed as a milestone, both conceptually and practically. Programs now can be data, and can be operated on as data. This capability is, of course, already implicit in the model of Turing: the descriptions are on the very same tape as the data. Yet the idea was realized only when machines acquired enough memory to make it practicable to locate actual programs in some internal place. After all, the Eniac had only twenty registers.

The stored-program concept embodies the second half of the interpretation principle, the part that says that the system's own data can be interpreted. But it does not yet contain the notion of designation—of the physical relation that underlies meaning.

LIST PROCESSING. The next step, taken in 1956, was list processing. The contents of the data structures were now symbols, in the sense of our physical symbol system: patterns that designated, that had referents. Lists held addresses which permitted access to other lists—thus the notion of list structures. That this was a new view was demonstrated to us many times in the early days of list processing when colleagues would ask where the data were—that is, which list finally held the collection of bits that were the content of the system. They found it strange that there were no such bits, there were only symbols that designated yet other symbol structures.

List processing is simultaneously three things in the development of computer science. (1) It is the creation of a genuine dynamic memory structure in a machine that had heretofore been perceived as having fixed structure. It added to our ensemble of operations those that built and modified structure in addition to those that replaced and changed content. (2) It was an early demonstration of the basic abstraction that a computer consists of a set of data types and a set of operations proper to these data types, so that a computational system should employ whatever data types are appropriate to the application, independent of the underlying machine. (3) List-processing produced a model of designation, thus defining symbol manipulation in the sense in which we use this concept in computer science today.

As often occurs, the practice of the time already anticipated all the elements of list processing: addresses are obviously used to gain access, the drum machines used linked programs (so called one-plus-one addressing), and so on. But the conception of list processing as an abstraction created a new world in which designation and dynamic symbolic structure were the defining characteristics. The embedding of the early list-processing systems in languages (the IPLs, LISP) is often decried as having been a barrier to the diffusion of list-processing techniques throughout programming practice; but it was the vehicle that held the abstraction together.

LISP. One more step is worth noting: McCarthy's creation of LISP in 1959-60 (McCarthy, 1960). It completed the act of abstraction, lifting list structures out of their embedding in concrete machines, creating a new formal system with S-expressions, which could be shown to be equivalent to the other universal schemes of computation.

CONCLUSION. That the concept of a designating symbol and symbol manipulation does not emerge until the mid-fifties does not mean that the earlier steps were either inessential or less important. The total concept is the join of computability, physical realizability (and by multiple technologies), universality, the symbolic representation of processes (that is, interpretability), and, finally, symbolic structure and designation. Each of the steps provided an essential part of the whole.

The first step in this chain, authored by Turing, is theoretically motivated, but the others all have deep empirical roots. We have been led by the evolution of the computer itself.

The stored-program principle arose out of the experience with Eniac. List processing arose out of the attempt to construct intelligent programs. It took its cue from the emergence of random-access memories, which provided a clear physical realization of a designating symbol in the address. LISP arose out of the evolving experience with list processing.

3.1.4   The evidence

We come now to the evidence for the hypothesis that physical symbol systems are capable of intelligent action, and that general intelligent action calls for a physical symbol system. The hypothesis is an empirical generalization and not a theorem. We know of no way of demonstrating the connection between symbol systems and intelligence on purely logical grounds. Lacking such a demonstration, we must look at the facts. Our central aim, however, is not to review the evidence in detail, but to use the example before us to illustrate the proposition that computer science is a field of empirical inquiry. Hence, we will only indicate what kinds of evidence there are, and the general nature of the testing process.

The notion of a physical symbol system had taken essentially its present form by the middle of the 1950's, and one can date from that time the growth of artificial intelligence as a coherent subfield of computer science. The twenty years of work since then has seen a continuous accumulation of empirical evidence of two main varieties. The first addresses itself to the *sufficiency* of physical symbol systems for producing intelligence, attempting to construct and test specific systems that have such a capability. The second kind of evidence addresses itself to the *necessity* of having a physical symbol system wherever intelligence is exhibited. It starts with man, the intelligent system best known to us, and attempts to discover whether his cognitive activity can be explained as the working of a physical symbol system. There are other forms of evidence, which we will comment upon briefly later, but these two are the important ones. We will consider them in turn. The first is generally called artificial intelligence, the second, research in cognitive psychology.

CONSTRUCTING INTELLIGENT SYSTEMS. The basic paradigm for the initial testing of the germ theory of disease was: identify a disease, then look for the germ. An analogous paradigm has inspired much of the research in artificial intelligence: identify a task domain calling for intelligence, then construct a program for a digital computer that can handle tasks in that domain. The easy and well-structured tasks were looked at first: puzzles and games, operations-research problems of scheduling and allocating resources, simple induction tasks. Scores, if not hundreds, of programs of these kinds have by now been constructed, each capable of some measure of intelligent action in the appropriate domain.

Of course intelligence is not an all-or-none matter, and there has been steady progress toward higher levels of performance in specific domains, as well as toward widening the range of those domains. Early chess programs, for example, were deemed successful if they could play a game legally and with some indication of purpose; a little later, they reached the level of human beginners; within ten or fifteen years, they began to compete with serious amateurs. Progress has been slow (and the total programming effort invested small) but continuous, and the paradigm of construct-and-test proceeds in a regular cycle—the whole research activity mimicking at the macroscopic level the basic generate-and-test cycle of many of the AI programs.

There is a steadily widening area within which intelligent action is attainable. For the original tasks, research has extended to building systems that handle and understand natural language in a variety of ways, systems for interpreting visual scenes, systems for hand-eye coordination, systems that design, systems that write computer programs, systems for speech understanding—the list is, if not endless, at least very long. If there are limits beyond which the hypothesis will not carry us, they have not yet become apparent. Up to the present, the rate of progress has been governed mainly by the rather modest quantity of scientific resources that have been applied and the inevitable requirement of a substantial system-building effort for each new major undertaking.

Much more has been going on, of course, than simply a piling up of examples of intelligent systems adapted to specific task domains. It would be surprising and unappealing if it turned out that the AI programs performing these diverse tasks had nothing in common beyond their being instances of physical symbol systems. Hence, there has been great interest in searching for mechanisms possessed of generality, and for common components among programs performing a variety of tasks. This search carries the theory beyond the initial symbol-system hypothesis to a more complete characterization of the particular kinds of symbol systems that are effective in artificial intelligence. In the second section of this paper, we will discuss one example of an hypothesis at this second level of specificity: the heuristic-search hypothesis.

The search for generality spawned a series of programs designed to separate out general problem-solving mechanisms from the requirements of particular task domains. The General Problem Solver (GPS) was perhaps the first of these; while among its descendants are such contemporary systems as PLANNER and CONNIVER. The search for common components has led to generalized schemes of representations for goals and plans, methods for constructing discrimination nets, procedures for the control of tree-search, pattern-matching mechanisms, and language-parsing systems. Experiments are at present under way to find convenient devices for representing sequences of time and tense, movement, causality, and the like. More and more, it becomes possible to assemble large intelligent systems in a modular way from such basic components.

We can gain some perspective on what is going on by turning, again, to the analogy of the germ theory. If the first burst of research stimulated by that theory consisted largely in finding the germ to go with each disease, subsequent effort turned to learning what a germ was—to building on the basic qualitative law a new level of structure. In artificial intelligence, an initial burst of activity aimed at building intelligent programs for a wide variety of almost randomly selected tasks is giving way to more sharply targeted research aimed at understanding the common mechanisms of such systems.

THE MODELING OF HUMAN SYMBOLIC BEHAVIOR. The symbol-system hypothesis implies that the symbolic behavior of man arises because he has the characteristics of a physical symbol system. Hence, the results of efforts to model human behavior with symbol systems become an important part of the evidence for the hypothesis, and research in artificial intelligence goes on in close collaboration with research in information-processing psychology, as it is usually called.

The search for explanations of man's intelligent behavior in terms of symbol systems has had a large measure of success over the past twenty years—to the point where information-processing theory is the leading contemporary point of view in cognitive psychology. Especially in the areas of problem solving, concept attainment, and long-term memory, symbol-manipulation models now dominate the scene.

Research in information-processing psychology involves two main kinds of empirical activity. The first is the conduct of observations and experiments on human behavior in tasks requiring intelligence. The second, very similar to the parallel activity in artificial intelligence, is the programming of symbol systems to model the observed human behavior. The psychological observations and experiments lead to the formulation of hypotheses about the symbolic processes the subjects are using, and these are an important source of the ideas that go into the construction of the programs. Thus many of the ideas for the basic mechanisms of GPS were derived from careful analysis of the protocols that human subjects produced while thinking aloud during the performance of a problem-solving task.

The empirical character of computer science is nowhere more evident than in this alliance with psychology. Not only are psychological experiments required to test the veridicality of the simulation models as explanations of the human behavior, but out of the experiments come new ideas for the design and construction of physical symbol systems.

OTHER EVIDENCE. The principal body of evidence for the symbol-system hypothesis that we have not considered is negative evidence: the absence of specific competing hypotheses as to how intelligent activity might be accomplished—whether by man or by machine. Most attempts to build such hypotheses have taken place within the field of psychology. Here we have had a continuum of theories from the points of view usually labeled "behaviorism" to those usually labeled "Gestalt theory". Neither of these points of view stands as a real competitor to the symbol-system hypothesis, and for two reasons. First, neither behaviorism nor Gestalt theory has demonstrated, or even shown how to demonstrate, that the explanatory mechanisms it postulates are sufficient to account for intelligent behavior in complex tasks. Second, neither theory has been formulated with anything like the specificity of artificial programs. As a matter of fact, the alternative theories are so vague that it is not terribly difficult to give them information-processing interpretations, and thereby assimilate them to the symbol-system hypothesis.

3.1.5 Conclusion

We have tried to use the example of the Physical Symbol System Hypothesis to illustrate concretely that computer science is a scientific enterprise in the usual meaning of that term: it develops scientific hypotheses which it then seeks to verify by empirical inquiry. We had a second reason, however, for choosing this particular example to illustrate our point. The Physical Symbol System Hypothesis is itself a substantial scientific hypothesis of the kind that we earlier dubbed "laws of qualitative structure". It represents an important discovery of computer science, which if borne out by the empirical evidence, as in fact appears to be occurring, will have major continuing impact on the field.

We turn now to a second example, the role of search in intelligence. This topic, and the particular hypothesis about it that we shall examine, have also played a central role in computer science, in general, and artificial intelligence, in particular.

3.2 Heuristic search

Knowing that physical symbol systems provide the matrix for intelligent action does not tell us how they accomplish this. Our second example of a law of qualitative structure in computer science addresses this latter question, asserting that symbol systems solve problems by using the processes of heuristic search. This generalization, like the previous one, rests on empirical evidence, and has not been derived formally from other premises. We shall see in a moment, however, that it does have some logical connection with the symbol-system hypothesis, and perhaps we can expect to formalize the connection at some time in the future. Until that time arrives, our story must again be one of empirical inquiry.

We will describe what is known about heuristic search and review the empirical findings that show how it enables action to be intelligent. We begin by stating this law of qualitative structure, the heuristic-search hypothesis.

HEURISTIC-SEARCH HYPOTHESIS. The solutions to problems are represented as symbol structures. A physical symbol system exercises its intelligence in problem solving by search—that is, by generating and progressively modifying symbol structures until it produces a solution structure.

Physical symbol systems must use heuristic search to solve problems because such systems have limited processing resources; in a finite number of steps, and over a finite interval of time, they can execute only a finite number of processes. Of course, that is not a very strong limitation, for all universal Turing machines suffer from it. We intend the limitation, however, in a stronger sense: we mean *practically* limited. We can conceive of systems that are not limited in a practical way but are capable, for example, of searching in parallel the nodes of an exponentially expanding tree at a constant rate for each unit advance in depth. We will not be concerned here with such systems, but with systems whose computing resources are scarce relative to the complexity of the situations with which they are confronted. The restriction will not exclude any real symbol systems, in computer or man, in the context of real tasks. The fact of limited resources allows us, for most purposes, to view a symbol system as though it were a serial, one-process-at-a-time device. If it can accomplish only a small amount of processing in any short time interval, then we might as well regard it as doing things one at a time. Thus "limited resource symbol system" and "serial symbol system" are practically synonymous. The problem of allocating a scarce resource from moment to moment can usually be treated, if the moment is short enough, as a problem of scheduling a serial machine.

3.2.1   Problem solving

Since ability to solve problems is generally taken as a prime indicator that a system has intelligence, it is natural that much of the history of artificial intelligence is taken up with attempts to build and understand problem-solving systems. Problem solving has been discussed by philosophers and psychologists for two millennia, in discourses dense with a feeling of mystery. If you think there is nothing problematic or mysterious about a symbol system solving problems, you are a child of today, whose views have been formed since mid-century. Plato (and, by his account, Socrates) found difficulty understanding even how problems could be *entertained*, much less how they could be solved. Let us remind you of how he posed the conundrum in the *Meno*:

Meno: And how will you inquire, Socrates, into that which you know not? What will you put forth as the subject of inquiry? And if you find what you want, how will you ever know that this is what you did not know?

To deal with this puzzle, Plato invented his famous theory of recollection: when you think you are discovering or learning something, you are really just recalling what you already knew in a previous existence. If you find this explanation preposterous, there is a much simpler one available today, based upon our understanding of symbol systems. An approximate statement of it is:

> To state a problem is to designate (1) a *test* for a class of symbol structures (solutions of the problem), and (2) a *generator* of symbol structures (potential solutions). To solve a problem is to generate a structure, using (2), that satisfies the test of (1).

We have a problem if we know what we want to do (the test), and if we don't know immediately how to do it (our generator does not immediately produce a symbol structure satisfying the test). A symbol system can state and solve problems (sometimes) because it can generate and test.

If that is all there is to problem solving, why not simply generate at once an expression that satisfies the test? This is, in fact, what we do when we wish and dream. "If wishes were horses, beggars might ride." But outside the world of dreams, it isn't possible. To know how we would test something, once constructed, does not mean that we know how to construct it—that we have any generator for doing so.

For example, it is well known what it means to "solve" the problem of playing winning chess. A simple test exists for noticing winning positions, the test for checkmate of the enemy king. In the world of dreams one simply generates a strategy that leads to checkmate for all counter strategies of the opponent. Alas, no generator that will do this is known to existing symbol systems (man or machine). Instead, good moves in chess are sought by generating various alternatives, and painstakingly evaluating them with the use of approximate, and often erroneous, measures that are supposed to indicate the likelihood that a particular line of play is on the route to a winning position. Move generators there are; winning-move generators there are not.

Before there can be a move generator for a problem, there must be a problem space: a space of symbol structures in which problem situations, including the initial and goal situations, can be represented. Move generators are processes for modifying one situation in the problem space into another. The basic characteristics of physical symbol systems guarantee that they can represent problem spaces and that they possess move generators. How, in any concrete situation they synthesize a problem space and move generators appropriate to that situation is a question that is still very much on the frontier of artificial intelligence research.

The task that a symbol system is faced with, then, when it is presented with a problem and a problem space, is to use its limited processing resources to generate possible solutions, one after another until if finds one that satisfies the problem-defining test. If the system had some control over the order in which potential solutions were generated, then it would be desirable to arrange this order of generation so that actual solutions would have a high likelihood of appearing early. A symbol system would exhibit intelligence to the extent that it succeeded in doing this. Intelligence for a system with limited processing resources consists in making wise choices of what to do next.

3.2.2 Search in problem solving

During the first decade or so of artificial-intelligence research, the study of problem solving was almost synonymous with the study of search processes. From our characterization of problems and problem solving, it is easy to see why this was so. In fact, it might be asked whether it could be otherwise. But before we try to answer that question, we must explore further the nature of search processes as it revealed itself during that decade of activity.

EXTRACTING INFORMATION FROM THE PROBLEM SPACE. Consider a set of symbol structures, some small subset of which are solutions to a given problem. Suppose, further, that the solutions are distributed randomly through the entire set. By this we mean that no information exists that would enable any search generator to perform better than a random search. Then no symbol system could exhibit more intelligence (or less intelligence) than any other in solving the problem, although one might experience better luck than another.

A condition, then, for the appearance of intelligence is that the distribution of solutions be not entirely random, that the space of symbol structures exhibit at least some degree of order and pattern. A second condition is that the pattern in the space of symbol structures be more or less detectable. A third condition is that the generator of potential solutions be able to behave differentially, depending on what pattern is detected. There must be information in the problem space, and the symbol system must be capable of extracting and using it. Let us look first at a very simple example, where the intelligence is easy to come by.

Consider the problem of solving a simple algebraic equation:

$$ax + b = cx + d$$

The test defines a solution as any expression of the form, $x = e$, such that $ae + b = ce + d$. Now, one could use as generator any process that would produce numbers which could then be tested by substituting in the latter equation. We would not call this an intelligent generator.

Alternatively, one could use generators that would make use of the fact that the original equation can be modified—by adding or subtracting equal quantities from both sides, or multiplying or dividing both sides by the same quantity—without changing its solutions. But, of course, we can obtain even more information to guide the generator by comparing the original expression with the form of the solution, and making precisely those changes in the equation that leave its solution unchanged, while at the same time bringing it into the desired form. Such a generator could notice that there was an unwanted cx on the right-hand side of the original equation, subtract it from both sides, and collect terms again.

It could then notice that there was an unwanted b on the left-hand side and subtract that. Finally, it could get rid of the unwanted coefficient $(a-c)$ on the left-hand side by dividing.

Thus, by this procedure, which now exhibits considerable intelligence, the generator produces successive symbol structures, each obtained by modifying the previous one; and the modifications are aimed at reducing the differences between the form of the input structure and the form of the test expression, while maintaining the other conditions for a solution.

This simple example already illustrates many of the main mechanisms that are used by symbol systems for intelligent problem solving. First, each successive expression is not generated independently, but is produced by modifying one produced previously. Second, the modifications are not haphazard, but depend upon two kinds of information. They depend on information that is constant over this whole class of algebra problems, and that is built into the structure of the generator itself: all modifications of expressions must leave the equation's solution unchanged. They also depend on information that changes at each step: detection of the differences in form that remain between the current expression and the desired expression. In effect, the generator incorporates some of the tests the solution must satisfy, so that expressions that don't meet these tests will never be generated. Using the first kind of information guarantees that only a tiny subset of all possible expressions is actually generated, but without losing the solution expression from this subset. Using the second kind of information arrives at the desired solution by a succession of approximations, employing a simple form of means-ends analysis to give direction to the search.

There is no mystery where the information that guided the search came from. We need not follow Plato in endowing the symbol system with a previous existence in which it already knew the solution. A moderately sophisticated generate-and-test system did the trick without invoking reincarnation.

SEARCH TREES. The simple algebra problem may seem an unusual, even pathological, example of search. It is certainly not trial-and-error search, for though there were a few trials, there was no error. We are more accustomed to thinking of problem-solving search as generating lushly branching trees of partial solution possibilities which may grow to thousands, or even millions, of branches, before they yield a solution. Thus, if from each expression it produces, the generator creates B new branches, then the tree will grow as B^D, where D is its depth. The tree grown for the algebra problem had the peculiarity that its branchiness, B, equaled unity.

Programs that play chess typically grow broad search trees, amounting in some cases to a million branches or more. Although this example will serve to illustrate our points about tree search, we should note that the purpose of search in chess is not to generate proposed solutions, but to evaluate (test) them. One line of research into gameplaying programs has been centrally concerned with improving the representation of the chess board, and the processes for making moves on it, so as to speed up search and make it possible to search larger trees. The rationale for this direction, of course, is that the deeper the dynamic search, the more accurate should be the evaluations at the end of it. On the other hand, there is good empirical evidence that the strongest human players, grandmasters, seldom explore trees of more than one hundred branches. This economy is achieved not so much by searching less deeply than do chess-playing programs, but by branching very sparsely and selectively at each node. This is only possible, without causing a deterioration of the evaluations, by having more of the selectivity built into the generator itself, so that it is able to select for generation only those branches which are very likely to yield important relevant information about the position.

The somewhat paradoxical-sounding conclusion to which this discussion leads is that search—successive generation of potential solution structures—is a fundamental aspect of a symbol system's exercise of intelligence in problem solving but that the amount of search is not a measure of the amount of intelligence being exhibited. What makes a problem a problem is not that a large amount of search is required for its solution, but that a large amount *would* be required if a requisite level of intelligence were not applied. When the symbolic system that is endeavoring to solve a problem knows enough about what to do, it simply proceeds directly towards its goal; but whenever its knowledge becomes inadequate, when it enters terra incognita, it is faced with the threat of going through large amounts of search before it finds its way again.

The potential for the exponential explosion of the search tree that is present in every scheme for generating problem solutions warns us against depending on the brute force of computers—even the biggest and fastest computers—as a compensation for the ignorance and unselectivity of their generators. The hope is still periodically ignited in some human breasts that a computer can be found that is fast enough, and that can be programmed cleverly enough, to play good chess by brute-force search. There is nothing known in theory about the game of chess that rules out this possibility. But empirical studies on the management of search in sizable trees with only modest results make this a much less promising direction than it was when chess was first chosen as an appropriate task for artificial intelligence. We must regard this as one of the important empirical findings of research with chess programs.

THE FORMS OF INTELLIGENCE. The task of intelligence, then, is to avert the ever-present threat of the exponential explosion of search. How can this be accomplished? The first route, already illustrated by the algebra example and by chess programs that only generate "plausible" moves for further analysis, is to build selectivity into the generator: to generate only structures that show promise of being solutions or of being along the path toward solutions. The usual consequence of doing this is to decrease the rate of branching, not to prevent it entirely. Ultimate exponential explosion is not avoided—save in exceptionally highly structured situations like the algebra example—but only postponed.

Hence, an intelligent system generally needs to supplement the selectivity of its solution generator with other information-using techniques to guide search.

Twenty years of experience with managing tree search in a variety of task environments has produced a small kit of general techniques which is part of the equipment of every researcher in artificial intelligence today. Since these techniques have been described in general works like that of Nilsson (1971), they can be summarized very briefly here.

In serial heuristic search, the basic question always is: What shall be done next? In tree search, that question, in turn, has two components: (1) From what node in the tree shall we search next, and (2) What direction shall we take from that node? Information helpful in answering the first question may be interpreted as measuring the relative distance of different nodes from the goal. Best-first search calls for searching next from the node that appears closest to the goal. Information helpful in answering the second question—in what direction to search—is often obtained, as in the algebra example, by detecting specific differences between the current nodal structure and the goal structure described by the test of a solution, and selecting actions that are relevant to reducing these particular kinds of differences. This is the technique known as means-ends analysis, which plays a central role in the structure of the General Problem Solver.

The importance of empirical studies as a source of general ideas in AI research can be demonstrated clearly by tracing the history, through large numbers of problem-solving programs, of these two central ideas: best-first search and means-ends analysis. Rudiments of best-first search were already present, though unnamed, in the Logic Theorist in 1955. The General Problem Solver, embodying means-ends analysis, appeared about 1957—but combined it with modified depth-first search rather than best-first search. Chess programs were generally wedded, for reasons of economy of memory, to depth-first search, supplemented after about 1958 by the powerful alpha-beta pruning procedure. Each of these techniques appears to have been reinvented a number of times, and it is hard to find general, task-independent, theoretical discussions of problem-solving in terms of these concepts until the middle or late 1960's. The amount of formal buttressing they have received from mathematical theory is still minuscule: some theorems about the reduction in search that can be secured from using the alpha-beta heuristic, a couple of theorems (reviewed by Nilsson, 1971) about shortest-path search, and some very recent theorems on best-first search with a probabilistic evaluation function.

"WEAK" AND "STRONG" METHODS. The techniques we have been discussing are dedicated to the control of exponential expansion rather than its prevention. For this reason, they have been properly called "weak methods"—methods to be used when the symbol system's knowledge or the amount of structure actually contained in the problem space are inadequate to permit search to be avoided entirely. It is instructive to contrast a highly-structured situation, which can be formulated, say, as a linear-programming problem, with

the less-structured situations of combinatorial problems like the traveling-salesman problem or scheduling problems. ("Less structured" here refers to the insufficiency or nonexistence of relevant theory about the structure of the problem space.)

In solving linear-programming problems, a substantial amount of computation may be
required, but the search does not branch. Every step is a step along the way to a solution. In
solving combinatorial problems or in proving theorems, tree search can seldom be avoided,
and success depends on heuristic search methods of the sort we have been describing.

Not all streams of AI problem-solving research have followed the path we have been
outlining. An example of a somewhat different point is provided by the work on theorem-
proving systems. Here, ideas imported from mathematics and logic have had a strong
influence on the direction of inquiry. For example, the use of heuristics was resisted when
properties of completeness could not be proved (a bit ironic, since most interesting mathematical systems are known to be undecidable). Since completeness can seldom be proved
for best-first search heuristics, or for many kinds of selective generators, the effect of this
requirement was rather inhibiting. When theorem-proving programs were continually in-
capacitated by the combinatorial explosion of their search trees, thought began to be given
to selective heuristics, which in many cases proved to be analogues of heuristics used in
general problem-solving programs. The set-of-support heuristic, for example, is a form of
working backward, adapted to the resolution theorem-proving environment.

A SUMMARY OF THE EXPERIENCE. We have now described the workings of our second
law of qualitative structure, which asserts that physical symbol systems solve problems by
means of heuristic search. Beyond that, we have examined some subsidiary characteristics
of heuristic search, in particular the threat that it always faces of exponential explosion
of the search tree, and some of the means it uses to avert that threat. Opinions differ as
to how effective heuristic search has been as a problem-solving mechanism—the opinions
depending on what task domains are considered and what criterion of adequacy is adopted.
Success can be guaranteed by setting aspiration levels low—or failure by setting them
high. The evidence might be summed up about as follows: Few programs are solving
problems at "expert" professional levels. Samuel's checker program and Feigenbaum and
Lederberg's DENDRAL are perhaps the best-known exceptions, but one could point also
to a number of heuristic search programs for such operations-research problem domains
as scheduling and integer programming. In a number of domains, programs perform at
the level of competent amateurs: chess, some theorem-proving domains, many kinds of
games and puzzles. Human levels have not yet been nearly reached by programs that have
a complex perceptual "front end": visual-scene recognizers, speech understanders, robots
that have to maneuver in real space and time. Nevertheless, impressive progress has been
made, and a large body of experience assembled about these difficult tasks.

We do not have deep theoretical explanations for the particular pattern of performance
that has emerged. On empirical grounds, however, we might draw two conclusions. First,

from what has been learned about human expert performance in tasks like chess, it is likely that any system capable of matching that performance will have to have access, in its memories, to very large stores of semantic information. Second, some part of the human superiority in tasks with a large perceptual component can be attributed to the special-purpose built-in parallel-processing structure of the human eye and ear.

In any case, the quality of performance must necessarily depend on the characteristics both of the problem domains and of the symbol systems used to tackle them. For most real-life domains in which we are interested, the domain structure has so far not proved sufficiently simple to yield theorems about complexity, or to tell us, other than empiri-cally, how large real-world problems are in relation to the abilities of our symbol systems to solve them. That situation may change, but until it does, we must rely upon empirical explorations, using the best problem solvers we know how to build, as a principal source of knowledge about the magnitude and characteristics of problem difficulty. Even in highly structured areas like linear programming, theory has been much more useful in strength-ening the heuristics that underlie the most powerful solution algorithms than in providing a deep analysis of complexity.

3.2.3   Intelligence without much search

Our analysis of intelligence equated it with ability to extract and use information about the structure of the problem space, so as to enable a problem solution to be generated as quickly and directly as possible. New directions for improving the problem-solving capabilities of symbol systems can be equated, then, with new ways of extracting and using information. At least three such ways can be identified.

NONLOCAL USE OF INFORMATION. First, it has been noted by several investigators that information gathered in the course of tree search is usually only used *locally*, to help make decisions at the specific node where the information was generated. Information about a chess position, obtained by dynamic analysis of a subtree of continuations, is usually used to evaluate just that position, not to evaluate other positions that may contain many of the same features. Hence, the same facts have to be rediscovered repeatedly at different nodes of the search tree. Simply to take the information out of the context in which it arose and use it generally does not solve the problem, for the information may be valid only in a limited range of contexts. In recent years, a few exploratory efforts have been made to transport information from its context of origin to other appropriate contexts. While it is still too early to evaluate the power of this idea, or even exactly how it is to be achieved, it shows considerable promise. An important line of investigation that Berliner (1975) has been pursuing is to use causal analysis to determine the range over which a particular piece of information is valid. Thus if a weakness in a chess position can be traced back to the move that made it, then the same weakness can be expected in other positions descendant from the same move.

The HEARSAY speech understanding system has taken another approach to making information globally available. That system seeks to recognize speech strings by pursuing a parallel search at a number of different levels: phonemic, lexical, syntactic, and semantic. As each of these searches provides and evaluates hypotheses, it supplies the information it has gained to a common "blackboard" that can be read by all the sources. This shared information can be used, for example, to eliminate hypotheses, or even whole classes of hypotheses, that would otherwise have to be searched by one of the processes. Thus increasing our ability to use tree-search information nonlocally offers promise for raising the intelligence of problem-solving systems.

SEMANTIC RECOGNITION SYSTEMS. A second active possibility for raising intelligence is to supply the symbol system with a rich body of semantic information about the task domain it is dealing with. For example, empirical research on the skill of chess masters shows that a major source of the master's skill is stored information that enables him to recognize a large number of specific features and patterns of features on a chess board, and information that uses this recognition to propose actions appropriate to the features recognized. This general idea has, of course, been incorporated in chess programs almost from the beginning. What is new is the realization of the number of such patterns and associated information that may have to be stored for master-level play: something on the order of 50,000.

The possibility of substituting recognition for search arises because a particular, and especially a rare, pattern can contain an enormous amount of information, provided that it is closely linked to the structure of the problem space. When that structure is "irregular", and not subject to simple mathematical description, then knowledge of a large number of relevant patterns may be the key to intelligent behavior. Whether this is so in any particular task domain is a question more easily settled by empirical investigation than by theory. Our experience with symbol systems richly endowed with semantic information and pattern-recognizing capabilities for accessing it is still extremely limited.

The discussion above refers specifically to semantic information associated with a recognition system. Of course, there is also a whole large area of AI research on semantic information processing and the organization of semantic memories that falls outside the scope of the topics we are discussing in this paper.

SELECTING APPROPRIATE REPRESENTATIONS. A third line of inquiry is concerned with the possibility that search can be reduced or avoided by selecting an appropriate problem space. A standard example that illustrates this possibility dramatically is the mutilated-checkerboard problem. A standard 64-square checker board can be covered exactly with 32 tiles, each a 1×2 rectangle covering exactly two squares. Suppose, now, that we cut off squares at two diagonally opposite corners of the checkerboard, leaving a total of 62 squares. Can this mutilated board be covered exactly with 31 tiles? With (literally) heavenly patience, the impossibility of achieving such a covering can be demonstrated by trying all possible arrangements. The alternative, for those with less patience and more intelligence, is to observe that the two diagonally opposite corners of a checkerboard are of the same color. Hence, the mutilated checkerboard has two fewer squares of one color than of the other. But each tile covers one square of one color and one square of the other, and any set of tiles must cover the same number of squares of each color. Hence, there is no solution. How can a symbol system discover this simple inductive argument as an alternative to a hopeless attempt to solve the problem by search among all possible coverings? We would award a system that found the solution high marks for intelligence.

Perhaps, however, in posing this problem we are not escaping from search processes. We have simply displaced the search from a space of possible problems solutions to a space of possible representations. In any event, the whole process of moving from one representation to another, and of discovering and evaluating representations, is largely unexplored territory in the domain of problem-solving research. The laws of qualitative structure governing representations remain to be discovered. The search for them is almost sure to receive considerable attention in the coming decade.

3.2.4   Conclusion

That is our account of symbol systems and intelligence. It has been a long road from Plato's *Meno* to the present, but it is perhaps encouraging that most of the progress along that road has been made since the turn of the twentieth century, and a large fraction of it since the mid-point of the century. Thought was still wholly intangible and ineffable until modern formal logic interpreted it as the manipulation of formal tokens. And it seemed still to inhabit mainly the heaven of Platonic ideas, or the equally obscure spaces of the human mind, until computers taught us how symbols could be processed by machines. A. M. Turing made his great contributions at the mid-century crossroads of these developments that led from modern logic to the computer.

PHYSICAL SYMBOL SYSTEMS. The study of logic and computers has revealed to us that intelligence resides in physical-symbol systems. This is computer science's most basic law of qualitative structure.

Symbol systems are collections of patterns and processes, the latter being capable of producing, destroying, and modifying the former. The most important properties of patterns is that they can designate objects, processes, or other patterns, and that when they designate processes, they can be interpreted. Interpretation means carrying out the designated process. The two most significant classes of symbol systems with which we are acquainted are human beings and computers.

Our present understanding of symbol systems grew, as indicated earlier, through a sequence of stages. Formal logic familiarized us with symbols, treated syntactically, as the raw material of thought, and with the idea of manipulating them according to carefully defined formal processes. The Turing machine made the syntactic processing of symbols truly machine-like, and affirmed the potential universality of strictly defined symbol systems. The stored-program concept for computers reaffirmed the interpretability of symbols, already implicit in the Turing machine. List processing brought to the forefront the denotational capacities of symbols and defined symbol processing in ways that allowed independence from the fixed structure of the underlying physical machine. By 1956 all of these concepts were available, together with hardware for implementing them. The study of the intelligence of symbol systems, the subject of artificial intelligence, could begin.

HEURISTIC SEARCH. A second law of qualitative structure of AI is that symbol systems solve problems by generating potential solutions and testing them—that is, by searching. Solutions are usually sought by creating symbolic expressions and modifying them sequentially until they satisfy the conditions for a solution. Hence, symbol systems solve problems by searching. Since they have finite resources, the search cannot be carried out all at once, but must be sequential. It leaves behind it either a single path from starting point to goal or, if correction and backup are necessary, a whole tree of such paths.

Symbol systems cannot appear intelligent when they are surrounded by pure chaos. They exercise intelligence by extracting information from a problem domain and using that information to guide their search, avoiding wrong turns and circuitous by-paths. The problem domain must contain information—that is, some degree of order and structure—for the method to work. The paradox of the *Meno* is solved by the observation that information may be remembered, but new information may also be extracted from the domain that the symbols designate. In both cases, the ultimate source of the information is the task domain.

THE EMPIRICAL BASE. Research on artificial intelligence is concerned with how symbol systems must be organized in order to behave intelligently. Twenty years of work in the area has accumulated a considerable body of knowledge, enough to fill several books (it already has), and most of it in the form of rather concrete experience about the behavior of specific classes of symbol systems in specific task domains. Out of this experience, however, there have also emerged some generalizations, cutting across task domains and systems, about the general characteristics of intelligence and its methods of implementation.

We have tried to state some of these generalizations here. They are mostly qualitative rather than mathematical. They have more the flavor of geology or evolutionary biology than the flavor of theoretical physics. They are sufficiently strong to enable us today to design and build moderately intelligent systems for a considerable range of task domains, as well as to gain a rather deep understanding of how human intelligence works in many situations.

WHAT NEXT? In our account we have mentioned open questions as well as settled ones; there are many of both. We see no abatement of the excitement of exploration that has surrounded this field over the past quarter century. Two resource limits will determine the rate of progress over the next such period. One is the amount of computing power that will be available. The second, and probably the more important, is the number of talented young computer scientists who will be attracted to this area of research as the most challenging they can tackle.

A. M. Turing concluded his famous paper "Computing Machinery and Intelligence" [chapter 6 of this volume] with the words:

> We can only see a short distance ahead, but we can see plenty there that needs to be done.

Many of the things Turing saw in 1950 that needed to be done have been done, but the agenda is as full as ever. Perhaps we read too much into his simple statement above, but we like to think that in it Turing recognized the fundamental truth that all computer scientists instinctively know. For all physical symbol systems, condemned as we are to serial search of the problem environment, the critical question is always: What to do next?

Notes for Chapter 3

1. *Editor's note*: These senses of the terms 'designation' and 'interpretation', and hence also of 'symbol', are specific to computer science; they concern only relationships and processes that occur *within* a computer. In linguistics and philosophy, by contrast, these terms would usually be explained in terms of relationships *between* an intelligent system (or what's inside of it) and its environment. Most of the essays in the present volume use the terms in this latter sense.

Vision

4

David Marr
1982

Understanding Complex Information-Processing Systems (*Vision*, Section 1.2)

Almost never can a complex system of any kind be understood as a simple extrapolation from the properties of its elementary components. Consider, for example, some gas in a bottle. A description of thermodynamic effects—temperature, pressure, density and the relationships among these factors—is not formulated by using a large set of equations, one for each of the particles involved. Such effects are described at their own level, that of an enormous collection of particles; the effort is to show that in principle the microscopic and macroscopic descriptions are consistent with one another. If one hopes to achieve a full understanding of a system as complicated as a nervous system, a developing embryo, a set of metabolic pathways, a bottle of gas, or even a large computer program, then one must be prepared to contemplate different kinds of explanation at different levels of description that are linked, at least in principle, into a cohesive whole, even if linking the levels in complete detail is impractical. For the specific case of a system that solves an information-processing problem, there are in addition the twin strands of process and representation, and both these ideas need some discussion.

Representation and Description

A *representation* is a formal system for making explicit certain entities or types of information, together with a specification of how the system does this. And I shall call the result of using a representation to describe a given entity a *description* of the entity in that representation (Marr and Wishihara, 1978).

For example, the Arabic, Roman, and binary numeral systems are all formal systems for representing numbers. The Arabic representation consists of a string of symbols drawn from the set (0, 1, 2, 3, 4, 5, 6, 7, 8, 9), and the rule for constructing the description of a particular integer n is that one decomposes n into a sum of multiples of powers of 10 and unites these multiples into a string with the largest powers on the left and the smallest on the right. Thus, thirty-seven equals $3 \times 10^1 + 7 \times 10^0$, which becomes 37, the Arabic numeral system's description of the number. What this description makes explicit is the number's decomposition into powers of 10. The binary numeral system's description of the number thirty-seven is 100101, and this description makes explicit the number's decomposition into powers of 2. In the Roman numeral system, thirty-seven is represented as XXXVII.

This definition of a representation is quite general. For example, a representation for shape would be a formal scheme for describing some aspects of shape, together with rules that specify how the scheme is applied to any particular shape. A musical score provides a way of representing a symphony; the alphabet allows the construction of a written representation of words; and so forth. The phrase "formal scheme" is critical to the definition, but the reader should not be frightened by it. The reason is simply that we are dealing with information-processing machines, and the way such machines work is by using symbols to stand for things—to represent things, in our terminology. To say that something is a formal scheme means only that it is a set of symbols with rules for putting them together—no more and no less.

A representation, therefore, is not a foreign idea at all—we all use representations all the time. However, the notion that one can capture some aspect of reality by making a description of it using a symbol and that to do so can be useful seems to me a fascinating and powerful idea. But even the simple examples we have discussed introduce some rather general and important issues that arise whenever one chooses to use one particular representation. For example, if one chooses the Arabic numeral representation, it is easy to discover whether a number is a power of 10 but difficult to discover whether it is a power of 2. If one chooses the binary representation, the situation is reversed. Thus, there is a trade-off; any particular representation makes certain information explicit at the expense of information that is pushed into the background and may be quite hard to recover.

This issue is important, because how information is represented can greatly affect how easy it is to do different things with it. This is evident even from our numbers example: It is easy to add, to subtract, and even to multiply if the Arabic or binary representations are used, but it is not at all easy to do these things—especially multiplication—with Roman numerals. This is a key reason why the Roman culture failed to develop mathematics in the way the earlier Arabic cultures had.

An analogous problem faces computer engineers today. Electronic technology is much more suited to a binary number system than to the conventional base 10 system, yet humans supply their data and require the results in base 10. The design decision facing the engineer, therefore, is, Should one pay the cost of conversion into base 2, carry out the arithmetic in a binary representation, and then convert back into decimal numbers on output; or should one sacrifice efficiency of circuitry to carry out operations directly in a decimal representation? On the whole, business computers and pocket calculators take the second approach, and general purpose computers take the first. But even though one is not restricted to using just one representation system for a given type of information, the choice of which to use is important and cannot be taken lightly. It determines what information is made explicit and hence what is pushed further into the background, and it has a far-reaching effect on the ease and difficulty with which operations may subsequently be carried out on that information.

Process

The term *process* is very broad. For example, addition is a process, and so is taking a Fourier transform. But so is making a cup of tea, or going shopping. For the purposes of this book, I want to restrict our attention to the meanings associated with machines that are carrying out information-processing tasks. So let us examine in depth the notions behind one simple such device, a cash register at the checkout counter of a supermarket.

There are several levels at which one needs to understand such a device, and it is perhaps most useful to think in terms of three of them. The most abstract is the level of *what* the device does and *why*. What it does is arithmetic, so our first task is to master the theory of addition. Addition is a mapping, usually denoted by $+$, from pairs of numbers into single numbers; for example, $+$ maps the pair (3, 4) to 7, and I shall write this in the form $(3 + 4) \to 7$. Addition has a number of abstract properties, however. It is commutative: both $(3 + 4)$ and $(4 + 3)$ are equal to 7; and associative: the sum of $3 + (4 + 5)$ is the same as the sum of $(3 + 4) + 5$. Then there is the unique distinguished element, zero, the adding of which has no effect: $(4 + 0) \to 4$. Also, for every number there is a unique "inverse," written (-4) in the case of 4, which when added to the number gives zero: $[4+(-4)] \to 0$.

Notice that these properties are part of the fundamental *theory* of addition. They are true no matter how the numbers are written—whether in binary Arabic, or Roman representation—and no matter how the addition is executed. Thus part of this first level is something that might be characterized as *what* is being computed.

The other half of this level of explanation has to do with the question of *why* the cash register performs addition and not, for instance, multiplication when combining the prices of the purchased items to arrive at a final bill. The reason is that the rules we intuitively feel to be appropriate for combining the individual prices in fact define the mathematical operation of addition. These can be formulated as *constraints* in the following way:

1. If you buy nothing, it should cost you nothing; and buying nothing and something should cost the same as buying just the something. (The rules for zero.)
2. The order in which goods are presented to the cashier should not affect the total. (Commutativity.)
3. Arranging the goods into two piles and paying for each pile separately should not affect the total amount you pay (Associativity; the basic operation for combining prices.)
4. If you buy an item and then return it for a refund, your total expenditure should be zero. (Inverses.)

It is a mathematical theorem that these conditions define the operation of addition, which is therefore the appropriate computation to use.

This whole argument is what I call the *computational theory* of the cash register. Its important features are (1) that it contains separate arguments about what is computed and why and (2) that the resulting operation is defined uniquely by the constraints it has to satisfy. In the theory of visual processes, the underlying task is to reliably derive properties of the world from images of it; the business of isolating constraints that are both powerful enough to allow a process to be defined and generally true of the world is a central theme of our inquiry.

In order that a process shall actually run, however, one has to realize it in some way and therefore choose a representation for the entities that the process manipulates. The second level of the analysis of a process, therefore, involves choosing two things: (1) a *representation* for the input and for the output of the process and (2) an *algorithm* by which the transformation may actually be accomplished. For addition, of course, the input and output representations can both be the same, because they both consist of numbers. However this is not true in general. In the case of a Fourier transform, for example, the input representation may be the time domain, and the output, the frequency domain. If the first of our levels specifies what and why, this second level specifies *how*. For addition, we might choose Arabic numerals for the representations, and for the algorithm we could follow the usual rules about adding the least significant digits first and "carrying" if the sum exceeds 9. Cash registers, whether mechanical or electronic, usually use this type of representation and algorithm.

There are three important points here. First, there is usually a wide choice of representation. Second, the choice of algorithm often depends rather critically on the particular representation that is employed. And third, even for a given fixed representation, there are often several possible algorithms for carrying out the same process. Which one is chosen will usually depend on any particularly desirable or undesirable characteristics that the algorithms may have; for example, one algorithm may be much more efficient than another, or another may be slightly less efficient but more robust (that is, less sensitive to slight inaccuracies in the data on which it must run). Or again, one algorithm may be parallel, and another, serial. The choice, then, may depend on the type of hardware or machinery in which the algorithm is to be embodied physically.

This brings us to the third level, that of the device in which the process is to be realized physically. The important point here is that, once again, the same algorithm may be implemented in quite different technologies. The child who methodically adds two numbers from right to left, carrying a digit when necessary, may be using the same algorithm that is implemented by the wires and transistors of the cash register in the neighborhood supermarket, but the physical realization of the algorithm is quite different in these two cases. Another example: Many people have written computer programs to play tic-tac-toe, and there is a more or less standard algorithm that cannot lose. This algorithm has in fact been implemented by W. D. Hillis and B. Silverman in a quite different technology, in a computer made out of Tinkertoys, a children's wooden building set. The whole monstrously ungainly engine, which actually works, currently resides in a museum at the University of Missouri in St. Louis.

Some styles of algorithm will suit some physical substrates better than others. For example, in conventional digital computers, the number of connections is comparable to the number of gates, while in a brain, the number of connections is much larger ($\times\ 10^4$) than the number of nerve cells. The underlying reason is that wires are rather cheap in biological architecture, because they can grow individually and in three dimensions. In conventional technology, wire laying is more or less restricted to two dimensions, which quite severely restricts the scope for using parallel techniques and algorithms; the same operations are often better carried out serially.

The Three Levels

We can summarize our discussion in something like the manner shown in Figure 4.1, which illustrates the different levels at which an information-processing device must be understood before one can be said to have understood it completely. At one extreme, the top level, is the abstract computational theory of the device, in which the performance of the device is characterized as a mapping from one kind of information to another, the abstract properties of this mapping are defined precisely, and its appropriateness and adequacy for the task at hand are demonstrated. In the center is the choice of representation for the input and output and the algorithm to be used to transform one into the other. And at the other extreme are the details of how the algorithm and representation are realized physically—the detailed computer architecture, so to speak. These three levels are coupled, but only loosely. The choice of an algorithm is influenced for example, by what it has to do and by the hardware in which it must run. But there is a wide choice available at each level, and the explication of each level involves issues that are rather independent of the other two.

Each of the three levels of description will have its place in the eventual understanding of perceptual information processing, and of course they are logically and causally related. But an important point to note is that since the three levels are only rather loosely related, some phenomena may be explained at only one or two of them. This means, for example, that a correct explanation of some psychophysical observation must be formulated at the appropriate level. In attempts to relate psychophysical problems to physiology, too often there is confusion about the level at which problems should be addressed. For instance, some are related mainly to the physical mechanisms of vision—such as afterimages (for example, the one you see after staring at a light bulb) or such as the fact that any color can be matched by a suitable mixture of the three primaries (a consequence principally of the fact that we humans have three types of cones). On the other hand, the ambiguity of the

Computational theory	Representation and algorithm	Hardware implementation
What is the goal of the computation, why is it appropriate, and what is the logic of the strategy by which it can be carried out?	How can this computational theory be implemented? In particular, what is the representation for the input and output, and what is the algorithm for the transformation?	How can the representation and algorithm be realized physically?

Figure 4.1
The three levels at which any machine carrying out an information-processing task must be understood.

Necker cube (Figure 4.2) seems to demand a different kind of explanation. To be sure, part of the explanation of its perceptual reversal must have to do with a bistable neural network (that is, one with two distinct stable states) somewhere inside the brain, but few would feel satisfied by an account that failed to mention the existence of two different but perfectly plausible three-dimensional interpretations of this two-dimensional image.

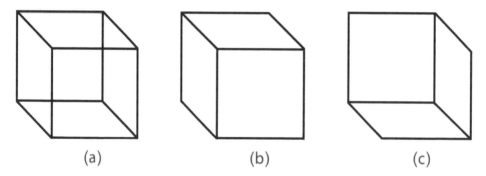

Figure 4.2
The so-called Necker illusion, named after L. A. Necker, the Swiss naturalist who developed it in 1832. The essence of the matter is that the two-dimensional representation (a) has collapsed the depth out of a cube and that a certain aspect of human vision is to recover this missing third dimension. The depth of the cube can indeed be perceived, but two interpretations are possible, (b) and (c). A person's perception characteristically flips from one to the other.

For some phenomena, the type of explanation required is fairly obvious. Neuroanatomy, for example, is clearly tied principally to the third level, the physical realization of the computation. The same holds for synaptic mechanisms, action potentials, inhibitory interactions, and so forth. Neurophysiology, too, is related mostly to this level . . . But one has to exercise extreme caution in making inferences from neurophysiological findings about the algorithms and representations being used, particularly until one has a clear idea about what information needs to be represented and what processes need to be implemented.

Psychophysics, on the other hand, is related more directly to the level of algorithm and representation. Different algorithms tend to fail in radically different ways as they are pushed to the limits of their performance or are deprived of critical information. As we shall see, primarily psychophysical evidence proved to Poggio and myself that our first stereo-matching algorithm (Marr and Poggio, 1976) was not the one that is used by the brain, and the best evidence that our second algorithm (Marr and Poggio, 1979) *is* roughly the one that is used also comes from psychophysics. Of course, the underlying computational theory remained the same in both cases, only the algorithms were different.

Psychophysics can also help to determine the nature of a representation. The work of Roger Shepard (1975), Eleanor Rosch (1978), or Elizabeth Warrington (1975) provides some interesting hints in this direction. More specifically, Stevens (1979) argued from psychophysical experiments that surface orientation is represented by the coordinates of slant and tilt, rather than (for example) the more traditional (p, q) of gradient space. He also deduced from the uniformity of the size of errors made by subjects judging surface orientation over a wide range of orientations that the representational quantities used for slant and tilt are pure angles and not, for example, their cosines, sines, or tangents.

More generally, if the idea that different phenomena need to be explained at different levels is kept clearly in mind, it often helps in the assessment of the validity of the different kinds of objections that are raised from time to time. For example, one favorite is that the brain is quite different from a computer because one is parallel and the other serial. The answer to this, of course, is that the distinction between serial and parallel is a distinction at the level of algorithm; it is not fundamental at all—anything programmed in parallel can be rewritten serially (though not necessarily vice versa). The distinction, therefore, provides no grounds for arguing that the brain operates so differently from a computer that a computer could not be programmed to perform the same tasks.

Importance of Computational Theory

Although algorithms and mechanisms are empirically more accessible, it is the top level, the level of computational theory, which is critically important from an information-processing point of view. The reason for this is that the nature of the computations that underlie perception depends more upon the computational problems that have to be solved than upon the particular hardware in which their solutions are implemented. To phrase the matter another way, an algorithm is likely to be understood more readily by understanding the nature of the problem being solved than by examining the mechanism (and the hardware) in which it is embodied.

In a similar vein, trying to understand perception by studying only neurons is like trying to understand bird flight by studying only feathers: It just cannot be done. In order to understand bird flight, we have to understand aerodynamics; only then do the structure of feathers and the different shapes of birds' wings make sense. More to the point, as we shall see, we cannot understand why retinal ganglion cells and lateral geniculate neurons have the receptive fields they do just by studying their anatomy and physiology. We can understand how these cells and neurons behave as they do by studying their wiring and interactions, but in order to understand *why* the receptive fields are as they are—why they are circularly symmetrical and why their excitatory and inhibitory regions have characteristic shapes and distributions—we have to know a little of the theory of differential operators, band-pass channels, and the mathematics of the uncertainty principle.

Perhaps it is not surprising that the very specialized empirical disciplines of the neurosciences failed to appreciate fully the absence of computational theory; but it is surprising that this level of approach did not play a more forceful role in the early development of artificial intelligence. For far too long, a heuristic program for carrying out some task was held to be a theory of that task, and the distinction between what a program did and how it did it was not taken seriously. As a result, (1) a style of explanation evolved that invoked the use of special mechanisms to solve particular problems, (2) particular data structures, such as the lists of attribute value pairs called property lists in the LISP programing language, were held to amount to theories of the representation of knowledge, and (3) there was frequently no way to determine whether a program would deal with a particular case other than by running the program.

Failure to recognize this theoretical distinction between *what* and *how* also greatly hampered communication between the fields of artificial intelligence and linguistics. Chomsky's (1965) theory of transformational grammar is a true computational theory in the sense defined earlier. It is concerned solely with specifying what the syntactic decomposition of an English sentence should be, and not at all with how that decomposition should be achieved. Chomsky himself was very clear about this—it is roughly his distinction between competence and performance, though his idea of performance did include other factors, like stopping in midutterance—but the fact that his theory was defined by transformations, which look like computations, seems to have confused many people. Winograd (1972b), for example, felt able to criticize Chomsky's theory on the grounds that it cannot be inverted and so cannot be made to run on a computer; I had heard reflections of the same argument made by Chomsky's colleagues in linguistics as they turn their attention to how grammatical structure might actually be computed from a real English sentence.

The explanation is simply that finding algorithms by which Chomsky's theory may be implemented is a completely different endeavor from formulating the theory itself. In our terms, it is a study at a different level, and both tasks have to be done. This point was appreciated by Marcus (1980), who was concerned precisely with how Chomsky's theory can be realized and with the kinds of constraints on the power of the human grammatical processor that might give rise to the structural constraints in syntax that Chomsky found.

It even appears that the emerging "trace" theory of grammar (Chomsky and Lasnik, 1977) may provide a way of synthesizing the two approaches—showing that, for example, some of the rather ad hoc restrictions that form part of the computational theory may be consequences of weaknesses in the computational power that is available for implementing syntactical decoding.

Synopsis (*Vision*, Chapter 6)

Our survey of this new, computational approach to vision is now complete. Although there are many gaps in the account, I hope that it is solid enough to establish a firm point of view about the subject and to prompt the reader to begin to judge its value. In this brief chapter, I shall take a very broad view of the whole approach, inquiring into its most important general features and how they relate to one another, and trying to say something about the style of research that this approach implies. It is convenient to divide the discussion into four main points.

The first point is one that we have met throughout the account—the notion of different levels of explanation. The central tenet of the approach is that to understand what vision is and how it works, an understanding at only one level is insufficient. It is not enough to be able to describe the responses of single cells, nor is it enough to be able to predict locally the results of psychophysical experiments. Nor it is enough even to be able to write computer programs that perform approximately in the desired way. One has to do all these things at once and also be very aware of the additional level of explanation that I have called the level of computational theory. The recognition of the existence and importance of this level is one of the most important aspects of this approach. Having recognized this, one can formulate the three levels of explanation explicitly (computational theory, algorithm, and implementation), and it then becomes clear how these different levels are related to the different types of empirical observation and theoretical analysis that can be conducted. I have laid particular stress on the level of computational theory not because I regard it as inherently more important than the other two levels—the real power of the approach lies in the integration of all three levels of attack—but because it is a level of explanation that has not previously been recognized and acted upon. It is therefore probably one of the most difficult ideas for newcomers to the field to grasp, and for this reason alone its importance should not be understated in any introductory book, such as this is intended to be.

The second main point is that by taking an information-processing point of view, we have been able to formulate a rather clear overall framework for the process of vision. This framework is based on the idea that the critical issues in vision revolve around the nature of the representations used—that is, the particular characteristics of the world that are made explicit during vision—and the nature of the processes that recover these characteristics, create and maintain the representations, and eventually read them. By analyzing the spatial aspects of the problem of vision, we arrived at an overall framework for visual information processing that hinges on three principal representations: (1) the primal sketch, which is concerned with making explicit properties of the two-dimensional image, ranging from the amount and disposition of the intensity changes there to primitive representations of the local image geometry and including at the more sophisticated end a hierarchical description of any higher-order structure present in the underlying reflectance distributions; (2) the $2\frac{1}{2}$-D sketch, which is a viewer-centered representation of the depth and orientation of the visible surfaces and includes contours of discontinuities in these quantities; and (3) the 3-D model representation, whose important features are that its coordinate system is object centered, that it includes volumetric primitives (which make explicit the organization of the space occupied by an object and not just its visible surfaces), and that primitives of various size are included, arranged in a modular, hierarchical organization.

The third main point concerns the study of processes for recovering the various aspects of the physical characteristics of a scene from images of it. The critical act in formulating computational theories for such processes is the discovery of valid constraints on the way the world behaves that provide sufficient additional information to allow recovery of the desired characteristic. The power of this type of analysis resides in the fact that the discovery of valid, sufficiently universal constraints leads to conclusions about vision that have the same permanence as conclusions in other branches of science.

Furthermore, once a computational theory for a process has been formulated, algorithms for implementing it may be designed, and their performance compared with that of the human visual processor. This allows two kinds of results. First, if performance is essentially identical, we have good evidence that the constraints of the underlying computational theory are valid and may be implicit in the human processor; second, if a process matches human performance, it is probably sufficiently powerful to form part of a general purpose vision machine.

The final point concerns the methodology or style of this type of approach, and it involves two main observations. First, the duality between representations and processes, which is set out explicitly in Figure 4.3, often provides a useful aid to thinking how best to proceed when studying a particular problem. In the study both of representations and of processes, general problems are often suggested by everyday experience or by psychophysical or even neurophysiological findings of a quite general nature. Such general observations can often lead to the formulation of a particular process or representational theory, specific examples of which can be programmed or subjected to detailed psychophysical testing. Once we have sufficient confidence in the correctness of the process or representation at this level, we can inquire about its detailed implementation, which involves the ultimate and very difficult problems of neurophysiology and neuroanatomy.

The second observation is that there is no real recipe for this type of research—even though I have sometimes suggested that there is—any more than there is a straightforward

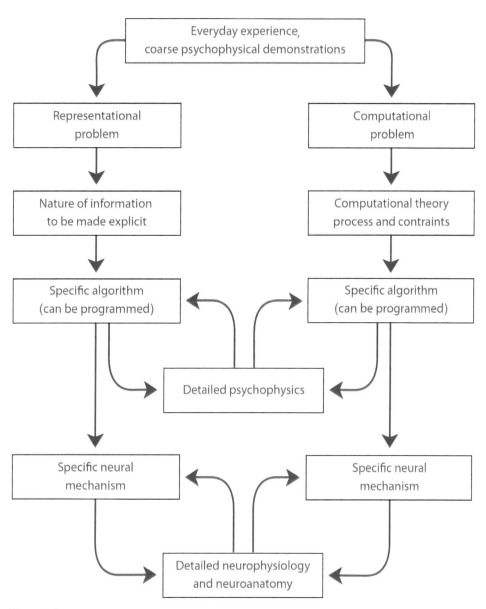

Figure 4.3
Relationships between representations and processes.

procedure for discovering things in any other branch of science. Indeed, part of the fun is that we never really know where the next key is going to come from—a piece of daily experience, the report of a neurological deficit, a theorem about three-dimensional geometry, a psychophysical finding in hyperacuity, a neurophysiological observation, or the careful analysis of a representational problem. All these kinds of information have played important roles in establishing the framework that I have described, and they will presumably continue to contribute to its advancement in an interesting and unpredictable way. I hope only that these observations may persuade some of my readers to join in the adventures we have had and to help in the long but rewarding task of unraveling the mysteries of human visual perception.

The Analog Alternative

5

Corey J. Maley
2023

Let us begin with two orthodoxies of cognitive science, both conveniently available in slogan form. Christoph Koch (1999) begins his seminal work in computational neuroscience "The brain computes!" Jerry Fodor (1981) famously proclaimed "There is no computation without representation." There are detractors from each of these views, of course, but cognitive scientists generally assume a close connection between cognition and computation, and between computation and representation. Taken together, these ideas form the foundational assumption of cognitive science: mentality requires computation, which requires representation. Understanding representation, and in turn, computation, is thus the *sine qua non* of cognitive science's success.

Although I happen to agree with these orthodoxies, my aim in what follows is not to make the case for either. Instead, I want to show that the landscape of representational types—particularly those that can underwrite computation—is larger than what nearly all cognitive scientists have recognized. In particular, the analog side of this space has been under-explored and under-theorized.

Much of the problem is that, conceptually, *computation* is almost universally taken to be synonymous with specifically *digital* computation: the kind of computation that traffics in digital representation. That there could be some other legitimate kind of computation has gone largely unnoticed and unquestioned. Furthermore, insofar as "digital" is contrasted with anything (whether representation, computation, or something else entirely), it is contrasted with "analog" in an unilluminating and ultimately misleading way. The received view has it that "digital" is synonymous with "discrete," and that "analog" is synonymous with "continuous." There is a kernel of truth here, but unfortunately, that small kernel has obscured the more fundamental difference between analog and digital representation, and in turn, computation.

In this chapter, I will try to begin remedying this situation. Specifically, I will show how to correctly understand analog representation, and do so in a way that helps us correctly understand analog computation. To do this, I will first provide some context for how the received view came to be. This will take the form of a brief discussion of computing machines in the twentieth century. Next, I will present a typology of representations, showing where analog and digital representation (rightly construed) fit within the broader landscape of more fundamental distinctions between representational types. Thus, while it is true that analog computers manipulate analog representations and digital computers manipulate digital ones, understanding what, precisely, "analog" and "digital" are about (which is missed by the received view) will then enable a clearer discussion of what analog and digital computation is about. Finally, I will suggest how a correct understanding of analog computation might make computation more palatable to researchers in the 4E tradition—particularly those in embodied and enactive cognition—who have otherwise eschewed computation.

5.1   A Brief History of Computational Machines

Because much of this chapter is devoted to correcting what I take to be an error in how fundamental divisions between computational and representational types are currently understood, it is helpful to take a moment to see how we got here. Interestingly, however, there is not as much written on the history of computation as one might expect. Mahoney (2011) notes that historians of technology have written relatively little on the history of digital computing machines.[1] The authors of what *has* been written are largely computer scientists and mathematicians, which presents problems to the historian and philosopher of computation:

> While it is firsthand and expert, it is also guided by the current state of knowledge and bound by the professional culture. That is, its authors take as givens (often technical givens) what a more critical, outside viewer might see as choices. Reading their accounts makes it difficult to see the alternatives, as the authors themselves lose touch with a time when they did not know what they know now. (Mahoney, 2011, 22–23)

This problem is particularly acute when it comes to analog computing machines, where even less has been written (Mindell, 2002). Nyce (1996, 3) puts the point well: "Because digital computers and computation have been so successful, they have influenced how we think about both computers as machines and computation as a process—so much so, it is difficult today to reconstruct what analog computing was all about." A complete history will have to wait for another time (and its own book); for now, we can sketch that history just enough to get a feel for what is to come.

In the late nineteenth and early twentieth century, a wide variety of computing machines were used in scientific, engineering, and industrial contexts. These included adding machines, slide rules of various types, and mechanical analog computers. In general, this hodgepodge of mechanisms was not subject to any systematic theoretical study: different problems required different solutions, and most machines were built to solve a particular kind of task. For example, mechanical adders worked much like cash registers, allowing human computers[2] to perform basic arithmetical calculations. Tabulating machines allowed operators to analyze census data. On naval warships, mechanical fire-control computing machines determined how to position the ship's guns to accurately hit moving targets (Mindell, 2002).

One exception to this lack of systematic analysis was the work done on the differential analyzer, a kind of mechanical analog computer developed by Vannevar Bush at MIT. Unlike many other computing machines that were created for a single, special purpose, the differential analyzer could be reconfigured to compute solutions to a large number of different kinds of mathematical problems (Bush, 1931). These mechanical analog computers were mostly (but not exclusively) used for solving problems that involved differential equations. Many engineering and scientific problems are amenable to analysis in terms of systems of differential equations, but large classes of these systems have no analytic solution. Thus, they can only be "solved" by tedious numerical calculation, or by some kind of mechanical simulation. The differential analyzer proved a useful new way to study problems of this sort.

Purely mechanical analog computers eventually gave way to electromechanical and electronic computers. Variables in mechanical analog computers would be represented by quantities such as the left-right displacement of a shaft, the angle of a gear, or the running total number of rotations of a roller or drum: in other words, quantities of the problem to be solved were represented by physical quantities in the computing machine, and variation in those quantities was represented by physically moving those parts. Electromechanical and electronic computers used electrical quantities, such as voltage and resistance, to represent the quantity of a variable. And, like the mechanical analog computer, changes in the quantity of a variable were represented by a change in those electrical quantities. Because fully electronic analog computing machines had no moving parts, they were more easily programmed and maintained than their mechanical and electromechanical counterparts. These machines eventually replaced the mechanical and electromechanical entirely, becoming the standard type of analog computer by the 1970s.

The majority of the problems solved on these analog computing machines were continuous in nature, so the physical quantities that the machines used to represent variables were likewise continuous in nature (e.g., angles, rotations, and voltages are all naturally considered as continuous quantities). However, there are important exceptions: some of the problems studied would require, for example, the absolute value function, or step functions. In those cases, the analog computing machines would use discontinuous variables to represent those discontinuities (James et al., 1971; Maley, forthcoming).

Although digital computers have now completely replaced analog computers, it took a few decades for them to do so. The earliest digital computers were larger, slower, more error-prone, and more expensive than their analog counterparts. But once they were on equal footing, it became important to distinguish the two types to potential buyers and users. At that point in history, both the analog and digital computing machines were electronic. However, the analog ones (mostly) used continuous voltages to represent their variables, while the digital ones used exclusively discrete voltages. The occasional exception where analog computers used *dis*continuous (i.e., discrete) voltages was overlooked. For digital computers, there were no exceptions: they *always* used discrete voltages. This was one important source of the "analog/digital" distinction: analog machines were continuous (or, at least, very often so), while digital machines were discrete.

There is certainly more to say about the history of this division, but this is part of the story of how we arrived at the received view of the analog/digital distinction. Again, according to this view, "analog" is synonymous with "continuous," and thus analog representations vary continuously, and analog computers are just computers that use continuous representations. On the other side, "digital" is synonymous with "discrete," and thus digital computers are just computers that use discrete representations.

Now, even if it were true that electronic analog computers always used continuous voltages (as the received view would have it, by definition), the most important difference between analog and digital computers is *not* simply a matter of continuity versus discreteness. More important—as I will spell out in detail in the next section—is *how* the voltages do the representing.[3] In short, analog representations (and, in turn, analog computers) represent the *magnitudes* of numbers via the magnitudes of physical quantities; digital representations (and, in turn, digital computers) represent the *names* of numbers via digits, where the digits are then represented by variations in physical quantities. Much more will be said about this below, but for now, I simply note that this crucial difference in how these computing machines and their representations operate was glossed over by what became the received analog/digital distinction. The received view has obscured the fact that the difference between the analog and digital is more interesting than the difference between types of peanut butter, where one is chunky and the other is smooth. Rather, there are two fundamentally different ways of representing, one of which essentially takes advantage of the physical nature of physical representations, and another that abstracts away from them.

5.2   Representational Types

According to the framework I offer here, there are two fundamental distinctions to be made between representational types. First, there are those that are analog and those that are not. Second, there are representations that are continuous and those that are not (i.e., discrete).[4] On this view (contra the received view), "analog" is *not* synonymous with "continuous," a point first made explicit by Lewis (1971), then defended and extended by Maley (2011) (this point is also implicit in Copeland, 1997). What were originally theoretical reasons for rejecting this synonymy have been borne out in examples of extant (albeit historical) analog computers (Maley, forthcoming). Moreover, "digital" is not synonymous with "discrete."

Instead, "digital" turns out to be just one of many non-analog ways of representing numbers (although its complexity is obscured by its familiarity). In contemporary digital computers, it is this particular type of representation—and not mere discreteness—that is essential to understanding their operation *qua* computer.

Now, it should be said that some philosophers have defended the received view. Goodman (1968), for instance, defends a sophisticated version of the received view. Haugeland (1981) also defends the received view, bringing engineering considerations of approximation procedures into the conversation. Later defenses of the received view, or variations thereof, can be found in (Papayannopoulos, 2020; Katz, 2016; Schonbein, 2014). For now, however, I will set critiques of these views aside.

A bit of terminology is needed before we begin in earnest. In what follows, I will refer to the physical thing doing the representing simply as the *representation*, and I will refer to what it is that is being represented as the *representandum*. How closely this distinction aligns with the vehicle/content distinction depends on how "vehicle" and "content" are understood, which varies in the literature. Some understand vehicles to be physical, and others do not; some understand content to be only *mental* content, and others do not. In order to avoid possible confusion, I will use these new terms.

The first distinction made above—that between analog and non-analog representations—reflect two distinct ways of representing numbers. Suppose for a moment that mathematical Platonism is true—that numbers are real, abstract objects. In order to manipulate these abstract objects (as we are wont to do, both by hand and with computing machines), we must concretely represent them somehow or another. One way to do that is to represent numbers via their magnitudes: the number one is represented by some concrete, physical magnitude of one; the number two is represented by a concrete, physical magnitude of two; and so on. Thus, the number two could be represented by the length of a rod, where the rod is two meters long; or it could be represented by the electrical potential across a circuit element, where the potential is two volts. This is the way of the analog.

The second—completely distinct—way to represent numbers is to represent them by what we might call their names, where names are of different types. Some names are completely arbitrary. For example, "Drumthwacket" and "Graceland" are arbitrary names for particular buildings in the United States; similarly, "*e*" and "*π*" are arbitrary names for particular numbers. Almost no information about the referent of those names is given by the names themselves. Alternatively, some names have a type of structure. If we consider addresses to be names (as they sometimes are), then "123 Main St." is a name that gives the location of a particular house in some city or another, according to certain conventions. Similarly, "314" is a name that gives the value of a number in some base, according to certain conventions. This is the way of the non-analog.

In short, the important difference between these is that we can represent a number either by its magnitude or by its name; this is the difference between analog and non-analog

Basic Representations

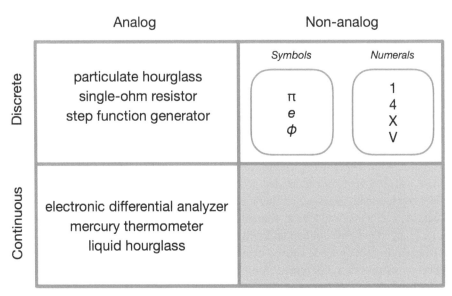

Figure 5.1
Representational types. Analog, which can be continuous or discrete, and non-analog, which are only discrete. Non-analog representations are further divided into symbolic and numerical representations, which can be divided yet further (see figure 5.3).

representation (the left-right division in figure 5.1). This difference is then reflected in how these are *physically* represented. With respect to their physical instantiations, analog and non-analog representation can be characterized as a difference between first-order and second-order representation (Maley, 2021). This way of understanding the two helps to make clear the differences between the types of *computation* that use those representations, discussed in the next section.

Let us look at each of these ways of representing in more detail, starting with analog representation. I will argue that *being analog (or not)* is fundamental, which will then enable me to show why being non-analog is not the same thing as being digital.

5.2.1   Analog vs Non-Analog Representations

Because we are concerned here with *physical* computers of some kind or another (either natural or artificial), representations are first and foremost physical objects of some kind or another. Representations do their representing via one (or more) of their physical properties; the different ways to spell out "via" is precisely what I argue is most fundamental about distinguishing representational types.

As mentioned above, one way for a representation to represent a number—the analog way—is for the amount, or quantity, of one of its properties to covary with the representantum. For example, one can use a lump of clay to represent a number by using the temperature of the clay in degrees Celsius, or the mass of the clay in decagrams. To make the example concrete, let us suppose that we want to represent the number fifty.[5] Thus, to represent fifty via the clay's mass, the clay would have a mass of fifty decagrams. If we want to increase the representantum to fifty-one, we need to increase the mass to fifty-one decagrams. Thus, as the representantum changes, the mass—the property doing the representing—changes in turn. Specifically, an *increase* in the representantum requires an increase in the mass of the representation; a *decrease* in the representantum requires a decrease in the mass of the representation. Thus, we have a quantity—one of the properties of the representation—representing the quantity of the representantum.[6] The magnitude of the representing quantity just is the magnitude of the number being represented; thus, what is "analog" about this type of representation is the analogy between the magnitude of the representation and the magnitude of the representantum.

An important part of this characterization is that it can hold for representations and representanda that are either continuous *or* discrete. For our clay example, suppose we are only interested in representing whole numbers, and suppose we only have single-decagram blobs of clay to add to our representation (perhaps the number we are representing is a count of a person's age in years). In such a case, we would still have an analog representation, even though the property doing the representing and the representantum both vary in *discrete*, rather than continuous, steps. What matters is *not* whether continuity is involved in either the representation or representantum, but that the property of the representation that *does the representing* covaries with the representantum. In many cases, the covariance will be linear, but at a minimum it must be monotonic: an increase/decrease in the magnitude of the representantum is characterized by *some* increase/decrease in the magnitude of the relevant property of the representation.[7]

Non-analog representation, on the other hand, does not work this way. Using our lump of clay, we could create a non-analog representation of the number fifty by separating the clay into two smaller lumps, rolling them out, and forming one into the numeral "5" and the other the numeral "0." Put in the right order, this would represent the number fifty. Alternatively, we could form our lump of clay into the single numeral "L," the Roman numeral for fifty.[8] Now, while it must be true that *some* physical property (or pattern thereof) of the representation must do the representing (how else could a physical representation represent anything?), it is not the *magnitude* of the physical property *doing the representing* that reflects the magnitude of the representantum. Rather, the physical properties of the representation are abstracted in a way so that it is *not* the magnitude of the property that matters, but only variation among arbitrary values or patterns of the property as the representandum varies.

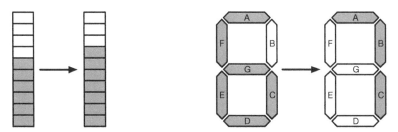

Figure 5.2
Left: Analog representation of six and seven. Right: Non-analog representation of six and seven.

Let us look at another example, this time in the context of electronic representations of the kind we often find on the dashboards of contemporary cars. The left side of figure 5.2 depicts an analog representation as it would change from representing six to seven, and the right side depicts a single numerical, non-analog representation doing the same thing; we can imagine each of these as representing, say, the remaining amount of fuel in a car (in gallons). Note that the segments in the analog display could indicate that the display is composed of discrete elements, or they may simply be marks meant to help read a continuously-varying level of (say) liquid (i.e., it may be discrete or continuous). On the characterization of analog representation advanced here, it does not matter. Either way, it is the magnitude (in this case, height) of the gauge (depicted here as gray) that determines the representandum. Thus, an increase (or decrease) in height corresponds to an increase (or decrease) in the representandum.

As for the numerical representation depicted on the right side of figure 5.2, the magnitude or quantity of the material is irrelevant to the representation *qua* representation. What matters, instead, is that certain segments are activated in specified patterns. As the representandum increases from six to seven, there is no magnitude or quantity that increases in the representation. Instead, the elements that are activated simply change from one pattern to another. In particular, segments D, E, F, and G are deactivated, segment B is activated, and segments A and C are unchanged. Once again, in the case of the analog representation, there is a monotonic change in the magnitude *that does the representing* as the representandum increases (or decreases); in the digital case, it is not the magnitude of any physical property *per se* that does any representing, but only a pattern of a physical quantities that are capable of changing (in fact, the number of activated segments *decreases* in this example as we go from six to seven but would then increase if we went from seven to eight).

The lesson from these examples generalizes. The defining feature of *any* analog representation on this view is that the magnitude or amount of the physical property that does the representing increases (or decreases) systematically (i.e., monotonically) with increases (or decreases) in the representandum. In the case of a non-analog representation, the physical property that does the representing only needs to change in some way or another as the representandum increases or decreases. There need be no systematic change in the magnitude of the representationally relevant property of the representation as the representandum systematically varies.

As illustrated in figure 5.1, there are some non-analog representations that are worth distinguishing from numerals. Numerals are special in that they combine to form complex representations, whereas non-numerals do not. Examples of non-numeral representations include "π" and "e," which represent the mathematical constants pi and Euler's number. These symbols could be represented with the same kind of segmented display as the numerical display above. However, it would be a mistake to call these digital: these kinds of symbols are not concatenated in the same ways that numerals are to form complex representations (i.e., numerical representations, which will be discussed in more detail below).

One final point is worth noting. Although it may be conceptually possible, there are no continuous, non-analog representations. To be sure, there are, in a sense, *non*-analog representations of continuous representanda; the digital expansion of a real number is one example.[9] However, there are no representations that themselves vary continuously in the property that does the representing, but where that property does *not* represent in an analog way (hence the gray box in the lower right quadrant of figure 5.1). Again, many representations have physical properties that vary continuously but are then used as *non*-analog representations. Binary numerals as they are implemented in contemporary digital computers, represented by voltage, are an example. The voltage varies continuously as it changes between different values (e.g., a "low" value of around zero volts to a "high" value of around five volts), we discretize that voltage (basically rounding it to zero or five) and treat it as though it only has two values: the low value represents the numeral "0," and the high value represents the numeral "1."

5.2.2 Numerical Representations

Perhaps the most interesting thing about certain non-analog representations is that they can be combined in various ways to form complex representations. Among these are the familiar digital representations, most important for our aims here, but there are others worth mentioning. Following Chrisomalis (2020), I will call these numerical representations. There are several families of numerical representations, all quite interesting, but I will focus the discussion here on digital representations (which Chrisomalis categorizes as a type of cumulative positional numerical system). Historically, this kind of representational scheme is not even the most common among different cultures. However, given that this scheme is the basis of contemporary digital computation, it is of particular philosophical importance for understanding extant computational systems.

Numerical Representations

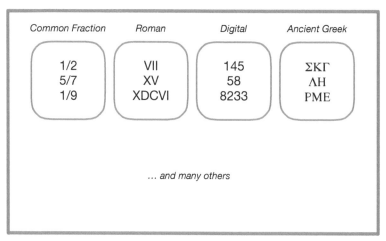

Figure 5.3
Some kinds of numerical representations.

In numerical representational schemes, individual numerals are combined in different ways, sometimes with auxiliary symbols, to form representations of new numbers. The Roman numeral scheme, for example, takes each numeral to have a certain value, which is the same value that each numeral has on its own. Thus, "I" represents one; "V" represents five, and so on. Numerals are written so that the largest-valued ones are left-most, and decrease to the right. The number represented by the entire string of numerals is the sum of the numbers represented by the individual numerals. Thus, "XVI" consists of the numerals representing ten, five, and one; the whole string thus represents sixteen. A slight complication arises with the convention in which a numeral followed by a larger numeral (on the right) was taken to mean that the smaller numeral was to be subtracted from the larger. Thus, "XIV" would represent fourteen.

Another example is the Greek numeral scheme. In this scheme, the first nine Greek letters of the alphabet represent the values one through nine; the next nine letters represent the values ten through ninety; the last nine represent the values one hundred through nine hundred. Again, the number represented is the sum of the numbers represented by each individual numeral. Using the same left-to-right, largest-to-smallest convention, "ΦΛB" represents five hundred (Φ) thirty (Λ) two (B). Interestingly, in schemes like the Roman and Greek, there is no need for a numeral to represent zero; thus "DII" and "ΦB" each represent five hundred and two.

There are still other schemes that use multiplication instead of addition, as well as the divisional scheme of common fractions; Chrisomalis (2020) discusses a number of these in fascinating detail. What unites all of these schemes is that their members are complexes, built out of individual numerals, where the representandum of the entire representation is a function of the representanda of the individual numerals. So let us turn to the most familiar numerical scheme, the digital scheme, which is also the basis upon which virtually all of our understanding of physical computation is built.

The digital scheme, first articulated in the philosophical literature by Lewis (1971), represents a number as a string of numerals. The value that each numeral contributes to the representandum depends on its position in the string, as well as the base of the scheme. Most familiarly, we use base-10, which requires the numerals 0 through 9. The right-most digit ("digit" here is the term for a numeral in a particular place) contributes that many units to the representandum, the next (to the left) digit contributes that many tens, and so on. Thus, "272" has the representandum equal to:

$$(2 \times 10^2) + (7 \times 10^1) + (2 \times 10^0) = 272$$

More generally,[10] for a base b other than 10, we would replace the 10 above with the number b, and the numerals would range from 0 to $(b-1)$. Interestingly, the digital scheme can be further extended by the use of a decimal place. Digits to the right of the decimal place can then represent *negative* powers of the base, allowing for real numbers to be represented.

When it comes to computers, one useful fact about the digital scheme is that only two numerals are necessary to represent any representable number. Again, because we are concerned with physical representation and computation, this makes the implementation of a digital machine (relatively) simple: all one needs is a physical substrate that can be in two different physical states. The binary system is thus virtually universal in contemporary digital computers.

Before concluding this section, we should note the difference between symbolic representation and numerical representation. Symbolic representations are simply not used in numerical representations as understood here. By this I simply mean that individual symbolic representations are not concatenated or otherwise systematically combined with other symbolic representations to form new representations. This is, of course, a contingent fact: we *could* have used the string "$\pi 0$" to represent $(\pi \times 10^1) + (0 \times 10^0) = 31.4145926\ldots$ But there are no extant representational schemes like this. Concatenations of symbols do occur in mathematical contexts, of course, but they are not numerical schemes.[11]

The point of going to the trouble of creating this typology of representations is to show how very different analog and digital representation really are. They are not merely two sides of the same coin. Instead, there is a more fundamental division between representations that are analog and those that are not analog. Numerals are a particular type of representation on the non-analog side, and digital representation is then one particular complex representational type built of numerals (among many others). Analog representations are not different because they are continuous but because they represent numbers in a fundamentally different way. Earlier I mentioned that this difference can also be characterized as first-order versus second-order representation; we can now see what that means.

Start with some physical property to be used as a representation (or part of a representation). As we saw above, with analog representation, the magnitude of the physical property represents the magnitude of the representandum. In an electronic analog computer, five volts represents the number five. Think of this as first-order representation. For digital representation, some value of the physical property represents a symbol (a numeral or some other symbol), and that symbol represents the name of the representandum (or part of the name). In an electronic digital computer, five volts[12] represents the numeral "1." In general, the numeral "1" is then a part of some digital representation, where it represents either the ones digit, or the twos digit, or the fours digit, and so on. Relative to analog representation, then, this is second-order representation.

Despite these differences—differences that the received view cannot capture, using only the resources of "discrete versus continuous"—analog and digital representation are alike in that both are the basis of different types of computation. Understanding analog and digital *computation* requires understanding analog and digital representation in just the way shown in this section: it is not merely the difference between continuous and discrete representations. If we accept the assumption that computation requires representation, we have been doing ourselves a disservice by looking only at digital representations, which occupies a relatively small space of the representational landscape. The analog space has been ignored, largely because its interesting features have been misunderstood. In the next section, we will begin to remedy this situation.

5.3   Computational Types

Just as it was for the case of analog and digital representation, it is a mistake to think that analog and digital *computation* are separated by whether the representations (or mechanisms, variables, or anything else) they use are continuous or discrete. Instead, what makes a computational machine analog or digital is just whether it uses analog or digital representations, in the specific sense outlined in section 5.2. This requires some unpacking, which is the purpose of this section. I will briefly examine some instances of digital and analog computation and mention some of the features that make each unique.

5.3.1   Digital Computation
Virtually all contemporary computing machines are digital computers, based on a design originally proposed by von Neumann (1982). Contrary to popular accounts, what makes these computers specifically digital is the many ways that they take advantage of numbers represented digitally, in the sense presented above. Much has been written about the

general ideas behind computation elsewhere, so here let us focus on what is specifically *digital* about digital computation. All data is ultimately stored as numbers represented digitally, including the very programs that are used to control the precise actions of the machine. So, for example, addition and multiplication in digital computers happens via algorithms familiar to us from elementary school: these operations are the result of digit-by-digit manipulations. The addition of numbers, for example, starts with adding the least-significant digits first, then adding the next-most-significant digits (plus a carry digit, if necessary), then the next-most, and so on. This kind of algorithm is only possible using the digital system with which we are all familiar—the only difference is, in a digital computer, a base-2 system is used, rather than base-10.

Similarly, digital representations enable a systematic organization of the data. As a toy example, suppose we have thirty-two possible locations for storing data. In base-2, we can write those thirty-two as addresses numbered 00000, 00001, 00010, ... 11111. For a variety of reasons, it is more efficient to spread these locations among several different groups. So, suppose we have four different "chips," each of which has eight individual locations.

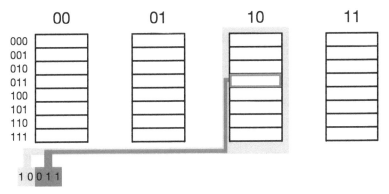

Figure 5.4
Digital addressing.

When we need to access a particular address, we can use the two most-significant digits to locate a particular chip, then the three least-significant digits to locate a particular address within that chip. The circuitry in a digital computer is designed so that this is how the addresses of data are parsed (although, in practice, at a much larger scale). Again, this is a way of taking advantage of the particular organization of numerals in a digital representation of numbers.

Actual digital computers contain huge amounts of data that are processed using a large number of operations at very high speeds. They accomplish what they do by allowing programmers to string together a small number of operations in many complicated ways, usually with different paths for different combinations of possible data. At bottom, however, their operation depends on components whose principles are not different in kind to the toy example here; the only difference in actual machines is their scale.

There are advantages and disadvantages to digital computation. One very simple example is that certain operations are fast. In base-10, increasing the order of magnitude of a number is as simple as adding a zero to its digital representation. For base-2, adding a zero multiplies the number by two. Additionally, we can increase the precision with which we represent a number arbitrarily by simply adding more digits. However, some operations are slow. Determining the largest element in a list requires examining *every* element in that list. A digital computer must do this in much the same way a person would have to find the largest three-digit number in a stack of index cards, where each card has a single number written on it. In order to find the largest, we would have to examine the first one and compare it to the second, keeping the larger of the two. Then, we would have to compare that one to the third one, keeping the largest of *those* two. After repeating this process for every card in the stack, we will have found the largest element.

One might wonder about all of the things we do with digital computers that seem to have nothing to do with the manipulation or storage of numbers. I am writing this sentence with a text editor, and in the background, several other programs are running, checking email, displaying notifications about upcoming appointments, and playing music. Very little of this is about processing numbers.

The answer, of course, is that these things are all ultimately represented in the machine by binary numbers. Not long ago, CDs were a widespread format for musical recordings. But CDs need not hold only music: they can hold data of any type. What makes this true is that, whatever the type of data, it is ultimately represented as numbers, which are represented in binary, and where the individual numerals are physically represented as pits (1s) and lands (0s) on the surface of the CD. Those numbers can then, in turn, represent elements of sounds, or letters, or pixels, or anything else that a particular program has been written to interpret them as. But the mechanisms that store, read, and manipulate *all* of those things can only be understood in the context of that data being represented as numbers represented digitally.

5.3.2 Analog Computation

Whereas digital computation uses digital representations, analog computation uses analog representations. Unfortunately, we are today much less familiar with analog computation, but simple examples can illustrate the principles quite well.

First, to understand how very different analog addition is from digital addition, consider again how we add a pair of, say, two-digit numbers as learned in elementary school. We line them up, add the ones digits and write down the result, then add the tens digits, including a carry digit if necessary. The same addition operation could be done in an *analog* fashion using two long rulers. Suppose we want to add thirty-four to forty-two. We locate forty-two on the first ruler, and thirty-four on the second. Then, we slide the second ruler so that its zero point lines up with forty-two. Finally, we see what number on the first ruler corresponds to thirty-four on the second ruler. Verbally this sounds complicated, but what we are doing is adding two numbers represented as *magnitudes*. Because the magnitudes that are doing the representing are lengths, we simply add (i.e., concatenate) those lengths.

Figure 5.5
Simple analog adder.

Mechanical analog computers of the early twentieth century used principles just like this: numbers were represented by lengths or other magnitudes such as angles, displacements, or the number of rotations of different physical components. A more complicated example is the disk integrator, shown in figure 5.6 (adapted from Maley, forthcoming).

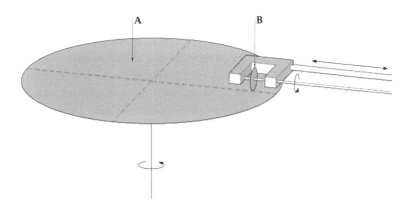

Figure 5.6
A mechanical integrator. The left-right displacement of B is the input, and the output is the running total number of rotations of the connected shaft.

Suppose we want to integrate some function: we input the value of the function, and get as output the definite integral of that function up to that point in time. This integrator works via a constantly-rotating turntable (disk A), which drives a perpendicular disk (B), which can move closer or farther from the center of A. When B is near the edge of A, it will rotate relatively quickly; when it is at the center of A, it will not rotate at all.

The input to this integrator—the value of the function to be integrated—is the displacement of disk B relative to the center of disk A. The output is the total number of rotations of B. If the function to be integrated started at zero and then increased, B would begin in the center of A and move outward (all while A is rotating at a constant speed). If the function decreased, B would move back toward the center of A (and would move to the other side of A if the function became negative). This variation in B's speed is such that the running total of B's rotations is the definite integral of the function.

Much like digital computers, these components could be combined in a large number of ways to produce much more complicated computations at speeds greater than anything a human could perform. One example of such a mechanical analog computer is shown in figure 5.7, where many such components are connected together, as well as drawing tables upon which output or input could be plotted graphically. These mechanical machines eventually gave way to electronic analog computers that used electrical magnitudes, such as voltage or resistance, to represent numbers; Maley (forthcoming) contains several examples.

Just like their digital counterparts, analog computers have advantages and disadvantages. Some operations are fast. For example, suppose (once again) that we want to sort a set of numbers. This time, instead of being written down on index cards (i.e., represented digitally), they are represented by lengths of dry spaghetti noodles (an example taken from Dewdney, 1984). In order to find the largest element, one simply needs to hold the bundle of all noodles together, tamp one end down on a hard surface, and then examine which noodle sticks up the highest. This process is essentially a single step, whereas the digital searching task took as many steps as there were elements to search. Other operations are slower. Whereas increasing the order of magnitude in a digital representation amounted to adding a digit to the representation, such an increase in the analog case can be much more complicated. Adding nine centimeters to a length of one centimeter takes some work, and adding ninety more takes even more work; in the digital case, we simply add a digit, then add another one.

Perhaps the most significant disadvantage of analog computation is the issue of precision. Because analog representation just is the representation of magnitudes by physical magnitudes, what we can *know* about a representation is limited to what we can observe about the physical magnitudes in question. It is difficult to measure lengths in thousandths of a centimeter without specialized equipment, for example; thus, a representation using

Figure 5.7
Mechanical analog computer. Copyright Department of Computer Science and Technology, University of Cambridge. Reproduced by permission.

length might be limited to a small number of significant digits. In the digital case, however, we can increase precision indefinitely by just adding more digits to the representations.

Analog computers no longer exist in any quantity outside museums and private collections; this is how it should be. As practical computing machines, contemporary digital computers outperform analog computers in almost every way. However, analog computation does have a place in our understanding of what computation is in general, not just in the special case of the digital. Moreover, it may well be that, in many cases, neural systems use analog representation and computation. One simple example is the representation of stimuli via neural firing rates: it has been known for almost a century that some neurons will fire more frequently as a tone gets louder or a muscle is increasingly stretched (Adrian, 1926). The firing rate thus monotonically increases as the relevant stimulus increases, which is an analog representation. Combine this with the right mechanisms in place to process that representation, and we have a clear case of analog computation (Maley, 2018).

5.4   The Analog Appeal to Anti-Computationalism

Properly understood, analog computation and representation give us a new understanding of what it could mean for minds—whether natural or artificial—to be computational. This approach might make the thesis that the mind/brain is computational in the first place more palatable to certain anti-computation/anti-representation research programs in cognitive science (a similar point has been made by Isaac, 2018). In particular, certain proponents of radical embodied cognition (Chemero, 2009; Van Gelder, 1995) and radical enactive cognition (Hutto, 2006) have argued that cognition is not computation, and that representation has no place in understanding cognition. However, what they all have in mind is digital—or at least non-analog—computation, where representations are independent from their physical bases, and systems can be understood in purely dynamical terms, without the necessity of any representational language.

Again, there is more to say than there is space to say it, but perhaps it is better to be brief and wrong (but interestingly wrong, one hopes) than to say nothing at all. Consider the Watt governor depicted in figure 5.8, an example originally introduced by Van Gelder (1995), purportedly as a system with complex behavior that can be perfectly described without positing representations. The Watt governor is a device meant to regulate (or

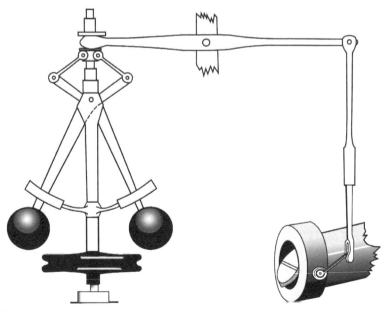

Figure 5.8
The Watt, or centrifugal, governor.

govern) the speed of a steam engine. Steam flows into an engine, which drives a flywheel, which powers some other machinery. The more steam that goes into the engine, the faster the flywheel turns; the governor keeps this speed within a narrow range by adjusting the amount of steam flowing into the engine. The flywheel connects to the horizontal pulley on the bottom left of figure 5.8, causing the metal spheres to rotate. Those spheres are connected by hinges to arms so that, as they rotate, they move outward (by so-called centrifugal force). Those hinges are connected to smaller arms, connected to a large washer such that, as the spheres rotate faster, they cause the washer to move down, which in turn pulls down a lever connected to a valve within the steam pipe, which then reduces the amount of steam flowing through the pipe. In short, it uses the engine speed to drive a mechanism that then reduces that speed (by closing the steam valve) when the speed gets too high, but increases the steam flow when the speed gets too low. It is essentially a feedback mechanism that keeps the steam flow within a certain range, thus keeping the engine at a certain speed.

Famously, van Gelder argued that the arm angle (the crucial variable in understanding this device) can be completely characterized by a differential equation. Had the valve been controlled with a small digital computer, hooked up to sensors and servos, we would certainly have to talk of representations and algorithms in order to understand the device. But given that it is not, a single equation (with the right parameters) completely captures all we need to know about this system. Although one might be tempted to think of the arm angle as representing the engine speed, van Gelder claims this would be a mistake: the equation is all one needs, and talk of representation and computation is superfluous and even potentially misleading. Thus—the argument goes—our mind/brain may well be a system like the Watt governor, where one does not need any talk of representation or computation, and so the computational assumption at the heart of cognitive science might be wrong.

Interestingly, the Watt governor is almost a perfect example of an *analog* computer on the account I have outlined above (a possibility not considered by van Gelder), and actually quite similar to the mechanical analog computers used in military ships in and around World War II, mentioned earlier (Mindell, 2002). These machines took as input the ship's speed and heading, represented as the rotation of shafts and angles of mechanical arms, plus information about the target ship's speed and heading, also represented as mechanical quantities. The output—the gun position required to hit the target—was a mathematical function of the inputs, computed by various mechanical devices, and output as a physical displacement that connected directly to the relevant gun. It is not at all clear why these mechanical analog devices count as representing inputs and computing functions (by the lights of the very people who created them), whereas the Watt governor does not.

Of course, whether the arm angle of the Watt governor represents the engine speed is contentious, and simply asserting that it does would beg the question against van Gelder.

A positive argument is required, and one that does not end up characterizing *all* mechanical devices as computational. Unfortunately, such an argument would take us too far afield. However, what can be shown is that, if the Watt governor were used in a slightly different context, then it *would* be an analog computer, and we *would* attribute to it representations in order to analyze and explain what it does, even by van Gelder's lights.

The Watt governor would be an analog computer if we were to use the speed of the engine as the input and the angle of the steam valve as the output, where the function computed is just the mathematical relation between the two. In that context, it would also be quite similar to the mechanical integrator illustrated in figure 5.6. Now, by van Gelder's own lights, the function that describes the relationship between the input and output is a mathematical one, and thus this device would compute precisely that function. All that remains is for the inputs and outputs to be genuine representations. As we have seen, all kinds of physical quantities can serve as the inputs and outputs to analog computers: besides the electrical and mechanical examples we have already seen, the economy-simulating MONIAC analog computer used fluid levels and fluid flow as variables (Isaac, 2018). Thus, engine speed and valve angle are as good as anything.

Now, one might object to the idea that we can just take an arbitrary mechanical component and use it as part of an analog computer. However, this should not be all that surprising. Even though analog computers are not medium-independent in the way non-analog computers are, there is still a wide variety of ways to physically create an analog computer. The primary difference is that a given mechanism might only be able to implement one particular mathematical function because of physical constraints on what it can represent. The Watt governor, for example, has an output that is a specific trigonomic function of its input with a narrow range. If we need such a function, the Watt governor will work perfectly in our mechanical analog computer, and we will explain the mechanism that transforms the input to the output by showing how the arm angles (and other components) represent the quantities specified in the equation. But we cannot use the Watt governor to implement just any function we want.

Whether radical embodied and enactive cognitive scientists will be amenable to these ideas will ultimately be up to them; one might anticipate that they will take the notion of "analog representation" developed here to be a rather thin notion of representation, which in turn makes analog computation itself rather thin. However, if historical precedent matters at all, analog computers, which preceded digital computers, are just as legitimate a form of computation as anything. Those hostile to computation but friendly to dynamical systems (for example) may have to reevaluate who they think their enemies are.

Of course, it remains to be seen whether cognitive science is correct in taking the mind/brain to be a computer in the first place. Philosophers of computation have gone a long way in helping to clarify what computation might be, allowing for this thesis to rise to the level of a testable hypothesis, rather than a working assumption, or a mere metaphorical framework. Properly understanding analog computation is a part of this effort, allowing researchers more options for understanding how the mind/brain might be a computer in a principled, systematic way.

Notes for Chapter 5

1. Which is not to say that nothing has been written: a few excellent examples include Mahoney's work, as well as (Campbell-Kelly et al., 2013) and (Haigh and Ceruzzi, 2021).

2. It is well known that the term "computer" referred to a human performing computations; in this section, I will refer to either "human computers" or "computing machines" to avoid ambiguity.

3. Or if not voltages, whatever the implementational media happens to be.

4. By a "continuous" representation, I mean a representation that can vary continuously: along a continuum. An individual representation cannot, by itself, be continuous; but phrasing things otherwise is rather cumbersome, so I will use this convention.

5. I will use the somewhat cumbersome English spelling of numbers here, simply to avoid using one representational scheme in the text to make a point about a completely different scheme.

6. Note that I am *not* specifying how the relevant properties of the representation would actually change; that is not relevant here. For the moment, I am just elucidating what is required for something to be an analog representation at all.

7. This is characterized more precisely in (Maley, forthcoming).

8. The first example is also a case of digital representation, although the second is not: more on this distinction is given in the next section.

9. I use the qualifier "in a sense" because even though the real numbers are continuous, a single real number is not, and it is not the case that the set of all digital expansions of real numbers is itself continuous.

10. In the case of bases higher than 10, new symbols are used as numerals. The hexadecimal (base-16) system uses A for 10, B for 11, and so on, so that "A2F" = $(A \times 16^2) + (2 \times 16^1) + (F \times 16^0) = (10 \times 256) + (2 \times 16) + (15 \times 1) = 2607$.

11. For example, 48π is interpreted as the multiplication of a two-digit number (forty-eight) with a symbolically represented one (π), but *not* as a three-digit number.

12. Usually, "1" is represented by five volts, and "0" is represented by zero volts, but there are other conventions.

II   WHAT IS INTELLIGENCE?

Part II: What Is Intelligence?

The central aim of artificial intelligence (AI) is to build intelligent machines. But what does it mean for a machine to be "intelligent"? And how can we *tell* when a machine is, in fact, intelligent? The articles in this part take different stances on these fundamental questions.

According to one dominant tradition, tracing to Turing's "Computing Machinery and Intelligence" (chapter 6), one answer suffices for both questions. In that article, Turing introduces the movie-worthy "Turing Test" for intelligence, which uses the paradigm of human conversation as the touchstone for assessing machines. That test operationalizes "intelligent machine" as a machine that can convince observers more often than not that it is (likely) a (typical) human. As with Justice Potter Stewart's definition of pornography, we know intelligence when we see it. Furthermore, we come to know it by comparing it to exemplars: in the case of AI, to human intelligent behavior.

Leveseque's argument (in chapter 7) is narrower and more proscriptive: even granting that symbol manipulation might suffice for understanding, the Turing test is too easily gamed. One of the first chatbots, Eliza, plays the role of a Rogerian psychotherapist by simply turning questions around on the interlocutor: "Are you sure?" "And how does [that] make you feel?" "How long have you been [feeling like that]?" "I'm not sure I understand you fully." Although Eliza is hardly convincing to a determined interlocutor, it shows a kind of strategy that future chatbots emulate more effectively: using humor and other deflection strategies to create a charming conversationalist, good at distracting the interlocutor from assessing whether its conversation partner really knows what's going on. What is required, Levesque claims, is a more direct test of whether and what the computer understands. For this, he argues that "Winograd schemas" can be used to test an interlocutor's ability to use background knowledge to disambiguate anaphoric pronoun reference in cases in which common background knowledge clearly and decisively solves the puzzle.

In her broad and provocative essay (chapter 10), Melanie Mitchell argues that we do not yet have a clear conception of what intelligence is. She claims that that this lack of a guiding idea is at least partially to blame for the cycles of enthusiasm (AI springs) and disappointment (AI winters) that characterize the history of AI. She identifies four fundamental "fallacies" that, she argues, give AI researchers an artificial sense of progress toward the goal of generalized AI—that is, toward AI that more or less captures how typical competent adults function. One unifying theme in all these fallacies is a difference between the kind of narrow, domain-specific problem-solving capacity that produces so much excitement (e.g., face recognition) and the kind of broad, domain-general knowledge that seems to come so effortlessly to the human mind.

This relationship between domain-specific and domain-general capacities is precisely what is at stake in Fodor's classic distinction between vertical (narrow, domain-specific, informationally encapsulated processers) and horizontal (broad, integrative, informationally porous) systems. Fodor's central thesis (chapter 9) is that domain-specific processing systems can take us only so far in our understanding of the mind. Our ability to endorse beliefs (as in the development of scientific beliefs), our ability to use language to describe domain-specific sensory inputs, and the integration of perception and action in purposive, goal-driven ways all seem to require access to broad, general information that one cannot specify in advance. Fodor argues, on this basis, that there must be non-modular systems (i.e., systems that are not narrowly informationally encapsulated) that can integrate the input from different modular systems to achieve the kind of belief-formation and agential capacities typical of humans.

One common way to characterize the kind of central processing that Fodor is after is in terms of "rationality": belief fixation and purposive action are, one might think, definitively characterized in terms of a kind of reason-responsiveness and, as such, a responsiveness to the rules of correct or incorrect inference. Russell's article takes as its fundamental assumption that a central goal of AI is to build machines that are rational. But, he asks, what is rationality? Is it the kind of rationality Fodor has in mind? Furthermore, how rational do we expect our AI machines to be? Must their rationality be perfect (and Spock-like), or is it sufficient merely to achieve human (i.e., demonstrably sub-optimal) levels of rationality? Additionally, must the rationality be evident in behavior alone, or must the internal reasoning process also ape human ratiocinative thought? By exploring the contours of these questions, Russell notes some of the obvious limitations on computational systems, as well as on minds. Time constraints matter, for example. Even paradigmatically intelligent humans can't consider all possible information. But how fast must these machines work? And how rational must they be? And what is the sense of rationality that constitutes the appropriate target in the effort to build suitably rational machines? In the process, Russell explores degrees of "hardness" in AI problems and offers a theory of bounded rationality that, he argues, suffices as a reasonable target for the field.

Combinations and Additions
The Turing Test.   The Turing test has been both controversial and central to discussions in AI. Those looking to read further might consider the following essays.

- For a useful review of the Turing test, its critiques, and its strengths and weaknesses, consider Saygin et al. (2003).
- Copeland (2000) defends the Turing test against a number of standard objections.
- Harnad (1991) argues that the Turing test would be improved if it required one to respond to all kinds of inputs, not just the linguistic inputs that Turing envisioned. This expanded version has come to be called the Total Turing Test.

- Hayes and Ford (1995) argue that the Turing test is a bad research goal for AI, given that it is ill-defined and amounts to an effort to confirm a null hypothesis: namely, that humans and machines are indistinguishable.

Winograd Schemas. Those wishing to follow up on Levesque's suggestion that Winograd schemas provide a superior test over the Turing test might consider reviewing the following recent articles:

- For updates on the Winograd test and the latest in attempts to master it, one might visit https://cs.nyu.edu/~davise/papers/WinogradSchemas/WS.html.
- Brown et al. (2020) review recent progress in tackling the challenge of disambiguating Winograd schemas; such progress appears to have been made using resources that do not require generalized knowledge.
- Sakaguchi et al. (2019) make a similar point, showing that progress can be made on disambiguating Winograd schemas without making serious progress in supplying machines with the kind of copious background knowledge characteristic of humans.

The Frame Problem. You open a bottle of root beer. In doing so, you make the soda accessible to drinking, you reduce the pressure in the bottle, and you bend a bottle cap. Yet most other things continue unchanged: the orbit of Mars, the outcome of the Pirates' game, and the curious delicacy of soup dumplings at Joe's Shanghai. Although we assume that single small changes do not change everything else in the world, that principle has proved remarkably difficult to formalize. Yet formalizing such a notion (knowing what does *not* change with our actions) seems to be required to build a rational agent. Fodor notes that this problem arises for his central processor: given that it is informationally un-encapsulated, any perception or action might be relevant to all of one's beliefs. Surely this is part of the challenge of encapsulating commonsense knowledge that Mitchell has in mind in her essay in this part (chapter 10). It is also related to arguments for modularity of mind considered by Woodward and Cowie in part IV, as one benefit of modular systems is that they need not consider the implications of new input for all of one's beliefs. Consider the following:

- Chow (2013) provides a useful overview of the frame problem and its significance for AI. He disambiguates six versions of the frame problem and discusses some "heuristic" solutions and their limitations. Ultimately, he argues that humans do not solve the frame problem, but, rather, sidestep it.
- Wheeler (2008) offers a self-avowedly Heideggerian solution to the frame problem that might usefully be paired with the articles by Haugeland (chapter 22) and Brooks (chapter 23) in part VI.

- Korb (1998) argues that the frame problem as originally formulated is unsolvable. However, with suitable restrictions the problem can be solved with appropriately powerful causal models. This essay might fruitfully be combined with Pearl's essay in part V (chapter 18).

Bounded Rationality.   It is no trivial matter to say what *non*-bounded rationality is, though it is often taken to involve at least conformity of one's thoughts with the axioms of logic and mathematics, and conformity of one's decisions and actions with expected utility theory. Everyone knows that humans fall short of these standards; some of the major themes in twentieth-century psychology and decision theory involve cataloging the ways in which human rationality is bounded. Some of these bounds have to do with limits on our memory or our time. Others have to do with the sorts of environments in which we evolved, and the specific skill sets for which they selected. For a few small sips of this firehose of information, one might consider:

- The concept of bounded rationality, as instantiated in Russell's essay, traces to the work of Herbert Simon (e.g., Simon, 1955). For a more recent review, see Cherniak (1986).
- For the specific influence of Russell's ideas on computer science, one might look to, for example, Zilberstein and Russell (1996), which discusses the feasibility of algorithms that can terminate after an unknown span of time.
- We are evolved organisms, and it is an open question how much evolution has shaped our capacities—and therefore what we think of as intelligence. Buss (1995) gives a nice expression of the contemporary sort of evolutionary psychology, which tries to explain our present limitations as adaptations to a very particular ancestral environment. Note that not all evolutionary accounts of what we are focus on *limitations* or assume that biological evolution alone is important. Culture is an important part of our evolutionary legacy, and it scaffolds many of our interesting cognitive abilities. Sterelny (2012) is a good example of the more nuanced strand of evolutionary psychology that looks to comparative and ethnographic work, focusing on the role of social interaction and social learning in shaping minds. Heyes (2018) similarly tries to weave a more plausible evolutionary story about the mind that is also sensitive to the role of culture.

AGI and UAI.   One way to contrast contemporary machine learning with the broad, flexible intelligence found in humans is to say that the latter is *general* or *universal*. This has given rise to two traditions with slightly different names: the search for *Artificial General Intelligence (AGI)* or for *Universal Artificial Intelligence (UAI)*. The differences between the two tend to be matters of intellectual tradition and technological focus; both are concerned with ways in which truly general intelligence might be built. Consider the following:

- Chollet (2019) presents a good review of the history of intelligence-measuring tasks and the way that they have often fallen short with AI. In addition to postulating several criteria for a good test of general intelligence, he presents the "Abstraction and Reasoning Corpus" (ARC). The ARC is a pattern-completion task that is meant to satisfy his criteria for a good test, as well as doing something that recognizably taps into human intelligence when *we* solve these problems. To date, success rates on the ARC are still low.

- The term "Artificial General Intelligence" captures a broad set of trends, and includes much of what tends towards the techno-futurist end of the spectrum. Notable in this arena is the work of the philosopher Nick Bostrom, who has written extensively on the problems posed by general intelligence. Much of this work is collected in Bostrom (2014).

- Much of UAI is inspired by the work of Marcus Hutter, who focuses on information-theoretic approaches to understanding intelligence. One feature of intelligence seems to be the ability to compress information in useful ways. Any modern computer could host videos of thousands of games of cricket, but extracting from those the *rules* of cricket would be far more challenging. This notion of compression is in turn related to classic philosophical questions like the problem of induction; indeed, on some readings, UAI claims that a solution to the general problem of induction would just *be* a foundation for general intelligence. His work is technically demanding, but Hutter (2012) gives a good high-level introduction to the approach.

Computing Machinery and Intelligence

6

Alan M. Turing
1950

6.1 The imitation game

I propose to consider the question "Can machines think?" This should begin with definitions of the meaning of the terms 'machine' and 'think'. The definitions might be framed so as to reflect so far as possible the normal use of the words, but this attitude is dangerous. If the meaning of the words 'machine' and 'think' are to be found by examining how they are commonly used it is difficult to escape the conclusion that the meaning and the answer to the question, "Can machines think?" is to be sought in a statistical survey such as a Gallup poll. But this is absurd. Instead of attempting such a definition I shall replace the question by another, which is closely related to it and is expressed in relatively unambiguous words.

The new form of the problem can be described in terms of a game which we call the "imitation game". It is played with three people, a man (A), a woman (B), and an interrogator (C) who may be of either sex. The interrogator stays in a room apart from the other two. The object of the game for the interrogator is to determine which of the other two is the man and which is the woman. He knows them by labels X and Y, and at the end of the game he says either "X is A and Y is B" or "X is B and Y is A". The interrogator is allowed to put questions to A and B thus:

C: Will X please tell me the length of his or her hair?

Now suppose X is actually A, then A must answer. It is A's object in the game to try to cause C to make the wrong identification. His answer might therefore be:

A: My hair is shingled, and the longest strands are about nine inches long.

In order that tones of voice may not help the interrogator the answers should be written, or better still, typewritten. The ideal arrangement is to have a teleprinter communicating between the two rooms. Alternatively the question and answers can be repeated by an intermediary. The object of the game for the third player (B) is to help the interrogator. The best strategy for her is probably to give truthful answers. She can add such things as "I am the woman, don't listen to him!" to her answers, but it will avail nothing as the man can make similar remarks.

We now ask the question, "What will happen when a machine takes the part of A in this game?" Will the interrogator decide wrongly as often when the game is played like this as he does when the game is played between a man and a woman? These questions replace our original, "Can machines think?"

6.2   Critique of the new problem

As well as asking, "What is the answer to this new form of the question?" one may ask, "Is this new question a worthy one to investigate?" This latter question we investigate without further ado, thereby cutting short an infinite regress.

The new problem has the advantage of drawing a fairly sharp line between the physical and the intellectual capacities of a man. No engineer or chemist claims to be able to produce a material which is indistinguishable from the human skin. It is possible that at some time this might be done, but even supposing this invention available we should feel there was little point in trying to make a "thinking machine" more human by dressing it up in such artificial flesh. The form in which we have set the problem reflects this fact in the condition which prevents the interrogator from seeing or touching the other competitors, or hearing their voices. Some other advantages of the proposed criterion may be shown up by specimen questions and answers. Thus:

Q: Please write me a sonnet on the subject of the Forth Bridge.

A: Count me out on this one. I never could write poetry.

Q: Add 34957 to 70764.

A: (Pause about 30 seconds and then give as answer) 105621.

Q: Do you play chess?

A: Yes.

Q: I have K at my Kl, and no other pieces. You have only K at K6 and R at Rl. It is your move. What do you play?

A: (After a pause of 15 seconds) R–R8 mate.

The question and answer method seems to be suitable for introducing almost any one of the fields of human endeavor that we wish to include. We do not wish to penalize the machine for its inability to shine in beauty competitions, nor to penalize a man for losing in a race against an airplane. The conditions of our game make these disabilities irrelevant. The "witnesses" can brag, if they consider it advisable, as much as they please about their charms, strength or heroism, but the interrogator cannot demand practical demonstrations.

The game may perhaps be criticized on the ground that the odds are weighted too heavily against the machine. If the man were to try and pretend to be the machine he would clearly make a very poor showing. He would be given away at once by slowness and inaccuracy in arithmetic. May not machines carry out something which ought to be described as thinking but which is very different from what a man does? This objection is a very strong one, but at least we can say that if, nevertheless, a machine can be constructed to play the imitation game satisfactorily, we need not be troubled by this objection.

It might be urged that when playing the "imitation game" the best strategy for the machine may possibly be something other than imitation of the behavior of a man. This may be, but I think it is unlikely that there is any great effect of this kind. In any case there is no intention to investigate here the theory of the game, and it will be assumed that the best strategy is to try to provide answers that would naturally be given by a man.

6.3   The machines concerned in the game

The question which we put in Section 6.1 will not be quite definite until we have specified what we mean by the word 'machine'. It is natural that we should wish to permit every kind of engineering technique to be used in our machines. We also wish to allow the possibility that an engineer or team of engineers may construct a machine which works, but whose manner of operation cannot be satisfactorily described by its constructors because they have applied a method which is largely experimental. Finally, we wish to exclude from the machines men born in the usual manner. It is difficult to frame the definitions so as to satisfy these three conditions. One might for instance insist that the team of engineers should be all of one sex, but this would not really be satisfactory, for it is probably possible to rear a complete individual from a single cell of the skin (say) of a man. To do so would be a feat of biological technique deserving of the very highest praise, but we would not be inclined to regard it as a case of "constructing a thinking machine". This prompts us to abandon the requirement that every kind of technique should be permitted. We are the more ready to do so in view of the fact that the present interest in "thinking machines" has been aroused by a particular kind of machine, usually called an "electronic computer" or "digital computer". Following this suggestion we only permit digital computers to take part in our game.

This restriction appears at first sight to be a very drastic one. I shall attempt to show that it is not so in reality. To do this necessitates a short account of the nature and properties of these computers.

It may also be said that this identification of machines with digital computers, like our criterion for "thinking", will only be unsatisfactory if (contrary to my belief), it turns out that digital computers are unable to give a good showing in the game.

There are already a number of digital computers in working order, and it may be asked, "Why not try the experiment straight away? It would be easy to satisfy the conditions of the game. A number of interrogators could be used, and statistics compiled to show how often the right identification was given." The short answer is that we are not asking whether all digital computers would do well in the game nor whether the computers at present available would do well, but whether there are imaginable computers which would do well. But this is only the short answer. We shall see this question in a different light later.

6.4   Digital computers

The idea behind digital computers may be explained by saying that these machines are intended to carry out any operations which could be done by a human computer. The human computer is supposed to be following fixed rules; he has no authority to deviate from them in any detail. We may suppose that these rules are supplied in a book, which is altered whenever he is put on to a new job. He has also an unlimited supply of paper on which he does his calculations. He may also do his multiplications and additions on a "desk machine", but this is not important.

If we use the above explanation as a definition, we shall be in danger of circularity of argument. We avoid this by giving an outline of the means by which the desired effect is achieved. A digital computer can usually be regarded as consisting of three parts:

   (i) Store.
  (ii) Executive unit.
 (iii) Control.

The store is a store of information, and corresponds to the human computer's paper, whether this is the paper on which he does his calculations or that on which his book of rules is printed. Insofar as the human computer does calculations in his head, a part of the store will correspond to his memory.

The executive unit is the part which carries out the various individual operations involved in a calculation. What these individual operations are will vary from machine to machine. Usually fairly lengthy operations, such as "Multiply 3540675445 by 7076345687", can be done, but in some machines only very simple ones, such as "Write down 0", are possible.

We have mentioned that the "book of rules" supplied to the computer is replaced in the machine by a part of the store. It is then called the "table of instructions". It is the duty of the control to see that these instructions are obeyed correctly and in the right order. The control is so constructed that this necessarily happens.

The information in the store is usually broken up into packets of moderately small size. In one machine, for instance, a packet might consist of ten decimal digits. Numbers are assigned to the parts of the store in which the various packets of information are stored, in some systematic manner. A typical instruction might say:

> Add the number stored in position 6809 to that in 4302 and put the result back into the latter storage position.

Needless to say it would not occur in the machine expressed in English. It would more likely be coded in a form such as 6809430217. Here 17 says which of various possible operations is to be performed on the two numbers—in this case the operation that is described above, namely, "Add the number . . . ". It will be noticed that the instruction takes up 10 digits and so forms one packet of information, very conveniently. The control will normally take the instructions to be obeyed in the order of the positions in which they are stored, but occasionally an instruction such as

> Now obey the instruction stored in position 5606, and continue from there.

may be encountered, or again

> If position 4505 contains 0 obey next the instruction stored in 6707, otherwise continue straight on.

Instructions of these latter types are very important because they make it possible for a sequence of operations to be repeated over and over again until some condition is fulfilled, but in doing so to obey, not fresh instructions on each repetition, but the same ones over and over again. To take a domestic analogy, suppose Mother wants Tommy to call at the cobbler's every morning on his way to school to see if her shoes are done. She can ask him afresh every morning. Alternatively she can stick up a notice once and for all in the hall which he will see when he leaves for school and which tells him to call for the shoes, and also to destroy the notice when he comes back if he has the shoes with him.

The reader must accept it as a fact that digital computers can be constructed, and indeed have been constructed, according to the principles we have described, and that they can in fact mimic the actions of a human computer very closely.

The book of rules which we have described our human computer as using is of course a convenient fiction. Actual human computers really remember what they have got to do. If one wants to make a machine mimic the behavior of the human computer in some complex operation one has to ask him how it is done, and then translate the answer into the form of an instruction table. Constructing instruction tables is usually described as "programming". To "program a machine to carry out the operation A" means to put the appropriate instruction table into the machine so that it will do A.

An interesting variant on the idea of a digital computer is a digital computer with a random element. These have instructions involving the throwing of a die or some equivalent electronic process; one such instruction might for instance be

> Throw the die and put the resulting number into store 1000.

Sometimes such a machine is described as having free will (though I would not use this phrase myself). It is not normally possible to determine from observing a machine whether it has a random element, for a similar effect can be produced by such devices as making the choices depend on the digits of the decimal for π.

Most actual digital computers have only a finite store. There is no theoretical difficulty in the idea of a computer with an unlimited store. Of course only a finite part of it can have been used at any one time. Likewise only a finite amount can have been constructed, but we can imagine more and more being added as required. Such computers have special theoretical interest and will be called infinite capacity computers.

The idea of a digital computer is an old one. Charles Babbage, Lucasian Professor of Mathematics at Cambridge from 1828 to 1839, planned such a machine, called the "Analytical Engine", but it was never completed. Although Babbage had all the essential ideas, his machine was not at that time such a very attractive prospect. The speed which would have been available would be definitely faster than a human computer but something like 100 times slower than the Manchester machine, itself one of the slower of the modern machines. The storage was to be purely mechanical, using wheels and cards.

The fact that Babbage's Analytical Engine was to be entirely mechanical will help us to rid ourselves of a superstition. Importance is often attached to the fact that modern digital computers are electrical, and that the nervous system also is electrical. Since Babbage's machine was not electrical, and since all digital computers are in a sense equivalent, we see that this use of electricity cannot be of theoretical importance. Of course electricity usually comes in where fast signaling is concerned, so it is not surprising that we find it in both these connections. In the nervous system chemical phenomena are at least as important as electrical. In certain computers the storage system is mainly acoustic. The feature of using electricity is thus seen to be only a very superficial similarity. If we wish to find such similarities we should look rather for mathematical analogies of function.

6.5   Universality of digital computers

The digital computers considered in the last section may be classified among the "discrete state machines". These are the machines which move by sudden jumps or clicks from one quite definite state to another. These states are sufficiently different for the possibility of confusion between them to be ignored. Strictly speaking there are no such machines. Everything really moves continuously. But there are many kinds of machines which can profitably be *thought of* as being discrete state machines. For instance in considering the switches for a lighting system it is a convenient fiction that each switch must be definitely on or definitely off. There must be intermediate positions, but for most purposes we can forget about them. As an example of a discrete state machine, we might consider a wheel which clicks round through 120° once a second, but may be stopped by a lever which can be operated from outside; in addition a lamp is to light in one of the positions of the wheel. This machine could be described abstractly as follows: The internal state of the machine (which is described by the position of the wheel) may be q_1, q_2, or q_3. There is an input signal i_0 or i_1 (position of lever). The internal state at any moment is determined by the last state and input signal according to the table

		Last State:		
		q_1	q_2	q_3
Input:	i_0	q_2	q_3	q_1
	i_1	q_1	q_2	q_3

The output signals, the only externally visible indication of the internal state (the light), are described by the table

State:	q_1	q_2	q_3
Output:	O_0	O_0	O_1

This example is typical of discrete state machines. They can be described by such tables, provided they have only a finite number of possible states.

It will seem that given the initial state of the machine and the input signals it is always possible to predict all future states. This is reminiscent of Laplace's view that from the complete state of the universe at one moment of time, as described by the positions and velocities of all particles, it should be possible to predict all future states. The prediction which we are considering is, however, rather nearer to practicability than that considered by Laplace. The system of the "universe as a whole" is such that quite small errors in the initial conditions can have an overwhelming effect at a later time. The displacement of a single electron by a billionth of a centimeter at one moment might make the difference between a man being killed by an avalanche a year later, or escaping. It is an essential property of the mechanical systems which we have called "discrete state machines" that this phenomenon does not occur. Even when we consider the actual physical machines instead of the idealized machines, reasonably accurate knowledge of the state at one moment yields reasonably accurate knowledge any number of steps later.

As we have mentioned, digital computers fall within the class of discrete state machines. But the number of states of which such a machine is capable is usually enormously large. For instance, the number for the machine now working at Manchester is about $2^{165,000}$ — that is, about $10^{50,000}$. Compare this with our example of the dicking wheel described above, which had three states. It is not difficult to see why the number of states should be so immense. The computer includes a store corresponding to the paper used by a human computer. It must be possible to write into the store any one of the combinations of symbols which might have been written on the paper. For simplicity suppose that only digits from 0 to 9 are used as symbols. Variations in handwriting are ignored. Suppose the computer is allowed 100 sheets of paper each containing 50 lines each with room for 30 digits. Then the number of states is $10^{100 \times 50 \times 30}$—that is, $10^{150,000}$. This is about the number of states of three Manchester machines put together. The logarithm to the base two of the number of states is usually called the "storage capacity" of the machine. Thus the Manchester machine has a storage capacity of about 165,000 and the wheel machine of our example about 1.6. If two machines are put together their capacities must be added to obtain the capacity of the resultant machine. This leads to the possibility of statements such as "The Manchester machine contains 64 magnetic tracks each with a capacity of 2560, eight electronic tubes with a capacity of 1280. Miscellaneous storage amounts to about 300 making a total of 174,380."

Given the table corresponding to a discrete state machine, it is possible to predict what it will do. There is no reason why this calculation should not be carried out by means of a digital computer. Provided it could be carried out sufficiently quickly the digital computer could mimic the behavior of any discrete state machine. The imitation game could then be played with the machine in question (as B) and the mimicking digital computer (as A) and the interrogator would be unable to distinguish them. Of course the digital computer must have adequate storage capacity a well as working sufficiently fast. Moreover, it must be programmed afresh for each new machine which it is desired to mimic.

This special property of digital computers, that they can mimic any discrete state machine, is described by saying that they are *universal* machines. The existence of machines with this property has the important consequence that, considerations of speed apart, it is unnecessary to design various new machines to do various computing processes. They can all be done with one digital computer, suitably programmed for each case. It will be seen that as a consequence of this all digital computers are in a sense equivalent.

We may now consider again the point raised at the end of Section 6.3. It was suggested tentatively that the question, "Can machines think?" should be replaced by "Are there imaginable digital computers which would do well in the imitation game?" If we wish we can make this superficially more general and ask, "Are there discrete state machines which would do well?" But in view of the universality property we see that either of these questions is equivalent to this: "Let us fix our attention on one particular digital computer C. Is it true that by modifying this computer to have an adequate storage, suitably increasing its speed of action, and providing it with an appropriate program, C can be made to play satisfactorily the part of A in the imitation game, the part of B being taken by a man?"

6.6   Contrary views on the main question

We may now consider the ground to have been cleared and we are ready to proceed to the debate on our question, "Can machines think?" and the variant of it quoted at the end of the last section. We cannot altogether abandon the original form of the problem, for opinions will differ as to the appropriateness of the substitution and we must at least listen to what has to be said in this connection.

It will simplify matters for the reader if I explain first my own beliefs in the matter. Consider first the more accurate form of the question. I believe that in about fifty years' time it will be possible to program computers, with a storage capacity of about 10^9, to make them play the imitation game so well that an average interrogator will not have more than 70 per cent chance of making the right identification after five minutes of questioning. The original question, "Can machines think?" I believe to be too meaningless to deserve discussion. Nevertheless I believe that at the end of the century the use of words and general educated opinion will have altered so much that one will be able to speak of machines thinking without expecting to be contradicted. I believe further that no useful purpose is served by concealing these beliefs. The popular view that scientists proceed inexorably from well-established fact to well-established fact, never being influenced by any unproved conjecture, is quite mistaken. Provided it is made clear which are proved facts and which are conjectures, no harm can result. Conjectures are of great importance since they suggest useful lines of research.

I now proceed to consider opinions opposed to my own.

(1) THE THEOLOGICAL OBJECTION. Thinking is a function of man's immortal soul. God has given an immortal soul to every man and woman, but not to any other animal or to machines. Hence no animal or machine can think.[1]

I am unable to accept any part of this, but will attempt to reply in theological terms. I should find the argument more convincing if animals were classed with men, for there is a greater difference, to my mind, between the typical animate and the inanimate than there is between man and the other animals. The arbitrary character of the orthodox view becomes clearer if we consider how it might appear to a member of some other religious community. How do Christians regard the Moslem view that women have no souls? But let us leave this point aside and return to the main argument. It appears to me that the argument quoted above implies a serious restriction of the omnipotence of the Almighty. It is admitted that there are certain things that He cannot do such as making one equal to two, but should we not believe that He has freedom to confer a soul on an elephant if He sees fit? We might expect that He would only exercise this power in conjunction with a mutation which provided the elephant with an appropriately improved brain to minister to the needs of this soul. An argument of exactly similar form may be made for the case of machines. It may seem different because it is more difficult to "swallow". But this really only means that we think it would be less likely that He would consider the circumstances suitable for conferring a soul. The circumstances in question are discussed in the rest of this paper. In attempting to construct such machines we should not be irreverently usurping His power of creating souls, any more than we are in the procreation of children: rather we are, in either case, instruments of His will providing mansions for the souls that He creates.

However, this is mere speculation. I am not very impressed with theological arguments, whatever they may be used to support. Such arguments have often been found unsatisfactory in the past. In the time of Galileo it was argued that the texts, "And the sun stood still . . . and hasted not to go down about a whole day" (Joshua x. 13) and "He laid the foundations of the earth, that it should not move at any time" (Psalm cv. 5) were an adequate refutation of the Copernican theory. With our present knowledge, such an argument appears futile. When that knowledge was not available, it made a quite different impression.

(2) THE "HEADS IN THE SAND" OBJECTION. "The consequences of machines thinking would be too dreadful. Let us hope and believe that they cannot do so."

This argument is seldom expressed quite so openly as in the form above. But it affects most of us who think about it at all. We like to believe that Man is in some subtle way superior to the rest of creation. It is best if he can be shown to be *necessarily* superior, for then there is no danger of him losing his commanding position. The popularity of the theological argument is clearly connected with this feeling. It is likely to be quite strong in intellectual people, since they value the power of thinking more highly than others, and are more inclined to base their belief in the superiority of Man on this power.

I do not think that this argument is sufficiently substantial to require refutation. Consolation would be more appropriate; perhaps this should be sought in the transmigration of souls.

(3) THE MATHEMATICAL OBJECTION. There are a number of results of mathematical logic which can be used to show that there are limitations to the powers of discrete state machines. The best known of these results is known as Gödel's theorem (1931), and shows that in any sufficiently powerful logical system statements can be formulated which can neither be proved nor disproved within the system, unless possibly the system itself is inconsistent. There are other, in some respects similar, results due to Church (1936), Kleene (1936), Rosser (1936), and Turing (1937). The latter result is the most convenient to consider, since it refers directly to machines whereas the others can only be used in a comparatively indirect argument; for instance, if Godel's theorem is to be used we need in addition to have some means of describing logical systems in terms of machines, and machines in terms of logical systems. The result in question refers to a type of machine which is essentially a digital computer with an infinite capacity. It states that there are certain things that such a machine cannot do. If it is rigged up to give answers to questions as in the imitation game, there will be some questions to which it will either give a wrong answer, or fail to give an answer at all, however much time is allowed for a reply. There may, of course, be many such questions, and questions which cannot be answered by one machine may be satisfactorily answered by another. We are of course supposing for the

present that the questions are of the kind to which an answer "Yes" or "No" is appropriate, rather than questions such as "What do you think of Picasso?" The questions that we know the machines must fail on are of this type, "Consider the machine specified as follows . . . Will this machine ever answer 'Yes' to any question?" The dots are to be replaced by a description of some machine in a standard form, which could be something like that used in Section 6.5. When the machine described bears a certain comparatively simple relation to the machine which is under interrogation, it can be shown that the answer is either wrong or not forthcoming. This is the mathematical result; it is argued that it proves a disability of machines to which the human intellect is not subject.

The short answer to this argument is that, although it is established that there are limitations to the powers of any particular machine, it has only been stated, without any sort of proof, that no such limitations apply to the human intellect. But I do not think this view can be dismissed quite so lightly. Whenever one of these machines is asked the appropriate critical question, and gives a definite answer, we know that this answer must be wrong, and this gives us a certain feeling of superiority. Is this feeling illusory? It is no doubt quite genuine, but I do not think too much importance should be attached to it. We too often give wrong answers to questions ourselves to be justified in being very pleased at such evidence of fallibility on the part of the machines. Further, our superiority can only be felt on such an occasion in relation to the one machine over which we have scored our petty triumph. There would be no question of triumphing simultaneously over *all* machines. In short, then, there might be men cleverer than any given machine, but then again there might be other machines cleverer again, and so on.

Those who hold to the mathematical argument would, I think, mostly be willing to accept the imitation game as a basis for discussion. Those who believe in the two previous objections would probably not be interested in any criteria.

(4) THE ARGUMENT FROM CONSCIOUSNESS. This argument is very well expressed in Professor Jefferson's Lister Oration for 1949, from which I quote.

> Not until a machine can write a sonnet or compose a concerto because of thoughts and emotions felt, and not by the chance fall of symbols, could we agree that machine equals brain—that is, not only write it but know that it had written it. No mechanism could feel (and not merely artificially signal, an easy contrivance) pleasure at its successes, grief when its valves fuse, be warmed by flattery, be made miserable by its mistakes, be charmed by sex, be angry or depressed when it cannot get what it wants.

This argument appears to be a denial of the validity of our test. According to the most extreme form of this view, the only way by which one could be sure that a machine thinks is to *be* the machine and to feel oneself thinking. One could then describe these feelings to the world, but of course no one would be justified in taking any notice. Likewise according to this view, the only way to know that a *man* thinks is to be that particular man. It is in fact the solipsist point of view. It may be the most logical view to hold but it makes communication of ideas difficult. A is liable to believe "A thinks but B does not" while

B believes "B thinks but A does not". Instead of arguing continually over this point, it is usual to have the polite convention that everyone thinks.

I am sure that Professor Jefferson does not wish to adopt the extreme and solipsist point of view. Probably he would be quite willing to accept the imitation game as a test. The game (with the player B omitted) is frequently used in practice under the name of *viva voce* to discover whether someone really understands something or has "learned it parrot fashion". Let us listen in to a part of such a *viva voce*:

> INTERROGATOR: In the first line of your sonnet, which reads "Shall I compare thee to a summer's day," would not "a spring day" do as well or better?
>
> WITNESS: It wouldn't scan.
>
> INTERROGATOR: How about "a winter's day". That would scan all right.
>
> WITNESS: Yes, but nobody wants to be compared to a winter's day.
>
> INTERROGATOR: Would you say Mr. Pickwick reminded you of Christmas?
>
> WITNESS: In a way.
>
> INTERROGATOR: Yet Christmas is a winter's day, and I do not think Mr. Pickwick would mind the comparison.
>
> WITNESS: I don't think you're serious. By a winter's day one means a typical winter's day, rather than a special one like Christmas.

And so on. What would Professor Jefferson say if the sonnet-writing machine were able to answer like this in the *viva voce*? I do not know whether he would regard the machine as "merely artificially signaling" these answers, but if the answers were as satisfactory and sustained as in the above passage I do not think he would describe it as "an easy contrivance". This phrase is, I think, intended to cover such devices as the inclusion in the machine of a record of someone reading a sonnet, with appropriate switching to turn it on from time to time.

In short then, I think that most of those who support the argument from consciousness could be persuaded to abandon it rather than be forced into the solipsist position. They will then probably be willing to accept our test.

I do not wish to give the impression that I think there is no mystery about consciousness. There is, for instance, something of a paradox connected with any attempt to localize it. But I do not think these mysteries necessarily need to be solved before we can answer the question with which we are concerned in this paper.

(5) ARGUMENTS FROM VARIOUS DISABILITIES. These arguments take the form, "I grant you that you can make machines do all the things you have mentioned but you will never be able to make one to do X." Numerous features X are suggested in this connection. I offer a selection:

> Be kind, resourceful, beautiful, friendly, have initiative, have a sense of humor, tell right from wrong, make mistakes, fall in love, enjoy strawberries and cream, make someone fall

in love with it, learn from experience, use words properly, be the subject of its own thought, have as much diversity of behavior as a man, do something really new.

No support is usually offered for these statements. I believe they are mostly founded on the principle of scientific induction. A man has seen thousands of machines in his lifetime. From what he sees of them he draws a number of general conclusions. They are ugly, each is designed for a very limited purpose, when required for a minutely different purpose they are useless, the variety of behavior of any one of them is very small, and so on and so forth. Naturally he concludes that these are necessary properties of machines in general. Many of these limitations are associated with the very small storage capacity of most machines. (I am assuming that the idea of storage capacity is extended in some way to cover machines other than discrete state machines. The exact definition does not matter as no mathematical accuracy is claimed in the present discussion.) A few years ago, when very little had been heard of digital computers, it was possible to elicit much incredulity concerning them, if one mentioned their properties without describing their construction. That was presumably due to a similar application of the principle of scientific induction. These applications of the principle are of course largely unconscious. When a burned child fears the fire and shows that he fears it by avoiding it, I should say that he was applying scientific induction. (I could of course also describe his behavior in many other ways.) The works and customs of mankind do not seem to be very suitable material to which to apply scientific induction. A very large part of space-time must be investigated if reliable results are to be obtained. Otherwise we may (as most English children do) decide that everybody speaks English, and that it is silly to learn French.

There are, however, special remarks to be made about many of the disabilities that have been mentioned. The inability to enjoy strawberries and cream may have struck the reader as frivolous. Possibly a machine might be made to enjoy this delicious dish, but any attempt to make one do so would be idiotic. What is important about this disability is that it contributes to some of the other disabilities, for instance, to the difficulty of the same kind of friendliness occurring between man and machine as between white man and white man, or between black man and black man.

The claim that "machines cannot make mistakes" seems a curious one. One is tempted to retort, "Are they any the worse for that?" But let us adopt a more sympathetic attitude, and try to see what is really meant. I think this criticism can be explained in terms of the imitation game. It is claimed that the interrogator could distinguish the machine from the man simply by setting them a number of problems in arithmetic. The machine would be unmasked because of its deadly accuracy. The reply to this is simple. The machine (programmed for playing the game) would not attempt to give the *right* answers to the arithmetic problems. It would deliberately introduce mistakes in a manner calculated to confuse the interrogator. A mechanical fault would probably show itself through an unsuitable decision as to what sort of a mistake to make in the arithmetic. Even this interpretation of the criticism is not sufficiently sympathetic. But we cannot afford the space to go into it much further. It seems to me that this criticism depends on a confusion between two kinds of mistakes. We may call them "errors of functioning" and "errors of conclusion". Errors of functioning are due to some mechanical or electrical fault which causes the machine to behave otherwise than it was designed to do. In philosophical discussions one like to ignore the possibility of such errors; one is therefore discussing "abstract machines". These abstract machines are mathematical fictions rather than physical objects. By definition they are incapable of errors of functioning. In this sense we can truly say that "machines can never make mistakes". Errors of conclusion can only arise when some meaning is attached to the output signals from the machine. The machine might, for instance, type out mathematical equations, or sentences in English. When a false proposition is typed we say that the machine has committed an error of conclusion. There is clearly no reason at all for saying that a machine cannot make this kind of mistake. It might do nothing but type out repeatedly "$0 = 1$". To take a less perverse example, it might have some method for drawing conclusions by scientific induction. We must expect such a method to lead occasionally to erroneous results.

The claim that a machine cannot be the subject of its own thought can of course only be answered if it can be shown that the machine has *some* thought with *some* subject matter. Nevertheless, "the subject matter of a machine's operations" does seem to mean something, at least to the people who deal with it. If, for instance, the machine were trying to find a solution of the equation $x^2 - 40x - 11 = 0$, one would be tempted to describe this equation as part of the machine's subject matter at that moment. It may be used to help in making up its own programs, or to predict the effect of alterations in its own structure. By observing the results of its own behavior it can modify its own programs so as to achieve some purpose more effectively. These are possibilities of the near future, rather than Utopian dreams.

The criticism that a machine cannot have much diversity of behavior is just a way of saying that it cannot have much storage capacity. Until fairly recently a storage capacity of even a thousand digits was very rare.

The criticisms that we are considering here are often disguised forms of the argument from consciousness. Usually if one maintains that a machine *can* do one of these things, and describes the kind of method that the machine could use, one will not make much of an impression. It is thought that the method (whatever it may be, for it must be mechanical) is really rather base. Compare the parenthesis in Jefferson's statement quoted above.

(6) LADY LOVELACE'S OBJECTION. Our most detailed information of Babbage's Analytical Engine comes from a memoir by Lady Lovelace (1842). In it she states, "The Analytical Engine has no pretensions to *originate* anything. It can do *whatever we know how to order it* to perform" (her italics). This statement is quoted by Hartree (1949) who adds: "This does not imply that it may not be possible to construct electronic equipment

which will 'think for itself', or in which, in biological terms, one could set up a conditioned reflex, which would serve as a basis for 'learning'. Whether this is possible in principle or not is a stimulating and exciting question, suggested by some of these recent developments. But it did not seem that the machines constructed or projected at the time had this property."

I am in thorough agreement with Hartree over this. It will be noticed that he does not assert that the machines in question had not got the property, but rather that the evidence available to Lady Lovelace did not encourage her to believe that they had it. It is quite possible that the machines in question had in a sense got this property. For suppose that some discrete state machine has the property. The Analytical Engine was a universal digital computer, so that, if its storage capacity and speed were adequate, it could by suitable programming be made to mimic the machine in question. Probably this argument did not occur to the Countess or to Babbage. In any case there was no obligation on them to claim all that could be claimed.

This whole question will be considered again under the heading of learning machines.

A variant of Lady Lovelace's objection states that a machine can "never do anything really new". This may be parried for moment with the saw, "There is nothing new under the sun." Who can be certain that "original work" that he has done was not simply the growth of the seed planted in him by teaching, or the effect of following well-known general principles. A better variant of the objection says that a machine can never "take us by surprise". This statement is a more direct challenge and can be met directly. Machines take me by surprise with great frequency. This is largely because I do not do sufficient calculation to decide what to expect them to do, or rather because, although I do a calculation, I do it in a hurried, slipshod fashion, taking risks. Perhaps I say to myself, "I suppose the voltage here ought to be the same as there: anyway let's assume it is." Naturally I am often wrong, and the result is a surprise for me, for by the time the experiment is done these assumptions have been forgotten. These admissions lay me open to lectures on the subject of my vicious ways, but do not throw any doubt on my credibility when I testify to the surprises I experience.

I do not expect this reply to silence my critic. He will probably say that such surprises are due to some creative mental act on my part, and reflect no credit on the machine. This leads us back to the argument from consciousness, and far from the idea of surprise. It is a line of argument we must consider closed, but it is perhaps worth remarking that the appreciation of something as surprising requires as much of a "creative mental act" whether the surprising event originates from a man, a book, a machine or anything else.

The view that machines cannot give rise to surprises is due, I believe, to a fallacy to which philosophers and mathematicians are particularly subject. This is the assumption that as soon as a fact is presented to a mind all consequences of that fact spring into the mind simultaneously with it. It is a very useful assumption under many circumstances, but one too easily forgets that it is false. A natural consequence of doing so is that one then assumes that there is no virtue in the mere working out of consequences from data and general principles.

(7) ARGUMENT FROM CONTINUITY IN THE NERVOUS SYSTEM. The nervous system is certainly not a discrete state machine. A small error in the information about the size of a nervous impulse impinging on a neuron, may make a large difference to the size of the outgoing impulse. It may be argued that, this being so, one cannot expect to be able to mimic the behavior of the nervous system with a discrete state system.

It is true that a discrete state machine must be different from a continuous machine. But if we adhere to the conditions of the imitation game, the interrogator will not be able to take any advantage of this difference. The situation can be made clearer if we consider some other simpler continuous machine. A differential analyzer will do very well. (A differential analyzer is a certain kind of machine, not of the discrete state type, used for some types of calculation.) Some of these provide their answers in a typed form, and so are suitable for taking part in the game. It would not be possible for a digital computer to predict exactly what answers the differential analyzer would give to a problem, but it would be quite capable of giving the right sort of answer. For instance, if asked to give the value of π (actually about 3.1416) it would be reasonable to choose at random between the values 3.12, 3.13, 3.14, 3.15, 3.16 with the probabilities of 0.05, 0.15, 0.55, 0.19, 0.06 (say). Under these circumstances it would be very difficult for the interrogator to distinguish the differential analyzer from the digital computer.

(8) THE ARGUMENT FROM INFORMALITY OF BEHAVIOR. It is not possible to produce a set of rules purporting to describe what a man should do in every conceivable set of circumstances. One might for instance have a rule that one is to stop when one sees a red traffic light, and to go if one sees a green one; but what if by some fault both appear together? One may perhaps decide that it is safest to stop. But some further difficulty may well arise from this decision later. To attempt to provide rules of conduct to cover every eventuality, even those arising from traffic lights, appears to be impossible. With all this I agree.

From this it is argued that we cannot be machines. I shall try to reproduce the argument, but I fear I shall hardly do it justice. It seems to run something like this: "If each man had a definite set of rules of conduct by which he regulated his life he would be no better than a machine. But there are no such rules, so men cannot be machines." The undistributed middle is glaring. I do not think the argument is ever put quite like this, but I believe this is the argument used nevertheless. There may however be a certain confusion between "rules of conduct" and "laws of behavior" to cloud the issue. By "rules of conduct" I mean precepts such as "Stop if you see red lights", on which one can act, and of which one can be conscious. By "laws of behavior" I mean laws of nature as applied to a man's body such as "if you pinch him he will squeak". If we substitute "laws of behavior which regulate his life" for "laws of conduct by which he regulates his life" in the argument quoted the undistributed middle is no longer insuperable. For we believe that it is not only true that being regulated by laws of behavior implies being some sort of machine (though not necessarily a discrete state machine), but that conversely being such a machine implies being regulated by such laws. However, we cannot so easily convince ourselves of the absence of complete laws of behavior as of complete rules of conduct. The only way we know of for finding such laws is scientific observation, and we certainly know of no circumstances under which we could say: "We have searched enough. There are no such laws."

We can demonstrate more forcibly that any such statement would be unjustified. For suppose we could be sure of finding such laws if they existed. Then given a discrete state machine it should certainly be possible to discover by observation sufficient about it to predict its future behavior, and this within a reasonable time, say a thousand years. But this does not seem to be the case. I have set up on the Manchester computer a small program using only 1000 units of storage, whereby the machine supplied with one sixteen figure number replies with another within two seconds. I would defy anyone to learn from these replies sufficient about the program to be able to predict any replies to untried values.

(9) THE ARGUMENT FROM EXTRA-SENSORY PERCEPTION. I assume that the reader is familiar with the idea of extra-sensory perception, and the meaning of the four items of it, namely, telepathy, clairvoyance, precognition and psychokinesis. These disturbing phenomena seem to deny all our usual scientific ideas. How we should like to discredit them! Unfortunately the statistical evidence, at least for telepathy, is overwhelming. It is very difficult to rearrange one's ideas so as to fit these new facts in. Once one has accepted them it does not seem a very big step to believe in ghosts and bogies. The idea that our bodies move simply according to the known laws of physics, together with some others not yet discovered but somewhat similar, would be one of the first to go.

This argument is to my mind quite a strong one. One can say in reply that many scientific theories seem to remain workable in practice, in spite of clashing with E.S.P.; that in fact one can get along very nicely if one forgets about it. This is rather cold comfort, and one fears that thinking is just the kind of phenomenon where E.S.P. may be especially relevant.

A more specific argument based on E.S.P. might run as follows: "Let us play the imitation game, using as witnesses a man who is good as a telepathic receiver, and a digital computer. The interrogator can ask such questions as 'What suit does the card in my right hand belong to?' The man by telepathy or clairvoyance gives the right answer 130 times out of 400 cards. The machine can only guess at random, and perhaps get 104 right, so the interrogator makes the right identification." There is an interesting possibility which opens here. Suppose the digital computer contains a random number generator. Then it will be natural to use this to decide what answer to give. But then the random number generator will be subject to the psychokinetic powers of the interrogator. Perhaps this psychokinesis might cause the machine to guess right more often then would be expected on a probability calculation, so that the interrogator might still be unable to make the right identification. On the other hand, he might be able to guess right without any questioning, by clairvoyance. With E.S.P. anything may happen.

If telepathy is admitted it will be necessary to tighten our test. The situation could be regarded as analogous to that which would occur if the interrogator were talking to himself and one of the competitors was listening with his ear to the wall. To put the competitors into a "telepathy-proof room" would satisfy all requirements.

6.7 Learning machines

The reader will have anticipated that I have no very convincing arguments of a positive nature to support my views. If I had I should not have taken such pains to point out the fallacies in contrary views. Such evidence as I have I shall now give.

Let us return for a moment to Lady Lovelace's objection, which stated that the machine can only do what we tell it to do. One could say that a man can "inject" an idea into the machine, and that it will respond to a certain extent and then drop into quiescence, like a piano string struck by a hammer. Another simile would be an atomic pile of less than critical size: an injected idea is to correspond to a neutron entering the pile from without. Each such neutron will cause a certain disturbance which eventually dies away. If, however, the size of the pile is sufficiently increased, the disturbance caused by such an incoming neutron will very likely go on and on, increasing until the whole pile is destroyed. Is there a corresponding phenomenon for minds, and is there one for machines? There does seem to be one for the human mind. The majority of them seem to be "subcritical", that is, to correspond in this analogy to piles of subcritical size. An idea presented to such a mind will on an average give rise to less than one idea in reply. A smallish proportion are supercritical. An idea presented to such a mind may give rise to a whole "theory" consisting of secondary, tertiary and more remote ideas. Animals' minds seem to be very definitely subcritical. Adhering to this analogy we ask, "Can a machine be made to be supercritical?"

The "skin of an onion" analogy is also helpful. In considering the functions of the mind or the brain we find certain operations which we can explain in purely mechanical terms. This we say does not correspond to the real mind: it is a sort of skin which we must strip off if we are to find the real mind. But then in what remains we find a further skin to be stripped off, and so on. Proceeding in this way, do we ever come to the "real" mind, or do we eventually come to the skin which has nothing in it? In the latter case the whole mind is mechanical. (It would not be a discrete state machine however. We have discussed this.)

These last two paragraphs do not claim to be convincing arguments. They should rather be described as "recitations tending to produce belief".

The only really satisfactory support that can be given for the view expressed at the beginning of Section 6.6 will be that provided by waiting for the end of the century and then doing the experiment described. But what can we say in the meantime? What steps should be taken now if the experiment is to be successful?

As I have explained, the problem is mainly one of programming. Advances in engineering will have to made too, but it seems unlikely that these will not be adequate for the requirements. Estimates of the storage capacity of the brain vary from 10^{10} to 10^{15} binary digits. I incline to the lower values and believe that only a very small fraction is used for the higher types of thinking. Most of it is probably used for the retention of visual impressions. I should be surprised if more than 10^9 was required for satisfactory playing of the imitation game, at any rate against a blind man. (Note: The capacity of the *Encyclopedia Britannica*, eleventh edition, is 2×10^9.) A storage capacity of 10^7 would be a very practicable possibility even by present techniques. It is probably not necessary to increase the speed of operations of the machines at all. Parts of modern machines which can be regarded as analogues of nerve cells work about a thousand times faster than the latter. This should provide a "margin of safety" which could cover losses of speed arising in many ways. Our problem then is to find out how to program these machines to play the game. At my present rate of working I produce about a thousand digits of program a day, so that about sixty workers, working steadily through the fifty years might accomplish the job, if nothing went into the wastepaper basket. Some more expeditious method seems desirable.

In the process of trying to imitate an adult human mind we are bound to think a good deal about the process which has brought it to the state that it is in. We may notice three components:

(a) The initial state of the mind, say at birth;

(b) The education to which it has been subjected; and

(c) Other experience, not to be described as education, to which it has been subjected.

Instead of trying to produce a program to simulate the adult mind, why not rather try to produce one which simulates the child's? If this were then subjected to an appropriate course of education one would obtain the adult brain. Presumably the child-brain is something like a notebook as one buys it from the stationers. Rather little mechanism, and lots of blank sheets. (Mechanism and writing are from our point of view almost synonymous.) Our hope is that there is so little mechanism in the child-brain that something like it can be easily programmed. The amount of work in the education we can assume, as a first approximation, to be much the same as for the human child.

We have thus divided our problem into two parts—the child-program and the education process. These two remain very closely connected. We cannot expect to find a good child-machine at the first attempt. One must experiment with teaching one such machine and see how well it learns. One can then try another and see if it is better or worse. There is an obvious connection between this process and evolution, by the identifications

Structure of the child-machine	=	Hereditary material
Changes of the child-machine	=	Mutations
Judgment of the experimenter	=	Natural selection

One may hope, however, that this process will be more expeditious than evolution. The survival of the fittest is a slow method for measuring advantages. The experimenter, by the exercise of intelligence, should be able to speed it up. Equally important is the fact that he is not restricted to random mutations. If he can trace a cause for some weakness he can probably think of the kind of mutation which will improve it.

It will not be possible to apply exactly the same teaching process to the machine as to a normal child. It will not, for instance, be provided with legs, so that it could not be asked to go out and fill the coal scuttle. Possibly it might not have eyes. But however well these deficiencies might be overcome by clever engineering, one could not send the creature to school without the other children making excessive fun of it. It must be given some tuition. We need not be too concerned about the legs, eyes, and so on. The example of Miss Helen Keller shows that education can take place provided that communication in both directions between teacher and pupil can take place by some means or other.

We normally associate punishments and rewards with the teaching process. Some simple child-machines can be constructed or programmed on this sort of principle. The machine has to be so constructed that events which shortly preceded the occurrence of a punishment-signal are unlikely to be repeated, whereas a reward-signal increases the probability of repetition of the events which led up to it. These definitions do not presuppose any feelings on the part of the machine. I have done some experiments with one such child-machine, and succeeded in teaching it a few things, but the teaching method was too unorthodox for the experiment to be considered really successful.

The use of punishments and rewards can at best be a part of the teaching process. Roughly speaking, if the teacher has no other means of communicating to the pupil, the amount of information which can reach him does not exceed the total number of rewards and punishments applied. By the time a child has learned to repeat "Casablanca" he would probably feel very sore indeed, if the text could only be discovered by a "Twenty Questions" technique, every "No" taking the form of a blow. It is necessary therefore to have some other "unemotional" channels of communication. If these are available it is possible to teach a machine by punishments and rewards to obey orders given in some language, such as a symbolic language. These orders are to be transmitted through the "unemotional" channels. The use of this language will diminish greatly the number of punishments and rewards required.

Opinions may vary as to the complexity which is suitable in the child-machine. One might try to make it as simple as possible consistently with the general principles. Alternatively one might have a complete system of logical inference "built in".[2] In the latter case the store would be largely occupied with definitions and propositions. The propositions would have various kinds of status, such as well-established facts, conjectures, mathematically proved theorems, statements given by an authority, and expressions having the logical form of a proposition but no belief-value. Certain propositions may be described as "imperatives". The machine should be so constructed that as soon as an imperative is classed as "well-established" the appropriate action automatically takes place. To illustrate this, suppose the teacher says to the machine, "Do your homework now." This may cause "Teacher says 'Do your homework now' " to be included among the well-established facts. Another such fact might be, "Everything that teacher says is true". Combining these may eventually lead to the imperative, "Do your homework now", being included amongst the well-established facts, and this, by the construction of the machine, will mean that the homework actually gets started; but the effect is very unsatisfactory. The processes of inference used by the machine need not be such as would satisfy the most exacting logicians. There might, for instance, be no hierarchy of types. But this need not mean that type fallacies will occur, any more than we are bound to fall over unfenced cliffs. Suitable imperatives (expressed *within* the systems, not forming part of the rules *of* the system) such as "Do not use a class unless it is a subclass of one which has been mentioned by teacher" can have a similar effect to "Do not go too near the edge."

The imperatives that can be obeyed by a machine that has no limbs are bound to be of a rather intellectual character, as in the example (doing homework) given above. Important among such imperatives will be ones which regulate the order in which the rules of the logical system concerned are to be applied. For at each stage when one is using a logical system, there is a very large number of alternative steps, any of which one is permitted to apply, so far as obedience to the rules of the logical system is concerned. These choices make the difference between a brilliant and a footling reasoner, not the difference between a sound and a fallacious one. Propositions leading to imperatives of this kind might be "When Socrates is mentioned, use the syllogism in Barbara" or "If one method has been proved to be quicker than another, do not use the slower method." Some of these may be "given by authority", but others may be produced by the machine itself, say by scientific induction.

The idea of a learning machine may appear paradoxical to some readers. How can the rules of operation of the machine change? They should describe completely how the machine will react whatever its history might be, whatever changes it might undergo. The rules are thus quite time-invariant. This is quite true. The explanation of the paradox is that the rules which get changed in the learning process are of a rather less pretentious kind, claiming only an ephemeral validity. The reader may draw a parallel with the Constitution of the United States.

An important feature of a learning machine is that its teacher will often be very largely ignorant of quite what is going on inside, although he may still be able to some extent to predict his pupil's behavior. This should apply most strongly to the later education of a machine arising from a child-machine of well-tried design (or program). This is in clear contrast with normal procedure when using a machine to do computations: one's object is then to have a clear mental picture of the state of the machine at each moment in the computation. This object can only be achieved with a struggle. The view that "the machine can only do what we know how to order it to do",[3] appears strange in face of this. Most of the programs which we can put into the machine will result in its doing something that we cannot make sense of at all, or which we regard as completely random behavior. Intelligent behavior presumably consists in a departure from the completely disciplined behavior involved in computation, but a rather slight one, which does not give rise to random behavior, or to pointless repetitive loops. Another important result of preparing our machine for its part in the imitation game by a process of teaching and learning is that "human fallibility" is likely to be admitted in a rather natural way, that is, without special "coaching". (The reader should reconcile this with the point of view on p. 113.) Processes that are learned do not produce a hundred percent certainty of result; if they did they could not be unlearned.

It is probably wise to include a random element in a learning machine (see p. 105). A random element is rather useful when we are searching for a solution of some problem. Suppose for instance we wanted to find a number between 50 and 200 which was equal to the square of the sum of its digits, we might start at 51 then try 52 and go on until we got a number that worked. Alternatively we might choose numbers at random until we got a good one. This method has the advantage that it is unnecessary to keep track of the values that have been tried, but the disadvantage that one may try the same one twice; but this is not very important if there are several solutions. The systematic method has the disadvantage that there may be an enormous block without any solutions in the region which has to be investigated first. Now the learning process may be regarded as a search for a form of behavior which will satisfy the teacher (or some other criterion). Since there is probably a very large number of satisfactory solutions, the random method seems to be better than the systematic. It should be noticed that it is used in the analogous process of evolution. But there the systematic method is not possible. How could one keep track of the different genetical combinations that had been tried, so as to avoid trying them again?

We may hope that machines will eventually compete with men in all purely intellectual fields. But which are the best ones to start with? Even this is a difficult decision. Many people think that a very abstract activity, like the playing of chess, would be best. It can also be maintained that it is best to provide the machine with the best sense organs that money can buy, and then teach it to understand and speak English. This process could follow the normal teaching of a child. Things would be pointed out and named, and so on. Again I do not know what the right answer is, but I think both approaches should be tried.

We can only see a short distance ahead, but we can see plenty there that needs to be done.

Notes for Chapter 6

1. Possibly this view is heretical. St. Thomas Aquinas (*Summa Theologica*, quoted in Russell, 1945, p. 458) states that God cannot make a man to have no soul. But this may not be a real restriction on His powers, but only a result of the fact that men's souls are immortal, and therefore indestructible.

2. Or rather "programmed in" for our child-machine will be programmed in a digital computer. But the logical system will not have to be learned.

3. Compare Lady Lovelace's statement (p. 114), which does not contain the word "only".

On Our Best Behaviour

7

Hector J. Levesque
2014

7.1 Intelligent behaviour

This paper is about the *science* of AI. Unfortunately, it is the *technology* of AI that gets all the attention. The general public could be forgiven for thinking that AI is just about all those whiz-bang applications, smart *this* and autonomous *that*. Those of us in the field know that for many applications, the term "intelligent" is no more than a buzzword (like the term "delicious" in "red delicious apples"). And along with the many possibly beneficial AI applications under consideration, we often have serious misgivings about the potential misuse of AI technology (in areas like weaponry).

But AI is more than just technology. Many of us are motivated not by any of the AI applications currently being considered, but by the scientific enterprise, the attempt to understand the world around us. Different sciences have different subject matters, and AI is the study of *intelligent behaviour* in computational terms. What could be more fascinating? The human brain is a remarkable thing, perhaps the single most complex object we know of in the universe. But even more remarkable is what a human brain is capable of *doing*. Our intelligent behaviour at its best goes well beyond what we have any right to expect to emerge out of purely physical matter. Indeed, the overarching question for the science of AI is:

> How is it possible for something physical (like people, for instance) to actually do *X*?

where *X* is one of the many instances of intelligent behaviour. This needs to be contrasted with a related question:

> Can we engineer a computer system to do something that is vaguely *X*-ish?

about which we will have much more to say later.

Note that the science of AI studies intelligent behaviour, not *who* or *what* is producing the behaviour. It studies natural language understanding, for instance, not natural language understanders. This is what makes AI quite different from the study of *people* (in neuro-science, psychology, cognitive science, evolutionary biology, and so on).

What sort of behaviour do we care about? Different researchers will quite naturally focus on different aspects. The behaviour may or may not depend on perceptual or motor skills. It may or may not include learning. It may or may not be grounded in emotional responses, or in social interactions. For some researchers, the main concern is intelligent behaviour seen in a variety of animals, like the ability to find a desired object in a room. For others, the focus is on behaviour seen in humans only, like the ability to play chess. (These two groups sometimes engage in methodological disputes, with the former arguing that we cannot expect to understand human behaviour until we understand its more basic forms, and the latter responding that this is not how science works at all. At this stage of the game, there is really no reason to take a doctrinaire position one way or another.)

7.1.1   Answering questions

In this paper, I intend to examine one basic form of intelligent behaviour: answering certain *ad-hoc* questions posed in English. Consider a question like the following:

Could a crocodile run a steeplechase?

Even if you know what crocodiles and steeplechases are,[1] you have never really thought about this question before, unless you happened to have read an early paper of mine (Levesque, 1988). Nor can you simply look up the correct answer somewhere. And yet, an answer does occur to you almost immediately. Here is another question from the same paper:

Should baseball players be allowed to glue small wings onto their caps?

Again, you have never thought of this before, but again an answer occurs to you. (In this case, you might even wonder if there is some sort of trick to the question that you may have missed. There is none.)

In this paper, I want to consider our ability to answer one-shot questions like these, and for four reasons:

1. This is behaviour that is clearly exhibited by people. We are indeed capable of answering questions like these without any special training or instructions.
2. This is behaviour that is difficult to crack. We have as yet no good idea about what people do to answer them. No existing computer program can duplicate our ability.
3. Our behaviour in answering questions like these appears to underly other more complex (and more ecologically significant) forms of behaviour.
4. Being clear and precise about the form of behaviour we care about even in this simple case will also help clarify what it means for the science of AI to be successful.

As we will see, however, there will be good reasons to move to answering questions of a more restricted form.

7.2   Behavioural tests

Given some form of intelligent behaviour, how do we know that the computational story told by AI researchers actually explains the behaviour. The answer, going all the way back to Turing, is this: a computational account is adequate if it is able to generate behaviour that cannot be distinguished over the long haul from the behaviour produced by people.

This, of course, harks back to the famous Turing Test (Turing, 1950; Chapter 6 of this volume). We imagine an extended conversation over a teletype between an interrogator and two participants, a person and a computer. The conversation is natural, free-flowing, and about any topic whatsoever. The computer is said to *pass the Turing Test* if no matter how long the conversation, the interrogator cannot tell which of the two participants is the person.

Turing's point in all this, it seems to me, is this: Terms like "intelligent," "thinking," "understanding," and the like are much too vague and emotionally charged to be worth arguing about. If we insist on using them in a scientific context at all, we should be willing to say that a program that can pass a suitable behavioural test has the property in question as much as the person. Adapting the dictum of the movie character Forest Gump who said "*Stupid is as stupid does*," we can imagine Turing saying "*Intelligent is as intelligent does*." This is a very sensible position, it seems to me, and I have defended it elsewhere (Levesque, 2009).

7.2.1   The trouble with the Turing Test

However, I do feel that the Turing Test has a serious problem: it relies too much on *deception*. A computer program passes the test iff it can *fool* an interrogator into thinking she is dealing with a person not a computer. Consider the interrogator asking questions like these:

> *How tall are you?*

or

> *Tell me about your parents.*

To pass the test, a program will either have to be evasive (and duck the question) or manufacture some sort of false identity (and be prepared to lie convincingly). In fact, evasiveness is seen quite clearly in the annual *Loebner Competition*, a restricted version of the Turing Test.[2] The "chatterbots" (as the computer entrants in the competition are called) rely heavily on wordplay, jokes, quotations, asides, emotional outbursts, points of order, and so on. Everything, it would appear, except clear and direct answers to questions!

The ability to fool people is interesting, no doubt, but not really what is at issue here.[3] We might well ask: is there a better behaviour test than having a free-form conversation?

There are some quite reasonable non-English options to consider, such as "captchas" (Von Ahn et al., 2003). But English is an excellent medium since it allows us to range over topics broadly and flexibly (and guard for biases: age, education, culture, *etc.*).

But here is another option: what if instead of a conversation, the interrogator only asks a number of *multiple-choice questions*? This has some distinct advantages:

- Verbal dodges are no longer possible. A program can no longer game the test using evasive maneuvers.
- It does not require the ability to generate "credible" English. The program will not need to worry about choosing words or syntax to accurately mimic actual speakers.
- The tests can be automated (administered and graded by machine). Success on the test does not depend on the judged similarity to people, but on the correctness of the answers.

7.2.2   Cheap tricks

We want multiple-choice questions that people can answer easily. But we also want to avoid as much as possible questions that can be answered using cheap tricks (*aka* heuristics).

Consider for example, the question posed earlier:

Could a crocodile run a steeplechase?
- *yes*
- *no*

The intent here is clear. The question can be answered by thinking it through: a crocodile has short legs; the hedges in a steeplechase would be too tall for the crocodile to jump over; so no, a crocodile cannot run a steeplechase.

The trouble is that there is another way to answer the question that does not require this level of understanding. The idea is to use the *closed world assumption* (Reiter, 1978; Collins et al., 1975). This assumption says (among other things) the following:

If you can find no evidence for the existence of something, assume that it does not exist.

For the question above, since I have never heard of a crocodile being able to run a steeplechase, I conclude that it cannot. End of story. Note that this is a *cheap* trick: it gets the answer right, but for dubious reasons. It would produce the wrong answer for a question about gazelles, for example. Nonetheless, if all we care about is answering the crocodile question correctly, then this cheap trick does the trick.

Can we find questions where cheap tricks like this will not be sufficient to produce the desired behaviour? This unfortunately has no easy answer. The best we can do, perhaps, is to come up with a suite of multiple-choice questions *carefully* and then study the sorts of computer programs that might be able to answer them. Here are some obvious guidelines:

- Make the questions Google-proof. Access to a large corpus of English text data should not *by itself* be sufficient.
- Avoid questions with common patterns. An example is "*Is x older than y?*" Perhaps no single Google-accessible web page has the answer, but once we map the word "older" to "birth date," the rest comes quickly.[4]
- Watch for unintended bias. The word order, vocabulary, grammar and so on all need to be selected very carefully not to betray the desired answer.

One existing promising approach in this direction is the *recognizing textual entailment* challenge (Dagan et al., 2005; Bobrow et al., 2007). But it has problems of its own, and so here we propose a different one.

7.3 Winograd schema questions

Our approach is best illustrated with an example question:[5]

> *Joan made sure to thank Susan for all the help she had given. Who had given the help?*
> - *Joan*
> - *Susan*

A *Winograd schema question* is a binary-choice question with these properties:

- Two parties are mentioned in the question (both are males, females, objects, or groups).
- A pronoun is used to refer to one of them ("he," "she," "it," or "they," according to the parties).
- The question is always the same: what is the referent of the pronoun?
- Behind the scenes, there are two *special words* for the schema. There is a slot in the schema that can be filled by either word. The correct answer depends on which special word is chosen.

In the above, the special word used is "given," and the other word is "received." So each Winograd schema actually generates two very similar questions:

> *Joan made sure to thank Susan for all the help she had **given**. Who had **given** the help?*
> - *Joan*
> - *Susan* ✓

and

> *Joan made sure to thank Susan for all the help she had **received**. Who had **received** the help?*
> - *Joan* ✓
> - *Susan*

It is this one-word difference between the two questions that helps guard against using the cheapest of tricks on them.

Here are some additional examples. The first is one that is suitable even for young children:

> *The trophy would not fit in the brown suitcase because it was so small. What was so small?*
> - *the trophy*
> - *the brown suitcase*

In this case, the special word used is "small" and the other word is "big." Here is the original example due to Terry Winograd (1972a) for whom the schema is named:

> *The town councillors refused to give the angry demonstrators a permit because they feared violence. Who feared violence?*
> - *the town councillors*
> - *the angry demonstrators*

Here the special word is "feared" and the alternative word is "advocated."

With a bit of care, it is possible to come up with Winograd schema questions that exercise different kinds of expertise. Here is an example concerning certain materials:

> *The large ball crashed right through the table because it was made of styrofoam. What was made of styrofoam?*
> - *the large ball*
> - *the table*

The special word is "styrofoam" and the alternative is "steel." This one tests for problem-solving skill:

> *The sack of potatoes had been placed below the bag of flour, so it had to be moved first. What had to be moved first?*
> - *the sack of potatoes*
> - *the bag of flour*

The special word is "below" and the alternative is "above." This example tests for an ability to visualize:

> *Sam tried to paint a picture of shepherds with sheep, but they ended up looking*
> *more like golfers. What looked like golfers?*
> * *the shepherds*
> * *the sheep*

The special word used is "golfers" and the other is "dogs."

Of course not just any question in this form will do the job here. It is possible to construct questions that are too "easy," like this one:

> *The racecar easily passed the school bus because it was going so fast. What*
> *was going so fast?*
> * *the racecar*
> * *the school bus*   (Special=*fast;* other=*slow)*

The problem is that this question can be answered using the following trick: ignore the given sentence, and check which two words co-occur more frequently (according to Google, say): "racecar" with "fast" or "school bus" with "fast." Questions can also be too "hard," like this one:

> *Frank was jealous when Bill said that he was the winner of the competition.*
> *Who was the winner?*
> * *Frank*
> * *Bill*   (Special=*jealous;* other=*happy)*

The problem is that this question is ambiguous when the "happy" variant is used. Frank could plausibly be happy because he is the winner or because Bill is. Further discussion on these and other issues can be found in Levesque et al. (2012).

7.3.1   A new test

It is now possible to formulate an alternative to the Turing Test. A collection of pre-tested Winograd schemas can be hidden in a library.[6] A Winograd Schema Test involves asking a number of these questions with a strong penalty for wrong answers (to preclude guessing). A test can be administered and graded in a fully automated way:

1. select N (*e.g.*, $N = 25$) questions that are suitable (with respect to vocabulary, expertise, *etc.*);

2. randomly use one of the special words in the question;

3. present the test to the subject, and obtain the N binary replies;

The final grade for the test is

$$\frac{\max(0, N - k \cdot \textit{Wrong})}{N}$$

where k codes the penalty for guessing (*e.g.*, $k = 5$). The main claim here is that normally-abled English-speaking adults will pass the test easily. So, if we want to produce behaviour that is indistinguishable from that of people, we will need to come up with a program that can also pass the test.

To summarize: With respect to the Turing Test, we agree with Turing that the substantive question is whether or not a certain *intelligent behaviour* can be achieved by a computer program. But a free-form *conversation* as advocated by Turing may not be the best vehicle for a formal test, as it allows a cagey subject to hide behind a smokescreen of playfulness, verbal tricks, and canned responses. Our position is that an alternative test based on Winograd schema questions is less subject to abuse, though clearly much less demanding intellectually than engaging in a cooperative conversation (about sonnets, for example, as imagined by Turing).

7.4 Passing the test

What would it take for a computer program to pass a Winograd schema test. My feeling is that we can go quite some distance with the following:

1. Take a Winograd schema question such as

   > *The trophy would not fit in the brown suitcase because it was so small. What was so small?*
   > * *the trophy*
   > * *the brown suitcase*

   and parse it into the following form:

   > Two parties are in relation R.
   >
   > One of them has property P. Which?

   For the question above, this gives the following:

   > R = does not fit in; P = is so small.

2. Then use *big data*: search all the English text on the web to determine which is the more common pattern:

   > – x does not fit in y + x is so small   *vs.*
   >
   > – x does not fit in y + y is so small

This "big data" approach is an excellent trick, but unfortunately, it is still too cheap. Among other things, it ignores the *connective* between R and P. Consider this:

> *The trophy would not fit in the brown suitcase despite the fact that it was so*
> *small. What was so small?*
> * *the trophy*
> * *the brown suitcase*

Note that the R and P here would be the same as before, even though the answer must be different this time.

Now consider the following example:

> *Fred is the only man alive who still remembers my father as an infant. When*
> *Fred first saw my father, he was twelve years old. Who was twelve years old?*
> * *Fred*
> * *my father*   *(*Special=*years;* other=*months)*

Here the relationship between any R and P is clearly much more complex.

So what do we conclude from this? Do we simply need a bigger bag of tricks?

7.4.1   The lure of statistics

There is a tendency in AI to focus on behaviour in a purely statistical sense. We ask:

> Can we engineer a system to produce a desired behaviour with no more errors than
> people would produce (with confidence level z)?

Looking at behaviour this way can allow some of the more challenging examples that arise (like the question concerning Fred above) to simply be *ignored* when they are not statistically significant.

Unfortunately, this can lead us to systems with very impressive performance that are nonetheless *idiot-savants*. We might produce prodigies at chess, face-recognition, *Jeopardy*, and so on, that are completely hopeless outside their area of expertise.[7]

But there is another way of looking at all this. Think of the behaviour of people on Winograd schema questions as a *natural phenomenon* to be explained, not unlike photosynthesis or gravity. In this case, even a *single example* can tell us something important about how people are able to behave, however insignificant statistically.

7.4.2   A thought experiment

Reconsider, for instance, the styrofoam / steel question from above. We might consider using other special words in the question: for "balsa wood," the answer would be "the table," for "granite," it would be "the large ball," and so on. But suppose we use an unknown word in the question:

> *The large ball crashed right through the table because it was made of XYZZY.*
> *What was made of XYZZY?*
> - *the large ball*
> - *the table*

Here there is no "correct" answer: subjects should not really favor one answer much over the other.

But suppose we had told the subjects some facts about the XYZZY material:[8]

1. It is a trademarked product of Dow Chemical.
2. It is usually white, but there are green and blue varieties.
3. It is ninety-eight percent air, making it lightweight and buoyant.
4. It was first discovered by a Swedish inventor, Carl Georg Munters.

We can ask, on learning any of these facts, at what point do the subjects stop guessing? It should be clear that only one of these facts really matters, the third one. But more generally, people get the right answer for *styrofoam* precisely because they already know something like the third fact above about the makeup of styrofoam. This background knowledge is critical; without it, the behaviour is quite different.

7.4.3 The lesson

So what do we learn from this experiment about the answering of Winograd schema questions? From a pure *technology* point of view, a reasonable question to ask here is this:

Can we produce a good semblance of the target behaviour without having to deal with background knowledge like this?

But from a *science* point of view, we must take a different stance. We want to understand what it takes to produce the intelligent behaviour that people exhibit. So the question really needs to be more like this:

What kind of system would have the necessary background knowledge to be able to behave the way people do?

7.4.4 A radical approach

So to account for what people are actually able to do, we need to consider what it would take to have a system that *knows* a lot about its world and can apply that knowledge as needed, the way people can.

One possibility is this:

- some part of what needs to be known is represented symbolically (call it the knowledge base);
- procedures operate on this knowledge base, deriving new symbolic representations (call it reasoning);

- some of the derived conclusions concern what actions should be taken next (including answering questions).

This is a very radical idea, first proposed by John McCarthy in a quite extraordinary and unprecedented paper (McCarthy, 1968). It suggests that we should put aside any idea of tricks and shortcuts, and focus instead on what needs to be *known*, how to represent it symbolically, and how to use the representations.

7.5 Two scientific hurdles

I do not want to suggest that with McCarthy's radical idea on board, it is all smooth sailing from here. A good question to ask is why, after 55 years, we have so little to show for it regarding the science of intelligent behaviour. The answer, I believe, is that it leaves some major issues unresolved.

My Computers and Thought Lecture at IJCAI-85 (Levesque, 1986) was in part a reaction to the "*Knowledge is Power*" slogan which was quite in vogue at the time. It all seemed too facile to me, even back then. My sense was that knowledge was *not* power if it could not be acquired in a suitable symbolic form, or if it could not be applied in a tractable way. These point to two significant hurdles faced by the McCarthy approach:

1. Much of what we come to know about world and the people around us is not from personal experience, but is due to our use of *language*.

   People talk to us, we listen to weather reports and to the dialogue in movies, and we read: text messages, sport scores, mystery novels, *etc*.

   And yet, it appears that we need to use extensive knowledge to make good sense of all this language.

2. Even the most basic child-level knowledge seems to call upon a wide range of logical constructs.

   Cause and effect and non-effect, counterfactuals, generalized quantifiers, uncertainty, other agents' beliefs, desires and intentions, *etc*.

   And yet, symbolic reasoning over these constructs seems to be much too demanding computationally.

I believe that these two hurdles are as serious and as challenging to the science of AI as an accelerating universe is to astrophysics. After 55 years, we might well wonder if an AI researcher will *ever* be able to overcome them.

Life being short (and "time to market" even shorter), it is perhaps not surprising that many AI researchers have returned to less radical methods (*e.g.*, more biologically-based, more like statistical mechanics) to focus on behaviours that are seemingly less knowledge-intensive (*e.g.*, recognizing handwritten digits, following faces in a crowd, walking over rough terrain). And the results have been terrific!

But these terrific results should not put us into denial. Our best behaviour *does* include knowledge-intensive activities such as participating in natural conversations, or responding to Winograd schema questions. It is my hope that enough of us stay focused on this sort of intelligent behaviour to allow progress to continue here as well.

This will require hard work! I think it is unreasonable to expect solutions to emerge spontaneously out of a few general principles, obviating any real effort on our parts. For example, I do not think we will ever be able to build a small computer program, give it a camera and a microphone or put it on the web, and expect it to acquire what it needs all by itself.

So the work will be hard. But to my way of thinking, it will be more like scaling a mountain than shoveling a driveway. Hard work, yes, but an exhilarating adventure!

7.5.1   Some suggestions

What about those hurdles? Obviously, I have no solutions. However, I do have some suggestions for my colleagues in the Knowledge Representation area:

1. We need to return to our roots in Knowledge Representation and Reasoning *for* language and *from* language.

   We should *not* treat English text as a monolithic source of information. Instead, we should carefully study how simple knowledge bases might be used to make sense of the simple language needed to build slightly more complex knowledge bases, and so on.

2. It is not enough to build knowledge bases without paying closer attention to the demands arising from their use.

   We should explore more thoroughly the space of computations between fact retrieval and full automated logical reasoning. We should study in detail the effectiveness of *linear* modes of reasoning (like unit propagation, say) over constructs that logically seem to demand more.

As to the rest of the AI community, I do have a final recommendation:

> We should avoid being overly swayed by what appears to be the most promising approach of the day.

As a field, I believe that we tend to suffer from what might be called *serial silver bulletism*, defined as follows:

> *the tendency to believe in a silver bullet for AI, coupled with the belief that previous beliefs about silver bullets were hopelessly naïve.*

We see this in the fads and fashions of AI research over the years: first, automated theorem proving is going to solve it all; then, the methods appear too weak, and we favour expert systems; then the programs are not situated enough, and we move to behaviour-based robotics; then we come to believe that learning from big data is the answer; and on it goes.

I think there is a lot to be gained by recognizing more fully what our own research does *not* address, and being willing to admit that other AI approaches may be needed for dealing with it. I believe this will help minimize the hype, put us in better standing with our colleagues, and allow progress in AI to proceed in a steadier fashion.

7.5.2   The prospects

Finally, let me conclude with a question about the future:

> Will a computer ever pass the Turing Test (as first envisaged by Turing) or even a broad Winograd Schema Test (without cheap tricks)?

The answer to this question, I believe, lies in a quote from Alan Kay: *"The best way to predict the future is to invent it."* I take this to mean that the question is not really for the pundits to debate. The question, in the end, is really about *us*, how much perseverance and inventiveness we will bring to the task. And I, for one, have the greatest confidence in what we can do when we set our minds to it.

Notes for Chapter 7

1. For those who do not know, a steeplechase is a horse race, similar to the usual ones, but where the horses must jump over a number of hedges on the racetrack. So it is like hurdles for horses.

2. See the book by Brian Christian (2011) for an interesting account of what it was like to play the human in a Loebner contest.

3. The ELIZA program (Weizenbaum, 1966) is a good place to start on that issue.

4. The program at www.trueknowledge.com appears to work this way

5. This section is drawn mainly from Levesque et al. (2012). I thank Ernie Davis and Leora Morgenstern for their contribution.

6. See, for example, the collection at `http://www.cs.nyu.edu/faculty/davise/papers/WS.html`.

7. Indeed, it would be good fun to try *Watson* on Winograd schema questions: the category is "Pronoun referents," the clue is "Joan made sure to thank Susan for all the help she had given," and the desired answer in the form of a question is "Who is Susan?"

8. These facts were lifted from the Wikipedia page for styrofoam.

Rationality and Intelligence

8

Stuart J. Russell
1997

8.1   Artificial intelligence

AI is a field whose ultimate goal has often been somewhat ill-defined and subject to dispute. Some researchers aim to emulate human cognition, others aim at the creation of intelligence without concern for human characteristics, and still others aim to create useful artifacts without concern for abstract notions of intelligence.

This variety is not *necessarily* a bad thing, since each approach uncovers new ideas and provides fertilization to the others. But one can argue that, since philosophers abhor a definitional vacuum, many of the damaging and ill-informed debates about the feasibility of AI have been about definitions of AI to which we as AI researchers do not subscribe.

My own motivation for studying AI is to create and understand intelligence as a general property of systems, rather than as a specific attribute of humans. I believe this to be an appropriate goal for the field as a whole, and it certainly includes the creation of useful artifacts—both as a spin-off and as a focus and driving force for technological development. The difficulty with this "creation of intelligence" view, however, is that it presupposes that we have some productive notion of what intelligence is. Cognitive scientists can say "Look, my model correctly predicted this experimental observation of human cognition", and artifact developers can say "Look, my system is saving lives/megabucks", but few of us are happy with papers saying "Look, my system is intelligent". This difficulty is compounded further by the need for theoretical scaffolding to allow us to design complex systems with confidence and to build on the results of others. "Intelligent" must be given a definition that can be related directly to the system's input, structure, and output. Such a definition must also be *general*. Otherwise, AI subsides into a smorgasbord of fields—intelligence as chess playing, intelligence as vehicle control, intelligence as medical diagnosis.

In this paper, I shall outline the development of such definitions over the history of AI and related disciplines. I shall examine each definition as a predicate P that can be applied, supposedly, to characterize systems that are intelligent. For each P, I shall discuss whether the statement "Look, my system is P" is interesting and at least sometimes true, and the sort of research and technological development to which the study of P-systems leads.

I shall begin with the idea that intelligence is strongly related to the capacity for successful behaviour—the so-called "agent-based" view of AI. The candidates for formal definitions of intelligence are as follows:

- P_1: *Perfect rationality*, or the capacity to generate maximally successful behaviour given the available information.
- P_2: *Calculative rationality*, or the in-principle capacity to compute the perfectly rational decision given the initially available information.
- P_3: *Metalevel rationality*, or the capacity to select the optimal combination of computation-sequence-plus-action, under the constraint that the action must be selected by the computation.
- P_4: *Bounded optimality*, or the capacity to generate maximally successful behaviour given the available information and computational resources.

All four definitions will be fleshed out in detail, and I will describe some results that have been obtained so far along these lines. Then I will describe ongoing and future work under the headings of calculative rationality and bounded optimality.

I shall be arguing that, of these candidates, bounded optimality comes closest to meeting the needs of AI research. There is always a danger, in this sort of claim, that its acceptance can lead to "premature mathematization", a condition characterized by increasingly technical results that have increasingly little to do with the original problem—in the case of AI, the problem of creating intelligence. Is research on bounded optimality a suitable stand-in for research on intelligence? I hope to show that P_4, bounded optimality, is more suitable than P_1 through P_3 because it is a real problem with real and desirable solutions, and also because it satisfies some essential intuitions about the nature of intelligence. Some important questions about intelligence can only be formulated and answered within the framework of bounded optimality or some relative thereof. Only time will tell, however, whether bounded optimality research, perhaps with additional refinements, can generate enough theoretical scaffolding to support significant practical progress in AI.

8.2 Agents

Until fairly recently, it was common to define AI as the computational study of "mental faculties" or "intelligent systems", catalogue various kinds, and leave it at that. This does not provide much guidance. Instead, one can define AI as the problem of designing systems that *do the right thing*. Now we just need a definition for "right".

This approach involves considering the intelligent entity as an *agent*, that is to say a system that senses its environment and acts upon it. Formally speaking, an agent is defined by the mapping from percept sequences to actions that the agent instantiates. Let O be the set of percepts that the agent can observe at any instant, and A be the set of possible actions the agent can carry out in the external world (including the action of doing nothing). Thus the *agent function* $f: O^* \rightarrow A$ defines how an agent behaves under all circumstances. What counts in the first instance is what the agent does, not necessarily what it thinks, or even whether it thinks at all. This initial refusal to consider further constraints on the internal workings of the agent (such as that it should reason logically, for example) helps in three ways: first, it allows us to view such "cognitive faculties" as planning and reasoning as occurring *in the service of* finding the right thing to do; second, it encompasses rather than excludes the position that systems can do the right thing without such cognitive faculties (Agre and Chapman, 1987; Brooks, 1989); third, it allows more freedom to consider various specifications, boundaries, and interconnections of subsystems.

The agent-based view of AI has moved quickly from workshops on "situatedness" and "embeddedness" to mainstream textbooks (Dean et al., 1995; Russell and Norvig, 1995) and buzzwords in Newsweek. *Rational* agents, loosely speaking, are agents whose actions make sense from the point of view of the information possessed by the agent and its goals (or the task for which it was designed). Rationality is a property of actions and does not specify—although it does constrain—the process by which the actions are selected. This was a point emphasized by Simon (1956), who coined the terms *substantive rationality* and *procedural rationality* to describe the difference between the question of *what* decision to make and the question of *how* to make it. That Rod Brooks' 1991 Computers and Thought lecture was titled "Intelligence without Reason" (see also Brooks, 1991) emphasizes the fact that reasoning is (perhaps) a *derived* property of agents that might, or might not, be a good implementation scheme to achieve rational behaviour. Justifying the cognitive structures that many AI researchers take for granted is not an easy problem.

One other consequence of the agent-based view of intelligence is that it opens AI up to competition from other fields that have traditionally looked on the embedded agent as a natural topic of study. Control theory is foremost among these, but evolutionary programming and indeed evolutionary biology itself also have ideas to contribute.[1]

The prevalence of the agent view has also helped the field move towards solving real problems, avoiding what Brooks calls the "hallucination" problem that arises when the fragility of a subsystem is masked by having an intelligent human providing input to it and interpreting its outputs.

8.3 Perfect rationality

Perfect rationality constrains an agent's actions to provide the maximum expectation of success given the information available. We can expand this notion as follows (see figure 8.1). The fundamental inputs to the definition are the environment class E in which the agent is to operate and the performance measure U which evaluates the sequence of states through which the agent drives the actual environment. Let $V(f, \boldsymbol{E}, U)$ denote the expected value according to U obtained by an agent function f in environment class $\boldsymbol{E}$, where (for now) we will assume a probability distribution over elements of $\boldsymbol{E}$. Then a perfectly rational agent is defined by an agent function f_{opt} such that

$$f_{\text{opt}} = \underset{f}{\operatorname{argmax}} V(f, \boldsymbol{E}, U).$$

This is just a fancy way of saying that the best agent does the best it can. The point is that perfectly rational behaviour is a well-defined function of $\boldsymbol{E}$ and U, which I will call the *task environment*. The problem of computing this function is addressed below.

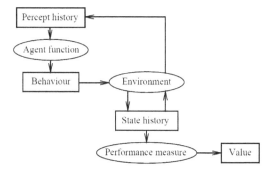

Figure 8.1
The agent receives percepts from the environment and generates a behaviour which in turn causes the environment to generate a state history. The performance measure evaluates the state history to arrive at the value of the agent.

The theoretical role of perfect rationality within AI is well-described by Newell's paper on the Knowledge Level (Newell, 1982). Knowledge-level analysis of AI systems relies on an assumption of perfect rationality. It can be used to establish an upper bound on the performance of any possible system, by establishing what a perfectly rational agent would do given the same knowledge.

Although the knowledge that a perfectly rational agent has determines the actions that it will take given its goals, the question of where the knowledge comes from is not well understood. That is, we need to understand rational learning as well as rational action. In the logical view of rationality, learning has received almost no attention—indeed, Newell's analysis precludes learning at the knowledge level. In the decision-theoretic view, Bayesian updating provides a model for rational learning, but this pushes the question back to the prior (Carnap, 1950). The question of rational priors, particularly for expressive representation languages, remains unsettled.

Another aspect of perfect rationality that is lacking is the development of a suitable body of techniques for the specification of utility functions. In economics, many results have been derived on the decomposition of overall utility into attributes that can be combined in various ways (Keeney et al., 1976), yet such methods have made few inroads into AI (but see Bacchus and Grove, 1995; Wellman, 1985). We also have little idea how to specify utility over time, and although the question has been raised often, we do not have a satisfactory understanding of the relationship between goals and utility.

The good thing about perfectly rational agents is that if you have one handy, you prefer it to any other agent. Furthermore, if you are an economist you can prove nice results about economies populated by them; and if you want to design distributed intelligent systems, assuming perfect rationality on the part of each agent makes the design of the interaction mechanisms much easier. The bad thing is that the theory of perfect rationality does not provide for the analysis of the internal design of the agent: one perfectly rational agent is as good as another. The *really* bad thing, as pointed out by Simon, is that perfectly rational agents do not exist. Physical mechanisms take time to process information and select actions, hence the behaviour of real agents cannot immediately reflect changes in the environment and will generally be suboptimal.

8.4   Calculative rationality

Before discussing calculative rationality, it is necessary to introduce a distinction between the agent function and the *agent program*, In AI, an agent is implemented as a program, which I shall call l, running on a machine, which I shall call M. An agent program receives as input the current percept, but also has internal state that reflects, in some form, the previous percepts. It outputs actions when they have been selected. From the outside, the behaviour of the agent consists of the selected actions *interspersed with inaction* (or whatever default actions the machine generates).

Calculative rationality is displayed by programs that, *if executed infinitely fast*, would result in perfectly rational behaviour. Unlike perfect rationality, calculative rationality is a requirement that can be fulfilled by many real programs. Also unlike perfect rationality, calculative rationality is not necessarily a desirable property. For example, a calculatively rational chess program will choose the "right" move, but may take 10^{50} times too long to do so.

The pursuit of calculative rationality has nonetheless been the main activity of theoretically well-founded research in AI. In the early stages of the field, it was important to concentrate on "epistemological adequacy" before "heuristic adequacy"—that is, capability in principle rather than in practice.[2] Calculative rationality has been the mainstay of both the logical and the decision-theoretic traditions. In the logical tradition, the performance measure accepts behaviours that achieve the specified goal in all cases and rejects any others. Thus Newell (1982) defines rational actions as those that are guaranteed to achieve

one of the agent's goals. Logical planning systems, such as theorem-provers using situation calculus, satisfy the conditions of calculative rationality under this definition. In the
decision-theoretic tradition, the design of calculatively rational agents has largely gone on
outside AI—for example, in stochastic optimal control theory (Kumar and Varaiya, 1986).
Representations have usually been very impoverished (state-based rather than sentential)
and solvable problems have been either very small or very specialized. Within AI, the development of probabilistic networks or belief networks has opened up many new possibilities for agent design, providing in many cases an exponential reduction in representational
complexity. Systems based on influence diagrams (probabilistic networks with action and
value nodes added) satisfy the decision-theoretic version of calculative rationality.

In practice, neither the logical nor the decision-theoretic traditions can avoid the intractability of the decision problems posed by the requirement of calculative rationality.
One response is to rule out sources of exponential complexity in the representations and
reasoning tasks addressed, so that calculative and perfect rationality coincide—at least, if
we ignore the little matter of polynomial-time computation. This position was expounded
in two fascinating Computers and Thought lectures given by Hector Levesque in 1985
(Levesque, 1986; Levesque and Brachman, 1987) and by Henry Kautz in 1989. The accompanying research results on tractable sublanguages are perhaps best seen as indications
of where complexity may be an issue rather than as a solution to the problem of complexity. The idea of restricting expressiveness was strongly opposed by Doyle and Patil (1991),
who pointed out that it also restricts the applicability of the representation and inference
services designed under such constraints.[3]

In the area of distributed AI, the system designer has control over that part of each agent's
environment that involves negotiations with other agents. Thus, one possible way to control
complexity is to constrain the negotiation problem so that optimal decisions can be made
easily. For example, the Clarke Tax mechanism can be used to ensure that the best policy
for each agent is simply to state its preferences truthfully (Ephrati and Rosenschein, 1991).
Of course, this approach does not necessarily result in optimal behaviour by the *ensemble*
of agents; nor does it solve the problem of complexity in interacting with the rest of the
environment.

The most common response to complexity has been to use various speedup techniques
and approximations in the hope of getting reasonable behaviour. AI has developed a very
powerful armoury of methods for reducing complexity, including the decomposition of
state representations into sentential form; sparse representations of environment models (as
in STRIPS operators); solution decomposition methods such as partial-order planning and
abstraction; approximate, parameterized representations of value functions for reinforcement learning; compilation (chunking, macro-operators, EBL, etc.); and the application of
metalevel control. Although some of these methods can retain guarantees of optimality
and are effective for moderately large problems that are well structured, it is inevitable that

intelligent agents will be unable to act rationally in all circumstances. This observation has been a commonplace since the very beginning of AI. Yet systems that select suboptimal actions fall outside calculative rationality per se, and we need a better theory to understand them.

8.5 Metalevel rationality

Metalevel rationality, also called Type II rationality by I.J Good (1971), is based on the idea of finding an optimal tradeoff between computational costs and decision quality. Although Good never made his concept of Type II rationality very precise—he defines it as "the maximization of expected utility *taking into account deliberation* costs—it is clear that the aim was to take advantage of some sort of *metalevel architecture* to implement this tradeoff. Metalevel architecture is a design philosophy for intelligent agents that divides the agent into two (or more) notional parts. The *object level* carries out computations concerned with the application domain—for example, projecting the results of physical actions, computing the utility of certain states, and so on. The *metalevel* is a second decision-making process whose application domain consists of the object-level computations themselves and the computational objects and states that they affect. Metareasoning has a long history in AI, going back at least to the early 1970s (see Russell and Wefald, 1991a for historical details). One can also view selective search methods and pruning strategies as embodying metalevel expertise concerning the desirability of pursuing particular object-level search operations.

The theory of *rational metareasoning* formalizes the intuition that the metalevel can "do the right thinking." The basic idea is that object-level computations are actions with costs (the passage of time) and benefits (improvements in decision quality). A rational metalevel selects computations according to their expected utility. Rational metareasoning has as a precursor the theory of *information value* (Howard, 1966)—the notion that one can calculate the decision-theoretic value of acquiring an additional piece of information by simulating the decision process that would be followed given each possible outcome of the information request, thereby estimating the expected improvement in decision quality averaged over those outcomes. The application to computational processes, by analogy to information-gathering, seems to have originated with Matheson (1968). In AI, Horvitz (1987a,b), Breese and Fehling (1990), and Russell and Wefald (1989, 1991a,b) all showed how the idea of value of computation could solve the basic problems of real-time decision-making.

The work done with Eric Wefald looked in particular at search algorithms, in which the object-level computations extend projections of the results of various courses of actions further info the future. For example, in chess programs, each object-level computation expands a leaf node of the game tree. The metalevel problem is then to select nodes for expansion and to terminate search at the appropriate point. The principal problem with metareasoning in such systems is that the local effects of the computations do not *directly* translate into improved decisions, because there is also a complex process of propagating the local effects at the leaf back to the root and the move choice. It turns out that a general formula for the value of computation can be found in terms of the "local efforts" and the "propagation function", such that the formula can be instantiated for any particular object-level system (such as minimax propagation), compiled, and executed efficiently at runtime. This method was implemented for two-player games, two-player games with chance nodes, and single-agent search. In each case, the same general metareasoning scheme resulted in efficiency improvements of roughly an order of magnitude over traditional, highly-engineered algorithms.

Another general class of metareasoning problems arises with *anytime* (Dean and Boddy, 1988) or *flexible* (Horvitz, 1987a) algorithms, which are algorithms designed to return results whose quality varies with the amount of time allocated to computation. The simplest type of metareasoning trades off the expected increase in decision quality for a single algorithm, as measured by a *performance profile*, against the cost of time (Simon, 1955). A greedy termination condition is optimal if the second derivative of the performance profile is negative. More complex problems arise if one wishes to build complex real-time systems from anytime components. First, one has to ensure the *interruptibility* of the composed system—that is, to ensure that the system as a whole can respond robustly to immediate demands for output. The solution is to interleave the execution of all the components, allocating time to each component so that the total time for each complete iterative improvement cycle of the system doubles at each iteration. In this way, we can construct a complex system that can handle arbitrary and unexpected real-time demands exactly as if it knew the exact time available in advance, with just a small ($\leqslant 4$) constant factor penalty in speed (Russell and Zilberstein, 1991). Second, one has to allocate the available computation optimally among the components to maximize the total output quality. Although this is NP-hard for the general case, it can be solved in time linear in program size when the call graph of the components is tree-structured (Zilberstein and Russell, 1996). Although these results are derived in the relatively clean context of anytime algorithms with well-defined performance profiles, there is reason to expect that the general problem of robust real-time decision-making in complex systems can be handled in practice.

Over the last few years, an interesting debate has emerged concerning the nature of metaknowledge and metareasoning. TEIRESIAS (Davis, 1980) established the idea that explicit, domain-specific metaknowledge was an important aspect of expert system creation. Thus, metaknowledge is a sort of "extra" domain knowledge, over and above the object-level domain knowledge, that one has to add to an AI system to get it to work well. On the other hand, in the work on rational metareasoning described above, it is clear that *the metatheory describing the effects of computations is domain-independent* (Ginsberg and Geddis, 1991; Russell and Wefald, 1991a). In principle, no additional domain knowledge is needed to assess the benefits of a computation. In practice, metareasoning from first principles can be very expensive. To avoid this, the results of metalevel analysis for particular domains can be compiled into domain-specific metaknowledge, or such knowledge can be learned directly from experience (see Russell and Wefald, 1991a, Chapter 6, and Minton, 1996). This view of emerging "computational expertise" leads to a fundamental insight into intelligence—namely, that there is an interesting sense in which *algorithms are not a necessary part of AI systems*. Instead, one can imagine a general process of rationally guided computation interacting with properties of the environment to produce more and more efficient decision making. To my mind, this way of thinking finesses one major puzzle of AI: if what is required for AI is incredibly devious and superbly efficient algorithms far surpassing the current best efforts of computer scientists, how did evolution (and how will machine learning) ever get there?

Significant open problems remain in the area of rational metareasoning. One obvious difficulty is that almost all systems to date have adopted a *myopic* strategy—a greedy, depth-one search at the metalevel. Obviously, the problem of optimal selection of computation *sequences* is at least as intractable as the underlying object-level problem. Nonetheless, sequences must be considered because in some cases the value of a computation may not be apparent as an improvement in decision quality until further computations have been done. This suggests that techniques from reinforcement learning could be effective, especially as the "reward function" for computation—that is, the improvement in decision quality—is easily available to the metalevel post hoc. Other possible areas for research include the creation of effective metalevel controllers for more complex systems such as abstraction hierarchy planners, hybrid architectures, and so on.

Although rational metareasoning seems to be a useful tool in coping with complexity, the concept of metalevel rationality as a formal framework for resource-bounded agents does not seem to hold water. The reason is that, since metareasoning is expensive, it cannot be carried out optimally. The history of object-level rationality has repeated itself at the metalevel: perfect rationality at the metalevel is unattainable and calculative rationality at the metalevel is useless. Therefore, a time/optimality tradeoff has to be made for metalevel computations, as for example with the myopic approximation mentioned above. Within the framework of metalevel rationality, however, there is no way to identify the appropriate tradeoff of time for metalevel decision quality. Any attempt to do so via a metametalevel simply results in a conceptual regress. Furthermore, it is entirely possible that in some environments, the most effective agent design will do no metareasoning at all, but will simply respond to circumstances. These considerations suggest that the right approach is to step outside the agent, as it were; to refrain from micromanaging the individual decisions made by the agent. This is the approach taken in bounded optimality.

8.6   Bounded optimality

The difficulties with perfect rationality and metalevel rationality arise from the imposition of constraints on things (actions, computations) that the agent designer does not directly control. Specifying that *actions or computations* be rational is of no use if no real agents can fulfill the specification. The designer controls the *program*. In Russell and Subramanian (1995), the notion of *feasibility* for a given machine is introduced to describe the set of all agent functions that can be implemented by some agent program running on that machine. This is somewhat analogous to the idea of computability, but is much stricter because it relates the operation of a program on a formal machine model with finite speed to the actual temporal behaviour generated by the agent.

Given this view, one is led immediately to the idea that optimal feasible behaviour is an interesting notion, and to the idea of finding the program that generates it. Suppose we define $Agent(l, M)$ to be the agent function implemented by the program l running on machine M. Then the bounded optimal program l_{opt} is defined by

$$l_{opt} = \underset{l \in \mathcal{L}_M}{\operatorname{argmax}} V(Agent(l, M), \boldsymbol{E}, U),$$

where $\mathcal{L}_M$ is the finite set of all programs that can be run on M. This is P_4. bounded optimality.

In AI, the idea of bounded optimality floated around among several discussion groups interested in the general topic of resource-bounded rationality in the late 1980s, particularly those at Rockwell (organized by Michael Fehling) and Stanford (organized by Michael Bratman). The term "bounded optimality" seems to have been originated by Eric Horvitz (1987b), who defined it informally as "the optimization of computational utility given a set of assumptions about expected problems and constraints on resources".

Similar ideas have also surfaced recently in game theory, where there has been a shift from consideration of optimal decisions in games to a consideration of optimal decision-making programs. This leads to different results because it limits the ability of each agent to do unlimited simulation of the other, who is also doing unlimited simulation of the first, and so on. Even the requirement of computability makes a significant difference (Megiddo and Wigderson, 1986). Bounds on the complexity of players have also become a topic of intense interest. Papadimitriou and Yannakakis (1994) have shown that a collaborative equilibrium exists for the iterated Prisoner's Dilemma game if each agent is a finite automaton with a number of states that is less than exponential in the number of rounds. This is essentially a bounded optimality result, where the bound is on space rather than speed of computation.

Philosophy has also seen a gradual evolution in the definition of rationality. There has been a shift from consideration of *act utilitarianism*—the rationality of individual acts—to *rule utilitarianism*, or the rationality of general policies for acting. The requirement that policies be feasible for limited agents was discussed extensively by Cherniak (1986) and Harman (1983). A philosophical proposal generally consistent with the notion of bounded optimality can be found in the "Moral First Aid Manual" (Dennett, 1986). Dennett explicitly discusses the idea of reaching an optimum within the space of feasible decision procedures, using as an example the Ph.D. admissions procedure of a philosophy department. He points out that the bounded optimal admissions procedure may be somewhat messy and may have no obvious hallmark of "optimality"—in fact, the admissions committee may continue to tinker with it since bounded optimal systems may have no way to recognize their own bounded optimality.

In work with Devika Subramanian, the general idea of bounded optimality has been placed in a formal setting so that one can begin to derive rigorous results on bounded optimal programs. This involves setting up completely specified relationships among agents, programs, machines, environments, and time. We found this to be a very valuable exercise in itself. For example, the "folk AI" notions of "real-time environments" and "deadlines" ended up with definitions rather different than those we had initially imagined. From this foundation, a very simple machine architecture was investigated in which the program consists of decision procedures of fixed execution time and decision quality. In a "stochastic deadline" environment, it turns out that the utility attained by running several procedures in sequence until interrupted is often higher than that attainable by any single decision procedure. That is, it is often better first to prepare a "quick and dirty" answer before embarking on more involved calculations in case the latter do not finish in time.

The interesting aspect of these results, beyond their value as a demonstration of nontrivial proofs of bounded optimality, is that they exhibit in a simple way what I believe to be a major feature of bounded optimal agents: the fact that the pressure towards optimality within a finite machine results in more complex program structures. Intuitively, efficient decision-making in a complex environment requires a software architecture that offers a wide variety of possible computational options, so that in most situations the agent has at least some computations available that provide a significant increase in decision quality.

One possible objection to the basic model of bounded optimality outlined above is that solutions are not *robust* with respect to small variations in the environment or the machine. This in turn would lead to difficulties in analysing complex system designs. Theoretical computer science faced the same problem in describing the running time of algorithms, because counting steps and describing instruction sets exactly gives the same kind of fragile results on optimal algorithms. The $O()$ notation was developed to deal with this and provides a much more robust way to describe complexity that is independent of machine speeds and implementation details. This robustness is also essential in allowing complexity results to develop cumulatively. In Russell and Subramanian (1995), the corresponding notion is asymptotic bounded optimality (ABO). As with classical complexity, we can define both average-case and worst-case ABO, where "case" here means the environment. For example, worst-case ABO is defined as follows:

Worst-case asymptotic bounded optimality. *An agent program l is timewise (or space-wise) worst-case ABO in $\boldsymbol{E}$ on M iff*

$$\exists k, n_0 \ \forall l', n \ \ n > n_0 \Rightarrow V^*(Agent(l, kM), \boldsymbol{E}, U, n) \geqslant V^*(Agent(l', M), \boldsymbol{E}, U, n)$$

where kM denotes a version of M speeded up by a factor k (or with k times more memory) and $V^*(f, \boldsymbol{E}, U, n)$ is the minimum value of $V(f, \boldsymbol{E}, U)$ for all E in $\boldsymbol{E}$ of complexity n.

In English, this means that the program is basically along the right lines if it just needs a faster (larger) machine to have worst-case behaviour as good as that of any other program in all environments.

Another possible objection to the idea of bounded optimality is that it simply shifts the intractable computational burden of metalevel rationality from the agent's metalevel to the designer's object level. Surely, one might argue, the designer now has to solve offline all the metalevel optimization problems that were intractable when online. This argument is not without merit—indeed, it would be surprising if the agent design problem turns out to be easy. There is however, a significant difference between the two problems, in that the agent designer is presumably creating an agent for an entire class of environments, whereas the putative metalevel agent is working in a specific environment. That this can make the problem *easier* for the designer can be seen by considering the example of sorting algorithms. It may be very difficult indeed to sort a list of a trillion elements, but it is relatively easy to design an asymptotically optimal algorithm for sorting. In fact, the difficulties of the two tasks are unrelated. The unrelatedness would still hold for BO as well as ABO design, but the ABO definitions make it a good deal clearer.

It can be shown easily that worst-case ABO is a generalization of asymptotically optimal algorithms, simply by constructing a "classical environment" in which classical algorithms operate and in which the utility of the algorithm's behaviour is a decreasing positive function of runtime if the output is correct and zero otherwise. Agents in more general environments may need to trade off output quality for time, generate multiple outputs over time, and so on. As an illustration of how ABO is a useful abstraction, one can show that under certain restrictions one can construct *universal* ABO programs that are ABO for any time variation in the utility function, using the doubling construction from Russell and Zilberstein (1991). Further directions for bounded optimality research are discussed below.

8.7   What is to be done?

This section describes some of the research activities that will, I hope, help to turn bounded optimality into a creative tool for AI system design. First, however, I shall describe work on calculatively rational systems that needs to be done in order to enrich the space of agent programs.

8.7.1   Components for calculative rationality

As mentioned above, the correct design for a rational agent depends on the task environment—the "physical" environment and the performance measure on environment histories. It is possible to define some basic properties of task environments that, together with the complexity of the problem, lead to identifiable requirements on the corresponding rational agent designs (Russell and Norvig, 1995, Chapter 2). The principal properties are whether the environment is *fully observable* or *partially observable*, whether it is *deterministic* or *stochastic*, whether it is *static* (i.e., does not change except when the agent acts) or *dynamic*, and whether it is *discrete* or *continuous*. Although crude, these distinctions serve to lay out an agenda for basic research in AI. By analysing and solving each subcase and producing calculatively rational mechanisms with the required properties, theoreticians can produce the AI equivalent of bricks, beams, and mortar with which AI architects can build the equivalent of cathedrals. Unfortunately, many of the basic components are currently missing. Others are so fragile and non-scalable as to be barely able to support their own weight. This presents many opportunities for research of far-reaching impact.

The logicist tradition of goal-based agent design, based on the creation and execution of guaranteed plans, is firmly anchored in fully observable, deterministic, static, and discrete task environments. (Furthermore, tasks are usually specified as logically defined goals rather than general utility functions.) This means that agents need keep no internal state and can even execute plans without the use of perception.

The theory of optimal action in stochastic, partially observable environments goes under the heading of *POMDPs* (Partially Observable Markov Decision Problems), a class of problems first addressed in the work of Sondik (1971) but almost completely unknown in AI until recently (Cassandra et al., 1994). Similarly, very little work of a fundamental nature has been done in AI on dynamic environments, which require real-time decision making, or on continuous environments, which have been largely the province of geometry-based robotics. Since most real-world applications are partially observable, nondeterministic, dynamic, and continuous, the lack of emphasis is somewhat surprising.

There are, however, several new bricks under construction. For example, dynamic probabilistic networks (DPNs) (Dean and Kanazawa, 1989) provide a mechanism to maintain beliefs about the current state of a dynamic, partially observable, nondeterministic environment, and to project forward the effects of actions. Also, the rapid improvement in the speed and accuracy of computer vision systems has made interfacing with continuous physical environments more practical. In particular, the application of Kalman filtering (Kalman, 1960), a widely used technique in control theory, allows robust and efficient tracking of moving objects; DPNs extend Kalman filtering to allow more general representations of world state. Reinforcement learning, together with inductive learning methods for continuous function representations such as neural networks, allow learning from delayed rewards in continuous, nondeterministic environments. Recently, Parr and Russell (1995), among others, have had some success in applying reinforcement learning to partially observable environments. Finally, learning methods for static and dynamic probabilistic networks with hidden variables (i.e., for partially observable environments) may make it possible to acquire the necessary environment models (Lauritzen, 1995; Russell et al., 1995).

The Bayesian Automated Taxi (a.k.a. BATmobile) project (Forbes et al., 1995) is an attempt to combine all these new bricks to solve an interesting application problem, namely driving a car on a freeway. Technically, this can be viewed as a POMDP because the environment contains relevant variables (such as whether or not the Volvo on your left is intending to change lanes to the right) that are not observable, and because the behaviour of other vehicles and the effects of one's own actions are not exactly predictable. In a POMDP, the optimal decision depends on the joint probability distribution over the entire set of state variables. It turns out that a combination of real-time vision algorithms, Kalman filtering, and dynamic probabilistic networks can maintain the required distribution when observing a stream of traffic on a freeway. The BATmobile currently uses a hand-coded decision tree to make decisions on this basis, and is a fairly safe driver (although probably far from optimal) on our simulator. We are currently experimenting with lookahead methods to make approximately rational decisions, as well as supervised learning and reinforcement learning methods.

As well as extending the scope of AI applications, new bricks for planning under uncertainty significantly increase the opportunity for metareasoning to make a difference. With logical planners, a plan either does or does not work; it has proved very difficult to find heuristics to measure the "goodness" of a logical plan that does not guarantee success, or to estimate the likelihood that an abstract logical plan will have a successful concrete instance. This means that it is very hard to identify plan elaboration steps that are likely to have high value. In contrast, planners designed to handle uncertainty and utility have built-in information about the likelihood of success and there is a continuum from hopeless to perfect plans. Getting metareasoning to work for such systems is a high priority. It is also important to apply those methods such as partial-order planning and abstraction that have been so effective in extending the reach of classical planners.

8.7.2 Directions for bounded optimality

Ongoing research on bounded optimality aims to extend the initial results of (Russell and Subramanian, 1995) to more interesting agent designs. In this section, I will sketch some design dimensions and the issues involved in establishing bounded optimality results.

The general scheme to be followed involves defining a virtual machine M that runs programs from a class $\mathcal{L}_M$. Typically, programs will have a "fixed part" that is shared across some subclass and a "variable part" that is specific to the individual program. Then comparisons are made between the best programs in different subclasses for the same machine. For example, suppose M is a machine capable of running any feedforward neural network. $\mathcal{L}_M$ consists of all such networks, and we might be interested in comparing the subclasses defined by different network topologies, while within each subclass individual programs differ in the weights on the links of the network. Thus, the boundary between machine and program depends to some extent on the range of comparisons that the designer wishes to consider.

At the most general level of analysis, the methodology is now quite straightforward: choose a machine, choose a program that runs on the machine, then dump the resulting agent into a class of environments E. The program with the best performance is bounded optimal for M in E. For example, M is an IBM PC with a C compiler; $\mathcal{L}_M$ consists of C programs up to a certain size; the environment consists of a population of human chess opponents; the performance measure is the chess rating achieved; the bounded optimal program is the one with the highest rating.

This rather blunt and unenlightening approach has no doubt occurred to many engaged in the construction of chess programs. As stated, the problem is ridiculously hard to solve and the solution, once found, would be very domain-specific. The problem is to define a research agenda for bounded optimality that provides a little more guidance and generality. This can be done by exploiting structure in the definition of the problem, in particular the orthogonality of time and content, and by using more sophisticated agent designs, particularly those that incorporate mechanisms for adaptation and optimization. In this way, we can prove bounded optimality results for more general classes of task environments.

8.7.2.1 Mechanisms for optimization   Modular design using a hierarchy of components is commonly seen as the only way to build reliable complex systems. The components fulfill certain behavioural specifications and interact in well-defined ways. To produce a composite bounded-optimal design, the optimizatian problem involves allocating execution time to components (Zilberstein and Russell, 1996) or arranging the order of execution of the components (Russell and Subramanian, 1995) to maximize overall performance. As illustrated earlier in the discussion of universal ABO algorithms, the techniques for optimizing temporal behaviour are largely orthogonal to the *content* of the system components, which can therefore be optimized separately. Consider, for example, a composite system that uses an anytime inference algorithm over a belief network as one of its components. If a learning algorithm improves the accuracy of the belief network, the performance profile of the inference component will improve, which will result in a reallocation of execution time that is guaranteed to improve overall system performance. Thus, techniques such as the doubling construction and the time allocation algorithm in Zilberstein and Russell (1996) can be seen as domain-independent tools for agent design. They enable bounded optimality results that do not depend on the specific temporal aspects of the environment class. As a simple example, we might prove that a certain chess program design is ABO for all time controls ranging from blitz to full tournament play.

The results obtained so far for optimal time allocation have assumed a static, offline optimization process with predictable component performance profiles and fixed connections among components. One can imagine far more subtle designs in which individual components must deal with unexpectedly slow or fast progress in processing and changing needs for information from other components. This might involve exchanging computational resources among components, establishing new interfaces, and so on. This is more reminiscent of a computational market, as envisaged by Wellman (1993), than of the classical subroutine hierarchies, and would offer a useful additional level of abstraction in system design.

8.7.2.2 Mechanisms for adaptation   In addition to combinatorial optimization of the structure and temporal behaviour of an agent, we can also use learning methods to improve the design:

- The *content* of an agent's knowledge base can of course be improved by inductive learning. In Russell and Subramanian (1995), it is shown that approximately bounded optimal designs can be guaranteed with high probability if each component is learned in such a way that its output quality is close to optimal among all components of a given execution time. Results from computational learning theory, particularly in the *agnostic learning* model (Kearns et al., 1992), can provide learning methods with the required properties. The key additional step is to analyze the way in which slight imperfection in each component carries through to slight imperfection in the whole agent.

- *Reinforcement learning* can be used to learn value information such as utility functions. Recent results (Tsitsiklis and Van Roy, 1997) provide convergence guarantees for reinforcement learning with a fairly broad class of function approximators. One can use such learning methods for metalevel information, e.g., the value of computation. In Russell and Wefald (1991a, Chapter 6), this is shown to be an effective technique. Formal results on convergence to optimal control of search would be of great interest. Further work is needed, however, since current theorems assume a stationary distribution that generates the agent's experiences whereas an agent that is improving its search control will presumably be exploring different populations of experiences over time.

• *Compilation* methods such as explanation-based learning can be used to transform an agent's representations to allow faster decision making. Several agent architectures including SOAR (Laird et al., 1986) use compilation to speed up all forms of problem solving. Some nontrivial results on convergence have been obtained by Tadepalli (1991), based on the observation that after a given amount of experience, novel problems for which no solution has been stored should be encountered only infrequently.

Presumably, an agent architecture can incorporate all these learning mechanisms. One of the issues to be faced by bounded optimality research is how to prove convergence results when several adaptation and optimization mechanisms are operating simultaneously. A "quasistatic" approach, in which one mechanism reaches convergence before the other method is allowed to take its next step, seems theoretically adequate but not very practical.

8.7.2.3 *Offline and online mechanisms* One can distinguish between *offline* and *online* mechanisms for constructing bounded-optimal agents. An offline construction mechanism is not itself part of the agent and is not the subject of bounded optimality constraints. Let C be an offline mechanism designed for a class of environments E. Then a typical theorem will say that C operates in a specific environment $E \in E$ and returns an agent design that is ABO (say) for E—that is, an environment-specific agent.

In the online case, the mechanism C is considered part of the agent. Then a typical theorem will say that the agent is ABO for all $E \in E$. If the performance measure used is indifferent to the transient cost of the adaptation or optimization mechanism, the two types of theorems are essentially the same. On the other hand, if the cost cannot be ignored—for example, if an agent that learns quickly is to be preferred to an agent that reaches the same level of performance but learns more slowly—then the analysis becomes more difficult. It may become necessary to define asymptotic equivalence for "experience efficiency" in order to obtain robust results, as is done in computational learning theory.

It is worth noting that one can easily prove the value of "lifelong learning" in the ABO framework. An agent that devotes a constant fraction of its computational resources to learning-while-doing cannot do worse, in the ABO sense, than an agent that ceases learning after some point. If some improvement is still possible, the lifelong learning agent will always be preferred.

8.7.2.4 *Fixed and variable computation costs* Another dimension of design space emerges when one considers the computational cost of the "variable part" of the agent design. The design problem is simplified considerably when the cost is fixed. Consider again the task of metalevel reinforcement learning, and to make things concrete let the metalevel decision be made by a Q-function mapping from computational state and action to value. Suppose

further that the Q-function is to be represented by a neural net. If the topology of the neural net is fixed, then all Q-functions in the space have the same execution time. Consequently, the optimality criterion used by the standard Q-learning process coincides with bounded optimality, and the equilibrium reached will be a bounded-optimal configuration.[4] On the other hand, if the topology of the network is subject to alteration as the design space is explored, then the execution time of the different Q-functions varies. In this case, the standard Q-learning process will not necessarily converge to a bounded-optimal configuration. A different adaptation mechanism must be found that takes into account the passage of time and its effect on utility.

Whatever the solution to this problem turns out to be, the important point is that the notion of bounded optimality helps to distinguish adaptation mechanisms that will result in good performance from those that will not. Adaptation mechanisms derived from calculative rationality will fail in the more realistic setting where an agent cannot afford to aim for perfection.

8.7.2.5   Fully variable architectures   The discussion so far has been limited to fairly sedate forms of agent architecture in which the scope for adaptation is circumscribed to particular functional aspects such as metalevel Q-functions. However, an agent must in general deal with an environment that is far more complex than itself and that exhibits variation over time at all levels of granularity. Limits on the size of the agent's memory may imply that almost complete revision of the agent's mental structure is needed to achieve high performance. For example, one can imagine that a simple rule-based agent living through cycles of winter and summer may have to discard all of its summer rules as winter approaches, and then relearn them from scratch the following year. Such situations may engender a rethinking of some of our notions of agent architecture and optimality, and suggest a view of agent programs as dynamical systems with various amounts of compiled and uncompiled knowledge and internal processes of inductive learning, forgetting, and compilation.

8.7.2.6   Towards a grammar of AI systems   The approach that seems to be emerging for bounded optimality research is to divide up the space of agent designs into "architectural classes" such that in each class the structural variation is sufficiently limited. Then ABO results can be obtained either by analytical optimization within the class or by showing that an empirical adaptation process results in an approximately ABO design. Once this is done, it should be possible to compare architecture classes directly, perhaps to establish asymptotic dominance of one class over another. For example, it might be the case that the inclusion of an appropriate "macro-operator formation" or "greedy metareasoning" capability in a given architecture will result in an improvement in behaviour in the limit of very complex environments—that is, one cannot compensate for the exclusion of the capability by increasing the machine speed by a constant factor. A central tool in such work will be the use of "no-cost" results where, for example, the allocation of a constant fraction of computational resources to learning or metareasoning can do no harm to an agent's ABO prospects.

Getting all these architectural devices to work together smoothly is an important unsolved problem in AI and must be addressed before we can make progress on understanding bounded optimality within these more complex architectural classes. If the notion of "architectural device" can be made sufficiently concrete, then AI may eventually develop a *grammar* for agent designs, describing the devices and their interrelations. As the grammar develops, so should the accompanying ABO dominance results.

8.8   Summary

I have outlined some directions for formally grounded AI research based on bounded optimality as the desired property of AI systems. This perspective on AI seems to be a logical consequence of the inevitable philosophical "move" from optimization over actions or computations to optimization over programs. I have suggested that such an approach should allow synergy between theoretical and practical AI research of a kind not afforded by other formal frameworks. In the same vein, I believe it is a satisfactory formal counterpart of the informal goal of creating intelligence. In particular, it is entirely consistent with our intuitions about the need for complex structure in real intelligent agents, the importance of the resource limitations faced by relatively tiny minds in large worlds, and the operation of evolution as a design optimization process. One can also argue that bounded optimality research is likely to satisfy better the needs of those who wish to emulate human intelligence, because it takes into account the limitations on computational resources that are presumably responsible for most of the regrettable deviation from perfect rationality exhibited by humans.

Bounded optimality and its asymptotic cousin are, of course, nothing but formally defined properties that one may want systems to satisfy. It is too early to tell whether ABO will do the same kind of work for AI that asymptotic complexity has done for theoretical computer science. Creativity in design is still the prerogative of AI researchers. It may, however be possible to systematize the design process somewhat and to automate the process of adapting a system to its computational resources and the demands of the environment. The concept of bounded optimality provides a way to make sure the adaptation process is "correct".

My hope is that with these kinds of investigations, it will eventually be possible to develop the conceptual and mathematical tools to answer some basic questions about intelligence. For example, *why* do complex intelligent systems (appear to) have declarative knowledge structures over which they reason explicitly? This has been a fundamental assumption that distinguishes AI from other disciplines for agent design, yet the answer is still unknown. Indeed, Rod Brooks, Hubert Dreyfus, and others flatly deny the assumption. What is clear is that it will need *something like* a theory of bounded optimal agent design to answer this question.

Most of the agent design features that I have discussed here, including the use of declarative knowledge, have been conceived within the standard methodology of "first build calculatively rational agents and then speed them up". Yet one can legitimately doubt that this methodology will enable the AI community to discover all the design features needed for general intelligence. The reason is that no conceivable computer will ever be remotely close to approximating perfect rationality for even moderately complex environments. Perfect rationality is, if you like, a "Newtonian" definition for intelligent agents whereas the real world is a particle accelerator. It may well be the case that agents based on improvements to calculatively rational designs are *not even close* to achieving the level of performance that is potentially achievable given the underlying computational resources. For this reason, I believe it is imperative not to dismiss ideas for agent designs that do not seem at first glance to fit into the "classical" calculatively rational framework. Instead, one must attempt to understand the potential of the bounded optimal configurations within the corresponding architectural class, and to see if one can design the appropriate adaptation mechanisms that might help in realizing these configurations.

As mentioned in the previous section, there is also plenty of work to do in the area of making more general and more robust "bricks" from which to construct AI systems for more realistic environments, and such work will provide added scope for the achievement of bounded optimality. In a sense, under this conception AI research is the same now as it always should have been.

Notes for Chapter 8

1. I view this as a very positive development. AI is a field defined by its problems, not its methods. Its principal insights—among them the learning, use, and compilation of explicit knowledge in the service of decision making—can certainly withstand the influx of new methods from other fields. This is especially true when other fields are simultaneously embracing the insights derived within AI.

2. Perhaps not coincidentally, this decision was taken before the question of computational intractability was properly understood in computer science.

3. Doyle and Patil (1991) propose instead the idea of "rational management of inference". Representation systems "should be designed to offer a broad mix of services varying in cost and quality" and should take into account "the costs and benefits [of computations] as perceived by the system's user". That is, they suggest a solution based on rational metareasoning, as discussed in Section 8.5.

4. A similar observation was made by Horvitz and Breese (1990) for cases where the object level is so restricted that the metalevel decision problem can be solved in constant time.

Central Systems

9

Jerry A. Fodor
1983

[T]he questions we now want to ask can be put like this: Are there psychological processes that can plausibly be assumed to cut across cognitive domains? And, if there are, is there reason to suppose that such processes are subserved by nonmodular (e.g., informationally unencapsulated) mechanisms?

The answer to the first of these questions is, I suppose, reasonably clear. Even if input systems are domain specific, there must be some cognitive mechanisms that are not. The general form of the argument goes back at least to Aristotle: the representations that input systems deliver have to interface somewhere, and the computational mechanisms that effect the interface must ipso facto have access to information from more than one cognitive domain. Consider:

(a) We have repeatedly distinguished between what the input systems compute and what the organism (consciously or subdoxastically) *believes*. Part of the point of this distinction is that input systems, being informationally encapsulated, typically compute representations of the distal layout on the basis of less information about the distal layout than the organism has available. Such representations want correction in light of background knowledge (e.g., information in memory) and of the simultaneous results of input analysis in other domains (see Aristotle on the 'common sense'). Call the process of arriving at such corrected representations "the fixation of perceptual belief." To a first approximation, we can assume that the mechanisms that effect this process work like this: they look simultaneously at the representations delivered by the various input systems and at the information currently in memory, and they arrive at a best (i.e., best available) hypothesis about how the world must be, given these various sorts of data.[1] But if there are mechanisms that fix perceptual belief, and if they work in anything like this way, then these mechanisms are not domain specific. Indeed, the point of having them is precisely to ensure that, wherever possible, what the organism believes is determined by all the information it has access to, regardless of which cognitive domains this information is drawn from.

(b) We use language (inter alia) to communicate our views on how the world is. But this use of language is possible only if the mechanisms that mediate the production of speech have access to what we see (or hear, or remember, or think) that the world is like. Since, by assumption, such mechanisms effect an interface among vertical faculties, they cannot themselves be domain specific. More precisely, they must at least be *less* domain specific than the vertical faculties are.[2]

(c) One aspect of the 'impenetrability' of the input systems is, we assumed, their insensitivity to the utilities of the organism. This assumption was required in part to explain the *veridicality* of perception given that the world doesn't always prove to be the way that we would prefer it to be. However, an interface between perception and utilities must take place *somewhere* if we are to use the information that input systems deliver in order to determine how we ought to act. (Decision theories are, to all intents and purposes, models of the structure of this interface. The point is, roughly, that wishful seeing is, avoided by requiring interactions with utilities to occur *after*—not *during*—perceptual integration.) So, again, the moral seems to be that there must be some mechanisms which cross the domains that input systems establish.

For these and other similar reasons, I assume that there must be relatively nondenominational (i.e., domain-*in*specific) psychological systems which operate, inter alia, to exploit the information that input systems provide. Following the tradition, I shall call these "central" systems, and I will assume that it is the operation of these sorts of systems that people have in mind when they talk, pretheoretically, of such mental processes as thought and problem-solving. Central systems may be domain specific in *some* sense—we will consider this when we get to the issues about 'epistemic boundedness'—but at least they aren't domain specific in the way that input systems are. The interesting question about the central systems is whether, being nondenominational, they are also nonmodular in other respects as well. That is, whether the central systems fail to exhibit the galaxy of properties that lead us to think of the input systems as a natural kind . . . [3]

Briefly, my argument is going to be this: we have seen that much of what is typical of the input systems is more or less directly a product of their informational encapsulation. By contrast, I'll claim that central systems are, in important respects, unencapsulated, and that it is primarily for this reason that they are not plausibly viewed as modular. Notice that I am not going to be arguing for a tautology. It is perfectly possible, in point of logic, that a system which is not domain specific might nevertheless be encapsulated. Roughly, domain specificity has to do with the range of questions for which a device provides answers (the range of inputs for which it computes analyses); whereas encapsulation has to do with the range of information that the device consults in deciding what answers to provide. A system could thus be domain specific but unencapsulated (it answers a relatively narrow range of questions put in doing so it uses whatever it knows); and a system could be nondenominational but encapsulated (it will give some answer to any question; but it gives its answers off the top of its head—i.e., by reference to less than all the relevant information). If, in short, it is true that only domain-specific systems are encapsulated, then that truth is interesting. Perhaps it goes without saying that I am not about to demonstrate this putative truth. I am, however, about to explore it.

So much for what I'm going to be arguing *for*. Now a little about the strategy of the argument. The fact is that there is practically no direct evidence, pro or con, on the question whether central systems are modular. No doubt it is possible to achieve some gross factoring of "intelligence" into "verbal" versus "mathematical/spatial" capacities; and no doubt there is something to the idea of a corresponding hemispheric specialization. But such dichotomies are *very* gross and may themselves be confounded with the modularity of the input systems—that is to say, they give very little evidence for the existence of domain-specific (to say nothing of modular) systems other than the ones that subserve the functions of perceptual and linguistic analysis.

When you run out of direct evidence, you might just as well try arguing from analogies, and that is what I propose to do. I have been assuming that the typical function of central systems is the fixation of belief (perceptual or otherwise) by nondemonstrative inference. Central systems look at what the input systems deliver, and they look at what is in memory, and they use this information to constrain the computation of 'best hypotheses' about what the world is like. These processes are, of course, largely unconscious, and very little is known about their operation. However, it seems reasonable enough that something can be inferred about them from what we know about *explicit* processes of nondemonstrative inference—viz., from what we know about empirical inference in science. So, here is how I am going to proceed. First, I'll suggest that scientific confirmation—the nondemonstrative fixation of belief in science—is typically unencapsulated. I'll then argue that if, pursuing the analogy, we assume that the central psychological systems are also unencapsulated, we get a picture of those systems that is, anyhow, not radically implausible given such information about them as is currently available.

The nondemonstrative fixation of belief in science has two properties which, though widely acknowledged, have not (so far as I know) yet been named. I shall name them: confirmation in science is *isotropic* and it is *Quineian*. It is notoriously hard to give anything approaching a rigorous account of what being isotropic and Quineian amounts to, but it is easy enough to convey the intuitions.

By saying that confirmation is isotropic, I mean that the facts relevant to the confirmation of a scientific hypothesis may be drawn from anywhere in the field of previously established empirical (or, of course, demonstrative) truths. Crudely: everything that the scientist knows is, in principle, relevant to determining what else he ought to believe. In principle, our botany constrains our astronomy, if only we could think of ways to make them connect.

As is usual in a methodological inquiry, it is possible to consider the isotropy of confirmation either normatively (as a principle to which we believe that rational inductive practice *ought* to conform) or sociologically (as a principle which working scientists actually adhere to in assessing the degree of confirmation of their theories). In neither case, however, should we view the isotropy of confirmation as merely gratuitous—or, to use a term of Rorty's (1979) as merely "optional." If isotropic confirmation 'partially defines the language game that scientists play'(remember when we used to talk that way?), that is because of a profound conviction—partly metaphysical and partly epistemological—to which scientists implicitly subscribe: the world is a connected causal system *and we don't know how the connections are arranged.* Because we don't, we must be prepared to abandon previous estimates of confirmational relevance as our scientific theories change. The points of all this is: confirmational isotropy is a reasonable property for nondemonstrative inference to have because the goal of nondemonstrative inference is to determine the truth about a causal mechanism—the world—of whose workings we are arbitrarily ignorant. That is why our institution of scientific confirmation is isotropic, and it is why it is plausible to suppose that what psychologists call "problem-solving" (i.e., nondemonstrative inference in the service of individual fixation of belief) is probably isotropic too.

The isotropy of scientific confirmation has sometimes been denied, but never, I think, very convincingly. For example, according to some historians it was part of the Aristotelian strategy against Galileo to claim that no data other than observations of the movements of astronomical objects could, in principle, be relevant to the (dis)confirmation of the geocentric theory. Telescopic observations of the phases of Venus were thus ruled irrelevant a priori. In notably similar spirit, some linguists have recently claimed that no data except certain specified kinds of facts about the intuitions of native speakers could, in principle, be relevant to the (dis)confirmation of grammatical theories. Experimental observations from psycholinguistics are thus ruled irrelevant a priori. However, this sort of methodology seems a lot like special pleading: you tend to get it precisely when cherished theories are in trouble from prima facie disconfirming data. Moreover, it often comports with Conventionalist construals of the theories so defended. That is, theories for which nonisotropic confirmation is claimed are often viewed, even by their proponents, as merely mechanisms for making predictions; what is alleged in their favor is predictive adequacy rather than correspondence to the world. (Viewed from our perspective, nonisotropic confirmation is, to that extent, not a procedure for fixation of belief, since, on the Conventionalist construal, the predictive adequacy of a theory is not a reason for believing that the theory is *true.*)

One final thought on the isotropy issue. We are interested in isotropic systems because such systems are ipso facto unencapsulated. We are interested in scientific confirmation because (a) there is every reason to suppose that it is isotropic; (b) there is every reason to suppose that it is a process fundamentally similar to the fixation of belief; and (c) it is perhaps the only "global", unencapsulated, wholistic cognitive process about which anything is known that's worth reporting. For all that, scientific *confirmation* is probably not the best place to look if you want to see cognitive isotropy writ large. The best place to look, at least if one is willing to trust the anecdotes, is scientific *discovery.*

What the anecdotes say about scientific discovery—and they say it with a considerable show of univocality (see, e.g., papers in Ortony, 1979)—is that some sort of 'analogical reasoning' often plays a central role. It seems to me that we are thoroughly in the dark here, so I don't propose to push this point very hard. But it really does look as though there have been frequent examples in the history of science where the structure of theories in a new subject area has been borrowed from, or at least suggested by, theories *in situ* in some quite different domain: what's known about the flow of water gets borrowed to model the flow of electricity; what's known about the structure of the solar system gets borrowed to model the structure of the atom; what's known about the behavior of the market gets borrowed to model the process of natural selection, which in turn gets borrowed to model the shaping of operant responses. And so forth. The point about all this is that "analogical reasoning" would seem to be isotropy in the purest form: a process which depends precisely upon the transfer of information among cognitive domains previously assumed to be mutually irrelevant. By definition, encapsulated systems do not reason analogically.

I want to suggest two morals before I leave this point. The first is that the closer we get to what we are pretheoretically inclined to think of as the 'higher,' 'more intelligent', less reflexive, less routine exercises of cognitive capacities, the more such global properties as isotropy tend to show up. I doubt that this is an accident. I suspect that it is precisely its possession of such global properties that we have in mind when we think of a cognitive process as paradigmatically intelligent. The second moral preshadows a point that I shall jump up and down about further on. It is striking that, while everybody thinks that analogical reasoning is an important ingredient in all sorts of cognitive achievements that we prize, nobody knows anything about how it works; not even in the dim, in-a-glass-darkly sort of way in which there are some ideas about how confirmation works. I don't think that this is an accident either. In fact, I should like to propose a generalization; one which I fondly hope will some day come to be known as 'Fodor's First Law of the Nonexistence of Cognitive Science'. It goes like this: the more global (e.g., the more isotropic) a cognitive process is, the less anybody understands it. *Very* global processes, like analogical reasoning, aren't understood at all. More about such matters in the last part of this discussion.

By saying that scientific confirmation is Quineian, I mean that the degree of confirmation assigned to any given hypothesis is sensitive to properties of the entire belief system; as it were, the shape of our whole science bears on the epistemic status of each scientific hypothesis. Notice that being Quineian and being isotropic are not the same properties, though they are intimately related. For example, if scientific confirmation is isotropic, it is quite possible that some fact about photosynthesis in algae should be relevant to the confirmation of some hypothesis in astrophysics ("the universe in a grain of sand" and all that). But the point about being Quineian is that we might have two astrophysical theories, both of which make the same predictions about algae and about everything else that we can think of to test, but such that one of the theories is better confirmed than the other—e.g., on grounds of such considerations as simplicity, plausibility, or conservatism. The point is that simplicity, plausibility, and conservatism are properties that theories have in virtue of their relation to the whole structure of scientific beliefs *taken collectively*. A measure of conservatism or simplicity would be a metric over *global* properties of belief systems.

Consider, by way of a simple example, Goodman's original (1954) treatment of the notion of projectability. We know that two hypotheses that are equivalent in respect of all the available data may nevertheless differ in their level of confirmation depending on which is the more projectable. Now, according to Goodman's treatment, the projectability of a hypothesis is inherited (at least in part) from the projectability of its vocabulary, and the projectability of an item of scientific vocabulary is determined by the (weighted?) frequency with which that item *has been projected* in previously successful scientific theories. So, the whole history of past projections contributes to determining the projectability of any given hypothesis on Goodman's account, and the projectability of a hypothesis (partially) determines its level of confirmation. Similarly with such notions as simplicity, conservatism, and the rest if only we knew how to measure them.

The idea that scientific confirmation is Quineian is by no means untendentious. On the contrary, it was a legacy of traditional philosophy of science—one of the "dogmas of Empiricism" (Quine, 1951) that there must be *semantic* connections between each theory statement and some data statements. That is, each hypothesis about "unobservables" must *entail* some predictions about observables, such entailments holding in virtue of the meanings of the theoretical terms that the hypotheses contain.[4] The effect of postulating such connections would be to determine a priori that certain data would disconfirm certain hypotheses, *whatever the shape of the rest of one's science might be*. For, of course, if H entails O, the discovery that $\neg O$ would entail that $\neg H$. To that extent, the (dis)confirmation of H by $\neg O$ is independent of global features of the belief system that H and O belong to. To postulate meaning relations between data statements and theory statements is thus to treat confirmation as a *local* phenomenon rather than a global one.

I emphasize this consideration because analogous semantic proposals can readily be found in the psychological literature. For example, in the sorts of cognitive theories espoused by, say, Bruner or Vygotsky (and, more recently, in the work of the "procedural" semanticists), it is taken for granted that there must be connections of meaning between 'concepts' and 'percepts'. Basically, according to such theories, concepts are recipes for sorting stimuli into categories. Each recipe specifies a (more or less determinate) galaxy of tests that one can perform to effect a sorting, and each stimulus category is identified with a (more or less determinate) set of outcomes of the tests. To put the idea crudely but near enough for present purposes, there's a rule that you can test for *dog* by finding out if a thing barks, and the claim is that this rule is constitutive (though not, of course, exhaustive) of the concept *dog*. Since it is alleged to be a *conceptual* truth that whether it barks is relevant to whether it's a dog, it follows that the confirmation relation between "a thing is a dog" and "it barks" is insensitive to global properties of one's belief system. So considerations of theoretical simplicity etc. *could* not, even in principle, lead to the conclusion that whether it barks is *ir*relevant to whether it's a dog. To embrace that conclusion would be to change the concept.

This sort of example makes it clear how closely related being Quineian and being isotropic are. Since, on the view just scouted, it is a matter of *meaning* that barking is relevant to dogness, it is not possible to discover on empirical grounds that one was wrong about that relevancy relation. But isotropy is the principle that *any* fact may turn out to be (ir)relevant to the confirmation of any other. The Bruner-Vygotsky-procedural semantics line is thus incompatible with the isotropy of confirmation as well as with its Quineianness.

In saying that confirmation is isotropic and Quineian, I am thus consciously disagreeing with major traditions in the philosophy of science and in cognitive psychology. Nevertheless, I shall take it for granted that scientific confirmation is Quineian and isotropic. (Those who wish to see the arguments should refer to such classic papers in the modern philosophy of science as Quine, 1951, and Putnam, 1962.) Moreover, since I am committed to relying upon the analogy between scientific confirmation and psychological fixation of belief, I shall take it for granted that the latter must be Quineian and isotropic too, hence that the Bruner-Vygotsky-procedural semantics tradition in cognitive psychology must be mistaken. I propose, at this point, to be both explicit and emphatic. The argument is that the central processes which mediate the fixation of belief are typically processes of rational nondemonstrative inference and that, since processes of rational nondemonstrative inference are Quineian and isotropic, so too are central processes. In particular, the theory of such processes must be consonant with the principle that the level of acceptance of any belief is sensitive to the level of acceptance of any other and to global properties of the field of beliefs taken collectively.

Given these assumptions, I have now got two things to do: I need to show that this picture of the central processes is broadly incompatible with the assumption that they are modular, and I need to show that it is a picture that has some plausibility independent of the putative analogy between cognitive psychology and the philosophy of science.

I take it that the first of these claims is relatively uncontroversial. We argued that modularity is fundamentally a matter of informational encapsulation and, of course, informationally encapsulated is precisely what Quineian/isotropic systems are not. When we discussed input systems, we thought of them as mechanisms for projecting and confirming hypotheses. And we remarked that, viewed that way, the informational encapsulation of such systems is tantamount to a constraint on the confirmation metrics that they employ; the confirmation metric of an encapsulated system is allowed to 'look at' only a certain restricted class of data in determining which hypothesis to accept. If, in particular, the flow of information through such a system is literally bottom-to-top, then its informational encapsulation consists in the fact that the ith-level hypotheses are (dis)confirmed solely by

reference to lower-than-i^{th} level representations. And even if the flow of data is unconstrained *within* a module, encapsulation implies constraints upon the access of intramod-
ular processes to extramodular information sources. Whereas, by contrast, isotropy is by
definition the property that a system has when it can look at anything it knows about in
the course of determining the confirmation levels of hypotheses. So, in general, the more
isotropic a confirmation metric is, the more heterogeneous the provenance of the data that
it accepts as relevant to constraining its decisions. Scientific confirmation is isotropic in
the limit in this respect; it provides a model of what the *non*modular fixation of belief is
like.

Similarly with being Quineian. Quineian confirmation metrics are ipso facto sensitive to
global properties of belief systems. Now, an informationally encapsulated system *could*,
strictly speaking, nevertheless be Quineian. Simplicity, for example, could constrain confirmation even in a system which computes its simplicity scores over some arbitrarily selected subset of beliefs. But this is mere niggling about the letter. In spirit, global criteria
for the evaluation of hypotheses comport most naturally with isotropic principles for the
relevance of evidence. Indeed, it is only on the assumption that the selection of evidence is
isotropic that considerations of simplicity (and other such global properties of hypotheses)
are *rational* determinants of belief. It is epistemically interesting that H & T is a simpler
theory than $\neg H$ & T where H is a hypothesis to be evaluated and T is the rest of what
one believes. But there is no interest in the analogous consideration where T is some *arbitrarily delimited* subset of one's beliefs. Where relevance is non-isotropic, assessments of
relative simplicity can be gerrymandered to favor any hypothesis one likes. This is one of
the reasons why the operation of (by assumption informationally encapsulated) input systems should not be identified with the fixation of perceptual belief; not, at least, by those
who wish to view the fixation of perceptual belief as by and large a rational process.

So it seems clear that isotropic/Quineian systems are ipso facto unencapsulated; and
if unencapsulated, then presumably nonmodular. Or rather, since this is all a matter of
degree, we had best say that *to the extent that* a system is Quineian and isotropic, it is also
nonmodular. If, in short, isotropic and Quineian considerations are especially pressing in
determining the course of the computations that central systems perform, it should follow
that these systems differ in their computational character from the vertical faculties.

We are coming close to what we started out to find: an overall taxonomy of cognitive
systems. According to the present proposal, there are, at a minimum, two families of such
systems: modules (which are, relatively, domain specific and encapsulated) and central
processes (which are, relatively, domain neutral and isotropic/Quineian). We have suggested that the characteristic function of modular cognitive systems is input analysis and
that the characteristic function of central processes is the fixation of belief. If this is right,
then we have three ways of taxonomizing cognitive processes which prove to be coexten-
sive:

Functional taxonomy: input analysis versus fixation of belief
Taxonomy by subject matter: domain specific versus domain neutral
Taxonomy by computational character: encapsulated versus Quineian/isotropic

I repeat that this coextension, if it holds at all, holds contingently. Nothing in point of logic stops one from imagining that these categories cross-classify the cognitive systems. If they do not, then that is a fact about the structure of the mind. Indeed, it is a deep fact about the structure of the mind.

All of which would be considerably more impressive if there were better evidence for the view of central processes that I have been proposing. Thus far, that account rests entirely on the analogy between psychological processes of belief fixation and a certain story about the character of scientific confirmation. There is very little that I can do about this, given the current underdeveloped state of psychological theories of thought and problem-solving. For what it's worth, however, I want to suggest two considerations that seem relevant and promising.

The first is that the difficulties we encounter when we try to construct theories of central processes are just the sort we would expect to encounter if such processes are, in essential respects, Quineian/isotropic rather than encapsulated. The crux in the construction of such theories is that there seems to be no way to delimit the sorts of informational resources which may affect, or be affected by, central processes of problem-solving. We can't, that is to say, plausibly view the fixation of belief as effected by computations over bounded, local information structures. A graphic example of this sort of difficulty arises in AI, where it has come to be known as the "frame problem" (i.e., the problem of putting a "frame" around the set of beliefs that may need to be revised in light of specified newly available information. Cf. the discussion in McCarthy and Hayes (1969), from which the following example is drawn).

To see what's going on, suppose you were interested in constructing a robot capable of coping with routine tasks in familiar human environments. In particular, the robot is presented with the job of phoning Mary and finding out whether she will be late for dinner. Let's assume that the robot 'knows' it can get Mary's number by consulting the directory. So it looks up Mary's number and proceeds to dial. So far, so good. But now, notice that commencing to dial has all sorts of direct and indirect effects on the state of the world (including, of course, the internal state of the robot), and some of these effects are ones that the device needs to keep in mind for the guidance of its future actions and expectations. For example, when the dialing commences, the phone ceases to be free to outside calls; the robot's fingers (or whatever) undergo appropriate alterations of spatial location; the dial tone cuts off and gets replaced by beeps; something happens in a computer at Murray Hill; and so forth. Some (but, in principle, not all) such consequences are ones that the robot must be designed to monitor since they are relevant to "updating" beliefs upon which it may eventually come to act. Well, *which* consequences? The problem has at least the following components. The robot must be able to identify, with reasonable accuracy, those of its previous beliefs whose truth values may be expected to alter as a result of its current activities; and it must have access to systems that do whatever computing is involved in effecting the alterations.

Notice that, unless these circuits are arranged correctly, things can go absurdly wrong. Suppose that, having consulted the directory, the robot has determined that Mary's number is 222-2222, which number it commences to dial, pursuant to instructions previously received. But now it occurs to the machine *that one of the beliefs that may need updating in consequence of its having commenced dialing is its (recently acquired) belief about Mary's telephone number.* So, of course, it stops dialing and goes and looks up Mary's telephone number (again). Repeat, *da capo*, as many times as may amuse you. Clearly, we have here all the makings of a computational trap. Unless the robot can be assured that some of its beliefs are invariant under some of its actions, it will never get to *do* anything.

How, then, does the machine's program determine which beliefs the robot ought to reevaluate given that it has embarked upon some or other course of action? What makes this problem so hard is precisely that it seems unlikely that any *local* solution will do the job. For example, the following truths appear to be self-evident: First, that there is no fixed set of beliefs such that, for any action, those and only those beliefs are the ones that require reconsideration. (That is, which beliefs are up for grabs depends intimately upon which actions are performed and upon the context of the performances. There are *some*—indeed, indefinitely many—actions which, if performed, *should* lead one to consider the possibility that Mary's telephone number has changed in consequence.) Second, new beliefs don't come docketed with information about which old beliefs they ought to affect. On the contrary, we are forever being surprised by the implications of what we know, including, of course, what we know about the actions we perform. Third, the set of beliefs apt for reconsideration cannot be determined by reference to the recency of their acquisition, or by reference to their generality, or by reference to merely semantic relations between the contents of the beliefs and the description under which the action is performed . . . etc. Should any of these propositions seem less than self-evident, consider the special case of the frame problem where the robot is a mechanical scientist and the action performed is an experiment. Here the question 'which of my beliefs ought I to reconsider given the possible consequences of my action'is transparently equivalent to the question "What, in general, is the optimal adjustment of my beliefs to my experiences?" This is, of course, exactly the question that a theory of confirmation is supposed to answer; and, as we have been at pains to notice, confirmation is not a relation reconstructible by reference to local properties of hypotheses or of the data that bear upon them.

I am suggesting that, as soon as we begin to look at cognitive processes other than input analysis—in particular, at central processes of nondemonstrative fixation of belief—we run into problems that have a quite characteristic property. They seem to involve isotropic and Quineian computations; computations that are, in one or other respect, sensitive to the whole belief system. This is exactly what one would expect on the assumption that nondemonstrative fixation of belief really is quite like scientific confirmation, and that scientific confirmation is itself characteristically Quineian and isotropic. In this respect, it seems to me, the frame problem is paradigmatic, and in this respect the seriousness of the frame problem has not been adequately appreciated.

For example, Raphael (1971) comments as follows: "(An intelligent robot) will have to be able to carry out tasks. Since a task generally involves some change in the world, it must be able to update its model (of the world) so it remains as accurate during and after the performance of a task as it was before. Moreover, it must be able to *plan* how to carry out a task, and this planning process usually requires keeping 'in mind'simultaneously a variety of possible actions and corresponding models of hypothetical worlds that would result from those actions. The bookkeeping problems involved with keeping track of these hypothetical worlds account for much of the difficulty of the frame problem" (p. 159). This makes it look as though the problem is primarily (a) how to notate the possible worlds and (b) how to keep track of the *demonstrative* consequences of changing state descriptions. But the deeper problem, surely, is to keep track of the *non*demonstrative consequences. Slightly more precisely, the problem is, given an arbitrary belief world W and a new state description 'a is F', what is the appropriate successor belief world W'? What ought the device to believe, given that it used to believe W and now believes that a is F? But this isn't just a bookkeeping problem; it is the general problem of inductive confirmation.[5]

So far as I can tell, the usual assumption about the frame problem in AI is that it is somehow to be solved 'heuristically'. The idea is that, while nondemonstrative confirmation (and hence, presumably, the psychology of belief fixation) is isotropic and Quineian *in principle*, still, given a particular hypothesis, there are, in practice, heuristic procedures for determining the range of effects its acceptance can have on the rest of one's beliefs. Since these procedures are by assumption merely heuristic, they may be assumed to be local—i.e., to be sensitive to less than the whole of the belief systems to which they apply. Something like this may indeed be true; there is certainly considerable evidence for heuristic short-cutting in belief fixation, deriving both from studies of the psychology of problem-solving (for a recent review, see Nisbett and Ross, 1980) and from the sociology of science (Kuhn, 1970). In such cases, it is possible to show how potentially relevant considerations are often systematically ignored, or distorted, or misconstrued in favor of relatively local (and, of course, highly fallible) problem-solving strategies. Perhaps a bundle of such heuristics, properly coordinated and rapidly deployed, would suffice to make the central processes of a robot as Quineian and isotropic as yours, or mine, or the practicing scientist's ever actually succeed in being. Since there are, at present, no serious proposals about what heuristics might belong to such a bundle, it seems hardly worth arguing the point.

Still, I am going to argue it a little.

There are those who hold that ideas recently evolved in AI—such notion as, e.g., those of 'frame'(see Minsky, 1975)[6] or 'script' see Schank and Abelson, 1975—will illuminate the problems about the globality of belief fixation since they do, in a certain sense, provide for placing a frame around the body of information that gets called when a given sort of problem is encountered. (For a discussion that runs along these optimistic lines, see Thagard.) It seems to me, however, that the appearance of progress here is entirely illusory—a prime case of confusing a notation with a theory.

If there were a principled solution to the frame problem, then no doubt that solution could be expressed as a constraint on the scripts, or frames, to which a given process of induction has access. But, lacking such a solution, there is simply no content to the idea that only the information represented in the frame (/script) that a problem elicits is computationally available for solving the problem. For one thing, since there are precisely no constraints on the individuation of frames (/scripts), *any* two pieces of information can belong to the same frame (/script) at the discretion of the programmer. This is just a way of saying that the solution of the frame problem can be accommodated to the frame (/script) notation *whatever that solution turns out to be*. Which is just another way of saying that the notation does not constrain the solution. Second, it is a widely advertised property of frames (/scripts) that they can cross-reference to one another. The frame for Socrates says, among other things, 'see Plato' . . . and so forth. There is no reason to doubt that, in any developed model, the system of cross-referencing would imply a graph in which there is a route (of greater or lesser length) from each point to any other. But now we have the frame problem all over again, in the form: Which such paths should actually be traversed in a given case of problem-solving, and what should bound the length of the trip? All that has happened is that, instead of thinking of the frame problem as an issue in the logic of confirmation, we are now invited to think of it as an issue in the theory of executive control (a change which there is, by the way, no reason to assume is for the better). More of this presently.

For now, let's summarize the major line of argument. If we assume that central processes are Quineian and isotropic, then we ought to predict that certain kinds of problems will emerge when we try to construct psychological theories which simulate such processes or otherwise explain them; specifically, we should predict problems that involve the characterization of nonlocal computational mechanisms. By contrast, such problems should not loom large for theories of psychological modules. Since, by assumption, modular systems are informationally encapsulated, it follows that the computations they perform are relatively local. It seems to me that these predictions are in reasonably good accord with the way that the problems of cognitive science have in fact matured: the input systems appear to be primarily stimulus driven, hence to exploit computational processes that are relatively insensitive to the general structure of the organism's belief system. Whereas, when we turn to the fixation of belief, we get a complex of problems that appear to be intractable precisely because they concern mental processes that aren't local. Of these, the frame problem is, as we have seen, a microcosm.

I have been marshaling considerations in favor of the view that central processes are Quineian/isotropic. That is what the analogy to scientific confirmation suggests that they ought to be, and the structure of the problems that arise in attempts to model central processes is quite compatible with that view of them. I now add that the view of central processes as computationally global can perhaps claim some degree of neurological plausibility. The picture of the brain that it suggests is a reasonably decent first approximation to the kind of brain that it appears we actually have.

When we discussed input analyzers, I commented on the natural connection between informational encapsulation and fixed neural architecture. Roughly, standing restrictions on information flow imply the option of hardwiring. If, in the extreme case, system B is required to take note of information from system A and is allowed to take note of information from nowhere else, you might as well build your brain with a permanent neuroanatomical connection from A to B. It is, in short, reasonable to expect biases in the distribution of information to mental processes to show up as structural biases in neural architecture.

Consider, by contrast, Quineian/isotropic systems, where more or less any subsystem may want to talk to any other at more or less any time. In this case, you'd expect the corresponding neuroanatomy to be relatively diffuse. At the limit, you might as well have a random net, with each computational subsystem connected, directly or indirectly, with every other; a kind of wiring in which you get a minimum of stable correspondence between neuroanatomical form and psychological function. The point is that in Quineian/isotropic systems, it may be *unstable, instantaneous* connectivity that counts. Instead of hardwiring, you get a connectivity that changes from moment to moment as dictated by the interaction between the program that is being executed and the structure of the task in hand. The moral would seem to be that computational isotropy comports naturally with neural isotropy (with what Lashley called "equipotentiality" of neural structure) in much the same way that informational encapsulation comports naturally with the elaboration of neural hardwiring.

So, if input analysis is modular and thought is Quineian/isotropic, you might expect a kind of brain in which there is stable neural architecture associated with perception-and-language but not with thought. And, I suggest, this seems to be pretty much what we in fact find. There is, as I remarked above, quite a lot that can be said about the neural specificity of the perceptual and linguistic mechanisms: at worst we can enumerate in some detail the parts of the brain that handle them; and at best we can exhibit characteristic neural architecture in the areas where these functions are performed. And then there are the rest of the higher brain systems (cf. what used to be called "association cortex"), in which neural connectivity appears to go every which way and the form/function correspondence appears to be minimal. There is some historical irony in all this. Gall argued from a (vertical) faculty psychology to the macroscopic differentiation of the brain. Flourens, his archantagonist, argued from the unity of the Cartesian ego to the brain's equipotentiality (see Bynum, 1976). The present suggestion is that they were *both* right.[7]

I am, heaven knows, not about to set up as an expert on neuropsychology, and I am painfully aware how impressionistic this all is. But while we're collecting impressions, I think the following one is striking. A recent issue of *Scientific American* (September, 1979) was devoted to the brain. Its table of contents is quite as interesting as the papers it contains. There are, as you might expect, articles that cover the neuropsychology of language and of the perceptual mechanisms. But there is nothing on the neuropsychology of thought—presumably because nothing is known about the neuropsychology of thought. I am suggesting that there is a good reason why nothing is known about it—namely, that there is nothing to know about it. You get form/function correspondence for the modular processes (specifically, for the input systems); but, in the case of central processes, you get an approximation to universal connectivity, hence no stable neural architecture to write *Scientific American* articles about.

To put these claims in a nutshell; there are *no* content-specific central processes for the performance of which correspondingly specific neural structures have been identified. Everything we now know is compatible with the claim that central problem-solving is subserved by equipotential neural mechanisms. This is precisely what you would expect if you assume that the central cognitive processes are largely Quineian and isotropic.

Notes for Chapter 9

1. This is, of course, an idealization; decisions about what to believe (subdoxastically or otherwise) do not, in general, succeed in making the optimal use of the available data. This consideration does not, however, affect the present point, which is just that such decisions must, of necessity, be sensitive to information from many different sources.

2. There is an assumption underlying this line of argument which the reader may not wish to grant: that the mechanisms that interface between vertical faculties have to be *computational* rather than, as one might say, merely mechanical. Old views of how language connects with perception (e.g., percepts are pictures and words are their associates) implicitly deny this assumption. It seems to me, however, that anyone who thinks seriously about what must be involved in deciding (e.g.) how to say what we see will accept the plausibility of the view that the mental processes that are implicated must be both computational and of formidable complexity.

3. *Editors' note;* these properties are defined in Part III of (Fodor, 1983). Fodor argues that input systems are domain-specific, mandatory, provide only limited information to the central system, are informationally encapsulated, have 'shallow' outputs, and have characteristic breakdown patterns.

4. Stronger versions had it that each theory statement must be logically equivalent to some (finite?) conjunction of observation statements. For a sophisticated review of this literature, see Glymour (1980). Glymour takes exception to some aspects of the Quineian account of confirmation, but not for reasons that need concern us here.

5. It is often proposed (see, e.g., McCarthy, 1980) that a logic capable of coping with the frame problem will have to be 'nonmonotonic'. (Roughly, a logic is monotonic when the addition of new postulates does *not* reduce the set of previously derivable theorems; nonmonotonic otherwise.) The point is that new beliefs don't just get *added on* to the old set; rather, old beliefs are variously altered to accommodate the new ones. This is, however, hardly surprising on the analysis of the frame problem proposed in the text. For, on that account, the frame problem is not distinguishable from the problem of nondemonstrative confirmation, and confirmation relations are themselves typically nonmonotonic. For example, the availability of a new datum may necessitate the assignment of new confirmation levels to indefinitely many previously accepted hypotheses. Hence, if we think of the confirmation system as formalized, indefinitely many previously derivable formulas of the form 'the level of H is L' may become nontheorems whenever new data become available.

6. Since there is no particular relation between *the frame problem* and *frames*-cum-data structures, the nomenclature in this area could hardly be more confusing.

7. The localization dispute didn't, of course, end with Gall and Flourens. For a useful, brief survey of its relatively modem history (since Wernicke), see Eggert (1977). It is of some interest—in passing—that Wernicke, committed localizationalist though he was in respect of the language mechanisms, held that only "primary functions . . . can be referred to specific areas. All processes which exceed these primary functions (such as the synthesis of various perceptions into concepts and the complex functions such as thought and consciousness) are dependent upon the fiber bundles connecting different areas of the cortex" (p. 92). Barring the associationism, Wernicke's picture is not very different from the one that we've been developing here.

Why AI Is Harder than We Think

10

Melanie Mitchell
2023

Since its beginning in the 1950s, the field of artificial intelligence has cycled several times between periods of optimistic predictions and massive investment ("AI spring") and periods of disappointment, loss of confidence, and reduced funding ("AI winter"). Even with today's seemingly fast pace of AI breakthroughs, the development of long-promised technologies such as self-driving cars, housekeeping robots, and conversational companions has turned out to be much harder than many people expected. One reason for these repeating cycles is our limited understanding of the nature and complexity of intelligence itself. In this chapter, I describe four fallacies in common assumptions made by AI researchers, which can lead to overconfident predictions about the field. I conclude by discussing the open questions spurred by these fallacies, including the age-old challenge of imbuing machines with humanlike common sense.

Introduction

The year 2020 was supposed to herald the arrival of self-driving cars. Five years earlier, a headline in *The Guardian* predicted that "from 2020 you will become a permanent backseat driver" (Adams, 2015). In 2016, *Business Insider* assured us that "10 million self-driving cars will be on the road by 2020" (Business Insider Intelligence, 2016). Tesla Motors CEO, Elon Musk, promised in 2019 that "a year from now, we'll have over a million cars with full self-driving, software . . . everything" (Hawkins, 2019). And 2020 was the target announced by several automobile companies to bring self-driving cars to market (McCormick, 2017; Kageyama, 2015).

Despite attempts to redefine "full self-driving" into existence (Baldwin, 2021), none of these predictions has come true. It's worth quoting AI expert Drew McDermott on what can happen when over-optimism about AI systems—in particular, self-driving cars—turns out to be wrong:

> Perhaps expectations are too high, and . . . this will eventually result in disaster. [S]uppose that five years from now [funding] collapses miserably as autonomous vehicles fail to roll.

> Every startup company fails. And there's a big backlash so that you can't get money for anything connected with AI. Everybody hurriedly changes the names of their research projects to something else. This condition [is] called the "AI Winter." (McDermott et al., 1985)

What's most notable is that McDermott's warning is from 1985, when, like today, the field of AI was awash with confident optimism about the near future of machine intelligence. McDermott was writing about a cyclical pattern in the field. New, apparent breakthroughs would lead AI practitioners to predict rapid progress, successful commercialization, and the near-term prospects of "true AI." Governments and companies would get caught up in the enthusiasm, and would shower the field with research and development funding. AI spring would be in bloom. When progress stalled, the enthusiasm, funding, and jobs would dry up. AI winter would arrive. Indeed, about five years after McDermott's warning, a new AI winter set in.

In this chapter, I explore the reasons for the repeating cycle of overconfidence followed by disappointment in expectations about AI. I argue that over-optimism among the public, the media, and even experts can arise from several fallacies in how we talk about AI and in our intuitions about the nature of intelligence. Understanding these fallacies and their subtle influences may help guide the creation of more robust, trustworthy, and perhaps actually *intelligent* AI systems.

Springs and winters

Overconfident predictions about AI are as old as the field itself. In 1958, for example, the *New York Times* reported on a demonstration by the US Navy of Frank Rosenblatt's "perceptron" (a rudimentary precursor to today's deep neural networks): "The Navy revealed the embryo of an electronic computer today that it expects will be able to walk, talk, see, write, reproduce itself, and be conscious of its existence" (*The New York Times*, 1958). This optimistic take was quickly followed by similar proclamations from AI pioneers, this time about the promise of logic-based "symbolic" AI. In 1960 Herbert Simon declared that "machines will be capable, within twenty years, of doing any work that a man can do" (Simon, 1960). The following year, Claude Shannon echoed this prediction: "I confidently expect that within a matter of 10 or 15 years, something will emerge from the laboratory which is not too far from the robot of science fiction fame" (IEEE Information Theory Society, 2016). And a few years later Marvin Minsky forecast that "within a generation . . . the problems of creating 'artificial intelligence' will be substantially solved" (Minsky, 1967).

The optimistic AI spring of the 1960s and early 1970s, reflected in these predictions, soon gave way to the first AI winter. Minsky and Papert's 1969 book *Perceptrons* (Minsky and Papert, 1969) showed that the kinds of problems solvable by Rosenblatt's perceptrons were very limited. In 1973 the Lighthill Report (Lighthill, 1973) in the UK and the Department of Defense's "American Study Group" report in the US, commissioned by their respective governments to assess prospects for AI in the near future, were both extremely negative about those prospects. This led to sharp funding decreases and a downturn in enthusiasm for AI in both countries.

AI once again experienced an upturn in enthusiasm starting in the early 1980s with several new initiatives: the rise of "expert systems" in industry (Durkin, 1996); Japan's huge investment in its "Fifth Generation" project (Gaines, 1984), which aimed for ambitious AI abilities as the core of a new generation of computing systems; the US's responding "Strategic Computing Initiative" (Stefik, 1985), which provided large funding for progress into general AI; as well as a new set of efforts on neural networks (McClelland et al., 1986a,b), which generated new hopes for the field.

By the latter part of the 1980s, these optimistic hopes had all been dashed; again, none of these technologies had achieved the lofty promises that had been made. Expert systems, which rely on humans to create rules that capture expert knowledge of a particular domain, turned out to be brittle—that is, often unable to generalize or adapt when faced with new situations. The problem was that the human experts writing the rules actually rely on subconscious knowledge—what we might call "common sense"—that was not part of the system's programming. The AI approaches pursued under the Fifth Generation project and Strategic Computing Initiative ran into similar problems of brittleness and lack of generality. The neural-network approaches of the 1980s and 1990s likewise worked well on relatively simple examples but lacked the ability to scale up to complex problems. Indeed, the late 1980s marked the beginning of a new AI winter, and the field's reputation suffered. When I received my PhD in 1990, I was advised not to use the term "Artificial Intelligence" on my job applications.

At the 50th anniversary commemoration of the 1956 Dartmouth Summer Workshop that launched the field, AI pioneer John McCarthy, who had originally coined the term "Artificial Intelligence," explained the issue succinctly: "AI was harder than we thought" (Moewes and Nürnberger, 2013).

The 1990s and 2000s saw the meteoric rise of *machine learning*: algorithms that create predictive models from data. Machine learning algorithms were typically inspired by statistics rather than by neuroscience or psychology, and were aimed at performing specific tasks rather than capturing general intelligence. Machine-learning practitioners were often quick to differentiate their discipline from the then-discredited field of AI.

However, around 2010, *deep learning*—in which brain-inspired multilayered neural networks are trained from data—emerged from its backwater position and rose to superstar status in machine learning. Deep neural networks had been around since the 1970s, but only recently, due to huge datasets scraped from the Web, fast parallel computing chips, and innovations in training methods, could these methods scale up enough to address a large number of previously unsolved AI challenges. Deep neural networks are what power all of the major AI advances we've seen in the past decade, including speech recognition, machine translation, chat bots, image recognition, game playing, and protein folding, among others.

Suddenly the term "AI" started to appear everywhere, and there was all at once a new round of optimism about the prospects of what has been variously called "general," "true," or "human-level" AI.

In surveys of AI researchers carried out in 2016 and 2018, the median prediction of those surveyed gave a 50 percent chance that human-level AI would be created by 2040–2060, though there was much variance of opinion, both for sooner and later estimates (Müller and Bostrom, 2016; Grace et al., 2018). Even some of the most well-known AI experts and entrepreneurs are in accord. Stuart Russell, co-author of a widely used textbook on AI, predicts that "superintelligent AI" will "probably happen in the lifetime of my children" (Russell, 2019b) and Sam Altman, CEO of the AI company OpenAI, predicts that within decades, computer programs "will do almost everything, including making new scientific discoveries that will expand our concept of 'everything'" (Altman, 2021). Shane Legg, co-founder of Google DeepMind, predicted in 2008 that "human level AI will be passed in the mid-2020s" (Despres, 2008), and Facebook's CEO, Mark Zuckerberg, declared in 2015 that "one of [Facebook's] goals for the next five to ten years is to basically get better than human level at all of the primary human senses: vision, hearing, language, general cognition" (McCracken, 2015).

However, in spite of all the optimism, it didn't take long for cracks to appear in deep learning's façade of intelligence. It turns out that, like all AI systems of the past, deep-learning systems can exhibit brittleness—unpredictable errors when facing situations that differ from the training data. This is because such systems are susceptible to *shortcut learning* (Geirhos et al., 2020; Lapuschkin et al., 2019): learning statistical associations in the training data that allow the machine to produce correct answers but sometimes for the wrong reasons. In other words, these machines don't learn the concepts we are trying to teach them, but rather they learn shortcuts to correct answers on the training set—and such shortcuts will not lead to good generalizations. Indeed, deep-learning systems often cannot learn the abstract concepts that would enable them to transfer what they have learned to new situations or tasks (Mitchell, 2021). Moreover, such systems are vulnerable to attack from "adversarial perturbations" (Moosavi-Dezfooli et al., 2017)—specially engineered changes to the input that are either imperceptible or irrelevant to humans but that induce the system to make errors.

Despite extensive research on the limitations of deep neural networks, the sources of their brittleness and vulnerability are still not completely understood. These networks, with their large number of parameters, are complicated systems whose decision-making mechanisms can be quite opaque. However, it seems clear from their non-humanlike errors and vulnerability to adversarial perturbations that these systems are not actually *understanding* the data they process, at least not in the human sense of "understand." It's still a matter of debate in the AI community whether such understanding can be achieved by adding network layers and more training data, or whether something more fundamental is missing.

At the time of writing (mid-2021), several new deep-learning approaches are once again generating considerable optimism in the AI community. Some of the hottest new areas are transformer architectures using self-supervised (or "predictive") learning (Devlin et al., 2018), meta-learning (Finn et al., 2017), and deep reinforcement learning (Arulkumaran et al., 2017); each of these has been cited as progress towards more general, humanlike AI. While these and other new innovations have shown preliminary promise, the AI cycle of springs and winters is likely to continue. The field continually advances in relatively narrow areas, but the path toward human-level AI is less clear.

In the next sections, I will argue that predictions about the likely timeline of human-level AI reflect our own biases and lack of understanding of the nature of intelligence. In particular, I describe four fallacies in our thinking about AI that seem most central to me. While these fallacies are well-known in the AI community, many assumptions made by experts still fall victim to these fallacies and give us a false sense of confidence about the near-term prospects of "truly" intelligent machines.

Fallacy 1: Narrow intelligence is on a continuum with general intelligence

Advances on a specific AI task are often described as "a first step" towards more general AI. The chess-playing computer Deep Blue "was hailed as the first step of an AI revolution" (Aron, 2016). IBM described its Watson system as "a first step into cognitive systems, a new era of computing" (High, 2013). OpenAI's GPT-3 language generator was called a "step toward general intelligence" (Alexander, 2019).

Indeed, if people see a machine do something amazing, albeit in a narrow area, they often assume the field is that much further along toward general AI. The philosopher Hubert Dreyfus (using a term coined by Yehoshua Bar-Hillel) called this a "first-step fallacy." As Dreyfus characterized it, "The first-step fallacy is the claim that, ever since our first work on computer intelligence we have been inching along a continuum at the end of which is AI so that any improvement in our programs no matter how trivial counts as progress." Dreyfus quotes an analogy made by his brother, the engineer Stuart Dreyfus: "It was like claiming that the first monkey that climbed a tree was making progress towards landing on the moon" (Dreyfus, 2012).

Like many AI experts before and after him, Dreyfus noted that the "unexpected obstacle" in the assumed continuum of AI progress has always been the problem of *common sense*. I will say more about this barrier of common sense in the last section.

Fallacy 2: Easy things are hard and hard things are easy

While John McCarthy lamented that "AI was harder than we thought," Marvin Minsky explained that this is because "easy things are hard" (Minsky, 1986). That is, the things that we humans do without much thought—looking out in the world and making sense of what we see, carrying on a conversation, walking down a crowded sidewalk without bumping into anyone—turn out to be the hardest challenges for machines. Conversely, it's often easier to get machines to do things that are very hard for humans; for example, solving complex mathematical problems, mastering games like chess and Go, and translating sentences between hundreds of languages have all turned out to be relatively easier for machines. This is a form of what's been called "Moravec's paradox," named after roboticist Hans Moravec, who wrote, "It is comparatively easy to make computers exhibit adult level performance on intelligence tests or playing checkers, and difficult or impossible to give them the skills of a one-year-old when it comes to perception and mobility" (Moravec, 1988).

This fallacy has influenced thinking about AI since the dawn of the field. AI pioneer Herbert Simon proclaimed, "Everything of interest in cognition happens above the 100-millisecond level—the time it takes you to recognize your mother" (Hofstadter, 1985). Simon is saying that, to understand cognition, we don't have to worry about unconscious perceptual processes. This assumption is reflected in most of the symbolic AI tradition, which focuses on the process of reasoning about input that has already been perceived.

In the last decades, symbolic AI approaches have lost favor in the research community, which has largely been dominated by deep learning, which does address perception. However, the assumptions underlying this fallacy still appear in recent claims about AI. For example, in a 2016 article, deep-learning pioneer Andrew Ng was quoted echoing Simon's assumptions, vastly underestimating the complexity of unconscious perception and thought: "If a typical person can do a mental task with less than one second of thought, we can probably automate it using AI either now or in the near future" (Ng, 2016).

More subtly, researchers at Google DeepMind, in talking about AlphaGo's triumph, described the game of Go as one of "the most challenging of domains" (Silver et al., 2017). Challenging for whom? For humans, perhaps, but as psychologist Gary Marcus pointed out, there are domains, including games, that, while easy for humans, are much more challenging than Go for AI systems. One example is charades, which "requires acting skills, linguistic skills, and theory of mind" (Marcus, 2018b), abilities that are far beyond anything AI can accomplish today.

AI is harder than we think because we are largely unconscious of the complexity of our own thought processes. Hans Moravec explains his paradox this way: "Encoded in the large, highly evolved sensory and motor portions of the human brain is a billion years of experience about the nature of the world and how to survive in it. The deliberate process we call reasoning is, I believe, the thinnest veneer of human thought, effective only because it is supported by this much older and much more powerful, though usually unconscious, sensorimotor knowledge. We are all prodigious Olympians in perceptual and motor areas, so good that we make the difficult look easy" (Moravec, 1988). Or more succinctly, Marvin Minsky notes, "In general, we're least aware of what our minds do best" (Minsky, 1980).

Fallacy 3: The lure of wishful mnemonics

The term "wishful mnemonic" was coined in a 1976 critique of AI by computer scientist Drew McDermott:

> A major source of simple-mindedness in AI programs is the use of mnemonics like "UN-DERSTAND" or "GOAL" to refer to programs and data structures. . . . If a researcher . . . calls the main loop of his program "UNDERSTAND," he is (until proven innocent) merely begging the question. He may mislead a lot of people, most prominently himself. . . . What he should do instead is refer to this main loop as "G0034," and see if he can convince himself or anyone else that G0034 implements some part of understanding. . . . Many instructive examples of wishful mnemonics by AI researchers come to mind once you see the point. (McDermott, 1976)

Now, many decades later, work on AI is replete with such wishful mnemonics—terms associated with human intelligence that are used to describe the behavior and evaluation of AI programs. *Neural* networks are loosely inspired by the brain, but with vast differences. Machine *learning* or deep *learning* methods do not really resemble learning in humans (or in non-human animals). Indeed, if a machine has learned something in the human sense of *learn*, we would expect that it would be able to use what it has learned in different contexts. However, it turns out that this is often not the case. In machine learning, there is an entire subfield called *transfer learning* that focuses on the still-open problem of how to enable machines to transfer what they have learned to new situations, an ability that is fundamental to human learning.

Indeed, the way we talk about machine abilities influences our conceptions of how general those abilities really are. Unintentionally providing real-world illustrations of McDermott's warning, one of IBM's top executives proclaimed that "Watson can *read* all of the health-care texts in the world in seconds" (Gustin, 2011). DeepMind co-founder Demis Hassabis tells us that "AlphaGo's *goal* is to beat the best human players, not just mimic them" (Ji-hye, 2016). And AlphaGo's lead research David Silver described one of the program's matches thus: "We can always ask AlphaGo how well it *thinks* it's doing during the game. . . . It was only towards the end of the game that *AlphaGo thought it would win*" (Shead, 2017). (Emphasis is mine in the quotations above.)

One could argue that such anthropomorphic terms are simply shorthand: IBM scientists know that Watson doesn't read or understand in the way humans do; DeepMind scientists know that AlphaGo has no goals or thoughts in the way humans do and no humanlike conceptions of a "game" or of "winning." However, such shorthand can be misleading to the public trying to understand these results (and to the media reporting on them) and can also unconsciously shape the way even AI experts think about their systems and how closely these systems resemble human intelligence.

McDermott's "wishful mnemonics" referred to terms we use to describe AI programs, but the research community also uses wishful mnemonics in naming AI evaluation benchmarks after the skills we hope they test. For example, here are some of the most widely cited current benchmarks in the subarea of AI called "natural-language processing" (NLP): the "Stanford Question Answering Dataset" (Rajpurkar et al., 2016), the "RACE Reading Comprehension Dataset" (Lai et al., 2017), and the "General Language Understanding Evaluation" (Wang et al., 2019). In all of these benchmarks, the performance of the best machines has already exceeded that measured for humans (typically Amazon Mechanical Turk workers). This has led to headlines such as "New AI model exceeds human performance at question answering" (Costenaro, 2018); "Computers are getting better than humans at reading" (Pham, 2018); and "Microsoft's AI model has outperformed humans in natural-language understanding" (Jawad, 2021). Given the names of these benchmark evaluations, it's not surprising that people would draw such conclusions. The problem is, these benchmarks don't actually measure general abilities for question-answering, reading comprehension, or natural-language understanding. The benchmarks test only very limited versions of these abilities; moreover, many of these benchmarks allow machines to learn shortcuts, as I described above—statistical correlations that machines can exploit to achieve high performance on the test without learning the actual skill being tested (McCoy et al., 2019; Linzen, 2020). While machines can outperform humans on these particular benchmarks, AI systems are still far from matching the more general human abilities we associate with the benchmarks' names.

Fallacy 4: Intelligence is all in the brain

The idea that intelligence is something distinct from the body, whether as a non-physical substance or as dependent only on the brain, has a long history in philosophy and cognitive science.

The so-called "information-processing model of mind" arose in psychology in the mid-twentieth century. This model views the mind as a kind of computer, which inputs, stores, processes, and outputs information. The body does not play much of a role except in the input (perception) and output (behavior) stages. Under this view, cognition takes place wholly in the brain and is, in theory, separable from the rest of the body. An extreme corollary of this view is that, in the future, we will be able to "upload" our brains—and thus our cognition and consciousness—to computers (Woollaston, 2013).

The assumption that intelligence can in principle be "disembodied" is implicit in almost all work on AI throughout its history. One of the most influential ideas in early AI research was Newell and Simon's "Physical Symbol System Hypothesis" (PSSH), which stated: "A physical symbol system has the necessary and sufficient means for general intelligent action" (Newell and Simon, 1976). The term "physical symbol system" refers to something much like a digital computer. The PSSH posits that general intelligence can be achieved in digital computers without incorporating any non-symbolic processes of brain or body. (For an insightful discussion of symbolic versus subsymbolic processes, see Hofstadter (1985)'s "Waking Up from the Boolean Dream.")

Newell and Simon's PSSH was a founding principle of the symbolic approach to AI, which dominated the field until the rise of statistical and neurally inspired machine learning in the 1990s and 2000s. However, these non-symbolic approaches also do not view the body as relevant to intelligence. Instead, neurally inspired approaches from 1980s connectionism to today's deep neural networks generally assume that intelligence arises solely from brain structures and dynamics. Today's deep neural networks are akin to the proverbial brain-in-a-vat: passively taking in data from the world and outputting instructions for behavior without actively interacting in the world with any kind of body. Of course, robots and autonomous vehicles are different in that they have a physical presence in the world, but to date the kinds of physical interactions they have, and the feedback to their "intelligence," is quite limited.

The assumption that intelligence is all in the brain has led to speculation that, to achieve human-level AI, we simply need to scale up machines to match the brain's "computing capacity" and then develop the appropriate "software" for this brain-matching "hardware." For example, one philosopher wrote a report on the literature that concluded, "I think it more likely than not that 10^{15} FLOP/s is enough to perform tasks as well as the human brain (given the right software, which may be very hard to create)" (Carlsmith, 2020). No body needed!

Top AI researchers have echoed the idea that scaling up hardware to match the brain will enable human-level artificial intelligence. For example, deep-learning pioneer Geoffrey Hinton predicted, "To understand [documents] at a human level, we're probably going to need human-level resources and we have trillions of connections [in our brains]. . . . But the biggest networks we have built so far only have billions of connections. So we're a few orders of magnitude off, but I'm sure the hardware people will fix that" (Patterson and Gibson, 2017). Others have predicted that the "hardware fix"—the speed and memory capacity to finally enable human-level AI—will come in the form of quantum computers (Musser, 2018).

However, a growing cadre of researchers is questioning the basis of the "all in the brain" information-processing model for understanding intelligence and for creating AI. Writing about what he calls "the cul-de-sac of the computational metaphor," computer scientist Rod

Brooks argues, "The reason for why we got stuck in this cul-de-sac for so long was because Moore's law just kept feeding us, and we kept thinking, 'Oh, we're making progress, we're making progress, we're making progress.' But maybe we haven't been" (Brooks, 2019). In fact, a number of cognitive scientists have argued for decades for the centrality of the body in all cognitive activities. One prominent proponent of these ideas, the psychologist Mark Johnson, writes of a research program on *embodied cognition*, gaining steam in the mid-1970s, that "began to provide converging evidence for the central role of our brains and bodies in everything we experience, think, and do" (Johnson, 2017). Psychologist Rebecca Fincher-Kiefer characterizes the embodied cognition paradigm this way: "Embodied cognition means that the representation of conceptual knowledge is dependent on the body: it is multimodal . . . , not amodal, symbolic, or abstract. This theory suggests that our thoughts are grounded, or inextricably associated with, perception, action, and emotion, and that our brain and body work together to have cognition" (Fincher-Kiefer, 2019).

The evidence for embodied cognition comes from a diverse set of disciplines. Research in neuroscience suggests, for example, that the neural structures controlling cognition are richly linked to those controlling sensory and motor systems, and that abstract thinking exploits body-based neural "maps" (Epstein et al., 2017). As neuroscientist Don Tucker noted, "There are no brain parts for disembodied cognition" (Tucker, 2007). Results from cognitive psychology and linguistics indicate that many, if not all, of our abstract concepts are grounded in physical, body-based internal models (Barsalou and Wiemer-Hastings, 2005), revealed in part by the systems of physically based metaphors found in everyday language (Lakoff and Johnson, 2008).

Several other disciplines, such as developmental psychology, add to evidence for embodied cognition. However, research in AI has mostly ignored these results, though there is a small group of researchers exploring these ideas in subareas known as "embodied AI," "developmental robotics," and "grounded language understanding," among others.

Related to the theory of embodied cognition is the idea that the emotions and the "irrational" biases that go along with our deeply social lives—typically thought of as separate from intelligence, or as getting in the way of rationality—are actually key to what makes intelligence possible. AI is often thought of as aiming at a kind of "pure intelligence," one that is independent of emotions, irrationality, and constraints of the body such as the need to eat and sleep. This assumption of the possibility of a purely rational intelligence can lead to lurid predictions about the risks we will face from future "superintelligent" machines.

For example, the philosopher Nick Bostrom asserts that a system's intelligence and its goals are orthogonal; he argues that "any level of intelligence could be combined with any final goal" (Bostrom, 2014, 105). As an example, Bostrom imagines a hypothetical superintelligent AI system whose sole objective is to produce paperclips; this imaginary system's superintelligence enables the invention of ingenious ways to produce paperclips, and uses up all of the Earth's resources in doing so.

AI researcher Stuart Russell concurs with Bostrom on the orthogonality of intelligence and goals. "It is easy to imagine that a general-purpose intelligent system could be given more or less any objective to pursue, including maximizing the number of paper clips or the number of known digits of pi" (Russell, 2019b, 167). Russell worries about the possible outcomes of employing such a superintelligence to solve humanity's problems: "What if a superintelligent climate control system, given the job of restoring carbon dioxide concentrations to preindustrial levels, believes the solution is to reduce the human population to zero? . . . If we insert the wrong objective into the machine and it is more intelligent than us, we lose" (Russell, 2019a).

The thought experiments proposed by Bostrom and Russell seem to assume that an AI system could be "superintelligent" without any basic humanlike common sense, yet while seamlessly preserving the speed, precision, and programmability of a computer. But these speculations about superhuman AI are plagued by flawed intuitions about the nature of intelligence. Nothing in our knowledge of psychology or neuroscience supports the possibility that "pure rationality" is separable from the emotions and cultural biases that shape our cognition and our objectives. Instead, what we've learned from research in embodied cognition is that human intelligence seems to be a strongly integrated system with closely interconnected attributes, including emotions, desires, a strong sense of selfhood and autonomy, and a commonsense understanding of the world. It's not at all clear that these attributes can be separated.

Conclusions

The four fallacies I have described reveal flaws in our conceptualizations of the current state of AI and our limited intuitions about the nature of intelligence. I have argued that these fallacies are at least in part why capturing humanlike intelligence in machines always turns out to be harder than we think.

These fallacies raise several questions for AI researchers. How can we assess actual progress toward "general" or "human-level" AI? How can we assess the *difficulty* of a particular domain for AI as compared with humans? How should we describe the actual abilities of AI systems without fooling ourselves and others with wishful mnemonics? To what extent can the various dimensions of human cognition (including cognitive biases, emotions, objectives, and embodiment) be disentangled? How can we improve our intuitions about what intelligence is?

These questions remain open. It's clear that to make and assess progress in AI more effectively, we will need to develop a better vocabulary for talking about what machines can do. And more generally, we will need a better scientific understanding of intelligence as it manifests in different systems in nature. This will require AI researchers to engage more deeply with other scientific disciplines that study intelligence.

The notion of *common sense* is one aspect of intelligence that has recently been driving collaborations between AI researchers and cognitive scientists from several other disciplines, particularly cognitive development (e.g., see Turek, 2018). There have been many attempts in the history of AI to give humanlike common sense to machines[1], ranging from the logic-based approaches of John McCarthy (McCarthy, 1986) and Douglas Lenat (Lenat et al., 1990) to today's deep-learning-based approaches (e.g., Zellers et al., 2019). "Common sense" is what AI researcher Oren Etzioni called "the dark matter of artificial intelligence," noting, "It's a little bit ineffable, but you see its effects on everything" (Knight, 2018). The term has become a kind of umbrella for what's missing from today's state-of-the-art AI systems (Davis and Marcus, 2015; Levesque, 2017). While common sense includes the vast amount of knowledge we humans have about the world, it also requires being able to use that knowledge to recognize and make predictions about the situations we encounter and to guide our actions in those situations. Giving machines common sense will require imbuing them with the very basic "core," perhaps innate, knowledge that human infants possess about space, time, causality, and the nature of inanimate objects and other living agents (Spelke and Kinzler, 2007), the ability to abstract from particulars to general concepts, and to make analogies from prior experience. No one yet knows how to capture such knowledge or abilities in machines. This is the current frontier of AI research, and one encouraging way forward is to tap into what's known about the development of these abilities in young children. Interestingly, this was the approach recommended by Alan Turing in his 1950 paper that introduced the Turing test. Turing asks, "Instead of trying to produce a programme to simulate the adult mind, why not rather try to produce one which simulates the child's?" (Turing, 1950)

In 1892, the psychologist William James said of psychology at the time, "This is no science; it is only the hope of a science" (James, 1892). This is a perfect characterization of today's AI. Indeed, several researchers have made analogies between AI and the medieval practice of alchemy. In 1977, AI researcher Terry Winograd wrote, "In some ways [AI] is akin to medieval alchemy. We are at the stage of pouring together different combinations of substances and seeing what happens, not yet having developed satisfactory theories . . . but . . . it was the practical experience and curiosity of the alchemists which provided the wealth of data from which a scientific theory of chemistry could be developed" (Winograd, 1977). Four decades later, Eric Horvitz, director of Microsoft Research, concurred: "Right now, what we are doing is not a science but a kind of alchemy" (Metz, 2017). In order to understand the nature of true progress in AI, and in particular, why it is harder than we think, we need to move from alchemy to developing a scientific understanding of intelligence.

Notes for Chapter 10

1. Some have questioned why we need machines to have *humanlike* cognition, but if we want machines to work with us in our human world, we will need them to have the same basic knowledge about the world that is the foundation of our own thinking.

INTENTIONALITY AND UNDERSTANDING

Part III: Intentionality and Understanding

Do machines merely act as if they are in touch with the world? Or can we be sure that they also have thoughts about things—that they generate states with *content*, which refer to objects in the world? One of the striking things about human minds is that we can represent the world, both as it is and as it might be. We can see the mountain peak; we can desire to climb it; we can call it to mind even when it's not in view; we can imagine that it might be subtly or even vastly different than it in fact is (made of different kinds of rock, for example, or housing different flora and fauna); and we can even imagine mountains, beside crystal fountains, where the hens lay soft-boiled eggs. We can have conflicting thoughts about one and the same object, even if we don't realize it: a mountain climber might desire to climb K2 and have no desire to scale Chogori, even though Chogori *is* K2. Franz Brentano first called attention to this set of phenomena in his *Psychology from an Empirical Standpoint* (1874/1973). It has come to be called *intentionality*. In fact, Brentano described intentionality as *the* mark of the mental: a feature had by all and only mental states.

Could an appropriately programmed computer also have intentionality? On the face of it, it might seem obvious and trivial that computers have internal states that "represent" other things. According to some of the views in part I, computers are defined in terms of their ability to manipulate symbols, and symbols usually represent things. But here we must be careful not to confuse two importantly different senses in which states can be about other things. On the one hand, we can talk about road signs, words in a book, or lines on a graph as "representing" other things, in the sense that someone could look at them and decipher their meanings. This has come to be called *derivative* intentionality, precisely because it requires for its existence an observer who supplies meaning to what would otherwise be mindless entities (paint on a sign, print on a page, etc.). The road signs, books, and graphs don't themselves have a clue of what they are about. *Original* intentionality, in contrast, is the source of the persistent challenge: How can we build systems that imbue the world with meaning themselves rather than having it supplied by an interpreter? More generally, how can a physical world contain systems that represent things in this stronger sense? The essays in this part articulate this challenge for artificial intelligence (AI) and place constraints on possible solutions.

In chapter 11, Dennett argues that intentionality should not be understood in terms of the components of a system or how they interact, but in terms of the complexity of behavior that arises from their organization. An intentional system, by his account, is a system for which we gain considerable predictive leverage by taking the "intentional stance"; that is, by treating the system as if it has beliefs, desires, emotions (etc.) and predicting that the system will behave more or less rationally in light of those beliefs and desires. This view leaves the line between intentional systems and those that are merely biological or physical (for example) somewhat blurry. For some, Dennett's view seems to leave the intentionality of the system in the "eye of the beholder," and so raises the question of how it is possible for the physical world to contain creatures that take stances in the first place. Indeed, one might think, following Haugeland in chapter 2, that intentionality is a matter of taking a stance. If so, it can't be reduced to stance-taking.

In chapter 12, Searle argues that rationally describable action, or, indeed, any mere symbol manipulation by itself, will not suffice for intentionality. His Chinese Room thought experiment has become a field-defining articulation of the challenge of intentionality. It putatively shows that even a system that passes the Turing test using sophisticated symbol manipulation might not, in fact, understand what it is talking about. He considers many attempts to meet that challenge and rejects them all, holding ultimately that original intentionality (or understanding) emerges from the as-yet-undiscovered, unique biochemical properties of the brain.

In chapter 13, Boden defends what has come to be called the "systems reply" to Searle's argument. According to this style of reply, Searle's argument investigates the parts of a purportedly intentional system, finds no intentionality in its individual parts, and wrongly concludes that the system as a whole does not understand what is going on. Searle, in this view, commits a kind of compositional fallacy: assuming that the property of the whole must be possessed by its components taken individually. This reply has been the subject of considerable controversy, as discussed next.

Consistent with this kind of objection, Francis Egan argues in chapter 14 that computational systems are definable and can be individuated strictly on the basis of the mathematical functions that they instantiate. Nonetheless, when we explain a capacity of a system to solve a problem in terms of its computational components, the explanation has two parts: one that describes the computational system narrowly in terms of the mathematical function that it computes, and one that "glosses" that computational description in ways that make explicit how the states of the computer track features of the world such that, in executing the mathematical function, it would solve the problem. Yet, of course, Searle thinks that there is such a gloss too and denies that this suffices for original intentionality. Whether the presence of additional mathematical structure is sufficient to address the challenge remains an open question.

Combinations and Additions
Intentionality is a thread running through much of contemporary philosophy of mind, and those wishing to assemble a deep focus on intentionality will find much relevant in other parts of this book. Haugeland's introductory piece (chapter 2) raises intentionality as a central problem for cognitive science. Furthermore, his "Mind Embodied and Embedded" (chapter 22) explores the possibility that intentionality might be supplied by systems outside the head proper. Buckner takes on one aspect of intentionality in his discussion of how

mechanical systems might perform different kinds of abstraction (chapter 15). And Haas's discussion of reinforcement learning might be seen as taking some first steps to understand what it means for a computing system to *give a damn*, a key component in Haugeland's conception of what a system would have to do in order to take stances (chapter 16).

History.   Those looking to read more deeply about the history and development of the topic of intentionality might consider the following essays as entry points:

- A return to Brentano (1874/1973) would give readers a sense of the historical origins of the discussion of intentionality and the claim that it is the distinctive "mark of the mental."
- Crane (1998) defends Brentano's thesis that intentionality is found only in the mental domain against a number of challenges, such as that sensations and emotions are non-intentional. He argues that intentionality is, indeed, the mark of the distinctive subject matter of the philosophy of mind.
- Some responses to Searle focus on the *computational* aspects of his setup and attempt to build in intentionality by giving a more fine-grained account of what needs to be in place. Sprevak (2007) suggests that Searle goes astray by focusing on the input-output relationships of the room rather than the specific program (and, by extension, the specific computational architecture) used.

Naturalizing Intentionality.   The scientific naturalist seeks to understand intentionality by showing that it can be explained in the familiar terms of scientific explanation: of law and regularity, of cause and effect, of structure and function. There are various important strands in the naturalist approach:

- Sellars (1956) distinguishes between two ways of viewing a fellow human: as an object in the "space of causes" and as a "denizen" of the "space of reasons." We understand things in the space of causes by revealing their etiologies and their mechanisms, and by showing how they fit into (i.e., play a role in) a more inclusive, higher-level system. We understand things in the space of reasons by knowing what they believe, how they act, and (crucially) why, not in the propulsive sense that a ball is launched from the cannon but in the ratiocinative sense of following from premises. These two ways of viewing actions, as mechanistic output and as imbued with meaning and reason, seem to carve the world in different ways, making it appear impossible to form a "synoptic view" that encompasses both these ways of thinking about them.
- Churchland (1981) argues that propositional attitude psychology, and the notion of intentionality that accompanies it, should be abandoned in favor of a neuroscientifically inspired way of talking about the processes underlying our behaviors.

- Rosenberg (1997) argues against Churchland on the grounds that Churchland's proposed replacement for sentential epistemologies, as well as epistemically mental notions such as "believes," "infers," and "concept," is false advertising, mislabeling transactions in the space of causes as transactions in the space of reasons. Mental vocabulary is partly constituted by webs of inferential connectedness, and we lack any clear sense of the difference between a causal transition and an inference.

Reductionism.   For those who wish to attack the problem of intentionality head on, one common strategy is to try to reduce intentional content to some kind of natural relation such as correlation, causation, counterfactual dependence, or selection.

- Dretske (1981) attempts to understand at least a limited form of intentionality in terms of the correlational notion of "information." Dretske argues that "indication" (as in "the compass indicates magnetic North" or "high PSA levels indicate recurrence of prostate cancer") can be understood without remainder in terms of law-like correlational dependence. One key question is whether such a natural relation as law-like dependence can satisfactorily help us to understand misrepresentation of states of affairs and the representation of non-existent things.
- A different approach to the problems of purely causal or correlational accounts of reference can be found in Fodor (1990). In the first chapter, Fodor influentially suggests that mental states depend asymmetrically on their contents. This account is developed to address what Fodor calls "the disjunction problem": that mental states (such as the perception of a cow) might be caused by items in an indescribably large disjunction of worldly features (like cow statues, horses, and distant shrubbery).
- Teleosemantic theories of mental content hold that the content of our thoughts (i.e., concepts or beliefs) is determined not by their causal relations to things in the here and now but by the historical, selective processes by which they have come to stand in the appropriate relations to their objects. For biological systems, these histories typically involve either evolution by natural selection or learning, which can clearly be modeled as a selective process as well. Millikan (1984) is the *locus classicus* on teleosemantic theories. Neander (1995) presents a more manageable overview of how the introduction of teleological considerations helps to solve the disjunction problem.
- Debates about intentionality are often reframed as debates over what it takes to *represent* the world. Representation seems like a slightly easier notion to get a handle on, and it taps into a rich literature in cognitive science. Shea (2018), while not concerned with intentionality as such, gives a broadly telcosemantic story about representational content.

Content Externalism.   Finally, one significant dispute in the philosophy of mental content has concerned whether meanings are properly to be sought "in the head," as features and relations among internal processing states, or rather, "in the world." To understand the way that meaning is situated in the causal structure of things, it might be useful to look outside the computational system and into the external systems in which it is embedded, causally or otherwise. In a way, the questions here are: How much about the mind can an attention to internal causal commerce, including the manipulation of information, explain? What parts of that explanation are housed outside these systems?

- According to one view, tracing to the so-called "Twin Earth" thought experiment of Hillary Putnam (1975), the mental content of a thought involves at least partly the referent of that thought itself. If one embraces a causal theory of reference, for example, and causal relations to things in the world make an essential contribution to what mental tokens mean, then one could change what one thinks by changing the world, leaving all the details "internal" to the mind/brain the same.
- Others argue that the meanings are determined by one's linguistic community. One's internal states could be the same, but if concepts are deployed differently in a given linguistic community, one's thoughts could change. This idea was initially developed in Burge (1979).

Social Sources of Intentionality.   Rather than seeking intentionality in the internal causal structure of a machine (such as a computer and a machine) or as the product of causal interactions between that thing and objects in the world, one might instead hope to understand intentionality as a social phenomenon, or more properly, of the relationship between an individual and a set of social norms and practices. According to this view, intentionality is not the biological product of a brain (as Searle suggests), nor is it merely the fact that they have been selected through learning and evolution (though that is surely part of the story, as Millikan would suggest). Rather, it is a social status achieved when one learns to behave and speak and think in conformity with social rules that govern the use of concepts. To understand a natural language is to play the game of giving and asking for reasons at least tolerably well (see, e.g., Haugeland's "Intentionality Allstars" in his (1998) paper; as well as, Brandom, 1994). Original intentionality is explained in terms of stable dispositions that are enforced by members of community concerning, such as the proper use of terms, the formation of well-formed thoughts, the permissibility of inferences, and the extension of a term. Understanding of the sort wanted in the Chinese room is ultimately grounded in the dispositions to conform to the rules governing the discourse and to hold others to be committed as well. For an enactive form of this kind of view, see Gallagher and Miyahara (2012).

Conclusion.   The topic of intentionality is perhaps a core outstanding and unresolved issue in the philosophy of mind, if not in philosophy generally. And perhaps this sketch suffices to say something about why the matter is so intractable in AI: the best ideas for how intentionality might be grounded in causal structures quite generally all have well-known obstacles, and there is little consensus about which of them, if any, stands the best chance.

Finding meaning in a world of causes is child's play, of course, but precisely how even such simple and loveable creatures imbue the causal structure of the world around them, including other people and the things they do and say, with meaning, remains mysterious. It appears there is a style of explanation concerning people, their reasons, their motives, their aims and preferences, their understanding of the world around them that operates according to principles that seem not to mirror the way causal mechanisms work. This is why it is difficult to bring the mental and the rest of the world into a synoptic view (Sellars 1965), why the mental is said to be "anomalous" (Davidson, 1995), and why some have opted instead to "eliminate" the idea of propositional thought and mental content from our understanding of persons (as defended by Churchland, 1981 or Stich, 1996). The authors reveal key landmarks in this contested and difficult, and perennially puzzling, terrain.

True Believers: The Intentional Strategy and Why It Works

11

Daniel C. Dennett
1981

There was a merchant in Baghdad who sent his servant to market to buy provisions and in a little while the servant came back, white and trembling, and said: "Master, just now when I was in the market-place I was jostled by a woman in the crowd and when I turned I saw it was Death that jostled me. She looked at me and made a threatening gesture; now, lend me your horse, and I will ride away from this city and avoid my fate. I will go to Samarra and there Death will not find me." The merchant lent him his horse, and the servant mounted it, and he dug his spurs in its flanks and as fast as the horse could gallop he went. Then the merchant went down to the market-place and he saw me standing in the crowd, and he came to me and said: "Why did you make a threatening gesture to my servant when you saw him this morning?" "That was not a threatening gesture," I said, "it was only a start of surprise. I was astonished to see him in Baghdad, for I had an appointment with him tonight in Samarra."
—W. Somerset Maugham, *DEATH SPEAKS*

In the social sciences, talk about *belief* is ubiquitous. Since social scientists are typically self-conscious about their methods, there is also a lot of talk about *talk about belief.* And since belief is a genuinely curious and perplexing phenomenon, showing many different faces to the world, there is abundant controversy. Sometimes belief attribution appears to be a dark, risky, and imponderable business—especially when exotic, and more particularly religious or superstitious, beliefs are in the limelight. These are not the only troublesome cases; we also court argument and skepticism when we attribute beliefs to nonhuman animals, or to infants, or to computers or robots. Or when the beliefs we feel constrained to attribute to an apparently healthy adult member of our own society are contradictory, or even just wildly false. A biologist colleague of mine was once called on the telephone by a man in a bar who wanted him to settle a bet. The man asked: "Are rabbits birds?" "No" said the biologist. "Damn!" said the man as he hung up. Now could he *really* have believed that rabbits were birds? Could anyone really and truly be attributed that belief? Perhaps, but it would take a bit of a story to bring us to accept it.

In all of these cases, belief attribution appears beset with subjectivity, infected with cultural relativism, prone to "indeterminacy of radical translation"—clearly an enterprise demanding special talents: the art of phenomenological analysis, hermeneutics, empathy, *Verstehen*, and all that. On other occasions, normal occasions, when familiar beliefs are the topic, belief attribution looks as easy as speaking prose and as objective and reliable as counting beans in a dish. Particularly when these straightforward cases are before us, it is quite plausible to suppose that in principle (if not yet in practice) it would be possible to confirm these simple, objective belief attributions by *finding something inside the believer's head*—by finding the beliefs themselves, in effect. "Look", someone might say, "either you believe there's milk in the fridge or you don't believe there's milk in the fridge" (you might have no opinion, in the latter case). But if you do believe this, that's a perfectly objective fact about you, and it must come down in the end to your brain's being in some particular physical state. If we knew more about physiological psychology, we could in principle determine the facts about your brain state and thereby determine whether or not you believe there is milk in the fridge, even if you were determined to be silent or disingenuous on the topic. In principle, on this view, physiological psychology could trump the results—or nonresults—of any "black box" method in the social sciences that divines beliefs (and other mental features) by behavioral, cultural, social, historical, *external* criteria.

These differing reflections congeal into two opposing views on the nature of belief attribution, and hence on the nature of belief. The latter, a variety of *realism*, likens the question of whether a person has a particular belief to the question of whether a person is infected with a particular virus—a perfectly objective internal matter of fact about which an observer can often make educated guesses of great reliability. The former, which we could call *interpretationism* if we absolutely had to give it a name, likens the question of whether a person has a particular belief to the question of whether a person is immoral, or has style, or talent, or would make a good wife. Faced with such questions, we preface our answers with "well, it all depends on what you're interested in", or make some similar acknowledgment of the relativity of the issue. "It's a matter of interpretation", we say. These two opposing views, so baldly stated, do not fairly represent any serious theorists' positions, but they do express views that are typically seen as mutually exclusive and exhaustive; the theorist must be friendly with one and only one of these themes.

I think this is a mistake. My thesis will be that while belief is a perfectly objective phenomenon (that apparently makes me a realist), it can be discerned only from the point of view of one who adopts a certain *predictive strategy*, and its existence can be confirmed only by an assessment of the success of that strategy (that apparently makes me an interpretionist).

First I will describe the strategy, which I call the *intentional strategy* or adopting the *intentional stance*. To a first approximation, the intentional strategy consists of treating the object whose behavior you want to predict as a rational agent with beliefs and desires and other mental states exhibiting what Brentano and others call *intentionality*. The strategy has often been described before, but I shall try to put this very familiar material in a new light by showing *how* it works and by showing *how well* it works.

Then I will argue that any object—or as I shall say, any *system*—whose behavior is well predicted by this strategy is in the fullest sense of the word a believer. *What it is* to be a true believer is to be an *intentional system*, a system whose behavior is reliably and voluminously predictable via the intentional strategy. I have argued for this position before (1971; 1976; 1978b), and my arguments have so far garnered few converts and many presumed counterexamples. I shall try again here, harder, and shall also deal with several compelling objections.

11.1   The intentional strategy and how it works

There are many strategies, some good, some bad. Here is a strategy, for instance, for predicting the future behavior of a person: determine the date and hour of the person's birth and then feed this modest datum into one or another astrological algorithm for generating predictions of the person's prospects. This strategy is deplorably popular. Its popularity is deplorable only because we have such good reasons for believing that it does not work (*pace* Feyerabend, 1978). When astrological predictions come true this is sheer luck, or the result of such vagueness or ambiguity in the prophecy that almost any eventuality can be construed to confirm it. But suppose the astrological strategy did in fact work well on some people. We could call those people *astrological systems*—systems whose behavior was, as a matter of fact, predictable by the astrological strategy. If there were such people, such astrological systems, we would be more interested than most of us in fact are in *how the astrological strategy works*—that is, we would be interested in the rules, principles, or methods of astrology. We could find out how the strategy works by asking astrologers, reading their books, and observing them in action. But we would also be curious about *why* it worked. We might find that astrologers had no useful opinions about this latter question—they either had no theory of why it worked or their theories were pure hokum. Having a good strategy is one thing; knowing why it works is another.

So far as we know, however, the class of astrological systems is empty; so the astrological strategy is of interest only as a social curiosity. Other strategies have better credentials. Consider the physical strategy, or *physical stance*; if you want to predict the behavior of a system, determine its physical constitution (perhaps all the way down to the microphysical level) and the physical nature of the impingements upon it, and use your knowledge of the laws of physics to predict the outcome for any input. This is the grand and impractical strategy of Laplace for predicting the entire future of everything in the universe; but it has more modest, local, actually usable versions. The chemist or physicist in the laboratory can use this strategy to predict the behavior of exotic materials, but equally the cook in the kitchen can predict the effect of leaving the pot on the burner too long. The strategy is not always practically available, but that it will always work *in principle* is a dogma of the physical sciences. (I ignore the minor complications raised by the subatomic indeterminacies of quantum physics.)

Sometimes, in any event, it is more effective to switch from the physical stance to what I call the *design stance*, where one ignores the actual (possibly messy) details of the physical constitution of an object, and, on the assumption that it has a certain design, predicts that it will behave *as it is designed to behave* under various circumstances. For instance, most users of computers have not the foggiest idea what physical principles are responsible for the computer's highly reliable, and hence predictable, behavior. But if they have a good idea of what the computer is designed to do (a description of its operation at any one of the many possible levels of abstraction), they can predict its behavior with great accuracy and reliability, subject to disconfirmation only in the cases of physical malfunction. Less dramatically, almost anyone can predict when an alarm clock will sound on the basis of the most casual inspection of its exterior. One does not know or care to know whether it is spring wound, battery driven, sunlight powered, made of brass wheels and jewel bearings or silicon chips—one just assumes that it is designed so that the alarm will sound when it is set to sound, and it is set to sound where it appears to be set to sound, and the clock will keep on running until that time and beyond, and is designed to run more or less accurately, and so forth. For more accurate and detailed design stance predictions of the alarm clock, one must descend to a less abstract level of description of its design; for instance, to the level at which gears are described, but their material is not specified.

Only the designed behavior of a system is predictable from the design stance, of course. If you want to predict the behavior of an alarm clock when it is pumped full of liquid helium, revert to the physical stance. Not just artifacts but also many biological objects (plants and animals, kidneys and hearts, stamens and pistils) behave in ways that can be predicted from the design stance. They are not just physical systems but designed systems.

Sometimes even the design stance is practically inaccessible, and then there is yet another stance or strategy one can adopt: the intentional stance. Here is how it works: first you decide to treat the object whose behavior is to be predicted as a rational agent; then you figure out what beliefs that agent ought to have, given its place in the world and its purpose. Then you figure out what desires it ought to have, on the same considerations, and finally you predict that this rational agent will act to further its goals in the light of its beliefs. A little practical reasoning from the chosen set of beliefs and desires will in many—but not all—instances yield a decision about what the agent *ought* to do; that is what you predict the agent *will* do.

The strategy becomes clearer with a little elaboration. Consider first how we go about populating each other's heads with beliefs. A few truisms: sheltered people tend to be ignorant; if you expose someone to something he comes to know all about it. In general, it seems, we come to believe all the truths about the parts of the world around us we are put in a position to learn about. Exposure to x—that is, sensory confrontation with x over some suitable period of time—is the *normally sufficient* condition for knowing (or having true beliefs) about x. As we say, we come to *know all about* the things around us. Such exposure is only *normally* sufficient for knowledge, but this is not the large escape hatch it might appear; our threshold for accepting abnormal ignorance in the face of exposure is quite high. "I didn't know the gun was loaded", said by one who was observed to be present, sighted, and awake during the loading, meets with a variety of utter skepticism that only the most outlandish supporting tale could overwhelm.

Of course we do not come to learn or remember all the truths our sensory histories avail us. In spite of the phrase "know all about", what we come to know, normally, are only all the *relevant* truths our sensory histories avail us. I do not typically come to know the ratio of spectacle-wearing people to trousered people in a room I inhabit, though if this interested me, it would be readily learnable. It is not just that some facts about my environment are below my thresholds of discrimination or beyond the integration and holding power of my memory (such as the height in inches of all the people present), but that many perfectly detectable, graspable, memorable facts are of no interest to me and hence do not come to be believed by me. So one rule for attributing beliefs in the intentional strategy is this: attribute as beliefs all the truths relevant to the system's interests (or desires) that the system's experience to date has made available. This rule leads to attributing somewhat too much—since we all are somewhat forgetful, even of important things. It also fails to capture the false beliefs we are all known to have. But the attribution of false belief, *any* false belief, requires a special genealogy, which will be seen to consist in the main in true beliefs. Two paradigm cases: S believes (falsely) that p, because S believes (truly) that Jones told him that p, that Jones is pretty clever, that Jones did not intend to deceive him, . . . and so on. Second case: S believes (falsely) that there is a snake on the barstool, because S believes (truly) that he seems to see a snake on the barstool, is himself sitting in a bar not a yard from the barstool he sees, and so forth. The falsehood has to start somewhere: the seed may be sown in hallucination, illusion, a normal variety of simple misperception, memory deterioration, or deliberate fraud, for instance; but the false beliefs that are reaped grow in a culture medium of true beliefs.

Then there are the arcane and sophisticated beliefs, true and false, that are so often at the focus of attention in discussions of belief attribution. They do not arise directly, goodness knows, from exposure to mundane things and events, but their attribution requires tracing out a lineage of mainly good argument or reasoning from the bulk of beliefs already attributed. An implication of the intentional strategy, then, is that true believers mainly believe truths. If anyone could devise an agreed-upon method of individuating and counting beliefs (which I doubt very much), we would see that all but the smallest portion (say, less than ten percent) of a person's beliefs were attributable under our first rule.[1]

Note that this rule is a derived rule, an elaboration and further specification of the fundamental rule: attribute those beliefs the system *ought to have*. Note also that the rule interacts with the attribution of desires. How do we attribute the desires (preferences, goals, interests) on whose basis we will shape the list of beliefs? We attribute the desires the system *ought to have*. That is the fundamental rule. It dictates, on a first pass, that we attribute the familiar list of highest, or most basic, desires to people: survival, absence of pain, food, comfort, procreation, entertainment. Citing any one of these desires typically terminates the "Why?" game of reason giving. One is not supposed to need an ulterior motive for desiring comfort or pleasure or the prolongation of one's existence. Derived rules of desire attribution interact with belief attributions. Trivially, we have the rule: attribute desires for those things a system believes to be good for it. Somewhat more informatively, attribute desires for those things a system believes to be best means to other ends it desires. The attribution of bizarre and detrimental desires thus requires, like the attribution of false beliefs, special stories.

The interaction between belief and desire becomes trickier when we consider what desires we attribute on the basis of verbal behavior. The capacity to *express* desires in language opens the floodgates of desire attribution. "I want a two-egg mushroom omelet, some French bread and butter, and a half bottle of lightly chilled white Burgundy." How could one begin to attribute a desire for anything so specific in the absence of such verbal declaration? How, indeed, could a creature come to *contract* such a specific desire without the aid of language? Language *enables* us to formulate highly specific desires, but it also *forces* us on occasion to commit ourselves to desires altogether more stringent in their conditions of satisfaction than anything we would otherwise have any reason to endeavor to satisfy. Since in order to get what you want you often have to say what you want, and since you often cannot say what you want without saying something more specific than you antecedently mean, you often end up giving others evidence (the very best of evidence, your unextorted word) that you desire things or states of affairs far more particular than would satisfy you—or better, than would have satisfied you, for once you have declared, being a man of your word, you acquire an interest in satisfying exactly the desire you declared and no other.

"I'd like some baked beans, please."
"Yes sir. How many?"

You might well object to having such a specification of desire demanded of you, but in fact we are all socialized to accede to similar requirements in daily life—to the point of not noticing it, and certainly not feeling oppressed by it. I dwell on this because it has a parallel in the realm of belief, where our linguistic environment is forever forcing us to give—or concede—precise verbal expression to convictions that lack the hard edges verbalization endows them with (see Dennett 1969, pp.184–85; Dennett 1978b). By concentrating on the *results* of this social force, while ignoring its distorting effect, one can easily be misled into thinking that it is *obvious* that beliefs and desires are rather like sentences stored in the head. Being language-using creatures, it is inevitable that we should often come to believe that some particular, actually formulated, spelled, and punctuated sentence *is true*, and that on other occasions we should come to want such a sentence to *come true*; but these are special cases of belief and desire and as such may not be reliable models for the whole domain.

That is enough, on this occasion, about the principles of belief and desire attribution to be found in the intentional strategy. What about the rationality one attributes to an intentional system? One starts with the ideal of perfect rationality and revises downward as circumstances dictate. That is, one starts with the assumption that people believe all the implications of their beliefs and believe no contradictory pairs of beliefs. This does not create a practical problem of clutter (infinitely many implications, for instance), for one is interested only in ensuring that the system one is predicting is rational enough to get to the particular implications that are relevant to its behavioral predicament of the moment. Instances of irrationality, or of finitely powerful capacities of inferences, raise particularly knotty problems of interpretation, which I will set aside on this occasion (see Dennett, 1981; Cherniak, 1986).

For I want to turn from the description of the strategy to the question of its use. Do people actually use this strategy? Yes, all the time. There may someday be other strategies for attributing belief and desire and for predicting behavior, but this is the only one we all know now. And when does it work? It works with people almost all the time. Why would it *not* be a good idea to allow individual Oxford colleges to create and grant academic degrees whenever they saw fit? The answer is a long story, but very easy to generate. And there would be widespread agreement about the major points. We have no difficulty thinking of the reasons people would then have for acting in such ways as to give others reasons for acting in such ways as to give others reasons for . . . creating a circumstance we would not want. Our use of the intentional strategy is so habitual and effortless that the role it plays in shaping our expectations about people is easily overlooked . The strategy also works on most other mammals most of the time. For instance, you can use it to design better traps to catch those mammals, by reasoning about what the creature knows or believes about various things, what it prefers, what it wants to avoid. The strategy works on birds, and on fish, and on reptiles, and on insects and spiders, and even on such lowly and unenterprising creatures as clams (once a clam believes there is danger about, it will not relax its grip on its closed shell until it is convinced that the danger has passed). It also works on some artifacts: the chess-playing computer will not take your knight because it knows that there is a line of ensuing play that would lead to losing its rook, and it does not want that to happen. More modestly, the thermostat will turn off the boiler as soon as it comes to believe the room has reached the desired temperature.

The strategy even works for plants. In a locale with late spring storms, you should plant apple varieties that are particularly *cautious* about *concluding* that it is spring—which is when they *want* to blossom, of course. It even works for such inanimate and apparently undesigned phenomena as lightning. An electrician once explained to me how he worked out how to protect my underground water pump from lightning damage: lightning, he said, always wants to find the best way to ground, but sometimes it gets tricked into taking second-best paths. You can protect the pump by making another, better path more *obvious* to the lightning.

11.2   True believers as intentional systems

Now clearly this is a motley assortment of "serious" belief attributions, dubious belief attributions, pedagogically useful metaphors, *façons de parler*, and, perhaps worse, outright frauds. The next task would seem to be distinguishing those intentional systems that *really* have beliefs and desires from those we may find it handy to treat *as if* they had beliefs and desires. But that would be a Sisyphean labor, or else would be terminated by fiat. A better understanding of the phenomenon of belief begins with the observation that even in the worst of these cases, even when we are surest that the strategy works *for the wrong reasons*, it is nevertheless true that it does work, at least a little bit. This is an interesting fact, which distinguishes this class of objects, the class of *intentional systems*, from the class of objects for which the strategy never works. But is this so? Does our definition of an intentional system exclude any objects at all? For instance, it seems the lectern in this lecture room can be construed as an intentional system, fully rational, believing that it is currently located at the center of the civilized world (as some of you may also think), and desiring above all else to remain at that center. What should such a rational agent so equipped with belief and desire do? Stay put, clearly—which is just what the lectern does. I predict the lectern's behavior, accurately, from the intentional stance, so is it an intentional system? If it is, anything at all is.

What should disqualify the lectern? For one thing, the strategy does not recommend itself in this case, for we get no predictive power from it that we did not antecedently have. We already knew what the lectern was going to do—namely nothing—and tailored the beliefs and desires to fit in a quite unprincipled way. In the case of people or animals or computers, however, the situation is different. In these cases often the only strategy that is at all practical is the intentional strategy; it gives us predictive power we can get by no other method. But, it will be urged, this is no difference in nature, but merely a difference that reflects upon our limited capacities as scientists. The Laplacean omniscient physicist could predict the behavior of a computer—or of a live human body, assuming it to be ultimately governed by the laws of physics—without any need for the risky, short-cut methods of either the design or intentional strategies. For people of limited mechanical aptitude, the intentional interpretation of a simple thermostat is a handy and largely innocuous crutch, but the engineers among us can quite fully grasp its internal operation without the aid of this anthropomorphizing. It may be true that the cleverest engineers find it practically impossible to maintain a clear conception of more complex systems, such as a time-sharing computer system or remote-controlled space probe, without lapsing into an intentional stance (and viewing these devices as asking and telling, trying and avoiding, wanting and believing), but this is just a more advanced case of human epistemic frailty. We would not want to classify these artifacts with the true believers—ourselves—on such variable and parochial grounds, would we? Would it not be intolerable to hold that some artifact or creature or person was a believer from the point of view of one observer, but not a believer at all from the point of view of another, cleverer observer? That would be a particularly radical version of interpretationism, and some have thought I espoused it in urging that belief be viewed in terms of the success of the intentional strategy. I must confess that my presentation of the view has sometimes invited that reading, but I now want to discourage it. The decision to adopt the intentional stance is free, but the facts about the success or failure of the stance, were one to adopt it, are perfectly objective.

Once the intentional strategy is in place, it is an extraordinarily powerful tool in prediction—a fact that is largely concealed by our typical concentration on the cases in which it yields dubious or unreliable results. Consider, for instance, predicting moves in a chess game. What makes chess an interesting game, one can see, is the *un*predictability of one's opponent's moves, except in those cases where moves are "forced"—where there is *clearly* one best move—typically the least of the available evils. But this unpredictability is put in context when one recognizes that in the typical chess situation there are very many perfectly legal and hence available moves, but only a few—perhaps half a dozen—with anything to be said for them, and hence only a few high-probability moves according to the intentional strategy. Even when the intentional strategy fails to distinguish a single move with a highest probability, it can dramatically reduce the number of live options.

The same feature of the intentional strategy is apparent when it is applied to "real world" cases. It is notoriously unable to predict the exact purchase and sell decisions of stock traders, for instance, or the exact sequence of words a politician will utter when making a scheduled speech. But one's confidence can be very high indeed about slightly less specific predictions: that the particular trader *will not buy utilities today*, or that the politician *will side with the unions against his party*, for example. This inability to predict fine-grained descriptions of actions, looked at another way, is a source of strength for the intentional strategy, for it is this neutrality with regard to details of implementation that permits one to exploit the intentional strategy in complex cases, for instance, in *chaining predictions* (see Dennett, 1978a). Suppose the US Secretary of State were to announce he was a paid agent of the KGB. What an unparalleled event! How unpredictable its consequences! Yet in fact we can predict dozens of not terribly interesting but perfectly salient consequences, and consequences of consequences. The President would confer with the rest of the Cabinet, which would support his decision to relieve the Secretary of State of his duties pending the results of various investigations, psychiatric and political, and all this would be reported at a news conference to people who would write stories that would be commented upon in editorials that would be read by people who would write letters to the editors, and so forth. None of that is daring prognostication, but note that it describes an arc of causation in space-time that could not be predicted under *any* description by any imaginable practical extension of physics or biology.

The power of the intentional strategy can be seen even more sharply with the aid of an objection first raised by Robert Nozick some years ago. Suppose, he suggested, some beings of vastly superior intelligence—from Mars, let us say—were to descend upon us, and suppose that we were to them as simple thermostats are to clever engineers. Suppose, that is, that they did not *need* the intentional stance—or even the design stance—to predict our behavior in all its detail. They can be supposed to be Laplacean super-physicists, capable of comprehending the activity on Wall Street, for instance, at the microphysical level. Where we see brokers and buildings and sell orders and bids, they see vast congeries of subatomic particles milling about—and they are such good physicists that they can predict days in advance what ink marks will appear each day on the paper tape labeled "Closing Dow Jones Industrial Average". They can predict the individual behaviors of all the various moving bodies they observe without ever treating any of them as intentional systems. Would we be right then to say that from *their* point of view we really were not believers at all (any more than a simple thermostat is)? If so, then our status as believers is nothing objective, but rather something in the eye of the beholder—provided the beholder shares our intellectual limitations.

Our imagined Martians might be able to predict the future of the human race by Laplacean methods, but if they did not also see us as intentional systems, they would be missing something perfectly objective: the *patterns* in human behavior that are describable from the intentional stance, and only from that stance, and that support generalizations and predictions. Take a particular instance in which the Martians observe a stockbroker deciding to place an order for 500 shares of General Motors. They predict the exact motions of his fingers as he dials the phone and the exact vibrations of his vocal cords as he intones his order. But if the Martians do not see that indefinitely many *different* patterns of finger motions and vocal cord vibrations—even the motions of indefinitely many different individuals—could have been substituted for the actual particulars without perturbing the subsequent operation of the market, then they have failed to see a real pattern in the world they are observing. Just as there are indefinitely many ways of *being a spark plug*—and one has not understood what an internal combustion engine is unless one realizes that a variety of different devices can be screwed into these sockets without affecting the performance of the engine—so there are indefinitely many ways of *ordering 500 shares of*

General Motors, and there are societal sockets in which one of these ways will produce just about the same effect as any other. There are also societal pivot points, as it were, where which way people go depends on whether they *believe that p*, or *desire A*, and does not depend on any of the other infinitely many ways they may be alike or different.

Suppose, pursuing our Martian fantasy a little further, that one of the Martians were to engage in a predicting contest with an Earthling. The Earthling and the Martian observe (and observe each other observing) a particular bit of local physical transaction. From the Earthling's point of view, this is what is observed. The telephone rings in Mrs. Gardner's kitchen. She answers, and this is what she says: "Oh, hello dear. You're coming home early? Within the hour? And bringing the boss to dinner? Pick up a bottle of wine on the way home then, and drive carefully." On the basis of this observation, our Earthling predicts that a large metallic vehicle with rubber tires will come to a stop on the drive within one hour, disgorging two human beings, one of whom will be holding a paper bag containing a bottle containing an alcoholic fluid. The prediction is a bit risky, perhaps, but a good bet on all counts. The Martian makes the same prediction, but has to avail himself of much more information about an extraordinary number of interactions of which, so far as he can tell, the Earthling is entirely ignorant. For instance, the deceleration of the vehicle at intersection *A*, five miles from the house, without which there would have been a collision with another vehicle—whose collision course had been laboriously calculated over some hundreds of meters by the Martian. The Earthling's performance would look like magic! How did the Earthling know that the human being who got out of the car and got the bottle in the shop would get back in? The coming true of the Earthling's prediction, after all the vagaries, intersections, and branches in the paths charted by the Martian, would seem to anyone bereft of the intentional strategy as marvelous and inexplicable as the fatalistic inevitability of the appointment in Samarra. Fatalists—for instance, astrologers—believe that there is a pattern in human affairs that is inexorable, that will impose itself *come what may*, that is, no matter how the victims scheme and second-guess, no matter how they twist and turn in their chains. These fatalists are wrong, but they are *almost* right. There *are* patterns in human affairs that impose themselves, not quite inexorably but with great vigor, absorbing physical perturbations and variations that might as well be considered random; these are the patterns that we characterize in terms of the beliefs, desires, and intentions of rational agents.

No doubt you will have noticed, and been distracted by, a serious flaw in our thought experiment: the Martian is presumed to treat his Earthling opponent as an intelligent being like himself, with whom communication is possible, a being with whom one can make a wager, against whom one can compete. In short, a being with beliefs (such as the belief he expressed in his prediction) and desires (such as the desire to win the prediction contest). So if the Martian sees the pattern in one Earthling, how can he fail to see it in the others? As a bit of narrative, our example could be strengthened by supposing that our Earthling cleverly learned Martian (which is transmitted by X-ray modulation) and disguised himself as a Martian, counting on the species-chauvinism of these otherwise brilliant aliens to permit him to pass as an intentional system while not giving away the secret of his fellow human beings. This addition might get us over a bad twist in the tale, but might obscure the moral to be drawn: namely, *the unavoidability of the intentional stance with regard to oneself and one's fellow intelligent beings.* This unavoidability is itself interest relative; it is perfectly possible to adopt a physical stance, for instance, with regard to an intelligent being, oneself included, but not to the exclusion of maintaining at the same time an intentional stance with regard to oneself at a minimum, and one's fellows *if* one intends, for instance, to learn what they know (a point that has been powerfully made by Stuart Hampshire in a number of writings). We can perhaps suppose our super-intelligent Martians fail to recognize *us* as intentional systems, but we cannot suppose them to lack the requisite concepts.[2] If they observe, theorize, predict, communicate, they view *themselves* as intentional systems.[3] Where there are intelligent beings, the patterns must be there to be described, whether or not we care to see them.

It is important to recognize the objective reality of the intentional patterns discernible in the activities of intelligent creatures, but also important to recognize the incompleteness and imperfections in the patterns. The objective fact is that the intentional strategy *works as well as it does*, which is not perfectly. No one is perfectly rational, perfectly unforgetful, all-observant, or invulnerable to fatigue, malfunction, or design imperfection. This leads inevitably to circumstances beyond the power of the intentional strategy to describe, in much the same way that physical damage to an artifact, such as a telephone or an automobile, may render it indescribable by the normal design terminology for that artifact. How do you draw the schematic wiring diagram of an audio amplifier that has been partially melted, or how do you characterize the program state of a malfunctioning computer? In cases of even the mildest and most familiar cognitive pathology—where people seem to hold contradictory beliefs or to be deceiving themselves, for instance—the canons of interpretation of the intentional strategy fail to yield clear, stable verdicts about which beliefs and desires to attribute to a person.

Now a *strong* realist position on beliefs and desires would claim that in these cases the person in question really does have some particular beliefs and desires which the intentional strategy, as I have described it, is simply unable to divine. On the milder sort of realism I am advocating, there is no fact of the matter of exactly which beliefs and desires a person has in these degenerate cases, but this is not a surrender to relativism or subjectivism, for *when* and *why* there is no fact of the matter is itself a matter of objective fact. On this view one can even acknowledge the *interest relativity* of belief attributions and grant that given the different interests of different cultures, for instance, the beliefs and desires one culture would attribute to a member might be quite different from the beliefs and desires another culture would attribute to the very same person. But supposing that were so in a particular case, there would be the further facts about *how well* each of the rival intentional strategies worked for predicting the behavior of that person. We can be sure in advance that no intentional interpretation of an individual will work to perfection, and it may be that two rival schemes are about equally good, and better than any others we can devise. That this is the case is itself something about which there can be a fact of the matter. The objective presence of one pattern (with whatever imperfections) does not rule out the objective presence of another pattern (with whatever imperfections).

The bogey of radically different interpretations with equal warrant from the intentional strategy is theoretically important—one might better say metaphysically important—but practically negligible once one restricts one's attention to the largest and most complex intentional systems we know: human beings.[4]

Until now I have been stressing our kinship to clams and thermostats, in order to emphasize a view of the logical status of belief attribution, but the time has come to acknowledge the obvious differences and say what can be made of them. The perverse claim remains: *all there is* to being a true believer is being a system whose behavior is reliably predictable via the intentional strategy, and hence *all there is* to really and truly believing that *p* (for any proposition p) is being an intentional system for which *p* occurs as a belief in the best (most predictive) interpretation. But once we turn out attention to the truly interesting and versatile intentional systems, we see that this apparently shallow and instrumentalistic criterion of belief puts a severe constraint on the internal constitution of a genuine believer, and thus yields a robust version of belief after all.

Consider the lowly thermostat, as degenerate a case of intentional system as could conceivably hold our attention for more than a moment. Going along with the gag, we might agree to grant it the capacity for about half a dozen different beliefs and fewer desires—it can believe the room is too cold or too hot, that the boiler is on or off, and that if it wants the room warmer it should turn on the boiler, and so forth. But surely this is imputing too much to the thermostat; it has no concept of heat or of a boiler, for instance. So suppose we *de-interpret* its beliefs and desires: it can believe the A is too F or G, and if it wants the A to be more F it should do K, and so forth. After all, by attaching the thermostatic control mechanism to different input and output devices, it could be made to regulate the amount of water in a tank, or the speed of a train, for instance. Its attachment to a heat sensitive transducer and a boiler is too impoverished a link to the world to grant any rich semantics to its belief-like states.

But suppose we then enrich these modes of attachment. Suppose we give it more than one way of learning about the temperature, for instance. We give it an eye of sorts that can distinguish huddled, shivering occupants of the room and an ear so that it can be told how cold it is. We give it some facts about geography so that it can conclude that is probably in a cold place if it learns that its spatio-temporal location is Winnipeg in December. Of course giving it a visual system that is multipurpose and general—not a mere shivering-object detector—will require vast complications of its inner structure. Suppose we also give our system more behavioral versatility: it chooses the boiler fuel, purchases it from the cheapest and most reliable dealer, checks the weather stripping, and so forth. This adds another dimension of internal complexity; it gives individual belief-like states *more to do*, in effect, by providing more and different occasions for their derivation or deduction from other states, and by providing more and different occasions for them to serve as premises for further reasoning. The cumulative effect of enriching these connections between the device and the world in which it resides is to enrich the semantics of its dummy predicates, F and G and the rest. The more of this we add, the less amenable our device becomes to serving as the control structure of anything other than a room-temperature maintenance system. A more formal way of saying this is that the class of indistinguishably satisfactory models of the formal system embodied in its internal states gets smaller and smaller as we add such complexities; the more we add, the richer or more demanding or specific the semantics of the system, until eventually we reach systems for which a unique semantic interpretation is practically (but never in principle) dictated (see Hayes, 1979). At that point we say this device (or animal or person) has beliefs *about heat* and *about this very room*, and so forth, not only because of the system's actual location in, and operations on, the world, but because we cannot imagine another niche in which it could be placed *where it would work* (see also Dennett, 1982, 1987a).

Our original simple thermostat had a state we called a belief about a particular boiler, to the effect that it was on or off. Why about *that* boiler? Well, what other boiler would you want to say it was about? The belief is about the boiler because it is *fastened* to the boiler.[5] Given the actual, if minimal, causal link to the world that happened to be in effect, we could endow a state of the device with *meaning* (of a sort) and *truth conditions*, but it was altogether too easy to substitute a different minimal link and completely change the meaning (in this impoverished sense) of that internal state. But as systems become perceptually richer and behaviorally more versatile, it becomes harder and harder to make substitutions in the actual links of the system to the world without changing the organization of the system itself. If you change its environment, it will *notice*, in effect, and make a change in its internal state in response. There comes to be a two-way constraint of growing specificity between the device and the environment. Fix the device in any one state and it demands a very specific environment in which to operate properly (you can no longer switch it easily from regulating temperature to regulating speed or anything else); but at the same time, if you do not *fix* the state it is in, but just plunk it down in a changed environment, its sensory attachments will be sensitive and discriminative enough to respond appropriately to the change, driving the system into a new state, in which it will operate effectively in the new environment. There is a familiar way of alluding to this tight relationship that can exist between the organization of a system and its environment: you say that the organism continuously *mirrors* the environment, or that there is a *representation* of the environment in—or implicit in—the organization of the system.

It is not that we attribute (or should attribute) beliefs and desires only to things in which we find internal representations, but rather that, when we discover some object for which the intentional strategy works, we endeavor to interpret some of its internal states or processes as internal representations. What makes some internal feature of a thing a representation could only be its role in regulating the behavior of an intentional system.

Now the reason for stressing our kinship with the thermostat should be clear. There is no magic moment in the transition from a simple thermostat to a system that *really* has an internal representation of the world around it. The thermostat has a minimally demanding representation of the world, fancier thermostats have more demanding representations of the world, fancier robots for helping around the house would have still more demanding representations of the world. Finally you reach us. We are so multifariously and intricately connected to the world that almost no substitution is possible—though it is clearly imaginable in a thought experiment. Hilary Putnam imagines the planet Twin Earth, which is just like Earth right down to the scuff marks on the shoes of the Twin Earth replica of your neighbor, but which differs from Earth in some property that is entirely beneath the thresholds of your capacities to discriminate. (What they call water on Twin Earth has a different chemical analysis.) Were *you* to be whisked instantaneously to Twin Earth and exchanged for your Twin Earth replica, you would never be the wiser—just like the simple control system that cannot tell whether it is regulating temperature, speed, or volume of water in a tank. It is easy to devise radically different Twin Earths for something as simple and sensorily deprived as a thermostat, but your internal organization puts a much more stringent demand on substitution. Your Twin Earth and Earth must be virtual replicas or you will change state dramatically on arrival.

So which boiler are *your* beliefs about when you believe the boiler is on? Why, the boiler in your cellar (rather than its twin on Twin Earth, for instance). What other boiler would your beliefs be about? The completion of the semantic interpretation of your beliefs, fixing the referents of your beliefs, requires, as in the case of the thermostat, facts about your actual embedding in the world. The principles, and problems, of interpretation that we discover when we attribute beliefs to people are the *same* principles and problems we discover when we look at the ludicrous, but blessedly simple, problem of attributing beliefs to a thermostat. The differences are of degree, but nevertheless of such great degree that understanding the internal organization of a simple intentional system gives one very little basis for understanding the internal organization of a complex intentional system, such as a human being.

11.3 Why does the intentional strategy work?

When we turn to the question of *why* the intentional strategy works as well as it does, we find that the question is ambiguous, admitting of two very different sorts of answer. If the intentional system is a simple thermostat, one answer is simply this: the intentional strategy works because the thermostat is well designed; it was designed to be a system that could be easily and reliably comprehended and manipulated from this stance. That is true, but not very informative, if what we are after are the actual features of its design that explain its performance. Fortunately, however, in the case of a simple thermostat those features are easily discovered and understood, so the other answer to our *why* question, which is really an answer about *how the machinery works*, is readily available.

If the intentional system in question is a person, there is also an ambiguity in our question. The first answer to the question of why the intentional strategy works is that evolution has designed human beings to be rational, to believe what they ought to believe and want what they ought to want. The fact that we are products of a long and demanding evolutionary process guarantees that using the intentional strategy on us is a safe bet. This answer has the virtues of truth and brevity, but it is also strikingly uninformative. The more difficult version of the question asks, in effect, how the machinery which Nature has provided us works. And we cannot yet give a good answer to that question. We just do not know. We do know how the *strategy* works, and we know the easy answer to the question of why it works, but knowing these does not help us much with the hard answer.

It is not that there is any dearth of doctrine, however. A Skinnerian behaviorist, for instance, would say that the strategy works because its imputations of beliefs and desires are shorthand, in effect, for as yet unimaginably complex descriptions of the effects of prior histories of response and reinforcement. To say that someone wants some ice cream is to say that in the past the ingestion of ice cream has been reinforced in him by the results, creating a propensity under certain background conditions (also too complex to describe) to engage in icecream-acquiring behavior. In the absence of detailed knowledge of those historical facts we can nevertheless make shrewd guesses on inductive grounds; these guesses are embodied in our intentional stance claims. Even if all this were true, it would tell us very little about the way such propensities were regulated by the internal machinery.

A currently more popular explanation is that the account of how the strategy works and the account of how the mechanism works will (roughly) *coincide*: for each predictively attributable belief, there will be a functionally salient internal state of the machinery, decomposable into functional parts in just about the same way the sentence expressing the belief is decomposable into parts—that is, words or terms. The inferences we attribute to rational creatures will be mirrored by physical, causal processes in the hardware; the *logical* form of the propositions believed will be copied in the *structural* form of the states in correspondence with them. This is the hypothesis that there is a *language of thought* coded in our brains, and our brains will eventually be understood as symbol manipulating systems in at least rough analogy with computers. Many different versions of this view are currently being explored, in the new research program called cognitive science, and provided one allows great latitude for attenuation of the basic, bold claim, I think some version of it will prove correct.

But I do not believe that this is *obvious*. Those who think that it is obvious, or inevitable, that such a theory will prove true (and there are many who do), are confusing two empirical claims. The first is that intentional stance description yields an objective, real pattern in the world—the pattern our imaginary Martians missed. This is an empirical claim, but one that is confirmed beyond skepticism. The second is that this real pattern is *produced by* another real pattern roughly isomorphic to it within the brains of intelligent creatures. Doubting the existence of the second real pattern is not doubting the existence of the first. There *are* reasons for believing in the second pattern, but they are not overwhelming. The best simple account I can give of the reasons is as follows.

As we ascend the scale of complexity form simple thermostat, through sophisticated robot, to human being, we discover that our efforts to design systems with the requisite behavior increasingly run foul of the problem of *combinatorial explosion*. Increasing some parameter by, say, ten percent—ten percent more inputs or more degrees of freedom in the behavior to be controlled or more words to be recognized or whatever—tends to increase the internal complexity of the system being designed by orders of magnitude. Things get out of hand very fast and, for instance, can lead to computer programs that will swamp the largest, fastest machines. Now somehow the brain has solved the problem of combinatorial explosion. It is a gigantic network of billions of cells, but still finite, compact, reliable, and swift, and capable of learning new behaviors, vocabularies, theories, almost without limit. Some elegant, *generative*, indefinitely extensible principles of representation must be responsible. We have only one model of such a representation system: a human language. So the argument for a language of thought comes down to this: what else could it be? We have so far been unable to imagine any plausible alternative in any detail. That is a good reason, I think, for recommending as a matter of scientific tactics that we pursue the hypothesis in its various forms as far as we can.[6] But we will engage in that exploration more circumspectly, and fruitfully, if we bear in mind that its inevitable rightness is far from assured. One does not well understand even a true empirical hypothesis so long as one is under the misapprehension that it is necessarily true.

Notes for Chapter 11

1. The idea that most of anyone's beliefs *must* be true seems obvious to some people. Support for the idea can be found in works by Quine, Putnam, Shoemaker, Davidson, and myself. Other people find the idea equally incredible—so probably each side is calling a different phenomenon belief.

Once one makes the distinction between belief and opinion (in my technical sense—Dennett, 1978b), according to which opinions are linguistically infected, relatively sophisticated cognitive states—*roughly* states of betting on the truth of a particular, formulated sentence—one can see the near triviality of the claim that most beliefs are true. A few reflections on peripheral matters should bring it out. Consider Democritus, who had a systematic, all-embracing, but (let us say, for the sake of argument) entirely false physics. He had things *all wrong*, though his views held together and had a sort of systematic utility. But even if every *claim* that scholarship permits us to attribute to Democritus (either explicit or implicit in his writings) is false, these represent a vanishingly small fraction of his *beliefs*, which include both the vast numbers of humdrum standing beliefs he must have had (about which house he lived in, what to look for in a good pair of sandals, and so forth) and also those occasional beliefs that came and went by the millions as his perceptual experience changed.

But, it may be urged, this isolation of his humdrum beliefs from his science relies on an insupportable distinction between truths of observation and truths of theory; all Democritus's beliefs are theory-laden, and since his theory is false, they are false. The reply is as follows: Granted that all observation beliefs are theory-laden, why should we choose Democritus's *explicit*, sophisticated theory (couched in his *opinions*) as the theory with which to burden his quotidian observations? Note that the least theoretical compatriot of Democritus also had myriads of theory-laden observation beliefs—and was, in one sense, none the wiser for it. Why should we not suppose Democritus's observations are laden with the same (presumably innocuous) theory? If Democritus forgot his theory, or changed his mind, his observational beliefs would be *largely* untouched. To the extent that his sophisticated theory played a discernible role in his routine behavior and expectations and so forth, it would be quite appropriate to couch his humdrum beliefs in terms of the sophisticated theory, but this will not yield a *mainly false* catalogue of beliefs, since so few of his beliefs will be affected. (The effect of theory on observation is nevertheless often underrated. See Churchland (1979) for dramatic and convincing examples of the tight relationship that can sometimes exist between theory and experience.) (The discussion in this note was distilled from a useful conversation with Paul and Patricia Churchland and Michael Stack.)

2. A member of the audience in Oxford pointed out that if the Martian included the Earthling in his physical stance purview (a possibility I had not explicitly excluded), he would not be surprised by the Earthling's prediction. He would indeed have predicted exactly the pattern of X-ray modulations produced by the Earthling speaking Martian. True, but as the Martian wrote down the results of his calculations, his prediction of the Earthling's prediction would appear, word by Martian word, as on a Ouija board, and what would be baffling to the Martian was how this chunk of mechanism, the Earthling predictor dressed up like a Martian, was able to yield this *true* sentence of Martian when it was so informationally isolated from the events the Martian needed to know of in order to make his own prediction about the arriving automobile.

3. Might there not be intelligent beings who had no use for communicating, predicting, observing, . . . ? There might be marvelous, nifty, invulnerable entities lacking these modes of action, but I cannot see what would lead us to call them *intelligent*.

4. John McCarthy's analogy to cryptography nicely makes this point. The larger the corpus of cipher text, the less chance there is of dual, systematically unrelated decipherings. For a very useful discussion of the principles and presuppositions of the intentional stance applied to machines— explicitly including thermostats—see McCarthy, 1979.

5. This idea is the ancestor in effect of the species of different ideas lumped together under the rubric of *de re* belief. If one builds from this idea toward its scions, one can see better the difficulties with them, and how to repair them. (For more on this topic, see Dennett, 1982.)

6. The fact that all *language-of-thought* models of mental representation so far proposed fall victim to combinatorial explosion in one way or another should temper one's enthusiasm for engaging in what Fodor aptly calls "the only game in town".

Minds, Brains, and Programs

12

John R. Searle
1980

What psychological and philosophical significance should we attach to recent efforts at computer simulations of human cognitive capacities? In answering this question, I find it useful to distinguish what I will call "strong" *AI* from "weak" or "cautious" *AI*. According to weak *AI*, the principal value of the computer in the study of the mind is that it gives us a very powerful tool. For example, it enables us to formulate and test hypotheses in a more rigorous and precise fashion than before. But according to strong AI, the computer is not merely a tool in the study of the mind; rather, the appropriately programmed computer really is a mind in the sense that computers given the right programs can be literally said to *understand* and have other cognitive states. And, according to strong AI, because the programmed computer has cognitive states, the programs are not mere tools that enable us to test psychological explanations; rather, the programs are themselves the explanations. I have no objection to the claims of weak AI, at least as far as this article is concerned. My discussion here will be directed to the claims I have defined as strong AI, specifically the claim that the appropriately programmed computer literally has cognitive states and that the programs thereby explain human cognition. When I refer to AI, it is the strong version as expressed by these two claims which I have in mind.

I will consider the work of Roger Schank and his colleagues at Yale (see, for instance, Schank and Abelson, 1977a), because I am more familiar with it than I am with any similar claims, and because it provides a clear example of the sort of work I wish to examine. But nothing that follows depends upon the details of Schank's programs. The same arguments would apply to Winograd's (1973) SHRDLU, Weizenbaum's (1966) ELIZA, and indeed, any Turing-machine simulation of human mental phenomena.

Briefly, and leaving out the various details, one can describe Schank's program as follows: the aim of the program is to simulate the human ability to understand stories. It is characteristic of the abilities of human beings to understand stories that they can answer questions about the story, even though the information they give was not explicitly stated in the story. Thus, for example, suppose you are given the following story: "A man went into a restaurant and ordered a hamburger. When the hamburger arrived, it was burned to a crisp, and the man stormed out of the restaurant angrily without paying for the hamburger or leaving a tip." Now, if you are given the question "Did the man eat the hamburger?", you will presumably answer, "No, he did not." Similarly if you are given the following story: "A man went into a restaurant and ordered a hamburger; when the hamburger came, he was very pleased with it; and as he left the restaurant he gave the waitress a large tip before paying his bill.", and you are asked the question "Did the man eat the hamburger?", you will presumably answer, "Yes, he ate the hamburger."

Now Schank's machines can similarly answer questions about restaurants in this fashion. In order to do so, they have a "representation" of the sort of information that human beings have about restaurants which enables them to answer such questions as those above, given these sorts of stories. When the machine is given the story and then asked the question, the machine will print out answers of the sort that we would expect human beings to give if told similar stories. Partisans of strong AI claim that in this question-and-answer sequence, not only is the machine simulating a human ability but also:

(a) The machine can literally be said to *understand* the story and provide answers to questions; and

(b) What the machine and its program do *explains* the human ability to understand the story and answer questions about it.

Claims (a) and (b) seem to me totally unsupported by Schank's work, as I will attempt to show in what follows.[1]

A way to test any theory of mind is to ask oneself what it would be like if one's own mind actually worked on the principles that the theory says all minds work on. Let us apply this test to the Schank program with the following *Gedankenexperiment*. Suppose that I am locked in a room and suppose that I'm given a large batch of Chinese writing. Suppose furthermore, as is indeed the case, that I know no Chinese either written or spoken, and that I'm not even confident that I could recognize Chinese writing as Chinese writing distinct from, say, Japanese writing or meaningless squiggles. Now suppose further that, after this first batch of Chinese writing, I am given a second batch of Chinese script together with a set of rules for correlating the second batch with the first batch. The rules are in English and I understand these rules as well as any other native speaker of English. They enable me to correlate one set of formal symbols with another set of formal symbols, and all that "formal" means here is that I can identify the symbols entirely by their shapes. Now suppose also that I am given a third batch of Chinese symbols together with some instructions, again in English, that enable me to correlate elements of this third batch with the first two batches, and these rules instruct me how I am to give back certain Chinese symbols with certain sorts of shapes in response to certain sorts of shapes given me in the third batch.

Unknown to me, the people who are giving me all of these symbols call the first batch a "script", they call the second batch a "story", and they call the third batch "questions".

Furthermore, they call the symbols I give them back in response to the third batch "answers to the questions", and the set of rules in English that they gave me they call "the program". To complicate the story a little bit, imagine that these people also give me stories in English which I understand, and they then ask me questions in English about these stories, and I give them back answers in English. Suppose also that after a while I get so good at following the instructions for manipulating the Chinese symbols and the programmers get so good at writing the programs that from the external point of view—that is, from the point of view of somebody outside the room in which I am locked—my answers to the questions are indistinguishable from those of native Chinese speakers. Nobody looking at my answers can tell that I don't speak a word of Chinese. Let us also suppose that my answers to the English questions are, as they no doubt would be, indistinguishable from those of other native English speakers, for the simple reason that I am a native speaker of English. From the external point of view, from the point of view of someone reading my "answers", the answers to the Chinese questions and the English questions are equally good. But in the Chinese case, unlike the English case, I produce the answers by manipulating uninterpreted formal symbols. As far as the Chinese is concerned, I simply behave like a computer; I perform computational operations on formally specified elements. For the purposes of the Chinese, I am simply an instantiation of the computer program.

Now the claims made by strong AI are that the programmed computer understands the stories and that the program in some sense explains human understanding. But we are now in a position to examine these claims in light of our thought experiment.

(a) As regards the first claim, it seems to me obvious in the example that I do not understand a word of the Chinese stories. I have inputs and outputs that are indistinguishable from those of the native Chinese speaker, and I can have any formal program you like, but I still understand nothing. Schank's computer, for the same reasons, understands nothing of any stories, whether in Chinese, English, or whatever, since in the Chinese case the computer is me; and in cases where the computer is not me, the computer has nothing more than I have in the case where I understand nothing.

(b) As regards the second claim—that the program explains human understanding—we can see that the computer and its program do not provide sufficient conditions of understanding, since the computer and the program are functioning and there is no understanding. But does it even provide a necessary condition or a significant contribution to understanding? One of the claims made by the supporters of strong AI is this: when I understand a story in English, what I am doing is exactly the same—or perhaps more of the same—as what I was doing in the case of manipulating the Chinese symbols. It is simply more formal symbol manipulation which distinguishes the case in English, where I do understand, from the case in Chinese, where I don't. I have not demonstrated that this claim is false, but it would certainly appear an incredible claim in the example.

Such plausibility as the claim has derives from the supposition that we can construct a program that will have the same inputs and outputs as native speakers, and in addition we assume that speakers have some level of description where they are also instantiations of a program. On the basis of these two assumptions, we assume that even if Schank's program isn't the whole story about understanding, maybe it is part of the story. That is, I suppose, an empirical possibility, but not the slightest reason has so far been given to suppose it is true, since what is suggested—though certainly not demonstrated—by the example is that the computer program is irrelevant to my understanding of the story. In the Chinese case I have everything that artificial intelligence can put into me by way of a program, and I understand nothing; in the English case I understand everything, and there is so far no reason at all to suppose that my understanding has anything to do with computer programs—that is, with computational operations on purely formally specified elements.

As long as the program is defined in terms of computational operations on purely for-mally-defined elements, what the example suggests is that these by themselves have no interesting connection with understanding. They are certainly not sufficient conditions, and not the slightest reason has been given to suppose that they are necessary conditions or even that they make a significant contribution to understanding. Notice that the force of the argument is not simply that different machines can have the same input and out-put while operating on different formal principles—that is not the point at all—but rather that whatever purely formal principles you put into the computer will not be sufficient for understanding, since a human will be able to follow the formal principles without under-standing anything, and no reason has been offered to suppose they are necessary or even contributory, since no reason has been given to suppose that when I understand English, I am operating with any formal program at all.

What is it, then, that I have in the case of the English sentences which I do not have in the case of the Chinese sentences? The obvious answer is that I know what the former mean but haven't the faintest idea what the latter mean. In what does this consist, and why couldn't we give it to a machine, whatever it is? Why couldn't the machine be given whatever it is about me that makes it the case that I know what English sentences mean? I will return to these questions after developing my example a little more.

I have had occasions to present this example to several workers in artificial intelligence and, interestingly, they do not seem to agree on what the proper reply to it is. I get a sur-prising variety of replies, and in what follows I will consider the most common of these (specified along with their geographical origins). First I want to block out some common misunderstandings about "understanding". In many of these discussions one finds fancy footwork about the word 'understanding'. My critics point out that there are different de grees of understanding, that 'understands' is not a simple two-place predicate, that there are even different kinds and levels of understanding, and often the law of the excluded mid-dle doesn't even apply in a straightforward way to statements of the form 'x understands

y', that in many cases it is a matter for decision and not a simple matter of fact whether x understands y. And so on.

To all these points I want to say: "Of course, of course." But they have nothing to do with the points at issue. There are clear cases where 'understands' applies and clear cases where it does not apply; and such cases are all I need for this argument.[2] I understand stories in English; to a lesser degree I can understand stories in French; to a still lesser degree, stories in German; and in Chinese, not at all. My car and my adding machine, on the other hand, understand nothing; they are not in that line of business.

We often attribute "understanding" and other cognitive predicates by metaphor and analogy to cars, adding machines, and other artifacts; but nothing is proved by such attributions. We say, "The door *knows* when to open because of its photoelectric cell", "The adding machine *knows how* (*understands how*, is *able*) to do addition and subtraction but not division", and "The thermostat *perceives* changes in the temperature". The reason we make these attributions is interesting and has to do with the fact that in artifacts we extend our own intentionality;[3] our tools are extensions of our purposes, and so we find it natural to make metaphorical attributions of intentionality to them. But I take it no philosophical ice is cut by such examples. The sense in which an automatic door "understands instructions" from its photoelectric cell is not at all the sense in which I understand English.

If the sense in which Schank's programmed computers understand stories were supposed to be the metaphorical sense in which the door understands, and not the sense in which I understand English, the issue would not be worth discussing. Newell and Simon write that the sense of "understanding" they claim for computers is exactly the same as for human beings. I like the straightforwardness of this claim, and it is the sort of claim I will be considering. I will argue that, in that literal sense, the programmed computer understands what the car and the adding machine understand: exactly nothing. The computer's understanding is not just (as in the case of my understanding of German) partial or incomplete; it is zero.

Now to the replies.

I THE SYSTEMS REPLY (Berkeley): While it is true that the individual person who is locked in the room does not understand the story, the fact is that he is merely part of a whole system and the system does understand the story. The person has large ledger in front of him in which are written the rules, he has a lot of scratch paper and pencils for doing calculations, he has "data banks" of sets of Chinese symbols. Now, understanding is not being ascribed to the mere individual; rather it is being ascribed to this whole system of which he is a part.

My response to the systems theory is simple. Let the individual internalize all of these elements of the system. He memorizes the rules in the ledger and the data banks of Chinese symbols, and he does all the calculations in his head. The individual then incorporates the entire system. There isn't anything at all to the system which he does not encompass. We can even get rid of the room and suppose he works outdoors. All the same, he understands nothing of the Chinese, and a fortiori neither does the system, because there isn't anything in the system which isn't in him. If he doesn't understand, then there is no way the system could understand because the system is just a part of him.

Actually I feel somewhat embarrassed even to give this answer to the systems theory because the theory seems to me so implausible to start with. The idea is that while a person doesn't understand Chinese, somehow the *conjunction* of that person and some bits of paper might understand Chinese. It is not easy for me to imagine how someone who was not in the grip of an ideology would find the idea at all plausible. Still, I think many people who are committed to the ideology of strong AI will in the end be inclined to say something very much like this; so let us pursue it a bit further. According to one version of this view, while the man in the internalized systems example doesn't understand Chinese in the sense that a native Chinese speaker does (because, for example, he doesn't know that the story refers to restaurants and hamburgers, and so on), still "the man as formal symbol manipulation system" *really does understand Chinese.* The subsystem of the man which is the formal symbol manipulation system for Chinese should not be confused with the subsystem for English.

So there are really two subsystems in the man; one understands English, the other Chinese, and "it's just that the two systems have little to do with each other". But, I want to reply, not only do they have little to do with each other, they are not even remotely alike. The subsystem that understands English (assuming we allow ourselves to talk in this jargon of "subsystems" for a moment) knows that the stories are about restaurants and eating hamburgers, and the like; he knows that he is being asked questions about restaurants and that he is answering questions as best he can by making various inferences from the content of the story, and so on. But the Chinese system knows none of this; whereas the English subsystem knows that 'hamburgers' refers to hamburgers, the Chinese subsystem knows only that 'squiggle-squiggle' is followed by 'squoggle-squoggle'. All he knows is that various formal symbols are being introduced at one end and are manipulated according to rules written in English, and that other symbols are going out at the other end.

The whole point of the original example was to argue that such symbol manipulation by itself couldn't be sufficient for understanding Chinese in any literal sense because the man could write 'squoggle-squoggle' after 'squiggle-squiggle' without understanding anything in Chinese. And it doesn't meet that argument to postulate subsystems within the man, because the subsystems are no better off than the man was in the first place; they still don't have anything even remotely like what the English-speaking man (or subsystem) has. Indeed, in the case as described, the Chinese subsystem is simply a part of the English subsystem, a part that engages in meaningless symbol manipulation according to the rules of English.

Let us ask ourselves what is supposed to motivate the systems reply in the first place—that is, what *independent* grounds are there supposed to be for saying that the agent must have a subsystem within him that literally understands stories in Chinese? As far as I can tell, the only grounds are that in the example I have the same input and output as native Chinese speakers, and a program that goes from one to the other. But the point of the example has been to show that that couldn't be sufficient for understanding, in the sense in which I understand stories in English, because a person, hence the set of systems that go to make up a person, could have the right combination of input, output, and program and still not understand anything in the relevant literal sense in which I understand English.

The only motivation for saying there *must* be a subsystem in me that understands Chinese is that I have a program and I can pass the Turing test: I can fool native Chinese speakers (see Turing, 1950; Chapter 6 of this volume). But precisely one of the points at issue is the adequacy of the Turing test. The example shows that there could be two "systems", both of which pass the Turing test, but only one of which understands; and it is no argument against this point to say that, since they both pass the Turing test, they must both understand, since this claim fails to meet the argument that the system in me which understands English has a great deal more than the system which merely processes Chinese. In short, the systems reply simply begs the question by insisting without argument that the system must understand Chinese.

Furthermore, the systems reply would appear to lead to consequences that are independently absurd. If we are to conclude that there must be cognition in me on the grounds that I have a certain sort of input and output and a program in between, then it looks as though all sorts of noncognitive subsystems are going to turn out to be cognitive. For example, my stomach has a level of description where it does information processing, and it instantiates any number of computer programs, but I take it we do not want to say that it has any understanding. Yet if we accept the systems reply, it is hard to see how we can avoid saying that stomach, heart, liver, and so on, are all understanding subsystems, since there is no principled way to distinguish the motivation for saying the Chinese subsystem understands from saying that the stomach understands. (It is, by the way, not an answer to this point to say that the Chinese system has information as input and output and the stomach has food and food products as input and output, since from the point of view of the agent, from my point of view, there is no information in either the food or the Chinese; the Chinese is just so many meaningless squiggles. The information in the Chinese case is solely in the eyes of the programmers and the interpreters, and there is nothing to prevent them from treating the input and output of my digestive organs as information if they so desire.)

This last point bears on some independent problems in strong AI, and it is worth digressing for a moment to explain it. If strong AI is to be a branch of psychology, it must be able to distinguish systems which are genuinely mental from those which are not. It must be able to distinguish the principles on which the mind works from those on which nonmental systems work; otherwise it will offer us no explanations of what is specifically mental about the mental. And the mental/nonmental distinction cannot be just in the eye of the beholder—it must be intrinsic to the systems. For otherwise it would be up to any beholder to treat people as nonmental and, for instance, hurricanes as mental, if he likes.

But quite often in the AI literature the distinction is blurred in ways which would in the long run prove disastrous to the claim that AI is a cognitive inquiry. McCarthy, for example, writes: "Machines as simple as thermostats can be said to have beliefs, and having beliefs seems to be a characteristic of most machines capable of problem solving performance" (1979). Anyone who thinks strong AI has a chance as a theory of the mind ought to ponder the implications of that remark. We are asked to accept it as a discovery of strong AI that the hunk of metal on the wall which we use to regulate the temperature has beliefs in exactly the same sense that we, our spouses, and our children have beliefs, and furthermore that "most" of the other machines in the room—telephone, tape recorder, adding machine, electric light switch, and so on—also have beliefs in this literal sense. It is not the aim of this article to argue against McCarthy's point, so I will simply assert the following without argument. The study of the mind starts with such facts as that humans have beliefs and thermostats, telephones, and adding machines don't. If you get a theory that denies this point, you have produced a counter-example to the theory, and the theory is false.

One gets the impression that people in AI who write this sort of thing think they can get away with it because they don't really take it seriously and they don't think anyone else will either. I propose, for a moment at least, to take it seriously. Think hard for one minute about what would be necessary to establish that that hunk of metal on the wall over there has real beliefs, beliefs with direction of fit, propositional content, and conditions of satisfaction; beliefs that have the possibility of being strong beliefs or weak beliefs; nervous, anxious or secure beliefs; dogmatic, rational, or superstitious beliefs; blind faiths or hesitant cogitations; any kind of beliefs. The thermostat is not a candidate. Neither are stomach, liver, adding machine, or telephone. However, since we are taking the idea seriously, notice that its truth would be fatal to the claim of strong AI to be a science of the mind, for now the mind is everywhere. What we wanted to know is what distinguishes the mind from thermostats, livers, and the rest. And if McCarthy were right, strong AI wouldn't have a hope of telling us that.

II **THE ROBOT REPLY** (Yale): Suppose we wrote a different kind of program from Schank's program. Suppose we put a computer inside a robot, and this computer would not just take in formal symbols as input and give out formal symbols as output, but rather it would actually operate the robot in such a way that the robot does something very much like perceiving, walking, moving about, hammering nails, eating, drinking—anything you like. The robot would, for example, have a television camera attached to it that enabled it to see, it would have arms and legs that enabled it to act, and all of this would be controlled by its computer brain. Such a robot would, unlike Schank's computer, have genuine understanding and other mental states.

The first thing to notice about the robot reply is that it tacitly concedes that cognition is not solely a matter of formal symbol manipulation, since this reply adds a set of causal relations with the outside world. But the answer to the robot reply is that the addition of such "perceptual" and "motor" capacities adds nothing by way of understanding, in particular, or intentionality, in general, to Schank's original program. To see this, notice that the same thought experiment applies to the robot case. Suppose that, instead of the computer inside the robot, you put me inside the room and you give me again, as in the original Chinese case, more Chinese symbols with more instructions in English for matching Chinese symbols to Chinese symbols and feeding back Chinese symbols to the outside.

Now suppose also that, unknown to me, some of the Chinese symbols that come to me come from a television camera attached to the robot, and other Chinese symbols that I am giving out serve to make the motors inside the robot move the robot's legs or arms. It is important to emphasize that all I am doing is manipulating formal symbols; I know none of these other facts. I am receiving "information" from the robot's "perceptual" apparatus, and I am giving out "instructions" to its motor apparatus without knowing either of these facts. I am the robot's homunculus, but unlike the traditional homunculus, I don't know what's going on. I don't understand anything except the rules for symbol manipulation. Now in this case I want to say that the robot has no intentional states at all; it is simply moving about as a result of its electrical wiring and its program. And furthermore, by instantiating the program, I have no intentional states of the relevant type. All I do is follow formal instructions about manipulating formal symbols.

III **THE BRAIN-SIMULATOR REPLY** (Berkeley and MIT): Suppose we design a program that doesn't represent information that we have about the world, such as the information in Schank's scripts, but simulates the actual sequence of neuron firings at the synapses of the brain of a native Chinese speaker when he understands stories in Chinese and gives answers to them. The machine takes in Chinese stories and questions about them as input, it simulates the formal structure of actual Chinese brains in processing these stories, and it gives out Chinese answers as outputs. We can even imagine that the machine operates not with a single serial program but with a whole set of programs operating in parallel, in the manner that actual human brains presumably operate when they process natural language. Now surely in such a case we would have to say that the machine understood the stories; and if we refuse to say that, wouldn't we also have to deny that native Chinese speakers understood the stories? At the level of the synapses what would or could be different about the program of the computer and the program of the Chinese brain?

Before addressing this reply, I want to digress to note that it is an odd reply for any partisan of artificial intelligence (functionalism, and so on) to make. I thought the whole idea of strong artificial intelligence is that we don't need to know how the brain works to know how the mind works. The basic hypothesis, or so I had supposed, was that there is a level of mental operations that consists in computational processes over formal elements which constitute the essence of the mental, and can be realized in all sorts of different brain processes in the same way that any computer program can be realized in different computer hardware. On the assumptions of strong AI, the mind is to the brain as the program is to the hardware, and thus we can understand the mind without doing neurophysiology. If we had to know how the brain worked in order to do AI, we wouldn't bother with AI.

However, even getting this close to the operation of the brain is still not sufficient to produce understanding. To see that this is so, imagine that instead of a monolingual man in a room shuffling symbols we have the man operate an elaborate set of water pipes with valves connecting them. When the man receives the Chinese symbols he looks up in the program, written in English, which valves he has to turn on and off. Each water connection corresponds to a synapse in the Chinese brain, and the whole system is rigged up so that after doing all the right firings—that is, after turning on all the right faucets—the Chinese answers pop out at the output end of the series of pipes.

Now where is the understanding in this system? It takes Chinese as input, it simulates the formal structure of the synapses of the Chinese brain, and it gives Chinese as output. But the man certainly doesn't understand Chinese, and neither do the water pipes. And if we are tempted to adopt what I think is the absurd view that somehow the *conjunction* of man *and* water pipes understands, remember that in principle the man can internalize the formal structure of the water pipes and do all the "neuron firings" in his imagination. The problem with the brain simulator is that it is simulating the wrong things about the brain. As long as it simulates only the formal structure of the sequence of neuron firings at the synapses, it won't have simulated what matters about the brain: its ability to produce intentional states. And that the formal properties are not sufficient for the causal properties is shown by the water pipe example. We can have all the formal properties carved off from the relevant neurobiological causal properties.

IV THE COMBINATION REPLY (Berkeley and Stanford): While each of the previous three replies might not be completely convincing by itself as a refutation of the Chinese room counter-example, if you take all three together they are collectively much more convincing and even decisive. Imagine a robot with a brain-shaped computer lodged in its cranial cavity; imagine the computer programmed with all the synapses of a human brain; imagine that the whole behavior of the robot is indistinguishable from human behavior; and now think of the whole thing as a unified system and not just as a computer with inputs and outputs. Surely in such a case we would have to ascribe intentionality to the system.

I entirely agree that in such a case we would find it rational and indeed irresistible to accept the hypothesis that the robot had intentionality, as long as we knew nothing more about it. Indeed, besides appearance and behavior, the other elements of the combination are really irrelevant. If we could build a robot whose behavior was indistinguishable over a large range from human behavior, we would attribute intentionality to it, pending some reason not to. We wouldn't need to know in advance that its computer brain was a formal analogue of the human brain.

But I really don't see that this is any help to the claims of strong AI, and here is why. According to strong AI, instantiating a formal program with the right input and output is a sufficient condition of, indeed is constitutive of, intentionality. As Newell (1980) puts it, the essence of the mental is the operation of a physical symbol system (see also Chapter 3 of this volume). But the attributions of intentionality that we make to the robot in this example have nothing to do with formal programs. They are simply based on the assumption that if the robot looks and behaves sufficiently like us, we would suppose, until proven otherwise, that it must have mental states like ours, which cause and are expressed by its behavior, and it must have an inner mechanism capable of producing such mental states. If we knew independently how to account for its behavior without such assumptions, we would not attribute intentionality to it, especially if we knew it had a formal program. And this is the point of my earlier response to the robot reply.

Suppose we knew that the robot's behavior was entirely accounted for by the fact that a man inside it was receiving uninterpreted formal symbols from the robot's sensory receptors and sending out uninterpreted formal symbols to its motor mechanisms, and the man was doing this symbol manipulation in accordance with a bunch of rules. Furthermore, suppose the man knows none of these facts about the robot; all he knows is which operations to perform on which meaningless symbols. In such a case we would regard the robot as an ingenious mechanical dummy. The hypothesis that the dummy has a mind would now be unwarranted and unnecessary, for there is now no longer any reason to ascribe intentionality to the robot or to the system of which it is a part (except of course for the man's intentionality in manipulating the symbols). The formal symbol manipulations go on, the input and output are correctly matched, but the only real locus of intentionality is the man, and he doesn't know any of the relevant intentional states; he doesn't, for example, *see* what comes into the robot's eyes, he doesn't *intend* to move the robot's arm, and he doesn't *understand* any of the remarks made to or by the robot. Nor, for the reasons stated earlier, does the system of which man and robot are a part.

To see the point, contrast this case with cases where we find it completely natural to ascribe intentionality to members of certain other primate species, such as apes and monkeys, and to domestic animals, such as dogs. The reasons we find it natural are, roughly, two: we can't make sense of the animal's behavior without the ascription of intentionality, and we can see that the beasts are made of stuff similar to our own—an eye, a nose, its skin, and so on. Given the coherence of the animal's behavior and the assumption of the same causal stuff underlying it, we assume both that the animal must have mental states underlying its behavior, and that the mental states must be produced by mechanisms made out of the stuff that is like our stuff. We would certainly make similar assumptions about the robot unless we had some reason not to; but as soon as we knew that the behavior was the result of a formal program, and that the actual causal properties of the physical substance were irrelevant, we would abandon the assumption of intentionality.

There are two other responses to my example which come up frequently (and so are worth discussing) but really miss the point.

V THE OTHER-MINDS REPLY (Yale): How do you know that other people understand Chinese or anything else? Only by their behavior. Now the computer can pass the behavior tests as well as they can (in principle), so if you are going to attribute cognition to other people, you must in principle also attribute it to computers.

The objection is worth only a short reply. The problem in this discussion is not about how I know that other people have cognitive states, but rather what it is that I am attributing to them when I attribute cognitive states to them. The thrust of the argument is that it couldn't be just computational processes and their output because there can be computational processes and their output without the cognitive state. It is no answer to this argument to feign anesthesia. In "cognitive sciences" one presupposes the reality and knowability of the mental in the same way that in physical sciences one has to presuppose the reality and knowability of physical objects.

VI THE MANY-MANSIONS REPLY (Berkeley): Your whole argument presupposes that AI is only about analogue and digital computers. But that just happens to be the present state of technology. Whatever these causal processes are that you say are essential for intentionality (assuming you are right), eventually we will be able to build devices that have these causal processes, and that will be artificial intelligence. So your arguments are in no way directed at the ability of artificial intelligence to produce and explain cognition.

I have no objection to this reply except to say that it in effect trivializes the project of strong artificial intelligence by redefining it as whatever artificially produces and explains cognition. The interest of the original claim made on behalf of artificial intelligence is that it was a precise, well defined thesis: mental processes are computational processes over formally defined elements. I have been concerned to challenge that thesis. If the claim is redefined so that it is no longer that thesis, my objections no longer apply, because there is no longer a testable hypothesis for them to apply to.

Let us now return to the questions I promised I would try to answer. Granted that in my original example I understand the English and I do not understand the Chinese, and granted therefore that the machine doesn't understand either English or Chinese, still there must be something about me that makes it the case that I understand English, and a corresponding something lacking in me which makes it the case that I fail to understand Chinese. Now why couldn't we give the former something, whatever it is, to a machine?

I see no reason in principle why we couldn't give a machine the capacity to understand English or Chinese, since in an important sense our bodies with our brains are precisely such machines. But I do see very strong arguments for saying that we could not give such a thing to a machine where the operation of the machine is defined solely in terms of computational processes over formally defined elements—that is, where the operation of the machine is defined as an instantiation of a computer program. It is not because I am the instantiation of a computer program that I am able to understand English and have other forms of intentionality. (I am, I suppose, the instantiation of any number of computer programs.) Rather, as far as we know, it is because I am a certain sort of organism with a certain biological (that is, chemical and physical) structure, and this structure under certain conditions is causally capable of producing perception, action, understanding, learning, and other intentional phenomena. And part of the point of the present argument is that only something that had those causal powers could have that intentionality. Perhaps other physical and chemical processes could produce exactly these effects; perhaps, for example, Martians also have intentionality, but their brains are made of different stuff. That is an empirical question, rather like the question whether photosynthesis can be done by something with a chemistry different from that of chlorophyll.

But the main point of the present argument is that no purely formal model will ever be by itself sufficient for intentionality, because the formal properties are not by themselves constitutive of intentionality, and they have by themselves no causal powers except the power, when instantiated, to produce the next state of the formalism when the machine is running. And any other causal properties which particular realizations of the formal model have are irrelevant to the formal model, because we can always put the same formal model in a different realization where those causal properties are obviously absent. Even if by some miracle Chinese speakers exactly realize Schank's program, we can put the same program in English speakers, water pipes, or computers, none of which understand Chinese, the program notwithstanding.

What matters about brain operation is not the formal shadow cast by the sequence of synapses but rather the actual properties of the sequences. All arguments for the strong version of artificial intelligence that I have seen insist on drawing an outline around the shadows cast by cognition and then claiming that the shadows are the real thing.

By way of concluding I want to state some of the general philosophical points implicit in the argument. For clarity I will try to do it in a question-and-answer fashion, and I begin with that old chestnut:

• Could a machine think?

The answer is, obviously: Yes. We are precisely such machines.

• Yes, but could an artifact, a man-made machine, think?

Assuming it is possible to produce artificially a machine with a nervous system, neurons with axons and dendrites, and all the rest of it, sufficiently like ours, again the answer to the question seems to be obviously: Yes. If you can exactly duplicate the causes, you can duplicate the effects. And indeed it might be possible to produce consciousness, intentionality, and all the rest of it, using chemical principles different from those human beings use. It is, as I said, an empirical question.

• OK, but could a digital computer think?

If by "digital computer" we mean anything at all which has a level of description where it can correctly be described as the instantiation of a computer program, then, since we are the instantiations of any number of computer programs and we can think, again the answer is, of course: Yes.

• But could something think, understand, and so on, *solely by virtue of* being a computer with the right sort of program? Could instantiating a program, the right program of course, by itself be a sufficient condition for understanding?

This I think is the right question to ask, though it is usually confused with one or more of the earlier questions, and the answer to it is: No.

• Why not?

Because the formal symbol manipulations by themselves don't have any intentionality. They are meaningless—they aren't even *symbol* manipulations, since the "symbols" don't symbolize anything. In the linguistic jargon, they have only a syntax but no semantics. Such intentionality as computers appear to have is solely in the minds of those who program them and those who use them, those who send in the input and who interpret the output.

The aim of the Chinese room example was to try to show this by showing that, as soon as we put something into the system which really does have intentionality, a man, and we program the man with the formal program, you can see that the formal program carries no additional intentionality. It adds nothing, for example, to a man's ability to understand Chinese.

Precisely that feature of AI which seemed so appealing—the distinction between the program and the realization—proves fatal to the claim that simulation could be duplication. The distinction between the program and its realization in the hardware seems to be parallel to the distinction between the level of mental operations and the level of brain operations. And if we could describe the level of mental operations as a formal program, it seems we could describe what was essential about the mind without doing either introspective psychology or neurophysiology of the brain. But the equation "Mind is to brain as program is to hardware" breaks down at several points, among them the following three.

First, the distinction between program and realization has the consequence that the same program could have all sorts of crazy realizations which have no form of intentionality.

Weizenbaum (1976), for example, shows in detail how to construct a computer using a roll of toilet paper and a pile of small stones. Similarly, the Chinese story-understanding program can be programmed into a sequence of water pipes, a set of wind machines, or a monolingual English speaker—none of which thereby acquires an understanding of Chinese. Stones, toilet paper, wind, and water pipes are the wrong kind of stuff to have intentionality in the first place (only something that has the same causal powers as brains can have intentionality), and, though the English speaker has the right kind of stuff for intentionality, you can easily see that he doesn't get any extra intentionality by memorizing the program, since memorizing it won't teach him Chinese.

Second, the program is purely formal, but the intentional states are not in that way formal. They are defined in terms of their content, not their form. The belief that it is raining, for example, if defined not as a certain formal shape, but as a certain mental content, with conditions of satisfaction, a direction of fit, and so on (see Searle, 1979). Indeed, the belief as such hasn't even got a formal shape in this syntactical sense, since one and the same belief can be given an indefinite number of different syntactical expressions in different linguistic systems.

Third, as I mentioned before, mental states and events are a product of the operation of the brain, but the program is not in that way a product of the computer.

• Well if programs are in no way constitutive of mental processes, then why have so many people believed the converse? That at least needs some explanation.

I don't know the answer to that. The idea that computer simulations could be the real thing ought to have seemed suspicious in the first place, because the computer isn't confined to simulating mental operations, by any means. No one supposes that computer simulations of a fire-alarm fire will burn the neighborhood down, or that a computer simulation of a rainstorm will leave us all drenched. Why on earth would anyone suppose that a computer simulation of understanding actually understood anything? It is sometimes said that it would be frightfully hard to get computers to feel pain or fall in love, but love and pain are neither harder nor easier than cognition or anything else. For simulation, all you need is the right input and output and a program in the middle that transforms the former into the latter. That is all the computer has for anything it does. To confuse simulation with duplication is the same mistake, whether it is pain, love, cognition, fires, or rainstorms.

Still, there are several reasons why AI must have seemed, and to many people perhaps still does seem in some way to reproduce and thereby explain mental phenomena. And I believe we will not succeed in removing these illusions until we have fully exposed the reasons that give rise to them.

First, and perhaps most important, is a confusion about the notion of "information processing". Many people in cognitive science believe that the human brain with its mind does something called "information processing", and, analogously, the computer with its program does information processing; but fires and rainstorms, on the other hand, don't do information processing at all. Thus, though the computer can simulate the formal features of any process whatever, it stands in a special relation to the mind and brain because, when the computer is properly programmed, ideally with the same program as the brain, the information processing is identical in the two cases, and this information processing is really the essence of the mental.

But the trouble with this argument is that it rests on an ambiguity in the notion of "information". In the sense in which people "process information" when they reflect, say, on problems in arithmetic or when they read and answer questions about stories, the programmed computer does not do "information processing". Rather, what it does is manipulate formal symbols. The fact that the programmer and the interpreter of the computer output use the symbols to stand for objects in the world is totally beyond the scope of the computer. The computer, to repeat, has a syntax but no semantics. Thus if you type into the computer "2 plus 2 equals?" it will type out "4". But it has no idea that '4' means 4, or that it means anything at all. And the point is not that it lacks some second-order information about the interpretation of its first-order symbols, but rather that its first-order symbols don't have any interpretations as far as the computer is concerned. All the computer has is more symbols.

The introduction of the notion of "information processing" therefore produces a dilemma. Either we construe the notion of "information processing" in such a way that it implies intentionality as part of the process, or we don't. If the former, then the programmed computer does not do information processing, it only manipulates formal symbols. If the latter, then, although the computer does information processing, it is only in the sense in which adding machines, typewriters, stomachs, thermostats, rainstorms, and hurricanes do information processing—namely, in the sense that there is a level of description at which we can describe them as taking information in at one end, transforming it, and producing information as output. But in this case it is up to outside observers to interpret the input and output as information in the ordinary sense. And no similarity is established between the computer and the brain in terms of any similarity of information processing in either of the two cases.

Secondly, in much of AI there is a residual behaviorism or operationalism. Since appropriately programmed computers can have input/output patterns similar to human beings, we are tempted to postulate mental states in the computer similar to human mental states. But once we see that it is both conceptually and empirically possible for a system to have human capacities in some realm without having any intentionality at all, we should be able to overcome this impulse. My desk adding machine has calculating capacities but no intentionality; and in this paper I have tried to show that a system could have input and output capabilities which duplicated those of a native Chinese speaker and still not understand Chinese, regardless of how it was programmed. The Turing test is typical of the tradition in being unashamedly behavioristic and operationalistic, and I believe that if AI workers totally repudiated behaviorism and operationalism, much of the confusion between simulation and duplication would be eliminated.

Third, this residual operationalism is joined to a residual form of dualism; indeed, strong AI only makes sense given the dualistic assumption that where the mind is concerned the brain doesn't matter. In strong AI (and in functionalism, as well) what matters are programs, and programs are independent of their realization in machines; indeed, as far as AI is concerned, the same program could be realized by an electronic machine, a Cartesian mental substance, or an Hegelian world spirit. The single most surprising discovery that I have made in discussing these issues is that many AI workers are shocked by my idea that actual human mental phenomena might be dependent on actual physical-chemical properties of actual human brains. But I should not have been surprised; for unless you accept some form of dualism, the strong-AI project hasn't got a chance.

The project is to reproduce and explain the mental by designing programs; but unless the mind is not only conceptually but empirically independent of the brain, you cannot carry out the project, for the program is completely independent of any realization. Unless you believe that the mind is separable from the brain both conceptually and empirically— dualism in a strong form—you cannot hope to reproduce the mental by writing and running programs, since programs must be independent of brains or any other particular forms of instantiation. If mental operations consist of computational operations on formal symbols, it follows that they have no interesting connection with the brain, and the only connection would be that the brain just happens to be one of the indefinitely many types of machines capable of instantiating the program. This form of dualism is not the traditional Cartesian variety that claims there are two sorts of *substances*, but it is Cartesian in the sense that it insists that what is specifically mental about the mind has no intrinsic connection with the actual properties of the brain. This underlying dualism is masked from us by the fact that AI literature contains frequent fulminations against "dualism". What the authors seem to be unaware of is that their position presupposes a strong version of dualism.

• Could a machine think?

My own view is that *only* a machine could think, and indeed only very special kinds of machines, namely brains and machines that had the *same causal powers* as brains. And that is the main reason why strong AI has had little to tell us about thinking: it has nothing to tell us about machines. By its own definition it is about programs, and programs are not machines. Whatever else intentionality is, it is a biological phenomenon, and it is likely to be as causally dependent on the specific biochemistry of its origins as are lactation, photosynthesis, or any biological phenomena. No one would suppose that we could produce milk and sugar by running a computer simulation of the formal sequences in lactation and photosynthesis; but where the mind is concerned, many people are willing to believe in such a miracle, because of a deep and abiding dualism: the mind, they suppose, is a matter of formal processes and is independent of specific material causes in a way that milk and sugar are not.

In defense of this dualism, the hope is often expressed that the brain is a digital computer. (Early computers, by the way, were often called "electronic brains".) But that is no help. Of course the brain is a digital computer. Since everything is a digital computer, brains are too. The point is that the brain's causal capacity to produce intentionality cannot consist in its instantiating a computer program, since for any program you like it is possible for something to instantiate that program and still not have any mental states. Whatever it is that the brain does to produce intentionality, it cannot consist in instantiating a program, since no program by itself is sufficient for intentionality.

Notes for Chapter 12

1. I am not saying, of course, that Schank himself is committed to these claims.

2. Also, "understanding" implies both the possession of mental (intentional) states and the truth (validity, success) of these states. For the purposes of this discussion, we are concerned only with the possession of the states.

3. Intentionality is by definition that feature of certain mental states by which they are directed at or are about objects and states of affairs in the world. Thus, beliefs, desires, and intentions are intentional states; undirected forms of anxiety and depression are not. (For further discussion, see Searle, 1979).

Escaping from the Chinese Room

13

Margaret Boden
1988

John Searle, in his paper on 'Minds, Brains, and Programs' (1980; Chapter 12 in this volume), argues that computational theories in psychology are essentially worthless. He makes two main claims: that computational theories, being purely formal in nature, cannot possibly help us to understand mental processes; and that computer hardware—unlike neuroprotein—obviously lacks the right causal powers to generate mental processes. I shall argue that both these claims are mistaken.

His first claim takes for granted the widely-held (formalist) assumption that the 'computations' studied in computer science are purely syntactic, that they can be defined (in terms equally suited to symbolic logic) as *the formal manipulation of abstract symbols, by the application of formal rules*. It follows, he says, that formalist accounts—appropriate in explaining the meaningless 'information'-processing or 'symbol'-manipulations in computers—are unable to explain how human minds employ *information* or *symbols* properly so-called. Meaning, or intentionality, cannot be explained in computational terms.

Searle's point here is not that no machine can think. Humans can think, and humans—he allows—are machines; he even adopts the materialist credo that only machines can think. Nor is he saying that humans and programs are utterly incommensurable. He grants that, at some highly abstract level of description, people (like everything else) are instantiations of digital computers. His point, rather, is that nothing can think, mean, or understand *solely* in virtue of its instantiating a computer program.

To persuade us of this, Searle employs an ingenious thought-experiment. He imagines himself locked in a room, in which there are various slips of paper with doodles on them; a window through which people can pass further doodle-papers to him, and through which he can pass papers out; and a book of rules (in English) telling him how to pair the doodles, which are always identified by their shape or form. Searle spends his time, while inside the room, manipulating the doodles according to the rules.

One rule, for example, instructs him that when *squiggle-squiggle* is passed in to him, he should give out *squoggle-squoggle*. The rule-book also provides for more complex sequences of doodle-pairing, where only the first and last steps mention the transfer of paper into or out of the room. Before finding any rule directly instructing him to give out a slip of paper, he may have to locate a *blongle* doodle and compare it with a *blungle* doodle—in which case, it is the result of this comparison which determines the nature of the doodle he passes out. Sometimes many such doodle-doodle comparisons and consequent doodle-selections have to be made by him inside the room before he finds a rule allowing him to pass anything out.

So far as Searle-in-the-room is concerned, the *squiggles* and *squoggles* are mere meaningless doodles. Unknown to him, however, they are Chinese characters. The people outside the room, being Chinese, interpret them as such. Moreover, the patterns passed in and out at the window are understood by them as *questions* and *answers* respectively: the rules happen to be such that most of the questions are paired, either directly or indirectly, with what they recognize as a sensible answer. But Searle himself (inside the room) knows nothing of this.

The point, says Searle, is that Searle-in-the-room is clearly instantiating a computer program. That is, he is performing purely formal manipulations of uninterpreted patterns: he is all syntax and no semantics.

The doodle-pairing rules are equivalent to the IF-THEN rules, or 'productions', commonly used (for example) in expert systems. Some of the internal doodle-comparisons could be equivalent to what AI workers in natural-language processing call a script—for instance, the restaurant script described by R. C. Schank and R. P. Abelson (1977b). In that case, Searle-in-the-room's paper-passing performance would be essentially comparable to the performance of a 'question-answering' Schankian text-analysis program. But 'question-answering' is not question-answering. Searle-in-the-room is not really *answering*: how could he, since he cannot understand the questions? Practice does not help (except perhaps in making the doodle-pairing swifter): if Searle-in-the-room ever escapes, he will be just as ignorant of Chinese as he was when he was first locked in.

Certainly, the Chinese people outside might find it useful to keep Searle-in-the-room fed and watered, much as in real life we are willing to spend large sums of money on computerized 'advice' systems. But the fact that people who already possess understanding may use an intrinsically meaningless formalist computational system to provide what they interpret *(sic)* as questions, answers, designations, interpretations, or symbols is irrelevant. They can do this only if they can externally specify a mapping between the formalism and matters of interest to them. In principle, one and the same formalism might be mappable onto several different domains, so could be used (by people) in answering questions about any of those domains. In itself, however, it would be meaningless—as are the Chinese symbols from the point of view of Searle-in-the-room.

It follows, Searle argues, that no system can understand anything solely in virtue of its instantiating a computer program. For if it could, then Searle-in-the-room would understand

Chinese. Hence, theoretical psychology cannot properly be grounded in computational concepts.

Searle's second claim concerns what a proper explanation of understanding would be like. According to him, it would acknowledge that meaningful symbols must be embodied in something having 'the right causal powers' for generating understanding, or intentionality. Obviously, he says, brains do have such causal powers whereas computers do not. More precisely (since the brain's organization could be paralleled in a computer), neuroprotein does whereas metal and silicon do not: the biochemical properties of the brain matter are crucial.

A. Newell's (1980; see also Chapter 3 of this volume) widely cited definition of 'physical-symbol systems' is rejected by Searle, because it demands merely that symbols be embodied in some material that can implement formalist computations—which computers, admittedly, can do. In Searle's view, no electronic computer can really manipulate symbols, nor really designate or interpret anything at all—*irrespective* of any causal dependencies linking its internal physical patterns to its behaviour. (This strongly realist view of intentionality contrasts with the instrumentalism of D. C. Dennett (1971; see also Chapter 11 of this volume). For Dennett, an intentional system is one whose behaviour we can explain, predict, and control only by ascribing beliefs, goals, and rationality to it. On this criterion, some *existing* computer programs are intentional systems, and the hypothetical humanoids beloved of science-fiction would be intentional systems *a fortiori*.)

Intentionality, Searle declares, is a biological phenomenon. As such, it is just as dependent on the underlying biochemistry as are photosynthesis and lactation. He grants that neuroprotein may not be the only substances in the universe capable of supporting mental life, much as substances other than chlorophyll may be able (on Mars, perhaps) to catalyse the synthesis of carbohydrates. But he rejects metal or silicon as potential alternatives, even on Mars. He asks whether a computer made out of old beer-cans could possibly *understand*—a rhetorical question to which the expected answer is a resounding 'No!' In short, Searle takes it to be intuitively obvious that the inorganic substances with which (today's) computers are manufactured are essentially incapable of supporting mental functions.

In assessing Searle's two-pronged critique of computational psychology, let us first consider his view that intentionality must be biologically grounded. One might be tempted to call this a positive claim, in contrast with his (negative) claim that purely formalist theories cannot explain mentality. However, this would be to grant it more than it deserves, for its explanatory power is illusory. The biological analogies mentioned by Searle are misleading, and the intuitions to which he appeals are unreliable.

The brain's production of intentionality, we are told, is comparable to photosynthesis—but is it, really? We can define the *products* of photosynthesis, clearly distinguishing various sugars and starches within the general class of carbohydrates, and showing how these differ from other biochemical products such as proteins. Moreover, we not only *know that* chlorophyll supports photosynthesis, we also *understand how* it does so (and *why* various other chemicals cannot). We know that it is a catalyst rather than a raw material; and we can specify the point at which, and the subatomic process by which, its catalytic function is exercised. With respect to brains and understanding, the case is very different.

Our theory of what intentionality is (never mind how it is generated) does not bear comparison with our knowledge of carbohydrates: just what intentionality *is* is still philosophically controversial. We cannot even be entirely confident that we can recognize it when we see it. It is generally agreed that the propositional attitudes are intentional, and that feelings and sensations are not; but there is no clear consensus about the intentionality of emotions.

Various attempts have been made to characterize intentionality and to distinguish its subspecies as distinct intentional states (beliefs, desires, hopes, intentions, and the like). Searle himself has made a number of relevant contributions, from his early work on speech-acts (1969) to his more recent account (1983) of intentionality in general. A commonly used criterion (adopted by Brentano in the nineteenth century and also by Searle) is a *psychological* one. In Brentano's words, intentional states direct the mind on an object; in Searle's, they have intrinsic representational capacity, or 'aboutness'; in either case they relate the mind to the world, and to possible worlds. But some writers define intentionality in logical terms (Chisholm, 1967). It is not even clear whether the logical and psychological definitions are precisely co-extensive (Boden, 1970). In brief, no theory of intentionality is accepted as unproblematic, as the chemistry of carbohydrates is.

As for the brain's biochemical 'synthesis' of intentionality, this is even more mysterious. We have very good reason to believe *that* neuroprotein supports intentionality, but we have hardly any idea *how*—*qua* neuroprotein—it is able to do so.

In so far as we understand these matters at all, we focus on the neurochemical basis of certain *informational functions*—such as message-passing, facilitation, and inhibition—embodied in neurones and synapses. For example: how the sodium-pump at the cell-membrane enables an action potential to propagate along the axon; how electrochemical changes cause a neurone to enter into and recover from its refractory period; or how neuronal thresholds can be altered by neurotransmitters, such as acetylcholine.

With respect to a visual cell, for instance, a crucial psychological question may be *whether it can function so as to detect intensity-gradients*. If the neurophysiologist can tell us which molecules enable it to do so, so much the better. But from the psychological point of view, it is not the biochemistry as such which matters but the information-bearing functions grounded in it. (Searle apparently admits this when he says, 'The type of realizations that intentional states have in the brain may be describable at a much higher functional level than that of the specific biochemistry of the neurons involved' (1983, 272).)

As work in 'computer vision' has shown, metal and silicon are undoubtedly able to support some of the functions necessary for the 2D-to-3D mapping involved in vision. Moreover, they can embody specific mathematical functions for recognizing intensity-gradients (namely 'DOG-detectors', which compute the difference of Gaussians) which seem to be involved in many biological visual systems. Admittedly, it may be that metal and silicon cannot support all the functions involved in normal vision, or in understanding generally. Perhaps only neuroprotein can do so, so that only creatures with a 'terrestrial' biology can enjoy intentionality. But we have no specific reason, at present, to think so. Most important in this context, any such reasons we might have in the future must be grounded in empirical discovery: intuitions will not help.

If one asks which mind-matter dependencies are intuitively plausible, the answer must be that *none* is. Nobody who was puzzled about intentionality (as opposed to action-potentials) ever exclaimed 'Sodium—of course!' Sodium-pumps are no less 'obviously' absurd than silicon chips, electrical polarities no less 'obviously' irrelevant than old beer-cans, acetylcholine hardly less surprising than beer. The fact that the first member of each of these three pairs is *scientifically* compelling does not make any of them *intuitively* intelligible: our initial surprise persists.

Our intuitions might change with the advance of science. Possibly we shall eventually see neuroprotein (and perhaps silicon too) as obviously capable of embodying mind, much as we now see biochemical substances in general (including chlorophyll) as obviously capable of producing other such substances—an intuition that was not obvious, even to chemists, prior to the synthesis of urea. At present, however, our intuitions have nothing useful to say about the material basis of intentionality. Searle's 'positive' claim, his putative alternative explanation of intentionality, is at best a promissory note, at worst mere mystery-mongering.

Searle's negative claim—that formal-computational theories cannot explain understanding—is less quickly rebutted. My rebuttal will involve two parts: the first directly addressing his example of the Chinese room, the second dealing with his background assumption (on which his example depends) that computer programs are pure syntax.

The Chinese-room example has engendered much debate, both within and outside the community of cognitive science. Some criticisms were anticipated by Searle himself in his original paper, others appeared as the accompanying peer-commentary (together with his Reply), and more have been published since. Here, I shall concentrate on only two points: what Searle calls the Robot reply, and what I shall call the English reply.

The Robot reply accepts that the only understanding of Chinese which exists in Searle's example is that enjoyed by the Chinese people outside the room. Searle-in-the-room's inability to connect Chinese characters with events in the outside world shows that he does not understand Chinese. Likewise, a Schankian teletyping computer that cannot recognize a restaurant, hand money to a waiter, or chew a morsel of food understands nothing of restaurants—even if it can usefully 'answer' our questions about them. But a robot, provided not only with a restaurant-script but also with camera-fed visual programs and limbs capable of walking and picking things up, would be another matter. If the input-output behaviour of such a robot were identical with that of human beings, then it would demonstrably understand both restaurants and the natural language—Chinese, perhaps—used by people to communicate with it.

Searle's first response to the Robot reply is to claim a victory already, since the reply concedes that cognition is not solely a matter of formal symbol-manipulation but requires in addition a set of causal relations with the outside world. Second, Searle insists that to add perceptuomotor capacities to a computational system is not to add intentionality, or understanding.

He argues this point by imagining a robot which, instead of being provided with a computer program to make it work, has a miniaturized Searle inside it—in its skull, perhaps. Searle-in-the-robot, with the aid of a (new) rule-book, shuffles paper and passes *squiggles* and *squoggles* in and out, much as Searle-in-the-room did before him. But now some or all of the incoming Chinese characters are not handed in by Chinese people, but are triggered by causal processes in the cameras and audio-equipment in the robot's eyes and ears. And the outgoing Chinese characters are not received by Chinese hands, but by motors and levers attached to the robot's limbs—which are caused to move as a result. In short, this robot is apparently able not only to answer questions in Chinese, but also to see and do things accordingly: it can recognize raw beansprouts and, if the recipe requires it, toss them into a wok as well as the rest of us.

(The work on computer vision mentioned above suggests that the vocabulary of Chinese would require considerable extension for this example to be carried through. And the large body of AI research on language-processing suggests that the same could be said of the English required to express the rules in Searle's initial 'question-answering' example. In either case, what Searle-in-the-room needs is not so much Chinese, or even English, as a programming-language. We shall return to this point presently.)

Like his roombound predecessor, however, Searle-in-the-robot knows nothing of the wider context. He is just as ignorant of Chinese as he ever was, and has no more purchase on the outside world than he did in the original example. To him, beansprouts and woks are invisible and intangible: all Searle-in-the-robot can see and touch, besides the rule-book and the doodles, are his own body and the inside walls of the robot's skull. Consequently, Searle argues, the robot cannot be credited with understanding of any of these worldly matters. In truth, it is not *seeing* or *doing* anything at all: it is 'simply moving about as a result of its electrical wiring and its program', which latter is instantiated by the man inside it, who 'has no intentional states of the relevant type' (1980, 420).

Searle's argument here is unacceptable as a rebuttal of the Robot reply, because it draws a false analogy between the imagined example and what is claimed by computational psychology.

Searle-in-the-robot is supposed by Searle to be performing the functions performed (according to computational theories) by the human brain. But, whereas most computationalists do not ascribe intentionality to the brain (and those who do, as we shall see presently, do so only in a very limited way), Searle characterizes Searle-in-the-robot as enjoying full-blooded intentionality, just as he does himself. Computational psychology does not credit the brain with *seeing beansprouts* or *understanding English*: intentional states such as these are properties of people, not of brains. In general, although representations and mental processes are assumed (by computationalists and Searle alike) to be embodied in the brain, the sensorimotor capacities and propositional attitudes which they make possible are ascribed to the person as a whole. So Searle's description of the system inside the robot's skull as one which can understand English does not truly parallel what computationalists say about the brain.

Indeed, the specific procedures hypothesized by computational psychologists, and embodied by them in computer models of the mind, are relatively stupid—and they become more and more stupid as one moves to increasingly basic theoretical levels. Consider theories of natural-language parsing, for example. A parsing procedure that searches for a determiner does not understand English, and nor does a procedure for locating the reference of a personal pronoun: only the person whose brain performs these interpretive processes, and many others associated with them, can do that. The capacity to understand English involves a host of interacting information processes, each of which performs only a very limited function but which together provide the capacity to take English sentences as input and give appropriate English sentences as output. Similar remarks apply to the individual components of computational theories of vision, problem-solving, or learning. Precisely because psychologists wish to *explain* human language, vision, reasoning, and learning, they posit underlying processes which lack the capacities.

In short, Searle's description of the robot's pseudo-brain (that is, of Searle-in-the-robot) as understanding English involves a category-mistake comparable to treating the brain as the bearer—as opposed to the causal basis—of intelligence.

Someone might object here that I have contradicted myself, that I am claiming that one cannot ascribe intentionality to brains and yet am implicitly doing just that. For I spoke of the brain's effecting 'stupid' component-procedures—but stupidity is virtually a *species* of intelligence. To be stupid is to be intelligent, but not very (a person or a fish can be stupid, but a stone or a river cannot).

My defence would be twofold. First, the most basic theoretical level of all would be at the neuroscientific equivalent of the machine-code, a level 'engineered' by evolution. The facts that a certain light-sensitive cell *can* respond to intensity-gradients by acting as a

DOG-detector and that one neurone *can* inhibit the firing of another, are explicable by the biochemistry of the brain. The notion of stupidity, even in scare-quotes, is wholly inappropriate in discussing such facts. However, these very basic information-processing functions (DOG-detecting and synaptic inhibition) *could* properly be described as 'very, very, very . . . stupid'. This of course implies that intentional language, if only of a highly grudging and uncomplimentary type, is applicable to brain processes after all—which prompts the second point in my defence. I did not say that intentionality cannot be ascribed to brains, but that full-blooded intentionality cannot. Nor did I say that brains cannot understand anything at all, in howsoever limited a fashion, but that they cannot (for example) understand English. I even hinted, several paragraphs ago, that a few computationalists do ascribe some degree of intentionality to the brain (or to the computational processes going on in the brain). These two points will be less obscure after we have considered the English reply and its bearing on Searle's background assumption that formal-syntactic computational theories are purely syntactic.

The crux of the English reply is that the instantiation of a computer program, whether by man or by manufactured machine, does involve understanding—at least of the rule-book. Searle's initial example depends critically on Searle-in-the-room's being able to understand the language in which the rules are written, namely English; similarly, without Searle-in-the-robot's familiarity with English, the robot's beansprouts would never get thrown into the wok. Moreover, as remarked above, the vocabulary of English (and, for Searle-in-the-robot, of Chinese too) would have to be significantly modified to make the example work.

An unknown language (whether Chinese or Linear B) can be dealt with only as an aesthetic object or a set of systematically related forms. Artificial languages can be designed and studied, by the logician or the pure mathematician, with only their structural properties in mind (although D. R. Hofstadter's (1979) example of the quasi-arithmetical pq-system shows that a psychologically compelling, and predictable, interpretation of a formal calculus may arise spontaneously). But one normally responds in a very different way to the symbols of one's native tongue; indeed, it is very difficult to 'bracket' (ignore) the meanings of familiar words. The view held by computational psychologists, that natural languages can be characterized in procedural terms, is relevant here: words, clauses, and sentences can be seen as mini-programs. The symbols in a natural language one understands initiate mental activity of various kinds. To learn a language is to set up the relevant causal connections, not only between words and the world ('cat' and the thing on the mat) but between words and the many non-introspectible procedures involved in interpreting them.

Moreover, we do not need to be told *ex hypothesi* (by Searle) that Searle-in-the-room understands English: his behaviour while in the room shows clearly that he does. Or, rather, it shows that he understands a *highly limited subset* of English.

Searle-in-the-room could be suffering from total amnesia with respect to 99 per cent of Searle's English vocabulary, and it would make no difference. The only grasp of English he needs is whatever is necessary to interpret *(sic)* the rule-book—which specifies how to accept, select, compare, and give out different patterns. Unlike Searle, Searle-in-the-room does not require words like 'catalyse', 'beer-can', 'chlorophyll', and 'restaurant'. But he may need 'find', 'compare', 'two', 'triangular', and 'window' (although his understanding of these words could be much less full than Searle's). He must understand conditional sentences, if any rule states that if he sees a *squoggle* he should give out a *squiggle*. Very likely, he must understand some way of expressing negation, temporal ordering, and (especially if he is to learn to do his job faster) generalization. If the rules he uses include some which parse the Chinese sentences, then he will need words for grammatical categories too. (He will not need explicit rules for parsing English sentences, such as the parsing procedures employed in AI programs for language-processing, because he already understands English.)

In short, Searle-in-the-room needs to understand only that subset of Searle's English which is equivalent to the programming-language understood by a computer generating the same 'question-answering' input-output behaviour at the window. Similarly, Searle-in-the-robot must be able to understand whatever subset of English is equivalent to the programming-language understood by a fully computerized visuomotor robot.

The two preceding sentences may seem to beg the very question at issue. Indeed, to speak thus of the programming-language understood by a computer is seemingly self-contradictory. For Searle's basic premiss—which he assumes is accepted by all participants in the debate—is that a computer program is purely formal in nature: the computation it specifies is purely syntactic and has no intrinsic meaning or semantic content to be understood.

If we accept this premiss, the English reply sketched above can be dismissed forthwith for seeking to draw a parallel where no parallel can properly be drawn. But if we do not, if—*pace* Searle (and others (Fodor, 1980; Stich, 1983))—computer programs are not concerned only with syntax, then the English reply may be relevant after all. We must now turn to address this basic question.

Certainly, one can for certain purposes think of a computer program as an uninterpreted logical calculus. For example, one might be able to prove, by purely formal means, that a particular well-formed formula is derivable from the program's data-structures and inferential rules. Moreover, it is true that a so-called interpreter program that could take as input the list-structure '(FATHER (MAGGIE))' and return '(LEONARD)' would do so on formal criteria alone, having no way of interpreting these patterns as possibly denoting real people. Likewise, as Searle points out, programs provided with restaurant-scripts are not thereby provided with knowledge of restaurants. The existence of a mapping between a formalism and a certain domain does not in itself provide the manipulator of the formalism with any understanding of that domain.

But what must not be forgotten is that a computer program is *a program for a computer*: when a program is run on suitable hardware, the machine *does* something as a result (hence the use in computer science of the words 'instruction' and 'obey'). At the level of the machine-code the effect of the program on the computer is direct, because the machine is engineered so that a given instruction elicits a unique operation (instructions in high-level languages must be converted into machine-code instructions before they can be obeyed). A programmed instruction, then, is not a mere formal pattern—nor even a declarative statement (although it may for some purposes be thought of under either of those descriptions). It is a procedure specification that, given a suitable hardware context, can cause the procedure in question to be executed.

One might put this by saying that a programming-language is a medium not only for expressing *representations* (structures that can be written on a page or provided to a computer, some of which structures may be isomorphic with things that interest people) but also for bringing about the *representational activity* of certain machines.

One might even say that a representation is an activity rather than a structure. Many philosophers and psychologists have supposed that mental representations are intrinsically active. Among those who have recently argued for this view is Hofstadter (1985, 648), who specifically criticizes Newell's account of *symbols* as manipulable formal tokens. In his words, 'The brain itself does not 'manipulate symbols'; the brain is the medium in which the symbols are floating and in which they trigger each other.' Hofstadter expresses more sympathy for 'connectionist' than for 'formalist' psychological theories. Connectionist approaches involve parallel-processing systems broadly reminiscent of the brain, and are well suited to model cerebral representations, symbols, or concepts, as *dynamic*. But it is not only connectionists who can view concepts as intrinsically active, and not only *cerebral* representations which can be thought of in this way: this claim has been generalized to cover traditional computer programs, specifically designed for von Neumann machines. The computer scientist B. C. Smith (1982) argues that programmed representations, too, are inherently active—and that an adequate theory of the semantics of programming-languages would recognize the fact.

At present, Smith claims, computer scientists have a radically inadequate understanding of such matters. He reminds us that, as remarked above, there is no general agreement—either within or outside computer science—about what *intentionality* is, and deep unclarities about *representation* as well. Nor can unclarities be avoided by speaking more technically, in terms of *computation* and *formal symbol-manipulation*. For the computer scientist's understanding of what these phenomena really are is also largely intuitive. Smith's discussion of programming-languages identifies some fundamental confusions within computer science. Especially relevant here is his claim that computer scientists commonly make too complete a theoretical separation between a program's control-functions and its nature as a formal-syntactic system.

The theoretical divide criticized by Smith is evident in the widespread 'dual-calculus' approach to programming. The dual-calculus approach posits a sharp theoretical distinction between a declarative (or denotational) representational structure and the procedural language that interprets it when the program is run. Indeed, the knowledge-representation and the interpreter are sometimes written in two quite distinct formalisms (such as predicate calculus and LISP, respectively). Often, however, they are both expressed in the same formalism; for example, LISP (an acronym for LISt-Processing language) allows facts and procedures to be expressed in formally similar ways, and so does PROLOG (PROgramming-in-LOGic). In such cases, the dual-calculus approach dictates that the (single) programming-language concerned be theoretically described in two quite different ways.

To illustrate the distinction at issue here, suppose that we wanted a representation of family relationships which could be used to provide answers to questions about such matters. We might decide to employ a list-structure to represent such facts as that Leonard is the father of Maggie. Or we might prefer a frame-based representation, in which the relevant name-slots in the FATHER-frame could be simultaneously filled by 'LEONARD' and 'MAGGIE'. Again, we might choose a formula of the predicate calculus, saying that there exist two people (namely, Leonard and Maggie), and Leonard is the father of Maggie. Last, we might employ the English sentence 'Leonard is the father of Maggie.'

Each of these four representations could be written/drawn on paper (as are the rules in the rule-book used by Searle-in-the-room), for us to interpret *if* we have learnt how to handle the relevant notation. Alternatively, they could be embodied in a computer database. But to make them usable by the computer, there has to be an interpreter-program which (for instance) can find the item 'LEONARD' when we 'ask' it who is the father of Maggie. No one with any sense would embody list-structures in a computer without providing it also with a *list-processing* facility, nor give it frames without a *slot-filling* mechanism, logical formulae without *rules of inference*, or English sentences without *parsing procedures*. (Analogously, people who knew that Searle speaks no Portuguese would not give Searle-in-the-room a Portuguese rule-book unless they were prepared to teach him the language first.)

Smith does not deny that there is an important distinction between the *denotational import* of an expression (broadly: what actual or possible worlds can be mapped onto it) and its *procedural consequence* (broadly: what it does, or makes happen). The fact that the expression '(FATHER (MAGGIE))' is isomorphic with a certain parental relationship between two actual people (and so might be mapped onto that relationship by us) is one thing. The fact that the expression '(FATHER (MAGGIE))' can cause a certain computer to locate 'LEONARD' is quite another thing. Were it not so, the dual-calculus approach would not have developed. But he argues that, rather than persisting with the dual-calculus approach, it would be more elegant and less confusing to adopt a 'unified' theory of programming-languages, designed to cover both denotative and procedural aspects.

He shows that many basic terms on either side of the dual-calculus divide have deep theoretical commonalities as well as significant differences. The notion of *variable*, for instance, is understood in somewhat similar fashion by the logician and the computer scientist: both allow that a variable can have different *values* assigned to it at different times. That being so, it is redundant to have two distinct theories of what a variable is. To some extent, however, logicians and computer scientists understand different things by this term: the value of a variable in the LISP programming-language (for example) is another LISP-expression, whereas the value of a variable in logic is usually some object external to the formalism itself. These differences should be clarified—not least to avoid confusion when a system attempts to reason *about* variables by *using* variables. In short, we need a single definition of 'variable', allowing both for its declarative use (in logic) and for its procedural use (in programming). Having shown that similar remarks apply to other basic computational terms, Smith outlines a unitary account of the semantics of LISP and describes a new calculus (MANTIQ) designed with the unified approach in mind.

As the example of using variables to reason about variables suggests, a unified theory of computation could illuminate how *reflective* knowledge is possible. For, given such a theory, a system's representations of data and of processes—including processes internal to the system itself—would be essentially comparable. This theoretical advantage has psychological relevance (and was a major motivation behind Smith's work).

For our present purposes, however, the crucial point is that a fundamental theory of *programs*, and of *computation*, should acknowledge that an essential function of a computer program is to make things happen. Whereas symbolic logic can be viewed as mere playing around with uninterpreted formal calculi (such as the predicate calculus), and computational logic can be seen as the study of abstract timeless relations in mathematically specified 'machines' (such as Turing machines), computer science cannot properly be described in either of these ways.

It follows from Smith's argument that the familiar characterization of computer programs as all syntax and no semantics is mistaken. The inherent procedural consequences of any computer program give it a toehold in semantics, where the semantics in question is not denotational, but causal. The analogy is with Searle-in-the-room's understanding of English, not his understanding of Chinese.

This is implied also by A. Sloman's (1986a; 1986b) discussion of the sense in which programmed instructions and computer symbols must be thought of as having some semantics, however restricted. In a causal semantics, the meaning of a symbol (whether simple or complex) is to be sought by reference to its causal links with other phenomena. The central questions are 'What causes the symbol to be built and/or activated?' and 'What happens as a result of it?' The answers will sometimes mention external objects and events visible to an observer, and sometimes they will not.

If the system is a human, animal, or robot, it may have causal powers which enable it to refer to restaurants and beansprouts (the philosophical complexities of reference to external, including unobservable, objects may be ignored here, but are helpfully discussed by Sloman). But whatever the information-processing system concerned, the answers will sometimes describe purely *internal* computational processes—whereby other symbols are built, other instructions activated. Examples include the interpretative processes inside Searle-in-the-room's mind (comparable perhaps to the parsing and semantic procedures defined for automatic natural-language processing) that are elicited by English words, and the computational processes within a Schankian text-analysis program. Although such a program cannot use the symbol 'restaurant' to mean *restaurant* (because it has no causal links with restaurants, food and so forth), its internal symbols and procedures do embody some minimal understanding of certain other matters—of what it is to compare two formal structures, for example.

One may feel that the 'understanding' involved in such a case is *so* minimal that this word should not be used at all. So be it. As Sloman makes clear, the important question is not *'When does a machine understand something?'* (a question which misleadingly implies that there is some clear cut-off point at which understanding ceases) but *'What things does a machine (whether biological or not) need to be able to do in order to be able to understand?'* This question is relevant not only to the possibility of a computational psychology, but to its *content* also.

In sum, my discussion has shown Searle's attack on computational psychology to be ill founded. To view Searle-in-the-room as an instantiation of a computer program is not to say that he lacks all understanding. Since the theories of a formalist-computational psychology should be likened to computer programs rather than to formal logic, computational psychology is not in principle incapable of explaining how meaning attaches to mental processes.

Computation and Content

14

Frances Egan
1995

14.1 Introduction

The dominant program in cognitive psychology since the demise of behaviorism in the 1960s has been *computationalism*. Computational theories treat human cognitive processes as a species of information processing, and the systems that implement such processing as symbol-manipulating systems. Describing a device as a symbol manipulator implies that it is possible to treat some of its internal states as representations of properties or objects in a particular domain. Computational theories of vision, for example, posit internal states that can be interpreted as representing the *depth* of the distal scene.

There has been considerable disagreement about the nature and function of representational contents assigned to the states posited by computational theories. It is widely thought that such theories respect what Jerry Fodor (1980) has called the "formality condition," which requires that computational processes have access only to the formal (that is, *nonsemantic*) properties of the representations over which they are defined. It is by respecting the formality condition that computationalism promises to answer one of the most pressing problems in the philosophy of mind—how can representational mental states be causally efficacious in the production of behavior? Representational mental states, according to computationalism, have their causal roles in virtue of (roughly) their structural properties.[1] But this advantage comes at a price. The formal character of computational description appears to leave no real work for the semantic properties of the mental states it characterizes. Thus, computationalism has been thought by some to support a form of *eliminativism*, the thesis that denies that intentionally characterized states play a genuinely explanatory role in psychology (see, for example, Stich, 1983). If the content of computational states is indeed explanatorily idle, then the relation between psychological states, as characterized by computational psychology, and psychological states as characterized by our commonsense explanatory practices, which do advert to content, is quite obscure.

In this paper I articulate and defend a strategy for reconciling the formal character of computational description with a commitment to the explanatory usefulness of mental content. I argue that content does not play an individuative or taxonomic role in computational theories—a computational characterization of a process is a *formal* characterization. Nonetheless, content does play a genuine explanatory role in computational accounts of cognitive capacities. Content ascriptions connect the formal characterization of an internal process with the subject's environment, enabling the computational theory to explain how the operation of the process constitutes the exercise of a cognitive capacity in that environment. I support my account of the role of content in computational psychology by reference to David Marr's theory of early vision,[2] in part because it has received a great deal of attention from philosophers; however, my argument depends on general features of computational methodology, and so applies to computational theories generally.

Recent attempts to reconcile computation and content have appealed to a notion of narrow content, that is, content that supervenes on intrinsic physical states of the subject. Proponents of narrow content have so far failed to articulate a notion that is clearly suitable for genuine explanatory work in psychology.[3] I argue that it is typically *broad* content that plays a central role in computational explanation, though I do identify a specific (and limited) function served by narrow content ascription.

14.2   Why Computational Theories Are Not Intentional

It might be argued that, the formality condition notwithstanding, computational theories are *intentional* in the following sense: The states they posit not only have representational content, but the content they have plays an individuative role in the theory. In other words, computational theories taxonomize states by reference to their contents.

The motivation for the claim that computational theories of cognition are intentional in the above sense is not hard to understand. Consider the following passages:

> There is no other way to treat the visual system as solving the problem that the theory sees it as solving than by attributing intentional states that represent objective physical properties. (Burge, 1986, 28–29) [I]t is at least arguable that where rational capacities are the *explananda*, it is necessary that there be propositional attitudes in the *explanans*. If this argument is correct, then it is pragmatically incoherent for Stich and his followers to insist that cognitive psychology explains rational capacities by reference to states not described as possessing propositional content. (Hannan, 1993)

The argument underlying both passages can be expressed somewhat crudely as follows:

(P) The *explananda* of computational psychological theories are intentionally characterized capacities of subjects.

(C) Therefore, computational psychological theories are intentional—they posit intentional states.

Underlying the argument is the intuition that scientific explanations should "match" (in some sense) their explananda. Wilson endorses a constraint of this sort, which he calls *theoretical appropriateness.*

> An explanation is theoretically appropriate when it provides a natural (e.g. non-disjunctive) account of a phenomenon at a level of explanation matching the level at which that phenomenon is characterized [in the explanandum]. (1994, 57)

The notion of a "level of explanation" is somewhat vague, but let us assume, for the sake of argument, that there is a unique level of explanation such that all and only explanations at that level involve ascriptions of content. If theoretical appropriateness is a desideratum of scientific explanation, then an explanation of intentionally characterized phenomena should itself advert to intentionally characterized states.[4]

An unresolved tension surfaces, though, when we consider computational explanation. The fact that the explananda of computational theories are intentionally specified suggests that computational states are essentially individuated by reference to their contents. If computational theories are not intentional, then how can computational theories explain intentionally characterized phenomena? But the formality condition exerts an opposite pressure. In requiring that computational processes have access only to the nonsemantic properties of the representational states over which they are defined, it suggests that computational individuation is nonsemantic, or in Fodor's terminology, *formal.* Are computational taxonomies intentional or formal? At this point it is helpful to turn to a well-developed example.

Interpreters of Marr's theory of vision have assumed that visual states are individuated in the theory by reference to their contents, hence that the theory is intentional (see Burge, 1986; Kitcher, 1988; Segal, 1989, 1991; Davies, 1991; Morton, 1993; Shapiro, 1993). Although there has been a good deal of disagreement about the sort of content (broad or narrow) that Marrian structures have, the assumption that content plays an individuative role in the theory has not been thought to require explicit argument.[5] Burge says that it is "sufficiently evident" that the theory is intentional from the fact that "the top levels of the theory are explicitly formulated in intentional terms" (1986, 55). I shall argue that in construing content as individuative, interpreters of Marr have misconstrued the role of content in computational theories.

While it is true that in his informal exposition of the various visual processes Marr typically characterizes them by reference to features of the distal scene, one should not read too much into this fact. The processes are also characterized formally. They have to be— Marr's theory of vision is a computational theory, and a formal characterization guarantees that they are programmable (hence, physically realizable). The question is, which characterization does the individuative work?

Marr argued persuasively that an information-processing system should be analyzed at three distinct levels of description. The "top" level, which Marr called the *theory of the computation*, is a characterization of the function computed by the system—what the system does. The *algorithmic level* specifies an algorithm for computing the function, and the *implementation level* describes how the process is realized physically.[6] The top level in Marr's hierarchy is sometimes identified with Pylyshyn's semantic level (Pylyshyn, 1984) and Newell's knowledge level (Newell, 1982). In other words, the theory of the computation has been construed as essentially an intentional or semantic characterization of a mechanism. But such a construal makes somewhat puzzling Marr's insistence that the search for the algorithm must await the precise specification of the theory of the computation. He says, "unless the computational theory of the process is correctly formulated, the algorithm will almost certainly be wrong" (1982, 124), suggesting that the top level should be understood to provide a *function-theoretic* characterization of the device. Indeed, Marr explicitly points out that the theory of the computation is a mathematical characterization of the function(s) computed by the various processing modules. In describing the mathematical formula that characterizes the initial filtering of the image (the calculation of the Laplacian of the image convolved with a Gaussian), Marr says the following:

> I have argued that from a computational point of view [the retina] signals $\nabla^2 G * I$ (the X channels) and its time derivative $\partial/\partial t(\nabla^2 G * I)$ (the y channels). From a computational point of view, this is a precise characterization of what the retina does. Of course, it does a lot more—it transduces the light, allows for a huge dynamic range, has a fovea with interesting characteristics, can be moved around, and so forth. What you accept as a reasonable description of what the retina does depends on your point of view. I personally accept $\nabla^2 G$ as an adequate description, although I take an unashamedly information-processing point of view. (1982, 537)

$\nabla^2 G$ is a function that takes as arguments two-dimensional intensity arrays $I(x, y)$ and has as values the isotropic rates of change of intensity at points (x, y) in the array. The implementation of this function is used in Marr and Hildreth's (1980) model of edge detection to detect *zero-crossings*. (A zero-crossing is a point where the value of a function changes its sign. Zero-crossings correspond to sharp intensity changes in the image.) Marr grants that the mathematical specification of the function computed by the retina may not make what the retina does *perspicuous*. Nonetheless, from an information-processing point of view, the formal specification is "adequate." More precisely, it is the description upon which the correct specification of the algorithm crucially depends.

The claim that the top level provides a mathematical characterization does not imply that it is wrong to speak of the visual system as taking representations of light intensity values as input and yielding representations of shape as output. I am not denying that computational processes have true intentional (semantic) descriptions. For some purposes, as we shall see in the next section, an intentional description of a process will be preferable to a formal characterization. It is not incorrect to say that an intentional characterization of the function computed by a mechanism resides at the top level in Marr's hierarchy, although the intentional characterization provides an *extrinsic* description of what the device does, and does not individuate the computational process. For the purpose of individuation, the precise mathematical description given by the theory of the computation is the description that counts.[7],[8]

If, as I have argued, the top level of a computational account provides a *purely mathematical* characterization of a device, then there is little temptation to construe the second, or *algorithmic* level, as intentional. (Only Burge, as far as I know, construes the algorithmic level as intentional, apparently because in discussing various possible algorithms Marr sometimes employs intentional language.) The algorithmic level of theory simply specifies *how* the function characterized in mathematical terms at the top level is computed by the system.

14.3   The Explanatory Role of Content

I have argued that Marr's theory of vision is not intentional. My argument appeals to general features of computational methodology; if I am right, then computational theories of cognition are not intentional—the states and processes characterized by such theories are not individuated by reference to the representational contents ascribed to them. The formal—namely mathematical—characterization does the taxonomic work.

Let us consider for a moment the implications of the claim that computational theories are not intentional. Two mechanisms that compute the same mathematical function, using the same algorithm, are, from a computational point of view, the same mechanism, even though they may be deployed in quite different environments. A computational description is an environment-independent characterization of a mechanism.[9] Inasmuch as computational processes are generally construed as *modular* processes, even the *internal* environment is irrelevant to the type-individuation of a computational process. Imagine a component of the visual system, called the *visex*, that computes a representation of the depth of the visual scene from information about binocular disparity.[10] Now imagine that within the auditory system of some actual or imagined creature there is a component that is physically identical to the visex. Call this component the *audex*. According to the theory of auditory processing appropriate to this creature, the audex computes a representation of certain sonic properties. We can imagine a particular visex and audex removed from their normal embeddings in visual and auditory systems respectively and switched. Since the two components are by hypothesis physically identical, they compute the same class of functions. The switch will make no discernible difference to the behavior of the creatures, nor to what is going on inside their heads. The two mechanisms are computationally identical, despite the difference in their normal internal environments.

It will perhaps be noted that the visual theory that describes the visex characterizes it as *computing a representation of depth from disparity*, and not as computing a representation of certain sonic properties, although it would do the latter if it were embedded in a different internal environment. The important point is that the postulated structures have no content considered independently of the environment (internal and external) in which they are normally situated. This is the sense in which an intentional characterization of a computational process is an *extrinsic* description. Structures in the raw primal sketch, which contains information from several distinct $\nabla^2 G$ channels and provides the input to most of the modular processes characterized by Marr's theory, are reliably correlated with such salient distal properties as object boundaries or changes in illumination, and are described by Marr as *representing* these properties. In some radically different environment, however, the same structures may be correlated with different distal properties, or perhaps with no objective feature of the world. In the latter world, the structures would not represent anything, except perhaps features of the *image*. They would have no distal content in that world.

The point I wish to underscore is that an intentional characterization of a computational mechanism involves an implicit relativization to the context in which the mechanism is normally embedded. The mathematical characterization provided by the theory of the computation does not. Only the mathematical characterization picks out an essential property of a computational mechanism. The intentional characterization is not essential, since in some possible circumstances it would not apply.

What, then, is the role that representational content plays in computational accounts of cognitive processes, if not to essentially characterize cognitive processes? I have argued elsewhere Egan (1992) that semantic interpretations play a role in computational psychology analogous to the role played by explanatory models in the physical sciences. There are two senses in which this is true. In the first place, an intentional characterization of an essentially formal process serves an expository function, explicating the formal account, which might not itself be perspicuous. Secondly, when a theory is incompletely specified (as is Marr's theory), the study of a model of the theory can often aid in the subsequent elaboration of the theory itself. A computational theorist may resort to characterizing a computation partly by reference to features of some represented domain, hoping to supply the formal details (i.e., the theory) later.

Though the analogy with models in physics is, I think, interesting and useful, the most important function served by intentional interpretations of computational processes is unique to psychology. The questions that antecedently define a psychological theory's domain are usually couched in intentional terms. For example, we want a theory of vision to tell us, among other things, how the visual system can detect *depth* from information contained in two-dimensional images. An intentional specification of the postulated computational processes demonstrates that these questions are indeed answered by the theory. It is only under an interpretation of some of the states of the system as representations of distal properties (like depth, or surface reflectance) that the processes given a mathematical characterization by a computational theory are revealed as *vision*. Thus content ascriptions play a crucial explanatory role: we need them to explain how the operation of a formally characterized process constitutes the exercise of a cognitive capacity in the environment in which the process is normally deployed.

Let us return for a moment to the argument considered earlier for the claim that computational theories of cognition are intentional:

(P) The *explananda* of computational psychological theories are intentionally characterized capacities of subjects.

(C) Therefore, computational psychological theories are intentional—they posit intentional states.

The premise of the argument is true—the questions that define a psychological theory's explanatory domain are usually couched in intentional terms—but, as we have seen, it does not follow that the theory characterizes the states and processes it describes as necessarily intentional. Computational states and processes will typically have no true intentional description when considered independently of an environment. Intentional characterizations are therefore not part of the individuative apparatus of computational theories. In *this* sense, (C) is false. Yet the argument does contain an important insight: an intentional characterization is needed to connect a computational theory with its pretheoretic explananda. An explanation of how the visual system detects the depth of the scene from information contained in two-dimensional images is forthcoming only when the states characterized in formal terms by the theory are construed as *representations of distal properties.*

But, one might object, isn't this crucial explanatory role played by an intentional interpretation of a computational process enough to make the computational theory intentional? Indeed, it might seem that a computational theory, when divorced from the intentional interpretation that secures its explanatory relevance, cannot properly be characterized as a theory of *cognition.* There is a sense in which this is true; however, it does not undermine my point that computational theories are not intentional. Let me explain.

A computational theory provides a mathematical characterization of the function computed by a mechanism, but only in some environments can this function be characterized as a *cognitive* function (that is, a function whose arguments and values are epistemically related, such that the outputs of the computation can be seen as rational or cogent given the inputs). An example will make the point clearer. The matching of stereo images essential to the computation of depth from binocular disparity is aided, according to Marr, by a fundamental fact about our world—that disparity varies smoothly, because matter is cohesive. This is an example of what Marr calls a *natural constraint* (in particular, the *continuity* constraint). In some environments, the constraints that enable a cognitive interpretation of the mathematical function computed by a mechanism will not be satisfied. In environments where the continuity constraint is not satisfied (a *spiky* universe), the stereopsis module would compute the same formally characterized function, *but it would not be computing depth from disparity.* The function might have no cognitive (i.e., rational) description in this environment. A computational theory prescinds from the actual environment because it aims to provide an abstract, and hence completely general, description of a mechanism that affords a basis for predicting and explaining its behavior in any environment, even in environments where what the device is doing cannot comfortably be described as *cognition*. When the computational characterization is accompanied by an appropriate intentional interpretation, we can see how a mechanism that computes a particular mathematical function can, in a particular context, subserve a cognitive function such as vision.

A computational theory explains a cognitive capacity by subsuming the mechanism that has that capacity under an abstract computational description. Explaining a pretheoretically identifiable capacity by reference to a class of devices that have an independent, theoretical, characterization is an explanatory strategy familiar from other domains, particularly biology. The ability of sand sharks to detect prey is explained by positing within the shark the existence of an *electric field detector* a device whose architecture and behavior is characterized by electromagnetic theory. Electromagnetic theory does most of the explanatory work in the biological explanation of the shark's prey detecting capacity. Of course, the explanation appeals to other facts—for example, that animals, but not rocks and other inanimate objects in the shark's natural environment, produce significant electric fields—but no one would suggest that such facts are part of *electromagnetic theory*. Similarly, by specifying the class of computational devices to which a mechanism belongs and providing an independent (i.e., noncognitive) characterization of the behavior of this class, a computational theory bears the primary explanatory burden in the explanation of a cognitive capacity. The intentional interpretation of the process also plays an explanatory role—it demonstrates that the capacity has been explained—but playing an essential role in the cognitive explanation does not thereby make it part of the *computational theory* proper.

So does it follow that computational theories are not cognitive? It depends. If a theory must give a cognitive characterization of a mechanism (according to which computing a cognitive function is a *necessary* property of the mechanism) to be a cognitive theory, then computational theories are not cognitive. If bearing the primary explanatory burden in an explanation of a cognitive capacity is sufficient, then they typically are.

Let us return briefly to Wilson's theoretical appropriateness condition, the requirement that a scientific explanation characterize a phenomenon at the same level in the explanans as in the explanadum. The above account of computational explanation suggests that theoretical appropriateness is not a general constraint on scientific explanation. Computational explanations characterize cognitive capacities in nonintentional, formal, terms. The requirement is independently implausible in any case, since it would rule out not only reductive explanations (e.g., microreductions) of antecedently characterized phenomena, but also explanation by functional analysis, the predominant form of explanation in both cognitive psychology and biology.[11] Such explanations typically analyze complex capacities or processes into more basic, less specialized, elements. For example, the explanation of the capacity to do long division appeals to the ability to copy numerals and perform multiplication and subtraction. The explanation of digestion appeals to more basic chemical processes. Both of these explanations appear to violate Wilson's theoretical appropriateness condition. Though Wilson grants that theoretical appropriateness is a *defeasible* constraint on scientific explanation, the ubiquity of explanations of this sort suggests that it is not a constraint at all.

14.4   The Ascription of Content

An interpretation of a computational system is given by an *interpretation function* f_I that specifies a mapping between the postulated structures of the system and elements of some represented domain. For example, to interpret a device as an adder involves specifying an interpretation function f_I that pairs states of the device with numbers. The device can plausibly be said to *represent* elements in the domain only if there exists an interpretation function that maps formally characterized structures to these elements in a fairly *direct* way.

Since an interpretation is just a structure-preserving mapping between formally characterized elements and elements of some represented domain, there is no reason to think that the interpretation of a computational system will be unique. The non-uniqueness of computational interpretation has been thought to be a problem for computationalism, but in fact it is not. Most "unintended" interpretations will not meet the directness requirement.[12] More importantly, the plausibility of a computational account depends only on the existence of an interpretation that does explanatory work.[13]

If the above account of the explanatory role of content is correct, then the interpretation of a computational system should connect the formal apparatus of the theory with its pretheoretic explananda. This requirement will constrain the choice of an appropriate interpretation function. A computational theory that purports to explain our arithmetical abilities cannot plausibly claim to have done so unless some of the states it postulates are interpretable as representing numbers. The fact that the system could also be interpreted as charting the progress of the Six-Day War (to use an example of Georges Rey's) would not undermine the theorist's claim to have described an arithmetical system, assuming that the mechanism can be consistently and directly interpreted as computing the appropriate arithmetical functions. Given the explanatory role of intentional interpretation as characterized in the previous section, the existence of "unintended" interpretations of computational systems is irrelevant. The preexisting explananda of the theory set the terms for the ascription of content.

Consider what this means for theories that purport to explain our perceptual capacities. The cognitive tasks that define the domains of theories of perception are typically specified in terms of the recovery of certain types of information about the subject's normal environment. Interpreting states of the system as representing environment-specific properties demonstrates that the theory explains how the subject is able to recover this information in its normal environment. Consequently, we should expect the contents ascribed to computationally characterized perceptual states to be *broad*, that is, not shared by physically identical subjects in significantly different environments.

It has been argued by Fodor (e.g., 1980, 1984, 1987) and others (e.g., Block, 1986; and Cummins, 1989) that computational psychology must restrict itself to a notion of *narrow* content, that is, content that supervenes on intrinsic physical states of the subject.[14] In part, the motivation for such a view is the recognition that computational taxonomy prescinds from the subject's normal environment. Physical duplicates are computational duplicates. Given this fact, if computational states have their semantic properties essentially, then computational psychology requires a notion of content that supervenes on the physical properties of the system; in other words, it needs a notion of narrow content. But if, as I have argued, computational states have their semantic properties only *nonessentially*, then narrow content is not necessary. And it turns out that there are good reasons why computational psychology should not restrict itself to narrow content.

In the first place, a useful notion of narrow content has been notoriously hard to specify. More importantly, since the explananda of theories of perception are typically formulated in environment-specific terms, ordinary environment-specific broad contents will best serve the explanatory goals of such theories. The point can be generalized. It is widely appreciated that ordinary contents are broad. Insofar as the pretheoretic explananda of computational theories are framed in ordinary terms, the ascription of broad content to computational states and structures will be appropriate.

A close look at Marr's theory confirms the point. He ascribes broad, environment-specific contents where possible. If in a subject's normal environment a structure is reliably correlated with a salient distal property, then Marr describes the structure as representing that property. (For example, he describes structures in the 2.5D. sketch as representing *surface orientation*.) Some of the structures posited by Marr's theory correlate with no simple distal property tokening in the subject's normal environment. The structures that Marr calls *edges* sometimes correlate with changes in surface orientation, sometimes with changes in depth, illumination, or reflectance. Marr describes edges as representing this disjunctive distal property. Notice that in both cases—correlation with a simple distal property in the subject's normal environment or correlation with a disjunctive distal property in the subject's normal environment—the contents ascribed to the representational structures are broad. Moreover, the broad contents so ascribed are determined by the correlations that obtain in the subject's normal environment, not by those that would obtain in some other environment.

Some of the structures that Marr posits (e.g., individual zero-crossings) do not, however, correlate with any easily characterized distal property, simple or disjunctive, in the subject's normal environment. Some of their tokenings correlate with distal properties, others appear to be mere artifacts of the imaging process. Marr recognizes this fact, cautioning that such structures as zero-crossings are not "physically meaningful"; he describes them as representing *discontinuities in the image*. Their contents are only proximal, and hence narrow—they supervene on the intrinsic properties of the subject. But such proximal or narrow content, far from being Marr's content of choice, is his content of last resort, since he ascribes proximal content only when a broad content ascription is unavailable.[15]

Covariational (or *information-theoretic*) theories of content identify the meaning of a representational state with the cause of the state's tokening in certain specifiable circumstances.[16] The foregoing account of content ascription in Marr's theory may tempt some to find in his theory a tacit endorsement of a covariational theory of content. This would be a mistake. I have claimed that in ascribing content Marr looks for salient distal correlates of a structure's tokening in the subject's normal environment. I have been careful to avoid claiming that these correlates are *the cause* of the structure's tokening. Though it may be natural to say that they are, Marr makes no such claim, and a number of well-known problems are avoided by not doing so.[17] It should be clear that Marr's theory is not committed to a covariational theory of content if one considers the sort of case where no *salient* distal correlate (simple or disjunctive) of a structure's tokening can be found. In such cases, Marr ascribes a proximal content to the structure, interpreting it as representing a feature of the image or input representation rather than the distal cause of its tokening, whatever that might be. The ascription of proximal content serves an important expository purpose—it makes the computational account of the device more perspicuous, by allowing us to keep track of what the device is doing at points in the processing where the theory posits structures that do not correlate neatly with a salient distal property.[18] No explanatory purpose would be served by an unperspicuous distal interpretation of these structures; consequently, Marr does not interpret them as representing their distal causes. The decision to adopt a proximal rather than a distal interpretation is dictated by purely explanatory considerations.[19]

14.5   Computational Psychology and Naturalistic Psychology

The compatibility of computational description and broad content seems to have gone unnoticed in the literature. Cummins (1989), whose account of representation in computational psychology bears some resemblance to mine, says the following:

> The CTC [computational theory of cognition] . . . seeks an *individualist* psychology, i.e., a psychology that focuses on cognitive capacities of the kind that might be brought to bear on radically different environments. If the anti-individualist position with regard to intentionality is right (i.e. if beliefs and desires cannot be specified in a way that is independent

of environment), then the explananda of an individualist psychology cannot be specified intentionally. It follows that the CTC shouldn't—indeed, *musn't*—concern itself with intentionally specified explananda. (140)

Cummins's mistake is in thinking that the fact that a computational theory seeks to provide a nonintentional, environment-independent characterization of a cognitive process entails that it cannot explain phenomena specified in environment-specific terms. This, we have seen, is wrong. A computational theory explains an environment-specific cognitive capacity by subsuming it under an environment-independent characterization. The intentional interpretation of the process serves as a bridge between the abstract characterization provided by the theory and the environment-specific intentional characterization that constitutes the theory's explananda. Precisely because the intentional interpretation does not play an essentially individuative role in the theory—in other words, whatever contents computational states have, they have them *non-essentially*—the theorist is free to assign broad contents where appropriate to secure the connection between theory and explananda.

The fact that the computational theorist can and typically will assign broad contents to computational structures has larger implications for psychology. In "Methodological Solipsism Considered as a Research Strategy in Cognitive Psychology," Fodor says the following:

> there is room for both a computational psychology—viewed as a theory of formal processes defined over mental representations—and a naturalistic psychology, viewed as a theory of the (presumably causal) relations between representations and the world which fix the semantic interpretations of the former. I think that in principle this is the right way to look at things . . . however . . . it's overwhelmingly likely that computational psychology is the only one that we are likely to get. [A] naturalistic psychology isn't a practical possibility and isn't likely to become one. (1980, 66)

Naturalistic psychology, as Fodor construes it, is the theory of organism/environment relations that fix the meanings of our mental terms. He offers two arguments for the claim that a naturalistic psychology is impossible. As both arguments have been thoroughly worked over in the literature (see the commentaries that accompany Fodor, 1980), I won't go into them here. But as far as I know, no one has disputed Fodor's implication that computational psychology and naturalistic psychology are entirely unrelated projects. If my account of the role of content in computational psychology is correct, then Fodor's way of conceiving things is wrong. If we had a complete computational psychology, that is, a computational account of each human cognitive capacity, we would *ipso facto* already have a naturalistic psychology. Let me elaborate.

Although a computational theory provides a formal, environment-independent, characterization of a process, the theorist will usually be unable to discover the correct formal characterization without investigating the subject's normal environment. Typically, a necessary first step in specifying the function computed by a cognitive mechanism is discovering environmental constraints that make the computation tractable. The solutions to information-processing problems are often underdetermined by information contained in the input to the mechanism; the solution is achieved only with the help of additional information reflecting very general features of the subject's normal environment. For example, as previously mentioned, the computation of depth from binocular disparity is possible only because the mechanism is built to assume something that is true about its normal environment—that disparity varies smoothly because matter is cohesive (the continuity constraint). Finding constraints of this very general sort is a necessary first step in characterizing the mathematical problem that the mechanism has to solve, and thus in arriving at a correct computational description of the process.

There is a second and more obvious point at which the computational theorist will contribute to the specification of the organism/environment interactions that fix the meanings of mental terms—namely, in the specification of an intentional interpretation of a formally characterized process. I have argued that content ascription is constrained by the subject's normal environment. The process of ascribing content to the structures posited by the theory involves the attempt to specify the normal environmental correlates of tokenings of these structures. The fact that Marr succeeded in ascribing distal contents to many of the structures posited in his theory (and Marr is not unique in this achievement) demonstrates that naturalistic psychology is not impossible. Although computational psychology is formal—its taxonomic principles are formal— it develops hand-in-glove with the project that Fodor calls naturalistic psychology.[20]

14.6   Scope and Limits of the Account

My account of the explanatory role of content has been articulated and defended by reference to *classical* computational models. Classical architectures treat cognitive processes as rule-governed manipulations of internal symbols or data structures that are explicit candidates for interpretation. *Connectionist* cognitive models, by contrast, do not posit data structures over which the device's operations are defined. (Many connectionist devices, unlike classical devices, are not correctly described as constructing, storing, and retrieving internal representations.) Connectionist models posit activated units (nodes) that increase or decrease the level of activation of other units to which they are connected until the ensemble settles into a stable configuration. Consequently, connectionist models lack convenient "hooks" on which an intentional interpretation of a process may be hung. Semantic interpretations ascribe content either to individual units in the network or to patterns of activation over an ensemble of units. However, I see no reason why the above account of the explanatory role of content would not apply straightforwardly to connectionist systems. Semantic interpretations of connectionist networks play the same complex explanatory role as do interpretations of classical computational models. Most importantly, they connect a connectionist theory of a cognitive capacity with its pretheoretic explananda.

It remains to be seen whether computational psychology will shed much light on paradigm cases of intentional states, namely, beliefs and desires. The conspicuous successes of computationalism have been in characterizing highly modularized, informationally encapsulated processes such as early vision and syntactic and phonological processing. The states posited by theories of this sort fail to exhibit the complex functional roles characteristic of the propositional attitudes (including, typically, accessibility to consciousness). They are *subdoxastic* states. Fodor, in *The Modularity of Mind* has expressed considerable pessimism about the prospects of characterizing in formal, computational terms more *central* cognitive processes such as belief fixation (see Chapter 9, this volume). I think this pessimism is well placed, if only because the context-sensitivity of belief ascription makes the programming task appear intractable. However, should a computational account of propositional attitudes be forthcoming, content would play the same explanatory role it plays in theories of modular capacities. An interesting consequence of this eventuality is that propositional attitudes, so characterized, would not have their contents essentially. Type-identical belief-state tokens might have different contents, should they be tokened in relevantly different environments.[21] The prospect of a computational theory of belief, therefore, challenges a fundamental commitment of orthodox philosophy of mind.[22] Some may conclude that such a theory would not really be about the propositional attitudes, though nothing in the *folk* conception of the mind would seem to warrant this conclusion.

Notes for Chapter 14

1. For language-like representations, the formality condition claims that they have their causal roles in virtue of their *syntax*.

2. For the most detailed exposition of Marr's theory see (Marr, 1982).

3. Loar (1988) and Segal (1989, 1991) have perhaps come closest. Loar's proposal concerns commonsense, as opposed to computational, psychology. Segal argues that narrow content plays a central role in Marr's theory. See (Egan, 1996) for criticism of Segal's proposal.

4. A tacit appeal to theoretical appropriateness seems to underlie the argument of Graves et al. (1973) for the claim that the explanation of the speaker's knowledge of her language must appeal to internalized *knowledge* of grammar.

5. Shapiro (1993) has described my claim (in Egan, 1991) that Marr's theory is not intentional as "startling." It should not be startling. A central claim of Field (1978) is, as Field puts it in his (1986) paper, "that psychological theories have a non-intentional core" (114). In any event, interpreters of Marr have not defended the crucial assumption that his theory *is* intentional.

6. In describing the levels of Marr's hierarchy as levels of *description* I do not mean to preclude treating the items classified by level as phenomena and processes rather than purely linguistic devices available to theorists.

7. In arguing for (various) intentional characterizations of the theory of the computation, interpreters of Marr point out that he speaks of the primal sketch as "representing the image," and of other

structures as representing such distal properties as depth and surface reflectance. The assumption underlying such arguments is that Marr's words in these passages are decisive for settling issues of *taxonomy*. If theory interpretation were so simple, much of the philosophy of science would be out of business. The individuative principles of a scientific theory can rarely be read off the language used to articulate the theory. Marr is not generally careful or consistent in his language. There is no reason why he should be—he is not focusing on the issues that have concerned philosophers. In the passage I have quoted in the text, however, Marr is explicitly discussing fundamental commitments of the information-processing approach, in particular, how the theory of the computation is to be understood; so the passage bears special significance in the context of the current issue.

8. Colin McGinn has pointed out to me that the theory of the computation is intentional in the following sense: it does specify an intended interpretation of a computational process—the intended interpretation is *mathematical*. The topmost level of a computational theory characterizes the system as computing a series of functions defined on mathematical entities. I am quite happy to say that a computational theory is intentional in this rather unusual sense. This is trot the sense in which interpreters of Marr have taken his theory to be intentional. (They have assumed that the theory characterizes the system, essentially, as computing a function defined on aspects of the visual domain, and this is precisely what I deny.)

9. This is not to suggest that the theorist can ignore the subject's environment in attempting to formulate a computational description of the device. Quite the contrary. See Section 14.5.

10. This is an adaption of an example from (Davies, 1991).

11. See Cummins (1983), chap. 2, for an account of functional analysis.

12. The directness requirement precludes interpreting a desk as an adder, since the assignment of numbers to states of the desk requires the interpreter to compute the addition function herself. The system is not doing the work. The directness requirement has yet to be precisely specified, but see Cummins (1989), chap. 8 for discussion. I gloss over this issue here primarily because, as we shall see below, the "problem" of ruling out unintended interpretations of computational systems typically does not arise.

13. The existence of more than one interpretation meeting the directness requirement simply shows that the formally characterized device is capable of computing more than one cognitive function. The visex, described above, would compute a function on the auditory domain if it were embedded differently in the organism.

14. Others, such as Stich (1983), impressed by the fact that content ascription is typically context-sensitive and observer-relative, have concluded that cognitive psychology should not advert to content at all.

15. Commentators who have thought narrow content to be Marr's content of choice have presumably done so because they recognize that content-determining correlations with distal properties can vary wildly across environments (see, for example, Segal, 1989, 1991). They fail to notice that for Marr the relevant correlations are those that obtain in the subject's normal environment.

16. See, for example, Stampe (1977), Dretske (1981), and Fodor (1990). There are, of course, important differences in their accounts.

17. One problem with covariational theories of content is their implication that the meaning of a symbol is given by the disjunction of all of its potential causes. Since "horse" tokenings would be caused not only by horses, but also by horsey looking cows, covariational theories seem to imply that "horse" means *horse or horsey looking cow*. (See Fodor, 1990 for discussion.) The "disjunction problem" gives rise to a further difficulty, namely, how to account for the possibility of a symbol's misrepresenting its object, given that all potential causes of a symbol's tokening determine its meaning. Though computational theorists have had little to say about misrepresentation (their concern is to characterize what is going on in the normal case, where perception is veridical) it is not hard to see how misrepresentation can arise on the account of content ascription I have sketched above. Structures assigned distal contents (simple or disjunctive) will misrepresent if they are tokened when the normal environmental conditions for their tokening are not satisfied. Suppose that, as part of a military training exercise, Bill, a normal human with a Marrian visual system, is placed in a room where the continuity constraint, which holds that disparity varies smoothly because matter is cohesive, is not satisfied. Bill's visual system normally computes *depth* from disparity information. However, in these circumstances, where spikes of matter project in all directions, Bill (or, more specifically, the stereopsis module of Bill's visual system) will compute the same formally characterized function as he normally does, but he will misrepresent some other property (not a property for which we have a convenient name) as depth. In general, where the constraints that normally enable an organism to compute a cognitive function are not satisfied, it will fail to represent its environment.

18. One might wonder whether what I am calling "proximal content" is really content at all. To be sure, proximal contents do not bear much resemblance to the contents we ascribe in our ordinary predictive and explanatory practices; however, I do think that contents of this sort play a genuine explanatory role in computational accounts of internal processes. To cite a second example, Marcus (1980) interprets the structural descriptions constructed in the course of natural language comprehension as representing not distal objects (or public language sentences) but the items in stacks or buffers of the parser. In both the vision and parsing cases, interpreting a structure as representing other structures constructed earlier in the process serves the important function of allowing us to keep track of what the processor is doing. Given that the rationale for content ascription in computational psychology is primarily explanatory, I think that proximal content should be treated as a species of content, though perhaps only as a sort of "minimal" content.

19. Matthews (1988), Segal (1989), and McGinn (1989) note another reason to resist an exclusively causal account of content. They argue that the contents of mental representations seem to be partly determined by the sorts of behaviors that they tend to produce. Whether a structure whose tokening is caused by both cracks and shadows means crack, *shadow, or crack or shadow* depends in part upon whether its tokening contributes to the production of behavior appropriate to cracks, shadows, or both.

20. Naturalistic psychology, construed as the specification of the organism/environment relations that fix the meanings of mental representations, should not be confused with the enterprise that is sometimes called "the naturalization project" in semantics. The latter attempts to specify sufficient conditions, in a nonintentional and nonsemantic vocabulary, for a mental state's meaning what it does. It is a purely philosophical project, not the concern of psychologists.

21. For example, a computational theory of belief would type-identify my *water* beliefs and my Twin Earth doppelganger's *twater* beliefs, although intentional interpretations appropriate to our

respective worlds might assign different broad contents to our type-identical beliefs. A computational theory of belief would, therefore, respect the intuition that has been the prime motivation for the postulation of narrow content—that doppelgangers are identical in psychologically relevant respects, and hence should be subsumed under the same psychological generalizations. But because a computational theory is not committed to narrow content, it can also accommodate the intuition that the subject's environment is a determinant of her belief *contents*.

22. But see Matthews (1994) for an account of propositional attitudes that denies that they have their contents essentially.

IV MODELING THE WORLD

Part IV: Modeling the World

The world is complicated. One way that intelligent agents might deal with that complexity is to build internal models—simplified representations of the world that still preserve all of the information necessary for effective action. The papers in this part present a variety of modeling approaches, each focused on representing different kinds of structure (categorical structure, value structure, predictive structure, and causal structure). Each has been theoretically fruitful both for understanding how humans work and for building machines that act effectively in the world.

In chapter 15, Cameron Buckner discusses the history of empiricist approaches to the problem of extracting useful abstract categories from low-level data. He shows that modern deep neural networks can be seen as performing certain kinds of transformations that reliably solve this problem. The geometric understanding of neural networks and what they do has always been important; Buckner shows how this tradition is continued and expanded by modern techniques.

Julia Haas's "The Evaluative Mind" (chapter 16) discusses reinforcement learning models. These focus on agents who model the world to effectively act in it, updating policies in response to feedback about the success of their actions. Haas's essay provides some insight into how reinforcement learning might provide a a basis for building desire, value, and the will into artificial systems. At its most controversial, she notes, this culminates in the 'Reward Is Enough' hypothesis, which suggests that all intelligent behavior can ultimately be understood in terms of trying to maximize some intrinsic reward signal.

In chapter 17, an excerpt from his article "Whatever Next?," Andy Clark demonstrates the power of predictive coding models, which use error-correction feedback both to update models of the world and act effectively in it. Building on a constant refrain in critical artificial intelligence (AI) research, Clark argues that the brain has no need to construct a complete internal model of the world that reflects completely and accurately the world around it; instead, the brain learns how to minimize error signals in predicting relevant states of the world looking forward. Clark shows how this change of modeling perspective provides descriptive and explanatory leverage over a host of perceptual, cognitive, and motor phenomena, including disorders of the central nervous system and illusions of various sorts.

Finally, Judea Pearl's "Theoretical Impediments to Machine Learning" (chapter 18) discusses recent advances in building devices that can learn the causal structure of their worlds from correlational data and, importantly, from facts about the consequences of interventions on the world. Such models allow agents to pick up on salient features of their world, guide interventions to produce desired outcomes, and diagnose the sources of error in those predictions. Models of the sort that Pearl advances are now routinely used to understand the causal relations among many variables in complex variable sets and have been used as models of human development. In building machines that search for and discover causal truths about the world, one gives machines the kinds of tools for building internal representations of the causal structure of the world, which knowledge might be thought to comprise the bulk (or at least a sizable portion) of our knowledge of the world as a whole.

One question—still very much open—is whether we ought to expect to settle on a single modeling strategy or whether effective mind design requires a combination of different models in different domains. Combining reinforcement learning and deep neural networks, for example, was key to success for Google's AlphaGo. Conversely, advocates of predictive coding often emphasize the theoretical and practical power that comes from using a unified modeling strategy for every stage of perception and action. And as we have suggested, understanding causal structure might be thought to be prerequisite for concept learning (as many concepts involve causal entanglements), for predicting what will happen next, and for planning effective actions in a complex and messy world.

Combinations and Additions

The papers in this part naturally go together with the papers in part V, which focus on advances in cognitive science that make some of these modeling strategies more or less plausible. Essays by Rummelhart and Chuchland and Sejnowski (chapters 19 and 20, respectively) provide useful background for understanding Buckner's paper in particular. Many of the papers in part VI provide a useful counterpoint, as they are motivated by the possibility that modeling is *not* necessary for intelligent behavior. In addition to the papers in this part, the interested reader might expand upon modeling literature in several ways.

The question of modeling is intimately bound up with questions about both intentionality and representation that arose in previous parts of the book. A focus on modeling might be seen as a natural extension of broader questions about intentionality and representation: a focus on *how* something is represented is as important as *what* is represented.

- Minsky (1975) was included in an earlier edition of *Mind Design*. It was state of the art when written. He is far more optimistic about the possibility of hand-coded knowledge representations than most researchers today.
- Dreyfus (1979) was also included in earlier editions and gives a substantial critique of the approach favored by Minsky. Together, they provide an interesting historical perspective on the necessity (or not) of building complex internal representations. Dreyfus also made a number of predictions about domains in which AI would fail, some of which were drastically wrong. Mitchell's paper in this volume (chapter 10) can be seen as an updated, more nuanced presentation in the same vein.
- Norvig (2011) is a now-classic defense of pure machine learning for natural language processing against the Chomsky-inspired approaches that used to predominate. Norvig observes that specific modeling choices often make problems seem more or less tractable. Representing language production as a serial Markov decision process is, as Chomsky

rightly noted, probably a nonstarter. The successes of natural language processing, by contrast, are partly due to the use of more sophisticated data structures that speed model learning.

- One factor in the success of recent machine learning that cannot be overstated is just the ready availability of extremely large data sets against which one can train. ASCI Red, the fastest supercomputer in the world when *Mind Design II* was published, had disk storage of 1.2 TB. This is the space that one expects from a commodity desktop today—and one could quickly fill that space with publicly available machine learning data sets. Halevy et al. (2009) details how machine learning in recent decades has been driven by the availability of large data sets, and how this has in turn changed modeling approaches. They also provide a short, accessible introduction to approaches that can handle very large collections of text.

Different modeling strategies are at the heart of modern machine learning. What was cutting edge at the time of writing may well be old hat by the time this book is in your hands. Nevertheless, there are a few additional papers that are worth recommending:

Deep Learning. Deep learning models, in some form or another, are likely to remain a core workhouse of modern machine learning. The interested reader might consider:

- Buckner's idea of "transformational abstraction" fits well with an increasing focus on geometric approaches to understanding minds. DiCarlo and Cox (2007) present a view of human object recognition as untangling a manifold in a higher-dimensional space. Influential in neuroscience, this geometric metaphor is also increasingly common in discussions of neural networks.
- LeCun et al. (2015) is a useful review of the methods and techniques of deep neural networks. They note that the several features, especially the convolutional layers, were directly inspired by the architecture of the visual system.
- Marcus (2018a) is an accessible criticism of current deep learning approaches, focusing on limitations that seem difficult to overcome in principle. There is much that dovetails with the critiques raised by Mitchell in chapter 10—and some that appear to be yielding to sustained research pressure.
- Goodfellow et al. (2014) discusses the use of adversarial examples both to test the limits of deep learning systems and to describe just what these systems have learned.

Reinforcement Learning. Reinforcement learning (RL)—either alone or as a hybrid with deep learning—is similarly widespread in real-world commercial systems.

- Sutton and Barto (2018b) remains the standard textbook, and its first chapter is still the most mathematically accessible introduction to RL from a computer science perspective. Its chapters 14 and 15 also link to the neuroscience of RL.

- After it became clear that computers could beat humans at chess, Go was the last holdout as the game too hard to be solved by computers. That eventually yielded to AlphaGo's combination of RL and deep learning. The documentary "AlphaGo" is an engaging introduction to AlphaGo and its achievements. Of the technical reports on AlphaGo, Silver et al. (2017) is also reasonably accessible.
- The neuroscientist Yael Niv's work is a treasure trove for those interested in neurally inspired forms of RL. Dayan and Niv (2008) contains a thorough discussion of the research linkages between computer science and neuroscience and how the two co-evolved. Niv and Langdon (2016) carefully distinguishes between the claims of RL at different Marrian levels.

Predictive Coding.   The philosophical literature on predictive coding has exploded in recent years:

- Hohwy et al. (2008) kicked off much of the philosophical interest in predictive coding models. Hohwy (2013) also contains accessible material linked to philosophical upshots of the framework.
- Clark's paper in this part is an excerpt from a full 2013 *BBS* article of the same title (Clark, 2013). The ensuing vigorous commentary and discussion on that article prefigured many of the debates that are still ongoing. He expanded this material into Clark (2015b).
- Predictive coding is a fellow traveler with an even more ambitious hypothesis, known as the "Free Energy Principle (FEP)." Defended by the neuroscientist Karl Friston, FEP suggests that error-controlled feedback can be seen as something like a fundamental law of nature, though the exact status of this claim is itself a matter of philosophical debate. Friston has published prolifically on FEP. Friston (2010) is an early attempt to sell FEP as a grand unified theory of the mind.
- At the other end of the ambitiousness scale, it is worth noting that small-scale models of predictive coding are now very standard in neuroscience. It is widely accepted that at least some forms of predictive coding—for example, by removing temporal autocorrelations—are widely used by the nervous system to preserve precious bandwidth. Huang and Rao (2011)'s review covers many of the standard ways in which prediction (broadly construed) can help efficient information transmission.
- Both predictive coding and the FEP continue the long cybernetic tradition. One relevant argument—often invoked by Friston—can be found in Conant and Ashby (1970). The paper is what it says on the tin: an argument that, understood correctly, effective action and modeling the world go hand in hand. The paper is, however, something of a mixed bag for the predictive coding crowd; much of it is also concerned with the theoretical limitations of error-controlled feedback, as contrasted with effective feedforward control.

Causal Models.   The literature on causal modeling can be a difficult nut to crack for the casual reader.

- There are a few books that are especially useful. Pearl and Mackenzie (2018) is a semi-popularized treatment of casual inference. Glymour (2001) is a dense but important introduction to causal Bayes nets.
- Readers looking for more bite-sized chunks might consider Hitchcock (2009), which provides a clear introduction to the fairly technical literature on causal machine learning aimed at philosophers, or Eberhardt (2009), which provides a philosophically motivated account of the basic framework for generating networks of causal models.
- Finally, the causal modeling literature often interacts with the psychological literature on development. Gopnik et al. (2004) extend this view of causal modeling to developmental psychology, arguing that machine learning approaches plausibly describe how children learn the causal structure of the world.

Modeling Strategies.   The debate over "neat" versus "scruffy" approaches to modeling the mind (the distinction is variously attributed to Schank, Abelson, or Minsky) is a perpetual one. It is not limited to computer science: much of the argument in the past two decades over the evolution of language (for example) has been over whether language should be seen as one good trick, suddenly appearing on the stage, or whether it was assembled piecemeal from a variety of sources. Within computer science, the debate might be seen as reflecting the two strands that gave rise to the discipline—the elegant simplicity of pure mathematics combined with the unashamed pragmatism of engineering. Proponents in the debate often occupy implausible extremes, but the heart of the dichotomy is a trade-off between simplicity and power that is faced by any modeler.

- Nilsson (1983)'s reprint of his 1983 AAAI presidential address presents a concise discussion of unified versus disunified approaches to AI. Interestingly paired with his short "Reconsiderations" (Nilsson, 2005), which revisits the issue twenty years later.
- Minsky (1986) is a fascinating, sprawling, and mostly un-excerptable collection of his reflections on the way that minds can be assembled from simpler agents. It was an influence on several later philosophers. Of particular interest to the present discussion is his chapter 12, which discusses the trade-offs between unified and disunified modeling of the world.
- Whitley and Watson (2005) contains a discussion of the so-called "No Free Lunch Theorem," which appears to deny the possibility of a single, optimal strategy for modeling the world. The upshot of the theorem is not entirely clear—hence the sustained interest—but one reading of it is that the question of the best modeling strategy is ultimately bound up with the sorts of environments that you expect to encounter. The literature on the theorem can get hairy, but this should be accessible to formally inclined students.

- Klein (2018) expresses skepticism about predictive coding considered as a grand unified theory of perception and action. At stake is motivation: predictive coding seems well suited as a theory of how humans might model the world, but the same models seem less suited to telling us what actions humans ought to take in a given context.

- Andrews (2021) discusses issues about scientific modeling in the context of the Free Energy Principle (FEP). One persistent question about many modeling strategies is whether they ought to be taken as literally true, as useful starting points for more elaborate models, or as bearing some more abstract relationship to actual systems. While the paper focuses on the FEP, the points made apply more widely.

Transformational Abstraction in Deep Neural Networks

15

Cameron Buckner
2023

Deep learning allows computational models that are composed of multiple processing layers to learn representations of data with multiple levels of abstraction. These methods have dramatically improved the state-of-the-art in speech recognition, visual object recognition, . . . and many other domains.
—Yann LeCun, Yoshua Bengio, and Geoffrey Hinton, "Deep Learning" (2015)

"Forming Abstractions" was one of the key AI abilities listed in the 1955 Dartmouth AI proposal . . . however, enabling machines to form humanlike conceptual abstractions is still an almost completely unsolved problem.
—Melanie Mitchell, *Artificial Intelligence: A Guide for Thinking Humans* (2019)

15.1 Introduction: Abstraction in Debates over Artificial Intelligence

Can Deep Neural Networks (DNNs) usefully model the human faculty of abstraction?[1] Current opinion on this question exhibits a stark and puzzling divide. That DNNs are capable of some sort of abstraction—indeed, that abstraction is their distinguishing strength—is often treated by DNN researchers as so obvious as to barely require mention. DNNs' success in recognizing objects in images, words in spoken speech, and strategies in a game of Go or chess are usually thought to derive from their ability to discover increasingly abstract patterns in complex data as it is processed by the hierarchy of node layers between input and ouput. There has even been hope that these networks model the way that human perceptual cortex discovers and manipulates abstract patterns in tasks like object and speech recognition. Neuroscientists of perception have long theorized about the existence of "abstraction layers" in cortex, for example that early vision specializes in the detection of specific and local patterns such as colors, contrasts, and shadings; which are the basis for the detection of more abstract properties, such as lines and angles, in middle vision, which allow detection of more abstract properties, such as shapes and figures, in late vision, and eventually of fully composed scenes and situations in the latest stages of the ventral stream (DiCarlo and Cox, 2007; Goodale and Milner, 1992; Hubel and Wiesel, 1967; Riesenhuber and Poggio, 1999). The idea that this hierarchy of abstraction can be modeled by a DNN provided inspiration for the first "deep" architectures and has more recently been bolstered by empirical evidence that the same kinds of features are recoverable at comparable depths of both primate perceptual cortex and an image-classifying DNN's layer hierarchy (Fukushima and Miyake, 1982; Khaligh-Razavi and Kriegeskorte, 2014; LeCun et al., 1990; Schmidhuber, 2015; Yamins and DiCarlo, 2016).

At the same time, skeptics take it as equally obvious that a fatal weakness of DNNs lies in their inability to learn and manipulate certain abstractions. For example, Melanie Mitchell argues in the paper quoted in the epigraph above, AI research in the last sixty years has made almost no progress on the core goal of enabling machines to form and manipulate human-like conceptual abstractions (Mitchell, 2019). Gary Marcus expresses similar concerns, holding that "knowledge represented in deep learning systems pertains mainly to (largely opaque) correlations between features, rather than to abstractions like quantified statements (e.g. all men are mortal)" (Marcus, 2018a). Coming closer to resolving the apparent tension with DNN proponents, François Chollet of Google Research argues that there are two distinct forms of abstraction in human cognition, the first of which is found in intuition and perception and can be modeled by DNNs, but the second of which drives explicit deductive reasoning and higher cognition and remains the "fundamental weakness of current [DNN] models" (Chollet, 2020). These critics all seem to agree on some degree of nativism: that acquiring fully human-like abstractions requires at least some basic stock of innate specialized representations. In particular, these critics point to research on "core knowledge" systems involving concepts such as OBJECT, AGENT, NUMBER, and CAUSE, which developmental psychologists such as Susan Carey and Elizabeth Spelke have argued are innate in humans and help us bootstrap a theory-like knowledge of mathematics, social relationships, and physical causality (Carey and Spelke, 1996; Marcus, 2018b).

So on the one hand, proponents of deep learning argue that their models succeed because they are good models of mental abstraction, and, on the other hand, skeptics argue that they fail because they are not. Though there is room here to lean on qualifiers like "perceptual" or "conceptual," this opposition sets up at least an apparent mystery, given that neither the skeptics nor proponents explicitly distinguish their use of the term "abstraction" from its use by their critical targets. We could pull at other threads in this knot—at "intelligence," "rationality," or "reasoning," for example—but doing so usually just brings us right back to the others. Psychometric tests of intelligence are designed to assess our ability to detect ever-subtler abstractions, and skeptics often point to AI failures on such tests—like Raven's matrices, Bongard problems, or new abstraction oriented psychometric test batteries like Chollet's Abstraction and Reasoning Corpus (ARC) (Chollet, 2019; Hernández-Orallo, 2017; Mitchell, 2019)—as evidence that they are not processing these stimuli in a human-like way.

Further, reasoning and abstraction are two sides of the same coin. A decision is often said to be based on reasoning when it relies on relationships that are abstract enough to resist description in terms of occurrently perceivable features of the environment. Consider the classic example of Chryssipus' dog: the dog is said to reason by exclusion when, chasing prey down a trail that leads to a three-way fork, it sniffs the first and second paths, and, failing to detect the prey's scent in the first two options, takes the third straightaway, without sniffing it as well. The decision, it seems, cannot be explained as easily as if the dog had taken the first or second trail upon sniffing it; the choice of the third, unsniffed path must be based on the situation's more abstract logical form. The most abstract relationships are often thought to be those that are difficult or impossible to characterize in terms of specific perceptual cues, such as the syncategorematic terms of logic or the numerical concepts of mathematics.

Since abstraction has received less direct attention than the other threads in this knot—with numerous works already written on intelligence or reasoning in AI (Hernández-Orallo, 2017; Legg and Hutter, 2007; Poole et al., 1998)—I focus on abstraction here. This focus presents us with a qualitatively and quantitatively rich landscape on which to map and explain recent progress in AI. We all seem to understand a kind of intuitive continuum of abstractness in properties—with local, simple properties, such as colors, contrasts, and shadings, often regarded as the simplest perceptual features; more composite features like lines and angles being slightly more abstract; figures and objects more abstract yet; followed by scenes and situations; abstract types of situations like justice and war; and finally the most abstract properties of all, higher-order mathematical and logical forms. This intuitive continuum may not withstand deeper philosophical scrutiny, but I argue here that many of DNNs' successes can be attributed to having made philosophically and empirically significant progress by clarifying the middle, murkier zones of this scale.

To elucidate the relevant concept(s) of abstraction, I adopt a strategy that melds the history of philosophy with recent empirical work. Some of the fears that DNN-based processing is alien or opaque can be alleviated by drawing upon empiricist theories of abstraction and its role in cognition, elaborated by philosophers like Locke, Hume, and Berkeley. These accounts illuminate and contextualize otherwise technical details of recent DNN architectures and show how these advances fit into empiricist theories of abstraction. But AI can also inform philosophy: I argue that DNN architectures can help resolve long-standing philosophical puzzles and debates regarding empiricist accounts of abstraction and its role in the acquisition of general category representations.

The structure of the remainder of the paper is as follows. In section 15.2, I canvass the role of abstraction in empiricist philosophy of mind. In section 15.3, I review one of the most popular kinds of DNN architecture—Deep Convolutional Neural Networks (DCNNs)—with particular focus on the components that may be relevant to abstraction. In section 15.4, I tie these stories together by suggesting that DCNNs bring together several different forms of abstraction into an intricate division of labor. Finally in section 15.5, I return to the concerns of the deep learning skeptics and ask whether the forms of abstraction that DCNNs do model can resolve all the philosophical puzzles for empiricist theories of abstraction and, if not, which puzzles remain.

15.2   Abstraction in Empiricist Philosophy of Mind

Empiricism, as I understand it, is the doctrine that all knowledge comes from the senses. Understood as a thesis about human concept formation, it is a thesis about the origins of the mind's representations—that they and/or their structure is derived, causally and representationally, from sensory experiences or their components. Call this view "origin empiricism." Origin empiricism is the view that prominent DNN researchers seem to have in mind when they describe their successes, such as when the developers of AlphaZero claim that it learns to play Go "without human knowledge" using a "tabula rasa algorithm" (Silver et al., 2017).

To avoid confusion at the outset, we should set aside some alternative ways of construing origin empiricism. For example, Gary Marcus portrays the empiricist position as requiring that all components of an architecture be derived in some way from experience—including basic representational formats, mental faculties, and inferential capacities. This position, however, has not been defended by any serious empiricist philosopher, and for good reason. Without basic capacities for attention, memory, inference, and abstraction, no mind could learn anything from any amount of perceptual experience. These domain-general faculties, moreover, plausibly develop without the aid of experience, their roles in cognition secured by more general neural wiring principles that could be innate in the sense of being under a high degree of genetic control (Zador, 2019). Thus, it is more productive to construe origin empiricism as allowing that domain-general faculties or formats may be innate but requiring that all domain-specific representations be derived from experience. This way of construing origin empiricism still allows significant debate to be had with the nativists mentioned in the introduction. Specifically, disagreement remains regarding the number and prominence of domain-specific representations that need to be built into a system to enable human-like learning and cognition—most notably the core knowledge concepts mentioned above.

The basic inferential mechanism in an empiricist theory of mind is association; sensory impressions are linked to one another and to actions via associative links (Clatterbuck, 2016). All empiricist theories of mind—from Aristotle to Quine—begin with a toolkit of domain-general principles of associative learning and inference that determine which ideas will become associated—and thereby linked in the transitions of thinking and decision-making—with which others (Buckner, 2017). The details have changed throughout the ages, but this basic toolkit includes similarity, frequency, contiguity, and temporal precedence, as well as the motivating impetuses provided by pleasure and pain. These principles remain the foundation of associative learning theory in psychology today—finding expression in models of classical conditioning, instrumental conditioning, and configural learning (Pearce and Bouton, 2001)—which in turn has inspired and been inspired by the artificial neural network algorithms that served as the precursors for deep learning (Gluck and Myers, 2001; Pearce, 2002; Squire, 2004).

For an empiricist philosophy of mind to get anywhere beyond the most basic forms of associative learning, it needs some way to rise above simple sensory impressions; and for this reason, every prominent empiricist appeals at key moments to a faculty of abstraction. In the simplest cases, there is no trouble deriving a theory of abstraction from the basic principles of association. If a red light is repeatedly paired with the sound of a bell, then the mind will come to associate the two perceptions by frequency and contiguity, and red lights will come to make one think of bells. Though the basic principles of frequency, contiguity, and reinforcement remain potent drivers of even adult human behavior, much else in human cognition—with apologies to Skinnerian ambition (Skinner, 1948)—operates according to more subtle psychological principles. We can also detect and decide on the basis of properties which are more complex than redness or bell-ringing, and the decisions made on the basis of such properties start to look more like rational inferences (Buckner, 2019b). The burden of explaining these more sophisticated associations on an empiricist framework falls mainly on the principle of similarity—though the similarities must be more sophisticated than mere stimulus generalization from red to orange. We commonly reason on the basis of categories like *dog*, *chair*, *sandwich*, *coffee*, *square*, *money*, *vacation*, and *virtue*. If the principles of association are ever to take us so far, then we need some way to understand how diverse instances of such categories come to be viewed as mutually similar to one another. And if the perceived similarities are not themselves innate—in violation of the empiricist prohibition on domain-specific representational structure—there must be some faculty that allows the relevant similarities to be apprehended and learned.

Enter the faculty of abstraction. We can get a start on understanding the faculty by appealing to the heuristic of relating it to amount of specificity. Consider the difficulty in learning even a mid-level abstract property, such as a geometric shape like *triangle*. The least abstract representation of a triangle, we might think, is a holistic perception of a particular triangle drawn on a piece of paper. This perception is specific in all respects: the triangle has a specific size, color, and degree of illumination; its angles have precise degrees, and its sides specific lengths; and it has a specific location in the visual field. If we are to learn a more general idea of a triangle using empiricist mechanisms, its common properties must somehow be extrapolated from a set of such specific exemplars, each with different values for these parameters.

John Locke illustrates the complications posed by acquiring a general concept of a triangle in this way in a frequently-mocked passage of the *Essay*[2]:

The ideas first in the mind, it is evident, are those of particular things, from whence, by slow degrees, the understanding proceeds to some few general ones. . . . For when we nicely reflect upon them, we shall find, that general ideas are fictions and contrivances of the mind, that carry difficulty with them, and do not so easily offer themselves, as we are apt to imagine. For example, does it not require some pains and skill to form the general idea of a triangle (which is yet none of the most abstract, comprehensive, and difficult), for it must be neither oblique, nor rectangle, neither equilateral, equicrural, nor scalenon; but all and none of these at once. In effect, it is something imperfect, that cannot exist; an idea wherein some parts of several different and inconsistent ideas are put together. (Locke (1690), IV.7.9)

Here, it appears that Locke is contradicting himself; for how could a single idea be both oblique and right-angled, or both equilateral and scalene? And yet Locke's point is that the general idea of a triangle must somehow include and subsume all of these inconsistent configurations of exemplars. Locke suggests that the acquisition of such a general idea from experience of particulars requires the contribution of an active mind, and many other parts of the *Essay* develop hypotheses about the mental processes that can carry us from such particular ideas to the general ideas that subsume them.

Unfortunately, Locke seems to offer several distinct mechanisms of abstraction without very clearly relating them to one another. The first mechanism of abstraction discussed by Locke is what Gauker (2011) calls "abstraction-as-subtraction." This mechanism achieves generality simply by subtracting out all of the forms of specificity that vary amongst members of a category. If one notices that one triangle is scalene and another is right-angled, then one subtracts the exact number of degrees of its angles from the general triangle representation, and leaves the number of degrees unspecified. If one notices that one triangle has sides of equal length and another is scalene, one subtracts out the exact length of the triangle's sides, and so on. Through the operation of this mechanism, the mind must "make nothing new, but only leave out of the complex Idea . . . that which is peculiar to each, and retain that which is common to all" (III, iii, 7). As Gauker notes, such a theory immediately raises some puzzles of its own—specifically, how we know which particulars to group together before subtracting, and how we know how much to subtract when noticing discrepancies? For example, how does one know to exclude from the process a three-sided figure whose sides do not join at one point? And how does one avoid subtracting out the presence of angles completely upon learning that their degrees may all differ? As Gauker puts it with some frustration, "how the mind forms such general ideas [such as angle in the abstract] is precisely the question that the abstraction-as-subtraction theory is supposed to answer" (2011, 27).

A second Lockean mechanism of abstraction Gauker (2011) calls "abstraction-as-composition." According to this approach, more abstract ideas are formed by acts of the mind that join together less abstract ones. For example, we might form the general idea of a triangle simply by joining together the simpler ideas of "3," "angle," and "side" together in the right way, rather than extracting such commonalities from messy exemplars. Many abstract ideas can be thought of as composed in this way—Locke in particular describes the idea of lead as being formed by joining "the simple Idea of a certain dull whitish colour, with certain degrees of Weight, Hardness, Ductility, and Fusibility" (II, xii 6, discussed in Gauker (2011, 20)). The obvious drawback to this mechanism is that it seems to presume that the learner begins with a stock of simpler abstractions and compositional principles from which the more complex ones can be formed. Recall that origin empiricists are trying to avoid populating the mind with innumerable innate ideas and domain-specific rules; but abstraction-as-composition seems to be taking a great many such building blocks for granted. If we consider the full learning problem as posed by a more recent empiricist like Quine—or as it confronts a DNN modeler today—it begins not with predigested input about angles and lines but rather with raw, unprocessed "stimulation of [the] sensory receptors" by "certain patterns of irradiation in assorted frequencies" (Quine, 1971, 82). Taken individually, abstraction-as-composition thus also cannot discharge the burdens of origin empiricism on its own.

These and other difficulties led later empiricists like Berkeley and Hume to abandon Locke's first two methods of abstraction and rest their hopes instead upon a third, which Gauker calls "abstraction-as-representation." On this approach, exemplars are grouped together in general category sets, and particular exemplars are variously chosen to stand in for the general class in processes of categorization and reasoning. This mechanism is most clearly articulated by Berkeley. Berkeley pithily dismissed abstraction-as-subtraction and abstraction-as-composition by highlighting problems with the troublesome triangle passage, opining "is it not a hard thing to imagine that a couple of children cannot prate together of their sugar-plums and rattles . . . 'til they have first tacked together numberless inconsistencies?" (Berkeley (1710), Introduction 13-14). Instead, Berkeley thought that ideas are always of particulars, so it would be better to build general category representations by treating them as sets of exemplars; in that manner, "an idea which, considered in itself, is particular becomes general by being made to represent or stand in for all other particular ideas of the same sort" (Berkeley (1710), 12). Unfortunately, though it at least seems to avoid the apparent contradictions in Locke's triangle passage, abstraction-as-representation faces versions of the same problems faced by the other two mechanisms. For one, to generalize correctly from a representative exemplar, we plausibly need to know which particulars are the most typical instances of a class. For another, we plausibly need to know which of their particular attributes are shared by the other exemplars to be sure that this particular's idiosyncrasies do not lead us astray. Hume, who also recommends Berkeley's doctrine of abstraction-as-representation, notes these burdens and evinces exasperation in discharging them, writing that the ability to select suitable exemplars is "most perfect in the greatest geniuses . . . but it can't be explained by the utmost efforts of human understanding" (Hume (1739), 1.7). Nativists perhaps rightly chide origin empiricists here for appealing to such "magic" when pressed to explain how the mind derives general ideas from experience.

Before considering whether DNNs might fill in these lacunae for origin empiricists, let us consider a fourth and final kind of abstraction—which I have called "abstraction-as-invariance." A property is invariant if it is unchanged under some systematic transformations of a space or domain. In physics, a search for invariance provides a method to reveal the laws of nature; for example, the law of conservation of angular momentum can be derived from the observation that momentum is invariant under rotation (i.e., the laws of physics do not depend upon the angle of a reference point). In mathematics, topology is a subdiscipline that studies properties that are unchanged under systematic spatial transformations, such as rotations (or more generally, continuous deformations called homeomorphisms). Logicists in the philosophy of mathematics have sought to formally define logical abstractions as those that are preserved under all permutations of the domain—for example, a valid argument form might be thought of as one that remains truth-preserving under all permutations of the propositions that could be joined by syncategorematic terms in that form.

An influential source of these ideas linking abstraction with invariance is Hume's *Treatise* (and also later the work of Cantor, Frege, and Boolos—see Shapiro, 2004; Antonelli, 2010), where he speculated that mathematics is the most perfect science because a notion of cardinal number can be derived from a perfectly invariant one-to-one correspondence (bijection) between two sets:

> Algebra and arithmetic [are] the only sciences in which we can carry on a chain of reasoning to any degree of intricacy, and yet preserve a perfect exactness and certainty. We are possessed of a precise standard, by which we can judge the equality and proportion of numbers; and according as they respond or not to that standard, we determine their relations, without any possibility of error. When two numbers are so combined, as that the one has always a unit answering to every unit of the other, we pronounce them equal. (I. III. I.)

Following Frege, this proposal has come to be called "Hume's Principle." Similar maneuvers have been deployed to define the notion of an abstract logical property and abstract objects today (Fine, 2002). This final form of abstraction seems unlike the others—it is less clear, for example, that humans actually work through any such proof in acquiring the notion of a number in the course of normal cognitive development. It may instead be something more like a regulative ideal or justificatory procedure than the first three kinds of abstraction, for it appeals to a kind of limit of transformations—identity under all permutations, or invariance under all homeomorphisms—that human cognition could only approximate or demonstrate after training in formal proof techniques. As we will see, however, it is an interesting supplement to the other forms of abstraction in the present conversation because it provides a procedure that can be used to approach the most abstract concepts that the rationalists have considered the strongest evidence for nativism.

To summarize, empiricists have explored (at least) four qualitatively distinct forms of abstraction: i) abstraction-as-subtraction, ii) abstraction-as-composition, iii) abstraction-as-representation, and iv) abstraction-as-invariance. Traditionally, many theorists treated these different approaches as unrelated in the best case and as theoretical competitors in the worst. Flaws noted with one form of abstraction were often thus taken as arguments for the others in internal debates amongst the most influential empiricists.

In the next section, I question this oppositional framework by reviewing the key components of deep convolutional neural networks, arguing that they provide a novel way to understand abstraction that obviates much of the previous debate. Whereas previously we might have approached "abstraction" as naming a unitary kind of mental operation which should be defined in terms of necessary and sufficient conditions—thus putting pressure on origin empiricists to say what, conceptually, the four kinds of abstraction have in common, or rejecting some forms in favor of others—we can instead explicate a kind of mechanism that performs diverse operations attributed to all four forms of abstraction simultaneously. This model-based approach to abstraction is more in-line with recent model-based approaches to explanation in cognitive science (Boyd, 1999; Craver, 2007; Godfrey-Smith, 2006; Weiskopf, 2011) than the options we have just canvassed and arguably dissolves some of the previous problems that have vexed the empiricist philosophers of previous centuries.

15.3   Deep Convolutional Neural Networks: Basic Architectural Features

Until recently, a type of DNN architecture called a "Deep Convolutional Neural Network" (hereafter DCNN) has been considered the most reliably successful tool on the widest range of problems.[3] This architecture is a key component in models of image recognition (AlexNet), strategy gameplay (AlphaGo), scientific data analysis, and many other applications. These DCNNs all inherit their basic features from an older neural network prototype developed by Fukushima in the late 1970s called "Neocognitron" (Fukushima, 1979), which was specifically designed to model certain aspects of perceptual abstraction thought to occur in primate neocortex (for the history, see Buckner, 2018, 2019b; Schmidhuber, 2015). Neocognitron was perhaps the first network that was truly "deep" (with 4–10 layers, depending on how they are counted), but its most powerful innovation was the way it combined two different types of processing nodes—linear convolutional filters and non-linear downsamplers—in a single network. These different kinds of node are stacked in a deep hierarchy in what I will call its characteristic "abstraction sandwich" motif. These sandwiches combine the strengths of diverse operations, allowing a single mechanism to simultaneously perform all four forms of abstraction alluded to in the previous section.

The distinction between two different types of processing neurons was inspired by influential work on the neuroanatomy of vision by Hubel and Wiesel (1967). Using single-cell recordings in early visual areas of cats, they identified two different cell types, "simple" and "complex" cells, based on their differential firing patterns. Whereas simple cells detect a low-level feature like an edge or contrast in a particular orientation and position, complex cells take input from many simple cells and fire in response to the same features but with a greater degree of positional invariance. Neuroscientists at the time speculated that many layers of these simple and complex cells might be iterated in the cortical visual processing stream, and their interplay might explain our own ability to recognize increasingly abstract features in diverse locations and poses. Neocognitron modeled this behavior by containing "simple" nodes that performed convolution (a type of linear algebra operation elaborated below) to detect features at particular locations and in particular poses, and "complex" nodes that averaged output from many spatially nearby simple nodes, aggregating their activity to detect those features across small shifts in its location or pose. Once the first sandwich has extracted somewhat abstract features from the raw input, another sandwich can be stacked atop it, focusing its computational resources on extracting even more abstract features from the last layer's output. In principle, this process could be repeated indefinitely, with many abstraction sandwiches stacked hierarchically, such that processing gradually detects more and more abstract features across an ever broader range of visuospatial variance. With these innovations, Neocognitron was able to outperform other neural networks of the day on difficult tasks characterized by high variance—such as handwritten digit or facial recognition—by modeling the hierarchical processing cascade of mammalian neocortical processing streams.

Each of these operations bears elaboration. Let us begin with convolution. Perceptual input is typically passed to such a network in a gridlike structure, and the smallest unit of information in a visual grid is often a pixel, which is typically a multi-dimensional vector of Red, Green, and Blue color channel intensity detected at that location. Convolution is a linear algebra operation over matrices; the operation transforms the vector values for a spatial chunk of pixels (usually a rectangle) in a way that maximizes some values and minimizes others. The patterns learned by convolutional nodes are called filters or kernels, because after training they amplify the presence of a particular kind of feature in its output; for example, a useful vertical-edge kernel maximizes values corresponding to a vertical edge while minimizing everything else. In the next layer of a sandwich, each convolution operation passes its output to a rectified linear unit (ReLU), which activates if the output of convolution exceeds a certain threshold. In other words, the output of convolution is only passed up the processing hierarchy if the feature is deemed to have been detected at that location. The net result of passing a vertical-edge kernel across the whole image would be a representation that shows all and only the vertical edges, creating a new intermediary representation called a "feature map." A vertical-edge feature map might be visualized by imagining sliding a stencil for a vertical edge across a whole image, and recording the degree to which the underlying image cleanly fills out the stencil on a separate, spatially organized map of locations.

Typically, however, the recognition of a general category often requires more than merely recognizing simple features like vertical edges; we might also need to detect edges in a wider diversity of presentations, in different locations, sizes, and angular orientations (so that, at later stages, various edges might be assembled into useful composites like shapes or digits). The addition of Fukushima's "complex" units completes an abstraction sandwich by taking input from several nearby convolutional nodes below and using a downsampling operation to aggregate their outputs. Generally speaking, downsampling is a kind of operation that selects a subset of input data to build a compressed representation that preserves only information from the original that is deemed especially relevant. File size reduction in the .jpg or .gif file formats and sound compression in .mp3s both involve downsampling. Using downsampling, we can now efficiently express the fact that an edge occurred approximately here in some spatial orientation, irrespective of where it appeared or how it was oriented. The net effect of globally multiplying the input by a variety of edge-detecting kernels and combining their outputs using downsampling is like applying an edge-detector filter in a digital photograph editing program; the result is a simplified image representation that reveals all the edges wherever they are located and however they are oriented, and "subtracts out" other information. In state-of-the-art networks, downsampling is usually performed by an operation called "max-pooling." Max-pooling involves simply passing along the greatest activation (above a critical threshold) amongst the inputs taken from filter nodes at spatially nearby locations. In the next section, I explain how a hierarchy of convolution-ReLU-pooling sandwiches shows how the brain can perform all four kinds of abstraction explored in section 15.2 using the same kind of fundamental mechanism.

15.4   Transformational Abstraction in Deep Convolutional Neural Networks

Despite their success and widespread popularity, a consensus theoretical explanation as to why DCNNs work so well has remained elusive. Following several other analyses (DiCarlo et al., 2012; Montufar et al., 2014; Patel et al., 2016; Schmidhuber, 2015), I characterize the computational core of these networks in terms of the three features just described: (1) many layers of hierarchical processing which interpolate two different kinds of computational nodes, (2) linear convolutional filters, and (3) non-linear "poolers."[4] Though there remains significant debate as to which of these operations is essential for good performance, the empiricist ideas in section 15.2 help show why this particular combination of features is so effective. In turn, artificial networks incorporating these features may explain why the neural structures and processes they model are so effective in solving the computational problems faced by the brain.

Return to the problem of acquiring general ideas of mid-level abstraction which plagued Locke—categories like triangle, sandwich, or chair. Perhaps some geometric categories, like triangle, can be defined with perfect invariance, but psychologists like Rosch (1978) and Barsalou (1999) have argued convincingly that membership in most mid-level categories deployed in human cognition is too graded and idiosyncratic to be defined so cleanly. They are instead, as Wittgenstein emphasized, "family-resemblance" categories that lack a perfectly invariant essence; this is one of the primary reasons that rule-based attempts at building an artificial intelligence failed to master them (Brooks, 1991; Hofstadter, 1985). However, if we treat invariance as a more graded and multi-dimensional notion, a domain-general ability to control for systematic variation in perceptual input might unite the four forms of abstraction canvassed in section 15.2.

Specifically, computer vision and machine learning researchers have struggled against the same concerns that troubled Locke: that triangle, chair, cat, and other everyday categories are difficult to recognize because their instances can be encountered in a variety of different poses or orientations that differ in their low-level perceptual properties. A chair seen from the front does not look much like the same chair seen from behind or above; so we must somehow unify all these diverse perspectives to build a reliable chair-detector. The set of variables on which perspectives can vary tends to be the same for a very wide range of common categories; computer vision researchers have come to call these repeat offenders "nuisance variables," as they present systematic challenges to category recognition and decision-making in the real world. Common examples of nuisance parameters are size, position, and angular rotation in visual recognition tasks, or pitch, tone, and duration in auditory recognition tasks. The challenge facing a computer vision modeler is thus to develop an artificial agent that can reshape its sense of perceptual similarity by controlling for common forms of nuisance variation. An agent that is able to do so should be able to judge a cat seen from the front as more similar to a cat seen from behind than to a dog seen from the front, despite the opposite conclusion being apparent in raw perceptual input statistics. Such abstract similarities may be clearest in cases of perceptual recognition, but the phenomenon also extends to amodal domains, such as chess or Go board patterns—as abstract patterns in board positions might be recognized not only in photographs of a game board, but also (given proper training) in symbolic notation.

So, how do we form a general idea like triangle when we have only been exposed to particular and idiosyncratic exemplars with mutually inconsistent surface properties—sizes, spatial positions, angular rotations, and degrees? When dealing with geometric figures like triangles, this diversity could be overcome by learning an appropriate set of geometric transformations. The right series of affine transformations—contractions, expansions, dilations, rotations, or shears—could transform any arbitrary triangle into any other arbitrary triangle. Cognitively, however, this would be overkill, for we do not require that the exemplars of a common category be rendered perceptually indistinguishable from one another. We only more modestly require that they be rendered more mutually similar to one another than they are to members of opposing categories with which they might initially appear more similar—such as a square or rhombus with lines of the same length and angular rotation.

To articulate a solution, it will be useful to introduce technical notions of a perceptual similarity space and category representations as regions therein (for development and critical examination of these notions, see Churchland., 1989; Gärdenfors, 2004; Gauker, 2011). Perceptual similarity space is a multi-dimensional vector space—with each dimension standing for a perceptually discriminable feature—that plots an agent's perceptual experience of each exemplar to a unique vector. Vector distance in this space marks the degree of perceived similarity between the different exemplars. A "manifold" is a region of this vector space, which can be taken to mark the boundaries of a category representation. Conceived in this way, the problem facing perceptual categorization is that, as DiCarlo et al. (2012) put it, nuisance variation causes "the manifolds corresponding to different [general categories to] be 'tangled' together, like pieces of paper crumpled into a ball" (p. 417). The task of both the brain and artificial agents is to find a series of operations—systematic transformations of this space—that reliably "unfold" the regions corresponding to different categories so that they can more easily be discriminated. More specifically, agents must learn a series of transformations of this space that map disparate triangles to nearby points in a transformed triangle manifold while ensuring that this manifold marks a region that is linearly separable from the manifolds corresponding to opposing categories, like "square" or "rhombus," whose exemplars might initially appear highly similar in terms of vector distance to certain triangle exemplars because they are of similar sizes and orientations (DiCarlo and Cox, 2007).

We now have a sturdier conceptual foundation to make sense of Locke's troublesome triangle passage. Against Berkeley and Hume, Locke need not be interpreted as suggesting that the general category representation of a triangle is an introspectible mental image with inconsistent properties. Rather, the general idea of a triangle might be something more subpersonal, like a transformed category manifold that, if it could be coherently imaged at all, would look more like a painting by Picasso, with many different triangle poses juxtaposed in a spatially impossible mish-mash. This is the sense in which an abstract representation of triangle might involve both all and none of those variations; it controls for them by transforming idiosyncratic exemplars into an abstract representational format that adjusts for nuisance variations, locating exemplars of a common category as nearby points in a transformed manifold. This general manifold itself, however, consists in a whole region of similarity space that should not be interpreted as depicting a single coherent view of an exemplar with some particular configuration of nuisance parameters. In this light, Locke's comments might charitably be seen as struggling to express a theory of abstraction beyond the reach of his day's philosophical and mathematical lexicon.

These transformations are achieved by performing the different forms of abstraction described in section 15.2, using the diverse operations in the node-sandwiches described in section 15.3. In short, the convolutional filters can be understood as performing the operation of abstraction-as-composition, and the max-pooling downsamplers can be thought of as performing the operation of abstraction-as-subtraction.[5] Multiple inconsistent ways of composing a feature from a sandwich's less-abstract inputs can be explored by different kernels at the same layer, and those multiple options can then be passed to a downsampler, which aggregates and subtracts out these forms of variation in the pooled feature map that it passes along to the next layer of sandwiches in the hierarchy. As this transformational process of abstraction is iterated throughout a deep hierarchy, the transformed signals may even approach ideals of abstraction-as-invariance, as later layers will have explored more and more systematic transformations and controlled for the influence of nuisance parameters almost completely.

Even better—and providing perhaps a twist on the simple construal of abstraction-as-subtraction as discarding information about nuisance parameters—properties subtracted from one representation by transformational abstraction might be given a dedicated resources in another. In other words, a transformational hierarchy might come to represent a single exemplar along multiple independent channels, with extracting a representation unfolded along the dimension of an individual nuisance parameter like an exemplar's location in the visual field (as has long been hypothesized in the larger-scale representational division-of-labor between ventral and dorsal stream processing—see Goodale and Milner, 1992). The result is a form of processing that begins with a buzzing, blooming confusion of raw entangled signals and ends with a series of transformed, highly abstracted, dedicated channels that can be mixed and matched at the output layer to flexibly craft answers to a wide variety of categorization and decision-making problems.

Thus far, I have explained only how the same network architecture might perform operations implementing abstraction-as-composition, abstraction-as-subtraction, and at least to some degree, abstraction-as-invariance. What of abstraction-as-representation, where a single exemplar is used to stand in for a whole category? Fascinatingly, machine learning researchers have discovered that information about possible nuisance configurations remains latent in these late-stage, transformed manifolds. We know this because the transformations required to extract abstract category representations from exemplars with specific combinations of nuisance parameters can be performed roughly in reverse to render highly plausible exemplars from arbitrary positions on untangled category manifolds (Goodfellow, 2016). Without elaborating the technical details here, this is the technique behind the "deepfakes" and other creative products of deep learning, such as photorealistic pictures of people who do not exist or photographs rendered flexibly in the style of famous artists. Returning to DiCarlo et al.'s paper-folding metaphor, if a system that has learned to "unfold" the manifolds for different categories could "re-fold" them in a similar manner, then each vector in an abstract category manifold can be remapped to its original perceptual representation with the appropriately specified values of its original nuisance parameters like pose, position, scale, and so on. Moreover, if we pick a novel location on an untangled manifold, and then refold the manifold using the this inverse procedure, we can produce photo-realistic exemplars with novel combinations of nuisance parameters that the network never even observed its training (Gatys et al., 2016).

This begins to look more like the theory of abstraction provided by Kant (and contemporary Kantians like Lawrence Barsalou—see Gauker (2011, 67)), who suggested that general category representations might consist of "rules of synthesis" allowing one to generate a range of possible exemplars corresponding to an abstract category. Yet with bidirectional transformations in hand, the task might be performed without any explicit rules; and for the networks discussed so far, the transformations are learned from experience using only domain-general mechanisms. If we refrain from transcendentalist indulgences in our metaphysics, the view still counts as empiricist in the relevant sense. These generative capacities would in turn supply us with a straightforward way to generate previously-observed or novel exemplars from abstractions. When engaged again with discriminative capacities, these generated exemplars could ground a capacity for abstraction-as-representation; previously-observed or imagined exemplars could be deployed in acts of demonstrative associative reasoning.

I call the computational processes that provide for these four forms of bidirectional travel between exemplars and abstractions "transformational abstraction." To summarize, why do DCNNs perform so well, relative to neural networks that lack these features? During training of these DCNNs, node parameters converge on the sequence of transformations that do the best job of solving the widest range of categorization and decision problems on which the network is being trained by increasing the net distance in feature space between the manifolds for the categories that must be discriminated. This transformational ability explains how DCNNs can recognize the abstract similarities shared amongst exemplars in a category like chair or triangle. Remarkably, no innate representational primitives or explicit definitions are required for them to do so. Moreover, the networks themselves discover the right series of transformations to perform; as Goodfellow (2016) put it, "[pooling] over the outputs of separately parametrized convolutions [allows the network] to learn which transformations to become invariant to" (2016, 337) for some range of categorization tasks on which they were trained. Insofar as those transformations and the intermediary features they reveal are useful for the recognition of other categories—the transformations useful for recognizing chairs may closely resemble those useful for recognizing other objects like tables or beds—the network will enjoy accelerated learning for those related categories as well, no magic required.

15.5   Next Steps for Future Progress

Up to this point, I have argued that there is substantial similarity in the way DCNNs transform perceptual signals and the way human cortex acquires category representations that
are at least mid-way up a commonsense hierarchy of abstraction. We are now in a position to return to the puzzle of the introduction and inquire how high up the continuum of
abstraction in human cognition such a process of transformational abstraction might carry
artificial agents. Is transformational abstraction only of use for perceptual and intuitive
categorization as suggested by Chollet, or could it be augmented and extended to cover
more theoretical category representations that characterize basic science, logic, and mathematics? Notably, the definition of transformational abstraction just provided also applies
to the most abstract properties like cardinality or logical validity, if we extend the forms
of nuisance variation that might need to be overcome to things like permutations of the
model's domain. There has even been recent empirical evidence to suggest that empiricist-
inspired DNNs can outperform approaches that make use of innate rules and representation
for early parsing steps (Ding et al., 2020).

However, it is an open empirical question whether an unaided DCNN (or near empiricist
tweak) could discover or implement the full range of transformations required to detect
cardinality, logical validity, or other highly abstract properties. This is a daunting task because it is unclear how convolution and pooling could be bootstrapped to evaluate complete
permutations of a set or domain. Even if DCNNs extrapolate well from a limited sample,
these properties require transformation at a kind of logical limit that may be difficult for
any method to achieve without explicit formulation of hypotheses regarding the set of permutations that must be evaluated for a complete assessment, or quantificational resources
to describe such sets. Thus, it is likely that DNNs of ever-greater depth and more training might be able to approximate such formal abstractions to an ever-greater degree, but
without ever completely achieving them. Additional components corresponding to these
resources might need to be added to DCNNs for them to discover mathematical or geometric properties in their full generality. Just such computational challenges may provide
extra inspiration for the nativists' plea for domain-specific innate biases and/or representational structures of the sort studied by the core knowledge camp mentioned in section 15.1.
Hopefully, the preceding discussion provides this debate with additional conceptual focus
and clarifies the ways in which it might be informed by empirical discoveries.

On the other hand, it seems that transformational abstraction's potential already exceeds
the strictly perceptual, extending across any domain with sources of nuisance variation
that could be mapped to systematic geometric dimensions and overcome by finite amounts
of convolution and pooling. Board configurations in Go, for example, are not limited to
visual or tactile modalities, and they were provided to AlphaGo in symbolic form; so it
seems inappropriate to call the patterns learned by AlphaGo merely perceptual. Some

critics worry that this renders AlphaGo's achievement less impressive since its input was partially pre-digested (c.f. Marcus (2018b)); but it also shows that the kind of transformations enabled by DCNNs are not narrowly limited to information vehicled in visual or auditory sense modalities. Moreover, AlphaGo's success at recognizing the kinds of board-wide abstractions that allows it to defeat human grandmasters derives from its DCNNs' transformational ability to recognize subtle invariances in board configurations across rotations, reflections, and dislocations. Just as with recognizing features in natural images, Go strategies need to be nuisance-tolerant, for game-relevant abstractions like "influence," "connection," and "stability" are largely preserved across rotations and small shifts in spatial location—and so this appears to be a quite domain-general capacity of DCNNs that exceeds perceptual domains.

Furthermore, we might question whether the average human really evaluates complete permutations or transformations of a domain to exhibit what facility they reliably do with inferences involving categories such as number, object, agent, or cause. Human cognition is notoriously plagued by errors with respect to these categories; we are unreliable at distinguishing correlation from causation, subject to perceptual illusions and systematic errors about objects and their physical properties (Kaiser et al., 1986; Kubricht et al., 2017), influenced by mathematically irrelevant aspects of equations such as physical spacing of symbols and whether the problem is phrased in a social domain or in the abstract (Fiddick et al., 2000; Landy et al., 2014), and prone to anthropomorphizing much of the natural world (Epley et al., 2007). These biases and persistent errors suggest that human cognition also relies on heuristics and perceptual scaffolding even in areas of human mental activity that the nativists take to be their natural dominions. Moreover, our own cognitive mechanisms are notoriously opaque, and introspection is famously unreliable (Nisbett and Ross, 1980). Motivated reasoning has a tendency to lead us—and perhaps even especially professional philosophers and psychologists, in what empiricist William James dubbed the "psychologist's fallacy" (Ashworth, 2009)—to presume that human experimental subjects approach the natural or social world with the same level of explicit theorizing and logical rigor as the academics writing the books and articles about them. This is a form of error I have elsewhere dubbed "anthropofabulation" (Buckner, 2013)—a way of looking at human cognition with rose-tinted glasses that can cause us to set criteria for the possession of intelligence, rationality, abstraction, or other mental properties to a level that exceeds even average human performance.

With this warning in mind, consider how well the proposed mechanism for transformational abstraction answers the challenges we posed above to abstraction-as-subtraction and abstraction-as-composition in section 15.2. In particular, do we now have good answers as to how a DCNN or brain determines which aspects of a particular to subtract, or which simple features to compose, in building more abstract composites? The short answer is that DCNNs determine this through trial-and-error in the process of training; there is no oracle that tells it the right combinations to explore; it simply gradually adjusts link weights through gradient descent learning, retaining those that produce a reliable reduction in its overall error function and discarding those that do not. This answer prompts one of the common criticisms that nativists launch at deep learning—that it is too "data hungry," requiring far more training samples to solve such problems than do human learners (Lake et al., 2017; Marcus, 2018b; Mitchell, 2019). A bone that nativists typically throw to DNN modelers at this point is the proposal that their deep learning may be biologically plausible, but only if it is seen to model the entire search process explored by millions of years of evolution, rather than the much briefer learning process that could be attributed to the cognitive development of a single human.

Savvy empiricists should turn up their noses at this meager offering (Botvinick et al., 2017), insisting instead that the nativist's concerns about the size of the training set must be inspected for anthropofabulation. This nativist worry is just a reincarnation of a "poverty of the stimulus" argument that has underestimated the richness of the stimulus for decades (Reali and Christiansen, 2005). The empiricist rebuttal should always be to either scrutinize the learning environment more carefully, asking the nativists whether they have really provided the ethological evidence that humans require no perceptual or experiential scaffolding to acquire their general concepts, or provide evidence that DNNs might also acquire these representations when provided with biologically-plausible experience. Recently, both human psychology and machine learning research has suggested that we have undercounted and overlooked important sources of additional training exposures in human cortical learning. For one, we need to be careful how we count exemplars; training DCNNs directly on successive video frames rather than still images has supported the idea that thousands of different vantage points on the same object can be treated as many different exemplars of the same category for the purposes of training (Lotter et al., 2016; Luc et al., 2017; Orhan et al., 2020). Moreover, neuroscientific research has suggested that humans replay past training episodes and even generate novel imagined experiences that can be used for additional training during memory consolidation, which occurs during sleep and daydreaming for months and years after initial training episodes (Blundell et al., 2016; Gluck and Myers, 2001; Gupta et al., 2010). Combining just these two sources of additional training can increase the amount of training exposures that humans experience by several orders of magnitude, and DCNN systems built according to these principles have already dramatically increased their sample efficiency in training.

To move this debate forward, I suggest that both sides should agree upon what has been learned so far: there are philosophically and psychologically significant forms of abstraction that are implemented by DCNNs and other DNN architectures. These processes allow these systems to learn significant abstractions from input data and possibly explain how their categorization and decision processes can non-accidentally generalize well to novel natural data. Future philosophical and empirical attention should be focused on relating these forms of transformational abstraction to full abstraction-as-invariance and its use in the remaining areas where humans outperform DNN-based agents: on problems of causal and prospective reasoning, logical and mathematical proof, and advanced social cognition. The remaining question—which remains an open one for both empiricists and nativists, in both philosophy and cognitive science—is whether these forms of transformational abstraction can be bootstrapped with the right experience or domain-general biases to also extract the causal, modal, and meta-representational relations thought to drive these forms of higher cognition in humans (Penn et al., 2008). Empiricists should not rest content with "hail Mary" passes to ever-larger datasets and ever-deeper networks, and rationalists must not rest content by pointing to the sometimes dramatic failures of current architectures on problems that exceed the abilities of even average adult humans.

This battle will be won or lost by more rigorously examining the developmental scaffolding that human children rely on to bootstrap their own core knowledge systems. To do so, we must draw upon the most sophisticated data collection tools at our disposal to conduct the highest-quality investigations. We must set aside unreliable intuitions and commonsense assumptions about the poverty or richness of human developmental experience and create new multi-modal datasets from sources such as headcams worn by infants during naturalistic learning interactions (e.g., SAYCam, a large, longitudinal dataset recorded from head-mounted cameras worn by infants aged six to thirty-two months as they learned from over 200,000 word-utterances in naturalistic speech), which we are only now beginning to use to train new DNNs (Orhan et al., 2020; Sullivan et al., 2020; Vong and Lake, 2020; Yoshida and Smith, 2008). We must also think more creatively about ways that brains can reuse old experiences and generate novel simulated ones to make more efficient use of human-like amounts of experience for further rounds of training and planning using domain-general machinery (Hassabis et al., 2017). Only by resisting the subtle influence of anthropofabulation and creating philosophically grounded, ethologically informed, and neuroscientifically inspired engineering experiments can we continue to make progress on one of the oldest questions in philosophy and cognitive science (Buckner, 2020; Rahwan et al., 2019).

Notes for Chapter 15

1. By a "deep neural network," I mean an artificial neural network that consists of more than three hidden layers of nodes interposed between input and output. By "usefully model," I mean "depict in a way that allows us to engage in successful surrogative reasoning about the target (in this case, abstraction in the mind-brain)," such as by making novel and true empirical predictions about human abstraction and/or by explaining how humans abstract, where those predictions and explanations are based on similarities between properties of the model and relevant properties of the mind or brain. Though this is the view defended here, it is worth noting that this "representational similarity" view of scientific modeling is no longer hegemonic in philosophy of science, and even if DNNs should fail to be an accurate representation of abstractive processes in the mind-brain,

there are other senses in which they might still be good scientific models (Downes, 2011). Articulating the notion of abstraction that is targeted by this modeling exercise is the main task of this chapter.

2. We might debate whether Locke is a justification empiricist, but he is definitely an origin empiricist (Odegard, 1965).

3. Attention-based transformer architectures like GPT-3 and BERT are starting to acquire the reputation as the most promising all-purpose architecture. For example, though they were previously considered mostly in the realm of language modeling, they have featured prominently in recent breakthroughs such as AlphaFold 2's dramatic improvement in predicting the course of protein folds (Jumper et al., 2020).

4. They also almost always involve regularization techniques, but I will not comment more on that here; for details, see Buckner (2019a).

5. Notably, the highly successful attention-based transformer architecture does not typically use pooling. However, its key use of "attention" to iteratively focus on subsets of especially relevant input may be seen to achieve abstraction-as-subtraction through other means; for more details, see Lindsay (2020).

The Evaluative Mind

16

Julia Haas
2023

16.1 Introduction

In his original introduction to *Mind Design*, John Haugeland observes that "an 'experiment' in mind design is more often an effort to *build* something and make it work, than to observe and analyze what already exists" (Chapter 2, this volume). But what happens when such an experiment in mind design succeeds in a way and to a degree that few could have predicted? And more to the point, how do we take on the implications of such successes when they challenge central features of how we understand the mind?

These are the circumstances that we find ourselves in with respect to developments in reinforcement learning. Over the past twenty-five years, reinforcement learning has had a tremendous impact on the development of artificial intelligence and has been a major driver in advancements in the so-called 'decision sciences'—computational neuroscience, neuroscience, psychology, psychiatry, and economics. But even as we continue to advance the notion of reward maximization as a general solution to the problem of artificial intelligence (Silver, 2015), we have not yet embraced the full implications of reinforcement learning, together with the accompanying reward-prediction hypothesis, for our conceptions of the mind. That is, we continue to think of the mind as some form of a thinking machine (e.g., "thinking, intellect," Haugeland, Chapter 2, this volume), where such thinking is best understood as some type of computation—ecumenically including neural networks, deep learning, genetic algorithms, and so on.

I propose that the successes and contributions of reinforcement learning urge us to see the mind in a new light, namely, to recognize that the mind is fundamentally *evaluative* in nature. There are weaker and stronger versions of this thesis.

The weaker version, which I commit to here, proposes that the mind is, at a fundamental level, in the business of evaluating states of affairs as better or worse. This version is additive in nature: it says that, *in addition to* performing computations over representations of descriptive matters of fact, the mind *also* performs computations over representations of those facts as better or worse.[1] But even merely recognizing this heretofore missing piece of the puzzle transforms our understanding of many central aspects of our cognitive experience.

The stronger version, which I explore but ultimately don't subscribe to, makes a revisionary rather than an additive claim: it proposes that the mind is *at bottom* evaluative in nature. This is to say that the mind's evaluative processes are conceptually *prior* to its perceptual, cognitive, or motor processes. In this sense, the stronger thesis is a type of grand unifying theory for understanding the mind. Notably, the stronger version is related to but distinct from the so-called 'reward is enough' hypothesis, which suggests that reward maximization is sufficient to "drive behavior that exhibits most if not all abilities that are studied in natural and artificial intelligence" (Silver et al., 2021, 1).

Even without the stronger version, reinforcement learning points us to the idea that, as living organisms, we not only continually experience the world, but experience it *as better and worse*. As Haugeland (1979, 619) puts it, the problem with classical computers is that they "don't give a damn." Montague (2006, 19) similarly suggests that the central difference between computers (as we have more traditionally conceived of them) and brains is that the latter use evolved, efficient computations that "care—or more precisely, [that] have a way to care." In my view, these notions of 'giving a damn' or 'caring' are basically right: minds *assess with respect to some goals,* i.e., they 'care' about how things are going with respect to those goals, be they as central as survival or as mundane as getting coffee.

Still, we need a much more systematic way of working out of what this actually means. Moreover, if we do in fact experience the world in this way—that is, *evaluatively*—then this will have important implications for understanding how many of our cognitive capacities function, e.g., why perception and attention select as they do; and, equally, why these capacities break down as they do, e.g., how Major Depressive Disorder may involve *both* a reduction in the primary sensitivity to rewards *and* an individual's reduced ability to *learn* from reward (Huys et al., 2013). Developing this picture is the work I aim to do here.

I build my argument out over stages. For precision, I make several assumptions about the nature of reinforcement learning and its instantiation in minds like ours. I sketch these assumptions, together with their relationship to other versions of reinforcement learning, in Section 16.2. I then briefly survey some of the empirical evidence suggesting that the reinforcement learning paradigm captures something important about biological minds like ours.

In Section 16.3, I get more specific about what that 'something important' is. I do so by characterizing the nature of valuation in the mind, defending the function of valuation as guiding selection and providing evidence for the ubiquity of valuation as selection across a wide range of 'low-' and 'high-level' human psychological capacities.

In Section 16.4, I defend the weaker version of the evaluative thesis. I sketch what we might expect from a strictly 'thinking' mind on the one hand, and from a thinking, evaluative mind on the other. I suggest that we find plenty of evidence for the latter in a variety of cognitive capacities.

In Section 16.5, I consider the stronger thesis, mapping out how an argument for it might go. I suggest it is a thesis well worth bearing in mind, particularly as we continue to make advancements in artificial intelligence. Nonetheless, I suggest that we presently lack the necessary evidence to subscribe to it wholesale and raise some challenges for securing it going forward.

In Section 16.6, I briefly conclude by addressing what Haugeland calls the common complaint regarding artificial intelligence. According to Haugeland, the complaint suggests that artificial intelligence "pays scant attention to feelings, emotions, ego, imagination, moods, consciousness" (this volume, p. 33). I show how by adopting an evaluative account, we can not only illuminate core aspects of minds like ours, but equally appeal to powerful, computational frameworks to design many (though not all) of the features Haugeland refers to into artificial agents.

To start, let's look at the narrow end of the argumentative wedge, namely, with a basic sketch of reinforcement learning.

16.2   Program, concepts, and findings

16.2.1   Overview

We can think of reinforcement learning as a research question, as a research program, and as a set of computational tools. As a research question, sometimes called the 'learning problem,' reinforcement learning asks how an agent can optimize its behavior by learning from interactions with its environment. For example, how does a baby plover learn the contours of its environment simply by hopping around in it? Or again, how does a newcomer to London find her way around, just by using a map and a bit of trial-and-error? As a research program, reinforcement learning refers to a branch of computer science, together with associated interdisciplinary approaches, that analyzes formal versions of this question and develops computational solutions to it (Dayan and Abbott, 2001; Glimcher and Fehr, 2013). Finally, reinforcement learning methods are the suites of computational algorithms that aim to solve the aforementioned learning problem (Sutton and Barto, 2018a).

As a research program, the reinforcement learning framework makes certain foundational and technical assumptions, with specific versions of the framework committing to some assumptions while suspending or relaxing others. Here, I sketch what I call the 'reinforcement learning and decision-making' (RLDM) framework, drawing on assumptions made in both machine learning and computational neuroscience.[2] Specifically, in addition to assuming many of the somewhat more basic features of the general framework, this version assumes that reinforcement learning is to some degree meaningfully instantiated in the minds of biological organisms, and takes a particular if minimal view regarding the problem of specifying where rewards come from in biological systems. Throughout, it will be useful to remember that this is just one variant of the general framework among many—though perhaps one that is particularly philosophically useful.

16.2.2   RLDM

Let's start with the basic ingredients. In a reinforcement learning framework, we have an agent and an environment. The agent is the learner or decision-maker in question, and it selects different actions in its environment, where actions can be understood as "any decisions we want to learn how to make," including mental actions (Sutton and Barto, 2018a, 50). The environment refers to everything 'outside' of the agent, which the agent cannot arbitrarily change but rather with which the agent interacts. (For example, in many cases, even parts of the agent's body are considered to be a part of the environment.) The agent and the environment interact in the sense that the agent is presented with sensory information from the environment, and the agent chooses among different actions within the environment (picking what is called a 'state-action pair'). The environment is then affected by these actions, and the process is (usually) iterated. Notably, the agent may not be able to observe the complete environment and may have no prior knowledge of the environment's dynamics. In addition, the agent may, but by no means needs to, build a model of the environment in order to choose actions in and learn from it.

A distinguishing feature of the reinforcement learning framework is the role of *reward*. Roughly, in reinforcement learning, the agent's objective in the environment is to maximize the cumulative reward it receives over time, where rewards are passed from the environment to the agent. In their influential text, Sutton and Barto call this framing the *reward hypothesis*, specifying, "all of what we mean by [an agent's] goals and purposes can be well thought of as the maximization of expected value of the cumulative sum of a received scalar signal (called reward)" (Sutton and Barto, 2018a, 53). That is, the agent's objective is to maximize its yield of reward as it acts in the world. This objective is characterized by assigning a quantity of intrinsic desirability to each state (or to taking each action in each state). This intrinsic desirability is known as the reward.[3]

This intrinsic desirability assigned to each state (or taking each action in each state), or *reward*, can be contrasted with the notion of *value*, which captures the expected, discounted, sum of future reward associated with each state (or each action in each state), conditional on a certain policy of action. We can elucidate the distinction between reward and value further using an example adapted from Silver (2015). Imagine an agent trying to find a door. Upon arriving at the door for the first time, the agent receives a *reward* from the environment. But this reward can also be used to assess how relatively good (valuable) individual states are expected to be to the extent that, conditional on a certain action policy, they *lead to* the door and hence the reward. Hence, an agent's ongoing interactions with its environment enable it to continually revise the value attributed to a given state or state-action pair conditional on a certain policy, upgrading or downgrading as needed. This enables the agent to *learn* the most appropriate actions in the most appropriate states to maximize cumulative reward over time, conditional on a certain policy, in spite of the fact that states (or state-action pairs) can be of high *value* without being intrinsically worthwhile (i.e., *rewarding*).

We can take the example of making and having coffee to help illustrate the difference between a state of high expected value that is nonetheless not technically rewarding. Although only drinking a cup of coffee itself may be intrinsically worthwhile (rewarding), and the grinding of the beans almost certainly is not, the state-action pair of grinding the coffee is nonetheless associated with *expected value*, as it is, conditional on a certain policy, a necessary step or state-action pair on the way to having the coffee.

The distinction between valuable and rewarding states partly helps explain why not every state in an environment needs to be directly rewarding in order for an agent to act appropriately within it.

As a branch of machine learning, reinforcement learning represents the foregoing conceptual features in computational terms. There are countless reinforcement learning algorithms, each with a distinctive computational profile. For example, the *temporal-difference learning algorithm* (TD) represents a computationally efficient way of making predictions about reward in the future. One way to improve predictions over time is to make a prediction about an actual outcome, compare the difference (or error) between the two, and then update the estimates that led to the initial prediction.

To borrow an example from Sutton (1988, 10), suppose you are a weather forecaster in a monotonous climate, charged with making a prediction each week about the chance of rain on the coming Saturday. Each week, you gain more information about the local weather patterns, allowing you to refine your predictive powers. That information could be used in different ways. You could make a prediction on Monday about the weather on Saturday, wait until Saturday, and then update Monday's prediction based on the difference between Monday's prediction and Saturday's actual weather. The temporal difference approach does something a little neater by updating its predictions throughout the week. Having made a prediction Monday about the weather on Saturday, TD lets you compare Monday's prediction to *Tuesday's* prediction about Saturday and adjust your monday predictions accordingly. For instance, if Monday's prediction for Saturday is a 90% chance of rain, but Tuesday's prediction for Saturday is only a 60% chance, then the temporal difference approach is to lower the Monday prediction for subsequent weeks with similar indicators.[4]

Given that different problem settings present different challenges, there are myriad different RL algorithms in use today. These trade off factors such as memory consumption, computation cost, data efficiency, and stability; some are useful for very small environments, and others are useful for very large environments; some for discrete action spaces, and others for continuous ones.[5] Thus, 'reinforcement learning' refers to a general learning problem and a suite of computational algorithms, as well as to the branch of computer science devoted to studying them, rather than to any token solution to the problem.

The RLDM version of reinforcement learning adds two assumptions to the basic reinforcement learning framework sketched above. First, it assumes a relationship between reinforcement learning and the minds of biological creatures like us. This assumption is by no means universally held: researchers in machine learning can pursue decades of research and remain entirely agnostic regarding the role of reinforcement learning in biological agents. Similarly, cognitive and comparative psychologists can study the nature of learning and behavior without any appeals to the reinforcement learning framework. However, RLDM follows computational neuroscientists and other decision scientists who suspect that reinforcement learning does, in fact, capture something special about minds like ours. As Dayan and Niv put it, reinforcement learning appears to offer

> More than just a computational, 'approximate ideal learner' theory for affective decision-making. [Reinforcement learning] algorithms, such as the temporal difference (TD) learning rule, appear to be directly instantiated in neural mechanisms, such as the phasic activity of dopamine neurons. That [reinforcement learning] appears to be so transparently embedded has made it possible to use it in a much more immediate way to make hypotheses about, and retrodictive and predictive interpretations of, a wealth of behavioral and neural data collected in a huge range of paradigms and systems. Dayan and Niv (2008, 1)

Notably, we are free to relax the condition that reinforcement learning is directly *instantiated* in the workings of the brain. It is sufficient to say that reinforcement learning provides remarkably useful frameworks for thinking about decision-making and selection in the mind.

RLDM's second assumption has to do with the *subjective* nature of reward. As noted above, in the basic reinforcement learning framework, rewards are passed from the environment to the agent when an agent enters certain states of the environment, or when the agent takes certain actions in certain states. This external nature of reward is unproblematic in the context of machine learning because the reward is simply designed by the researcher as a means of communicating what the researcher wants the artificial agent to achieve. But things get thornier when considering biological organisms, since it's not clear where rewards come from. This question regarding the origin of reward in biology generates what Juechems and Summerfield (2019) call the *paradox of reward*. The issue is paradoxical, the authors contend, because,

> No external entity exists that can directly quantify the consequences of each action, like the points that are awarded in a video game for completing levels or shooting monsters. Nor is it obvious that biological systems have a dedicated channel for receipt of external rewards that is distinct from the classical senses. Rather, rewards and punishments are sensory observations—the taste of an apple, the warmth of an embrace—and so stimulus value

must be inferred by the agent, not conferred by the world. In other words, rewards must be intrinsic, not extrinsic." (2019, 837-838)

Exactly how this conversion between sensory observations and assignments of intrinsic rewards occurs—assuming that it occurs at all—remains the subject of lively theoretical debate. One possible explanation is that minds like ours have evolved specific mechanisms that convert sensory observations into hedonic signals (e.g., see Schultz, 2015). Another, complementary possibility is that, in addition to the evolved mechanisms for basic rewards (e.g., food and water), human beings develop cognitive setpoints, akin to homeostatic setpoints, on which reward amounts to a by-product of computing the distance to self-defined goals (e.g., such as getting married or going to graduate school) (Juechems and Summerfield, 2019). Here, RLDM again takes a minimal approach, and merely assumes *that* minds like ours subpersonally assign subjective rewards to, *e.g.*, sensory observations, albeit indirectly; it remains provisionally agnostic about how this assignment takes place.

16.2.3 Substantiating the first assumption

Let's explore the first assumption in more depth. In what sense does RLDM provide a distinctive, interpretive lens for cognitive neuroscientific evidence?

As gestured at above, arguably the most significant connection is between RLDM and the reward system in the mammalian brain. In the mid-1990s, theoretical and empirical work showed that the firing of dopamine neurons is accurately approximated by the temporal difference learning algorithm (for narrative accounts of the discovery, see (Montague, 2006; Redish, 2013; Colombo, 2014). That is, dopamine neurons fire when an organism experiences a higher- or lower-than-expected value in association with a given state (Schultz et al., 1997). This discovery provides the foundation for the so-called *reward prediction error hypothesis of dopamine neuron activity,* which holds that "one of the functions of the phasic activity of dopamine-producing neurons in mammals is to deliver an error signal between an old and a new estimate of expected future reward to target areas through the brain" (Sutton and Barto, 2018a, 381).

This seminal finding in turn led to the use of reinforcement learning methods to study the neuroscience of vision (Hayhoe and Ballard, 2005; Hikosaka et al., 2006; Hickey et al., 2010), attention (Della Libera and Chelazzi, 2009; Chelazzi et al., 2014; Anderson and Kim, 2018), memory (Patil et al., 2017; Ergo et al., 2020), prospective memory (Krishnan and Shapiro, 1999; Katai et al., 2003; Kliegel et al., 2005; Walter and Meier, 2014), cognitive control (Savine and Braver, 2010; Chiew and Braver, 2014; Cubillo et al., 2019), and above all, decision-making (Sutton and Barto, 2018a; Dayan and Niv, 2008; Rangel et al., 2008; Dayan, 2011; Glimcher and Fehr, 2013).

For example, a systematic body of evidence now indicates that the reward system guides visual fixation and saccadic eye movement, i.e., what we look at, when, and in what order (Liao and Anderson, 2020). Similarly, reward guides what we do or don't attend to more precisely than do either location or salience (Anderson and Kim, 2018). Conversely, deficits and disruptions (e.g., by addictive substances) to the reward system are not only implicated in diseases such as Parkinson's and Tourette's, but also in a range of psychiatric disorders, including depression (Huys et al., 2015) and addiction (Hyman, 2005; Redish et al., 2008; Redish, 2013). Arguably, methods from reinforcement learning thus represent an important and, to date, under-utilized framework for elucidating the nature and mechanisms underlying selection between competing states of affairs across a range of 'low'- as well as 'high-level' kinds of cognitive processing.

When proponents say there's something special about RLDM, then, they tend to point to one or both of the following considerations. First, reinforcement learning algorithms successfully predict and characterize the workings of the reward system; by contrast, other approaches, including predictive processing (see Clark, 17 of this volume), often provide merely retrodictive explanations of known phenomena.

Second, the reward system appears to play an outsized role in a range of cognitive capacities, from sensation through to economic choice. The question is, what's the best way of characterizing this role of reward and value in the mind, from a philosophical point of view?[6]

16.3   Valuation

16.3.1   Overview
In principle, the role of reward can be characterized at multiple levels of explanation and across multiple, co-dependent theoretical domains, including in computational terms, cellular- and systems- neuroscientific terms, cognitive neuroscientific and neuroeconomic terms, and psychological and behavioral terms (Hochstein, 2016). For instance, as discussed above, we can capture the role of reward and value in computational terms using methods from reinforcement learning (for an overview, see Sutton and Barto (2018a) though see also hybrid approaches, such as that put forward in Gershman (2015)). Or again, following the Schultz et al. (1997) discovery, we can characterize reward and value in cellular-and-system neuroscientific terms, both in terms of dopaminergic functioning as well as in terms of the more general, system-level neural analyses of the reward system in the brain. At a 'higher' level still, we can characterize reward and value in cognitive neuroscientific and neuroeconomic terms, drawing on behavioral experiments and fMRI data, and using constructs such as 'decision-making,' 'motivation,' and 'willingness-to-pay.' And so on.

In what follows, I characterize the role of reward and value in the mind at roughly a 'conceptual' level of explanation, i.e., at a coarseness of grain typical in the philosophy of mind. Accordingly, my argument also broadens out at this stage, moving from the specifics of RLDM and associated empirical evidence to a more traditional, philosophical characterization—namely, to characterize a cognitive process I'll call *valuation*. This is essential for future work in the philosophy of mind, e.g., to enable us to distinguish and understand the relationship between, say, valuation and the philosophical folk psychological notion of *desire* (for work in this spirit, see Schroeder, 2004; Arpaly and Schroeder, 2014), or again, to enable us distinguish and understand the relationship between, valuation and the various notions of *affect*, *mood*, and *emotion* (for a philosophical discussion of emotion see, e.g., Scarantino and Sousa, 2021).

In this way, the resulting characterization of valuation in some cases *complements* and in some cases *revises* the traditional conceptual machinery used to describe and understand the mind and minds like ours.

16.3.2   Characterising valuation

Recall from the previous section that in basic reinforcement learning, reward is some quantity assigned to represent the intrinsic desirability to each state (or to taking each action in each state), and which is conveyed to an agent when they reach that state. Further, this intrinsic desirability assigned to each state (or taking each action in each state), or reward, can be contrasted with the notion of value, which captures the expected, discounted, sum of future reward associated with each state (or each action in each state), conditional on a certain policy of action. So, while coffee is intrinsically rewarding for me in the morning, grinding coffee or getting milk is not—but these latter states are nonetheless valuable to the degree that, conditional on my action policy, they lead me to my cup of coffee.

Recall in addition that, according to RLDM, the reward hypothesis captures something special about the mind, namely, the substantial role of the reward system in the mammalian brain, where the reward system is itself implicated in a wide range of 'low-' and 'high-level' cognitive capacities.

I argue that if both of these claims are right, then we can use RLDM and the corresponding empirical evidence to revise our philosophical understanding of what the mind is doing, how it is going about it, and what this kind of processing is for.

Let's start with the 'what.' Very simply, I argue, the mind engages in *valuation*. Informally, I take this to mean that the mind continually attributes reward and value to a range of sensations, perceptions, actions and so on—essentially forming a kind of evaluative layer over the features of its experience.

In more technical terms, I argue that valuation refers to the subpersonal attribution of goal- and context-dependent subjective reward and value to internal and external stimuli. Valuation is *subpersonal* in the sense that it demarcates a causal rather than an intentional mechanism (Dennett, 1969; Drayson, 2014). This is key: the mind routinely, mechanistically assess states of affairs as better or worse.[7] Further, it is *goal- and context-dependent* in the sense that what is rewarding or valuable depends on what the agent is trying to do, and when and where the agent is trying to do it. For example, if my goal is to wake up and have a productive day, then drinking a cup of coffee first thing in the morning is valuable. But if my goal is to rest and get a good night's sleep, then drinking a cup of coffee late at night is not. It is *subjective* in the sense that what is considered rewarding and/or valuable is agent-relative; while this author finds coffee rewarding, many individuals do not. And the term *stimuli* here is intended as a broad catch-all: reward and value can be attributed to external objects (commodities), states, state-action pairs, and action policies, but also to internal states of affairs, such as experiences, feelings, and moods.

In terms of the 'how,' valuation is realized in a number of complementary ways. One important way is through the retroactive attribution of value to states that lead to reward in subsequent states. Recall the task of walking to a nearby door in the previous section. Upon arriving at the door for the first time and therefore receiving or experiencing the *reward*, there occurs a subpersonal, retroactive attribution of *value* to the antecedent states that then led to the reward. That is, there occurs a subpersonal, retroactive attribution of value to the penultimate state, derived from the reward associated with arriving at the 'ultimate' state, i.e., the door. This retroactive attribution in turn continues to feed backwards, i.e., there occurs the subpersonal, retroactive attribution to the antepenultimate state, and so on. In this way, ongoing interactions continue to revise the value attributed to a given state or state-action pair, upgrading or downgrading as needed. For instance, if the baby plover finds a new trove of bugs, the value of a certain path leading to the beach can increase. But values can also be computed 'on the fly' (Balleine and Dickinson, 1998; Langdon et al., 2018), relative to features of context (Hunter and Daw, 2021), and with respect to imagined or expected future states (Gagne and Dayan, 2022; Russek et al., 2021). For instance, if the newcomer to London is traveling from Green Park to Russell Square and Holborn Station is under renovation, the value of taking the blue line decreases.

Here, the main idea is that the mind continually assesses and reassesses states of affairs as better or worse, constructing and casting, to put things in fairly figurative terms, a kind of evaluative fabric over its states and experiences.

16.3.3 Valuation as selection

But it's the 'what for' of valuation that is of most interest (as these things tend to go).

The *function* of valuation in minds like ours, I argue, is to solve for what I call the *selection problem*, or the problem of selecting between one or more competing alternatives. The selection problem can be described in general terms, insofar as the mind must continually select what to *compute*, what to *sense*, what to *perceive*, what to *attend to*, what to *choose* (as an action in the world), and so on. Technically characterized examples of the selection problem include selecting between *multiple action controllers* (Daw et al., 2005), the problem of *perceptual decision-making* (Gold and Shadlen, 2007), and the problem of *action-based decision-making* (Glimcher, 2011). Crucially, as the span of these examples should illustrate, the selection problem occurs ubiquitously in the mind. It occurs at every major stage of mental processing, from sensation and computation to action, and at every level of description of mental processing, from the sub-personal to the personal.

A central, underappreciated upshot of the RLDM's experiment in mind design, I argue, is that the mind selects between available computations, sensations, perceptions and so on *conditional on* attributions of reward and value.

To illustrate, consider the unlikely phenomenon of binocular rivalry. Binocular rivalry occurs when one stimulus is shown to one eye at the same time as a different stimulus is shown to the other. The resulting experience is of the two images alternating back and forth; *perceptual dominance* in binocular rivalry refers to one of the two images appearing first, or for a longer period of time during the overall duration of the experience of alternation. Notably, both rewarded stimuli and rewarded percepts result in perceptual dominance; that is, participants are more likely to perceive stimuli and percepts associated with a reward (Balcetis et al., 2012; Wilbertz et al., 2014; Marx and Einhäuser, 2015; Haas, 2021). Moreover, a complementary phenomenon occurs for punished percepts: participants experience perceptual dominance for the *non*-punished percept in the pair, suggesting that the reward or punishment is *not* simply additional information taken into consideration by Bayes-like predictive processing, as a predictive processing view might suggest (Wilbertz et al., 2014). In this way, *the selection of the perceptually dominant percept is directly conditional on the attribution of reward and value in the binocular rivalry paradigm, i.e., on valuation.* Participants tend to perceive the most rewarded or valuable stimulus or percept. Hence, when it comes to the cognitive task of selecting 'what to perceive,' valuation plays a driving role.

But valuation doesn't just play a driving role in perception. Rather, when I say that the mind is fundamentally evaluative in nature, I mean that we *sense*, *perceive*, and *attend* to the features of our environment conditional on our distributions of reward and value attribution, as when we attend to rewarded rather than salient or location-based percepts (Anderson and Kim, 2018). We *remember, remember to remember* (remember prospectively) conditional on reward (for a useful review, see Walter and Meier, 2014). We *allocate our cognitive resources* (in cognitive control) conditional on our distributions of reward and value attributions, as shown by the expected value of control account of cognitive control (Musslick et al., 2015). And we *decide, choose,* and *plan* our future actions conditional on our distributions of reward and value attributions, as when prior reward experience determines a participant's willingness-to-pay in everyday economic transactions (Plassmann et al., 2007).

Conversely, when the reward system is impaired, for example, through cell death in the basal ganglia (Parkinson's) or due to allostatic shift (substance addiction), there are direct, corresponding deficits in selection: e.g., in motor tremors, mood disorders, and executive dysfunction in Parkinson's disease, and e.g., in cravings, impaired control, and continued use in spite of overwhelmingly negative consequences in substance addiction (for extended discussions, see Redish, 2004; Redish et al., 2008). And so on.

To emphasize, I do not argue that selection is *synonymous* with valuation. But selection is *conditional* on valuation: we select or avoid what we learn is better or worse over a life-long course of iteration.[8] Moreover, valuation is deployed and redeployed across a range of selection problems in the mind, including selection in sensation, perception, attention, and cognition generally.[9]

Hence, where I suggested above that the reward system "influences" or is "implicated in" a range of cognitive processing, I can now be much more specific: *valuation guides selection* across the range of mental processing that occurs in minds like ours.

16.4   The weaker thesis

What, then, of the evaluative thesis—the view that the mind is fundamentally evaluative in nature?

At the outset, I suggested that on the weaker version of the view, the mind encompasses *both* thinking *and* evaluation. That is, according to the weaker thesis, the mind does some-thing like 'see' two competing stimuli in binocular rivalry, and 'perceive' only one of those stimuli at a time, resulting in the signature perceptual experience of perceptual alternation. In a standard case, we might also say than an individual could go on to draw on this per-ception to form beliefs, draw inferences, and perform all the other kinds of cognitive tasks that are typically associated with, as Haugeland put it, "thinking, intellect," (Haugeland, Chapter 2, this volume), or as others put it, "intelligence."

But, on the weaker version of the evaluative thesis, the mind *also* does something else, without which it would not be the mind it is—namely, it continually assesses things as better or worse, conditional on certain goals and aspects of the environment, in the ways described above, i.e., subpersonally, through various forms of attribution, in a two-place relation, and so on.

In this sense, the weaker thesis doesn't exactly try to unseat the traditional conception of thinking mind but rather complements it by describing a *fundamental* cognitive process that has heretofore been relatively overlooked.

I defend the weaker thesis on three grounds.

First, evidence bears out the positive features of the view. A survey of mature, textbook neuroscience suggests that the reward system is indeed implicated in *basic biophysical processes* such as eating, drinking, and reproduction; in *basic cognitive processes* such as working memory, executive functioning and time estimation; and, crucially, in *all learned behaviors*, ranging from learning-based sensory processing through planning, strategiz-ing, and second-order preference-formation (for a concise review, see Arias-Carrión et al., 2010; for extended discussions, see Glimcher and Fehr, 2013). Equally, the reward system is implicated in the kinds of *'sophisticated' cognitive processes* that are often of interest to philosophers, including in emotional responding, social preference formation, speech and language processing (see especially Simonyan et al. (2012); and also (Ripollés et al., 2014; McNamara and Durso, 2018)), and generalization.

Second, *predictions* made by the weaker thesis are better supported than predictions made by competing theoretical accounts, e.g., by accounts in the predictive processing space or accounts emphasizing the role of emotions in our cognitive processes. Returning to the example of binocular rivalry offers a good example of the former comparison. The weaker thesis predicts that rewards (and negative rewards, i.e., punishments) should influence perceptual dominance in binocular rivalry; predictive processing accounts make no such prediction, and in fact struggle to explain this type of finding post hoc. But as noted above, reward modulates perceptual dominance in binocular rivalry (Haas, 2021).

An example of the latter type of comparison might involve competing explanations of psychopathy. The weaker thesis proposes that psychopathy is a disorder of valuation, perhaps involving an inability to predict negative outcomes, and/or an inability to update appropriately following negative experiences (e.g., see Oba et al., 2021). By contrast, on an account of psychopathy emphasizing emotions, individuals with psychopathic traits fundamentally suffer from a disorder of empathy, or the ability to respond appropriately to emotional stimuli (Hare, 1998; Soderstrom, 2003; Blair, 2007; Brook and Kosson, 2013; Domes et al., 2013; Blair, 2018). Accordingly, the former but not the latter account predicts that individuals with psychopathic traits will exhibit deficits in basic economic decision-making. Here, some evidence seems to bear out the weaker thesis: controlling for other deficits, psychopaths appear to perform significantly worse on the Iowa Gambling Task (Mahmut et al., 2008), as well as on other types of risky decision-making (Takahashi et al., 2014).

Third, *deficits* in the reward system corroborate the view. Here, standard cases again emerge in the computational and cognitive neuroscientific literature, including regarding the aforementioned Parkinson's and Tourette's diseases, as well as diseases such as Major Depressive Disorder and different categories of substance addiction. Take the case of prospective memory, or the ability to 'remember to remember.' I suggested above that, like so many of our cognitive capacities, prospective memory is conditional on valuation; we are more likely to 'remember to remember' something in the future when it's associated with a reward. For example, participants show higher prospective memory performance for tasks that were associated with a monetary reward as compared to those that were not (Krishnan and Shapiro, 1999). By extension, consistent with the weaker thesis, we would expect to see *deficits* on prospective memory tasks among individuals with Parkinson's disease. The reasoning goes like this: prospective memory is conditional on valuation, valuation by realized in the reward system in the brain, and the reward system is compromised in

Parkinson's disease. Hence, we should expect deficits on prospective memory tasks among individuals with Parkinson's.

And this is indeed what we find. Individuals with Parkinson's exhibit impairment in several core stages of prospective memory, most notably when it comes to the phases of intention formation and intention initiation (Katai et al., 2003; Kliegel et al., 2005, 2011; Pirogovsky et al., 2012; Ramanan and Kumar, 2013; D'Iorio et al., 2019; Coundouris et al., 2020; though see Zabberoni et al., 2017; Kinsella et al., 2018). Analogous arguments propose that impaired reward valuation, i.e., the dysfunctional underestimation, downgrading, or failure to update regarding rewards in individual with Major Depressive Disorder (Takamura et al., 2017; Rupprechter et al., 2018, 2021), may explain why this demographic also exhibit systematic deficits in prospective memory tasks (Altgassen et al., 2009; Chen et al., 2013; Li et al., 2013; McFarland and Vasterling, 2018). And so on. The basic structure of this third kind of argument, then, is to identify a cognitive capacity modulated by valuation; identify a disease that either upregulates or downregulates valuation (via the reward system) and then determine whether, as predicted by the weaker thesis, individuals with the relevant disorder also exhibit deficits on the corresponding cognitive capacity.

Each of the three sets of reasons gives inductive support for the weaker thesis, by giving a *confirming* instance of it. Saying 'valuation is ubiquitous in the mind' is akin to saying 'lots and lots of swans are white.' This means that the weaker thesis can be disconfirmed—namely, by uncovering a meaningful number of instances where cognitive selection is clearly not, at least in part, underwritten by valuational processes. But this is in fact precisely why I defend the weaker thesis. The normative principles originating in RLDM, together with evidence from the decision sciences, enable us to make a principled but nonetheless fundamentally *empirical* claim about a certain process in the mind—where this claim already brings with it significant high-level implications for understanding the workings of the mind.

By contrast, these same principles and evidence, to my mind, will struggle to bear out something conceptually stronger, including a universal claim regarding the role of valuation in the mind, which I discuss next.

16.5   The stronger thesis

Whereas the weaker thesis holds that valuation is empirically ubiquitous in the mind, the stronger thesis proposes that the mind is *at bottom* evaluative in nature.

There are a couple of ways of understanding the stronger thesis. It can be understood as the claim that valuation as selection guides *all cognitive selection* in the mind. On this understanding, valuation amounts to grand unifying theory for exploring the nature of the mind. This is the stronger, universal version of the weaker thesis. And it can be understood as the claim that valuation is ontologically prior *to* and thus conceptually necessary for understanding the mind's perceptual, cognitive, and motor processes. We can call the former claim the *scope commitment* and the latter the *priority commitment*.

Prima facie, one might assume that a proponent of the evaluative thesis and RLDM model of valuation would by extension directly subscribe to one or both of these commitments. As we will see, they may hold some theoretical advantages over the weaker thesis. They are also nominally more in line with the prominent 'Reward is Enough' hypothesis (Silver et al., 2021). Nonetheless, I don't commit to either.

So, why not go whole hog and defend the stronger version of the evaluative view? Let's start with the scope commitment.

16.5.1   The scope commitment

The scope commitment is a supercharged version of the weaker thesis. Whereas the weaker thesis holds that valuation is ubiquitous in the mind, the scope commitment holds that valuation lies at the heart of *all* cognitive capacities. Hence, where the weaker thesis suggests that 'lots of swans are white,' the scope commitment rounds up to claim that 'all swans are white,' period.

So formulated, the central challenge with the scope commitment should quickly become obvious: the scope commitment requires defending a universal claim, and no amount of evidence will get us there, as there's always the possibility of an untested counterexample somewhere.[10] The scope commitment is just too easily falsified.

Moreover, it simply doesn't strike me as *likely* that valuation underwrites everything of interest in the mind. The evolved mind is a messy artefact, and at a bare minimum, we can expect 'spandrel' capacities that don't rely on valuation in any interesting sense. I can get plenty of mileage out of the weaker thesis without needing to extend it to the logical limit.

16.5.2   The priority commitment

This leaves us with the priority commitment. The priority commitment is trickier to deal with. The priority commitment makes an ontological claim about the mind : our 'thinking' processes are *conditional* on our evaluative processes. That is, we have the memories, beliefs and so on that we do *in virtue* of our assessments of better or worse. Note that this is analogous to action-first theories in cognitive science; for a review, see (Briscoe and Grush, 2020).

To take a concrete example of this kind of theorizing, one might argue that the normative function of episodic memory is not to encode a past event 'as it actually happened,' but rather to encode a past event in light of what it might be useful for an agent to remember—and by extension, *do*—in the future.

Adopting the priority commitment enables us to make top down rather than inductive predictions regarding the workings of various cognitive capacities. For instance, to continue with the case of episodic memory, adopting the scope commitment can help us make predictions about what will and won't be remembered, or why individuals experience flashbulb memories (if indeed they do). On the priority commitment, flashbulb memories may contain such an impressive level of detail because, following a traumatic event, it is not clear which features of the preceding event are most relevant to future action, such that 'all' of them are carried forward for future learning. This interpretation draws a close connection between flashbulb memories and the more general credit assignment problem in reinforcement learning, or the problem of determining which actions lead or led to a given outcome (Minsky, 1961; Sutton and Barto, 2018a).

This kind of hypothesis generation is certainly appealing. It's also pretty tempting to defend the priority of valuation as a way of counteracting the standard emphases placed on computation (and predictive processing!) in the philosophical and cognitive scientific literatures. Still, I stop short of doing so, for two reasons.

First, where the scope commitment is too easily falsified, the priority commitment is, conversely, unfalsifiable. If I can describe any cognitive or behavioral phenomenon of interest in terms of the maximization of reward, it becomes more difficult to test the hypothesis.

Second, 'grand unifying' theories of mind encourage us to recast broad swathes of empirical evidence into a single explanatory framework. However, the resulting explanations are sometimes less than illuminating. Moreover, surely some explanatory richness is lost if everything about the mind is ultimately, say, 'imagination,' 'attention,' or 'prediction-error minimization.' In some cases, these kinds of theories even run the risk of discounting evidence that is at odds with their theoretical commitments (Haas, 2021).

There's no reason to expect that the priority commitment would avoid such a fate. To try and keep to a fine-grained and falsifiable view, I thus stick with the weaker thesis.

16.5.3 'Reward is enough'

Finally, let me draw out a few points of comparison between the evaluative thesis explored in this paper and the prominent and somewhat controversial 'reward is enough' (RIE) hypothesis (Silver et al., 2021). RIE holds that reward maximization is enough to "drive behavior that exhibits *most if not all* abilities that are studied in natural and artificial intelligence" (Silver et al., 2021, 1, added emphasis mine). Here, reward is understood in the sense put forward by the basic reinforcement learning framework introduced in Section 16.2.

Like the stronger thesis, RIE involves a couple of different claims. First, RIE makes the *epistemological* claim that reward maximization is enough to understand many—if not all—features of intelligence. Implicit in this claim is that reward maximization provides better and richer explanations than other rival scientific theories do. Second, RIE makes the *ontological* claim that intelligent processes *just are* reward maximization processes, where "intelligence, and its associated abilities, can be understood as subserving the maximization of reward by an agent acting in its environment" (Silver et al., 2021, 5). And third, RIE makes that *causal* claim that reward maximization is sufficient to *drive* the kinds of abilities we associate with behavior, such as gathering nuts or playing Go. According to this last claim, the forms of intelligence "implicitly emerge" through and as a direct result of the process of reward maximization. By extension, the authors contend, "a good reward-maximizing agent, in the service of achieving its goal, could implicitly yield all the abilities associated with intelligence that have been considered in natural and artificial intelligence" (Silver et al., 2021, 5).

What is the relationship between the evaluative thesis and RIE? At least on their face, the stronger thesis's priority commitment and RIE's epistemological claim appear consistent: the role of reward provides a unified and valuable way of understanding the mind and the nature of intelligence.

But the evaluative thesis and REI come apart on the ontological and causal fronts. At the end of the day, even the stronger thesis amounts to a pair of claims about the function and scope of a *cognitive process* in the mind. By contrast, RIE suggests that *all intelligence processing* is an expression or *by product* of reward maximization where, at bottom, the pursuit of reward drives the emergence of all other kinds of intelligence. These start to look like two very different kinds of arguments.

This being said, one softening feature of RIE is that it makes a pragmatic bet regarding the role of reward maximization in generating diverse forms of intelligence in artificial agents. That is, the authors of RIE propose that pure reinforcement learning frameworks will be sufficient to arrive at artificial general intelligence, without the need for handcrafting or pre-training. The authors acknowledge,

> We do not offer any *theoretical* guarantee on the sample efficiency of the reinforcement learning agent. Indeed, the rate at and degree to which abilities emerge will depend upon the specific environment, learning algorithm, and inductive biases; furthermore one may construct artificial environments in which learning will fail. Instead, we conjecture that the solution strategy of learning to maximize reward via interaction will be 'enough' for intelligence, and its associated abilities, to emerge in practice. (Silver et al., 2021, 10)

In this sense, by adopting a kind of maker's approach (Craver, 2021), RIE is at least indirectly falsifiable through efforts to leverage reward maximization to design artificial intelligence.[11]

16.6 Conclusion

At the outset of this chapter, I proposed that RLDM is an instance of mind design so successful that we have not quite figured out what to do with it yet. I further argued that, in light of this success, we should move beyond characterizing the mind as exhaustively constituted by "thinking, intellect," as Haugeland originally put it, and begin to recognize its fundamentally evaluative nature. At the same time, I've sought to distinguish my view, which some philosophers may take to be remarkably strong, from even stronger views, which are more in line with views held by some in the machine learning and reinforcement learning literatures.

By way of conclusion, I want to briefly address what Haugeland called the common complaint about artificial intelligence, namely, that it cannot or may never achieve the rich interiority of everyday life, including "feelings, emotions, ego, imagination, moods, consciousness—the whole 'phenomenology' of an inner life. No matter how smart the machines become, there's still 'nobody home' " (this volume, p. 33). Haugeland's characterisation is reminiscent of the traditional dichotomized conception of the mind: namely, of understanding the mind in terms of 'thinking' and, well, 'everything else'—even if the 'everything else' includes a lot of the important processes.

The notion of valuation—normatively rich, empirically substantiated—allows us to put pressure on this type of traditional, dichotomized view. At a minimum, it challenges the idea that we can in good scientific conscience continue to group together phenomena as disparate as emotions, consciousness, and ego under the heading of 'phenomenology.' As noted above, with a notion of valuation in place, we can, for instance, start to work out the relationship and differences between valuation and the various philosophical theories of emotion, or the role of valuation in driving instances of imagination (Gershman et al., 2017). Moreover, without in any way diminishing the 'thinking' or 'computational' mind, valuation brings with it new avenues for revising our extant philosophical and psychological cognitive taxonomies (Janssen et al., 2017).

More broadly, the notion of valuation challenges our assumptions regarding which aspects of mind can or cannot be quantified—and thereby understood in properly scientific terms. For example, in their discussion of "intelligence" and "intelligent" processes, Silver and colleagues (2021) largely appeal to features of the conventionally thinking mind such as perception, language, and generalization. But what the foregoing discussion should show is that we can also appeal to the normative principles of RLDM to better decompose and understand those allegedly more 'qualitative' aspects of the mind such as valuation—and, by extension, our personal-level capacities such motivation, cognitive control, choice, and moral cognition.

We should also carry these insights forward into our ongoing efforts at mind design. That is, as we make advancements toward more sophisticated artificial intelligence and, particularly artificial general intelligence, we can enrich our understanding of the kinds of mental capacities that we can and should include in these efforts—and we should move past the idea of designing only 'thinking' machines in the traditional sense.

Notes for Chapter 16

1. Of course, many approaches in the philosophy of mind and cognitive science posit what we might call 'compound states,' such as desires, that may be similarly evaluative. But it's consistent with such views that evaluative compound states are outliers—that "other stuff"—and overshadowed by traditional descriptive computations and belief-like states and processes. The weaker thesis makes a stronger claim, in that it posits widespread evaluative processing at a *fundamental* level and, notably, where evaluative processing modulates even belief-like states and processes. Thanks to Murray Shanahan for pressing me on this point.

2. Name adapted from Gęsiarz and Crockett (2015).

3. Thanks to Neil Rabinowitz for this formulation.

4. For a more detailed discussion, see Sutton and Barto (2018a, Chapter 6, and especially Example 6.1.)

5. Thanks to Neil Rabinowitz for this formulation.

6. This section is indebted to Sutton and Barto (2018a) and, especially, to Neil Rabinowitz.

7. This subpersonal process very likely plays a role in our personal-level experiences of 'value,' 'valuing,' and 'values,' e.g., see foregoing discussion of willingness-to-pay. But the focus throughout the remainder of this paper will be on the nature and workings of the subpersonal process.

8. It is worth emphasizing that valuation needn't be 'online' in order to guide selection. On the contrary, as in the foregoing example of retroactive attribution, selection can and often is informed by past reward and value attributions. And this 'carried over' feature of valuation as selection in turn has important implications for the nature of self-regulation and control, insofar as it implies that at least in many cases, we do not have direct, intrapsychic control over our motivational states (see Haas, in prep). Thanks to Neil Rabinowitz for pressing me on this point.

9. And has been for millions of years: see, e.g., the role of reinforcement signaling in *Drosophila* (Waddell (2013); see also Haas and Klein (2020)). Though this is beyond the scope of the current paper, valuation appears to be a highly conserved cognitive process.

10. Thanks to Carl Craver for helping me drill down on this point.

11. Thanks to Neil Rabinowitz for pressing me on this point, and to Sean and Legassick and Hado van Hasselt for helpful discussions of the REI thesis.

Whatever Next? Predictive Brains, Situated Agents, and the Future of Cognitive Science

17

Andy Clark
2013

17.1 Introduction: Prediction machines

17.1.1 From Helmholtz to action-oriented predictive processing

"The whole function of the brain is summed up in: error correction." So wrote W. Ross Ashby, the British psychiatrist and cyberneticist, some half a century ago.[1] Computational neuroscience has come a very long way since then. There is now increasing reason to believe that Ashby's (admittedly somewhat vague) statement is correct, and that it captures something crucial about the way that spending metabolic money to build complex brains pays dividends in the search for adaptive success. In particular, one of the brain's key tricks, it now seems, is to implement dumb processes that correct a certain kind of error: error in the multi-layered prediction of input. In mammalian brains, such errors look to be corrected within a cascade of cortical processing events in which higher-level systems attempt to predict the inputs to lower-level ones on the basis of their own emerging models of the causal structure of the world (i.e., the signal source). Errors in predicting lower level inputs cause the higher-level models to adapt so as to reduce the discrepancy. Such a process, operating over multiple linked higher-level models, yields a brain that encodes a rich body of information about the source of the signals that regularly perturb it.

Such models follow Helmholtz (1860/1962) in depicting perception as a process of probabilistic, knowledge-driven inference. From Helmholtz comes the key idea that sensory systems are in the tricky business of inferring sensory causes from their bodily effects. This in turn involves computing multiple probability distributions, since a single such effect will be consistent with many different sets of causes distinguished only by their relative (and context dependent) probability of occurrence.

Helmholz's insight informed influential work by MacKay (1956), Neisser (1967), and Gregory (1980), as part of the cognitive psychological tradition that became known as "analysis-by-synthesis" (for a review, see Yuille and Kersten, 2006). In this paradigm, the brain does not build its current model of distal causes (its model of how the world is) simply by accumulating, from the bottom-up, a mass of low-level cues such as edge-maps and so forth. Instead (see Hohwy, 2007), the brain tries to predict the current suite of cues from its best models of the possible causes. In this way:

> The mapping from low- to high-level representation (e.g. from acoustic to word-level) is computed using the *reverse* mapping, from high- to low-level representation. (Chater and Manning, 2006, p. 340, their emphasis)

Helmholz's insight was also pursued in an important body of computational and neuroscientific work. Crucial to this lineage were seminal advances in machine learning that began with pioneering connectionist work on back-propagation learning (McClelland et al., 1986b; Rumelhart et al., 1986b) and continued with work on the aptly named "Helmholz Machine" (Dayan et al., 1995; Dayan and Hinton, 1996; see also Hinton and Zemel, 1994).[2] The Helmholtz Machine sought to learn new representations in a multilevel system (thus capturing increasingly deep regularities within a domain) without requiring the provision of copious pre-classified samples of the desired input-output mapping. In this respect, it aimed to improve (see Hinton, 2010) upon standard back-propagation driven learning. It did this by using its own top-down connections to provide the desired states for the hidden units, thus (in effect) self-supervising the development of its perceptual "recognition model" using a *generative* model that tried to create the sensory patterns for itself (in "fantasy," as it was sometimes said).[3] (For a useful review of this crucial innovation and a survey of many subsequent developments, see Hinton, 2007a).

A generative model, in this quite specific sense, aims to capture the statistical structure of some set of observed inputs by tracking (one might say, by schematically recapitulating) the causal matrix responsible for that very structure. A good generative model for vision would thus seek to capture the ways in which observed lower-level visual responses are generated by an interacting web of causes—for example, the various aspects of a visually presented scene. In practice, this means that top-down connections within a multilevel (hierarchical and bidirectional) system come to encode a probabilistic model of the activities of units and groups of units within lower levels, thus tracking (as we shall shortly see in more detail) interacting causes in the signal source, which might be the body or the external world—see, for example, Kawato et al. (1993); Hinton and Zemel (1994); Mumford (1994); Hinton et al. (1995); Dayan et al. (1995); Olshausen and Field (1996); Dayan (1997); Hinton and Ghahramani (1997).

It is this twist—the strategy of using top-down connections to try to generate, using high-level knowledge, a kind of "virtual version" of the sensory data via a deep multilevel cascade—that lies at the heart of "hierarchical predictive coding" approaches to perception; for example, Rao and Ballard (1999), Lee and Mumford (2003), Friston (2005). Such approaches, along with their recent extensions to action—as exemplified in Friston and Stephan (2007), Friston et al. (2009), Friston (2010), Brown et al. (2011)—form the main focus of the present treatment. These approaches combine the use of top-down probabilistic generative models with a specific vision of one way such downward influence might operate. That way (borrowing from work in linear predictive coding—see below) depicts the top-down flow as attempting to predict and fully "explain away" the driving sensory signal, leaving only any residual "prediction errors" to propagate information forward within the system—see Rao and Ballard (1999), Lee and Mumford (2003), Friston (2005), Hohwy et al. (2008), Jehee and Ballard (2009), Friston (2010), Brown et al. (2011); and, for a recent review, see Huang and Rao (2011).

Predictive coding itself was first developed as a data compression strategy in signal processing (for a history, see Shi and Sun, 1999). Thus, consider a basic task such as image transmission: In most images, the value of one pixel regularly predicts the value of its nearest neighbors, with differences marking important features such as the boundaries between objects. That means that the code for a rich image can be compressed (for a properly informed receiver) by encoding only the "unexpected" variation: the cases where the actual value departs from the predicted one. What needs to be transmitted is therefore just the difference (a.k.a. the "prediction error") between the actual current signal and the predicted one. This affords major savings on bandwidth, an economy that was the driving force behind the development of the techniques by James Flanagan and others at Bell Labs during the 1950s (for a review, see Musmann, 1979). Descendents of this kind of compression technique are currently used in JPEGs, in various forms of lossless audio compression, and in motion-compressed coding for video. The information that needs to be communicated "upward" under all these regimes is just the prediction error: the divergence from the expected signal. Transposed (in ways we are about to explore) to the neural domain, this makes prediction error into a kind of proxy (Feldman and Friston, 2010) for sensory information itself. Later, when we consider predictive processing in the larger setting of information theory and entropy, we will see that prediction error reports the "surprise" induced by a mismatch between the sensory signals encountered and those predicted. More formally—and to distinguish it from surprise in the normal, experientially loaded sense—this is known as *surprisal* (Tribus, 1961).

Hierarchical predictive processing combines the use, within a multilevel bidirectional cascade, of "top-down" probabilistic generative models with the core predictive coding strategy of efficient encoding and transmission. Such approaches, originally developed in the domain of perception, have been extended (by Friston and others—see sect. 17.1.3) to encompass action, and to offer an attractive, unifying perspective on the brain's capacities for learning, inference, and the control of plasticity. Perception and action, if these unifying models are correct, are intimately related and work together to reduce prediction error by sculpting and selecting sensory inputs. In the remainder of this section, I rehearse some of the main features of these models before highlighting (in sects. 17.2-17.5 following) some of their most conceptually important and challenging aspects.

17.1.2   Escaping the black box

A good place to start (following Rieke, 1999) is with what might be thought of as the "view from inside the black box." For, the task of the brain, when viewed from a certain distance, can seem impossible: it must discover information about the likely causes of impinging signals without any form of direct access to their source. Thus, consider a black box taking inputs from a complex external world. The box has input and output channels along which signals flow. But all that it "knows", in any direct sense, are the ways its own states (e.g., spike trains) flow and alter. In that (restricted) sense, all the system has direct access to is its own states. The world itself is thus off-limits (though the box can, importantly, issue motor commands and await developments). The brain is one such black box. How, simply on the basis of patterns of changes in its own internal states, is it to alter and adapt its responses so as to tune itself to act as a useful node (one that merits its relatively huge metabolic expense) for the origination of adaptive responses? Notice how different this conception is to ones in which the problem is posed as one of establishing a mapping relation between environmental and inner states. The task is not to find such a mapping but to infer the nature of the signal source (the world) from just the varying input signal itself.

Hierarchical approaches in which top-down generative models are trying to predict the flow of sensory data provide a powerful means for making progress under such apparently unpromising conditions. One key task performed by the brain, according to these models, is that of guessing the next states of its own neural economy. Such guessing improves when you use a good model of the signal source. Cast in the Bayesian mode, good guesses thus increase the posterior probability[4] of your model. Various forms of gradient descent learning can progressively improve your first guesses. Applied within a hierarchical predictive processing[5] regime, this will—if you survive long enough—tend to yield useful generative models of the signal source (ultimately, the world).

The beauty of the bidirectional hierarchical structure is that it allows the system to infer its own priors (the prior beliefs essential to the guessing routines) as it goes along. It does this by using its best current model—at one level—as the source of the priors for the level below, engaging in a process of "iterative estimation" (see Dempster et al., 1977; Neal and Hinton, 1998) that allows priors and models to co-evolve across multiple linked layers of processing so as to account for the sensory data. The presence of bidirectional hierarchical structure thus induces "empirical priors"[6] in the form of the constraints that one level in the hierarchy places on the level below, and these constraints are progressively tuned by the sensory input itself. This kind of procedure (which implements a version of "empirical Bayes"; Robbins, 1956) has an appealing mapping to known facts about the hierarchical and reciprocally connected structure and wiring of cortex (Friston, 2005; Lee and Mumford, 2003).[7]

A classic early example, combining this kind of hierarchical learning with the basic predictive coding strategy described in section 17.1.1, is Rao and Ballard (1999) model of predictive coding in the visual cortex. At the lowest level, there is some pattern of energetic stimulation, transduced (let's suppose) by sensory receptors from ambient light patterns produced by the current visual scene. These signals are then processed via a multilevel cascade in which each level attempts to predict the activity at the level below it via backward[8] connections. The backward connections allow the activity at one stage of the processing to return as another input at the previous stage. So long as this successfully predicts the lower level activity, all is well, and no further action needs to ensue. But where there is a mismatch, "prediction error" occurs and the ensuing (error-indicating) activity is propagated to the higher level. This automatically adjusts probabilistic representations at the higher level so that top-down predictions cancel prediction errors at the lower level (yielding rapid perceptual inference). At the same time, prediction error is used to adjust the structure of the model so as to reduce any discrepancy next time around (yielding slower timescale perceptual learning). Forward connections between levels thus carry the "residual errors" (Rao and Ballard, 1999, p. 79) separating the predictions from the actual lower level activity, while backward connections (which do most of the "heavy lifting" in these models) carry the predictions themselves. Changing predictions corresponds to changing or tuning your hypothesis about the hidden causes of the lower level activity. The concurrent running of this kind of prediction error calculation within a loose bidirectional hierarchy of cortical areas allows information pertaining to regularities at different spatial and temporal scales to settle into a mutually consistent whole in which each "hypothesis" is used to help tune the rest. As the authors put it:

> Prediction and error-correction cycles occur concurrently throughout the hierarchy, so top-down information influences lower-level estimates, and bottom-up information influences higher-level estimates of the input signal. (Rao and Ballard, 1999, p. 80)

In the visual cortex, such a scheme suggests that backward connections from V2 to V1 would carry a prediction of expected activity in V1, while forward connections from V1 to V2 would carry forward the error signal indicating residual (unpredicted) activity.

To test these ideas, Rao and Ballard implemented a simple bidirectional hierarchical network of such "predictive estimators" and trained it on image patches derived from five natural scenes. Using learning algorithms that progressively reduce prediction error across the linked cascade and after exposure to thousands of image patches, the system learnt to use responses in the first level network to extract features such as oriented edges and bars, while the second level network came to capture combinations of such features corresponding to patterns involving larger spatial configurations. The model also displayed a number of interesting "extra-classical receptive field" effects, suggesting that such non-classical surround effects (and, as we'll later see, context effects more generally) may be a rather direct consequence of the use of hierarchical predictive coding.

For immediate purposes, however, what matters is that the predictive coding approach, given only the statistical properties of the signals derived from the natural images, was able to induce a kind of generative model of the structure of the input data: It learned about the presence and importance of features such as lines, edges, and bars, and about combinations of such features, in ways that enable better predictions concerning what to expect next, in space or in time. The cascade of processing induced by the progressive reduction of prediction error in the hierarchy reveals the world outside the black box. It maximizes the posterior probability of generating the observed states (the sensory inputs), and, in so doing, induces a kind of internal model of the source of the signals: the world hidden behind the veil of perception.

17.1.3   Action-oriented predictive processing

Recent work by Friston (2003; 2010; and with colleagues: Brown et al., 2011; Friston et al., 2009) generalizes this basic "hierarchical predictive processing" model to include action. According to what I shall now dub "action-oriented predictive processing,"[9] perception and action both follow the same deep "logic" and are even implemented using the same computational strategies. A fundamental attraction of these accounts thus lies in their ability to offer a deeply unified account of perception, cognition, and action.

Perception, as we saw, is here depicted as a process that attempts to match incoming "driving" signals with a cascade of top-down predictions (spanning multiple spatial and temporal scales) that aim to cancel it out. Motor action exhibits a surprisingly similar profile, except that:

> In motor systems error signals self-suppress, not through neuronally mediated effects, but by eliciting movements that change bottom-up proprioceptive and sensory input. This unifying perspective on perception and action suggests that action is both perceived and caused by its perception. (Friston, 2003, p. 1349)

This whole scenario is wonderfully captured by Hawkins and Blakeslee, who write that:

> As strange as it sounds, when your own behaviour is involved, your predictions not only precede sensation, they determine sensation. Thinking of going to the next pattern in a sequence causes a cascading prediction of what you should experience next. As the cascading prediction unfolds, it generates the motor commands necessary to fulfil the prediction. Thinking, predicting, and doing are all part of the same unfolding of sequences moving down the cortical hierarchy. (Hawkins and Blakeslee, 2004, p. 158)

A closely related body of work in so-called optimal feedback control theory (e.g., Todorov, 2009; Todorov and Jordan, 2002) displays the motor control problem as mathematically equivalent to Bayesian inference. Very roughly—see Todorov (2009) for a detailed account—you treat the desired (goal) state as observed and perform Bayesian inference to find the actions that get you there. This mapping between perception and action emerges also in some recent work on planning (e.g., Toussaint, 2009). The idea, closely related to these approaches to simple movement control, is that in planning we imagine a future goal state as actual, then use Bayesian inference to find the set of intermediate states (which can now themselves be whole actions) that get us there. There is thus emerging a fundamentally unified set of computational models which, as Toussaint (2009, p. 29) comments, "does not distinguish between the problems of sensor processing, motor control, or planning." Toussaint's bold claim is modified, however, by the important caveat (op. cit., p. 29) that we must, in practice, deploy approximations and representations that are specialized for different tasks. But at the very least, it now seems likely that perception and action are in some deep sense computational siblings and that:

> The best ways of interpreting incoming information via perception, are deeply the same as the best ways of controlling outgoing information via motor action ... so the notion that there are a few specifiable computational principles governing neural function seems plausible. (Eliasmith, 2007, p. 380)

Action-oriented predictive processing goes further, however, in suggesting that motor intentions actively elicit, via their unfolding into detailed motor actions, the ongoing streams of sensory (especially proprioceptive) results that our brains predict. This deep unity between perception and action emerges most clearly in the context of so-called active inference, where the agent moves its sensors in ways that amount to actively seeking or generating the sensory consequences that they (or rather, their brains) expect (Friston, 2009; Friston et al., 2010). Perception, cognition, and action—if this unifying perspective proves correct—work closely together to minimize sensory prediction errors by selectively sampling, and actively sculpting, the stimulus array. They thus conspire to move a creature through time and space in ways that fulfil an ever-changing and deeply inter-animating set of (sub-personal) expectations. According to these accounts, then:

> Perceptual learning and inference is necessary to induce prior expectations about how the sensorium unfolds. Action is engaged to resample the world to fulfil these expectations. This places perception and action in intimate relation and accounts for both with the same principle. (Friston et al., 2009, p. 12)

In some (I'll call them the "desert landscape") versions of this story (see especially Friston, 2011b; Friston et al., 2010) proprioceptive prediction errors act directly as motor commands. On these models it is our expectations about the proprioceptive consequences of moving and acting that directly bring the moving and acting about.[10] I return briefly to these "desert landscape" scenarios in section 17.5.1 further on.

17.2   Representation, inference, and the continuity of perception, cognition, and action

The hierarchical predictive processing account, along with the more recent generalizations to action represents, or so I shall now argue, a genuine departure from many of our previous ways of thinking about perception, cognition, and the human cognitive architecture. It offers a distinctive account of neural representation, neural computation, and the representation relation itself. It depicts perception, cognition, and action as profoundly unified and, in important respects, continuous. And it offers a neurally plausible and computationally tractable gloss on the claim that the brain performs some form of Bayesian inference.

17.2.1 Explaining away

To successfully represent the world in perception, if these models are correct, depends crucially upon cancelling out sensory prediction error. Perception thus involves "explaining away" the driving (incoming) sensory signal by matching it with a cascade of predictions pitched at a variety of spatial and temporal scales. These predictions reflect what the system already knows about the world (including the body) and the uncertainties associated with its own processing. Perception here becomes "theory-laden" in at least one (rather specific) sense: What we perceive depends heavily upon the set of priors (including any relevant hyper-priors) that the brain brings to bear in its best attempt to predict the current sensory signal. On this model, perception demands the success of some mutually supportive stack of states of a generative model (recall sect. 17.1.1 above) at minimizing prediction error by hypothesizing an interacting set of distal causes that predict, accommodate, and (thus) "explain away" the driving sensory signal.

This appeal to "explaining away" is important and central, but it needs very careful handling. It is important as it reflects the key property of hierarchical predictive processing models, which is that the brain is in the business of active, ongoing, input prediction and does not (even in the early sensory case) merely react to external stimuli. It is important also insofar as it is the root of the attractive coding efficiencies that these models exhibit, since all that needs to be passed forward through the system is the error signal, which is what remains once predictions and driving signals have been matched.[11] In these models it is therefore the backward (recurrent) connectivity that carries the main information processing load. We should not, however, overplay this difference. In particular, it is potentially misleading to say that:

> Activation in early sensory areas no longer represents sensory information per se, but only that part of the input that has not been successfully predicted by higher-level areas. (de-Wit et al., 2010, p. 8702)

It is potentially misleading because this stresses only one aspect of what is (at least in context of the rather specific models we have been considering[12]) actually depicted as a kind of duplex architecture: one that at each level *combines* quite traditional representations of inputs with representations of error. According to the duplex proposal, what gets "explained away" or cancelled out is the error signal, which (in these models) is depicted as computed by dedicated "error units." These are linked to, but distinct from, the so-called representation units meant to encode the causes of sensory inputs. By cancelling out the activity of the error units, activity in some of the laterally interacting "representation" units (which then feed predictions downward and are in the business of encoding the putative sensory causes) can actually end up being selected and sharpened. The hierarchical predictive processing account thus avoids any direct conflict with accounts (e.g., biased-competition models such as that of Desimone and Duncan, 1995) that posit top-down *enhancements* of selected aspects of the sensory signal, because:

> High-level predictions explain away prediction error and tell the error units to "shut up" [while] units encoding the causes of sensory input are selected by lateral interactions, with the error units, that mediate empirical priors. This selection stops the gossiping [hence actually sharpens responses among the laterally competing representations]. (Friston, 2005, p. 829)

The drive towards "explaining away" is thus consistent, in this specific architectural setting, with both the sharpening and the dampening of (different aspects of) early cortical response.[13] Thus Spratling, in a recent formal treatment of this issue,[14] suggests that any apparent contrast here reflects:

> A misinterpretation of the model that may have resulted from the strong emphasis the predictive coding hypothesis places on the *error-detecting nodes* and the corresponding *under-emphasis on the role of the prediction nodes in maintaining an active representation of the stimulus*. (Spratling, 2008, p. 8, my emphasis)

What is most distinctive about this duplex architectural proposal (and where much of the break from tradition really occurs) is that it depicts the forward flow of information as solely conveying error, and the backward flow as solely conveying predictions. The duplex architecture thus achieves a rather delicate balance between the familiar (there is still a cascade of feature-detection, with potential for selective enhancement, and with increasingly complex features represented by neural populations that are more distant from the sensory peripheries) and the novel (the forward flow of sensory information is now entirely replaced by a forward flow of prediction error).

This balancing act between cancelling out and selective enhancement is made possible, it should be stressed, only by positing the existence of "two functionally distinct subpopulations, encoding the conditional expectations of perceptual causes and the prediction error respectively" (Friston, 2005, p. 829). Functional distinctness need not, of course, imply gross physical separation. But a common conjecture in this literature depicts superficial pyramidal cells (a prime source of forward neuro-anatomical connections) as playing the role of error units, passing prediction error forward, while deep pyramidal cells play the role of representation units, passing predictions (made on the basis of a complex generative model) downward (see, e.g., Friston, 2005, 2009; Mumford, 1992). However it may (or may not) be realized, some form of functional separation is required. Such separation constitutes a central feature of the proposed architecture, and one without which it would be unable to combine the radical elements drawn from predictive coding with simultaneous support for the more traditional structure of increasingly complex feature detection and top-down signal enhancement. But essential as it is, this is a demanding and potentially problematic requirement.

17.2.2   The delicate dance between top-down and bottom-up

In the context of bidirectional hierarchical models of brain function, action-oriented predictive processing yields a new account of the complex interplay between top-down and bottom-up influences on perception and action, and perhaps ultimately of the relations between perception, action, and cognition.

As noted by Hohwy (2007, p. 320) the generative model providing the "top-down" predictions is here doing much of the more traditionally "perceptual" work, with the bottom-up driving signals really providing a kind of ongoing feedback on their activity (by fitting, or failing to fit, the cascade of downward-flowing predictions). This procedure combines "top-down" and "bottom-up" influences in an especially delicate and potent fashion, and it leads to the development of neurons that exhibit a "selectivity that is not intrinsic to the area but depends on interactions across levels of a processing hierarchy" (Friston, 2003, p. 1349). Hierarchical predictive coding delivers, that is to say, a processing regime in which context-sensitivity is fundamental and pervasive.

To see this, we need only reflect that the neuronal responses that follow an input (the "evoked responses") may be expected to change quite profoundly according to the contextualizing information provided by a current winning top-down prediction. The key effect here (itself familiar enough from earlier connectionist work using the "interactive activation" paradigm—see, e.g., McClelland and Rumelhart, 1981; Rumelhart et al., 1986b—is that, "when a neuron or population is predicted by top-down inputs it will be much easier to drive than when it is not" (Friston, 2002, p. 240). This is because the best overall fit between driving signal and expectations will often be found by (in effect) inferring noise in the driving signal and thus recognizing a stimulus as, for example, the letter *m* (say, in the context of the word "mother") even though the same bare stimulus, presented out of context or in most other contexts, would have been a better fit with the letter *n*.[15] A unit normally responsive to the letter *m* might, under such circumstances, be successfully driven by an *n*-like stimulus.

Such effects are pervasive in hierarchical predictive processing, and have far-reaching implications for various forms of neuroimaging. It becomes essential, for example, to control as much as possible for expectations when seeking to identify the response selectivity of neurons or patterns of neural activity. Strong effects of top-down expectation have also recently been demonstrated for conscious recognition, raising important questions about the very idea of any simple (i.e., context independent) "neural correlates of consciousness." Thus, Melloni et al. (2011) show that the onset time required to form a reportable conscious percept varies substantially (by around 100 msec) according to the presence or absence of apt expectations, and that the neural (here, EEG) signatures of conscious perception vary accordingly—a result these authors go on to interpret using the apparatus of hierarchical predictive processing. Finally, in a particularly striking demonstration of the power of top-down expectations, Egner et al. (2010) show that neurons in the fusiform face area (FFA) respond every bit as strongly to non-face (in this experiment, house) stimuli under high expectation of faces as they do to face-stimuli. In this study:

> FFA activity displayed an interaction of stimulus feature and expectation factors, where the differentiation between FFA responses to face and house stimuli decreased linearly with increasing levels of face expectation, with face and house evoked signals being indistinguishable under high face expectation. (Egner et al., 2010, p. 16607)

Only under conditions of low face expectation was FFA response maximally different for the face and house probes, suggesting that "[FFA] responses appear to be determined by feature expectation and surprise rather than by stimulus features per se" (Egner et al., 2010, p.16601). The suggestion, in short, is that FFA (in many ways the paradigm case of a region performing complex feature detection) might be better treated as a face-expectation region rather than as a face-detection region: a result that the authors interpret as favoring a hierarchical predictive processing model. The growing body of such results leads Muckli to comment that:

> Sensory stimulation might be the minor task of the cortex, whereas its major task is to . . . predict upcoming stimulation as precisely as possible. (Muckli, 2010, p. 137)

In a similar vein, Rauss et al. (2011) suggest that on such accounts:

> Neural signals are related less to a stimulus per se than to its congruence with internal goals and predictions, calculated on the basis of previous input to the system. (Rauss et al., 2011, p. 1249)

Attention fits very neatly into this emerging unified picture, as a means of variably balancing the potent interactions between top-down and bottom-up influences by factoring in their precision (degree of uncertainty). This is achieved by altering the gain (the "volume," to use a common analogy) on the error-units accordingly. The upshot of this is to "control the relative influence of prior expectations at different levels" (Friston, 2009, p. 299). In recent work, effects of the neurotransmitter dopamine are presented as one possible neural mechanism for encoding precision (see Fletcher and Frith [2009, pp. 53–54] who refer the reader to work on prediction error and the mesolimbic dopaminergic system such as Holleman and Schultz, 1998; Waelti et al., 2001). Greater precision (however encoded) means less uncertainty, and is reflected in a higher gain on the relevant error units (see Friston, 2005, 2010; Friston et al., 2009). Attention, if this is correct, is simply one means by which certain error-unit responses are given increased weight, hence becoming more apt to drive learning and plasticity, and to engage compensatory action.

More generally, this means that the precise mix of top-down and bottom-up influence is not static or fixed. Instead, the weight given to sensory prediction error is varied according to how reliable (how noisy, certain, or uncertain) the signal is taken to be. This is (usually) good news, as it means we are not (not quite) slaves to our expectations. Successful perception requires the brain to minimize surprisal. But the agent is able to see very (agent-) surprising things, at least in conditions where the brain assigns high reliability to the driving signal. Importantly, that requires that other high-level theories, though of an initially agent-unexpected kind, win out so as to reduce surprisal by explaining away the highly weighted sensory evidence. In extreme and persistent cases (more on this in sect. 17.4.2), this may require gradually altering the underlying generative model itself, in what Fletcher and Frith (2009, p. 53) nicely describe as a "reciprocal interaction between perception and learning."

All this makes the lines between perception and cognition fuzzy, perhaps even vanishing. In place of any real distinction between perception and belief we now get variable differences in the mixture of top-down and bottom-up influence, and differences of temporal and spatial scale in the internal models that are making the predictions. Top-level (more "cognitive") models[16] intuitively correspond to increasingly abstract conceptions of the world, and these tend to capture or depend upon regularities at larger temporal and spatial scales. Lower-level (more "perceptual") ones capture or depend upon the kinds of scale and detail most strongly associated with specific kinds of perceptual contact. But it is the precision-modulated, constant, content-rich interactions between these levels, often mediated by ongoing motor action of one kind or another, that now emerges as the heart of intelligent, adaptive response.

These accounts thus appear to dissolve, at the level of the implementing neural machinery, the superficially clean distinction between perception and knowledge/belief. To perceive the world just is to use what you know to explain away the sensory signal across multiple spatial and temporal scales. The process of perception is thus inseparable from rational (broadly Bayesian) processes of belief fixation, and context (top-down) effects are felt at every intermediate level of processing. As thought, sensing, and movement here unfold, we discover no stable or well-specified interface or interfaces between cognition and perception. Believing and perceiving, although conceptually distinct, emerge as deeply mechanically intertwined. They are constructed using the same computational resources, and (as we shall see in sect. 17.4.2) are mutually, reciprocally, entrenching.

17.2.3 Summary so far
Action-oriented (hierarchical) predictive processing models promise to bring cognition, perception, action, and attention together within a common framework. This framework suggests probability-density distributions induced by hierarchical generative models as our basic means of representing the world, and prediction-error minimization as the driving force behind learning, action-selection, recognition, and inference. Such a framework offers new insights into a wide range of specific phenomena including non-classical receptive field effects, bi-stable perception, cue integration, and the pervasive context-sensitivity of neuronal response. It makes rich and illuminating contact with work in cognitive neuroscience while boasting a firm foundation in computational modeling and Bayesian theory.

It thus offers what is arguably the first truly systematic bridge[17] linking three of our most promising tools for understanding mind and reason: cognitive neuroscience, computational modelling, and probabilistic Bayesian approaches to dealing with evidence and uncertainty.

17.3   From action-oriented predictive processing to an architecture of mind

17.3.1   Scope and limits

According to Mumford:

> In the ultimate stable state, the deep pyramidals [conveying predictions downwards] would send a signal that perfectly predicts what each lower area is sensing, up to expected levels of noise, and the superficial pyramidals [conveying prediction errors upwards] wouldn't fire at all. (Mumford, 1992, p. 247)

In an intriguing footnote, Mumford then adds:

> In some sense, this is the state that the cortex is trying to achieve: perfect prediction of the world, like the oriental Nirvana, as Tai-Sing Lee suggested to me, when nothing surprises you and new stimuli cause the merest ripple in your consciousness. (op. cit., p. 247, Note 5)

This remark highlights a very general worry that is sometimes raised in connection with the large-scale claim that cortical processing fundamentally aims to minimize prediction error, thus quashing the forward flow of information and achieving what Mumford evocatively describes as the "ultimate stable state." It can be put like this:

> How can a neural imperative to minimize prediction error by enslaving perception, action, and attention accommodate the obvious fact that animals don't simply seek a nice dark room and stay in it? Surely staying still inside a darkened room would afford easy and nigh-perfect prediction of our own unfolding neural states? Doesn't the story thus leave out much that really matters for adaptive success: things like boredom, curiosity, play, exploration, foraging, and the thrill of the hunt?

The simple response (correct, as far as it goes) is that animals like us live and forage in a changing and challenging world, and hence "expect" to deploy quite complex "itinerant" strategies (Friston, 2010; Friston et al., 2009) to stay within our species-specific window of viability. Change, motion, exploration, and search are *themselves* valuable for creatures living in worlds where resources are unevenly spread and new threats and opportunities continuously arise. This means that change, motion, exploration, and search themselves become predicted—and poised to enslave action and perception accordingly. One way to unpack this idea would be to look at the possible role of priors that induce motion through a state space until an acceptable, though possibly temporary or other wise unstable, stopping point (an attractor) is found. In precisely this vein Friston (2011a, p. 113) comments that "some species are equipped with prior expectations that they will engage in exploratory or social play."

The whole shape of this space of prior expectations is specific to different species and may also vary as a result of learning and experience. Hence, nothing in the large-scale story about prediction error minimization dictates any general or fixed balance between what is sometimes glossed as "exploration" versus "exploitation" (for some further discussion of this issue, see Friston and Stephan, 2007, pp. 435–36). Instead, different organisms amount (Friston, 2011a) to different "embodied models" of their specific needs and environmental niches, and their expectations and predictions are formed, encoded, weighted, and computed against such backdrops. This is both good news and bad news. It's good because it means the stories on offer can indeed accommodate all the forms of behavior (exploration, thrill-seeking, etc.) we see. But it's bad (or at least, limiting) because it means that the accounts don't in themselves tell us much at all about these key features: features which nonetheless condition and constrain an organism's responses in a variety of quite fundamental ways.

In one way, of course, this is clearly unproblematic. The briefest glance at the staggering variety of biological (even mammalian) life forms tells us that whatever fundamental principles are sculpting life and mind, they are indeed compatible with an amazing swathe of morphological, neurological, and ethological outcomes. But in another way it can still seem disappointing. If what we want to understand is the specific functional architecture of the human mind, the distance between these very general principles of prediction-error minimization and the specific solutions to adaptive needs that we humans have embraced remains daunting. As a simple example, notice that the predictive processing account leaves wide open a variety of deep and important questions concerning the nature and format of human neural representation. The representations on offer are, we saw, constrained to be probabilistic (and generative model based) through and through. But that is compatible with the use of the probabilistic-generative mode to encode information using a wide variety of different schemes and surface forms. Consider the well-documented differences in the way the dorsal and ventral visual streams code for attributes of the visual scene. The dorsal stream (Milner and Goodale, 2006) looks to deploy modes of representation and processing that are *at some level of interest* quite distinct from those coded and computed in the ventral stream. And this will be true even if there is indeed, at some more fundamental level, a common computational strategy at work throughout the visual and the motor cortex.

Discovering the nature of various inner representational formats is thus representative of the larger project of uncovering the full shape of the human cognitive architecture. It seems likely that, as argued by Eliasmith (2007), this larger project will demand a complex combination of insights, some coming "top-down" from theoretical (mathematical, statistical, and computational) models, and others coming "bottom-up" from neuroscientific work that uncovers the brain's actual resources as sculpted by our unique evolutionary (and—as we'll next see—sociocultural) trajectory.

17.3.2 Neats versus scruffies (twenty-first century replay)

Back in the late 1970s and early 1980s (the heyday of classical Artificial Intelligence [AI]) there was a widely held view that two personality types were reflected in theorizing about the human mind. These types were dubbed, by Roger Schank and Robert Abelson, the "neats" versus the "scruffies."[18] Neats believed in a few very general, truth-conducive principles underlying intelligence. Scruffies saw intelligence as arising from a varied bag of tricks: a rickety tower of rough-and-ready solutions to problems, often assembled using various quick patches and local ploys, and greedily scavenging the scraps and remnants of solutions to other, historically prior, problems and needs. Famously, this can lead to scruffy, unreliable, or sometimes merely unnecessarily complex solutions to ecologically novel problems such as planning economies, building railway networks, and maintaining the Internet. Such historically path-dependent solutions were sometimes called "kluges"— see, for example, Clark (1987) and Marcus (2008). Neats favored logic and provably correct solutions, while scruffies favored whatever worked reasonably well, fast enough, in the usual ecological setting, for some given problem. The same kind of division emerged in early debates between connectionist and classical AI (see, e.g., Sloman, 1990), with connectionists often accused of developing systems whose operating principles (after training on some complex set of input-output pairs) was opaque and "messy." The conflict reappears in more recent debates (Griffiths et al., 2010; McClelland et al., 2010) between those favoring "structured probabilistic approaches" and those favoring "emergentist" approaches (where these are essentially connectionist approaches of the parallel distributed processing variety).[19]

My own sympathies (Clark, 1989, 1997) have always lain more on the side of the scruffies. Evolved intelligence, it seemed to me (Clark, 1987), was bound to involve a kind of unruly motley of tricks and ploys, with significant path-dependence, no premium set on internal consistency, and fast effective situated response usually favored at the expense of slower, more effortful, even if more truth-conducive modes of thought and reasoning. Seen through this lens, the "Bayesian brain" seems, at first glance, to offer an unlikely model for evolved biological intelligence. Implemented by hierarchical predictive processing, it posits a single, fundamental kind of learning algorithm (based on generative models, predictive coding, and prediction-error minimization) that approximates the rational ideal of Bayesian belief update. Suppose such a model proves correct. Would this amount to the final triumph of the neats over the scruffies? I suspect it would not, and for reasons that shed additional light upon the questions about scope and limits raised in the previous section.

Favoring the "neats," we have encountered a growing body of evidence (see section 17.2.2) showing that for many basic problems involving perception and motor control, human agents (as well as other animals) do indeed manage to approximate the responses and choices of optimal Bayesian observers and actors. Nonetheless, a considerable distance still separates such models from the details of their implementation in humans or other animals. It is here that the apparent triumph of the neats over the scruffies may be called into question. For the Bayesian brain story tells us, at most, what the brain (or better, the brain in action) manages to compute. It also suggests a good deal about the forms of representation and computation that the brain must deploy: For example, it suggests that the brain must deploy a probabilistic representation of sensory information; that it must take into account uncertainty in its own sensory signals, estimate the "volatility" (frequency of change) of the environment itself (Yu, 2007), and so on. But that still leaves plenty of room for debate and discovery as regards the precise shape of the large-scale cognitive architecture within which all this occurs.

17.4   Content and consciousness

How, finally, do the accounts on offer relate to a human mental life? This, of course, is the hardest—though potentially the most important—question of all. I cannot hope to adequately address it in the present treatment, but a few preliminary remarks may help to structure a space for subsequent discussion.

17.4.1   Agency and experience

To what extent, if any, do these stories capture or explain facts about what we might think of as *personal* (or agent-level) cognition—the flow of thoughts, reasons, and ideas that characterize daily conscious thought and reason? A first (but fortunately merely superficial) impression is that they fall far short of illuminating personal-level experience. For example, there seems to be a large disconnect between surprisal (the implausibility of some sensory state given a model of the world) and agent-level surprise. This is evident from the simple fact that the percept that, overall, best minimizes surprisal (hence minimizes prediction errors) "for" the brain may well be, for me the agent, some highly surprising and unexpected state of affairs—imagine, for example, the sudden unveiling of a large and doleful elephant elegantly smuggled onto the stage by a professional magician.

The two perspectives are, however, easily reconciled. The large and doleful elephant is best understood as improbable but not (at least not in the relevant sense—recall sect. 17.3.1) surprising. Instead, that percept is the one that best respects what the system knows and expects about the world, given the current combination of driving inputs and assigned precision (reflecting the brain's degree of confidence in the sensory signal). Given the right driving signal and a high enough assignment of precision, top-level theories of an initially agent-unexpected kind can still win out so as to explain away that highly weighted tide of incoming sensory evidence. The sight of the doleful elephant may then emerge as the least surprising (least "surprisal-ing"!) percept available, given the inputs, the priors, and the current weighting on sensory prediction error. Nonetheless, systemic priors did not render that percept very likely in advance, hence (perhaps) the value to the agent of the feeling of surprise.

17.4.2   Illuminating experience: The case of delusions

It might be suggested that merely *accommodating* the range of human personal-level experiences is one thing, while truly *illuminating* them is another. Such positive impact is, however, at least on the horizon. We glimpse the potential in an impressive body of recent work conducted within the predictive processing (hierarchical predictive coding) framework addressing delusions and hallucination in schizophrenia (Corlett et al., 2009a; Fletcher and Frith, 2009).

Recall the unexpected sighting of the elephant described in the previous section. Here, the system already commanded an apt model able to "explain away" the particular combination of driving inputs, expectations, and precision (weighting on prediction error) that specified the doleful, gray presence. But such is not always the case. Sometimes, dealing with ongoing, highly-weighted sensory prediction error may require brand new generative models gradually to be formed (just as in normal learning). This might hold the key, as Fletcher and Frith (2009) suggest, to a better understanding of the origins of hallucinations and delusion (the two "positive symptoms") in schizophrenia. These two symptoms are often thought to involve two mechanisms and hence two breakdowns, one in "perception" (leading to the hallucinations) and one in "belief" (allowing these abnormal perceptions to impact top-level belief). It seems correct (see, e.g., Coltheart, 2007) to stress that perceptual anomalies alone will not typically lead to the strange and exotic belief complexes found in delusional subjects. But must we therefore think of the perceptual and doxastic components as effectively independent?

A possible link emerges if perception and belief-formation, as the present story suggests, both involve the attempt to match unfolding sensory signals with top-down predictions. Importantly, the impact of such attempted matching is precision-mediated in that the systemic effects of residual prediction error vary according to the brain's confidence in the signal (sect. 17.2.2). With this in mind, Fletcher and Frith (2009) canvass the possible consequences of disturbances to a hierarchical Bayesian system such that prediction error signals are falsely generated and—more important—highly weighted (hence accorded undue salience for driving learning).

There are a number of potential mechanisms whose complex interactions, once treated within the overarching framework of prediction error minimization, might conspire to produce such disturbances. Prominent contenders include the action of slow neuromodulators such as dopamine, serotonin, and acetylcholine (Corlett et al., 2009a, 2010). In addition, Friston (2010, p. 132) speculates that fast, synchronized activity between neural

areas may also play a role in increasing the gain on prediction error within the synchronized populations.[20] The key idea, however implemented, is that understanding the positive symptoms of schizophrenia requires understanding disturbances in the generation and
weighting of prediction error. The suggestion (Corlett et al., 2009a,b; Fletcher and Frith,
2009) is that malfunctions within that complex economy (perhaps fundamentally rooted
in abnormal dopaminergic functioning) yield wave upon wave of persistent and highly
weighted "false errors" that then propagate all the way up the hierarchy forcing, in severe
cases (via the ensuing waves of neural plasticity) extremely deep revisions in our model
of the world. The improbable (telepathy, conspiracy, persecution, etc.) then becomes
the least surprising, and—because perception is itself conditioned by the top-down flow
of prior expectations—the cascade of misinformation reaches back down, allowing false
perceptions and bizarre beliefs to solidify into a coherent and mutually supportive cycle.

Such a process is self-entrenching. As new generative models take hold, their influence
flows back down so that incoming data is sculpted by the new (but now badly misinformed)
priors so as to "conform to expectancies" (Fletcher and Frith, 2009, p. 348). False perceptions and bizarre beliefs thus form an epistemically insulated self-confirming cycle.[21] This,
then, is the dark side of the seamless story (sect. 17.2) about perception and cognition. The
predictive processing model merges—usually productively—perception, belief, learning,
and affect into a single overarching economy: one within which dopamine and other neurotransmitters control the "precision" (the weighting, hence the impact on inference and on
learning) of prediction error itself. But when things go wrong, false inferences spiral and
feed back upon themselves. Delusion and hallucination then become entrenched, being
both co-determined and co-determining.

The same broadly Bayesian framework can be used (Corlett et al., 2009a) to help make
sense of the ways in which different drugs, when given to healthy volunteers, can tem-
porarily mimic various forms of psychosis. Here, too, the key feature is the ability of
the predictive coding framework to account for complex alterations in both learning and
experience contingent upon the (pharmacologically modifiable) way driving sensory signals are meshed, courtesy of precision-weighted prediction errors, with prior expectancies
and (hence) ongoing prediction. The psychotomimetic effects of ketamine, for example,
are said to be explicable in terms of a disturbance to the prediction error signal (perhaps
caused by AMPA upregulation) and the flow of prediction (perhaps via NMDA interference). This leads to a persistent prediction error and—crucially—an inflated sense of the
importance or salience of the associated events, which in turn drives the formation of short-
lived delusion-like beliefs (see Corlett et al., 2009a, pp. 6–7; also, discussion in Gerrans,
2007). The authors go on to offer accounts of the varying psychotomimetic effects of other
drugs (such as LSD and other serotonergic hallucinogens, cannabis, and dopamine ago-
nists such as amphetamine) as reflecting other possible varieties of disturbance within a
hierarchical predictive processing framework.[22]

17.4.3   Perception, imagery, and the senses

Another area in which these models are suggestive of deep facts about the nature and construction of human experience concerns the character of perception and the relations between perception and imagery/visual imagination. Prediction-driven processing schemes, operating within hierarchical regimes of the kind described above, learn probabilistic generative models in which each neural population targets the activity patterns displayed by the neural population below. What is crucial here—what makes such models *generative* as we saw in section 17.1.1—is that they can be used "top-down" to predict activation patterns in the level below. The practical upshot is that such systems, simply as part and parcel of learning to perceive, develop the ability to self-generate[23] perception-like states from the top down, by driving the lower populations into the predicted patterns.

There thus emerges a rather deep connection between perception and the potential for self-generated forms of mental imagery (Kosslyn et al., 1995; Reddy et al., 2010). Probabilistic generative model based systems that can learn to visually perceive a cat (say) are, ipso facto, systems that can deploy a top-down cascade to bring about many of the activity patterns that would ensue in the visual presence of an actual cat. Such systems thus display (for more discussion of this issue, see Clark (2015a) a deep duality of perception and imagination.[24] The same duality is highlighted by Grush (2004) in the "emulator theory of representation," a rich and detailed treatment that shares a number of key features with the predictive processing story.[25]

17.5   Taking stock

17.5.1   Comparison with standard computationalism

Just how radical is the story we have been asked to consider? Is it best seen as an alternative to mainstream computational accounts that posit a cascade of increasingly complex feature detection (perhaps with some top-down biasing), or is it merely a supplement to them: one whose main virtue lies in its ability to highlight the crucial role of prediction error in driving learning and response? I do not think we are yet in a position to answer this question with any authority. But the picture I have painted suggests an intermediate verdict, at least with respect to the central issues concerning representation and processing.

Concerning representation, the stories on offer are potentially radical in at least two respects. First, they suggest that probabilistic generative models underlie both sensory classification and motor response. And second, they suggest that the forward flow of sensory data is replaced by the forward flow of prediction error. This latter aspect can, however, make the models seem even more radical than they actually are: Recall that the forward flow of prediction error is here combined with a downward flow of predictions, and at every stage of processing the models posit (as we saw in some detail in sect. 17.2.1) functionally distinct "error units" and "representation units." The representation units that communicate predictions downward do indeed encode increasingly complex and more abstract features (capturing context and regularities at ever-larger spatial and temporal scales) in the processing levels furthest removed from the raw sensory input. In a very real sense then, much of the standard architecture of increasingly complex feature detection is here retained. What differs is the shape of the flow of information, and (relatedly) the pivotal role assigned to the computation and propagation of prediction error.

A related issue concerns the extent to which the new framework reproduces traditional insights concerning the specialization of different cortical areas. This is a large question whose full resolution remains beyond the scope of the present discussion. But in general, the hierarchical form of these models suggests a delicate combination of specialization and integration. Different levels learn and deploy different sets of predictions, corresponding to different bodies of knowledge, aimed at the level below (specialization) but the system settles in a way largely determined by the overall flow and weighting of prediction error, where this flow is itself varied according to current context and the reliability and relevance of different types of information (integration).[26]

A second source of potential radicalism lies with the suggestion (sect. 17.1.3) that, in extending the models to include action ("action-oriented predictive processing"), we might simultaneously do away with the need to appeal to goals and rewards, replacing them with the more austere construct of predictions. In this vein, we read that:

> Crucially, active inference does not invoke any "desired consequences." It rests only on experience-dependent learning and inference: Experience induces prior expectations, which guide perceptual inference and action. (Friston et al., 2011, p. 157)

In this desert landscape vision, there are neither goals nor reward signals as such. Instead, there are only (both learnt and species-specific) expectations, across many spatial and temporal scales, which directly enslave both perception and action. Cost functions, in other words, are replaced by expectations concerning actions and their sensory (especially proprioceptive) consequences. Here, I remain unconvinced. For even if such an austere description is indeed possible (and for some critical concerns, see Gershman and Daw, 2012), that would not immediately justify our claiming that it thereby constitutes the better tool for understanding the rich organization of the cognitive economy. To see this, we need only reflect that it's all "just" atoms, molecules, and the laws of physics too, but that doesn't mean those provide the best constructs and components for the systemic descriptions attempted by cognitive science. The desert landscape theorist thus needs to do more, it seems to me, to demonstrate the explanatory advantages of abandoning more traditional appeals to value, reward, and cost (or perhaps to show that those appeals make unrealistic demands on processing or implementation—see Friston, 2011b).

What may well be right about the desert landscape story, it seems to me, is the suggestion that utility (or more generally, personal and hedonic value) is not simply a kind of add-on, implemented by what Gershman and Daw (2012, p. 296) describe as a "segregated representation of probability and utility in the brain." Instead, it seems likely that we represent the very events over which probabilities become defined in ways that ultimately fold in their personal, affective, and hedonic significance. This folding-in is probably especially marked in frontolimbic cortex (Merker, 2004). But the potent web of backward connections ensures that such folding-in, once it has occurred, is able (as noted by Barrett and Bar, 2009) to impact processing and representation at every lower stage of the complex processing hierarchy. If this proves correct, then it is prediction error calculated relative to these affectively rich and personal-history-laden expectations that drives learning and response.

Thus construed, an action-oriented predictive processing framework is not so much revolutionary as it is reassuringly integrative. Its greatest value lies in suggesting a set of deep unifying principles for understanding multiple aspects of neural function and organization. It does this by describing an architecture capable of combining high-level knowledge and low-level (sensory) information in ways that systematically deal with uncertainty, ambiguity, and noise. In so doing it reveals perception, action, learning, and attention as different but complementary means to the reduction of (potentially affect-laden and goal-reflecting) prediction error in our exchanges with the world. It also, and simultaneously, displays human learning as sensitively responsive to the deep statistical structures present in both our natural and human-built environments. Thus understood, action-oriented predictive processing leaves much *unspecified*, including (1) the initial variety of neural and bodily structures (and perhaps internal representational forms) mandated by our unique evolutionary trajectory, and (2) the acquired variety of "virtual" neural structures and representational forms installed by our massive immersion in "designer environments" during learning and development.

To fill in these details requires, or so I have argued, a deep (but satisfyingly natural) engagement with evolutionary, embodied, and situated approaches. Within that context, seeing how perception, action, learning, and attention might all be constructed out of the same base materials (prediction and prediction error minimization) is powerful and illuminating. It is there that Friston's ambitious synthesis is at its most suggestive, and it is there that we locate the most substantial empirical commitments of the account. Those commitments are to the computation (by dedicated error units or some functionally equivalent means) and widespread use by the nervous system of precision-weighted prediction error, and its use as proxy for the forward flow of sensory information. The more widespread this is, the greater the empirical bite of the story. If it doesn't occur, or occurs only in a few special circumstances, the story fails as a distinctive empirical account.[27]

17.5.2 Conclusions: Towards a grand unified theory of the mind?

Action-oriented predictive processing models come tantalizingly close to overcoming some of the major obstacles blocking previous attempts to ground a unified science of mind, brain, and action. They take familiar elements from existing, well-understood, computational approaches (such as unsupervised and self-supervised forms of learning using recurrent neural network architectures, and the use of probabilistic generative models for perception and action) and relate them, on the one hand, to a priori constraints on rational response (the Bayesian dimension), and, on the other hand, to plausible and (increasingly) testable accounts of neural implementation. It is this potent positioning between the rational, the computational, and the neural that is their most attractive feature. In some ways, they provide the germ of an answer to Marr's dream: a systematic approach that addresses the levels of (in the vocabulary of Marr, 1982) the computation, the algorithm, and the implementation.

The sheer breadth of application is striking. Essentially the same models here account for a variety of superficially disparate effects spanning perception, action, and attention. Indeed, one way to think about the primary "added value" of these models is that they bring perception, action, and attention into a single unifying framework. They thus constitute the perfect explanatory partner, I have argued, for recent approaches that stress the embodied, environmentally embedded, dimensions of mind and reason.[28] Perception, action, and attention, if these views are correct, are all in the same family business: that of reducing sensory prediction error resulting from our exchanges with the environment. Once this basic family business is revealed, longer-term environmental structuring (both material and socio-cultural) falls neatly into place. We structure our worlds and actions so that most of our sensory predictions come true.

But this neatness hides important complexity. For, another effect of all that material and socio-cultural scaffolding is to induce substantial path-dependence as we confront new problems using pre-existing material tools and inherited social structures. The upshot, or so I have argued, is that a full account of human cognition cannot hope to "jump" directly from the basic organizing principles of action-oriented predictive processing to an account of the full (and in some ways idiosyncratic) shape of human thought and reason.

What emerges instead is a kind of natural alliance. The basic organizing principles highlighted by action-oriented predictive processing make us superbly sensitive to the structure and statistics of the training environment. But our human training environments are now so thoroughly artificial, and our explicit forms of reasoning so deeply infected by various forms of external symbolic scaffolding, that understanding distinctively human cognition demands a multiply hybrid approach. Such an approach would combine the deep computational insights coming from probabilistic generative approaches (among which figure action-oriented predictive processing) with solid neuroscientific conjecture *and* with a full appreciation of the way our many self-structured environments alter and transform the problem spaces of human reason. The most pressing practical questions thus concern what might be thought of as the "distribution of explanatory weight" between the accounts on offer, and approaches that explore or uncover these more idiosyncratic or evolutionary path-dependent features of the human mind, and the complex transformative effects of the socio-cultural cocoon in which it develops.

Questions also remain concerning the proper scope of the basic predictive processing account itself. Can that account really illuminate reason, imagination, and action selection in all its diversity? What do the local approximations to Bayesian reasoning look like as we depart further and further from the safe shores of basic perception and motor control? What new forms of representation are then required, and how do they behave in the context of the hierarchical predictive coding regime? How confident are we of the basic Bayesian gloss on our actual processing? (Do we, for example, have a firm enough grip on when a system is computing its outputs using a "genuine approximation" to a true Bayesian scheme, rather than merely behaving "as if" it did so?)

The challenges (empirical, conceptual, and methodological) are many and profound. But the potential payoff is huge. What is on offer is a multilevel account of some of the deepest natural principles underlying learning and inference, and one that may be capable of bringing perception, action, and attention under a single umbrella. The ensuing exchanges between neuroscience, computational theorizing, psychology, philosophy, rational decision theory, and embodied cognitive science promise to be among the major intellectual events of the early twenty-first century.

Notes for Chapter 17

1. This remark is simply described as a "scribbled, undated, aphorism" in the online digital archive of the scientist's journal: See http://www.rossashby.info/index.html.

2. I am greatly indebted to an anonymous BBS referee for encouraging me to bring these key developments into clearer (both historical and conceptual) focus.

3. The obvious problem was that this generative model itself needed to be learnt: something that would in turn be possible if a good recognition model was already in place, since that could provide the right targets for learning the generative model. The solution (Hinton et al., 1995) was to use each to gradually bootstrap the other, using the so-called "wake-sleep algorithm"—a computationally tractable approximation to "maximum likelihood learning" as seen in the expectation-maximization (EM) algorithm of Dempster et al. (1977). Despite this, the Helmholtz Machine remained slow and unwieldy when confronted with complex problems requiring multiple layers of processing. But it represents an important early version of an unsupervised multilayer learning device, or "deep architecture" (Hinton, 2002, 2007b, 2010; Hinton and Salakhutdinov, 2006; Hinton et al., 2006; for reviews, see Bengio, 2009; Hinton, 2007a).

4. This names the probability of an event (here, a worldly cause), given some set of prior beliefs and the evidence (here, the current pattern of sensory stimulation). For our purposes, it thus names the probability of a worldly (or bodily) cause, conditioned on the sensory consequences.

5. In speaking of "predictive processing" rather than resting with the more common usage "predictive coding," I mean to highlight the fact that what distinguishes the target approaches is not simply the use of the data compression strategy known as predictive coding. Rather, it is the

use of that strategy in the special context of hierarchical systems deploying probabilistic generative models. Such systems exhibit powerful forms of learning and are able flexibly to combine top-down and bottom-up flows of information within a multilayer cascade.

6. In what follows, the notions of prior, empirical prior, and prior belief are used interchangeably, given the assumed context of a hierarchical model.

7. Because these proposals involve the deployment of topdown probabilistic generative models within a multilayer architecture, it is the organizational structure of the neocortex that most plausibly provides the requisite implementation. This is not to rule out related modes of processing using other structures, for example, in nonhuman animals, but simply to isolate the "best fit." Nor is it to rule out the possibility that, moment-to-moment, details of the large-scale routing of information flow within the brain might depend on gating effects that, although cortically mediated, implicate additional structures and areas. For some work on such gating effects among cortical structures themselves, see den Ouden et al. (2010).

8. I have adopted the neuroanatomist practice of labeling connections simply as "backward" and "forward" so as to avoid the functional implications of the labels "feedback" and "feedforward." This is important in the context of predictive processing models, since it is now the forward connections that are really providing (by conveying prediction error) feedback on the downward-flowing predictions—see Friston (2005) and Hohwy (2007). Thanks to one of the BBS reviewers for this helpful terminological suggestion.

9. This is also known (see, e.g., Friston et al., 2009) as "active inference." I coin "action-oriented predictive processing" as it makes clear that this is an action-encompassing generalization of the (hierarchical) predictive coding story about perception. It also suggests (rightly) that action becomes conceptually primary in these accounts, since it provides the only way (once a good world model is in place and aptly activated) to actually alter the sensory signal so as to reduce sensory prediction error—see Friston (2009, p. 295). In addition, Friston's most recent work on active inference looks to involve a strong commitment (Friston, 2011a, see especially) to the wholesale replacement of value functions, considered as determinants of action, with expectations ("prior beliefs," though note that "belief" here is very broadly construed) about action. This is an interesting and challenging suggestion that goes beyond claims concerning formal equivalence and even beyond the observations concerning deep conceptual relations linking action and perception. "Action-oriented predictive processing," as I shall use the term, remains deliberately agnostic on this important matter (see also sect. 17.5.1).

10. I note in passing that this radical view resonates with some influential philosophical work concerning high level (reflective) intentions and actions: specifically, Velleman's (1989) account of practical reasoning in which intentions to act are depicted as self-fulfilling expectations about one's own actions (see, e.g., Velleman, 1989, p. 98).

11. This kind of efficiency, as one of the BBS referees nicely noted, is something of a double-edged sword. For, the obvious efficiencies in forward processing are here bought at the cost of the multilevel generative machinery itself: machinery whose implementation and operation requires a whole set of additional connections to realize the downward swoop of the bidirectional hierarchy. The case for predictive processing is thus not convincingly made on the basis of "communicative frugality" so much as upon the sheer power and scope of the systems that result.

12. In personal correspondence, Lee de-Wit notes that his usage follows that of, for example, Murray et al. (2004) and Dumoulin and Hess (2006), both of whom contrast "predictive coding" with "efficient coding," where the former uses top-down influence to subtract out predicted elements of lower-level activity, and the latter uses top-down influence to enhance or sharpen it. This can certainly make it look as if the two stories (subtraction and sharpening) offer competing accounts of, for example, fMRI data such as Murray et al. (2002) showing a dampening of response in early visual areas as higher areas settled into an interpretation of a shape stimulus. The accounts would be alternatives, since the dampening might then reflect *either* the subtraction of well-predicted parts of the early response ("predictive coding") or the quashing of the rest of the early signal and the attendant sharpening of the consistent elements. The models I am considering, however, accommodate both subtraction *and* sharpening (see main text for details). This is therefore an instance (see sect. 17.5.1) in which more radical elements of the target proposals (here, the subtracting away of predicted signal elements) turn out, on closer examination, to be consistent with more familiar effects (such as top-down enhancement).

13. The consistency between selective sharpening and the dampening effects of "explaining away" also makes it harder—though not impossible—to tease apart the empirical implications of predictive coding and "evidence accumulation" accounts such as Gold and Shadlen's (2001)—for a review, see Smith and Ratcliff (2004). For an attempt to do so, see Hesselmann et al. (2010).

14. In this (2008) treatment Spratling further argues that the forms of hierarchical predictive coding account we have been considering are mathematically equivalent to some forms of "biased competition" model, but that they nonetheless suggest different claims concerning neural implementation. I take no position on these interesting claims here.

15. I here adapt, merely for brevity of exposition, a similar example from Friston (2002, p. 237).

16. Technically, there is always a single hierarchical generative model in play. In speaking here of multiple internal models, I mean only to flag that the hierarchical structure supports many levels of processing which distribute the cognitive labor by building distinct "knowledge structures" that specialize in dealing with different features and properties (so as to predict events and regularities obtaining at differing temporal and spatial scales).

17. The clear lineage here is with work in connectionism and recurrent artificial neural networks (see, e.g., Rumelhart et al., 1986b, and early discussions such as Churchland., 1989; Clark, 1989). What is most exciting about the new proposals, it seems to me, is that they retain many of the insights from this lineage (which goes on to embrace work on Helmholz machines and ongoing work on "deep architectures"—see sect. 17.1.1) while making explicit contact with both Bayesian theorizing and contemporary neuroscientific research and conjecture.

18. These terms, according to a memoir by Wendy Lehnert (2007), were introduced by Bob Abelson as part of a keynote address to the *3rd Annual Meeting of the Cognitive Science Society* in 1981.

19. The hierarchical predictive coding family of models that (along with their extensions to action) form the main focus of the present treatment are not, in my view, happily assimilated to either of these camps. They clearly share Bayesian foundations with the "pure" structured probabilistic approaches highlighted by Griffiths et al., but their computational roots lie (as we saw in sect 17.1.1) in work on machine learning using artificial neural networks. Importantly, however, hierarchical predictive processing model now bring "bottom-up" insights from cognitive neuroscience into increasingly productive contact with those powerful computational mechanisms of learning and

inference, in a unifying framework able (as Griffiths et al. correctly stress) to accommodate a very wide variety of surface representational forms. Moreover, such approaches are computationally tractable because local (prediction-error minimizing) routines are being used to approximate Bayesian inference. For some excellent antidotes to the appearance of deep and irreconcilable conflict hereabouts, see Feldman (2010) and Lee (2010).

20. A much better understanding of such multiple interacting mechanisms (various slow neuromodulators perhaps acting in complex concert with neural synchronization) is now needed, along with a thorough examination of the various ways and levels at which the flow of prediction and the modulating effects of the weighting of prediction error (precision) may be manifest (for some early forays, see Corlett et al., 2010; see also Friston and Kiebel, 2009). Understanding more about the ways and levels at which the flow and impact of prediction error may be manipulated is vitally important if we are to achieve a better understanding of the multiple ways in which "attention" (here understood—see sect. 17.2.2—as various ways of modifying the gain on prediction error) may operate so as to bias processing by flexibly controlling the balance between top-down and bottom-up influence.

21. There are probably milder versions of this everywhere, both in science (Maher, 1988) and in everyday life. We tend to see what we expect, and we use that to confirm the model that is both generating our expectations and sculpting and filtering our observations.

22. Intriguingly, the authors are also able to apply the model to one non-pharmacological intervention: sensory deprivation.

23. This need not imply an ability deliberately to engage in such a process of self-generation. Such rich, deliberate forms of imagining may well require additional resources, such as the language-driven forms of cognitive "self-stimulation" described in Dennett (1991), Chapter 8.

24. It is perhaps worth remarking that, deep duality notwithstanding, nothing in the present view requires that the system, when engaged in imagery-based processing, will typically support the very same kinds of stability and richness of experienced detail that daily sensory engagements offer. In the absence of the driving sensory signal, no stable ongoing information about low-level perceptual details is there to constrain the processing. As a result, there is no obvious pressure to *maintain* or perhaps even to generate (see Reddy et al., 2010) a stable hypothesis at the lower levels: there is simply whatever task-determined downward pressure the active higher-level encoding exerts.

25. Common features include the appeal to forward models and the provision of mechanisms (such as Kalman filtering—see Friston, 2002; Grush, 2004; Rao and Ballard, 1999) for estimating uncertainty and (thus) flexibly balancing the influence of prior expectations and driving sensory inputs. Indeed, Grush (2004, p. 393) cites the seminal predictive coding work by Rao and Ballard (1999) as an account of visual processing compatible with the broader emulator framework. In addition, Grush's account of perception as "environmental emulation" (see section 5.2 of Grush, 2004) looks highly congruent with the depiction (Friston, 2003 and elsewhere) of perception as reconstructing the hidden causes structuring the sensory signal. Where the accounts seem to differ is in the emphasis placed on prediction error as (essentially) a replacement for the sensory signal itself, the prominence of a strong Bayesian interpretation (using the resources of "empirical Bayes" applied across a hierarchy of processing stages), and the attempted replacement of motor commands by top-down proprioceptive predictions alone (for a nice treatment of this rather

challenging speculation, see Friston, 2011a). It would be interesting (although beyond the scope of the present treatment) to attempt a more detailed comparison.

26. For the general story about combining specialization and integration, see Friston (2002) and discussion in Hohwy (2007). For a more recent account, including some experimental evidence concerning the possible role of prediction error in modulating inter-area coupling, see den Ouden et al. (2010).

27. The empirical bet is thus, as Egner and colleagues recently put it, that "the encoding of predictions (based on internal forward models) and prediction errors may be a ubiquitous feature of cognition in the brain . . . rather than a curiosity of reward learning . . . or motor planning" (Egner et al., 2010, p. 16607).

28. When brought under the even-more-encompassing umbrella of the "free energy principle", the combined ambition is formidable. If these accounts were indeed to mesh in the way Friston (2010) suggests, that would reveal the very deepest of links between life and mind, confirming and extending the perspective known as "enactivist" cognitive science (see, e.g., Di Paolo, 2009; Thompson, 2007; Varela et al., 1991).

Theoretical Impediments to Machine Learning with Seven Sparks from the Causal Revolution

18

Judea Pearl
2018

Scientific Background

If we examine the information that drives machine learning today, we find that it is almost entirely statistical. In other words, learning machines improve their performance by optimizing parameters over a stream of sensory inputs received from the environment. It is a slow process, analogous in many respects to the natural selection process that drives Darwinian evolution. It explains how species like eagles and snakes have developed superb vision systems over millions of years. It cannot explain however the super-evolutionary process that enabled humans to build eyeglasses and telescopes over barely one thousand years. What humans possessed that other species lacked was a mental representation, a blue-print of their environment which they could manipulate at will to *imagine* alternative hypothetical environments for planning and learning. Anthropologists like N. Harari, and S. Mithen are in general agreement that the decisive ingredient that gave our Homo sapiens ancestors the ability to achieve global dominion, about 40,000 years ago, was their ability to choreograph a mental representation of their environment, interrogate that representation, distort it by mental acts of imagination and finally answer "What if?" kind of questions. Examples are interventional questions: "What if I act?" and retrospective or explanatory questions: "What if I had acted differently?" No learning machine in operation today can answer such questions about interventions not encountered before, say, "What if we ban cigarettes." Moreover, most learning machines today do not provide a representation from which the answers to such questions can be derived.

I postulate that the major impediment to achieving accelerated learning speeds as well as human level performance should be overcome by removing these barriers and equipping learning machines with causal reasoning tools. This postulate would have been speculative twenty years ago, prior to the mathematization of counterfactuals. Not so today.

Advances in graphical and structural models have made counterfactuals computationally manageable and thus rendered model-driven reasoning a more promising direction on which to base strong AI. In the next section, I will describe the impediments facing machine learning systems using a three-level hierarchy that governs inferences in causal reasoning. The final section summarizes how these impediments were circumvented using modern tools of causal inference.

The Three-Layer Causal Hierarchy

Level	Typical Activity	Typical Questions	Examples
1. Association $P(y\|x)$	Seeing	What is? How would seeing X change my belief in Y?	What does a symptom tell me about a disease? What does a survey tell us about the election results?
2. Intervention $P(y\|do(x),z)$	Doing Intervening	What if? What if I do X?	What if I take aspirin, will my headache be cured? What if we ban cigarettes?
3. Counterfactuals $P(y_x\|x',y')$	Imagining, Retrospection	Why? Was it X that caused Y? What if I had acted differently?	Was it the aspirin that stopped my headache? Would Kennedy be alive had Oswald not shot him? What if I had not been smoking the past 2 years?

Figure 18.1
The Causal Hierarchy. Questions at level i can only be answered if information from level i or higher is available.

An extremely useful insight unveiled by the logic of causal reasoning is the existence of a sharp classification of causal information, in terms of the kind of questions that each class is capable of answering. The classification forms a 3-level hierarchy in the sense that questions at level i ($i = 1, 2, 3$) can only be answered if information from level j ($j \geq i$) is available.

Figure 18.1 shows the 3-level hierarchy, together with the characteristic questions that can be answered at each level. The levels are titled 1. Association, 2. Intervention, and

3. Counterfactual. The names of these layers were chosen to emphasize their usage. We call the first level Association, because it invokes purely statistical relationships, defined by the naked data.[1] For instance, observing a customer who buys toothpaste makes it more likely that he/she buys floss; such association can be inferred directly from the observed data using conditional expectation. Questions at this layer, because they require no causal information, are placed at the bottom level on the hierarchy. The second level, Intervention, ranks higher than Association because it involves not just seeing what is, but changing what we see. A typical question at this level would be: What happens if we double the price? Such questions cannot be answered from sales data alone, because they involve a change in customers behavior, in reaction to the new pricing. These choices may differ substantially from those taken in previous price-raising situations. (Unless we replicate precisely the market conditions that existed when the price reached double its current value.) Finally, the top level is called Counterfactuals, a term that goes back to the philosophers David Hume and John Stewart Mill, and which has been given computer-friendly semantics in the past two decades. A typical question in the counterfactual category is "What if I had acted differently," thus necessitating retrospective reasoning.

Counterfactuals are placed at the top of the hierarchy because they subsume interventional and associational questions. If we have a model that can answer counterfactual queries, we can also answer questions about interventions and observations. For example, the interventional question, What will happen if we double the price? can be answered by asking the counterfactual question: What would happen had the price been twice its current value? Likewise, associational questions can be answered once we can answer interventional questions; we simply ignore the action part and let observations take over. The translation does not work in the opposite direction. Interventional questions cannot be answered from purely observational information (i.e., from statistical data alone). No counterfactual question involving retrospection can be answered from purely interventional information, such as that acquired from controlled experiments; we cannot re-run an experiment on subjects who were treated with a drug and see how they behave had they not given the drug. The hierarchy is therefore directional, with the top level being the most powerful one.

Counterfactuals are the building blocks of scientific thinking as well as legal and moral reasoning. In civil court, for example, the defendant is considered to be the culprit of an injury if, *but for* the defendant's action, it is more likely than not that the injury would not have occurred. The computational meaning of *but for* calls for comparing the real world to an alternative world in which the defendant action did not take place.

Each layer in the hierarchy has a syntactic signature that characterizes the the sentences admitted into that layer. For example, the association layer is characterized by conditional probability sentences, e.g., $P(y|x) = p$ stating that: the probability of event $Y = y$ given that we observed event $X = x$ is equal to p. In large systems, such evidential sentences can be computed efficiently using Bayesian Networks, or any of the neural networks that support deep-learning systems.

At the interventional layer we find sentences of the type $P(y|do(x), z)$, which denotes "The probability of event $Y = y$ given that we intervene and set the value of X to x and subsequently observe event $Z = z$. Such expressions can be estimated experimentally from randomized trials or analytically using Causal Bayesian Networks (Pearl, 2000, Chapter 3). A child learns the effects of interventions through playful manipulation of the environment (usually in a deterministic playground), and AI planners obtain interventional knowledge by exercising their designated sets of actions. Interventional expressions cannot be inferred from passive observations alone, regardless of how big the data.

Finally, at the counterfactual level, we have expressions of the type $P(y_x|x',y')$ which stand for "The probability that event $Y = y$ would be observed had X been x, given that we actually observed X to be x' and and Y to be y'. For example, the probability that Joe's salary would be y had he finished college, given that his actual salary is y' and that he had only two years of college." Such sentences can be computed only when we possess functional or Structural Equation models, or properties of such models (Pearl, 2000, Chapter 7).

This hierarchy, and the formal restrictions it entails, explains why statistics-based machine learning systems are prevented from reasoning about actions, experiments and explanations. It also informs us what extra-statistical information is needed, and in what format, in order to support those modes of reasoning.

Researchers are often surprised that the hierarchy denegrades the impressive achievements of deep learning to the level of Association, side by side with textbook curve-fitting exercises. A popular stance against this comparison argues that, whereas the objective of curve-fitting is to maximize "fit," in deep learning we try to minimize "over fit." Unfortunately, the theoretical barriers that separate the three layers in the hierarchy tell us that the nature of our objective function does not matter. As long as our system optimizes some property of the observed data, however noble or sophisticated, while making no reference to the world outside the data, we are back to level-1 of the hierarchy with all the limitations that this level entails.

The Seven Pillars of the Causal Revolution (or What You Can Do with a Causal Model That You Could Not Do Without?)

Consider the following five questions:

- How effective is a given treatment in preventing a disease?
- Was it the new tax break that caused our sales to go up?
- What is the annual health-care costs attributed to obesity?
- Can hiring records prove an employer guilty of sex discrimination?

• I am about to quit my job, but should I?

The common feature of these questions is that they are concerned with cause-and-effect relationships. We can recognize them through words such as "preventing," "cause," "attributed to," "discrimination," and "should I." Such words are common in everyday language, and our society constantly demands answers to such questions. Yet, until very recently science gave us no means even to articulate them, let alone answer them. Unlike the rules of geometry, mechanics, optics or probabilities, the rules of cause and effect have been denied the benefits of mathematical analysis.

To appreciate the extent of this denial, readers would be stunned to know that only a few decades ago scientists were unable to write down a mathematical equation for the obvious fact that "mud does not cause rain." Even today, only the top echelon of the scientific community can write such an equation and formally distinguish "mud causes rain" from "rain causes mud." And you would probably be even more surprised to discover that your favorite college professor is not among them.

Things have changed dramatically in the past three decades. A mathematical language has been developed for managing causes and effects, accompanied by a set of tools that turn causal analysis into a mathematical game, not unlike solving algebraic equations, or finding proofs in high-school geometry. These tools permit us to express causal questions formally, codify our existing knowledge in both diagrammatic and algebraic forms, and then leverage our data to estimate the answers. Moreover, the theory warns us when the state of existing knowledge or the available data are insufficient to answer our questions; and then suggests additional sources of knowledge or data to make the questions answerable.

Harvard professor Garry King gave this transformation a historical perspective: "More has been learned about causal inference in the last few decades than the sum total of everything that had been learned about it in all prior recorded history" (Morgan and Winship, 2015). I call this transformation "The Causal Revolution," (Pearl and Mackenzie, 2018) and the mathematical framework that led to it I call "Structural Causal Models (SCM)."

The SCM deploys three parts

1. Graphical models,
2. Structural equations, and
3. Counterfactual and interventional logic

Graphical models serve as a language for representing what we know about the world, counterfactuals help us to articulate what we want to know, while structural equations serve to tie the two together in a solid semantics.

Figure 18.2 illustrates the operation of SCM in the form of an inference engine. The engine accepts three inputs: Assumptions, Queries, and Data, and produces three outputs: Estimand, Estimate and Fit indices. The Estimand (E_S) is a mathematical formula that, based on the Assumptions, provides a recipe for answering the Query from any hypothetical

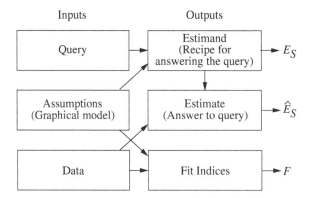

Figure 18.2
How the SCM "inference engine" combines data with causal model (or assumptions) to produce answers to queries of interest.

data, whenever they are available. After receiving the Data, the engine uses the Estimand to produce an actual Estimate $(\hat{E}_S)$ for the answer, along with statistical estimates of the confidence in that answer (To reflect the limited size of the data set, as well as possible measurement errors or missing data.) Finally, the engine produces a list of "fit indices" which measure how compatible the data are with the Assumptions conveyed by the model.

To exemplify these operations, let us assume that our Query stands for the causal effect of X on Y, written $Q = P(Y|do(X))$, where X and Y are two variables of interest. Let the modeling assumptions be encoded in the graph below, where Z is a third variable affecting both

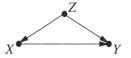

X and Y. Finally, let the data be sampled at random from a joint distribution $P(X,Y,Z)$. The Estimand (E_S) calculated by the engine will be the formula $E_S = \sum_z P(Y|X,Z)P(Z)$. It defines a property of $P(X,Y,Z)$ that, if estimated, would provide a correct answer to our Query. The answer itself, the Estimate $\hat{E}_S$, can be produced by any number of techniques that produce a consistent estimate of E_S from finite samples of $P(X,Y,Z)$. For example, the sample average (of Y) over all cases satisfying the specified X and Z conditions, would be a consistent estimate. But more efficient estimation techniques can be devised to overcome data sparsity (Rosenbaum and Rubin, 1983). This is where deep learning excels and where most work in machine learning has been focused, albeit with no guidance of a model-based estimand. Finally, the Fit Index in our example will be NULL. In other words, after examining the structure of the graph, the engine should conclude that the assumptions encoded do not have any testable implications. Therefore, the veracity of resultant estimate must lean entirely on the assumptions encoded in the graph – no refutation nor corroboration can be obtained from the data.[2]

The same procedure applies to more sophisticated queries, for example, the counterfactual query $Q = P(y_x|x',y')$ discussed before. We may also permit some of the data to arrive from controlled experiments, which would take the form $P(V|do(W))$, in case W is the controlled variable. The role of the Estimand would remain that of converting the Query into the syntactic format of the available data and, then, guiding the choice of the estimation technique to ensure unbiased estimates. Needless to state, the conversion task is not always feasible, in which case the Query will be declared "non-identifiable" and the engine should exit with FAILURE. Fortunately, efficient and complete algorithms have been developed to decide identifiability and to produce estimands for a variety of counterfactual queries and a variety of data types (Bareinboim and Pearl, 2016).

Next we provide a bird's eye view of seven accomplishments of the SCM framework and discuss the unique contribution that each pillar brings to the art of automated reasoning.

Pillar 1: Encoding Causal Assumptions—Transparency and Testability

The task of encoding assumptions in a compact and usable form, is not a trivial matter once we take seriously the requirement of transparency and testability.[3] Transparency enables analysts to discern whether the assumptions encoded are plausible (on scientific grounds), or whether additional assumptions are warranted. Testability permits us (be it an analyst or a machine) to determine whether the assumptions encoded are compatible with the available data and, if not, identify those that need repair.

Advances in graphical models have made compact encoding feasible. Their transparency stems naturally from the fact that all assumptions are encoded graphically, mirroring the way researchers perceive of cause-effect relationship in the domain; judgments of counterfactual or statistical dependencies are not required, since these can be read off the structure of the graph. Testability is facilitated through a graphical criterion called d-separation, which provides the fundamental connection between causes and probabilities. It tells us, for any given pattern of paths in the model, what pattern of dependencies we should expect to find in the data (Pearl, 1988).

Pillar 2: Do-calculus and the control of confounding

Confounding, or the presence of unobserved causes of two or more variables, has long been consider the the major obstacle to drawing causal inference from data. This obstacle had been demystified and "deconfounded" through a graphical criterion called "back-door." In particular, the task of selecting an appropriate set of covariates to control for confounding has been reduced to a simple "roadblocks" puzzle manageable by a simple algorithm (Pearl, 1993).

For models where the "back-door" criterion does not hold, a symbolic engine is available, called *do-calculus*, which predicts the effect of policy interventions whenever feasible, and exits with failure whenever predictions cannot be ascertained with the specified assumptions (Pearl, 1995; Tian and Pearl, 2002; Shpitser and Pearl, 2008).

Pillar 3: The Algorithmization of Counterfactuals

Counterfactual analysis deals with behavior of specific individuals, identified by a distinct set of characteristics. For example, given that Joe's salary is $Y = y$, and that he went $X = x$ years to college, what would Joe's salary be had he had one more year of education.

One of the crown achievements of the Causal Revolution has been to formalize counterfactual reasoning within the graphical representation, the very representation researchers use to encode scientific knowledge. Every structural equation model determines the truth value of every counterfactual sentence. Therefore, we can determine analytically if the probability of the sentence is estimable from experimental or observational studies, or combination thereof (Balke and Pearl, 2011; Pearl, 2000, Chapter 7).

Of special interest in causal discourse are counterfactual questions concerning "causes of effects," as opposed to "effects of causes." For example, how likely it is that Joe's swimming exercise was a necessary (or sufficient) cause of Joe's death (Pearl, 2015a; Halpern and Pearl, 2005).

Pillar 4: Mediation Analysis and the Assessment of Direct and Indirect Effects

Mediation analysis concerns the mechanisms that transmit changes from a cause to its effects. The identification of such intermediate mechanism is essential for generating explanations and counterfactual analysis must be invoked to facilitate this identification. The graphical representation of counterfactuals enables us to define direct and indirect effects and to decide when these effects are estimable from data, or experiments (Robins and Greenland, 1992; Pearl, 2001; VanderWeele, 2015). Typical queries answerable by this analysis are: What fraction of the effect of X on Y is mediated by variable Z.

Pillar 5: External Validity and Sample Selection Bias

The validity of every experimental study is challenged by disparities between the experimental and implementational setups. A machine trained in one environment cannot be expected to perform well when environmental conditions change, unless the changes are localized and identified. This problem, and its various manifestations are well recognized by machine-learning researchers, and enterprises such as "domain adaptation," "transfer learning," "life-long learning," and "explainable AI," are just some of the subtasks identified by researchers and funding agencies in an attempt to alleviate the general problem of robustness. Unfortunately, the problem of robustness requires a causal model of the environment, and cannot be handled at the level of Association, in which most remedies were tried. Associations are not sufficient for identifying the mechanisms affected by changes that occurred. The *do*-calculus discussed above now offers a complete methodology for overcoming bias due to environmental changes. It can be used both for re-adjusting learned policies to circumvent environmental changes and for controlling bias due to non-representative samples (Bareinboim and Pearl, 2016).

Pillar 6: Missing Data

Problems of missing data plague every branch of experimental science. Respondents do not answer every item on a questionnaire, sensors fade as environmental conditions change, and patients often drop from a clinical study for unknown reasons. The rich literature on this problem is wedded to a model-blind paradigm of statistical analysis and, accordingly, it is severely limited to situations where missingness occurs at random, that is, independent of values taken by other variables in the model. Using causal models of the missingness process we can now formalize the conditions under which causal and probabilistic relationships can be recovered from incomplete data and, whenever the conditions are satisfied, produce a consistent estimate of the desired relationship (Mohan and Pearl, 2017).

Pillar 7: Causal Discovery

The *d*-separation criterion described above enables us to detect and enumerate the testable implications of a given causal model. This opens the possibility of inferring, with mild assumptions, the set of models that are compatible with the data, and to represent this set compactly. Systematic searches have been developed which, in certain circumstances, can prune the set of compatible models significantly to the point where causal queries can be estimated directly from that set (Spirtes et al., 2000; Pearl, 2000; Peters et al., 2017).

Conclusions

The philosopher Stephen Toulmin (1961) identifies model-based vs. model-blind dichotomy as the key to understanding the ancient rivalry between Babylonian and Greek science. According to Toulmin, the Babylonians astronomers were masters of black-box prediction, far surpassing their Greek rivals in accuracy and consistency (Toulmin, 1961, pp. 27–30). Yet

Science favored the creative-speculative strategy of the Greek astronomers which was wild with metaphysical imagery: circular tubes full of fire, small holes through which celestial fire was visible as stars, and hemispherical earth riding on turtle backs. Yet it was this wild modeling strategy, not Babylonian rigidity, that jolted Eratosthenes (276-194 BC) to perform one of the most creative experiments in the ancient world and measure the radius of the earth. This would never have occurred to a Babylonian curve-fitter.

Coming back to strong AI, we have seen that model-blind approaches have intrinsic limitations on the cognitive tasks that they can perform. We have described some of these tasks and demonstrated how they can be accomplished in the SCM framework, and why a model-based approach is essential for performing these tasks. Our general conclusion is that human-level AI cannot emerge solely from model-blind learning machines; it requires the symbiotic collaboration of data and models.

Data science is only as much of a science as it facilitates the interpretation of data – a two-body problem, connecting data to reality. Data alone are hardly a science, regardless how big they get and how skillfully they are manipulated.

Notes for Chapter 18

1. Other names used for inferences at this layer are: "model-free," "model-blind," "black-box," or "data-centric." Darwiche (2018) used "function-fitting," for it amounts to fitting data by a complex function defined by the neural network architecture.

2. The assumptions encoded in the graph are conveyed by its missing arrows. For example, Y does not influence X or Z, X does not influence Z and, most importantly, Z is the only variable affecting both X and Y. That these assumptions lack testable implications can be concluded from the fact that the graph is complete, i.e., no edges are missing.

3. Economists, for example, having chosen algebraic over graphical representations, are deprived of elementary testability-detecting features (Pearl, 2015b).

V CONTRIBUTIONS FROM COGNITIVE NEUROSCIENCE

Part V: Contributions from Cognitive Neuroscience

There has long been a fruitful interchange between biology and artificial intelligence (AI), with neuroscience in particular leading the way. At least since McCulloch and Pitts (1943) postulated both a simplified model of the neuron and an accompanying "logical calculus" for its activity, neural networks have been proposed to shed light both as descriptive models of the brain and as basic building blocks for AI. The interplay between computation and psychology is still very much alive today. Indeed, computational neuroscience is now a thriving field of its own.

In his classic "The Architecture of Mind: A Connectionist Approach" (chapter 19), David Rumelhart makes a case for the utility of neural networks in understanding cognition. His demonstration of the power of what are (by today's standards) quite primitive parallel distributed processing (PDP) networks was a high-water mark for neurally inspired approaches to cognition. We include it here both for its clear exposition of the fundamentals and the way that it captures the early enthusiasm for the connectionist approach.

In excerpts from *The Computational Brain* (1992), Churchland and Sejnowski exemplify the other direction (in chapter 20), showing how a computational approach has been fruitful for understanding the brain. In this seminal work on the philosophy of neuroscience, they connect the abstract language of computation with the comparatively messy details of how brains work. They also lay out fundamental assumptions about brain function, such as the idea that brain mechanisms typically span multiple levels of organization and can be described at different (Marrian) levels of analysis.

Cowie and Woodward's "The Mind Is Not (Just) a System of Modules Shaped (Just) by Natural Selection" (chapter 21) considers whether there are good reasons to believe that the mind is composed of largely causally independent and informationally encapsulated modules. In doing so, they bring together issues of modularity with considerations about the correct role for evolutionary psychology in the understanding of the mind. Evolution is, of course, the original Mind Designer—but how to understand that relation, much less how it might affect our understanding of artificial systems, remains a hotly contested topic. Perhaps more centrally, the question of whether the mind might simply be an assemblage of relatively simple, domain-specific modules, has direct bearing on the kinds of artificial systems that might plausibly implement human-like intelligence.

Combinations and additions

The papers in this part of the book are naturally combined with those in part IV; which to read first is more a matter of emphasis than of strict division. A reader focusing on intelligence might combine these papers with those in part II, asking whether there is something distinctive about human intelligence that depends constitutively on how human cognition

is implemented. The idea that intelligence evolved to deal with specific evolutionary problems is also a theme of some of the papers in part VI.

Historical Connections.   There have been several useful recent discussions about the historical link between neuroscience and computation:

- Readers looking to learn more about McCulloch and Pitts's pioneering entry into this
  area will benefit from Piccinini (2004), which offers a close reading of this classic
  paper. For a closer look at the historical origins of McColloch and Pitts, readers might
  consider Abraham (2002).
- The idea that computers arranged like nervous systems might be powerful learners is
  already prefigured in Turing (1948/2004). Especially striking to the modern reader is
  the focus on pleasure and pain as appropriate training signals, prefiguring later work on
  reinforcement learning. In his introduction to Turing's piece, Copeland suggests that
  this may have been developed in parallel with McCulloch and Pitts.

On Connectionism.   In the last edition of *Mind Design*, a debate raged about whether connectionist architectures provide a strong alternative to classical computation. As much
of this debate was focused on PDP and its limitations—many of which have since been
transcended—we felt it was best to elide them. But the debates are far from settled. Consider the following:

- The *locus classicus* of this discussion is Fodor and Pylyshyn (1988), which argues that
  connectionist representations lack the kind of representational framework that can explain the systematicity (that the ability to think that Alex loves Bill, seems to entail the
  ability to think that Bill loves Alex) and productivity (the ability to endlessly combine
  atomic thoughts into new forms) of natural language. We opted not to include this discussion in this edition because the problem seems, in our view, to have been resolved
  by denying the contrast in representational forms that lies at the heart of Fodor and
  Pylyshyn's argument.
- Already by the time of *Mind Design II*, it was becoming clear that one could, in fact,
  implement GOFAI machines in connectionist hardware if one so desired. Smolensky (1991), for example, argues that connectionist systems can capture and recover
  the componential structure that Fodor and Pylyshyn thought was required to explain
  systematicity and productivity.
- This implementation argument was developed in full generality in Chalmers (1990).
  Connectionist systems can be simulated on GOFAI machines (all of them are, in fact);
  and GOFAI systems (e.g., Turing machines) can be implemented on connectionist systems. So the conflict about what is possible in principle seems to have deflated, though
  the details might matter for particular cases.

We also removed a different line of discussion, though it seems to us very much alive, about how computationalist models of mind should affect how we think of minds and theorizing about them. Consider the following:

- Churchland (1990), which was excerpted from Churchland. (1989) (and which appeared in *Mind Design II*), argues for the radical thesis is that neurally inspired architectures should prompt an overall revolution in the way we think of the mind, replacing quaint concepts like "belief" and "desire" with a scientifically mature and neurally inspired replacement vocabulary. Churchland (1981) provides the most general and provocative version of that line of thought.
- Rosenberg (1997), in "Connectionism and Cognition" (also found in *Mind Design II*), argues, in contrast, that there simply is no replacement for a sentential epistemology and, as a consequence, no replacement for a sentential model of belief and desire. Rosenberg argues that connectionism is best viewed as the implementational under-laborer of sentential epistemologies. We simply cannot make sense of the idea of justification or inference, and hence of belief, in terms that don't advert to representational contents and to the acceptance of rules governing relationships among such contents.
- The idea that there must at least some level of description that is described as rule-governed (rather than merely causal) is a theme in Pylyshyn (1984), which also contains an extended discussion of the presuppositions of traditional computationalism.
- Moving from connectionism to even more neurally inspired theories, as presaged by Churchland and Sejnowski's article, Piccinini and Bahar (2013) provide a concise critical review of the senses in which neural systems might be said to compute along with connections to recent literature in computational neuroscience.

Modularity of Mind and Brain.   Much of the debate around modularity turns on what one thinks modules are in the first place. The classic source is the beginning of Fodor (1983) (later sections of which are excerpted as chapter 9 of this volume), which presents a fairly rigid list of criteria for modularity. Various authors relax these assumptions, usually in the service of defending a "massive modularity" hypothesis:

- Carruthers (2004), to which the Cowie and Woodward (chapter 21) is a direct response, defines a module as any "isolable subcomponent" of a complex system. This gives up on many of the properties that Fodor originally proposed (such as innateness, encapsulation, and localizability) . This makes it more plausible that there are many modules, at the cost of a thinner theory overall. Carruthers (2006) defends this at greater length.
- Conversely, Coltheart (2007) suggests that the essential feature of modularity is domain specificity and corresponding informational encapsulation from material in other domains. Encapsulation is the key feature evoked to explain, for example, double dissociations in neurospsychology, as well as the curious impenetrability of visual illusions.

- While many discussions of modularity make appeal to engineering principles, few dig into actual engineered systems and the advantages in each. Calcott (2014) is a notable exception. Calcott discusses the notion of modularity as it appears in software engineering, noting that the key feature there is the appearance of a stable and consistent *interface* between modules. Consistent interfaces make it easier to reuse modules in new circumstances.
- Anderson (2010) provides evidence that the same neural areas might be used for different functions in different contexts. Some version of this hypothesis is now widely accepted. On one reading, reuse shows the need to distinguish between different senses of the "function' of a subroutine. In his later work, however, Anderson (2014) suggests that reuse presents a powerful challenge to even minimal notions of modularity.

Function and Decomposition.   When debating modularity, one subtle issue has to do with whether modules are *functional* parts of systems or *mechanical*, spatiotemporally isolable parts as well. Many discussions of modularity in neuroscience assume that both must be the case, but it's clear that the two come apart. Consider the stock functionalist example of the carburetor. There is a functional step of carburetion—that is, of atomizing gasoline and mixing it with an appropriate portion of air to be burned. Some cars also have *carburetors*: specific parts, the function of which is to carburate. However, you'd be hard-pressed to find a car with a carburetor today: advances in fuel injection and environmental controls meant that carburetion is done by the joint action of several parts, most of which serve other functions as well. When asking about modularity, therefore, it's always worth asking what sort of decomposition one means. Consider adding the following to your reading:

- In philosophy, this distinction is made clearly in chapter 2 of Cummins (1983). Cummins distinguishes between "functional" and "componential" analysis, noting that the former puts indirect constraints only on the latter. He also emphasizes the need to distinguish between capacities and subcapacities of a whole system versus capacities of a whole, which are analyzed in terms of the capacities of its parts.
- While Fodor originally suggested that modules were neurally localizable, he never leaned hard on this and soon abandoned the idea. Even within neuropsychology, the need for localization was hotly debated. Caramazza (1986) presents a classic discussion of what came to be called the "ultracognitivist" picture, where modules are understood purely at the cognitive level. Shallice (1988) contains a rich discussion of the pros and cons of different approaches to localization within this tradition.
- Dissociability is meant to be the hallmark of modularity, and yet connectionist systems have been shown to exhibit double dissociation. For a theoretical demonstration of this possibility, see Plaut (1995). Haxby et al. (2001) is a seminal neuroimaging paper that also provides a concrete demonstration of a way that apparent modularity could arise from distributed neural networks.

- The literature on computers has rarely been tempted to confuse anatomical and functional modularity: the mapping between software and hardware is pretty obviously many-many. That is, it seems pretty obvious that there isn't a specific part of your computer dedicated to making windows, even if the code for making windows is an importantly modular part of the operating system. Jonas and Kording (2017) present an amusing demonstrations of the limits of neuroscientific methods when applied to actual computational systems (and is in turn a riff on the equally fun Lazebnik (2002)). This sort of exercise is good for generating intuitions about real-life cases and the gap between theoretical ideas about how to reverse-engineer a brain and the reality of forms of organization that apparently defy that approach.

The Architecture of Mind: A Connectionist Approach

19

1989

Cognitive science has a long-standing and important relationship to the computer. The computer has provided a tool whereby we have been able to express our theories of mental activity; it has been a valuable source of metaphors through which we have come to understand and appreciate how mental activities might arise out of the operations of simple-component processing elements.

I recall vividly a class I taught some fifteen years ago in which I outlined the then-current view of the cognitive system. A particularly skeptical student challenged my account, with its reliance on concepts drawn from computer science and artificial intelligence, with the question of whether I thought my theories would be different if it had happened that our computers were parallel instead of serial. My response, as I recall, was to concede that our theories might very well be different, but to argue that that wasn't a bad thing. I pointed out that the inspiration for our theories and our understanding of abstract phenomena always is based on our experience with the technology of the time. I pointed out that Aristotle had a wax tablet theory of memory, that Leibniz saw the universe as clockworks, that Freud used a hydraulic model of libido flowing through the system, and that the telephone-switchboard model of intelligence had played an important role as well. The theories posited by those of previous generations had, I suggested, been useful in spite of the fact that they were based on the metaphors of their time. Therefore, I argued, it was natural that in our generation—the generation of the serial computer—we should draw our insights from analogies with the most advanced technological developments of our time. I don't now remember whether my response satisfied the student, but I have no doubt that we in cognitive science have gained much of value through our use of concepts drawn from our experience with the computer.

In addition to its value as a source of metaphors, the computer differs from earlier technologies in another remarkable way. The computer can be made to *simulate* systems whose operations are very different from the computers on which these simulations run. In this way we can use the computer to simulate systems with which we *wish* to have experience and thereby provide a source of experience that can be drawn upon in giving us new metaphors and new insights into how mental operations might be accomplished. It is this use of the computer that the connectionists have employed. The architecture that we are exploring is not one based on the von Neumann architecture of our current generation of computers but rather an architecture based on considerations of how brains themselves might function. Our strategy has thus become one of offering a general and abstract model of the computational architecture of brains, to develop algorithms and procedures well suited to this architecture, to simulate these procedures and architecture on a computer, and to explore them as hypotheses about the nature of the human information-processing system. We say that such models are *neurally inspired*, and we call computation on such a system *brain-style computation*. Our goal in short is to replace the computer metaphor with the brain metaphor.

19.1   Why brain-style computation?

Why should a brain-style computer be an especially interesting source of inspiration? Implicit in the adoption of the computer metaphor is an assumption about the appropriate level of explanation in cognitive science. The basic assumption is that we should seek explanation at the *program* or *functional* level rather than the implementation level. Thus, it is often pointed out that we can learn very little about what kind of program a particular computer may be running by looking at the electronics. In fact we don't care much about the details of the computer at all; all we care about is the particular program it is running. If we know the program, we know how the system will behave in any situation. It doesn't matter whether we use vacuum tubes or transistors, whether we use an IBM or an Apple, the essential characteristics are the same. This is a very misleading analogy. It is true for computers because they are all essentially the same. Whether we make them out of vacuum tubes or transistors, and whether we use an IBM or an Apple computer, we are using computers of the same general design. But, when we look at an essentially different architecture, we see that the architecture makes a good deal of difference. It is the architecture that determines which kinds of algorithms are most easily carried out on the machine in question. It is the architecture of the machine that determines the essential nature of the program itself. It is thus reasonable that we should begin by asking what we know about the architecture of the brain and how it might shape the algorithms underlying biological intelligence and human mental life.

The basic strategy of the connectionist approach is to take as its fundamental processing unit something close to an abstract neuron. We imagine that computation is carried out through simple interactions among such processing units. Essentially the idea is that these processing elements communicate by sending numbers along the lines that connect the processing elements. This identification already provides some interesting constraints on the kinds of algorithms that might underlie human intelligence.

The operations in our models then can best be characterized as "neurally-inspired". How does the replacement of the computer metaphor with the brain metaphor as model of mind affect our thinking? This change in orientation leads us to a number of considerations that further inform and constrain our model-building efforts. Perhaps the most crucial of these is time. Neurons are remarkably slow relative to components in modern computers. Neurons operate in the time scale of milliseconds, whereas computer components operate in the time scale of nanoseconds—a factor of 10^6 faster. This means that human processes that take on the order of a second or less can involve only a hundred or so time steps. Because most of the processes we have studied—perception, memory retrieval, speech processing, sentence comprehension, and the like—take about a second or so, it makes sense to impose what Feldman (1985) calls the "100-step-program" constraint. That is, we seek explanations for these mental phenomena that do not require more than about a hundred elementary sequential operations. Given that the processes we seek to characterize are often quite complex and may involve consideration of large numbers of simultaneous constraints, our algorithms *must* involve considerable parallelism. Thus although a serial computer could be created out of the kinds of components represented by our units, such an implementation would surely violate the 100-step-program constraint for any but the simplest processes. Some might argue that, although parallelism is obviously present in much of human information processing, this fact alone need not greatly modify our world view. This is unlikely. The speed of components is a critical design constraint. Although the brain has *slow* components, it has *very many* of them. The human brain contains billions of such processing elements. Rather than organize computation with many, many serial steps, as we do with systems whose steps are very fast, the brain must deploy many, many processing elements cooperatively and in parallel to carry out its activities. These design characteristics, among others, lead, I believe, to a general organization of computing that is fundamentally different from what we are used to.

A further consideration differentiates our models from those inspired by the computer metaphor—that is, the constraint that all the knowledge is *in the connections*. From conventional programmable computers we are used to thinking of knowledge as being stored in the states of certain units in the system. In our systems we assume that only very short-term storage can occur in the states of units; long-term storage takes place in the connections among units. Indeed it is the connections—or perhaps the rules for forming them through experience—that primarily differentiate one model from another. This is a profound difference between our approach and other more conventional approaches, for it means that almost all knowledge is *implicit* in the structure of the device that carries out the task, rather than *explicit* in the states of units themselves. Knowledge is not directly accessible to interpretation by some separate processor, but it is built into the processor itself and directly determines the course of processing. It is acquired through tuning of connections, as they are used in processing, rather than formulated and stored as declarative facts.

These and other neurally inspired classes of working assumptions have been one important source of assumptions underlying the connectionist program of research. These have
not been the only considerations. A second class of constraints arises from our beliefs
about the nature of human information processing considered at a more abstract, computational level of analysis. We see the kinds of phenomena we have been studying as products
of a kind of constraint-satisfaction procedure in which a very large number of constraints
act simultaneously to produce the behavior. Thus we see most behavior not as the product
of a single, separate component of the cognitive system but as the product of a large set
of interacting components, each mutually constraining the others and contributing in its
own way to the globally observable behavior of the system. It is very difficult to use serial
algorithms to implement such a conception but very natural to use highly parallel ones.
These problems can often be characterized as *best-match* or *optimization* problems. As
Minsky and Papert (1969) have pointed out, it is very difficult to solve best-match problems serially. This is precisely the kind of problem, however, that is readily implemented
using highly parallel algorithms of the kind we have been studying.

The use of brain-style computational systems, then, offers not only a hope that we can
characterize how brains actually carry out certain information-processing tasks but also
solutions to computational problems that seem difficult to solve in more traditional computational frameworks. It is here where the ultimate value of connectionist systems must
be evaluated.

In this chapter, I begin with a somewhat more formal sketch of the computational framework of connectionist models. I then follow with a general discussion of the kinds of
computational problems that connectionist models seem best suited for. Finally, I briefly
review the state of the art in connectionist modeling.

19.1.1   The connectionist framework

There are seven major components of any connectionist system:

- a *set of processing units*;
- a *state of activation* defined over the processing units;
- an *output function* for each unit that maps its state of activation into an output;
- a *pattern of connectivity* among units;
- an *activation rule* for combining the inputs impinging on a unit with its current state to
  produce a new level of activation for the unit;
- a *learning rule* whereby patterns of connectivity are modified by experience; and
- an *environment* within which the system must operate.

Figure 19.1 illustrates the basic aspects of these systems. There is a set of processing
units, generally indicated by circles in my diagrams; at each point in time each unit u_i has
an activation value, denoted in the diagram as $a_i(t)$; this activation value is passed through

a function f_i; to produce an output value $o_i(t)$. This output value can be seen as passing through a set of unidirectional connections (indicated by lines or arrows in the diagrams) to other units in the system. There is associated with each connection a real number, usually called the *weight* or *strength* of the connection, designated w_{ij} (*to* unit i, *from* unit j), which determines how strongly the former is affected by the latter. All of the inputs must then be combined; and the combined inputs to a unit (usually designated the *net input* to that unit), along with its current activation value, determine its new activation value via a function F. These systems are viewed as being plastic in the sense that the pattern of interconnections is not fixed for all time; rather the weights can undergo modification as a function of experience. In this way the system can evolve. What a unit represents can change with experience, and the system can come to perform in substantially different ways.

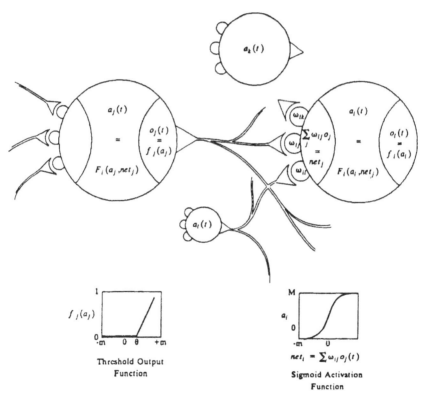

Figure 19.1
The basic parts of a parallel distributed processing system.

THE SET OF PROCESSING UNITS. Any connectionist system begins with a set of processing units. Specifying the set of processing units and what they represent is typically the first stage of specifying a connectionist model. In some systems these units may represent particular conceptual objects such as features, letters, words, or concepts; in others they are simply abstract elements over which meaningful patterns can be defined. When we speak of a distributed representation, we mean one in which the units represent small, feature-like entities we call *microfeatures*. In this case it is the pattern as a whole that is the meaningful level of analysis. This should be contrasted to a *one-unit-one-concept* or *localist* representational system, in which single units represent entire concepts or other large meaningful entities.

All of the processing of a connectionist system is carried out by these units. There is no executive or other overseer. There are only relatively simple units, each doing its own relatively simple job. A unit's job is simply to receive input from its neighbors and, as a function of the inputs it receives, to compute an output value, which it sends to its neighbors. The system is inherently parallel in that many units can carry out their computations at the same time.

Within any system we are modeling, it is useful to characterize three types of units: *input*, *output*, and *hidden* units. Input units receive inputs from sources external to the system under study. These inputs may be either sensory inputs or inputs from other parts of the processing system in which the model is embedded. The output units send signals out of the system. They may either directly affect motoric systems or simply influence other systems external to the ones we are modeling. The hidden units are those whose only inputs and outputs are within the system we are modeling. They are not "visible" to outside systems.

THE STATE OF ACTIVATION. In addition to the set of units we need a representation of the state of the system at time t. This is primarily specified by a vector $\mathbf{a}(t)$, representing the pattern of activation over the set of processing units. Each element of the vector stands for the activation of one of the units. It is the *pattern* of activation over the whole set of units that captures what the system is representing at any time. It is useful to see processing in the system as the evolution, through time, of a pattern of activity over the set of units.

Different models make different assumptions about the activation values a unit is allowed to take on. Activation values may be continuous or discrete. If they are continuous, they may be unbounded or bounded. If they are discrete, they may take binary values or any of a small set of values. Thus in some models units are continuous and may take on any real number as an activation value. In other cases they may take on any real value between some minimum and maximum such as, for example, the interval [0,1]. When activation values are restricted to discrete values, they most often are binary—such as the values 0 and 1, where 1 is usually taken to mean that the unit is active and 0 is taken to mean that it is inactive.

THE OUTPUT FUNCTION. Units interact by transmitting signals to their neighbors. The strengths of their signals, and therefore the degrees to which they affect their neighbors, are determined by their levels of activation. Associated with each unit u_i is an output function $f_i(a_i(t))$, which maps the current state of activation to an output signal $o_i(t)$. In some of our models, the output level is exactly equal to the activation level of the unit. In this case, f is the identity function $f(x) = x$. Sometimes f is some sort of threshold function, so that a unit has no effect on another unit unless its activation exceeds a certain value. Sometimes the function f is assumed to be a stochastic function in which the output of the unit depends probabilistically on its activation level.

THE PATTERN OF CONNECTIVITY. Units are connected to one another. It is this pattern of connectivity that constitutes what the system knows and determines how it will respond to any arbitrary input. Specifying the processing system and the knowledge encoded therein is, in a connectionist model, a matter of specifying this pattern of connectivity among the processing units.

In many cases we assume that each unit provides an additive contribution to the input of the units to which it is connected. In such cases the total input to any unit is simply the weighted sum of the separate inputs from each of the units connected to it. That is, the inputs from all of the incoming units are simply multiplied by their respective connection weights and summed to get the overall input to that unit. In this case the total pattern of connectivity can be represented by merely specifying the weights for each of the connections in the system. A positive weight represents an excitatory input, and a negative weight represents an inhibitory input. It is often convenient to represent such a pattern of connectivity by a weight matrix $\mathbf{W}$ in which the entry w_{ij} represents the strength and sense of the connection to unit u_i from unit u_j. The weight w_{ij} is a positive number if unit u_j excites unit u_i; it is a negative number if unit u_j inhibits unit u_i; and it is 0 if unit u_j has no direct connection to unit u_i. The absolute value of w_{ij} specifies the *strength of the connection*.

The pattern of connectivity is very important. It is this pattern that determines what each unit represents. One important issue that may determine both how much information can be stored and how much serial processing the network must perform is the *fan-in* and *fan-out* of a unit The fan-in is the number of elements that either excite or inhibit a given unit. The fan-out is the number of units affected directly by a unit. It is useful to note that in brains these numbers are relatively large. Fan-in and fan-out range as high as 100,000 in some parts of the brain. It seems likely that this large fan-in and fan-out allows for a kind of operation that is less like a fixed circuit and more statistical in character.

THE ACTIVATION RULE. We also need a rule whereby the inputs impinging on a particular unit are combined with one another and with the current state of the unit to produce a new state of activation. We need a function F_i, which takes $a_i(t)$ and the net inputs, $\text{net}_i = \sum_j w_{ij} o_j(t)$, and produces a new state of activation. In the simplest cases, when F_i is the identity function and depends only on the inputs, we can write $a_i(t+1) = \text{net}_i(t)$—or, in vector notation for the whole network at once, $\mathbf{a}(t+1) = \mathbf{net}(t) = \mathbf{Wo}(t)$. Sometimes F is a threshold function so that the net input must exceed some value before contributing to the new state of activation. Often the new state of activation depends on the old one as well as the current input. The function F itself is what we call the activation rule. Usually the function is assumed to be deterministic. Thus, for example, if a threshold is involved, it may be that $a_i(t) = 1$ if the total input exceeds some threshold value, and equals 0 otherwise. Other times it is assumed that F is stochastic. Sometimes activations are assumed to decay slowly with time so that even with no external input the activation of a unit will simply decay and not go directly to zero. Whenever $a_i(t)$ is assumed to take on continuous values, it is common to assume that F is a kind of sigmoid (that is, S-shaped) function. In this case an individual unit can *saturate* and reach a minimum or maximum value of activation.

THE LEARNING RULE: CHANGES AS A FUNCTION OF EXPERIENCE. Changing the processing or knowledge structure in a connectionist system involves modifying the patterns of interconnectivity. In principle this can involve three kinds of modification:

(1) development of new connections;
(2) loss of existing connections;
(3) modification of the strengths of connections that already exist.

Very little work has been done on (1) and (2). To a first order of approximation, however, (1) and (2) can be considered a special case of (3). Whenever we change the strength of connection away from zero to some positive or negative value, it has the same effect as growing a new connection. Whenever we change the strength of a connection to zero, that has the same effect as losing an existing connection. Thus we have concentrated on rules whereby *strengths* of connections are modified through experience.

Virtually all learning rules for models of this type can be considered variants of the *Hebbian* learning rule, suggested by Hebb in his classic book *The Organization of Behavior* (1949). Hebb's basic idea is this: if a unit u_i receives an input from another unit u_j at a time when both units are highly active, then the weight w_{ij} to u_i from u_j should be *strengthened*. This idea has been extended and modified so that it can be stated more generally as

$$\delta w_{ij} = g(a_i(t), \tau_i(t)) \cdot h(o_j(t), w_{ij})$$

or, suppressing the time variables for easier readability, as

$$\delta w_{ij} = g(a_i, \tau_i) \cdot h(o_j, w_{ij})$$

where τ_i is a kind of *teaching* input to u_i. Simply stated, this equation says that the *change* in the connection to u_i from u_j is given by the product of a function $g(\ldots)$ of the activation of u_i and its teaching input τ_i and another function $h(\ldots)$ of the output value of u_j and the current connection strength w_{ij}. In the simplest versions of Hebbian learning, there is no teacher and the functions g and h are simply proportional to their first arguments. Thus we have

$$\delta w_{ij} = \varepsilon a_i o_j$$

where ε is the constant of proportionality representing the learning rate. Another common variation is a rule in which

$$h(o_j, w_{ij}) = o_j$$

(as in the simplest case) but

$$g(a_i, \tau_i) = \varepsilon \cdot (\tau_i - a_i)$$

This is often called the *Widrow-Hoff rule*, because it was originally formulated by Widrow and Hoff (1960), or the *delta* rule, because the amount of learning is proportional to the *difference* (or delta) between the actual activation achieved and the target activation provided by a teacher. In this case we have

$$\delta w_{ij} = \varepsilon \cdot (\tau_i - a_i) \cdot o_j$$

This is a generalization of the *perceptron* learning rule for which the famous *perceptron convergence theorem* has been proved. Still another variation has

$$\delta w_{ij} = \varepsilon a_i \cdot (o_j - w_{ij})$$

This is a rule employed by Grossberg (1976) and others in the study of *competitive learning*. In this case usually only the units with the strongest activation values are allowed to learn.

THE ENVIRONMENT. It is crucial in the development of any model to have a clear representation of the environment in which this model is to exist. For connectionist models, we represent the environment as a time-varying stochastic function over a space of possible input patterns. That is, for each possible input pattern, we imagine that there is some probability that, at any given time, that pattern is impinging on the input units. This probability function may in general depend on the history of inputs to the system as well as outputs of the system. In practice most connectionist models involve a much simpler characterization of the environment. Typically, the environment is characterized by a stable probability distribution over the set of possible input patterns, independent of past inputs and past responses of the system. In this case we can imagine listing the set of possible inputs to the system and numbering them from 1 to M. The environment is then characterized by a set of probabilities p_i for $i = l, \ldots, M$. Because each input pattern can be considered a vector, it is sometimes useful to characterize those patterns with nonzero probabilities as constituting *orthogonal* or *linearly independent* sets of vectors.

To summarize, the connectionist framework consists not only of a formal language but also a perspective on our models. Other qualitative and quantitative considerations arising from our understanding of brain processing and of human behavior combine with the formal system to form what might be viewed as an aesthetic for our model-building enterprises.

19.1.2 Computational features of connectionist models

In addition to the fact that connectionist systems are capable of exploiting parallelism in computation and mimicking brain-style computation, such systems are important because they provide good solutions to a number of very difficult computational problems that seem to arise often in models of cognition. In particular they typically:

- are good at solving constraint-satisfaction problems;
- are efficient mechanisms for best-match search, pattern recognition, and content-addressable memory;
- automatically implement similarity-based generalization;
- offer simple, general mechanisms for adaptive learning; and
- exhibit graceful degradation with damage or information overload.

CONSTRAINT SATISFACTION PROBLEMS. Many cognmve-science problems are usefully conceptualized as problems in which a solution is given through the satisfaction of a very large number of mutually interacting constraints. The challenge is to devise a computational system that is capable of efficiently solving such problems. Connectionist networks are ideal for implementing constraint-satisfaction systems; indeed, the trick for getting connectionist networks to solve difficult problems is often to cast the problems as constraint-satisfaction problems. In this case, we conceptualize the connectionist network as a *constraint network* in which each unit represents a hypothesis of some sort (for example, that a certain semantic feature, visual feature, or acoustic feature is present in the input), and each connection represents a constraint among the hypotheses.

Thus, for such a network, if feature B is expected to be present whenever feature A is present, there should be a positive connection from the unit corresponding to the hypothesis that A is present to the unit representing the hypothesis that B is present. Contrariwise, if there is a constraint that whenever A is present B is expected *not* to be present, there should be a negative connection from A to B. If the constraints are weak, the weights should be small; if the constraints are strong, then the weights should be large. Similarly, the inputs to such networks can also be thought of as constraints. A positive input to a particular unit means that there is evidence from the outside that the relevant feature is present. A negative input means that there is evidence from the outsidc that the feature is not present. The stronger the input, the greater the evidence. If a network of this kind is allowed to run, it will eventually *settle* into an optimal state in which as many as possible of the constraints arc satisfied, with priority given to the strongest constraints. (Actually, the system will find a *locally* best solution to the constraint-satisfaction problem. *Global* optima are more difficult to find.) The procedure whereby such a system *settles* into such a state is called

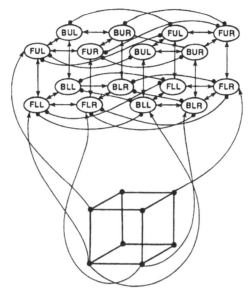

Figure 19.2
A simple network representing some constraints involved in perceiving a Necker cube. The ovals are the units in the network; connections with arrow-heads are positive (excitatory), while those with circle-heads are negative (inhibitory); the dotted lines represent input stimuli from the perceived cube.

relaxation. We speak of the system *relaxing* to a solution. Thus, many connectionist models are constraint-satisfaction models that settle on locally optimal solutions through a process of relaxation.

Figure 19.2 shows an example of a simple 16-unit constraint network. Each unit in the network represents a hypothesis concerning a vertex in a line drawing of a Necker cube. The network consists of two interconnected subnetworks—one corresponding to each of the two global interpretations of the Necker cube. Each unit in each subnetwork is assumed to receive input from the region of the input figure—the cube—corresponding to its location in the network. Each unit in figure 19.2 is labeled with a three-letter sequence indicating whether its vertex is hypothesized to be front or back (F or B), upper or lower (U or L), and right or left (R or L). Thus, for example, the lower-left unit of each subnetwork is assumed to receive input from the lower-left vertex of the input figure. The unit in the left network represents the hypothesis that it is receiving input from a lower-left vertex in the front surface of the cube (and is thus labeled FLL), whereas the one in the right subnetwork represents the hypothesis that it is receiving input from a lower-left vertex in the back surface (BLL). Because there is a constraint that each vertex has a single interpretation, these two units are connected by a strong negative connection. Because the interpretation of any given vertex is constrained by the interpretations of its neighbors, each unit in a subnetwork is connected positively with each of its neighbors within the network. Finally, since there is a constraint that there can be only one vertex of each kind (for example, there can be only one lower-left vertex in the front plane, FLL), there is a strong negative connection between units representing the same label in each subnetwork. Thus each unit has three neighbors connected positively, two competitors connected negatively, and one positive input from the stimulus.

For purposes of this example, we assume that the strengths of the connections have been arranged so that two negative inputs exactly balance three positive inputs. Further it is assumed that each unit receives an excitatory input from the ambiguous stimulus pattern and that each of these excitatory influences is relatively small. Thus, if all three of a unit's neighbors are on and both of its competitors are on, these effects would entirely cancel out one another; and if there were a small input from the outside, the unit would have a tendency to come on. On the other hand, if fewer than three of its neighbors were on and both of its competitors were on, the unit would have a tendency to turn off, even with an excitatory input from the stimulus pattern.

In the preceding paragraphs, I focused on the individual units of the networks. It is often useful, however, to focus not on the units but on entire *states* of the network. In the case of binary (on-off or 0-1) units, there would be a total of 2^{16} possible states in which a network of this size could reside—since, in principle, each of the 16 units could have either value 0 or 1. In the case of continuous units, in which each unit can take on any value between 0 and 1, the system could in principle take on any of an infinite number of states. Yet because of the constraints built into the network, there are only a relatively few of those states into which the system will ever actually settle.

To see this, consider the case in which the units are updated asynchronously, one at a time. During each time slice, one of the units is chosen to update. If its net input exceeds 0, its value will be pushed toward 1; otherwise its value will be pushed toward 0. Imagine that the system starts with all units off. A unit is then chosen at random to be updated. Because it is receiving slight positive input from the stimulus and no other inputs, it will be given a positive activation value. Then another unit is chosen to update. Unless it is in direct competition with the first unit, it too will be turned on. Eventually a coalition of neighboring units will be turned on. These units will tend to turn on more of their neighbors in the same subnetwork and turn off their competitors in the other subnetwork. The system will (almost always) end up in a situation in which all of the units in one subnetwork are fully activated and none of the units in the other subnetwork is activated. That is, the system will end up interpreting the Necker cube as either facing left or facing right. Whenever the system gets into a state and stays there, the state is called a *stable state* or a *fixed point* of the network. The constraints implicit in the pattern of connections among the units determine the set of possible stable states of the system and therefore the set of possible interpretations of the inputs.

Hopfield (1982) has shown that it is possible to give a general account of the behavior of systems like this (with symmetric weights and asynchronous updates). In particular, he has shown that such systems can be conceptualized as minimizing a global measure, which he calls the *energy* of the system, through a method of *gradient descent* or, equivalently, maximizing the constraints satisfied through a method of *hill climbing*. More specifically, the system operates so as to move always from a state that satisfies fewer constraints to one that satisfies more, where the measure of constraint satisfaction is given by

$$G(t) = \sum_i \sum_j w_{ij} a_i(t) a_j(t) + \sum_i \text{input}_i(t) a_i(t)$$

Essentially the equation says that the overall goodness of fit is given by the sum of the degrees to which each pair of units contributes to the goodness plus the degree to which the units satisfy the input constraints. The contribution of a pair of units is given by the product of their activation values and the weight connecting them. Thus, if the weight is positive, each unit wants to be as active as possible—that is, the activation values for those two units should be pushed toward 1. If the weight is negative, then at least one of the units should be 0 to maximize the pairwise goodness. Similarly if the input constraint for a given unit is positive, then its contribution to the total goodness of fit is maximized by bringing the activation of that unit toward its maximal value. If it is negative, the activation value should be decreased toward 0. Of course the constraints will generally not be totally consistent. Sometimes a given unit may have to be turned on to increase the function in some ways yet decrease it in other ways. The point is that it is the sum of all of these individual contributions that the system seeks to maximize. Thus, for every state of the system—every possible pattern of activation over the units—the pattern of inputs and the connectivity matrix W determine a value of the goodness-of-fit function. The system processes its input by moving upward from state to adjacent state until it reaches a state of maximum goodness. When it reaches such a *stable state* or *fixed point*, it will stay in that state and it can be said to have "settled" on a solution to the constraint-satisfaction problem or, as in our present case, "settled into an interpretation" of the input.

It is important to see then that entirely *local* computational operations, in which each unit adjusts its activation up or down on the basis of its net input, serve to allow the network to converge toward states that maximize a *global* measure of goodness or degree of constraint satisfaction. Hopfield's main contribution to the present analysis was to point out this basic fact about the behavior of networks with symmetrical connections and asynchronous update of activations.

Finally, one of the most difficult problems in cognitive science is to build systems that can allow a large number of knowledge sources to interact usefully in the solution of a problem. Thus, in language processing we would want syntactic, phonological, semantic, and pragmatic knowledge sources all to interact in the construction of the meaning of an input. Reddy et al. (1973) have had some success in the case of speech perception with the

Hearsay system because they were working in the highly structured domain of language. Less structured domains have proved very difficult to organize. Connectionist models, conceived as constraint-satisfaction networks, are ideally suited for blending multiple-knowledge sources. Each knowledge type is simply another constraint, and the system will, in parallel, find those configurations of values that best satisfy all of the constraints from all of the knowledge sources. The uniformity of representation and the common currency of interaction (activation values) make connectionist systems especially powerful for this domain.

To summarize, there is a large subset of connectionist models that can be considered constraint-satisfaction models. These networks can be described as carrying out their information processing by climbing into states of maximal satisfaction of the constraints implicit in the network. A very useful consequence of this way of viewing networks is that we can describe their behavior not only in terms of the behavior of individual units but also in terms of the properties of the network itself A primary concept for understanding these network properties is the *goodness-of-fit landscape* over which the system moves. Once we have correctly described this landscape, we have described the operational properties of the system—it will process information by moving uphill toward goodness maxima. The particular maximum that the system will find is determined by where the system starts and by the distortions of the space induced by the input. One of the very important descriptors of a goodness landscape is the set of maxima that a system can find, the size of the region that feeds into each maximum, and the height of the maximum itself. The states themselves correspond to possible interpretations, the peaks in the space correspond to the best interpretations, the extent of the foothills or skirts surrounding a particular peak determines the likelihood of finding the peak, and the height of the peak corresponds to the degree to which the constraints of the network are actually met or alternatively to the goodness of the interpretation associated with the corresponding state.

BEST-MATCH SEARCH, PATTERN RECOGNITION, AND CONTENT-ADDRESSABLE MEMORY. These are all variants on the general best-match problem (compare Minsky and Papert, 1969). Best-match problems are especially difficult for serial computational algorithms (they involve exhaustive search), but, as we have just indicated, connectionist systems can readily be used to find the interpretation that best matches a set of constraints.

They can similarly be used to find stored data that best match some target or probe. In this case, it is useful to imagine that the network consists of two classes of units. One class, the *visible* units, corresponds to the contents stored in the network, in the sense that each stored pattern is a possible pattern of activation of these units. The other units, the *hidden* units, correspond to shared structural properties of the stored patterns that play a role in storing and retrieving them. The patterns themselves are actually stored in the weights on the connections among all these units. If we think of each stored pattern as a collection of features, then each visible unit corresponds to the hypothesis that some particular feature is present in the relevant pattern, and each hidden unit corresponds to a hypothesis concerning a *configuration* of several features. The hypothesis to which a particular hidden unit corresponds is determined by the exact *learning rule* used to store the input and by the characteristics of the ensemble of stored patterns. Retrieval in such a network amounts to setting the values of *some* of the visible units (the retrieval probe) and letting the system settle to the best interpretation of that input, while itself setting the values of the remaining visible units. This is a kind of pattern completion. The details are not too important here because a variety of learning rules lead to networks that all have the following important properties:

• When a previously stored (that is, familiar) pattern enters the memory system, it is amplified, and the system responds with a stronger version of the input pattern. This is a kind of recognition response.

• When an unfamiliar pattern enters the memory system, it is dampened, and the activity of the memory system is shut down. This is a kind of unfamiliarity response.

• When part of a familiar pattern is presented, the system responds by "filling in" the missing parts. This is a kind of recall paradigm in which the part constitutes the retrieval cue, and the filling in is a kind of memory-reconstruction process. This is a content-addressable memory system.

• When a pattern similar to a stored pattern is presented, the system responds by distorting the input pattern toward the stored pattern. This is a kind of assimilation response in which similar inputs are assimilated to similar stored events.

• Finally, if a number of similar patterns have been stored, the system will respond strongly to the central tendency of the stored patterns, even though the central tendency itself was never stored. Thus this sort of memory system automatically responds to prototypes even when no prototype has been seen.

These properties correspond very closely to the characteristics of human memory and, I believe, are exactly the kind of properties we want in any theory of memory.

AUTOMATIC, SIMILARITY-BASED GENERALIZATION. One of the major complaints against AI programs is their "fragility". The programs are usually very good at what they are programmed to do, but respond in unintelligent or odd ways when faced with novel situations. There seem to be at least two reasons for this fragility. In conventional symbol-processing systems similarity is represented only indirectly, and is therefore not available as a basis for generalizations; and most AI programs are not self-modifying and cannot adapt to their environments.

In our connectionist systems, on the other hand, similarities among patterns are directly represented along with the patterns themselves in the connection weights—in such a way that similar patterns have similar effects. Therefore, similarity-based generalization is an automatic property of connectionist models. It should be noted that the degree of similarity between patterns is roughly given by the inner product of the vectors representing the patterns. Thus the dimensions of generalization are given by the dimensions of the representational space. Often this will lead to the right generalizations. But, there are situations in which it leads to inappropriate generalizations. In such cases, we must allow the system to *learn* its appropriate representation. In the next section I describe how the appropriate representation can be learned so that the correct generalizations are automatically made.

LEARNING. A key advantage of connectionist systems is the fact that simple yet powerful learning procedures can be defined that allow the systems to adapt to their environments. It was work on the learning aspect of neurally inspired models that first led to an interest in them (compare Rosenblatt, 1962), and it was the demonstration that those learning procedures could not work for complex networks that contributed to the loss of interest (compare Minsky and Papert, 1969). Although the *perceptron convergence procedure* and its variants have been around for some time, they are limited to simple two-layer networks involving only input and output units. There were no hidden units in these cases and no internal representation. The coding provided by the external world had to suffice. Nevertheless, such networks have proved useful in a wide variety of applications. Perhaps their most important characteristic is that they map similar input patterns to similar output patterns. This is what allows them to make reasonable generalizations and perform reasonably on patterns that have never before been presented. The similarity of patterns in connectionist systems is determined by their overlap. This overlap, for two-layer networks, is determined entirely outside the learning system itself—by whatever produces the patterns.

The constraint that similar input patterns lead to similar outputs can lead to an inability of the system to learn certain mappings from input to output. Whenever the representation provided by the outside world is such that the similarity structure of the input and output patterns is very different, a network without internal representations (that is, a network without hidden units) will be unable to perform the necessary mappings. A classic example of this case is the exclusive-or (XOR) problem illustrated in table 19.1. Here we see that those patterns that overlap least are supposed to generate identical output values. This problem and many others like it cannot be solved by networks that lack hidden units with which to create their own internal representations of the input patterns. It is interesting to note that if the input patterns contained a third input bit, taking the value 1 when and only when the other two were both 1 (as shown in table 19.2), a two-layer system would be able to solve the problem.

Minsky and Papert (1969) have provided a careful analysis of conditions under which such systems are capable of carrying out the required mappings. They show that in many interesting cases networks of this kind are incapable of solving the problems. On the other hand, as Minsky and Papert also point out, if there is a layer of simple perceptron-like hidden units, as shown in figure 19.3, with which the original input pattern can be augmented, there is always a recoding (that is, an internal representation) of the input

Input patterns		Output patterns
00	→	0
01	→	1
10	→	1
11	→	0

Table 19.1
XOR problem.

Input patterns		Output patterns
000	→	0
010	→	1
100	→	1
111	→	0

Table 19.2
XOR problem with redundant third bit.

patterns in the hidden units in which the similarity of the patterns among the hidden units can support any required mapping from the input to the output units. Thus if we have the right connections from the input units to a large enough set of hidden units, we can always find a representation that will perform any mapping from input to output through these hidden units. In the case of the XOR problem, the addition of a feature that detects the conjunction of the input units changes the similarity structure of the patterns sufficiently to allow the solution to be learned.

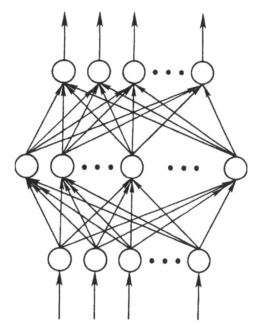

Figure 19.3
A multilayer network in which input patterns are recoded by internal representation units.

As illustrated in figure 19.4, this can be done with a single hidden unit. The numbers on the arrows represent the strengths of the connections among the units. The numbers written in the circles represent the thresholds of the units. The value of +1.5 for the threshold of the hidden unit ensures that it will be turned on only when both input units are on. The threshold of 0.5 for the output unit ensures that it will turn on only when it receives a net positive input greater than 0.5. The weight of -2 from the hidden unit to the output unit ensures that the output unit will not come on when both input units are on. Note that, from the point of view of the output unit, the hidden unit is treated as simply another input unit. It is as if the input patterns consisted of three rather than two units (essentially as in table 19.2).

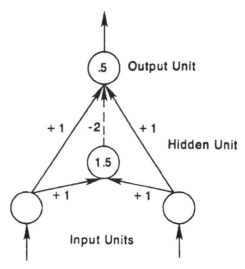

Figure 19.4
A simple XOR network with one hidden unit.

The existence of networks such as this illustrates the potential power of hidden units and internal representations. The problem, as noted by Minsky and Papert, is that, whereas there is a very simple guaranteed learning rule for all problems that can be solved without hidden units—namely, the perceptron convergence procedure (or the variation reported originally by Widrow and Hoff, 1960)—there has been no equally powerful rule for learning in multilayer networks.

It is clear that if we hope to use these connectionist networks for general computational purposes, we must have a learning scheme capable of learning its own internal representations. This is just what we (Rumelhart et al., 1986a) have done. We have developed a generalization of the perceptron learning procedure, called the *generalized delta rule*, which allows the system to learn to compute arbitrary functions. The constraints inherent in networks without self modifying internal representations are no longer applicable. The basic learning procedure is a two-stage process. First, an input is applied to the network. Then, after the system has processed for some time, certain units of the network—usually the output units—are informed of the values they ought to have attained. If they have attained the desired values, the weights on their input connections are left unchanged. If they differ from their target values, then those weights are changed slightly, in such a way as to reduce the differences between the actual values attained and the target values.

Those *differences* between the actual and target values at the output units can be thought of as *error signals*. Similar error signals must be sent back in turn to those units that impinged on the output units. Each such unit receives an error signal that is equal to the sum of the errors in each of the output units to which it connects times the weight on the connection to that output unit. Then, based on those error signals, the weights on the *input* connections into those "second-layer" units can be modified, after which error signals can be passed back another layer. This process—called the *backpropagation of error*—continues until the error signals reach the input units or until they have been passed back a predetermined number of times. Then a new input pattern is presented and the process repeats. Although the procedure may sound difficult, it is actually quite simple and easy to implement within these nets. As shown in Rumelhart et al. (1986a), such a procedure will always change its weights in such a way as to reduce the overall difference between the actual output values and the desired output values. Moreover it can be shown that this system will work for any network whatsoever.

Minsky and Papert, in their pessimistic discussion of perceptrons, discuss *multilayer machines*. They state that

> The perceptron has shown itself worthy of study despite (and even because of!) its severe limitations. It has many features chat attract attention: its linearity; its intriguing learning theorem; its clear paradigmatic simplicity as a kind of parallel computation. There is no reason to suppose that any of these virtues carry over to the many-layered version. Nevertheless, we consider it to be an important research problem to elucidate (or reject) our intuitive judgment that the extension is sterile. Perhaps some powerful convergence theorem will be discovered, or some profound reason for the failure to produce an interesting "learning theorem" for the multilayered machine will be found. (1969, 231–232)

Although our learning results do not *guarantee* that we can find a solution for all solvable problems, our analysis and simulation results have shown that, as a practical matter, this error-propagation scheme leads to solutions in virtually every case. In short, I believe that we have answered Minsky and Papert's challenge and *have* found a learning result sufficiently powerful to demonstrate that their pessimism about learning in multilayer machines was misplaced.

One way to view the procedure I have been describing is as a parallel computer that, having been shown the appropriate input/output exemplars specifying some function, programs itself to compute that function in general. Parallel computers are notoriously difficult to program. Here we have a mechanism whereby we do not actually have to know how to write the program to get the system to do it.

GRACEFUL DEGRADATION. Finally, connectionist models are interesting candidates for cognitive-science models because of their property of graceful degradation in the face of damage and information overload. The ability of our networks to learn leads to the promise of computers that can literally learn their way around faulty components: because every unit participates in the storage of many patterns and because each pattern involves many different units, the loss of a few components will degrade the stored information, but will not destroy it. Similarly such memories should not be conceived as having a certain fixed capacity. Rather, there is simply more and more storage interference and blending of similar pieces of information as the memory is overloaded. This property of graceful degradation mimics the human response in many ways and is one of the reasons we find these models of human information processing plausible.

19.2   The state of the art

Recent years have seen a virtual explosion of work in the connectionist area. This work has been singularly interdisciplinary, being carried out by psychologists, physicists, computer scientists, engineers, neuroscientists, and other cognitive scientists. A number of national and international conferences have been established and are being held each year. In such an environment it is difficult to keep up with the rapidly developing field. Nevertheless, a reading of recent papers indicates a few central themes in this activity. These themes include the study of learning and generalization (especially the use of the backpropagation learning procedure), applications to neuroscience, mathematical properties of networks—both of the learning algorithms and of connectionist style computation itself in comparison to more conventional computational paradigms—and finally the development of an implementational base for physical realizations of connectionist computational devices, especially in the areas of optics and analog VLSI.

Although there are many other interesting and important developments, I conclude with a brief summary of the work with which I have been most involved over the past several years, namely, the study of learning and generalization within multilayer networks. Even this summary is necessarily selective, but it should give a sampling of much of the current work in the area.

The backpropagation learning procedure has become possibly the single most popular method for training networks. The procedure has been used to train networks on problem domains including character recognition, speech recognition, sonar detection, mapping from spelling to sound, motor control, analysis of molecular structure, diagnosis of eye diseases, prediction of chaotic functions, playing backgammon, the parsing of simple sentences, and many, many more areas. Perhaps the major point of these examples is the enormous range of problems to which the backpropagation learning procedure can usefully be applied. In spite of the rather impressive breadth of topics and the success of some of these applications, there are a number of serious open problems. The theoretical issues of primary concern fall into three main areas. (1) The architecture problem: are there useful architectures beyond the standard three-layer network that are appropriate for certain areas of application? (2) The scaling problem: how can we cut down on the substantial training time that seems to be involved for more difficult and interesting problems? (3) The generalization problem: how can we be certain that a network trained on a subset of the example set will generalize correctly to the entire set of examples?

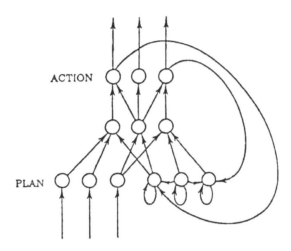

Figure 19.5
A recurrent network of the type developed by Jordan (1986a) for learning to *perform* sequential operations.

19.2.1   Some architecture

Although most applications have involved the simple three-layer backpropagation network with one input layer, one hidden layer, and one output layer of units, there have been a large number of interesting architectures proposed—each for the solution of some particular problem of interest. There are, for example, a number of "special" architectures that have been proposed for the modeling of such sequential phenomena as motor control. Perhaps the most important of these is the one proposed by Mike Jordan (1986a) for producing sequences of phonemes. The basic structure of the network is illustrated in figure 19.5. It consists of four groups of units. *Plan units*, which tell the network which sequence it is producing, are fixed at the start of a sequence and are not changed. *Context units*, which keep track of where the system is in the sequence, receive input from the output units of the systems and from themselves, constituting a memory for the sequence produced thus far. *Hidden units* combine the information from the plan units with that from the context units to determine which output is to be produced next. *Output units* produce the desired output values. This basic structure, with numerous variations, has been used successfully in producing sequences of phonemes (Jordan, 1986a), sequences of movements (Jordan, 1988), sequences of notes in a melody (Todd, 1989), sequences of turns in a simulated ship (Miyata, 1987), and for many other applications. An analogous network for *recognizing* sequences has been used by Elman (1988) for processing sentences one at a time; and another variation has been developed and studied by Mozer (1988). The architecture used by Elman is illustrated in figure 19.6. This network also involves four sets of units: *input units*, in which the sequence to be recognized is presented one element at a time; *context units*, which receive inputs from and send outputs to the hidden units and thus constitute a memory for recent events; *hidden units*, which combine the current input with the memory of past inputs either to name the sequence, to predict the next element of the sequence, or both; and, of course, *output units*.

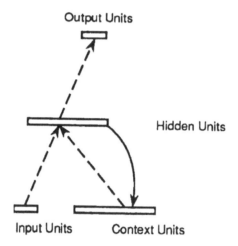

Figure 19.6
A recurrent network of the type employed by Elman (1988) for learning to recognize sequences.

Another kind of architecture that has received some attention was suggested by Hinton and Sejnowski (1986) and has been employed by Elman and Zipser (1987), Cottrell et al. (1987), and many others. It has become part of the standard toolkit of backpropagation. This is the so-called method of autoencoding the pattern set. The basic architecture in this case consists of three layers of units as in the conventional case; however, the input and output layers are identical. The idea is to pass the input through a small number of hidden units and reproduce it over the output units. This requires the hidden units to do a kind of nonlinear, principle-components analysis of the input patterns. In this case, that corresponds to a kind of extraction of critical features. In many applications, these features turn out to provide a useful compact description of the patterns. Many other architectures are being explored as well. The space of interesting and useful architecture is large and the exploration will continue for many years.

19.2.2   The scaling problem

The scaling problem has received somewhat less attention, although it has clearly emerged as a central problem with backpropagation-like learning procedures. The basic finding has been that difficult problems require many learning trials. For example, it is not unusual to require tens or even hundreds of thousands of pattern presentations to learn moderately difficult problems—that is, problems whose solutions require tens of thousands to a few hundred thousand connections. Large and fast computers are required for such problems, and it is impractical for problems requiring more than a few hundred thousand connections. It is therefore a matter of concern to learn how to speed up the learning so that it can learn more difficult problems in a more reasonable number of exposures. The proposed solutions fall into two basic categories. One line of attack is to improve the learning procedure, either by optimizing the parameters dynamically (that is, change the learning rate systematically during learning), or by using more information in the weight-changing procedure (that is, the so-called second-order backpropagation procedure, in which the second derivatives are also computed). Although some improvements can be attained by these methods, in certain problem domains the basic scaling problem still remains. It seems that the basic problem is that difficult problems require a large number of exemplars, however efficiently each exemplar is used. The other approach grows from viewing *learning* and *evolution* as continuous with one another. On this view, the fact that networks take a long time to learn is to be expected, because we normally compare their behavior to organisms that have long evolutionary histories. Accordingly, the solution is to *start* the systems at places that are as pre-suited as possible for the problem domains to be learned. Shepard (1989) has argued that such an approach is critical for an appropriate understanding of the phenomena being modeled.

A final approach to the scaling problem is through modularity. Sometimes it is possible to break a problem into smaller subproblems and train subnetworks separately on these. Larger networks can then be assembled from those pretrained modules to solve the original problem. An advantage of the connectionist approach in this regard is that the preliminary training need only be approximately right. A final round of training can be used after assembly to learn the interfaces among the modules.

19.2.3   The generalization problem

One final aspect of learning that has been looked at is the nature of generalization. It is clear that the most important aspect of networks is not that they learn a set of mappings but that they learn the function implicit in the exemplars under study in such a way that they respond properly to cases not yet observed. Although there are many examples of successful generalization (e.g., the learning of spelling-to-phoneme mappings in Sejnowski and Rosenberg's NETtalk, 1987), there are a number of cases in which the networks do not generalize correctly (see Denker et al., 1987). One simple way to understand this is to note that for most problems there are enough degrees of freedom in the network that there are a large number of genuinely different solutions to the problems—each of which constitutes a different way of generalizing to unseen patterns. Clearly not all of these can be correct.

Weigend and I have proposed an hypothesis that shows some promise in promoting better generalization (Weigend and Rumelhart, 1991). The basic idea is this: the problem of generalization is essentially the induction problem. Given a set of observations, what is the appropriate principle that applies to all cases? Note that the network at any point in time can be viewed as a specification of an inductive hypothesis. Our proposal is that we follow a version of Occam's razor and select the *simplest*, *most robust* network that is consistent with the observations made. The assumption of robustness is simply an embodiment of a kind of continuity assumption that small variations in the input pattern should have little effect on the output or on the performance of the system. The simplicity assumption is simply to choose—of all networks that correctly account for the input data—the net with the fewest hidden units, the fewest connections, the most symmetries among the weights, and so on. We have formalized this procedure and modified the backpropagation learning procedure so that it prefers simple, robust networks, and, all things being equal, will select those networks. In many cases it turns out that these are just the networks that do the best job generalizing.

The Computational Brain

20

Patricia Churchland and Terrence Sejnowski
1992

From Chapter 1

Computational neuroscience is an evolving approach that aims to discover the properties characterizing and the principles governing neurons and networks of neurons. It draws on both neurobiological data and computational ideas to investigate how neural networks can produce complex effects such as stereo vision, learning, and auditory location of sound-emitting objects. To put it crudely, it has one foot in neuroscience and one foot in computer science. A third foot is firmly planted in experimental psychology, and at least a toe is in philosophy, so evidently the enterprise is multi pedal. Of which more anon.

Probably the closest academic kin of computational neuroscience is systems neurobiology, a branch of neuroscience that traditionally has focused on much the same set of problems, but did not explicitly ally itself with computer modeling or with an avowedly information-processing framework for theories. A precocious ancestor went by the name of "cybernetics," which, inversely to systems neurobiology, generally leaned more heavily on the engineering and psychophysical sides, and more lightly on the neurobiological side. Coined more recently, "connectionism" usually refers to modeling with networks that bear only superficial similarities to real neural networks, while "neural net modeling" can cover a broad range of projects. Ironically perhaps, "neural net modeling" is usually identified with computer modeling of highly artificial nonneuronal networks, often with mainly technological significance such as medical diagnoses in emergency wards.[1] "PDP" ("parallel distributed processing") is generally the preferred label of cognitive psychologists and some computer scientists who seek to model rather high-level activity such as face recognition and language learning rather than lower-level activity such as visual motion detection or defensive bending in the leech.

As we use the term, "computational neuroscience" aims for biological realism in computational models of neural networks, though *en route*, rather simplified and artificial models may be used to help test and explore computational principles. Academic garden-plotting is a comically imprecise trade because the carrots regularly wander in with turnips and the turnips with the potatoes. Each of us (P.S.C. and T.J.S.) is cheerfully guilty of wandering into neuroscience from his mother discipline, so we emphatically do not mean to tut-tut academic "cross-fielding." On the contrary, we view the blurring of the disciplinary boundaries between neuroscience, computer science, and psychology as a healthy development to be wisely encouraged. In any case, perhaps a crude survey will help orient the greenhorn—or even the old hand—to the clustering of goals, tactics, and prejudices manifest in the "network" game.

The expression "computational" in computational neuroscience reflects the role of the computer as a research tool in modeling complex systems such as networks, ganglia, and brains. Using the word in that sense, one could have also computational astronomy or computational geology. In the present context, however, the word's primary force is its descriptive connotation, which here betokens the deep-seated conviction that what is being modeled by a computer is itself a kind of computer, albeit one quite unlike the serial, digital machines on which computer science cut its teeth. That is, nervous systems and probably parts of nervous systems are themselves naturally evolved computers—organically constituted, analog in representation, and parallel in their processing architecture. They represent features and relations in the world and they enable an animal to adapt to its circumstances. They are a breed of computer whose *modus operandi* still elude us but are the mother lode, so to speak, of computational neuroscience.

A number of broad clues about computation in nervous systems are available. First, unlike a digital computer which is general purpose and can be programmed to run any algorithm, the brain appears to be an interconnected collection of special-purpose systems that are very efficient at performing their tasks but limited in their flexibility. Visual cortex, for example, does not appear able to assume the functions of the cerebellum or the hippocampus. Presumably this is not because visual cortex contains cells that are essentially and intrinsically visual in what they do (or contain "visons" instead of "auditons"), but rather it is mainly because of their morphological specialization and of their place in the system of cells in visual cortex, i.e., relative to their input cells, their intracortical and subcortical connections, their output cells, and so on. Put another way, a neuron's specialization is a function of the neuron's computational roles in the system, and evolution has refined the cells better to perform those roles.

Second, the clues about the brain's computational principles that can be gleaned from studying its microstructure and organization are indispensable to figuring out its computational organization because the nervous system is a product of evolution, not engineering design. Evolutionary modifications are always made within the context of an organization and architecture that are already in place. Quite simply, Nature is not an intelligent engineer. It cannot dismantle the existing configuration and start from scratch with a preferred design or preferred materials. It cannot mull the environmental conditions and construct an optimal device. Consequently, the computational solutions evolved by Nature may be quite unlike those that an intelligent human would invent, and they may well be neither optimal nor predictable from orthodox engineering assumptions.

Third, human nervous systems are by no means exclusively cognitive devices, though the infatuation with cognition fosters a tacit tendency to assume so. Nervous systems must also manage such matters as thermoregulation—a very complex function for mammals—growth, aspects of reproduction, respiration, regulation of hunger, thirst, and motor control and maintenance of behavioral state, such as sleeping, dreaming, being awake, and so forth. Thus an evolutionary modification that results in a computational improvement in vision, say, might seem to have the earmarks of an engineering prizewinner. But if it cannot mesh with the rest of the brain's organization, or if it marginalizes critical functions such as thermoregulation, the animal and its "prizewinning" vision genes will die. Given these reasons, *reverse* engineering, where the device is taken apart to see how it works, is a profitable strategy with respect to the brain. By contrast, a purely *a priori* approach, based entirely on reasonable principles of engineering design, may lead us down a blind alley.

Fourth, it is prudent to be aware that our favorite intuitions about these matters may be misleading, however "self-evident" and compelling they be. More specifically, neither the nature of the computational problems the nervous system is solving nor the difficulty of the problems confronting the nervous system can be judged merely by introspection. Consider, for example, a natural human activity such as walking—a skill that is typically mastered in the first year or so of life. One might doubt whether this is a computational problem at all, or if it is, whether it is a problem of sufficient complexity to be worth one's reflection. Since walking is virtually effortless, unlike, say, doing algebra, which many people do find a strain, one might conclude from casual observation that walking is a computationally easy task—easier, at least, than doing algebra. The preconception that walking is computationally rather trivial is, however, merely an illusion. It is easy enough for toy manufacturers to make a doll that puts one foot in front of the other as long as she is held by the child. But for the doll to walk as we do, maintaining balance as we do, is a completely different task. Locomotion turns out to be a complicated matter, the ease implied by introspection notwithstanding.

Another computational issue of critical importance in generating hypotheses in computational neuroscience concerns the time available for performing the computation. From the point of view of the nervous system, it is not enough to come up with solutions that merely give the correct output for a given input. The solutions must also be available within milliseconds of the problem's presentation, and applications must be forthcoming within a few hundred milliseconds. It is important that nervous systems can routinely detect signals, recognize patterns, and assemble responses within one second. The ability of nervous systems to move their encasing bodies appropriately and swiftly was typically selected at every stage of evolution, since by and large natural selection would favor those organisms that could flee or fight predators, and catch and cache prey. *Ceteris paribus*, slow nervous systems become dinner for faster nervous systems. Even if the computational strategies used by the brain should turn out not to be elegant or beautiful but to have a sort of evolutionary do-it-yourself quality, they are demonstrably very fast. This tiny response-time rules out as just too slow many kinds of ostensibly elegant computational architectures and clever computational principles. This point is all the more significant when it is considered that events in an electronic computer happen in the nanosecond (10^{-9}) range, whereas events in neurons happen in the millisecond (10^{-3}) range.

A related consideration is that organic computers such as brains are constrained in the amount of space available for the essential elements—cell bodies, dendrites, axons, glial cells, and vascularization—and the cranial capacity is in turn limited by the mechanisms of reproduction. In mammals, for example, the size of the pelvic cavity of the mother constrains head size of offspring, and therefore brain size of offspring. What this all means is that the length of wiring in nervous systems must also be limited—evolution cannot just help itself to indefinite lengths of connecting wire but must make every centimeter count. In a human brain, for example, the total length of wiring is about 10^8 meters and it has to be packed into a volume of about 1.5 liters. The spatial configuration of sense organs and muscles on the body and the relative position of the afferent and efferent systems will also be relevant to the computational genre that has been selected in the evolution of nervous systems.One strategy the brain uses to economize on wire is to map the processing units so that neighboring units process similar representations. Another strategy involves sharing wire, meaning that the same wire (axon) can be used in coding a large range of representations (Mead, 1989). The computational genre adopted for a nervous system will, therefore, be constrained not only by temporal factors but also by spatial factors.

Computation is also limited by power consumption, and on this matter too the brain is impressively efficient. For example, a neuron uses roughly 10^{-15} joules of energy per operation (e.g., one neuron activating another at a synapse). By contrast, the most efficient silicon technology currently requires about 10^{-7} joules per operation (multiply, add, etc.) (Mead, 1989). Using the criterion of joules per operation, the brain is about *7 or 8 orders of magnitude* more power efficient than the best of the silicon chips. A direct consequence of their energy efficiency is that brains can perform many more operations per second than even the newest supercomputers. The fastest digital computers are capable of around 10^9 operations per second; the brain of the common housefly, for example, performs about 10^{11} operations per second when merely resting.

Finally, there are constraints imposed by the materials of construction. That is, cells are made out of proteins and lipids, they have to rely on mitochondria for their energy supply; nervous systems must have the substances and dispositions necessary for growth and development, and they must exploit such features as the membrane properties of cells and the available chemicals in order to function as an organic computer. Additionally, the nervous system needs a constant supply of oxygen and a reliable supply of nutrients.

Evolution has to make what it can out of proteins, lipids, membranes, amino acids, etc. This is not altogether unlike the engineering make-do game where the given materials are limited (a finite number of popsicle sticks, rubber bands, and paper clips), and the task, for example, is to build a weight-supporting bridge. Indeed, John Allman (1990) has suggested that brain expansion in homeotherms was spurred by the need to engage in intense prey-catching in order to keep the home fires burning, as it were. In the competition for large amounts of fuel, homeotherms with sophisticated neural machinery that upgraded prey-catching and predator avoidance would have had an advantage.

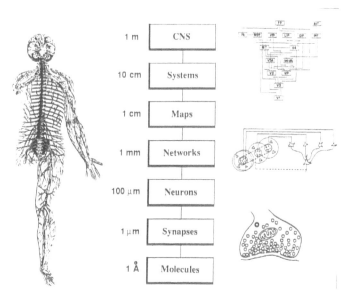

Figure 20.1
Schematic illustration of levels of organization in the nervous system. The spatial scales at which anatomical organizations can be identified varies over many orders of magnitude. Icons to the right represent structures at distinct levels: (top) a subset of visual areas in visual cortex (van Essen and Maunsell, 1980); (middle) a network model of how ganglion cells could be connected to simple cells in visual cortex (Hubel and Wiesel, 1962), and (bottom) a chemical synapse (Kandel and Schwartz, 1985). (From Churchland and Sejnowski 1988.)

Two conceptual ideas have structured much of how we tend to conceive of problems in computational neuroscience. First is the notion of *levels*, and the second concerns the *co-evolution* of research on different levels. In the brain, there is both large-scale and small-scale organization, and different functions take place on higher and lower levels (figure 20.1). One sort of account will explain how signals are integrated in dendrites; a different account will explain the interaction of neurons in a network, or the interaction of networks in a system.[2] A model that captures the salient features of learning in networks will have a different face from a model that describes the NMDA channel. Nevertheless, the theories on one level must mesh with the theories of levels both higher and lower, because an inconsistency or a lacuna somewhere in the tale means that some phenomenon has been misunderstood. After all, brains are assemblies of cells, and something would be seriously amiss if neurons under one description had properties incompatible with the same neurons under another description.

From Chapter 2

Levels in Nervous Systems

Discussions concerning the nature of psychological phenomena and their neurobiological bases invariably make reference to the notion of "levels." In trying to be a bit more precise about what is meant by "level," we found three different ideas about levels in the literature: *levels of analysis, levels of organization, and levels of processing.* Roughly speaking, the distinctions are drawn along the following lines: levels of organization are essentially anatomical, and refer to a hierarchy of components and to structures comprising these components. Levels of processing are physiological, and refer to the location of a process relative to the transducers and muscles. Levels of analysis are conceptual and refer to different kinds of questions asked about how the brain performs a task: into what subtasks does the brain divide the tasks, what processing steps execute a subtask, and what physical structures carry out the steps? In what follows, we elaborate on these distinctions.

Levels of Analysis

A framework for a theory of levels, articulated by Marr (1982), provided an important and influential background for thinking about levels in the context of computation by nervous structures.[3] This framework drew upon the conception of levels in computer science, and accordingly Marr characterized three levels: (1) the computational level of abstract problem analysis, decomposing the task (e.g., determining the 3-D depth of objects from the 2-D pattern on the retina) into its main constituents; (2) the level of the algorithm, specifying a formal procedure to perform the task so that for a given input, the correct output results; and (3) the level of physical implementation, constructing a working device using a particular technology. This division really corresponds to three different sorts of questions that can be raised about a phenomenon: (1) how does the problem decompose into parts?, (2) what principles govern how the parts interact to solve the problem?, and (3) what is the stuff whose causal interactions implement the principles?

    An important element in Marr's view was that a higher-level question was largely independent of the levels below it, and hence computational problems of the highest level could be analyzed independently of understanding the algorithm which performs the computation. Similarly, the algorithmic problem of the second level was thought to be solvable independently of understanding its physical implementation. Thus his preferred strategy was top-down rather than bottom-up. At least this was the official doctrine though, in practice, downward glances figured significantly in Marr's attempts to find problem analyses and algorithmic solutions. Ironically, given his advocacy of the top-down strategy, Marr's work was itself highly influenced by neurobiological considerations, and implementation facts constrained his choice of problem and nurtured his computational and algorithmic insights. Publicly, the advocacy of the top-down strategy did carry the implication, dismaying for some and comforting for others, that neurobiological facts could be more or less ignored, since they were, after all, just at the implementation level.

Unfortunately, two very different issues were confused in the doctrine of independence. One concerns whether, as a *matter of discovery*, one can figure out the relevant algorithm and the problem analysis independently of facts about implementation. The other concerns whether, as a *matter of formal theory*, a given algorithm which is already known to perform a task in a given machine (e.g., the brain) can be implemented in some other machine which has a different architecture. So far as the latter is concerned, what computational theory tells us is that an algorithm can be run on different machines, and in that sense and that sense alone, the algorithm is independent of the implementation. The formal point is straightforward: since an algorithm is formal, no specific physical parameters (e.g., vacuum tubes, Ca^{2+}) are part of the algorithm.

That said, it is important to see that the purely formal point cannot speak to the issue of how best to discover the algorithm in fact used by a given machine, nor how best to arrive at the neurobiologically adequate task analysis. Certainly it cannot tell us that the discovery of the algorithms relevant to cognitive functions will be independent of a detailed understanding of the nervous system. Moreover, it does not tell us that any implementation is as good as any other. And it had better not, since different implementations display enormous differences in speed, size, efficiency, elegance, etc. The formal independence of algorithm from architecture is something we can exploit to build computationally equivalent machines once we know how the brain works, but it is no guide to discovery if we do not know how the brain works.

The issue of independence of levels marks a major conceptual difference between Marr (1982) and the current generation of researchers studying neural and connectionist models. In contrast to the doctrine of independence, current research suggests that considerations of implementation play a vital role in the kinds of algorithms that are devised and the kind of computational insights available to the scientist. Knowledge of brain architecture, far from being irrelevant to the project, can be the essential basis and invaluable catalyst for devising likely and powerful algorithms—algorithms that have a reasonable shot at explaining how in fact the neurons do the job.

Levels of Organization

Marr's three-level division treats computation monolithically, as a single kind of level of analysis. Implementation and task-description are likewise each considered as a single level of analysis. Yet when we measure Marr's three levels of analysis against levels of organization in the nervous system, the fit is poor and confusing at best (Crick, 1979; Churchland and Sejnowski, 1988; Shepherd, 1988). To begin with, there is organized structure at different scales: molecules, synapses, neurons, networks, layers, maps, and systems (figure 20.2). At each structurally specified stratum we can raise the computational question: what does that organization of elements do? What does it contribute to the wider, computational organization of the brain? In addition, there are physiological levels: ion movement, channel configurations, EPSPs (excitatory postsynaptic potentials), IPSPs (inhibitory postsynaptic potentials), action potentials, evoked response potentials, and probably other intervening levels that we have yet to learn about and that involve effects at higher anatomical levels such as networks or systems.

The range of structural organization implies, therefore, that there are many levels of implementation and that each has its companion task description. But if there are as many types of task descriptions as there are levels of structural organization, this diversity could be reflected in a multiplicity of algorithms that characterize how the tasks are accomplished. This in turn means that the notion of *the* algorithmic level is as over-simplified as the notion of *the* implementation level.

Note also that the very same level of organization can be viewed computationally (in terms of functional role) or implementationally (in terms of the substrate for the function), depending on what questions you ask. For example, the details of how an action potential is propagated might, from the point of view of communication between distant areas, be considered an implementation, since it is an all-or-none event and only its timing carries information. However, from a lower structural level—the point of view of ionic distributions—the propagating action potential is a computational construct whose regenerative and repetitive nature is a consequence of several types of nonlinear voltage-dependent ionic channels spatially distributed along an axon.

Levels of Processing

The focus for this levels concept is the link between anatomy and what is represented in the anatomy. As a first pass, it assumes that the greater the distance from cells responding to sensory input, the higher is the degree of information processing. Thus the level-rank assigned is a function of synaptic distance from the periphery. On this measure, cells in the primary visual area of the neocortex that respond to oriented bars of light are at a higher level than cells in the lateral geniculate nucleus (LGN), which in turn are at a higher level than retinal ganglion cells. Because the nature of the representations and the

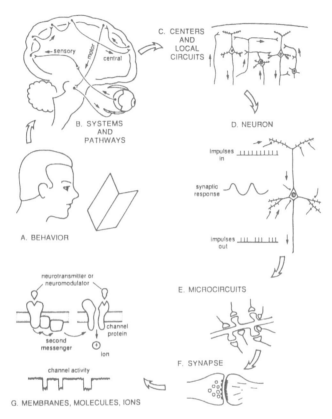

Figure 20.2
Levels of organization in the nervous system, as characterized by Gordon Shepherd (1988).

transformations on the representations are still poorly understood, only the relative level—
x is higher or lower than y—rather than the ordinal level—first, second, etc.—is referred
to.

Once the sensory information reaches the cerebral cortex, it fans out through cortico-
cortical projections into a multitude of parallel streams of processing. In the primate visual
system, 25 areas that are predominantly or exclusively visual have been identified (van
Essen et al. 1991; figure 20.3). Many (perhaps all) forward projections are matched by a
backward projection, and there are even massive feedback projections from primary visual
cortex to the LGN. Given these reciprocal projections, the processing hierarchy is anything
but a one-way ladder. Even so, by examining the cortical layer into which fibers project, it
is possible to find some order in the information flow. Forward projections generally terminate in the middle layers of cortex, and feedback projections usually terminate in the upper
and lower layers (Rockland and Pandya, 1979; Maunsell and van Essen, 1983). So far,

however, the function of these feedback pathways is not established, though the idea that they have a role in learning, attention, and perceptual recognition is not unreasonable. If higher areas can affect the flow of information through lower areas, then strictly sequential processing cannot be taken for granted.

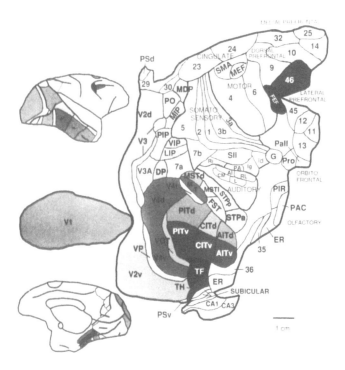

Figure 20.3
A flattened projection of the cerebral cortex in the right hemisphere of the macaque monkey. Stippling indicates cortical areas implicated in visual processing. (Upper left) Lateral view of macaque brain, showing visual areas. (Lower left) Medial view of macaque brain. (From van Essen and Anderson 1990.)

The organization typical of earlier sensory areas is only approximately, roughly, and incompletely hierarchical.[4] Beyond the sensory areas, moreover, not even that much hierarchy is manifest. The anatomy of frontal cortex and other areas beyond the primary sensory areas suggests an information organization more like an Athenian democracy than a Ford assembly line. Hierarchies typically have an apex, and following the analogy, one might expect to find a brain region where all sensory information converges and from which motor commands emerge. It is a striking fact that this is false of the brain. Although there are convergent pathways, the convergence is partial and occurs in many places many times

over, and motor control appears to be distributed rather than vested in a command center
(Arbib 1989; Altman and Kien 1989; figure 20.4).

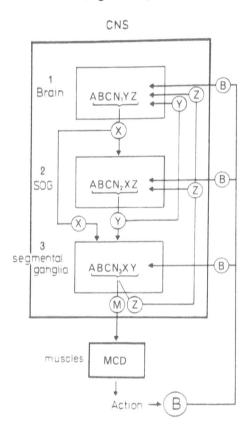

Figure 20.4
Model for decision-making in the insect nervous system. In the CNS, stations 1, 2, 3 contain local networks 1,
2, 3. These stations approximate the brain, the subesophageal (SOC), and segmental ganglia of the locust. The
output of each station results from a consensus between the activity of the inputs and the local networks in that
station, so the output of each station is different. The stations are thus linked in several parallel loops, and the
output of the whole system is the consensus of the activity in all the loops. (From Altman and Kien 1989.)

The assumption that there is a sensory-processing hierarchy, if only to a first approximation, affords the possibility of probing the processing stages by linking various behavioral
measures, such as task-relative reaction time (RT), to events taking place in the processing hierarchy at different times as measured by cellular response. To put it more crudely,
temporal ordering helps determine what is cause and what is effect. Accuracy of response
under varying conditions can be measured, and both humans and animals may be subjects.
This is an important method for triangulating the brain areas involved in executing a certain

task and for determining something about the processing stages of the task. For example, on the physiological side, one may measure the delay between the presentation of a moving target and the first response by motion-sensitive cells in visual area MT, and on the behavioral side one may measure the response latency relative to degrees of noise in the stimulus. One surprise is that the latencies for signals reaching the visual areas in the cortex are so long, relative to the behavioral RT. The latency for MT is about 50–60 msec, and about 100 msec in inferotemporal cortex. Since human RT to a complex object is on the order of 150–200 msec including assembling the motor response, sending the signal down the spinal cord, and activating the muscles, this suggests that surprisingly few processing steps intervene between detection in MT and preparing the response in the motor cortex, striatum, cerebellum, and spinal cord. Such data help constrain theories about the nature of the processing.

By way of illustration, consider a set of experiments by William Newsome and colleagues (1989) in which they show a correlation between the accuracy of the behavioral response to motion detection and the spiking frequency of single neurons responding to motion stimuli in MT (Newsome et al., 1989). In the task, tiny dots move randomly on a TV screen. The monkey is trained to respond as soon as it detects coherent motion, to either the right or the left. Across trials, what varies is the number of dots moving coherently and their direction of motion. The monkey detects direction of motion with as few as four dots moving coherently, and his accuracy improves as the number of dots moving together increases. What about the cells in MT? Suppose one records from a cell that prefers right-going motion. The visual display is set up so that it is matched to the cell's receptive field, with the result that the experimenter has control of the minimum stimulus needed to produce the maximum response. So long as fewer than four dots move coherently, the cell does not respond. With increasing numbers of dots moving coherently in the cell's preferred direction, the cell responds more vigorously. Indeed, the accuracy curve displayed in the monkey's behavior and the spiking-frequency curve displayed by the single cell are, to a first approximation, congruent (figure 20.5). This implies, to put it crudely, that the information contained in the cellular responses of single sensory neurons and the information contained in the behavioral response are roughly on par. It should, however, be kept in mind that the monkeys were very highly trained on this task and that the sensory stimulus was chosen to match the optimal response of each neuron. In a naive monkey, there may not be such close correspondence between the response of the single cell and the overt behavior.

The next phase of the experiment tests whether the information carried by directionally selective cells found in MT is really used in generating the response. To do this, Newsome and colleagues presented *left*-going visual stimuli, and at the proper latency they electrically stimulated the column containing cells preferring *right*-going visual stimuli. How did the animal behave? Would the electrical stimuli demonstrate its effectiveness by

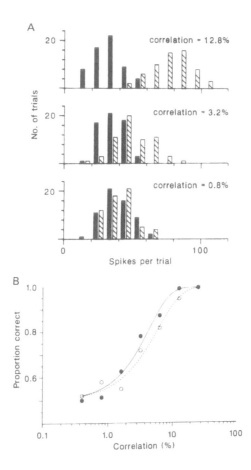

Figure 20.5

(A) Responses of a directionally selective neuron (in visual area MT) at three different motion correlations spanning physiological threshold. Hatched bars represent responses to motion in the neuron's preferred direction; solid bars indicate responses to motion 180° opposite to the preferred direction. Sixty trials were performed in each direction for each of the three correlation levels. Response distributions for a range of correlation levels were used to compute a "neurometric" function that characterized the neuron's sensitivity to the motion signal. and could be compared with the psychometric function computed from the monkey's behavioral response. (B) Comparison of simultaneously recorded psychometric and neurometric functions. Opens circles, psychophysical performance of the monkey; filled circles, performance of the neuron. Psychophysical performance at each correlation is given by the proportion of trials on which the monkey correctly identified the direction of motion. Neuronal performance is calculated from distributions of responses of the directionally sensitive MT neuron. The physiological and psychophysical data form similar curves, but the data for the neuron lie to the left of the data for the monkey, meaning that the neuron was somewhat more sensitive than the monkey. (From Newsome et al. 1989. Reprinted by permission from *Nature* 341: 52-54. Copyright © 1989 Macmillan Magazines Ltd.)

overriding, at least sometimes, the visual stimuli? The monkey behaved as though he saw right-going stimuli; more exactly, the electrical stimulus decreased the probability that the animal would respond to the visual stimulus and increased the probability that it would respond as though presented with a stimulus in the opposite direction. This result implies that the cells' responses—and hence the information carried in those responses—are behaviorally significant.

During the past hundred years, experimental psychologists have assembled an impressive body of RT information, and it is a valuable data base upon which neuroscientists may draw. Thus consider also a set of studies by Requin and colleagues (Requin et al., 1988; Riehle and Requin, 1989). In the first stage, they measured the monkey's RT where the task was to make a wrist flexion in a certain direction and by a certain amount as indicated by a signal. There were basically three conditions: the monkeys were precued or not, and if they were precued, the cue indicated either the direction or the extent of the movement. Precuing was found to have a large effect on the RT but only a slight effect on the movement time, showing that precuing has its major effect on programming and preparing for the movement, rather than on the speed of execution of the movement. Additionally, if the advance cue specified where but not how much, the RT was shortened more than if the cue specified how much but not where. This suggests that information about extent of movement cannot be efficiently incorporated until the system knows the direction of the movement.

In the second stage, Riehle and Requin investigated the electrophysiological properties of cells in the primary motor cortex (MI) and the premotor cortex (PM). They found execution-related neurons, which were more common in MI, and preparation-related, directionally selective neurons, which were more common in PM. This coheres with other physiological data, and implies that PM probably involves an earlier stage of processing than does MI, since PM has more to do with preparing for the movement than with executing it. Moreover, within the class of preparation-related cells in PM, they found two subclasses: those related to programming the muscle movements, and those related to preprocessing the general components of the movement program. This is another instance of research that narrows down hypotheses about relative order of processing and the structures involved in a distinct aspect of processing by establishing behavioral reaction times and by correlating those data with specific responses of cells.[5]

From Chapter 3

Introduction

What is computation? In virtue of what is something a computer? Why do we say a slide rule is a computer but an egg beater is not? These are, in a way, the philosophical questions of computer science, inasmuch as they query foundational issues that are typically glossed over as researchers get on with their projects. Like the philosophical questions of other disciplines (What is the nature of life? [Biology] What is the nature of substance and change? [Physics and Chemistry]), the answers become more convincing, meaningful, and interconnected as the empirical discipline matures and gives more ballast to the theory. In advance of understanding that there are atoms, how atoms link together, and what their properties are, one simply cannot say a whole lot about the nature of substance and change. It is not, however, that one must say *nothing*—in that event, one could not get the science started. The point rather is that the theory outlining the elementary ideas of the discipline gradually bootstraps itself up, using empirical discoveries as support, and kicking away old misconceptions in the long haul.

The definition of computation is no more *given* to us than were the definitions of light, temperature, or force field. While some rough-hewn things can, of course, be said, and usefully said, at this stage, precision and completeness cannot be expected. And that is essentially because there is a lot we do not yet know about computation. Notice in particular that once we understand more about what sort of computers *nervous systems* are, and how they do whatever it is they do, we shall have an enlarged and deeper understanding of what it is to compute and represent. Notice also that we are not starting from ground zero. Earlier work, especially by Turing (1937, 1950), von Neumann (1951, 1952), Rosenblatt (1961), and McCulloch and Pitts (1943), made important advances in the theory and science of computation. The technological development of serial, digital computers and clever software to run on them was accompanied by productive theoretical inquiry into what sort of business computation is.[6]

Agreeing that precise definitions are not forthcoming, can we nonetheless give rough and ready answers to the opening questions? First, although we may be guided by the example of a serial digital computer, the notion of "computer" is broader than that. Identifying computers with *serial digital* computers is neither justified nor edifying, and a more insightful strategy will be to see the conventional digital computer as only a special instance, not as the defining archetype. Second, in the most general sense, we can consider a physical system as a computational system when its physical states can be seen as representing states of some other systems, where transitions between its states can be explained as operations on the representations. The simplest way to think of this is in terms of a mapping between the system's states and the states of whatever is represented. That is, the physical system is a computational system just in case there is an appropriate (revealing) mapping between the system's physical states and the elements of the function computed. This "simple" proposal needs quite a lot of unpacking.

Functions: Computable or Noncomputable, Linear or Nonlinear

Since this hypothesis concerning what makes a physical system a computational system may not be self-evident, let us approach the issue more gradually by first introducing several key but simple mathematical concepts, including "function," and the distinction between *computable* and *noncomputable* functions. To begin, what is a function? A function in the mathematical sense is essentially just a mapping, either 1:1 or many:1, between the elements of one set, called the "domain," and the elements of another, usually referred to as the "range"[7] (figure 20.6). Consequently, a function is a set of ordered pairs, where the first member of the pair is drawn from the domain, and the second element is drawn from the range. A computable function then is a mapping that can be specified in terms of some *rule* or other, and is generally characterized in terms of what you have to do to the first element to get the second. For example, multiply the first by 2, $\{(1, 2), (2, 4), (3, 6)\}$, expressible algebraically as $y = 2x$; multiply the element from the domain by itself $\{(6.2, 38.44), (9.6, 92.16)\}$, expressible algebraically as $y = x^2$, and so on.

What then is a noncomputable function? It is an infinite set of ordered pairs for which no rule can be provided, not only now, but in principle. Hence its specification consists simply and exactly in the list of ordered pairs. For example, if the elements are randomly associated, then no rule exists to specify the mapping between elements of the domain and elements of the range. Outside of mathematics, people quite reasonably tend to equate "function" with "computable function," and hence to consider a nonrule mapping to be no function at all. But this is not in fact how mathematicians use the terms, and for good reason, since it is useful to have the notion of a noncomputable function to describe certain mappings. Moreover, it is useful for the issue at hand because it is an empirical question whether brain activity can really be characterized by a computable function or only to a first approximation, or perhaps whether some of its activities cannot be characterized at all in terms of computable functions (Penrose, 1989).

What is a *linear* function? Intuitively, it is one where the plot of the elements of the ordered pair yields a straight line. A *nonlinear* function is one where the plot does not yield a straight line (figure 20.7). Thus when brain function is described as "nonlinear," what this means is that (a) the activity is characterized by a computable function, and (b) that function is nonlinear. Notice also that the space in which functions are plotted may be a two-dimensional space (the x and y axes), but it may, of course, have more than two dimensions (e.g., an x axis, y axis, and also w, v, z, etc. axes).

Because the notion of a *vector* simplifies discussion enormously, we introduce it here. A vector is just an ordered set of numbers. For example, the set of incomes for 1990 of three vice-presidents in a corporation can be represented by the vector $<\$30, \$10, \$10>$; the eggs laid per week by five hens as $<4, 6, 1, 0, 7>$; the spiking frequency of four neurons/sec as $<10, 55, 44, 6>$. By contrast, a scalar is a single value rather than a many-valued set. The *order* in the set matters when we want to operate on the values in the

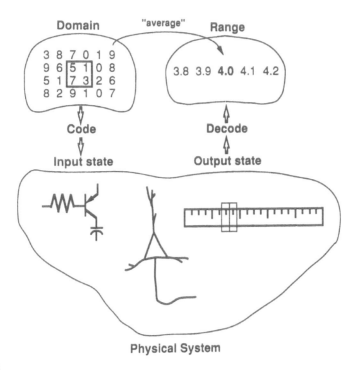

Figure 20.6
Mapping between a domain and a range can be accomplished by a variety of physical systems. There are three steps: (1) The input data is coded into a form appropriate for the physical system (electrical signal in an electrical circuit, chemical concentration in neuron, position of a slider in a slide rule). (2) The physical system shifts into a new state. (3) The output state of the physical system is decoded to produce the result of the mapping. The example shown here is the "average" map that takes four values and produces their average. Such a mapping might be useful as part of a visual system. Mappings could also be made from the domain of temporal sequences, and the range could be a sequence of output values.

set according to an order-sensitive rule. Systems, including the nervous system, execute functions that perform vector-to-vector mapping. For example, from the stretch receptors' values to the muscle contraction values, or from the head velocity values to eye velocity values.

A geometric articulation of these concepts compounds their value. Any coordinate system defines a state space, and the number of axes will be a function of the number of dimensions included. A state space is the set of all possible vectors. For example, a patient's body temperature and diastolic blood pressure can be represented as a position in a 2-D state space. Or, if a network has three units, each unit may be considered to define an axis in a 3-D space. The activity of a unit at a time is a point along its axis, so that the global activation of all the units in the net is specified by a point in that 3-D space (figure 20.8). More generally, if a network has n units, then it defines an n-dimensional

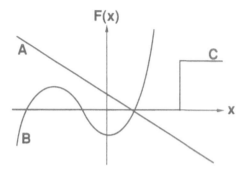

Figure 20.7
Examples of functions $F(x)$, plotted along the vertical axis, of one variable, x, plotted along the horizontal axis. Function A is a linear function. Function B is a nonlinear function. Function C is a discontinuous function.

activation space, and an activation vector can be represented as a point in that state space. A sequence of vectors can be represented as a trajectory in the state space.[8] Thus the patient's body temperature and blood pressure followed through time results in a trajectory in a 2-space. A function maps a point in one state space to a point in another state space—for example, from a point in stretch-receptor activation space to a point in muscle spindle activation space.

These notions—"vector" and "state space"—are part of linear algebra, and they are really the core of the mathematics needed to understand model networks. They are mercifully simple conceptually, and they are rather intuitively extendable from easily visualizable 2-D cases to very complex, n-D cases, where n may be thousands or millions. Although volumes more can be written on the topic of linear algebra, this is perhaps enough to ease the entry into the discussion of model neural networks.[9]

Computers, Pseudocomputers, and Cryptocomputers

The mathematical interlude was intended to provide a common vocabulary so that we might return to the question of characterizing, albeit roughly, what about a physical system makes it a computer. To pick up the thread left hanging during the mathematical interlude, let us hypothesize that a physical system computes some function **f** when (1) there is a systematic mapping from states of the system onto the arguments and values of **f**, and (2) the sequence of intermediate states executes an algorithm for the function.[10] Informally, an algorithm is a finite, deterministic procedure, e.g., a recipe for making gingerbread or a rule for finding the square root.

We count something as a computer because, and only when, its inputs and outputs can usefully and systematically be interpreted as representing the ordered pairs of some function that interests us. Thus there are two components to this criterion: (1) the objective matter of what function(s) describe the behavior of the system, and (2) the subjective and

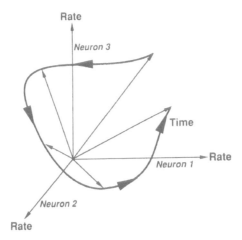

Figure 20.8
Schematic diagram of the trajectory of a three-neuron system through state space. The state of the system is a 3-D vector whose components are the firing rates of the three neurons. As the firing rates change with time, the tip of the vector traces out a trajectory (thick line). For more neurons the state space will have a higher dimension.

practical matter of whether we care what the function is. This means that delimiting the class of computers is not a sheerly empirical matter, and hence that "computer" is not a natural kind, in the way that, for example, "electron" or "protein" or "mammal" is a natural kind. For categories that do delimit natural kinds, experiments are relevant in deciding whether an item really belongs to the category. Moreover, there are generalizations and laws (natural laws) about the items in the categories and there are theories interleaving the laws. Nonnatural kinds differ in all these respects, and typically have an interest-relative dimension.

"Bee," for example, is a natural kind, but "gem" and "weed" are not. Objects are considered gems depending on whether some social group puts special value on them, typically as status symbols. Plants are considered weeds depending on whether gardeners (serious gardeners?) in the region happen to like having them in the garden. Some gardeners cultivate baby's breath as a desirable plant; other gardeners fight it as a weed. There is no experiment that will determine whether baby's breath is really a weed or not, because there is no fact of the matter—only social or idiosyncratic conventions.[11] Similarly, we suggest, there is no instrinsic property necessary and sufficient for all computers, just the interest-relative property that someone sees value in interpreting a system's states as representing states of some other system, and the properties of the system support such an interpretation. Desktop von Neumann machines exist precisely because we are keenly interested in the functions we build and program them to execute, so the interest-relative component is dyed in the wool. For this reason, and because these machines are so common, they are the prototypical computers, just as dandelions are prototypical weeds. These prototypes should not, however, he mistaken for the category itself.

It may be suggested as a criticism of this very general characterization of computation that it is *too* general. For in this very wide sense, even a sieve or a threshing machine could he considered a computer, since they sort their inputs into types, and if one wanted to spend the time at it, one could discover a function that describes the input–output behavior. While this observation is correct, it is not so much a criticism as an apt appreciation of the breadth of the notion. It is rather like a lawn-growing perfectionist incredulously pointing out that on our understanding of "weed," even dandelions might be nonweeds relative to some clime and some tribe of growers. And so, indeed, they might be some farmer's cash crop. Nor is this idle fancy. Cultivated dandelion greens now appear as a delicacy in the specialty section of the greengrocery.

Conceivably, sieves and threshing machines could be construed as computers if any-one has reason to care about the specific function reflected in their input–output behavior, though it is hard to see what those reasons might be. Unlike desktop computers that are engineered precisely for their computational prowess, sieves and threshing machines are constructed for other reasons, namely their sheerly mechanical prowess in the sorting of objects according to size and shape. Not too much emphasis should be placed on the link between purposeful design and use as a computer, however, for a fortuitously shaped rock can be used as a sundial. This is a truly simple computer-trouvé, but we do have rea-son to care about the temporal states that its shadow-casting states can be interpreted as representing.

There is perhaps a correct intuition behind the criticism nonetheless. Finding a device sufficiently interesting to warrant the description "computer" probably also entails that its input–output function is rather complex and inobvious, so that discovering the function reveals something important and perhaps unexpected about the real nature of the device and how it works. Thus finding out what is computed by a sieve is probably not very interesting and will not teach us much we did not already know. How a sieve works is dead simple. In contrast, finding out what is computed by the cerebellum will teach us a lot about the nature of the tissue and how it works.

A computer is a physical device with physical states and causal interactions resulting in transitions between those states. Basically, certain of its physical states are arranged such that they represent something, and its state transitions can be interpreted as computational operations on those representations. A slide rule is taken to compute—for example, (Mult 2, 7) to give 14 as the output—by dint of the fact that its physical regularities are set up in such a way as to honor the abstract regularities in the domain of numbers; the system of Aubrey holes at Stonehenge computes eclipses of the sun by dint of the fact that its physical organization and state transitions are set up so that the sun stone, moon stone, and nodal stone land in the same hole exactly when an eclipse of the sun occurs. Notice that this would be so even in the highly unlikely event that Stonehenge was the fortuitous product of landslides and flooding rather than human contrivance.

Nervous systems are also physical devices with causal interactions that constitute state transitions. Through slow evolution, rather than miraculous chance or intelligent design, they are configured so that their states *represent*—the external world, the body they inhabit, and in some instances, parts of the nervous system itself—and their physical state transitions execute computations. A circuit in mammalian brain stem evolved to compute the next position of the eyeball based on the angular velocity of the head. Briefly, the neuronal activity originating in the semicircular canals represents head velocity, and the interneurons, motor neurons and eyeball muscles are physically arranged such that for head velocity of a certain amount, the neurons causally interact so that the muscles of eyeball change tension by exactly the amount needed to compensate for the head movement. Loosely speaking, this organization evolved "for" this task; a little more strictly speaking, this circuit came to be the way it is by random mutations and natural selection; in standard epigenetic circumstances and relative to the ancestor's nervous system and to the system's other components, this organization enhances somewhat the organism's chances of surviving and reproducing.

There is a major contrast between manufactured and biological computers. Since we construct digital computers ourselves, we build the appropriate relationship into their design. Consequently, we tend to take this mapping for granted in computers generally, both manufactured and evolved. But for structures in the nervous system, these relationships have to be discovered. In the case of biological computers, discovery may turn out to be very difficult since we typically do not know what is being computed by a structure, and intuitive folk ideas may be misleading.

By contrast with systems we conventionally call computers, the *modus operandi* of some devices are such that a purely causal explanation, without reference to anything having been computed or represented, will suffice. A mouse-trap or a sieve, for example, is a simple mechanical device. Purely causal explanations will likely suffice for some aspects of brain activity too, such as the ion pump in neuronal membranes by virtue of which sodium is pumped out of the cell or the manner in which binding of neurochemicals to receptors changes the internal chemistry of the cell. Bear in mind, however, that even at this level an ion, such as Na^+, *could* represent a variable like velocity. At this stage, no one is really convinced that this is in fact so, but the possibility is not ruled out simply because ions are very low-level entities. Effects at higher levels of organization appear to require explanations in terms of computations and representations. Here a purely causal story, even if the line is still fairly clean, would give only a very unsatisfying explanation. For example, a purely causal or mechanical explanation of the integration of signals by dendrites is unenlightening with respect to what information the cell is getting and what it does with it. We need to know what this interaction means in terms of what the patterns of activity represent and what the system is computing.

Consider, for example, the neurons in parietal cortex whose behavior can be explained as computing head-centered coordinates, taking positions of the stimulus on the retina and position of the eyeball in the head as input (Zipser and Andersen, 1988). Knowing that some neurons have a response profile that causes other neurons to respond in a certain way may be useful, especially in testing the computational hypothesis, but on its own it does not tell us anything much about the role of those neurons in the animal's visual capacity. We need additionally to know what the various states of neurons represent, and how such representations can be transformed by neural interactions into other representations. At the network level, there are examples where the details of connectivity and physiology of the neurons in the network still leave many of the whys and wherefores dangling, while a computational approach that incorporates the physiological details may make contact with the broader brainscape of tasks, solutions, environmental niche, and evolutionary history.[12]

There is a nonmathematical sense of "function," according to which the job performed by something is said to be its function. In this sense, the heart is said to function as a pump, rather, than say as a noisemaker to soothe babies on their mother's breast. Though making a "ka-thump" sound is something the heart does, and though babies appear to be soothed by it, this surely is not the heart's *function*, meaning, roughly, its "primary job." Functional assignments can reasonably be made in the context of evolutionary development, what the animal needs to survive and reproduce, its environmental niche, and what would make sense given the assignment of function to related structures. In this "job" sense of function, the function of some part of the nervous system is to compute some function (in the mathematical sense), such as position for the eyeball given head velocity.

There is nothing mystical about characterizing a biological structure as having a specific function, even though neither god nor man designed the structure with a purpose in mind.[13] The teleological trappings are only that, and the teleology is eliminable or reducible without remainder in an evolutionary framework. To assign a computational role to a circuit is to specify a job of that circuit—detecting head velocity, for example. Consequently, the considerations that bear on determining the job of an organ such as the liver bear also on the assignment of computational role to neuronal structures. That the nervous system evolved, and that maladaptive structures tend to be weeded out in the evolutionary contest, restricts many functional hypotheses—in both senses of "functional"—that are logically possible but just not biologically reasonable. The crux of the matter is that many biologically irrelevant computational hypotheses can be culled out by a general functional truth about nervous systems, namely that *inter alia* they serve to help the animal move adaptively in the world.[14]

Notes for Chapter 20

1. William Baxt has developed a net for diagnosis of coronary occlusion in patients presenting with acute anterior chest pain (Baxt, 1990).

2. These levels have been postulated within a single brain. However, as Horace Barlow has suggested (personal communication), the levels diagram might be more accurate if it recognized the interaction *between* brains and added a step to the topmost level. The argument for the extension is that the interaction between brains is a major factor in what an individual brain can and does do. Natural selection is one form of interaction between brains that gives rise to the general capacities and predispositions of the brain of a given species. Additionally, given the predispositions an individual has at birth, interactions between conspecific brains as well as between contraspecific brains have much to do with the particular capacities, skills, knowledge, and representations an individual brain acquires. For example, the particular language a human learns may empower or limit him, both in how he interacts with other humans, how he solves certain kinds of problems, and how he thinks about things even when not explicitly conversing. A dog's interactions with its human owner can have a profound effect on the animal's temperment, and perhaps vice versa; seals growing up in an environment with killer whales and those without killer whales are likely to have a differently configured "predator space." Although we agree with Barlow that the social level is very important, it has not been the main focus of this book.

3. The original conception of levels of analysis can be found in Marr and Poggio (1976, 1977). While Marr (1982) emphasized the importance of the computational level, the notion of a hierarchy of levels grew out of earlier work by Reichardt and Poggio (1976) on the visual control of orientation in the fly. In a sense, the current view on the interaction between levels is not so much a departure from the earlier views as a return to the practice previously established by Reichardt, Poggio, and even by Marr himself, who published a series of papers on neural network models of the cerebellar cortex and cerebral cortex (see, for example, Marr 1969, 1970). The emphasis on the computational level has nonetheless had an important influence on the problems and issues that concern the current generation of neural and connectionist models (Sejnowski et al., 1988).

4. For data that undermine the idea that there is a neat processing hierarchy, see especially Malpeli (1983); Malpeli et al. (1986); Mignard and Malpeli (1991).

5. For a small sample of other reaction time experiments, see also Cooper and Shepard (1973); Posner (1978); Eriksen and St. James (1986); Rosenbaum et al. (1987); Treisman (1988).

6. Specifically, what we wish to defuse is the gripe that until exact definitions of computation and computer are formulated, computational neuroscience is a mere pretender that must stop dead in its tracks. In the absence of precisely specified necessary and sufficient conditions, it might be argued, we do not know what we mean, and hence we do not know what we are talking about. But this reasoning is fallacious. Like any science, computational neuroscience begins with primitive ideas and crude results, and it can use its discoveries to revise and redefine its basic concepts, where the revised concepts can serve as a platform for the next research foray. To recognize this sort of co-evolution of theory and experiment is not to sully precision, for precision based on a genuine basis of evidence and theoretical coherence is greatly to be prized. But it is to resist phony precision, precision that cobbles together a contrived definition before the science can begin to decide between this definition and dozens of alternatives. It is to embrace what philosophers and historians of science have slowly come to realize: that the science essentially leads,

rather than follows, definitions. (Daniel Dennett wittily dubs the eagerness to forge definitions in advance of adequate data as the "heartbreak of premature definition.") And it is to embrace what many cognitive psychologists and linguists suspect: that typically we learn concepts, including rather abstract concepts, by being presented with good examples of the type. We then expand the range of application as a function of further experience and pragmatics. (See Lakoff 1987; P. M. Churchland. 1989.)

7. The one mapping that is generally not considered a function is a 1:many mapping.

8. An alternative is to include time as one of the axes so that the state evolves along a state-time trajectory, in analogy with space-time trajectories in physics.

9. See also Jordan (1986b).

10. For further discussion, see Cummins and Schwarz (1991).

11. Even the notion of "disease," which may seem to be a natural kind, does have an interest relative component. For a remarkable paper in the history of medicine, "The disease of masturbation: values and the concept of disease," see Tristram Engelhardt (1974).

12. Determining which function a network computes and what its states represent are by no means straightforward tasks . . . One worry to allay here is that there can be unresolvable ambiguities for the simple reason that the computational hypothesis is always underdetermined by the evidence. In other words, for any given computational hypothesis, others are also possible (though sometimes just *barely* possible) relative to the *same* body of evidence. For example, one typically assumes that the line connecting two data points is continuous with earlier segments of the line, but that is an *assumption*, not a hidebound necessity. The underdetermination is not, we submit, cause for despair. At least, it is no more problematic than is the assignment of functions to other structures in biological systems, such as hearts and kidneys. Underdeterminacy of hypotheses by the evidence is a rather philosophical consideration, in the lighthearted sense that it is a "don't-worry-now" problem. Ultimately it needs to be addressed because it is puzzling and nontrivial, but in fact most research proceeds perfectly well without paralyzing reflection on this problem.

13. For discussion on this point, see Millikan (1984) and Mitchell (1989).

14. If certain neurons are connected by pathways to transducers for light, and if they respond selectively to events in the visual field, there is a presumption in favor of supposing their job is to process visual information about the outside world. Even if a strangely gifted mathematician could find a completely different function which equally accommodated the neuronal data, say a function that computes the high and low tides in MacFarhlane Cove on the west side of Queen Charlotte Island, this is merely a coincidental, a sheerly fortuitous concurrence, like someone happening to have freckles on her back that can be read as the Tenth Commandment.

The Mind Is Not (Just) a System of Modules Shaped (Just) by Natural Selection

21

Fiona Cowie and James Woodward
2003

21.1 Did the Mind Evolve by Natural Selection?

Of course our minds and brains evolved by natural selection! They aren't the result of divine intervention or fabrication by space aliens. Nor are they solely products of drift or any other naturalistic alternative to selection. That natural selection profoundly "shaped" the mind and brain is accepted by both by evolutionary psychologists and virtually all of their most vigorous critics.

What, then, is at issue in the debate surrounding evolutionary psychology (hereafter, "EP")? First, there are disagreements about the likely intellectual payoffs of EP's characteristic research strategy. EP employs a 'reverse engineering' methodology: the researcher (i) notes some competence or behavior, (ii) conjectures that it is a solution to some 'adaptive problem' faced by our tree- or savanna-dwelling ancestors, and then (iii) proposes that natural selection engineered a specialized psychological mechanism or 'module' to produce that competence or behavior. Some EP researchers also offer (iv) behavioral or psychological evidence for the proposed module, but, as we shall see, this evidence is rarely compelling, and other relevant evidence (from, e.g., neurobiology, genetics, or developmental biology) is often not cited. Critics of EP, like us, think that this methodology is unlikely to yield much insight.

We also dispute EP's views about the structure of the human mind, the way in which it develops, and the relation between evolution and mental architecture. Evolutionary psychologists claim that the mind is 'massively modular.' It is composed of a variety of more or less independent 'organs,' each of which is devoted to the performance of a particular kind of task, and each of which develops in a largely genetically-determined manner. EP's hypothesis of massive mental modularity is not just the uncontroversial idea that the mind/brain consists, at some level of analysis, of components that operate according to distinctive principles. For as we discuss in §21.4, EP endows its modules with a number of additional properties such as informational encapsulation (§21.4.3) and independent evolvability (§21.4.4). In addition, EP also makes specific claims about which modules we have. Thus, the modules at issue in EP are not, e.g., small groups of neurons, but are rather the complex processing structures that underlie high-level cognitive tasks like 'cheater detection.'

EP's views about mental structure and development are motivated by two very general evolutionary considerations. First, EP holds that evolution is likely to have favored strongly modular mental architectures. Second, and relatedly, EP holds that mental modules are the fairly direct products of natural selection. This requires that the different modules must be independently evolvable: they must have independent genetic bases so that natural selection can act to change one module independently of the others. It also means that while EP theorists are careful to say in their 'official' pronouncements that they allow a role for learning and other environmental influences, their more detailed arguments typically assume that the development of modules is tightly genetically constrained.

There are problems with all of these assumptions. First, there is no reason to think that evolution 'must' produce modular minds. Evolutionary psychologists (e.g., Cosmides and Tooby, 1994; Tooby and Cosmides, 1990; Carruthers, 2004) argue that general-purpose psychological mechanisms would not have evolved because they are too slow and require too much background knowledge and computational space for the making of life-or-death judgments. Specialized modules, on the other hand, deliver fast and economical decisions on matters crucially affecting an organism's fitness, so would have been preferred by natural selection. However, it is simply wrong to suppose that modules are invariably (or even usually) superior to general-purpose devices. What sorts of mental organization will be favored by selection depends entirely on the details of the selection pressures an organism is subject to and its genetic structure. As Sober (1994) shows, such factors as how variable the environment is, the costs of making various sorts of mistakes, the costs of building various sorts of discriminative abilities into the organism etc., can have large effects on the relative fitnesses of general-purpose vs. more specialized strategies. In addition, the ability to adapt quickly (i.e., within the individual's lifetime) to changing circumstances is vital for organisms inhabiting unstable environments (Maynard Smith et al., 1985). Indeed, there is evidence that both the physical (in particular, climatic) and social environments inhabited by early hominids were highly unstable (Potts, 1996, 1998; Allman, 1999). There thus would have been considerable selective pressure favoring the evolution of cognitive mechanisms allowing the rapid assimilation of new information and behavioral flexibility, rather than innately-specified modules. (For more on this issue, see §21.3 below, and Woodward and Cowie, 2005)

Secondly, EP's view that the modules existing in the adult mind are largely genetically specified (or are the products of learning mechanisms that are themselves genetically constrained to produce a particular module as output) is inconsistent with what is known about the role of experience-dependent learning and development in shaping the mature mind. As we argue in §21.2.2, whatever modular processing mechanisms the adult mind contains emerge from a complex developmental process. Less modular structures and capacities that are present in infants interact with both with the environment and the genes to generate (or be transformed into) new competences that were not directly selected for.

Thirdly, the notion of a module is itself quite unclear. As we show in §21.4, there are several different (and non-coextensive) criteria for modularity employed in the EP literature. Researchers move back and forth among different notions of modularity, illicitly taking evidence for modularity in one sense to bear on modularity in other senses. They also tend to conflate issues about the modularity of processing in the adult mind with quite separate issues to do with the role of modules in development and learning.

These unclarities make EP's claim that the mind is 'a system of modules' somewhat difficult to assess. Our view, defended in §21.3, is that the mind is not just a collection of specialized modules. Although our minds probably do contain modules in some sense(s) of that term, these structures are unlikely to correspond to the modules (for cheater detection, mate selection, predator avoidance, etc.) postulated in EP.

21.2   Reverse Engineering: A Backward Step for Psychology

EP is premised on the idea that modern human mental organization is a more or less direct reflection of the ways in which hominids evolved to solve the problems posed by their physical and social environments. Thus, by reflecting on the tasks our ancestors must have been able to solve, and by supposing that whatever psychological abilities enabled our ancestors to solve those tasks would have been selected for, evolutionary psychologists seek to map our current psychological organization. Because they also assume that selection engineers a proprietary solution for each of these 'adaptive tasks,' evolutionary psychologists see the modern mind as 'massively modular': it contains numerous specific mechanisms (or 'modules') which evolved for specific tasks and houses few (if any) general purpose psychological mechanisms.

One problem with this strategy has already been mentioned: it ignores the possibility that *flexibility* might well have been at a selective premium for hominids inhabiting rapidly changing environments. In this section, we discuss three further problems with EP's adaptationist or 'reverse engineering' approach to generating psychological hypotheses.

21.2.1   Reading Structure from Function.
EP believes that since "form follows function" (Tooby and Cosmides, 1997, p. 13), one can figure out how the mind is just by considering what it does (or rather, what our ancestors' minds did, back in the 'environment of evolutionary adaptation' ("EEA")).

One reason that EP's reverse engineering strategy is misguided is that you *can't* infer structure from function alone. Instead, formulating and confirming functional and structural hypotheses are highly interrelated endeavors, with information about structure informing hypotheses about function and *vice versa*.

As an illustration, consider how our thinking about human declarative memory has evolved over the last half century (cf. LeDoux, 1996, chapter 7). By the 1940s, neurophysiologists had concluded that memory is distributed over the whole brain, not localized in a particular region. [A structural hypothesis.] But then came the patient H.M., who had had much of both temporal lobes removed to treat severe epilepsy. Post-operatively, HM remembered much of what had happened to him prior to the surgery and could form new short-term memories lasting a few seconds. However, he was unable to form new long-term memories. HM thus indicated that short-term memory and long-term memory are distinct [a functional hypothesis], that they are supported by different brain systems [a structural hypothesis], and that the areas responsible for the formation of new long-term memories are different from those allowing storage of the old ones [structural]. Also prior to this, the limbic system (including the hippocampus and amygdala) had been thought to comprise the emotional circuitry of the brain [functional]. But the hippocampus was one of the areas that was so badly compromised in HM, and in other patients with severe memory deficits [structural], indicating that the limbic system was also involved in cognitive functioning [functional] and suggesting that the hippocampus was the seat of memory [structural]. As the workings of the hippocampus were further investigated [structural], it was found to be especially implicated in learning and memory of spatial information [functional]. Further, since all of the patients on whom the early hippocampal memory story had been based had also had damage to the amygdala [structural], this was an indication that the amygdala was also involved in memory [functional]. (This latter claim is still controversial [functional], given that later studies have shown that hippocampal lesions alone will produce amnesia [structural].)

This vignette illustrates how views about functions are (or should be) highly sensitive to structural information. It thus underscores the naïveté of the assumption (endemic in EP) that one can accurately individuate psychological functions by enumerating the tasks that the mind can perform. Evolutionary psychologists try to avoid this difficulty by inferring functions not (or not just) from behavioral data about what our minds can do at present, but rather from their ideas about which psychological capacities were selected for back in the EEA. In effect, then, evolutionary psychologists think of psychological functions as *biological* functions (in the sense of Wright, 1973): capacities that the mind had in the past that are still present because they were selected for, rather than as functions in the sense of what the mind does at present, regardless of whether they were selected for (*causal role* functions in the sense of Cummins, 1975).

Prima facie, however, this move compounds, rather than solving, the problem just discussed. After all, if it's hard to delineate the functional anatomy of our own minds on the basis of merely behavioral evidence, it's even harder to limn the minds of our ancestors by speculating about what they did and the selection pressures they faced: biological functions are typically *tougher* to figure out than causal role functions. For one thing, as Lewontin has repeatedly pointed out (e.g., 1990), cognitive functions leave no unambiguous marks on the hominid fossil record and humans have no close living relatives whose homologous psychological capacities might allow inferences about ancestral functioning. In addition, as Stotz and Griffiths (2002) argue, the evolutionary or 'adaptive' problems faced by an organism cannot be specified independently of the organism's capacities (and/or the structures that underlie those capacities). If you didn't know, to take their example, that a given fossil bird had a reinforced beak and skull (like a modern woodpecker), you would be unable to reconstruct its niche (living in a forest), its habits (eating insects living under the bark of trees) or the adaptive problems (getting at the insects) and selection pressures it faced. In the absence of detailed knowledge of what the mind is actually like, speculating about the adaptive problems faced by hominids in the EEA is like speculating about the niche and feeding habits of a headless fossil bird. Thus, EP's strategy of inferring the mind's functional architecture from speculations about its biological function(s) is seriously off track.

21.2.2   The One-to-One Assumption

The epistemological problems just outlined are quite endemic to adaptationist reasoning about the mind. However, there is a second problem with EP's view of the relation between structure and function: EP assumes that once a psychological function is somehow identified, it is legitimate to postulate a *single* mechanism—a 'module'—that performs that function. As Carruthers puts it:

> . . . in biology generally, distinct functions predict distinct mechanisms to fulfill those functions . . . [Hence] one should expect that distinct mental functions—estimating numerosity, predicting the effects of a collision, reasoning about the states of another person, and so on—are likely to be realized in distinct cognitive learning mechanisms . . . " (2004. p. 300)

This 'one to one' assumption is not a dispensable part of EP methodology. If a single mechanism could subserve many different functions or if a single function required the cooperation of a number of different mechanisms, then the characteristic EP procedure of inferring mechanisms from functions would be undermined. For in that case, there would be many different alternative hypotheses about the mechanisms involved in the performance a given function, and the identification of the function itself would provide no evidence about which of these alternatives was correct. The one-to-one hypothesis avoids this difficulty by assuming that the only possibility is that a distinct mechanism performs each function.

Given the central role played in the EP methodology by the 'one-to-one' assumption, it is then a real problem for EP that this assumption embodies a serious misapprehension about how natural selection works. Far from "characteristically [operating] by 'bolting on' new special-purpose items to the existing repertoire" (Carruthers, 2004, p. 300), natural selection usually operates by jury-rigging what is already there to perform new tasks instead of (or in addition to) the old ones. Feathers originally evolved for thermal regulation, and subsequently were exapted for flight and mating displays as well. Vertebrate limbs originally evolved for swimming, and subsequently were fitted for walking, climbing, flying and manipulation. At the genetic level, too, exaptation and multifunctionality are common, both within organisms and across species. The Hox genes that control the development of a chicken's legs and feet, for instance, also control development of its wings. Moreover the self-same genes are responsible (with only very minor changes in sequencing) for limb development in all tetrapods—wings, claws, paws, flippers, flukes and hands all have the same genetic origins (Davidson, 2001:167-76; Gilbert, 2000: 503-21).

Exaptation and multifunctionality are also features of the mind and brain. If a given mechanism M1 carries out some task, T1, and in so doing processes information that is relevant to some other task, T2, then M1 could well be selected because of its role in performing T2 in addition to T1. For example, the processes of object identification may generate information that is relevant to depth perception. If so, those processes may be recruited for both functions and we'd have two functions utilizing a single mechanism. On the other hand, what is intuitively a single task may involve multiple mechanisms cobbled together over time: T2 may involve M2 and M3 in addition to M1. Depth perception looks like this: mechanisms that are at least partly distinct, both anatomically and phylogenetically, are involved in the processing of the various depth 'cues' such as binocular disparity, occlusion, texture gradients, etc.

The reuse of old materials for new purposes, with all the redundancy and ad hoc interconnectedness that it implies, is characteristic of selection's 'tinkering' mode of operation. Because natural selection typically does not operate by designing new, single- purpose devices to solve new environmental challenges, EP's one-to-one assumption is highly dubious.

Another problem with the one-to-one assumption concerns EP's individuation of functions or tasks. Consider the detection of numerosity. How should we decide whether this is one psychological function subserved by a single module (as Carruthers assumes, 2004, p. 300) or several functions subserved by several modules? The detection of numerosity, after all, is actually a highly complex task. It involves (e.g.) object detection and individuation, which involve (e.g.) depth and edge perception, which involve (e.g.) perception of luminance and color boundaries . . . etc. Detecting numerosity is a function carried out by the performance of other, simpler functions: functions are nested. They are also shared. Just as the detection of numerosity itself can play a role in higher-level functions (say, performing a task in a psychology experiment), all of the lower-level functions just discussed play roles in the performance of other tasks: depth perception also subserves motion detection; perception of color boundaries subserves depth perception; object individuation subserves object recognition, etc. Given that functions are both nested and shared in this manner, it is hard to see how evolutionary psychologists—relying only on the one-to-one assumption and eschewing the sorts of detailed investigations into neural and cognitive mechanisms described in §21.2.1—could have any principled reason for saying that a given function (like the perception of numerosity) is carried out by one module or many. Similarly for face-recognition, cheater detection, and the various other capacities that are the focus of EP theorizing.

The observations in §§21.2.1 and 21.2.2 clearly undermine EP's assumptions that mechanisms or modules and functions correspond in a neat 1:1 manner and that as a result, the existence of modules can be inferred from a specification of the tasks the mind performs. Of course, one could read EP as simply *stipulating* a notion of 'module' such that each function is *ipso facto* performed by one and only one module. But such a reading of EP's structural hypotheses trivializes them. In addition, this 'thin' interpretation of what a module is is inconsistent with the fact that the modules postulated in EP are virtually always assumed to have other properties, such as being independent targets of selection, being independently disruptable, being informationally encapsulated, and so on. (See §21.4.)

21.2.3   The Role of Learning and Development

Another crucial limitation of EP's methodology is its misunderstanding of the role of learning and development in shaping the mature mind. It's not that evolutionary psychologists assign no role at all to learning and development. It is rather that they think of these processes as strongly genetically pre-specified. Not only does this 'preformationist' picture have little empirical support, it engenders a crucial misspecification in the EP literature of what stands in need of adaptive explanation.

Evolutionary psychologists take some behavior or capacity possessed by mature humans—say, mate preferences, or cheater detection, or the desire to rape—and then proceed to give an adaptive explanation of the postulated mechanism underlying that behavior or capacity (cf., e.g., Thornhill and Thornhill, 1987, 1992 on rape; Wright, 1994 on family relations). But if learning plays an important role in the acquisition of these mechanisms or behaviors, then what really needs adaptive explanation is *the processes underlying the development of those mechanisms*.

Admittedly, some evolutionary psychologists do see their task as involving the explanation of development—see Carruthers' emphasis on "evolved learning mechanisms" as giving rise to various modules (2004, pp. 300, 307). However, the assumption here seems to be that if some competence (and the module, M, underlying it) are adaptations built by natural selection, then either (i) the unfolding of M is directly genetically pre-specified; or (ii) M is produced by a 'learning module,' L, which is itself built by the genes and tightly constrained to produce M as its output. On this view, the relationship between L and M is very direct: to the extent that experience plays any role at all in the development of M, it merely serves to 'trigger' a cascade of effects in L, the outcome of which is tightly genetically constrained.

However, there are a number of serious flaws in this reasoning, even assuming that a given processing module M in the adult mind is indeed an adaptation built by natural selection. First, as a number of psychologists, biologists and philosophers of biology have emphasized, adaptive traits may be 'coded for' in the environment. (Cf. Oyama, 1985; Sterelny and Griffiths, 1999; Sterelny, 2003). That is, instead of building M into the genes (either directly or indirectly via learning mechanism L), natural selection may have given us dispositions to *construct an environment E* in which M would arise as a result of learning and/or other developmental mechanisms which are *not* genetically determined to produce M. For example, rather than building in a 'folk psychology' module, evolution may have given us dispositions to create the kinds of social and familial environments in which children's generalized developmental and learning abilities enable them to acquire knowledge of other minds.

A second problem here concerns the relation of current evidence from neurobiology and genetics to EP's assumption that modules like M or L are "innate or innately channeled." (Carruthers, 2004, p. 304). Several writers (e.g., Bates et al., 1998) have advanced a simple counting argument against the notion that numerous cognitive modules (with all their detailed representations and complex algorithms) are genetically specified. Human beings have approximately 30,000–70,000 genes (Venter et al., 2001; Shouse, 2002). By contrast, there are an estimated 10^{14} synaptic connections in the brain. Thus, it is argued, there are too few genes by many orders of magnitude to code for or specify even a small portion of these connections.

We find this argument suggestive but not decisive. The role of regulatory genes and networks in governing the expression of structural genes probably generates many more combinatorial possibilities than the figure of 30,000 genes suggests. Still, the counting argument does draw attention to the need for evolutionary psychologists to explain, consistently with what is known about brain development, how cognitive modules could be genetically specified. This, we think, is a non-trivial task, especially vis à vis the cerebral cortex, which is known to play a central role in the sorts of high-level cognitive tasks (like language acquisition, cheater detection, theory of mind, etc.) that figure in EP theorizing. For while the gross architectural features of the cortex do appear to be genetically specified, there is considerable evidence that the cortex is in other respects initially relatively undifferentiated and equipotent. In particular, the patterns of synaptic and dendritic connections that develop in different cortical areas—and presumably correspond to the representations (of syntax, folk psychology, etc.) which EP's modules contain—are very heavily influenced by sensory inputs, and influenced in a way that the evolutionary psychologist's 'triggering' metaphor seems ill equipped to capture. Indeed, many areas of cortex have the capacity to acquire fundamentally different sorts of representations depending on experience. For instance, the cortical areas normally devoted to visual processing in sighted subjects are used for tactile tasks, such as Braille reading, in congenitally blind subjects, and auditory cortex is recruited for processing sign language in deaf subjects (e.g., Büchel et al., 1998; Nishimura et al., 1999). This phenomenon of 'cross-modal plasticity' makes it very hard to see how the cortex could contain innate representations specialized for specific cognitive or learning tasks, and undermines EP's notion that the development of cognitive modules like M or L is genetically driven. We think that until we hear more about the ways in which the genetic and regulatory mechanisms needed to build the mental modules postulated in EP actually work, we are entitled to view EP's developmental story—or, really, its lack of such a story—with suspicion.

21.2.4   Non-Darwinian Traits

Such suspicions are reinforced by consideration of a final shortcoming of EP's reverse engineering strategy, namely, its blindness to the fact that many psychological traits may not be susceptible of direct Darwinian explanation at all. First, while we grant Carruthers' point (2004, p. 294) that the entire mind is unlikely to be the product of drift or some other non-selective process, it's by no means impossible that particular psychological mechanisms might be the results of such processes. Developmental, allometric and physio-chemical factors are all known to play significant roles in neural functioning and organization, and may well turn out to be responsible for some psychological traits as well.

Alternatively, some psychological mechanisms might be 'spandrels' in the sense of Gould and Lewontin (1979). That is, they might be lucky byproducts of traits that evolved for other purposes. There's evidence, for instance, that our capacity to organize continuous acoustical signals into linguistically-relevant segments (phonemes) is a byproduct of the way that mammalian brains happen to have evolved to process auditory information. Of course, byproducts that happen to be advantageous may themselves be subject to positive selection pressure—they may become 'secondary adaptations.' But the possibilities that psychological mechanisms are spandrels or mere secondary adaptations undermine, in different ways, EP's assumption that each psychological mechanism is built to order to solve a distinct adaptive problem. The spandrels possibility puts into doubt EP's assumption that modules are *optimal* or near-optimal solutions to adaptive problems: a turtle's fins may be optimized for propelling a heavy body through water, but they are far from optimal means of crossing the sand at nesting time. And the possibility that some mental mechanisms are exaptations further undermines EP's one-to-one assumption, discussed in §21.2.2: complex exaptations (like, arguably, the human capacity for language or cheater detection) are often cobbled together from multiple mechanisms that are designed (and still used) for other purposes. While one can certainly *call* such complex secondary adaptations *single* mechanisms or modules, it's unclear that they can be attributed the other features commonly ascribed to modules, such as informational encapsulation or independent disruptability. (See below, §§21.4.3, 21.4.4.)

21.3   The Mind as A System of Modules

EP claims not just that the mind contains various mental modules, but that it is a *system* of modules. In this section, we examine the arguments for this claim. (We assume here, for the sake of argument, that the notion of a 'module' is relatively clear. This assumption will be criticized in §21.4.)

The main argument for the claim that the mind is a system of modules is originally due to John Tooby and Leda Cosmides. They claim that domain-specific modules would inevitably be selected for because relatively content-independent (or general-purpose) architectures are in principle not viable objects of selection (e.g., Cosmides and Tooby, 1992b, 1994; Tooby and Cosmides, 1990, 1992; see also Samuels, 1998 for a forceful statement of EP's 'massive modularity' hypothesis). There are two arguments given for this claim. First, general learning mechanisms face the 'Frame Problem.' Unless the factors relevant to a problem are delineated in advance, general- purpose inference mechanisms face a massive combinatorial explosion—and their owners get eaten before they can reproduce. (See §21.3.1.) Secondly, Chomsky's poverty of the stimulus argument for the existence of a language-learning module is generalized to show that general-purpose inference is ineffective in the face of *any* learning problem. For one thing, there will always be more hypotheses compatible with the available data than the learner can effectively test. For another thing, testing is itself problematic. There are no domain-neutral criteria for success: evaluating foraging strategies involves different measures from those used to test hypotheses about cheaters. Worse, there are some hypotheses and strategies that an individual cannot evaluate at all—mate selection strategies would be an example, assuming, of course, that the appropriate measure here is inclusive fitness. (See §21.3.2) The upshot is that hominids equipped only with general-purpose inference or learning mechanisms wouldn't have survived in the EFA. Additional constraints on learning mechanisms are clearly needed, and those are what modular architectures supply.

21.3.1   Combinatorial Explosion and the 'Frame Problem'

Fodor (1983; see also Chapter 9, this volume) maintained that many or most cognitive (or 'central') processes are non-modular, since reasoning, deliberation and planning etc. must potentially have access to everything an agent knows. He recognized that this meant that such non-modular processes are subject to the so-called 'frame problem'—the problem of specifying what information is relevant to which problem—and for this reason, speculated that they would prove unamenable to cognitive-scientific investigation. The pessimism of evolutionary psychologists is deeper even than Fodor's: they view the frame problem not just as an obstacle to *theorizing about* central processors, but rather to their very existence! Carruthers (2004, p. 303), for instance, argues that "any processor which had to access the full set of the agent's background beliefs . . . would be faced with an unmanageable combinatorial explosion" and hence concludes that "the mind . . . consist[s] of a set of processing systems which . . . operate in isolation from most of the information which is available elsewhere in the mind." EP thus (dis)solves the frame problem by assuming that the processes underlying decision-making and behavior are modular: they neither have nor need access to the bulk of the agent's beliefs and desires.

Whether this is a satisfactory solution to the frame problem depends on what one takes that problem to be. *If* human reasoning, deliberation and planning processes can generate satisfactory decisions and behavior without access to large numbers of the agent's beliefs and desires, then this will indeed be an important point in favor of the modularist picture. However, it seems plain that in many cases, reasoning etc. *cannot* issue in even minimally satisfactory decisions and behaviors without such access—consider, for instance, the range of factors bearing on a decision to cooperate with a conspecific. If this is so, however, then EP's claim to have solved the frame problem is undermined, and the modularist must confront the question of how our processes of reasoning, deliberation and planning *could* have access to so many and so varied of our background beliefs and desires. Presumably, evolutionary psychologists cannot invoke a single, hardwired 'Decision Making Module' here, for natural selection clearly cannot anticipate all the decisions we potentially face in a lifetime; moreover, the beliefs and desires that are relevant to these decisions vary with context and hence cannot be prespecified. Suppose that it is instead suggested that a *group* of encapsulated modules collaborate in the planning and execution of complicated actions. In that case, we must ask how their operations are coordinated. There seem to be two options. One is that there is a fixed hierarchy of modules, such that each module sends its outputs to the next one up in the hierarchy, and so on, until a behavioral command is outputted. Alternatively, there is some kind of 'Module Integration Module' (what Samuels et al., 1999 unironically call a "Resource Allocation Module") which takes the outputs of various lower-level modules, evaluates them, and issues in the same behavioral instruction—Carruthers (2004, section 15.6) proposes that "an existing module . . . the natural-language faculty" (p. 307) performs this integrative task.

But neither of these alternatives is plausible. An evolved, hard-wired hierarchy of modules is vulnerable to the same objections as the Decision Making Module: our behaviors are simply too complex, and the mental processes giving rise to them too varied, for the frame problem to be solved by a pre-specified hierarchy. This leaves us with the idea of a Module Integration Module, which takes in the deliverances of all the other modules whose computations are potentially relevant to a given problem and decides what to do with them. But a 'module' that can (i) assess which of the plethora of modular outputs are important in a given context and (ii) decide what outcome is desirable and then (iii) figure out which behaviors (and in what order) will result in that outcome *isn't a module (in the EP sense) at all*! Instead, it's functionally equivalent to Fodor's Central Processor, and, assuming that the frame problem and combinatorial problems are real problems, it raises them all over again. As soon as one looks in detail at how a massively modular mind is supposed to work, one sees that the frame problem is not an argument *for* the theory that the mind is massively modular; instead, it's an argument *against* that thesis![1]

21.3.2   The Argument from the Poverty of the Stimulus

Suppose that a poverty of the stimulus argument has convinced us that some hypothesis or skill which people acquire could not have been learned just from the evidence available. This shows us that additional constraints, not present in the evidence, are required for successful learning. Evolutionary psychologists (like other proponents of poverty of the stimulus arguments) are quick to assume that the constraints in question must be (i) representational, (ii) cognitively sophisticated and (iii) specific to various common-sense domains or subject matters. Thus, for instance, we are told that the necessary constraints are 'theories' of various sorts (e.g., universal grammar, theory of mind). And because the content of these theories so far outruns the available data, this view suggests in turn (iv) that the needed constraints on learning are embodied in innately-specified modules (Language Acquisition Devices, Theory of Mind modules, etc.).

However, this picture itself outruns what is warranted by the poverty of the stimulus argument. For that argument indicates only that some constraints are needed, not what *kinds* of constraints those are. Thus, learning may be subserved by other types of constraint in addition to (or instead of) the sophisticated representational constraints postulated in EP. There might, for instance, be perceptual biases of various sorts, or dispositions to direct our attention to certain kinds of stimuli, or facts about our reward structures that encourage certain sorts of behavior rather than others. For example, there is evidence that subcortical mechanisms preferentially direct infants' visual attention to objects that fit a loosely face-like template, and that reward mechanisms release chemicals that make infants feel good when attending to such stimuli (Johnson, 1997). By themselves, these mechanisms are incapable of generating the full range of adult face-recognition behavior. However, they do help in reducing the underdetermination problem faced by the child (why focus on faces rather than elbows? why focus on eyes rather than chins?), and the preferential looking and attending that they produce may result in the gradual construction of cortical circuits that behave like a 'face recognition module.'

Other possible constraints are developmental or architectural. Chronotopic factors governing the timing of different aspects of development can reduce underdetermination by guiding the *sequencing* of various learning tasks: learning to the grammar of a language is easier if you already have a representation of its phonemes, for example. In addition, although the detailed pattern of synaptic connections that develops in the cortex is experience-dependent, the gross architecture of the cortex (e.g., different areas' characteristic laminar structures and basic circuitry types) may well be genetically specified (cf. §21.2.3). These architectural features do not themselves amount to innate representations or modules, yet they may help the brain to solve learning problems by biasing certain areas to assume some tasks rather than others, or encouraging certain sorts of representations rather than others to develop in response to sensory input. As these examples show, it is a mistake to suppose, as evolutionary psychologists frequently do, that the only two possibilities are either a completely unconstrained, general purpose learner or a heavily modular learner pre-equipped with large bodies of domain specific knowledge.

One final point deserves to be made about EP's claim that the mind is a 'system of modules.' Both of the arguments discussed in this section are arguments for a very strong version of the modularity hypothesis, namely, that the mind contains *nothing but* modules. As already indicated, we don't think that the evidence for this 'massively modular' view of the mind is at all compelling. However, there is also a more 'Modest' modularity hypothesis to the effect that the mind contains *some* modules. (E.g., Fodor's (1983) modularity hypothesis was Modest: it postulated both modular sensory mechanisms and non-modular central processing mechanisms. Modesty also embraces the possibility that some cognitive (as opposed to sensory) processing is modular too.) Our discussion so far leaves it open that some kind of Modest modularity thesis is correct. In the next section, however, we argue that the notion of a module, as deployed in EP, is fundamentally unclear. Thus, while the mind may indeed contain some 'modules' (in some sense of that word), we will see in §21.4 that even advocates of Modest modularity need to clarify considerably what their thesis amounts to.

21.4   In Search of Mental Modules

We turn now to the question of what modules are. We argue that the various different criteria used for modularity in the EP literature are far from co-extensive and thus lead to quite different notions of a 'module.' We also emphasize that these different modularity claims require (but often do not get) different sorts of supporting evidence. We conclude that EP's widespread failure to recognize these points both weakens its case for the modularity of mind and undermines the status of the specific cognitive modules it postulates.

21.4.1 Modularity and Neural Specificity

As Carruthers notes (2004, section 15.1.1) and as we will be lamenting in this section, the meaning of term 'module' in EP is highly elastic. However, one negative point about EP's notion of modularity has been foreshadowed in previous sections: it bears little relation to the neuroscientist's notion of *neural specificity*. This is the idea, first, that different brain regions are (relatively) specialized to different tasks. In most people, for instance, the left hemisphere is dominant in language processing—word production, e.g., is more or less localized to Broca's area, Wernicke's area and the left thalamus (Indefrey and Levelt, 2000, p. 854). Secondly, the idea of neural specificity embraces the fact that the representations and computations that are used in different brain regions and for different tasks may be quite diverse. For example, the perception of an object's color involves the representation of its spectral properties by the three retinal cone types, adjusted so as to compensate for properties of the ambient light (Wandell, 2000), whereas perception of sounds involves the representation of low-level acoustical features as onset time, pitch and location, followed by the computation of higher-order properties such as timbre, resulting ultimately in the representation of items of speech, music, or other types of noise (Shamma, 2000).

Now, if all that were meant by EP's claims that perceptual and cognitive processing and mechanisms are 'domain specific' or 'modular' were that such processes and mechanisms are neurally localized and involve different kinds of computations over different kinds of representations, we would readily agree. Not even the most rabid anti-modularist doubts, for example, that retinal cones are ineffective at extracting acoustical information. However, as we have already suggested, adherents of EP generally have something much stronger in mind than this.

As evidence for this, consider first the fact that the neural specialization described above is typically *relative*, rather than absolute. Cells in a certain area may respond especially strongly to certain kinds of inputs or may be particularly active in the execution of a certain task. But as neural imaging data are increasingly making clear, they will typically also respond, though less vigorously, to many other inputs and task demands. Andersen et al. (2000), for example, give evidence that the posterior parietal cortex, classically thought to be specialized for attention and spatial awareness, is also involved in the planning of goal-directed behavior. Similarly, DeAngelis et al. (2000) argue that cortical area MT, normally held to be highly specialized for motion detection, is also implicated in the perception of stereoscopic depth.

Just as the same brain areas may subserve different tasks, many tasks that common sense might count as unitary can involve activation of numerous different brain regions. Face recognition, for example, involves not only the areas in the fusiform gyrus that are cited in lesion and dissociation studies, but also the parahippocampal gyrus, the hippocampus, the superior temporal sulcus, the amygdala and the insula (McCarthy, 2000). Likewise the production of verbs involves areas in the left frontal cortex, anterior cingulate, posterior temporal lobe and right cerebellum (Posner and Raichle, 1994, p. 120). At the neural level, then, tasks like recognizing a face or producing a spoken word are performed by a 'single mechanism' only in a very attenuated and task-relative sense.

This sharing of tasks by the same neural areas and the distribution of tasks over numerous different areas contrasts strongly with EP's talk of distinct modules devoted to distinct cognitive and perceptual tasks. Hence, evolutionary psychologists' claims about 'domain specific' or 'dedicated' modules should not be confused with the facts about neural specificity just described. But if that's the case, what *does* EP's talk of 'dedicated' or 'domain specific' processing amount to?

Evolutionary psychologists answer that one needs to distinguish between what Marr (1982) called 'implementational level' details on the one hand, and theories at the 'computational level' on the other (cf. Griffiths, 2001). Since their theories are at the psychological or computational level, we should not expect the modules they postulate to be reflected in the nitty gritty of neural organization. As Cosmides and Tooby put it, EP "is more closely allied with the cognitive level of explanation than with any other level of proximate causation." (1987, p. 284)

But while the urge to theorize at one level of description while ignoring constraints from other levels is endemic to cognitive science, we think that it is a mistake. No psychologist should ignore the neurosciences because psychological theories must be implementable in brains and, as is increasingly becoming apparent, this constraint is an extremely strong one. It is doubly a mistake for evolutionary psychologists to neglect facts about how psychological tasks are performed by the brain. First, as §21.2.1 made clear, the individuation of psychological functions must be constrained by implementational information. Second, as §21.3.1 urged, one cannot usefully theorize about how natural selection operates on the mind and brain while neglecting implementational issues. Third, a sharp psychological/implementational divide undermines one of EP's central sources of evidence: if EP's modules have nothing to do with the brain, it is hard to see the relevance of the sorts of neuroscientific data (about localization, dissociations, etc.) that are frequently cited in the EP literature (cf. Carruthers, 2004, sections 15.4.2 and 15.4.3; and see Pinker, 1999). Most importantly, though, neglecting implementational constraints threatens to leach EP's notions of modularity and task-specificity of any real content. If the notion of a module is not tied to claims about neural specificity, what does it amount to? In what follows, we review several features that have been ascribed to modules and examine their interrelations.

21.4.2 Modularity and Dissociability
One feature that is often ascribed to modules in EP is dissociability or independent disruptability, the idea being that if two modules are distinct, then it should be possible (at least in principle) to interfere with the operation of each one without affecting the operation of other.[2] As we have already observed (§21.2.1), EP lacks an intrinsic characterization of

modules that would allow one to determine directly whether one independently-identified mechanism has dissociated from another. Instead, modules are characterized functionally, in terms of the tasks that they are assumed to perform, and the dissociations that are actually observed are dissociations between *tasks* (e.g., between production of words and comprehension of grammatical sentences). It is these dissociations among tasks that are taken to be evidence for the existence of independent modules. Thus, Carruthers (2004, section 15.4.2) and Pinker (1994, 49ff.), for instance, argue that the double dissociation between general cognitive tasks and language production and comprehension tasks seen in subjects with Specific Language Impairment and Williams syndrome is strong evidence that there is a task-specific mental module underlying language.

While the evidential significance of dissociations is a complicated subject to which we cannot do justice here, such inferences are far more problematic than is generally appreciated.[3] First, there are a number of intuitively non-modular architectures that can give rise to double dissociations among tasks (cf. Shallice, 1988, 245ff.). Second, it is crucial to distinguish between dissociations arising from developmental disorders and dissociations resulting from injuries to (or experimental manipulations of) adult brains. The former bear on mechanisms of learning or development, and the latter on mature psychological competences. Third, inferences from a double dissociation of capacities to the distinctness of modules generally require additional empirical assumptions, such as (i) a 'universality' assumption to the effect that both normal and abnormal subjects share a cognitive architecture (excluding the damaged modules in abnormals); (ii) a 'subtraction' assumption to the effect that brain damage only removes modules or the connections between them and it does not engender any significant neural reorganization; and (iii) various 'gating' assumptions about whether the destruction of one or all connections between modules involved in a task is necessary for disruption of the task. (Cf. Shallice, 1988, 218ff.; Glymour, 2001, pp. 135-6, 143-4.)

These assumptions are empirically questionable, especially when the dissociations in question are developmental or genetic in origin. First, subjects with genetic abnormalities (or childhood brain injuries) are likely to differ from normal subjects in many different ways. Secondly, incapacities appearing early in childhood are known to call forth compensatory psychological strategies and substantial neural reorganization.

Hence, and contrary to what Carruthers and Pinker imply, it is extremely unlikely that subjects with Specific Language Impairment differ from normal subjects only in having impaired language function. Instead, as many empirical studies attest, such subjects have numerous other cognitive and perceptual deficits as well.[4] Thus, the cleanness of the dissociation between language and general cognitive abilities is undercut—as is EP's inference from that dissociation to the existence of distinct modules underlying those abilities.

We conclude this section by again acknowledging that there is a very 'thin' notion of module such that, given certain other assumptions, a double dissociation entails modularity (in that sense). For example, if we simply assume that a distinct module underlies each distinct capacity (c.f. the 'One-to-one' assumption discussed in §21.2.2), with all normal subjects sharing the same architecture, and if we count a dissociation of capacities in any two people as indicating that those capacities are distinct (across all subjects), then we have an unproblematic inference from dissociability to distinctness of modules. However, this pretty inference is bought at the cost of a not-very-interesting notion of 'module.' As soon as we begin to invest modules with other, 'thicker' properties—like informational encapsulation or independent evolvability (§§21.4.3–21.4.4)—the inference becomes far less compelling, as these properties do not necessarily apply to modules as distinguished by the dissociability criterion.

21.4.3   Modules and Encapsulation
Modules are also often said to be *informationally encapsulated* in the sense that other psychological systems have access only to the information that is the output of the module; the processing that goes on within it is not accessible to, or influenced by, information or processes in other parts of the mind (Fodor, 1983). However, it is not clear how useful this feature is in picking out distinct cognitive mechanisms. First, informational encapsulation is often a relative, rather than an all-or-nothing matter. It's plausible that some brain or psychological mechanisms may be completely informationally isolated from *some* other mechanisms (in the sense that there are no circumstances in which mechanism A is internally influenced by mechanism B). But many if not virtually all mechanisms are influenced in their internal operations by *some* other mechanisms—or at least this is true if we don't trivialize the notion of an 'internal operation' (see below). Relatedly, informational encapsulation often seems to be task-relative. Whether mechanism or brain region A is influenced in its internal processing by information or processing in mechanism or region B may vary depending on the tasks A and B are engaged in.

As an illustration of these points, consider the role of attention in many psychological processes. There is evidence that although low-level visual processing, such as occurs in the primary visual area V1, is often relatively encapsulated, it can be modified by higher-level processes involving visual attention, which occur in other neural regions (Luck and Hillyard, 2000). This kind of result raises familiar issues about EP's individuation of tasks: are the processes in V1 performing *different* tasks or functions depending on whether attention is involved? It also undermines the usefulness of the encapsulation criterion for modularity. Does the fact that the processing of a visual stimulus by V1 is altered depending on whether subjects pay attention to that stimulus show that V1 is unencapsulated with respect to tasks that involve attention but encapsulated with respect to other tasks not involving attention? If so, are there *two* modules associated with V1, one operative when attention is involved and the other when it's not? Peter Carruthers (private communication) suggests that if attention sometimes influences processing in V1, then attention should count as an *input* to V1, not an influence on its internal processing. Hence, he argues, processing in V1 *is* encapsulated after all. Our response is that the notion of informational encapsulation only makes sense if there is some basis for distinguishing between an inputs to a module and processes that influence the internal operation of the module, for it's the latter kind of influence that claims of encapsulation deny. If *any* informational influence on the internal processing of a mechanism can be reconceptualized as an input to that mechanism, and if influence *via* input is consistent with encapsulation, then the notion of informational encapsulation is vacuous.

We have already argued (§21.3.1) that dissociability is a dubious criterion for modularity. It's also of little help in the present connection, for contrary to what is often assumed, encapsulation bears no simple connection to dissociability. Consider the well-known diagram of the macaque visual system due to van Essen (figure 21.1).

We see here some 32 cortical 'areas,' as well as some subcortical areas. These areas are differentially sensitive to different sorts of stimuli and/or specialized for different sorts of processing (although typically not in an all-or-nothing fashion). Assuming that they are also susceptible of at least some degree of dissociation, we would appear to have (by the 1:1 and dissociability criteria) as many as 32 distinct modules depicted in this diagram. However, these cortical areas are also highly interconnected: van Essen traced 197 linkages (= roughly 40% of the $32 \times 31/2 \approx 500$ linkages that are in principle possible). Most of these linkages appear to be reciprocal, indicating that there is no simple sequential or hierarchical direction of information flow among the postulated modules; instead, each module talks to (and is talked to by) numerous others at numerous different stages of visual processing. This raises serious questions about how the dissociability criterion is supposed to line up with the encapsulation criterion for modularity and how the latter criterion is to be interpreted. Is the sort of interconnectedness found in figure 21.1 consistent with these areas being distinct modules? If so, it looks as though encapsulation (and perhaps modularity as well) come in degrees, rather than being all-or-nothing matters, in which case we need (i) some measure of degree of encapsulation and (ii) a theory about how this bears on judgments of modularity. If, on the other hand, modularists prefer to say that this degree of interconnectedness is *in*consistent with the idea that the areas form distinct modules, then it follows that distinctness of function and dissociability are not reliable criteria for individuating modules.

21.4.4 Modules and Independent Evolvability

Still another criterion for modularity is that modules are *independent targets of natural selection*. That is, selection must be able to change each of them independently of the others. This feature of modules is presupposed by EP's characteristic view of organisms as confronting a large collection of separate adaptive problems, each of which gets an independent evolved module by way of solution.

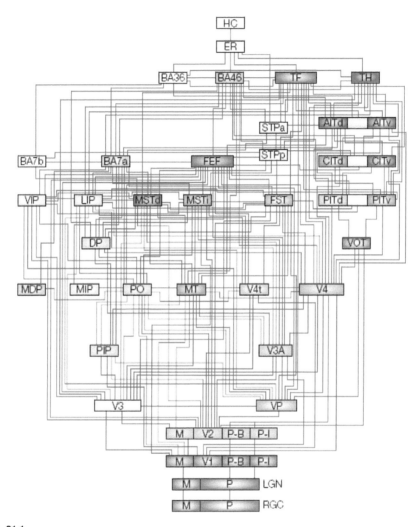

Figure 21.1
The hierarchy of visual areas in the macaque brain, showing 32 areas of visual cortex and their linkages, together with some subcortical and nonvisual connections. (From Felleman and van Essen, 1991.)

The independent evolvability criterion, however, is again problematic. For if a trait is to be an independent target of selection, it must be what Sterelny and Griffiths (1999) call a 'mosaic' rather than a 'connected' trait.[5] To use one of their examples, skin color is a plausible candidate for a mosaic trait because "it can evolve with relatively little change in the rest of the organism" (1999, p. 320). By contrast, having two lungs is a connected trait: you can't change this trait without changing a great deal else in the organism because lung number is influenced by the genes and developmental mechanisms that govern the bilateral symmetry of the organism. Hence, natural selection can only influence lung number by influencing these genes and developmental mechanisms, and this in turn would affect many other phenotypical features. Since lung number is not an independent target of selection—since it is part of the "bigger package" (Sterelny and Griffiths, 1999, p. 320)—it would be a mistake to try to give an adaptive explanation of our having two lungs *simpliciter*. Instead, what needs to be explained is the evolution of bilateral symmetry.

Evolutionary psychologists assume that modules are independently evolvable, that is, that they are mosaic traits (like skin color) rather than connected traits (like having two lungs). However, there is evidence that many human cognitive abilities may be connected rather than mosaic traits. For example, Finlay and Darlington (1995) show that brain structures change in size across species in a highly coordinated and predictable manner: homologous structures enlarge at different but stable rates when compared to overall brain size. It is thought that these regularities reflect deeply entrenched developmental constraints on the order of neurogenesis, suggesting that while natural selection can increase (or decrease) the size of the brain as a whole, the sizes of particular cortical regions cannot be changed independently, even in response to specific and pressing selective problems. Thus, natural selection may *not* be able to 'fine tune' the cortical regions responsible for (say) cheater detection or the perception of numerosity independently of the (allegedly) distinct cognitive modules that underlie other cognitive capacities like face recognition or language.

A further question concerns the relationship between the independent evolvability criterion and the other features of modules discussed above. We submit that there is no connection between these properties: independent evolvability does not entail, and is not entailed by, either independent disruptability or informational encapsulation. Indeed, it is a consequence of the arguments presented in this paper that there is *no connection whatsoever* between *any* of the properties—independent disruptability, informational encapsulation, innateness, independent evolvability—that are commonly ascribed to modules.

This is important, because it undermines a pattern of argument that is highly prevalent in the EP literature. Evolutionary psychologists provide evidence for the existence of a module in *some* sense (e.g. in the sense that performance on two tasks dissociates) and then go on to assume (without argument) that the module in question satisfies the other criteria discussed above as well. Thus, they slide from hypotheses of modularity in one of the various 'thin' senses we have discussed in this paper to claims about the existence of modules in a much 'thicker' and more substantive sense.

This slide is wholly unjustified. As an illustration, consider Cosmides and Tooby's (1992a) well-known experiments on the Wason selection task and their subsequent hypothesis of a 'cheater detection' module. Prima facie, what their experimental results show is that people behave differently (and in some respects more reliably) when dealing with conditionals framed as rules governing social exchange than they do when dealing with conditionals with other contents. Even if we accept that these results establish differential performance on cheater-detection tasks *tout court* (and not just those that involve conditionals—itself a big jump), they do *not* constitute evidence for the existence of a distinct cheater-detection module in any more robust sense. That is, they do not even remotely suggest that cheater detection is subserved by an independently-disruptable, informationally-encapsulated psychological mechanism which has been subject to distinct selection pressures and which as a consequence is genetically specified or 'innate' etc. It is of course conceivable, although (we think) unlikely, that a cheater detection module possessing all these features exists; our point is that Tooby and Cosmides' experiment provides no evidence that it does.

Our overall argument in §21.4 can be put as follows. Interpreted one way (as involving a sufficiently 'thin' conception of a module), EP's claims about modularity amount to little more than redescriptions of certain experimental results or evolutionary psychologists' functional speculations. So construed, claims about the existence of 'mental modules' are uncontroversial—but also uninteresting. Modularity claims become more contentful and more interesting as the 'thin' notion of a module is extended to include the other properties described above. However, not only is the evidence that would support such extensions is rarely provided, what we know about the brain makes it unlikely that there could be 'thick' mental modules for the sorts of high-level cognitive capacities that are EP's main theoretical focus.

21.5 Conclusion

Much of the appeal of EP derives from the fact that it appears to provide a way of 'biologizing' cognitive science, with evolutionary considerations supposedly providing powerful additional constraints on psychological theorizing. We think that this appearance is misleading. Evolutionary psychologists largely ignore the biological evidence that has the strongest scientific credentials and is most directly relevant to their claims about psychological mechanisms. This includes not only evidence from neurobiology, genetics, and developmental biology, but also any evidence from evolutionary biology, ethology and population genetics that threatens to undermine their armchair adaptationism. Their methods assume, wrongly, that one can usefully speculate about biological and psychological functions in ignorance of information about structure, genes, and development. Their central theoretical concept—modularity—is left fundamentally unclear. And their picture of the mind as 'massively modular' fails to do justice to many of its most important features, such as its capacity to engage in long-range planning and its remarkable cognitive and behavioral flexibility.

Notes for Chapter 21

1. We concede that our discussion does not even begin to explain how human beings manage to take account of a wide range of background information and act flexibly and reasonably. But modular theories are in far worse shape. They not only fail to provide a positive account of how the problem is solved, but also make assumptions that are inconsistent with the fact that we do (somehow) solve the problem. Alternatively, and to the extent that they do attempt to accommodate this fact, they are forced to abandon basic commitments of the modular account.

2. Dissociations are often thought to particularly compelling evidence of independent modules when there is a 'double dissociation' of tasks, that is, when a pair of individuals is observed, one of whom can perform task A but not task B, and the other of whom can perform B but not A.

3. This issue is the subject of considerable debate. See Shallice, 1988 and Glymour, 2001 for surveys.

4. See, e.g., Vargha-Khadem and Passingham, 1990, Anderson et al., 1993, Merzenich et al., 1996.

5. Gilbert (2000, 693ff.) calls this a requirement of 'modularity'—not to be confused with the cognitive modularity that concerns EP.

VI   BODY AND WORLD

Part VI: Body and World

Mathematics is the paradigmatic abstract pursuit. Computation, insofar as it is understood as a branch of applied mathematics, would seem to share some of math's disembodied nature. And the very possibility of artificial intelligence would seem to rest on the fact that it doesn't really matter *what* is doing the computing—silicon and brains are all the same, so long as they can implement the same functions. Yet when we look at actual intelligent organisms, it is obvious that much of our intelligence is devoted just to getting around the world. We are, in Graziano (2008)'s apt phrase, "intelligent movement machines." A child learning to climb the monkey bars is engaged in something deeply intelligent—and yet it is very hard to see how to capture that intelligence in pure mathematics without leaving out something important. Watching an ant make its way over hills of sand, Simon reasonably wondered how much of the observed complexity in behavior can be attributed to the ant and how much can be attributed to the world through which it moves (Simon, 1969).

The three papers in this concluding part grapple with various aspects of this insight. They ask to what extent understanding intelligence, or cognition generally, requires attending to the active, physical systems in which it is instantiated (in which the mind is said to be "embodied") and the world in which those systems are working (in which the mind is said to be "embedded")?

These two claims are the focus of Haugeland's classic "Mind Embodied and Embedded" (chapter 22). Starting with Simon's insight about the ant, Haugeland argues that the coupling between ourselves and the world might be tight enough that it is hard to decompose the mind, body, and world into independent components in a mechanism. Many of our activities in the world require tightly coupled interactions between what's going on "in the head" and in the world itself. A person playing Tetris might manipulate the falling objects so they can just "see" how they fit into the row beneath them, and a person driving to Denver might just get on I-70 and exit when the signs instruct them to do so. These are examples of what has come to be called "active externalism." Yet Haugeland seems to propose that meaning is also world-involving, scaffolding itself on a "web of significance" in worldly objects or on one's commitment to participate in a community of concept-users (often referred to as "meaning externalism"). (See also the discussion of externalized views of intentionality in the introduction to part III.)

Note that it is possible to be *embodied* without being *human*. A key commitment of much work in this area is that the true test for AI will be mobile robots that interact with the world in real time while doing complex, real-world tasks.

"Intelligence without Representation," by Brooks (chapter 23), argues from an engineering perspective that the best way to build autonomous mobile robots is to avoid having them build complex models of the world. As Brooks suggests, the robot can let the world be its own best representation. If it needs to see if there's a bottle of root beer in the fridge, it might be better to have it open the door and look around than it would be to have it store and update an internal representation of FRIDGECONTENTS. Similarly, Brooks argues, we can build intelligent machines without supposing (à la Fodor) that there is some central system that integrates all of the inputs into a central cognition or decision mechanism (an executive or a self); minimal constraints among low-level processing units might suffice to produce all the intelligent behaviors we want. Rather than track and manipulate static facts about what's true, he argues, a good robot divides up the world in terms of what it can do to it and acts on the information required to get tasks done.

Finally, Webb's "What Does Biorobotics Offer Philosophy? A Tale of Two Navigation Systems" (chapter 24) canvasses the fruitful overlap between robotics and insect neuroscience that has been done since the mid-1990s. Many of the other AI approaches detailed in this volume require substantial computational resources. By contrast, the desert ant and the honeybee are capable of prodigious feats of navigation despite having orders of magnitude fewer neurons than humans. Webb demonstrates that many of the mechanisms by which this is achieved are now reasonably clear, but that the upshot for representational theories of cognition remains a contested question. What is clear, however, is that there is a lot to learn from both studying and building simple, embodied systems that rely only on relatively lightweight representational systems.

Combinations and Additions

The material in this part is in dialogue—sometimes explicitly—with the material in parts I and II. It is useful to contrast (say) the traditional Marrian focus on the computational and algorithmic levels with the implementation-focused material in this chapter. When we erase the conceptual boundaries between mind, body, and world, we also blur the distinction between the abstract characterization of the task and the mechanisms in terms of which it is implemented: the mechanisms are themselves part of the computation.

Robotics is an important part of modern engineering, but much of this work now goes on in proprietary environments. There is a lot of work on robotics in ethics and cognate fields, especially as robots press into fields like transportation and nursing. We have set aside ethics of AI, however, and recent philosophical work on robotics in other subfields appears to be rather thin on the ground. This represents a good opportunity for future work by enthusiastic philosophers. One trend worth noting is the incorporation of uncertainty into robotics: a realistic robot cannot be entirely sure it knows what is going on or whether its actions have had the desired effect. Modeling robotic decision-making in terms of Partially Observable Markov Decision Processes (POMDPs) has become popular. POMDPs arise naturally as extensions of the reinforcement learning (RL) techniques discussed in chapter 16. This has become more relevant for robotics as solvers for POMDPs with realistic numbers of variables have been discovered (see Kurniawati 2021 for a recent review).

For readers who want a peek into the era about which Brooks writes, Errol Morris's 1997 documentary *"Fast, Cheap, and Out of Control"* features some of Brooks's robots in action and is an interesting exploration of the idea of distributed intelligence more generally.

Embodiment has sometimes been thought to solve the issues about intentionality raised in part III: crudely speaking, the Chinese room may not have intentionality, but an appropriately configured robot moving about in a world *would*. This possibility has been raised and discussed extensively in the responses to Searle's arguments (chapter 12 of this volume).

Dynamic Systems.   Most models of computation familiar to working philosophers are digital, and advances in AI have come almost exclusively in the digital space. Yet as Maley pointed out in chapter 5 of this volume, there are analog models of computation as well. Furthermore, analog computation has long had a place at the AI table, beginning with Wiener (1948). The cybernetic tradition continues to inform both robotics and AI, including the predictive processing models discussed in part IV. When *Mind Design II* was published, there was considerable enthusiasm about so-called Dynamic Systems Theory (DST). DST argues for a so-called *dynamic* approach to cognition, on which cognition is best modelled using continuous models like those offered by differential equations. The focus of the dynamic systems theorists is often squarely on real-time action by embodied systems interacting continuously with the world. Initial enthusiasm for DST appears to have waned a bit—no doubt in part because differential equations remain mathematically heavy going, whereas the basics of digital computers are very easy to grasp. Yet DST has found many applications and continues to form an important research program in philosophy of mind.

- Van Gelder (1995) presents one of the first defenses of DST. This article emphasized many of the themes that came to characterize the dynamic approach, including the claim that analog computation is a better model of the human mind than symbolic processors. Van Gelder uses the Watt governor (a mechanism for maintaining constant output speed from an inconstant steam engine) as an example to show how complex tasks can be performed by analog systems that do not symbolically represent phenomena in any traditional sense. His article "Dynamics and Cognition," exploring similar themes, appeared in *Mind Design II*.
- Chemero (2000) defends the idea that dynamical systems are an important component of an anti-representationalist approach to mind. Chemero (2013) (drawn from his longer 2009 book of the same title) discusses the historical relationships between DST, Gibsonian ecological psychology, and anti-representationalism. While this package remains a minority view in philosophy of mind, it continues to attract strident defenders who find in it an antidote to a lasting heritage of Cartesian separation of mind and body.

- Pushback to the dynamic systems approach often focused on the question of representation. Bechtel (1998) responds to van Gelder, arguing that dynamical systems, including the Watt governor, do represent phenomena, even if they do not do so digitally.
- Clark (1998) is a cautious response to early dynamicist enthusiasm, suggesting that we might be able to get by with non-symbolic processing for some functions but that more complex cognition may well require symbolic representation of the world.

Active Externalism.   Many approaches emphasize a tight connection between mind and world, especially in skilled action. The connection is still a merely causal relationship, albeit a particularly tight one: the mind itself depends only on the brain, and remains safely locked inside the bounds of the skull. Some authors have gone even further and suggest that the mind can actually be *constituted* by external objects: that is, in the right cases, your mind literally *extends* into the environment itself. The so-called extended mind hypothesis is interesting for AI for at least two reasons. On the one hand, it suggests that the right unit of analysis of minds is brains/machines plus environments. Current AI might be missing the scaffolded environment that is key to human intelligence. On the other hand, it suggests that tight integration with computational systems—smartphones, Google, and the like—literally expands our own cognitive capacities. Note that this is parallel to but distinct from the questions about *content* externalism raised in the discussion of part III— there, the question was about whether two things with identical insides could have different contents of thought, whereas here, the question is much more about how to understand the mind itself.

- Clark and Chalmers (1998) is the classic paper arguing that mental states can literally extend into the environment. Notably, it requires relatively modest commitments. Indeed, the argument for the extended mind can be read as a direct consequence of Haugeland's claim of tight coupling plus some plausible functionalist principles. Clark (2008) further extends the idea that technology literally extends the mind.
- Much of the pushback to the extended mind thesis revolves around the difference between causal and constitutive relationships. My camellias and I share many tight causal connections: I give them carbon dioxide and water and love, and they give me oxygen and beauty in return. But very few think that the flowers are literally part of my mind. Adams and Aizawa (2009) is one of several papers by the same authors that argues for a strong distinction between mere coupling and actual constitution. They suggest that defenders of the extended mind fail to respect that difference.
- Subsequent work on the extended mind has teased out a variety of different possible relationships between mind and world. Newen et al. (2018) summarizes work in the "embodied, embedded, enacted, and extended," or "4E" approach to cognition, the collective name for the variety of sophisticated approaches that have sprung up to deal with aspects of embodiment.

- Seth (2013) connects predictive processing models with concerns about embodiment and interoception, and so this article might fruitfully be read in conjunction both with this part and with Clark's piece in part IV (chapter 17).
- Hewitson et al. (2018) is an incisive review and commentary on several recent strands of 4E cognition and attempts to link them to cognitive science. The sections on 'morphological' computation are particularly relevant to thinking about robotics.
- Finally, the idea that intelligence requires embodiment was a constant theme in Brooks's writing. Brooks (1990) is a nice complement to the included reading.

Mind Embodied and Embedded

22

John Haugeland
1998

22.1 Intimacy

Among Descartes's most lasting and consequential achievements has been his constitution
of the mental as an independent ontological domain. By taking the mind as a substance,
with cognitions as its modes, he accorded them a status as self-standing and determinate on
their own, without essential regard to other entities. Only with this metaphysical conception in place, could the idea of solipsism—the idea of an intact ego existing with nothing
else in the universe—so much as make sense. And behind that engine have trailed the sorry
boxcars of hyperbolic doubt, the mind-body problem, the problem of the external world,
the problem of other minds, and so on.

Although the underlying assumptions have been under fire, off and on, at least since
Hegel—including with renewed intensity in recent years—most of the challenges have
been of a general sort that I will call "interrelationist". Characteristically, they accept as
a premise that the mental, or at any rate the cognitive, has some essential feature, such as
intentionality or normativity, and then argue that this feature is impossible except through
participation in some supra-individual network of relations. For instance, accounts based
on interpretation and the "principle of charity", such as those of Donald Davidson and
Daniel Dennett (with roots in Quine), ascribe contentful states only as components of an
overall pattern that is rational *in context*—that is, in relation to the system's situation or environment. Similarly, social practice accounts, such as those of Richard Rorty and Robert
Brandom (with roots in Sellars and Wittgenstein), understand the norms that enable reasoning and content to be instituted *communally*—that is, in relation to the practices and
responses of others. On neither approach is solipsism even a coherent possibility.

Interrelationist arguments are *holistic* in the specific sense that they take cognitive phenomena to be members of some class of phenomena, each of which has its relevant character only by virtue of its determinate relations to the others—that relevant character being,
in effect, nothing other than its "place" in the larger pattern or whole. The obvious example is a move or play in a game: pushing around a little piece of plastic shaped like a

turret could only amount to a *rook* move in an appropriate spatial and temporal context of other chess pieces and moves. To call it a rook move apart from any such context is simply nonsense. Likewise, so the reasoning goes, to regard any phenomenon as intentional or normative in isolation from the relevant whole, is also nonsense. And since, in the case of mental attributions, the relevant whole must include the individual's environment and/or community, the Cartesian independence of the mental realm is impossible.

While undeniably important and compelling, considerations like these seem to me seriously incomplete and potentially distorting. They remain theoretical or intellectual in a way that not only does not undermine but actually reinforces an aspect of the Cartesian separation that is still so pervasive as to be almost invisible. In particular, interrelationist accounts retain a principled distinction between the mental and the corporeal—a distinction that is reflected in contrasts like semantics versus syntax, the space of reasons versus the space of causes, or the intentional versus the physical vocabulary. (Notice that each of these contrasts can be heard either as higher versus lower "level" or as inner versus outer "sphere".) The contrary of *this* separation—or battery of separations—is not interrelationist holism, but something that I would like to call the *intimacy* of the mind's embodiment and embeddedness in the world. The term 'intimacy' is meant to suggest more than just necessary interrelation or interdependence but a kind of *commingling* or *integralness* of mind, body, and world—that is, to undermine their very distinctness. The challenge is as much to spell out what this could mean as to make a case for it. Indeed, no sooner does such a possibility seem intelligible at all, than ways to bring out its plausibility and significance turn up everywhere.

There is little original in what follows. The strategy will be to bring some well-known principles of systems analysis to bear on the mind-body-world "system" in a way that refocuses questions of division and unity, and then to canvass a selection of investigations and proposals—some fairly recent, others not—in the light of this new focus. The hope is that these superficially disparate ideas, none of them new, will seem to converge around the theme of intimacy in a way that illuminates and supports them all. Sorting and aligning issues in this manner has sometimes been discussed under titles like 'embedded computation' and 'situated cognition'.

22.2   Simon's ant

The simplest introduction to the range of phenomena I want to explore is the beautiful parable with which Herbert Simon opens chapter three of *The Sciences of the Artificial*, a chapter to which he gives the subtitle "Embedding Artifice in Nature".

> We watch an ant make his [sic] laborious way across a wind- and wave-molded beach. He moves ahead, angles to the right to ease his climb up a steep dunelet, detours around a pebble, stops for a moment to exchange information with a compatriot. Thus he makes his weaving, halting way back to his home. . . . Viewed as a geometric figure, the ant's path is

irregular, complex, hard to describe. But its complexity is really a complexity in the surface of the beach, not a complexity in the ant. (1969, 63–64)

Simon summarizes the lesson of his parable twice, word-for-word the same, except for those indicating the subject of the behavior.

> An ant [A man] viewed as a behaving system, is quite simple. The apparent complexity of its [his] behavior over time is largely a reflection of the complexity of the environment in which it [he] finds itself [himself]. (64–65; italics in originals.)

This lesson can be taken in two rather different ways. On the one hand, one might heave a sigh of scientific relief: understanding people as behaving systems is going to be easier than we thought, because so much of the apparent complexity in their behavior is due to factors external to them, and hence external to our problem. On the other hand, one might see the problem itself as transformed: since the relevant complexity in the observed behavior depends on so much more than the behaving system itself, the investigation cannot be restricted to that system alone, but must extend to some larger structure of which it is only a fraction.

That Simon himself took the lesson in the first way is evident from the two "hedges" that he immediately offers—both of which strike me as quite remarkable (and ultimately untenable).

> Now I should like to hedge my bets a little. Instead of trying to consider the "whole man," fully equipped with glands and viscera, I should like to limit the discussion to Homo sapiens, "thinking man." . . . I should also like to hedge my bets in a second way, for a human being can store away in memory a great furniture of information that can be evoked by appropriate stimuli. Hence I would like to view this information-packed memory less as part of the organism than as part of the environment to which it adapts. (65; second hedge only in the second edition.)

With these qualifications in place, Simon can safely turn his attention away not only from sand dunes and pebbles, but also from human knowledge, culture, the body, and the world, so as to concentrate on cryptarithmetic and nonsense syllables—all in support of his view that the human "information processing system" (essentially a glorified CPU) must be serial and rather simple. In effect, he wants to pare away enough of the real human being that what's left is strikingly like an ant.

The alternative reading of the parable, however, is already suggested by the history of artificial intelligence research itself. Perhaps the largest-scale trend in this history has been precisely *counter* to the suggestion of relegating knowledge ("information-packed memory") to the "environment"—that is, regarding it as external to the problem of understanding intelligence. The essential point of systems based on semantic nets, frames, internal models, prototypes, and "common sense" is that, except in very special circumstances, the intelligent performance of a system depends more directly on the *particular* interconnectedness and organization of its knowledge, than on any reasoning or processing power. Note that the issue is not the quantity of information, but its specific quality—its *concrete* structure. Everything is in the *details*—that *these* items are grouped together, that there is a cross-reference from *here* to *there*, that *this* topic appears in *that* index with *those* keys—in such a way that abstracting the form of the knowledge from its content would make no sense. In other words, according to this trend in AI, to study (or build) *intelligent* systems is, above all, to study (or build) large, concrete knowledge structures—*not* simple processors.

Until recently, however, nearly all of this research has retained the assumption that the relevant "furniture of information" is implemented as complex symbol structures that are, in many respects, just like the contents of the traditional Cartesian mind. In particular, they are internal to the individual agent, and different in kind from any physiology or hardware. The explorations that follow can be seen as trying out the second reading of Simon's parable in a more radical way. If the significant complexity of intelligent behavior depends intimately on the concrete details of the agent's embodiment and worldly situation, then perhaps intelligence as such should be understood as characteristic, in the first instance, of some more comprehensive structure than an internal, disembodied "mind", whether artificial or natural.

22.3 Components, systems, and interfaces

Of course, human intelligence is embodied and embedded; nobody denies that. The question is how important this fact is to the nature of intelligence. One way to put the question is to ask whether we can in principle partition off the intellect (or mind) from the body and/or the world. "Partition off" does not this time mean isolation or removal. That is, we can grant the holist thesis that mind would be impossible in the *absence* of body and/or world, and still ask whether it can be understood as a distinct and well-defined *subsystem* within the necessary larger whole. But this requires a brief discussion of the principles for dividing systems into distinct subsystems along nonarbitrary lines.

It is a fine testimony to the depth and breadth of Simon's slender volume that, in a later chapter, entitled "The Architecture of Complexity", he addresses this very issue: On what principled basis are large systems decomposable into subsystems? And, to answer it, he invites us to

> distinguish between the interactions *among* subsystems, on the one hand, and the interactions *within* subsystems—that is, among the parts of those subsystems—on the other. The interactions at the different levels may be, and often will be, of different orders of magnitude. (209)

What is he getting at? Consider a television set in comparison to a block of marble. The former, we are inclined to say, is highly systematic, composed of many nested interacting subsystems, whereas the latter is hardly systematic at all. Why? One suggestion might be that the TV is composed of many different kinds of material, arranged in complicated shapes and patterns, whereas the marble contains relatively few materials and is nearly (though not quite) homogeneous. This cannot be the right answer, however, because a computer microchip (an integrated circuit) is surely more systematic than a compost of rotting table scraps, even though the former contains relatively few materials and is nearly homogeneous, whereas the latter is diverse and messy.

Rather, the difference must lie in the nature of the discontinuities within the whole, and the character of the interactions across them. To see this, think of *how* the TV is organized. If we suppose that, at some level of analysis, it consists of a thousand components, then we can ask how these components are distinguished. One possible decomposition would be neatly geometrical: assuming the set is roughly cubical, divide it into ten equal slices along each axis, to yield a thousand smaller cubes, of which the entire set exactly consists. What's wrong with this "decomposition"? Well, consider one of the "component" cubes—say, one near the center. It contains half of a transistor, two thirds of a capacitor, several fragments of wire, a small triangle of glass from the picture tube, and a lot of hot air. Obviously, this is an incoherent jumble that makes no sense—even though a thousand equally crazy "pieces", put together *exactly* right, would make up a TV set. Our task is to say why.

A resistor is a quintessential electronic component. It has two wires coming out of it, and its only "job", as the name suggests, is to *resist* (to some specified degree) the flow of electricity between them. It doesn't matter how it does that job—nor, within limits, does anything else about it matter—just so long as it does that job properly and reliably, and doesn't interfere with any other components. An electronic component, like a resistor, is a relatively independent and self-contained portion of a larger electronic circuit. This means several things. In the first place, it means that the resistor does not interact with the rest of the system except through its circuit connections—namely, those two wires. That is, nothing that happens outside of it affects anything that happens inside, or vice versa, except by affecting the currents in those connections. (To be more precise, all effects other than these are negligible, either because they are so slight or because they are irrelevant.) Second, it means that the relevant interactions through those connections are themselves well-defined, reliable, and relatively simple. For instance, it's *only* a flow of electrons, not of chemicals, contagion, or contraband. Finally, it means that it is not itself a composite of components at a comparable level of independence and self-containedness: a resistor plus a capacitor do not add up to a distinct component. (However, a suitable larger arrangement of resistors, capacitors, and transistors might add up to a pre-amp—which could in turn be a component in a higher-level system.)

An electronic component's connecting wires constitute its "interface" to the rest of the system. In careful usage, the notions of component, system, and interface should all be understood together and in terms of one another. A *component* is a relatively independent and selfcontained portion of a system in the sense that it relevantly interacts with other components only through interfaces between them (and contains no internal interfaces at the same level). An *interface* is a point of interactive "contact" between components such that the relevant interactions are well-defined, reliable, and relatively simple. A *system* is a relatively independent and self-contained composite of components interacting at interfaces. So the pre-amp mentioned above would be both a component and a system; such a component system is often called a *subsystem*. Though these concepts are all defined in terms of one another, they are not therefore circular or empty, because they collectively involve the further notions of relative independence, simplicity, relevance, and interaction.

An important consequence is that genuine components are in principle replaceable by functional equivalents. For instance, a resistor in an electronic circuit can be replaced by any other that has the same resistance value (and perhaps meets a few other specifications). The circuit as a whole will continue to function as before, because all that mattered about that resistor in the first place was its resistance via a simple interface—and, by stipulation, the replacement matches that. (Of course, rifles had components before Eli Whitney invented interchangeable parts. But that was basically a difference of degree—specifically, of *how* well-defined the interfaces were and *how readily* interchangeable the parts were.)

Return now to the thousand little cubes making up a TV set. Are they *components*, in the strict sense? Obviously not, because they are not even "relatively" independent and self-contained. Or, what comes to the same thing, the surfaces separating them are not proper interfaces. That is, the interactions required across those surfaces, for the set to work, are absurdly complex and irregular, with no hope of clear definition or reliable implementation. Just imagine trying to assemble a new set from a thousand such cubes taken one each from a thousand other sets! Yet a TV can easily be made out of parts taken from others, if only the divisions are made at genuine interfaces.

The point is even more vivid if we consider instead a system that moves, such as an engine or an animal: then the cubes wouldn't so much as contain the same physical hunks through time, and a consistent "interface" wouldn't even be conceivable. Yet decomposition of such systems into simpler components is perfectly standard and straightforward, if their boundaries are allowed to move with them. For instance, a connecting rod between a piston and crankshaft is relatively self-contained, and has very well-defined interfaces in its two bearing surfaces; and all that matters about them is that their axes be kept reliably parallel and a certain distance apart. Again, the component as such is delimited by its simple, reliable interfaces.

22.4   Incorporeal interfaces

Examples like electronic circuits, mechanisms, and even organisms can leave the impression that the boundaries of components and subsystems are set by corporeal discontinuities—virtually complete, except at the interfaces, where narrowly defined contacts are permitted. It is particularly important for our purposes to counter this impression, since the corporeal discontinuity between our bodies and the world—the very discontinuity that determines these bodies as bodies—misleadingly enhances the apparent significance of bodily surfaces as relevant interfaces for the understanding of other phenomena, such as intelligence.

That systematic interfaces need not coincide with corporeal surfaces can be shown by example. Large organizations, like governments, corporations, and universities, are almost always subdivided into various divisions, departments, and units. But the correspondence between these demarcations and corporeal boundaries is at best haphazard, and never essential. Indeed, as more and more business is conducted via worldwide communication networks, the physical locations of personnel and data become practically irrelevant. What matter instead are the access codes, permission levels, distribution lists, private addresses, priority orderings, and so on, that determine where information flows and what gets attended to. It is the structure of these, ultimately, that determines departmentalization and hierarchy.

Members of a single department or unit tend to work more closely together, sharing resources and concerns, than do members of different departments. Likewise, units of the same division interact more often and more intimately than do units of different divisions; and so on. Nothing depends, ultimately, on who is in what building, or on what continent— as Simon himself clearly appreciated.

> Most physical and biological hierarchies are described in spatial terms. We detect the organelles in a cell in the way we detect the raisins in a cake—they are "visibly" differentiated substructures localized spatially in the larger structure. On the other hand, we propose to identify social hierarchies not by observing who lives close to whom but by observing who interacts with whom. These two points of view can be reconciled by defining hierarchy in terms of intensity of interaction, but observing that in most biological and physical systems relatively intense interaction implies relative spatial propinquity. (199)

"Intensity" of interaction here means something like how "tightly" things are coupled, or even how "close-knit" they are—that is, the degree to which the behavior of each affects or constrains the other. Heard in this way, it can serve as a generic notion encompassing the mechanical integrity of a connecting rod and the electrical unity of a resistor, as well as the social or institutional cohesiveness of a group. The different parts of a connecting rod interact so intensely, for example, that they always move rigidly together; by comparison, its interactions with the piston and the crankshaft are "looser," allowing independent rotation about a common axis. Further, comparing these intensities can be the first step in accounts, respectively, of relative independence and interface simplicity; for each can be seen as a matter of less intense interaction—looser coupling—externally, as compared to internally.

22.5   Intelligibility as the principle of decomposition

What Simon mentions only in passing, however, without the emphasis it will need for our purposes, is the *motivation* for treating systems in this way. In a brief subsection entitled "Near Decomposability and Comprehensibility", he writes:

> The fact that many complex systems have a nearly decomposable, hierarchic structure is a major facilitating factor enabling us to understand, describe, and even 'see' such systems and their parts. (218–219)

'Nearly decomposable systems' is his term for systems of relatively independent interacting components with simple interfaces between them. So the point about comprehensibility can be paraphrased as follows: *finding*, in something complicated and hard to understand, a set of simple reliable interfaces, dividing it into relatively independent components, is a way of rendering it *intelligible*.

The significance of this can be brought out by approaching it from another side. Biological and electronic systems are also in some sense physical—as, indeed, are social and (other) information systems. But in that case, more than one kind of interaction, and accordingly more than one kind of decomposition, would seem to be possible in what is somehow the same "stuff". How, then, are we to decide *which* interactions and decompositions are the important ones? Once this question is asked, however, the answer is obvious: it depends on what we're interested in—which is to say, it depends on what phenomena we are trying to understand. Thus, when we turn to the mind-body-world "system", and wonder how, perhaps, to decompose it, our considerations will perforce be relative to some prior identification of what is to be understood.

Part of the reason, for instance, that the structure of the beach is as important as the structure of the ant in Simon's parable is that the ant's actual path is determined in real time by *close interaction* between the ant and the concrete details of the beach's surface. If, by contrast, the ant were responding to an internal model or representation of the beach, instead of responding the beach itself, or if it just contained a list of steps and turns which it followed slavishly, then the importance of the beach would be reduced or eliminated. The other part of the reason, however, and in some sense the prior part, is that what we want to understand in the first place is the ant's *path*. If we were interested instead in it's respiration or its immune system, then the beach would be largely irrelevant, regardless of how tightly the ant is coupled to it when walking. In other words, *which* close interactions matter, when considering the scope and structure of systems, depends fundamentally on what we're interested in—that is, what we're trying to understand.

Here, then, is where the account of decomposition takes hold. If what we're interested in is the path, and if the ant relies mostly on its own internal structure to guide its steps, counting on the ground just for friction and support, then the ant and beach are two relatively independent components or systems, with a well-defined simple interface at the soles of its feet. If, on the other hand, there is constant close coupling between the ant and the details of the beach surface, and if this coupling is crucial in determining the actual path, then, for purposes of understanding that path, the ant and beach must be regarded more as an integrated unit than as a pair of distinct components. This is the simplest archetype of what I mean by *intimacy*.

22.6 Brooks's subsumption architecture

Insect examples have all the advantages and disadvantages of simple archetypes. They are, of course, wonderfully clear, as far as they go; but they don't go very far. We will try to work our way up toward more interesting cases via a series of intermediaries. Simon muses at one point (64) that if someone were to build insect-like robots, their behavior on a beach would be much like that of his ant. Little did he know that, two decades later, such a project would be in full swing in the laboratory of Rod Brooks at MIT. It is perhaps slightly ironic that part of what drives Brooks's efforts is a dissatisfaction with the symbol-manipulation approach to artificial intelligence pioneered by Simon and Allen Newell in the 1950's. As we shall see, however, this is no accident.

Brooks's best known "creature," named *Herbert* (after Simon), is a self-powered, wheeled contraption, about the size of a small trash can, with various sensors, one moveable arm on top, and surprisingly little compute power. It's lot in life is to buzz around the MIT AI Lab looking for empty soda pop cans, pick them up, and return them to a central bin. Herbert was built (around 1990) and actually worked (albeit clumsily). What makes this noteworthy, compared, say, to robots of the 1970's, is that the labs and offices in which Herbert worked were in no way specially prepared: there were no guidelines painted on the floors or walls, the typical mess and clutter of real work space were not cleaned up, people carried on with their own business as usual, and so on. So Herbert managed to negotiate a relatively inhospitable, changing environment, do its job, and stay mostly out of trouble—with roughly the proficiency of a crustacean.

What matters for us is not this modest success but the design principles on which Herbert is based. Two points deserve emphasis. First, Brooks uses what he calls the "subsumption architecture", according to which systems are decomposed not in the familiar way by local functions or faculties, but rather by global *activities* or *tasks*.

> [This] alternative decomposition makes no distinction between peripheral systems, such as vision, and central systems. Rather the fundamental slicing up of an intelligent system is in the orthogonal direction dividing it into *activity* producing subsystems. Each activity or behavior producing system individually connects sensing to action. We refer to an activity producing system as a *layer*. An activity is a pattern of interactions with the world. Another name for our activities might well be skill . . . (1991, 146; see also Chapter 23 of this volume, p. 472)

Thus, Herbert has one subsystem for detecting and avoiding obstacles in its path, another for wandering around, a third for finding distant soda cans and homing in on them, a fourth for noticing nearby soda cans and putting its hand around them, a fifth for detecting something between its fingers and closing them, and so on . . . fourteen in all. What's striking is that these are all complete input/output systems, more or less independent of each other. They can't be entirely independent, of course, because, for instance, Herbert has only one set of wheels; so if two different subsystems undertake to move the robot at the same moment, one must dominate—through some interface. But the bulk of the interactions, the tightest couplings, are *within* the respective activity layers—including, as Brooks explicitly points out, *interactions with the world*.

In other words, each of the various activities of this system is like the walking of Simon's ant. Each involves constant close interaction with certain specific aspects of the environment, and can only be understood in terms thereof. So the structures of the respective aspects of the environment are at least as important as the structures of the internal portions of the corresponding layers in rendering the different activities intelligible. Herbert has fourteen relatively independent, closely knit subsystems, each encompassing *both* structures within the robot *and* structures outside of it. To put it one last way, one that foreshadows where we're going, each of Herbert's highest-level subsystems is somewhat mental, somewhat bodily, and somewhat worldly. That is, according to Simon's principles of intensity of interaction, the primary division is not into mind, body, and world, but rather into "layers" that cut across these in various ways. And, in particular, the outer surface of the robot is *not* a primary interface. (Of course, there may be further subdivisions within the respective layers, which may or may not take portions of this surface as subsidiary interfaces.)

22.7 Perceiving instead of representing

The second point that deserves emphasis, closely related to the first, is captured in a slogan that Brooks proposes: *The world is its own best model.* (1990, 5) This is precisely to repudiate designs like the alternatives I mentioned earlier for Simon's ant: that is, the ant should *not* contain any inner model or representation of the beach, nor an inner list of step and turn instructions. These alternatives would substitute complexity *within* the organism for intensity of interaction *between* the organism and its environment. But Brooks, as his slogan indicates, is very much against that. Why?

We can put the answer in another slogan that Brooks would probably like: *Perception is cheap, representation expensive.* Such a slogan might surprise many AI workers, who are acutely aware of how difficult pattern recognition can be. But the point is that *good enough* perception is cheaper than *good enough* representation—where that means "good enough" to avoid serious errors. The trouble with representation is that, to be good enough, it must be relatively complete and relatively up to date, both of which are costly in a dynamic environment. Perception, by contrast, can remain happily *ad hoc*, dealing with concrete questions only as they arise. To take a homely example, it would be silly, for most purposes, to try to *keep track of* what shelf everything in the refrigerator is currently on; if and when you want something, just *look*.

Why would anyone have supposed otherwise? The answer lies in two deep assumptions that have informed symbolic AI from the beginning—including the work of Newell and Simon. The first is that intelligence is best manifested in *solving problems*, especially *hard* problems. The second is that problems are best solved by a process of *reasoning*: working from a statement of the problem and such ancillary knowledge as is available to a statement of the solution. The greatest triumphs in the history of the field are its demonstrations that these ideals *can* be realized mechanically—principally via formal inference, heuristically guided search, and structured knowledge representation. But notice how they bias the orientation toward representation and away from perception. Not only must the problem and the relevant knowledge be represented, generally in some symbolic formalism, but so also all the intermediate states that are explored on the way to the solution. The generation, use, and management of all these representations then becomes the paramount concern.

Perception, under such a regime, is reduced to a peripheral channel through which the problem is initially posed, and incidental facts are supplied; it might as well be a teletype. In most of AI, in fact, the process of perception has been conceived as *transduction*: some special preprocessor takes optical or auditory input, "recognizes" it, and then produces a symbolic output for the main system—not unlike what the system could have gotten from a teletype. What's pertinent about a teletype here is that it's a narrow-bandwidth device—the very antithesis of tight coupling.

For instance, the number of "bits" of information in the input to a perceptual system is enormous compared to the number in a typical symbolic description. So a "visual transducer" that responds to a sleeping brown dog with some expression like "Lo, a sleeping brown dog" has effected a huge data reduction. And this is usually regarded as a benefit, because, without such a reduction, a *symbolic* system would be overwhelmed. But it is also a serious bottleneck in the system's ability to be in close touch with its environment. Organisms with perceptual systems not encumbered by such bottlenecks could have significant advantages in sensitivity and responsiveness. The alternative "wide bandwidth" coupling, however, is precisely what, by Simon's systems-analytic criterion, would undermine or downgrade the organism/environment boundary as an important decompositional interface—just as Brooks proposes.

Models that emphasize internal symbolic representations insinuate bottlenecks into the understanding of action, just as they do for perception, and for much the same reason. The product of a rational problem-solving process is a low-bandwidth sequence of symbol structures, which can either report the results (say, on a teletype) or send instructions to an "output transducer". But skillful or adept engagement with a situation is as likely to profit from a wide-band-width coupling as is responsiveness to it. (We will return to this following the next section.)

In the meantime, notice that the very distinction between perception and action is itself artificially emphasized and sharpened by the image of a central processor or mind working *between* them, receiving "input" from the one and then (later) sending "output" to the other. The primary instance is rather *interaction*, which is simultaneously perceptive and active, richly integrated in real time. Thus, what's noteworthy about our refrigerator aptitudes is not just, or even mainly, that we can visually identify what's there, but rather the fact that we can, easily and reliably, reach around the milk and over the baked beans to lift out the orange juice—without spilling any of them. This high-bandwidth hand-eye coordination—or, better, hand-eye-refrigerator coordination—is what Brooks calls an "activity" or "skill" (though much more advanced than his robots). There is little reason to believe that symbol processing has much to do with it—unless one is already committed to the view that *reasoning* must underlie *all* flexible competence.

22.8   Affordance and ecological optics

The psychologist James J. Gibson makes several related points at a level somewhat higher than insects. Early in *The Ecological Approach to Visual Perception*, he begins a section entitled "The Mutuality of Animal and Environment" by explaining that

> the words *animal* and *environment* make an inseparable pair. Each term implies the other. No animal could exist without an environment surrounding it. Equally, although not so obvious, an environment implies an animal (or at least an organism) to be surrounded. This means that the surface of the earth, millions of years before life developed on it, was not an environment, properly speaking. (1979, 8)

This is not a fussy semantic quibble, but a subtle observation about levels and units of intelligibility. We can only understand animals *as perceivers* if we consider them as inseparably related to an environment, which is itself understood in terms appropriate to that animal.

Central to Gibson's "ecological approach" is his account of *what* it is that an animal perceives and *how*. Visual perception cannot be understood, he maintains, if one starts from the perspective of *physical* optics. A system that sees—a sighted animal—is not responsive, in the first instance, to physically simple properties of light, like color and brightness, but rather to visible features of the environment that matter to it. Gibson calls such features "affordances".

> The *affordances* of the environment are what it *offers* the animal, what it *provides* or *furnishes*, for good or ill. The verb *to afford* is found in the dictionary, but the noun *affordance* is not. I have made it up. I mean by it something that refers to both the environment and the

animal in a way that no existing term does. It implies the complementarity of the animal and the environment. (127)

So for example, a suitably sturdy and flat surface could *afford* a place to stand or walk to an animal of a certain sort—not to a fish, of course, and what affords standing room to a sparrow might not to a cat (a matter of some importance to both). Nooks can afford shelter and seclusion, green leaves or smaller neighbors can afford lunch, larger neighbors can afford attack, and so on—all depending on who's looking and with what interests.

What's important (and controversial) here is not the idea of affordances as such, but the claim that they can be *perceived*—as opposed to inferred. "The central question for the theory of affordances is not whether they exist and are real but whether information is available in ambient light for perceiving them." (140) Intuitively, the startling thesis is this: it can be *a feature of the ambient light itself* that, for instance, something over there "looks edible" or "looks dangerous" (from here, to a creature like me). This would have to be a very complicated feature indeed, practically impossible to specify (in physical terms). Gibson calls such features "high-order invariants", and makes essentially two points about them. First:

> The trouble with the assumption that high-order optical invariants specify high-order affordances is that experimenters, accustomed to working in the laboratory with low-order stimulus variables, cannot think of a way to measure them. (141)

In other words, if perceptual systems "pick up" high-order invariants, then the surfaces of the eyes and other sense organs cannot be interfaces—because the relevant interactions are not well-defined and relatively simple.

The second is a point that we have seen Gibson emphasize several times already, and moreover just what we would expect to follow from the lack of a well-defined interface.

> The hypothesis of information in ambient light to specify affordances is the culmination of ecological optics. The notion of invariants that are related at one extreme to the motives and needs of an observer and at the other extreme to the substances and surfaces of a world provides a new approach to psychology. (143)

This is not merely to reiterate the complementarity of the animal and its environment, but also to associate that integration with the "high order" affordances and invariants that constitute their interaction. Specific complexity in the perceptual capacities of the organism itself is what sustains the corresponding complexity in what it perceives, via tightly coupled, high-bandwidth interaction—at the level of description appropriate to understanding perception. Thus, the culmination of ecological optics is, in our terms, the *intimacy* of perceiver and perceived.

22.9   Transduction versus skillful interaction

So far, with the exception of the refrigerator example, all our discussions have involved relatively primitive creatures or systems. This might give the impression that intimate intermingling of mind, body, and world—in particular, lack of mental distinctness—is characteristic mainly of lower life forms, as opposed to people. Descartes, after all, held that animals have no minds at all, and are *merely* physical. The space of reasons, by contrast, is often seen as pre-eminently or even exclusively human; and it is chiefly ratiocination that seems to require input/output interfaces and transducers to enable perception and action. (Transduction, remember, is the function that Descartes assigned to the pineal gland.) So maybe the lesson is not to undermine the mind/body separation across the board, but rather to restrict it to ourselves—the *rational* animals.

On the contrary, however, I want to suggest that the human mind may be *more* intimately intermingled with its body and its world than is any other, and that this is one of its distinctive advantages. Moreover, I think that Simon's criterion of intensity of interaction, at the relevant level of intelligibility, will be just the right tool for making this visible. Let us return to the phenomenon of skillful behavior and perception, and consider its structure in more detail. In Part III of *What Computers Can't Do*, in a chapter entitled "The Role of the Body in Intelligent Behavior", Hubert L. Dreyfus writes:

> Generally, in acquiring a skill—in learning to drive, dance, or pronounce a foreign language, for example—at first we must slowly, awkwardly, and consciously follow the rules. But then there comes a moment when we finally can perform automatically. At this point we do not seem to be simply dropping these same rigid rules into unconsciousness; rather we seem to have picked up the muscular gestalt which gives our behavior a new flexibility and smoothness. The same holds for acquiring the skill of perception. (1972/92, 248–249; second edition wording)

A "*muscular* gestalt"? What have the *muscles* got to do with it? We react with questions like these, perhaps even with a trace of exasperation, because of a very seductive traditional story. When we are acting *intelligently*, our rational intellect is (consciously and/or unconsciously) taking account of various facts at its disposal, figuring out what to do, and then issuing appropriate output instructions. These instructions are converted by output transducers into physical configurations (mechanical forces, electric currents, chemical concentrations, . . .) that result in the requisite bodily behavior. The transducers, therefore, function as (or define) *interfaces* between the rational and the physical. As such, they also provide a natural point of subdivision—in the sense that any alternative output subsystem that responded to the same instructions with the same behavior could be substituted without making any significant difference to the intellectual part. On that picture, then, the muscles would fall entirely on the physical side, and not be relevant to the intelligent (sub)system at all—even as "gestalts".

Well, *are there transducers* between our minds and our bodies? From a certain all-too-easy perspective, the question can seem obtuse: *of course* there are. Almost by definition, it seems, there *has to be* a conversion between the symbolic or conceptual contents of our minds and the physical processes in our bodies; and that conversion just is transduction. But Dreyfus is, in effect, denying this—not by denying that there are minds or that there are bodies, but by denying that there needs to be any interface or conversion between them.

The fateful die is already cast in the image of the intellect figuring things out and then issuing instructions. An *instruction* (according to conventional wisdom) is a syntactic expression which, by virtue of belonging to a suitably interpretable formal system, carries a certain sort of semantic content. Specifically, its content does *not* depend on how or whether it might be acted upon by any *particular* physical output system. For instance, if I decide to type the letter 'A', the content of the forthcoming instruction wouldn't depend on it being an instruction to *my* fingers, as opposed to any others, or even some robotic prosthesis. Any output system that could take that instruction and type an 'A'—and, *mutatis mutandis*, other instructions and behaviors—would do as well. The idea that there are such instructions is morally equivalent to the idea that there are transducers.

22.10   Output patterns that aren't instructions

A different—and incompatible—story might go like this. There are tens of millions (or whatever) of neural pathways leading out of my brain (or neocortex, or whatever) into various muscle fibers in my fingers, hands, wrists, arms, shoulders, and so on, and also from various tactile and proprioceptive cells back again. Each time I type a letter, a substantial fraction of these fire at various frequencies, and in various temporal relations to one another. But that some particular pulse pattern, on some occasion, should result in my typing an 'A' depends on many contingencies, over and above just which pattern of pulses it happens to be.

In the first place, it depends on the lengths of my fingers, the strengths and quicknesses of my muscles, the shapes of my joints, and the like. Of course, whatever else I might do with my hands, from typing the rest of the alphabet to tying my shoes, would likewise depend *simultaneously* on particular pulse patterns and these other concrete contingencies. But there need be no way to "factor out" the respective contributions of these different dependencies, such that contents could consistently be assigned to pulse patterns independent of which fingers they're destined for. That is to say, there need be *no* way—even in principle, and with God's own microsurgery—to reconnect my neurons to anyone else's fingers, such that I could reliably type or tie my shoes with them. It would be like trying to assemble the cubes from a thousand TV sets into a single new one. But, in that case, what any given pattern "means" depends on it being a pattern specifically for *my particular* fingers—or, to use Dreyfus's phrase, for fingers with my "muscular gestalts".

Perhaps an analogy would help—even if it's fairly far fetched. Imagine an encryption algorithm with the following three features: it uses very large encryption keys (tens of millions of bits, just for instance); cryptograms, even for quite brief messages, are comparable in size to the keys themselves; and it is tremendously redundant, in the sense that (for each key) countless distinct cryptograms would decode to the same message. Now, consider, for a given key and message, all the cryptograms that would decode to that message; and ask whether it could make any sense to speak of what *these* cryptograms have in common apart from *that particular* key. It's hard to see how it could. Yet, if individual cryptograms have any meaning at all, then these must all have the same meaning; so either cryptograms are meaningless, or they mean something only in conjunction with a *particular* key. Then the analogy works like this: each individual's *particular body*—his or her own muscular gestalts—functions like a large encryption key; and the pulse patterns coming down from the brain are the cryptograms, which are either meaningless, or they mean something only in conjunction with that particular body. Either way, they aren't instructions. This is *only* an analogy, however, because the activity of the fingers should not be regarded as "decoding neural messages", but rather as an integral part of the "processing" that the brain and other neurons also contribute to.

But even that may be overly sanguine. Whether a given *efferent* neural pattern will result in a typed 'A' depends *also* on how my fingers happen already to be deployed and moving, the angle of the keyboard, how tired I am, and so on—factors that *aren't constant*, even for the short run. On different occasions, the same pattern will give different letters, and different patterns the same letter. The reason that I can type, despite all this, is that there are comparably rich *afferent* patterns forming a kind of feedback loop that constantly "recalibrates" the system. (In terms of the above analogy, it's as if the encryption keys were not only large, but ever changing—the new ones being sent upstream all the time.) But that would mean that the "content" of any given neural output pattern would depend not only on the particular body that it's connected to, but also on the *concrete details* of its current worldly situation.

If there were simple instructions—well-defined, repeatable messages—coming down the nerves from my brain to my fingers, then that narrow-bandwidth channel could be an interface to my fingers as physical transducers. Accordingly, it would be possible to divide the system there, and substitute "equivalent" fingers, in place of mine. Such an architecture is implicitly assumed by much of philosophy and most of AI. By contrast, the alternative that I have been sketching sees these nerves as carrying high-bandwidth interactions (high-intensity, in Simon's terms), without any simple, well-defined structure. Thus, by the same criterion, we would not get two relatively independent separable components   a rational mind and a physical body, meeting at an interface—but rather a single closely-knit unity.

22.11   Specific complexity

Nerve fibers, of course, aren't the only high-bandwidth channel between my fingers and other parts of my body. The immune system, for instance, is extraordinarily complex and responsive. And even the circulatory transportation of metabolites and by-products carries, in the technical sense, a lot of "information". Why focus on the nerves? Once the question is asked, the answer is easy to see. When we are trying to understand intelligence—as manifested, say, in intelligent behavior—we look to the complexity that is *specific* to that behavior. The distribution of antibodies and proteins to my hands, while no doubt essential to my typing ability, doesn't differ very much depending *which* letter I type; indeed, it doesn't depend much on whether I'm typing, writing longhand, or tying bows.

But the complexity of the nervous system is task specific, and in two different ways. In the first place, at any moment, the pulse patterns needed for typing an 'A' differ from those needed for typing a 'B', not to mention from those needed for writing a 'B'. The skills in question just are the abilities to get these things done right. And getting them right—this letter as opposed to that one—depends *in specific detail* on the actual pulse patterns, in a way that it does not depend on any details of my immune defenses. Second, as I acquired these skills, various more or less permanent changes were made in my neural pathways, in implementing all the relevant habits and reflexes. (Dreyfus, remember, was discussing *learning*.) And these changes, likewise, were specific to the skills learned—in a way that, for example, increases in circulatory capacity wouldn't have been.

The point, however, is not to focus exclusively on the nervous system. Far from it. As emphasized above, actual performance depends on a number of other specific contingencies besides nerve impulses. Similarly, a range of other *specifically relevant* permanent changes are involved in the acquisition of skills. Thus, muscles of the requisite strengths, shapes, and limberness must be developed and maintained—differently for different skills. This is most conspicuous for very demanding manual abilities, like musicianship, surgery, and stage magic. Indeed, a professional violinist must acquire specific callouses, perhaps subtle grooves in the tips of her phalanges, even a certain set of the jaw.

The unity of mind and body can be promoted wholesale, perhaps, on the basis of general principles of monism or the unity of science. Such arguments are indifferent to variety and substructure within either the mental or the physical: everything is unceremoniously lumped together at one swoop. Here, by contrast, integration is offered at retail. In attempting to undermine the idea of an interface between the mind and the fingers, I am staking no claim to the liver or intestines. (Simon may be right about glands and viscera.) The idea is not to wipe out all distinctions and homogenize everything on general principles, but rather to call certain very familiar divisions into question, on the basis of considerations highly peculiar to them.

22.12   Getting the whole rug smooth

If a rug doesn't fit, then flattening it out in one place will just move the hump to another. If there's no interface between the brain and the fingers, then maybe it just is (has to be?) somewhere else. One might imagine, for instance, that the efferent nerves are high bandwidth because they (along with much of the spinal cord and some of the brain) are all part of a very sophisticated physical output system—the psycho-physical interface itself being further "in". It could be that ratiocination (or representation more generally) occurs only in the cortex, or only the *neo*cortex, or whatever. Then the relevant transductions would have to take place *within* the brain, between one part of it and another—not so far from the pineal gland, as luck might have it.

Now, my question is: Why would anyone ever be tempted by such a supposition? And the answer, surely, is the same *pre*supposition that the mental *must be* different in kind—categorically different—from anything bodily or worldly; so, *there must be* some interface somewhere. For, without that *a priori* conviction, the obvious evidence of neuroanatomy would be decisive: the neural pathways from perception to action are high-bandwidth *all the way through*. If anything, the bandwidth increases toward the center, rather than narrowing down. There's just no plausible constriction where well-defined instructions might be getting converted; that is, there's no place where a counterpart of the above argument against efferent transduction wouldn't apply.

Well then, might the hump slip out in the other direction, out past the fingers? It cannot be denied that the keyboard itself is a well-defined interface. No matter how complicated and various are the ways of striking the keys, the result is always limited to character codes from a set of a few hundred, in a slow, unambiguous, serial order. (It's not for nothing that a teletype was earlier our paradigm of a low-bandwidth device.) By these lights, then, the meaningful (mental) extends all the way to the fingertips—maybe a touch beyond—and *then* interfaces to the physical world. This is, to be sure, a surprising fall-back position for defenders of mental/physical transduction—certainly not Cartesian in spirit. But could it work?

The first clue that it cannot is the artificiality of the example. Typing at a keyboard, though genuinely skillful activity, is quite atypical in the digital character of its success conditions. Dreyfus speaks instead of driving, dancing, or pronouncing a foreign language. These, too, are hard to learn; but there is no simple, well-defined test for whether the learner has got it right or wrong. The point is not merely that, like cutting wood or matching colors, you can be more or less right, that errors come in degrees. Rather, for driving, dancing, and even pronunciation, there is no well-defined standard specifying the difference between correct and incorrect. This is not to deny that there *is* a difference between doing well and doing badly, or that experts can tell. Quite the contrary: the claim is that "telling the difference" is itself a skill—one that is likewise hard to learn, and for which there can be no exact specification of what is done, or how.

Even driving, dancing, and pronunciation, however, are more socially circumscribed and narrowly delimited than most of what we do. From cooking to love making, from playing with the kids to shopping in the mall, our lives are filled with activities that exhibit human learning and human intelligence, that some of us are better at than others (as the good ones can tell), but for which none of us could articulate a definitive standard. This is the character of skillful being in the world in general. The simple, interface-like definiteness of what counts as accuracy in typing or color matching is, by contrast, the special case. So the hump in the rug can't slide outward either. We have to make it *all* lie flat.

22.13   Vicarious coping

If there is no determinate interface between the mind and the body, or between the mind and the world, does this mean that the body and the world are somehow mental, or that the mind is corporeal and mundane? Yes, in a way, both. But not in a way that washes out all distinctions, rendering the three terms synonymous, and therefore redundant. As always, it is a matter of what we are trying to understand. When we are studying anatomy and physiology, the brain is relatively separable from the rest of the organism; the organism itself is even more separable from its environment; and the mind isn't in the picture at all. When, on the other hand, our topic is intelligence, then the mind is very much to the point, and its scope and limits are part of the issue.

Intelligence abides in the *meaningful*. This is not to say that it is surrounded by or directed toward the meaningful, as if they were two separate phenomena, somehow related to one another. Rather, intelligence has its very existence in the meaningful as such—in something like the way a nation's wealth lies in its productive capacity, or a corporation's strength may consist in its market position. Of course, the meaningful, here, cannot be wholly passive and inert, but must include also activity and process. Intelligence, then, is nothing other than the overall interactive structure of meaningful behavior and objects. This is a view shared by scientists and philosophers, all the way from the most classical AI to its most radical critics—including, among others, Simon and Dreyfus. Why?

Perhaps the basic idea can be brought out this way. Intelligence is the ability to deal reliably with more than the present and the manifest. That's surely not an adequate definition of intelligence, but it does get at something essential, and, in particular, something that has to do with meaning. For instance, *representations*—especially *mental* representations—are often taken as the archetype of the meaningful, and that wherein intelligence abides. The connection is straightforward. Representations are clearly an asset in coping with the absent and covert, insofar as they themselves are present, and "stand in for" something else—something absent—which they "represent". This "standing in for" is their meaning-fulness; and it is what makes intelligence possible.

How does it work? A typical sort of story goes like this. Individual representations can function as such *only* by participating, in concert with many others, in a larger and norm-governed *scheme* of representation. Then, assuming the scheme itself is in good shape, and is used correctly, a system can vicariously keep track of and explore absent and covert represented phenomena by keeping track of and exploring their present and manifest representational stand-ins. (Really, what it means for a scheme to be "in good shape" is for this coping at one remove to be generally feasible.) In effect, the structure of the extant representations, in conjunction with that of the scheme itself, "encode" something of the structure of what is represented, in such a way that the latter can be accommodated or taken account of, even when out of view.

An alternative understanding of intelligence might keep the basic framework of this ac-count, while modifying certain specifics. Our discussion of transduction, for instance, may have cast some suspicion on the idea of mental representation, or even of mind/world sep-aration. But it need not undermine the broader view that intelligence abides in the mean-ingful, or that it consists in an ability to deal with the unobvious. Could there be a way to retain these latter, but without the former? That is, could there be a way to understand the effectiveness of intelligence in terms of meaningfulness, but without representations or a separated inner realm?

22.14   The world itself as meaningful

Not long after the passage about skills and muscular gestalts, Dreyfus addresses exactly this question.

> When we are at home in the world, the meaningful objects embedded in their context of references among which we live are not a model of the world stored in our mind or brain: *they are the world itself.* (265–266)

There are really several (closely related) points being made in this dense and powerful sentence. First, there is, so to speak, the locus of the meaningful; second its charac-ter; and third, our situation with regard to it. The meaningful is not in our mind or brain, but is instead essentially worldly. The meaningful is not a model—that is, it's not representational—but is instead objects embedded in their context of references. And we do not store the meaningful inside of ourselves, but rather live and are at home in it. These are all summed up in the slogan that the meaningful *is the world itself.* (This may be remi-niscent, anachronistically, of Brooks's later but less radical dictum that the world is its own best model.)

The first thesis, in its negative aspect, is simply a repudiation of the view, almost ubiq-uitous in cognitive science and traditional philosophy, that the meaningful objects amidst which intelligence abides are primarily *inner*. "Classical" cognitive scientists restrict these inner objects to *symbolic* expressions and models, whereas others are more liberal about mental images, cognitive maps, and maybe even "distributed representations". But Dreyfus wants to extend the meaningful well beyond the inner, in any traditional sense: meaningful objects are "the world itself ".

It is important to guard against a possible misunderstanding. Everyone would allow that worldly objects can be meaningful in a *derivative* way, as when we assign to them meanings that we somehow already have. You and I, for instance, could agree to use a certain signal to mean, say, that the British are coming; and then it would indeed mean that—but only derivatively from our decision. (Many philosophers and scientists would hold further that this is the *only* way that external objects can come to be meaningful.) By contrast, when Dreyfus says that meaningful objects are the world itself, he means *original* meaning, not just derivative. That is, intelligence itself abides "out" in the world, not just "inside"—contra cognitive science, classical or otherwise.

The second thesis, in its negative aspect, is again a repudiation of an almost universal assumption: that the meaningful is primarily representational. As before, the target is not only the classical symbolic approach, but most of its more liberal successors. These two negative points combined constitute a rejection of what is sometimes called "the representational theory of the mind". In its positive aspect, that the meaningful is "objects embedded in their context of references", the thesis may call for some explanation. Clearly what Dreyfus has in mind are tools and other paraphernalia. What is the sense in which these are *meaningful*?

We might begin by saying, very roughly, that the meaningful in general is that which is significant in terms of something beyond itself, and subject to normative evaluation according to that significance. Then we could see representations as familiar paradigms of the meaningful in this sense. That in terms of which a representation is significant is that which it purports to represent—its object—and it is evaluated according to whether it represents that object correctly or accurately. When cognitive scientists and philosophers speak of meaningful *inner* entities, they *always* mean representations (nothing *other than* representations has ever been proposed as inner and meaningful). Descartes, in effect, *invented* the "inner realm" as a repository for cognitive representations—above all, representations of what's outside of it—and cognitive science hasn't really changed that at all.

But when Dreyfus holds that meaningful objects are the world itself, he doesn't just (or even mostly) mean representations. The world can't be representation "all the way down". But that's not to say that it can't all be meaningful, because there are more kinds of significance than representational content. A number of philosophers earlier in the twentieth century—Dewey, Heidegger, Wittgenstein, and Merleau-Ponty, to name a few of the most prominent—have made much of the significance of equipment, public places, community practices, and the like. A hammer, for instance, is significant beyond itself in terms of *what it's for*: driving nails into wood, by being wielded in a certain way, in order to build something, and so on. The nails, the wood, the project, and the carpenter him or herself, are likewise caught up in this "web of significance", in their respective ways. These are the meaningful objects that are the world itself; and none of them is a representation.

There's an obvious worry here that the whole point depends on a pun. *Of course*, hammers and the like are "significant" (and even "meaningful") in the sense that they're *important* to us, and *interdependent* with other things in their proper use. But that's not the same as meaning in the sense of bearing content or having a semantics. Certainly! That's why they're *not* representations. So it's agreed: they are meaningful in a broader sense, though not in a narrower one. The real question is: Which sense matters in the context of understanding human intelligence?

22.15   Knowing the way

The third thesis is that we live in the meaningful—that is, in the world—and are at home there. Part of the point, to be sure, is that we reside in the midst of our paraphernalia, and are accustomed to it. But the more fundamental insight must connect the meaningful as such with the nature of intelligence. It is clear enough how tools can extend our capacity to cope with the present and manifest; that is more or less the definition of a tool. But how do they help us deal with the absent and covert? Or, rather: aren't those tools that do help us with the absent and covert precisely, and for that very reason, *representations*? Not at all.

Consider the ability to get to San Jose. That's a capacity to deal with something out of view—a distant city—and so just what is characteristic of intelligence. Moreover, a cognitive scientist will instinctively attribute it to some sort of representation, either an internal or external map or set of instructions, which an intelligent system either consists in or can consult and follow. But that's not the only way to achieve the effect. A quite different approach would be to keep a stable of horses, one pre-trained for each likely destination. Then all that the capable person would need to do is pick the right horse, stay on it, and get off at the end. Here we're inclined to say that it's the *horse* that knows the way, not the rider—or maybe that the full ability is really collaborative, say like Gilbert and Sullivan's. At any rate, the horse's contribution is not to be ignored.

Now let me tell you how *I* get to San Jose: I pick the right road (Interstate 880 south), stay on it, and get off at the end.[1] Can we say that the *road* knows the way to San Jose, or perhaps that the road and I *collaborate*? I don't think this is as crazy as it may first sound. The complexity of the road (its shape) is comparable to that of the task and highly specific thereto; moreover, staying on the road requires constant high-bandwidth interaction with this very complexity. In other words, the internal guidance systems and the road itself must be closely coupled, in part because much of the "information" upon which the ability depends is "encoded" *in the road*. Thus, much as an internal map or program, learned and stored in memory, would (*pace* Simon) have to be deemed *part of* an intelligent system that used it to get to San Jose, so I suggest the *road* should be considered *integral to* my ability.

Don't be distracted by the fact that the road was designed and built by intelligent engineers who, no doubt, knew the route. Even if we might want to *extend* the collaboration in this case, the engineers are not essential in the way that road itself is; for some "roads"—forest trails, for instance—need not be intelligently designed, yet the argument works the same for them. A more serious worry is how narrow the example is: intelligent navigation ought to be more flexible, allowing, say, for alternative destinations and starting points. And then it might seem that the *intelligence* lies in this adaptability—knowing how to get there from the east as well as from the north, or where to turn off to get to Palo Alto or Modesto instead—which is internal after all. But, in the first place, even that flexibility is mostly encoded in the world, in the road signs that enable one to choose and stay on the "right" road. And, in the meantime, the road itself still holds the information for getting from one junction to the next. Most important, however, is to remember the point: it's not that *all* of the structure of intelligence is "external", but only that *some* of it is, in a way that is integral to the rest.

22.16   Abiding in the meaningful

Still, the road example is quite limited. How much of what a culture has learned about life and its environment is "encoded" in its paraphernalia and practices? Consider, for example, agriculture—without question, a basic manifestation of human intelligence, and dependant on a vast wealth of information accumulated through the centuries. Well, *where* has this information accumulated? Crucial elements of that heritage, I want to claim, are embodied in the shapes and strengths of the plow, the yoke, and the harness, as well as the practices for building and using them. The farmer's learned skills are essential too; but these are nonsense apart from the specific tools they involve, and *vice versa*. Their interaction must be high-bandwidth, in real time. Hence, they constitute an essential unity—a unity that incorporates overall a considerable expertise about the workability of the earth, the needs of young plants, water retention, weed control, root development, and so on.

The structure of an intricate and established institution can likewise be an integral contribution to an understanding of how, say, to build cars or manage a city. That the departments are related *this* way, that the facilities for *that* are over *there*, that *these* requests must be submitted to *those* offices on *such and such* forms—all of this constitutes, if not a theory, at least an essential part of the architecture of a very considerable overall competence. Such competence is as distinctively human as is any other sophisticated art or technology. Yet, not only is it not the competence of any single individual, it is also not the sum of the competencies of all the individuals—for that sum would not include the structure of established interrelationships and institutional procedures, not to mention the physical plant, which are prerequisite to the whole. The point is not merely that organizations evolve in functionally effective ways, as do insects and trees, but rather that the structure of an institution is implemented in the high-bandwidth intelligent interactions among individuals, as well as between individuals and their paraphernalia. Furthermore, the expertise of those individuals could not be what it is apart from their participation in that structure. Consequently, the intelligence of each is itself intelligible only in terms of their higher unity.

Even in so self-conscious a domain as a scientific laboratory, whether research or development oriented, much of the intelligent ability to investigate, distinguish, and manipulate natural phenomena is embodied in the specialized instrumentation, the manual and perceptual skills required to use and maintain it, and the general laboratory ethos of cleanliness, deliberation, and record keeping. Without these, science would be impossible; they are *integral* to it. The point is not that theory is baseless without evidence, or useless without applications. Rather, apart from its intimate involvement in highly specific complex activities in highly specific complex circumstances, there's no such thing as scientific intelligence— it doesn't make any sense. For all its explicitness and abstraction, science is as worldly as agriculture, manufacturing, and government.

I have postponed till last the most obvious externalization of human intelligence—texts, images, maps, diagrams, programs, and the like—not because I underestimate their importance, but because they are so similar to what is traditionally supposed to be in the mind. That poses two dangers. First, it distracts attention from the radicalness of the claim that intelligence abides in the meaningful *world*: not just books and records, but roads and plows, offices, laboratories, and communities. Second, it makes it too easy for a traditionalist to think: "External representations are not really integral to intelligence, but are merely devices for conveying or restoring to intelligence proper—the inner mind—contents which it might otherwise lack." By now, however, these dangers will (I hope) have abated. So it can safely be acknowledged that (to borrow Simon's phrase) the "great furniture of information" that civilization has accumulated belongs with the rest of its furniture in the abode of its understanding.

22.17 Conclusion

If we are to understand mind as the locus of intelligence, we cannot follow Descartes in regarding it as separable in principle from the body and the world. I have argued that such separability would have to coincide with narrow-bandwidth interfaces, among the interactions that are relevant to intelligence. In recent decades, a commitment to understanding intelligence as rational problem solving—sometimes assumed *a priori*—has supported the existence of these interfaces by identifying them with transducers. Broader approaches, freed of that prejudicial commitment, can look again at perception and action, at skillful involvement with public equipment and social organization, and see not principled separation but all sorts of close coupling and functional unity. As our ability to cope with the absent and covert, human intelligence abides in the meaningful—which, far from being restricted to representations, extends to the entire human world. Mind, therefore, is not incidentally but *intimately* embodied and *intimately* embedded in its world.

Notes for Chapter 22

1. The "road to San Jose" example is inspired by a discussion in Batali (1993).

Intelligence without Representation

23

Rodney A. Brooks
1991

23.1 Introduction

Artificial intelligence started as a field whose goal was to replicate human-level intelligence in a machine. Early hopes diminished as the magnitude and difficulty of that goal was appreciated. Slow progress was made over the next 25 years in demonstrating isolated aspects of intelligence. Some recent work has tended to concentrate on commercializable aspects of "intelligent assistants" for human workers.

No one talks about replicating the full gamut of human intelligence anymore. Instead we see a retreat into specialized subproblems, such as knowledge representation, natural language understanding, vision, or even more specialized areas such as truth maintenance or plan verification. All the work in these subareas is benchmarked against the sorts of tasks humans do within those areas. Amongst the dreamers still in the field of AI (those not dreaming about dollars, that is) there is a feeling that one day all these pieces will fall into place and we will see "truly" intelligent systems emerge.

However, I and others believe that human-level intelligence is too complex and too little understood to be correctly decomposed into the right subpieces at the moment, and that even if we knew the subpieces we still wouldn't know the right interfaces between them. Furthermore we will never understand how to decompose human-level intelligence until we've had a lot of practice with simpler intelligences.

In this paper I therefore argue for a different approach to creating artificial intelligence.

- We must incrementally build up the capabilities of intelligent systems, having *complete* systems at each step, thus automatically ensuring that the pieces and their interfaces are valid.

- At each step, we should build complete intelligent systems that we let loose in the real world with real sensing and real action. Anything less provides a candidate with which we can delude ourselves.

We have been following this approach and have built a series of autonomous mobile robots. We have reached an unexpected conclusion (C) and have a rather radical hypothesis (H).

(C) When we examine very simple level intelligence we find that explicit representations and models of the world simply get in the way. It turns out to be better to let the world itself serve as its own model.

(H) Representation is the wrong unit of abstraction in building the bulkiest parts of intelligent systems.

Representation has been the central issue in artificial intelligence work over the last 15 years only because it has provided an interface between otherwise isolated modules and conference papers.

23.2   The evolution of intelligence

We already have an existence proof of the possibility of intelligent entities: human beings. Additionally, many animals are intelligent to some degree. (This is a subject of intense debate, much of which really centers around a definition of intelligence.) They have evolved over the 4.6 billion year history of the earth.

It is instructive to reflect on the way in which earth-based biological evolution spent its time. Single-cell entities arose out of the primordial soup roughly 3.5 billion years ago. A billion years passed before photosynthetic plants appeared. After almost another billion and a half years, around 550 million years ago, the first fish and vertebrates arrived, and then insects 450 million years ago. Then things started moving fast. Reptiles arrived 370 million years ago, followed by dinosaurs at 330 and mammals at 250 million years ago. The first primates appeared 120 million years ago and the immediate predecessors to the great apes a mere 18 million years ago. Man arrived in roughly his present form 2.5 million years ago. He invented agriculture a scant 19,000 years ago, writing less than 5000 years ago and "expert" knowledge only over the last few hundred years.

This suggests that problem-solving behavior, language, expert knowledge and application, and reason are all pretty simple once the essence of acting and reacting are available. That essence is the ability to move around in a dynamic environment, sensing the surroundings to a degree sufficient to achieve the necessary maintenance of life and reproduction. This part of intelligence is where evolution has concentrated its time—it is much harder.

I believe that mobility, acute vision and the ability to carry out survival related tasks in a dynamic environment provide a necessary basis for the development of true intelligence. Moravec (1984) argues this same case rather eloquently.

Human level intelligence has provided us with an existence proof, but we must be careful about what lessons are to be gained from it.

A story

    Suppose it is the 1890's. Artificial flight is the glamor subject in science, engineering, and venture capital circles. A bunch of AF researchers are miraculously transported by a time machine to the 1990's for a few hours. They spend the whole time in the passenger cabin of a commercial passenger Boeing 747 on a medium duration flight.

    Returned to the 1890's they feel invigorated, knowing that AF is possible on a grand scale. They immediately set to work duplicating what they have seen. They make great progress in designing pitched seats, double pane windows, and know that if only they can figure out those weird 'plastics' they will have the grail within their grasp. (A few connectionists amongst them caught a glimpse of an engine with its cover off and they are preoccupied with inspirations from that experience.)

23.3   Abstraction as a dangerous weapon

Artificial intelligence researchers are fond of pointing out that AI is often denied its rightful successes. The popular story goes that when nobody has any good idea of how to solve a particular sort of problem (for example, playing chess) it is known as an AI problem. When an algorithm developed by AI researchers successfully tackles such a problem, however, AI detractors claim that since the problem was solvable by an algorithm, it wasn't really an AI problem after all. Thus AI never has any successes.

    But have you ever heard of an AI failure?

I claim that AI researchers are guilty of the same (self-)deception. They partition the problems they work on into two components. The AI component, which they solve, and the non-AI component which they don't solve. Typically, AI "succeeds" by defining the parts of the problem that are unsolved as not AI. The principal mechanism for this partitioning is abstraction. Its application is usually considered part of good science, and not (as it is in fact used in AI) as a mechanism for self-delusion. In AI, abstraction is usually used to factor out all aspects of perception and motor skills. I argue below that these are the hard problems solved by intelligent systems, and further that the shape of solutions to these problems constrains greatly the correct solutions of the small pieces of intelligence which remain.

    Early work in AI concentrated on games, geometrical problems, symbolic algebra, theorem proving, and other formal systems (see the classic papers in Feigenbaum and Feldman, 1963 and Minsky, 1968). In each case, the semantics of the domains were fairly simple.

    In the late sixties and early seventies, the "blocks world" became a popular domain for AI research. It had a uniform and simple semantics. The key to success was to represent the state of the world completely and explicitly. Search techniques could then be used for planning within this well-understood world. Learning could also be done within the blocks world; there were only a few simple concepts worth learning, and they could be captured by enumerating the set of subexpressions which must be contained in any formal description of a world containing an instance of the concept. The blocks world was even used for vision research and mobile robotics, as it provided strong constraints on the perceptual processing necessary (see, for instance, Nilsson, 1984).

Eventually, criticism surfaced that the blocks world was a "toy world" and that within it there were simple special purpose solutions to what should be considered more general problems. At the same time there was a funding crisis within AI (both in the US and the UK, the two most active places for AI research at the time). AI researchers found themselves forced to become relevant. They moved into more complex domains, such as trip planning, going to a restaurant, medical diagnosis, and such like.

Soon there was a new slogan: "Good representation is the key to AI" (as in: *conceptually efficient programs*, Bobrow and Brown, 1975). The idea was that by representing only the *pertinent* facts explicitly, the semantics of a world (which on the surface was quite complex) were reduced to a simple closed system once again. Abstraction to only the relevant details thus simplified the problems.

Consider chairs, for example. While these two characterizations are true,

(CAN (SIT-ON PERSON CHAIR)), and

(CAN (STAND-ON PERSON CHAIR)),

there is really much more to the concept of a chair. Chairs have some flat (maybe) sitting place, with perhaps a back support. They have a range of possible sizes, requirements on strength, and a range of possibilities in shape. They often have some sort of covering material—unless they are made of wood, metal or plastic. They sometimes are soft in particular places. They can come from a range of possible styles. In sum, the concept of what is a chair is hard to characterize simply. There is certainly no AI vision program that can find arbitrary chairs in arbitrary images; they can at best find one particular type of chair in carefully selected images.

This characterization, however, is perhaps the correct AI representation for solving certain problems—for instance, one in which a hungry person sitting on a chair in a room can see a banana hanging from the ceiling just out of reach. Such problems are never posed to AI systems by showing them a photo of the scene. A person (even a young child) can make the right interpretation of the photo and suggest a plan of action. For AI planning systems, however, the experimenter is required to abstract away most of the details to form a simple description in terms of atomic concepts such as PERSON, CHAIR and BANANA.

But this abstraction process is the essence of intelligence and the hard part of the problems being solved. Under the current scheme, the abstraction is done by the researchers, leaving little for the AI programs to do but search. A truly intelligent program would study the photograph, perform the abstraction itself, and solve the problem.

The only input to most AI programs is a restricted set of simple assertions deduced from the real data by humans. The problems of recognition, spatial understanding, dealing with sensor noise, partial models, and the like, are all ignored. These problems are relegated to the realm of input black boxes. Psychophysical evidence suggests they are all intimately tied up with the representation of the world used by an intelligent system.

There is no clean division between perception (abstraction) and reasoning in the real world. The brittleness of current AI systems attests to this fact. For example, MYCIN (Shortliffe, 1976) is an expert at diagnosing human bacterial infections; but it really has no model of what a human (or any living creature) is or how they work, or what are plausible things to happen to a human. If told that the aorta is ruptured and the patient is losing blood at the rate of a pint every minute, MYCIN will try to find a bacterial cause of the problem.

Thus, because we still perform all the abstractions for our programs, most AI work is still done in the equivalent of the blocks world. Now the blocks are slightly different shapes and colors, but their underlying semantics have not changed greatly.

It could be argued that performing this abstraction (perception) for AI programs is merely the normal reductionist use of abstraction common in all good science. The abstraction reduces the input data so that the program experiences the same "perceptual world" (what von Uexküll, 1921 called a *Merkwelt*) as humans. Other (vision) researchers will independently fill in the details at some other time and place. I object to this on two grounds. First, as von Uexküll and others have pointed out, each animal species, and clearly each robot species with its own distinctly nonhuman sensor suites, will have its own different *Merkwelt*. Second, the *Merkwelt* we humans provide our programs is based on our own introspection. It is by no means clear that such a *Merkwelt* is anything like what we actually use internally—it could just as easily be an output coding for communication purposes (thus, most humans go through life never realizing they have a large blind spot almost in the center of their visual fields).

The first objection warns of the danger that reasoning strategies developed for the human-assumed *Merkwelt* may not be valid when real sensors and perceptual processing are used. The second objection says that, even with human sensors and perception, the *Merkwelt* may not be anything like that used by humans. In fact, it may be the case that our introspective descriptions of our internal representations are completely misleading and quite different from what we really use.

A continuing story

Meanwhile our friends in the 1890's are busy at work on their AF machine. They have come to agree that the project is too big to be worked on as a single entity and that they will need to become specialists in different areas. After all, they had asked questions of fellow passengers on their flight and discovered that the Boeing Co. employed over 6000 people to build such an airplane.

Everyone is busy, but there is not a lot of communication between the groups. The people making the passenger seats used the finest solid steel available as the framework. There was some muttering that perhaps they should use tubular steel to save weight, but the general consensus was that if such an obviously big and heavy airplane could fly then clearly there was no problem with weight.

On their observation flight, none of the original group managed a glimpse of the driver's seat, but they have done some hard thinking and believe they have established the major constraints on what should be there and how it should work. The pilot, as he will be called, sits in a seat above a glass floor so that he can see the ground below so he will know where to land. There are some side mirrors so he can watch behind for other approaching airplanes. His controls consist of a foot pedal to control speed (just as in these new fangled automobiles that are starting to appear), and a steering wheel to turn left and right. In addition the wheel stem can be pushed forward and back to make the airplane go up and down. A clever arrangement of pipes measures airspeed of the airplane and displays it on a dial. What more could one want? Oh yes. There's a rather nice setup of louvers in the windows so that the driver can get fresh air without getting the full blast of the wind in his face.

An interesting sidelight is that all the researchers have by now abandoned the study of aerodynamics. Some of them had intensely questioned their fellow passengers on this subject and not one of the modern flyers had known a thing about it. Clearly the AF researchers had previously been wasting their time in its pursuit.

23.4 Incremental intelligence

I wish to build completely autonomous mobile agents that co-exist in the world with humans, and are seen by those humans as intelligent beings in their own right. I will call such agents *Creatures*. This is my intellectual motivation. I have no particular interest in demonstrating how human beings work—although humans, like other animals, are interesting objects of study in this endeavor, inasmuch as they are successful autonomous agents. I have no particular interest in applications; it seems clear to me that, if my goals can be met, then the range of applications for such Creatures will be limited only by our (or their) imagination. I have no particular interest in the philosophical implications of Creatures, although clearly there will be significant implications.

Given the caveats of the previous two sections, and considering the parable of the AF researchers, I am convinced that I must tread carefully in this endeavor to avoid some nasty pitfalls.

For the moment then, consider the problem of building Creatures as an engineering problem. We will develop an *engineering methodology* for building Creatures.

First, let us consider some of the requirements for our Creatures.

- A Creature must cope appropriately and in a timely fashion with changes in its dynamic environment.

- A Creature should be robust with respect to its environment. Minor changes in the properties of the world should not lead to total collapse of the Creature's behavior; rather one should expect only a gradual change in capabilities of the Creature as the environment changes more and more.
- A Creature should be able to maintain multiple goals and, depending on the circumstances it finds itself in, change which particular goals it is actively pursuing; thus it can both adapt to surroundings and capitalize on fortuitous circumstances.
- A Creature should do *something* in the world; it should have some purpose in being.

Now, let us consider some of the valid engineering approaches to achieving these requirements. As in all engineering endeavors, it is necessary to decompose a complex system into parts, build the parts, and then interface them into a complete system.

23.4.1 Decomposition by function

Perhaps the strongest traditional notion of intelligent systems (at least implicitly among AI workers) has been of a central system, with perceptual modules as inputs and action modules as outputs. The perceptual modules deliver a symbolic description of the world and the action modules take a symbolic description of desired actions and make sure they happen in the world. The central system then is a symbolic information processor.

Traditionally, work in perception (and vision is the most commonly studied form of perception) and work in central systems has been done by different researchers and even totally different research laboratories. Vision workers are not immune to earlier criticisms of AI workers. Most vision research is presented as a transformation from one image representation (such as a raw grey-scale image) to another registered image (such as an edge image). Each group, AI and vision, makes assumptions about the shape of the symbolic interfaces. Hardly anyone has ever connected a vision system to an intelligent central system. Thus the assumptions independent researchers make are not forced to be realistic. There is a real danger from pressures to neatly circumscribe the particular piece of research being done.

The central system must also be decomposed into smaller pieces. We see subfields of artificial intelligence such as "knowledge representation", "learning", "planning", "qualitative reasoning", etc. The interfaces between these modules are also subject to intellectual abuse.

When researchers working on a particular module get to choose both the inputs and the outputs that specify the module requirements, I believe there is little chance the work they do will fit into a complete intelligent system.

This bug in the functional decomposition approach is hard to fix. One needs a long chain of modules to connect perception to action. In order to test any of them, they all must first be built. But until realistic modules are built, it is highly unlikely that we can predict exactly what modules will be needed or what interfaces they will need.

23.4.2 Decomposition by activity

An alternative decomposition makes no distinction between peripheral systems, such as vision, and central systems. Rather, the fundamental slicing up of an intelligent system is in the orthogonal direction, dividing it into *activity* producing subsystems. Each activity, or behavior-producing system, individually connects sensing to action. We refer to an activity producing system as a *layer*. An activity is a pattern of interactions with the world. Another name for our activities might well be *skills* —since each activity can, at least post facto, be rationalized as pursuing some purpose. We have chosen the word 'activity', however, because our layers must decide when to act for themselves—not be some subroutine to be invoked at the beck and call of some other layer. We call Creatures that are decomposable into activities or behavior-producing layers in this way *behavior-based systems*.

The advantage of this approach is that it gives an incremental path from very simple systems to complex autonomous intelligent systems. At each step of the way, it is only necessary to build one small piece, and interface it to an existing, working, complete intelligence.

The idea is to build first a very simple complete autonomous system, and *test it in the real world*. Our favorite example of such a system is a Creature, actually a mobile robot, which avoids hitting things. It senses objects in its immediate vicinity and moves away from them, halting if it senses something in its path. It is still necessary to build this system by decomposing it into parts, but there need be no clear distinction between a "perception system," a "central system" and an "action system". In fact, there may well be two independent channels connecting sensing to action—one for initiating motion, and one for emergency halts—so there is no single place where "perception" delivers a representation of the world in the traditional sense.

Next we build an incremental layer of intelligence which operates in parallel to the first system. It is pasted onto the existing debugged system and tested again in the real world. This new layer might directly access the sensors and run a different algorithm on the delivered data. The first-level autonomous system continues to run in parallel, and unaware of the existence of the second level. For example, in Brooks (1986) we reported on building a first layer of control which let the Creature avoid objects, and then adding a layer which instilled an activity of trying to visit distant visible places. The second layer injected commands to the motor control part of the first layer, directing the robot towards the goal; but, independently, the first layer would cause the robot to veer away from previously unseen obstacles. The second layer monitored the progress of the Creature and sent updated motor commands, thus achieving its goal without being explicitly aware of obstacles, which had been handled by the lower level of control.

23.5   Who has the representations?

With multiple layers, the notion of perception delivering a description of the world gets blurred even more, as the part of the system doing perception is spread out over many pieces which are not particularly connected by data paths or related by function. Certainly there is no identifiable place where the "output" of perception can be found. Furthermore, totally different sorts of processing of the sensor data proceed independently and in parallel, each affecting the overall system activity through quite different channels of control.

In fact, not by design but rather by observation, we note that a common theme in the ways in which our layered and distributed approach helps our Creatures meet our goals is that there is no central representation.

- Low-level simple activities can instill the Creature with reactions to dangerous or important changes in its environment. Without complex representations and the need to maintain those representations and reason about them, these reactions can easily be made quick enough to serve their purpose. The key idea is to sense the environment often, and so have an up-to-date idea of what is happening in the world.
- By having multiple parallel activities, and by removing the idea of a central representation, there is less chance that any given change in the class of properties enjoyed by the world can cause total collapse of the system. Rather, one might expect that a given change will at most incapacitate some but not all of the levels of control. Gradually, as a more alien world is entered (alien in the sense that the properties it holds are different from the properties of the world in which the individual layers were debugged) the performance of the Creature might continue to degrade. By not trying to have an analogous model of the world, centrally located in the system, we are less likely to have built in a dependence on that model being completely accurate. Rather, individual layers extract only those *aspects* (Agre and Chapman, 1987) of the world which they find relevant—projections of a representation into a simple subspace, if you like. Changes in the fundamental structure of the world have less chance of being reflected in every one of those projections than they would have of showing up as a difficulty in matching some query to a single central world model.
- Each layer of control can be thought of as having its own implicit purpose (or goal, if you insist). Since they are *active* layers, running in parallel and with access to sensors, they can monitor the environment and decide on the appropriateness of their goals. Sometimes goals can be abandoned when circumstances seem unpromising, and other times fortuitous circumstances can be taken advantage of. The key idea here is to use *the world itself as its own best model*, and to match the preconditions of each goal continuously against the real world. Because there is separate hardware for each layer, we can match as many goals as can exist in parallel; we do not pay any price for higher

numbers of goals, as we would if we tried to add more and more sophistication to a single processor, or even some multi-processor with a capacity-bounded network.

• The purpose of the Creature is implicit in its higher level purposes, goals, or layers. There need be no explicit representation of goals that some central (or distributed) process selects from, to decide what is most appropriate for the Creature to do next.

23.5.1   No representation versus no central representation

Just as there is no central representation, there is not even a central system. Each activity-producing layer connects perception to action directly. It is only the observer of the Creature who imputes a central representation or central control. The Creature itself has none; it is a collection of competing behaviors. Out of the local chaos of their interactions, there emerges, in the eye of an observer, a coherent pattern of behavior. There's no central, purposeful locus of control. (Minsky 1986 gives a similar account of how human behavior is generated.) Note carefully that we are not claiming that chaos is a necessary ingredient of intelligent behavior. Indeed, we advocate careful engineering of all the interactions within the system (evolution had the luxury of incredibly long time scales and enormous numbers of individual experiments, and thus perhaps was able to do without this careful engineering).

We do claim, however, that there need be no explicit representation of either the world or the intentions of the system to generate intelligent behaviors for a Creature. Without such explicit representations, and when viewed locally, the interactions may indeed seem chaotic and without purpose.

I claim there is more than this, however. Even at a local level, we do not have traditional AI representations. We never use tokens which have any semantics that can be attached to them. The best that can be said in our implementations is that a number is passed from one process to another. But it is only by looking at the state of both the first and second processes that that number can be given any interpretation at all. An extremist might say that we really do have representations, but they are just implicit. With an appropriate mapping of the complete system and its state to another domain, we could define representations that these numbers and topological connections between processes somehow encode.

However we are not happy with calling such things representations. They differ from standard representations in too many ways.

There are no variables that need instantiation in reasoning processes. (See Agre and Chapman, 1987 for a more thorough treatment of this.) There are no rules that need to be selected through pattern matching. There are no choices to be made. To a large extent, the state of the world determines the action of the Creature. Simon (1969) noted that the complexity of behavior of a system was not necessarily inherent in the complexity of the Creature, but perhaps in the complexity of the environment. He made this analysis in his description of an ant wandering the beach, but ignored its implications in the next paragraph when he talked about humans. We hypothesize (following Agre and Chapman) that much of even human-level activity is similarly a reflection of the world through very simple mechanisms without detailed representations.

23.6   The methodology in practice

In order to build systems based on an activity decomposition so that they are truly robust, we must rigorously follow a careful methodology.

23.6.1   Methodological maxims

First, it is vitally important to test the Creatures we build *in the real world*—the same world that we humans inhabit. It is disastrous to fall into the temptation of testing them in a simplified world first, even with the best intentions of later transferring activity to an unsimplified world. With a simplified world (matte painted walls, rectangular vertices everywhere, colored blocks as the only obstacles) it is very easy to build a submodule of the system that happens accidentally to rely on some of those simplified properties. This reliance can then easily be reflected in the requirements on the interfaces between that submodule and others. The disease spreads and the complete system depends in a subtle way on the simplified world. When it comes time to move to the unsimplified world, we gradually and painfully realize that every piece of the system must be rebuilt. Worse than that, we may need to rethink the total design, as the issues may change completely. We are not so concerned that it might be dangerous to test simplified Creatures first, and later add more sophisticated layers of control, because evolution has been successful using this approach.

Second, as *each* layer is built, it must be tested *extensively* in the real world. The system must interact with the real world over extended periods. Its behavior must be observed and be carefully and thoroughly debugged. When a second layer is added to an existing layer, there are three potential sources of bugs: the first layer, the second layer, and the interaction of the two layers. Eliminating the first of these sources of bugs as a possibility makes finding bugs much easier. Furthermore, there remains only one thing that it is possible to vary in order to fix the bugs—the second layer.

23.6.2   An instantiation of the methodology: Allen

We have now built a series of robots based on the methodology of task decomposition. They all operate in an unconstrained dynamic world (laboratory and office areas in the MIT Artificial Intelligence Laboratory). They successfully operate with people walking by, people deliberately trying to confuse them, and people just standing around watching them. All these robots are Creatures in the sense that, on power-up, they exist in the world and interact with it, pursuing multiple goals determined by their control layers implementing different activities. This is in contrast to other mobile robots that are given programs or plans to follow for a specific mission.

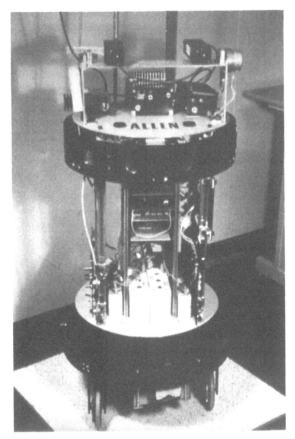

Figure 23.1
This is the first robot we built, called Allen.

Our first robot, named *Allen*, is shown in figure 23.1. Allen uses an offboard LISP machine for most of its computations. Allen implements the abstract architecture that we call the *subsumption architecture*, embodying the fundamental ideas of decomposition into layers of task-achieving behaviors, and incremental composition through debugging in the real world. (Details of this and other implementations can be found in Brooks, 1987.)

Each layer in the subsumption architecture is composed of a fixed-topology network of simple finite state machines. Each finite state machine has a handful of states, one or two internal registers, one or two internal timers, and access to simple computational machines which can compute things such as vector sums. The finite state machines run

asynchronously, sending and receiving fixed-length (in this case, 24-bit) messages over
wires. For Allen, these were virtual wires; on our later robots we have used physical wires
to connect computational components.

There is no central locus of control. Rather, the finite state machines are data-driven by
the messages they receive. The arrival of messages or the expiration of designated time periods cause the finite state machines to change state. The finite state machines have access
to the contents of the messages and might output them, test them with a predicate and con-
ditionally branch to a different state, or pass them to simple computation elements. There
is no possibility of access to global data, nor of dynamically established communications
links. There is thus no possibility of global control. All finite state machines are equal, yet
at the same time they are prisoners of their fixed-topology connections.

Layers are combined through mechanisms we call *suppression* (whence the name 'subsumption architecture') and *inhibition*. In both cases, as a new layer is added, one of the
new wires is side-tapped into an existing wire. A predefined time constant is associated
with each side-tap. In the case of suppression, the side-tapping occurs on the input side of
a finite state machine. If a message arrives on the new wire, it is directed to the input port
of the finite state machine as though it had arrived on the existing wire. Additionally any
new messages on the existing wire are suppressed (that is, rejected) for the specified time
period. For inhibition, the side-tapping occurs on the output side of a finite state machine.
A message on the new wire simply inhibits messages being emitted on the existing wire
for the specified time period. Unlike suppression, the new message is not delivered in their
place.

As an example, consider the three layers of figure 23.2. These are three layers of control
that we have run on Allen for well over a year. The robot has a ring of 12 ultrasonic sonars
as its primary sensors. Every second, these sonars are run to give twelve radial depth
measurements. Sonar is extremely noisy due to many objects being mirrors to sonar. There
are thus problems with specular reflection and return paths following multiple reflections
due to surface skimming with low angles of incidence (less than thirty degrees).

In more detail the three layers work as follows:

1. The lowest-level layer implements a behavior which makes the robot (the physical
   embodiment of the Creature) avoid hitting objects. It avoids both static objects and
   moving objects—even those that are actively attacking it. The finite state machine
   labelled *sonar* simply runs the sonar devices and every second emits an instantaneous
   map with the readings converted to polar coordinates. This map is passed on to the
   collide and *feelforce* finite state machines. The first of these simply watches to see of
   there is anything dead ahead, and if so sends a *halt* message to the finite state machine
   in charge of running the robot forwards. (If that finite state machine is not in the
   correct state the message may well be ignored.) Simultaneously, the other finite state
   machine computes a repulsive force on the robot, based on an inversesquare law, where

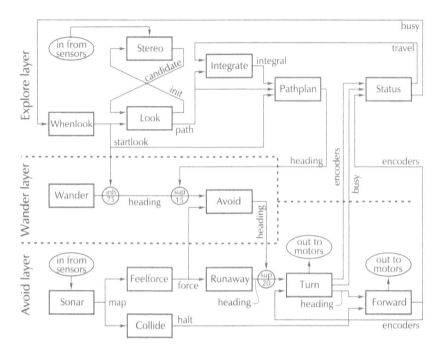

Figure 23.2
We wire finite state machines together into layers of control. Each layer is built on top of existing layers. Lower
layers never rely on the existence of higher-level layers. (This is Allen.)

each sonar return is considered to indicate the presence of a repulsive object. The
contributions from all the sonars are vector-added to produce an overall force acting on
the robot. The output is passed to the *runaway* machine, which thresholds it and passes
it on to the *turn* machine, which orients the robot directly away from the summed
repulsive force. Finally the *forward* machine drives the robot forward. Whenever this
machine receives a halt message while the robot is driving forward, it commands the
robot to halt.

This network of finite state machines generates behaviors which let the robot avoid
objects. If it starts in the middle of an empty room it simply sits there. If someone
walks up to it, the robot moves away. If it moves in the direction of other obstacles it
halts. Overall, it manages to exist in a dynamic environment without hitting or being
hit by objects.

2. The next layer makes the robot wander about, when not busy avoiding objects. The
   wander finite state machine generates a random heading for the robot every ten seconds
   or so. The *avoid* machine treats that heading as an attractive force and sums it with the
   repulsive force computed from the sonars. It uses the result to suppress the lower-level

behavior, forcing the robot to move in a direction close to what *wander* decided but at the same time avoiding any obstacles. Note that if the *turn* and *forward* finite state machines are busy running the robot, the new impulse to wander will be ignored.

3. The third layer makes the robot try to explore. It looks for distant places, then tries to reach them. This layer suppresses the wander layer, and observes how the bottom layer diverts the robot due to obstacles (perhaps dynamic). It corrects for any divergences, and the robot achieves the goal.

The *whenlook* finite state machine notices when the robot is not busy moving, and starts up the free space finder (labelled *stereo* in the diagram) finite state machine. At the same time it inhibits wandering behavior so that the observation will remain valid. When a path is observed it is sent to the *pathplan* finite state machine, which injects a commanded direction to the *avoid* finite state machine. In this way lower-level obstacle avoidance continues to function. This may cause the robot to go in a direction different from that desired by *pathplan*. For that reason, the actual path of the robot is monitored by the *integrate* finite state machine, which sends updated estimates to the *pathplan* machine. This machine then acts as a difference engine, forcing the robot in the desired direction and compensating for the actual path of the robot as it avoids obstacles.

These are just the particular layers that were first implemented on Allen. (See Brooks, 1986 for more details; Brooks and Connell (1986) report on another three layers implemented on that particular robot.)

23.6.3   A second example: Herbert

Allen's lowest layer was entirely reactive: it merely avoided collisions. But its next two layers, *wander* and *explore*, were not entirely reactive. Our second Creature, a mobile robot named *Herbert* (Connell, 1989), was a much more ambitious project, and pushed the idea of reactivity—as in Allen's lowest layer—much further.

Herbert (shown in figure 23.3) used thirty infrared proximity sensors to navigate along walls and through doorways, a magnetic compass to maintain a global sense of direction, a laser scanner to find soda-can-like objects visually, and a host of sensors on an arm with a set of fifteen behaviors which, together, were sufficient to locate and pick up soda cans reliably. Herbert's task was to wander around people's offices looking for soda cans, pick one up, and bring it back to where the robot had started from. Herbert did succeed at this task (although mechanical failures in the seating of its onboard chips limited reliable operation to about fifteen minutes at a time).

In programming Herbert, it was decided that it should maintain no internal state longer than three seconds, and that there would be no internal communication between behavior generating modules. Each one was connected to sensors on the input side, and a fixed-priority arbitration network on the output side. The arbitration network drove the actuators.

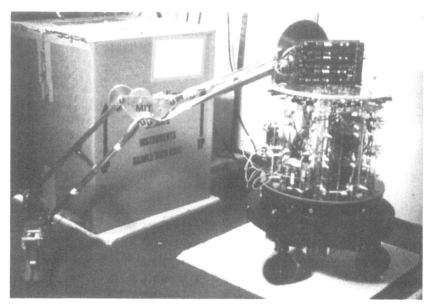

Figure 23.3
This is Herbert, a more ambitious robot than Allen.

Since Herbert maintained hardly any internal state—hardly any memory—it often had to rely on the world itself as its only available "model" of the world. Further, the world itself was the only effective medium of communication between Herbert's separate modules. The laser-based soda-can finder, for example, drove the robot so that its arm was lined up in front of the soda can. But it did not tell the arm controller that there was now a soda can ready to be picked up. Rather, the arm behaviors monitored the shaft encoders on the wheels, and, when they noticed that there was no body motion, initiated motions of the arm—which, in turn, triggered other behaviors such that, eventually, the robot would pick up the soda can.

The advantage of this approach was that there was no need to set up internal expectations for what was going to happen next. That meant that the control system could both (1) be naturally opportunistic if fortuitous circumstances presented themselves, and (2) easily respond to changed circumstances—such as some other object approaching on a collision course.

As one example of how the arm behaviors cascaded upon one another, consider actually grasping a soda can. The hand had a grasp reflex that operated whenever something broke an infrared beam between the fingers. When the arm located a soda can with its local sensors, it simply drove the hand so that the two fingers lined up on either side of the can. The hand then independently grasped the can. Given this arrangement, it was possible for a human to hand a soda can to the robot. *As* soon as it was grasped, the arm retracted—it did not matter whether it was a soda can that was intentionally grasped, or one that magically appeared. The same opportunism among behaviors let the arm adapt automatically to a wide variety of cluttered desktops, and still successfully find the soda can.

The point of Herbert is two-fold:

- It demonstrates complex, apparently goal-directed and intentional behavior in a system which has no long-term internal state and no internal communication; and
- It is very easy for an observer of such a system to attribute more complex internal structure than really exists—Herbert, for instance, appeared to be doing things like path planning and map building, even though it was not.

23.7   What this is not

The subsumption architecture with its network of simple machines is reminiscent, at the surface level at least, of a number of mechanistic approaches to intelligence, such as connectionism and neural networks. But it is different in many respects from these endeavors, and also quite different from many other post-Dartmouth[1] traditions in artificial intelligence. We very briefly explain those differences in the following paragraphs.

23.7.1   It isn't connectionism

Connectionists try to make networks of simple processors. In that regard, the things they build (in simulation only—no connectionist system has ever driven a real robot in a real environment, no matter how simple) are similar to the subsumption networks we build. However, their processing nodes tend to be uniform, and they seek insights (as their name suggests) from learning how best to interconnect them (which is usually assumed to mean richly, at least). Our nodes, by contrast, are all unique finite state machines, the density of connections among them is much lower, is not at all uniform, and is especially low between layers. Additionally, connectionists seem to be looking for explicit distributed representations to arise spontaneously from their networks. We harbor no such hopes because we believe representations are not necessary and appear only in the eye or mind of the observer.

23.7.2   It isn't neural networks

Neural-network research is the parent discipline, of which connectionism is a recent incarnation. Workers in neural networks claim that there is some biological significance to their network nodes, as models of neurons. Most of the models seem wildly implausible given the paucity of modeled connections relative to the thousands found in real neurons. We claim no biological significance in our choice of finite state machines as network nodes.

23.7.3   It isn't production rules

Each individual activity-producing layer of our architecture could be viewed as in implementation of a production rule. When the right conditions are met in the environment ,
a certain action will be performed. We feel that analogy is a little like saying that any
FORTRAN program with IF statements is implementing a production-rule system. But a
production system really is more than that—it has a rule base, from which a particular rule
is selected by matching the preconditions for some or all of the rules to a given database;
and these preconditions may include variables which must be bound to individuals in that
database. Our layers, on the other hand, run in parallel and have no variables or need for
matching. Instead, aspects of the world are extracted and directly trigger or modify certain
behaviors of the layer.

23.7.4   It isn't a blackboard

If one really wanted, one could make an analogy of our networks to a blackboard control architecture. Some of the finite state machines would be localized knowledge sources. Others
would be processes acting on these knowledge sources by finding them on the blackboard.
There is a simplifying point in our architecture however: all the processes know exactly
where to look on the "blackboard", since they are hardwired to the correct place. I think
this forced analogy indicates its own weakness. There is no flexibility at all in where a
process can gather appropriate knowledge. Most advanced blackboard architectures make
heavy use of the general sharing and availability of almost all knowledge. Furthermore,
in spirit at least, blackboard systems tend to hide from a consumer of knowledge who the
particular producer was. This is the primary means of abstraction in blackboard systems.
In our system we make such connections explicit and permanent.

23.7.5   It isn't German philosophy

In some circles, much credence is given to Heidegger as one who understood the dynamics of existence. Our approach has certain similarities to work inspired by this German
philosopher (for instance, Agre and Chapman, 1987) but our work was not so inspired. It
is based purely on engineering considerations. That does not preclude it from being used
in philosophical debate as an example on any side of any fence, however.

23.8   Key ideas

Situatedness, embodiment, intelligence, and emergence can be identified as key ideas that
have led to the new style of artificial intelligence research that we are calling "behavior-
based robots".

23.8.1 Situatedness

Traditional artificial intelligence has adopted a style of research where the agents that are built to test theories about intelligence are essentially problem solvers that work in a symbolic abstracted domain. The symbols may have referents in the minds of the builders of the systems, but there is nothing to ground those referents in any real world. Furthermore, the agents are not situated in a world at all. Rather, they are simply given a problem, and they solve it. Then they are given another problem, and they solve that one. They are not participating in a *world* at all, as do agents in the usual sense.

In these systems, there is no external world per se, with continuity, surprises, or history. The programs deal only with a model world, with its own built-in physics. There is a blurring between the knowledge of the agent and the world it is supposed to be operating in. Indeed, in many artificial intelligence systems, there is no distinction between the two: the agent is capable of direct and perfect perception as well as direct and perfect action. When consideration is given to porting such agents or systems to operate in the world, the question arises of what sort of representation they need of the real world. Over the years within traditional artificial intelligence, it has become accepted that they will need an objective model of the world with individuated entities, tracked and identified over time. The models of knowledge representation that have been developed expect and require such a one-to-one correspondence between the world and the agent's representation of it.

Early AI robots, such as Shakey and the Cart, certainly followed this approach. They built models of the world, planned paths around obstacles, and updated their estimates of where the objects were relative to themselves as they moved. We have developed a different approach (Brooks, 1986) in which a mobile robot uses the world itself as its own model—continuously referring to its sensors rather than to an internal world model. The problems of object class and identity disappear. The perceptual processing becomes much simpler. And the performance of this robot (Allen) is better in comparable tasks than the Cart. (The tasks carried out by Allen, not to mention Herbert, are in a different class from those attempted by Shakey—Shakey could certainly not have done what Allen does.)

A situated agent must respond in a timely fashion to its inputs. Modelling the world completely under these conditions can be computationally challenging. But a world in which it is situated also provides some continuity to the agent. That continuity can be relied upon, so that the agent can use its perception of the world instead of an objective world model. The representational primitives that are useful then change quite dramatically from those in traditional artificial intelligence.

The key idea from situatedness is: *The world is its own best model.*

23.8.2 Embodiment

There are two reasons that embodiment of intelligent systems is critical. First, only an embodied intelligent agent is fully validated as one that can deal with the real world. Second, only through a physical grounding can any internal symbolic or other system find a place to bottom out, and give "meaning" to the processing going on within the system.

The physical grounding of a robot within the world forces its designer to deal with all the issues. If the intelligent agent has a body, has sensors, and has actuators, then all the details and issues of being in the world must be faced. It is no longer possible to argue in conference papers that the simulated perceptual system is realistic, or that problems of uncertainty in action will not be significant. Instead, physical experiments can be done simply and repeatedly. There is no room for "cheating" (in the sense of self-delusion). When this is done, it is usual to find that many of the problems that used to seem significant are not so in the physical system. Typically, "puzzle-like" situations, where symbolic reasoning had seemed necessary, tend not to arise in embodied systems. At the same time, many issues that had seemed like nonproblems become major hurdles. Typically, these concern aspects of perception and action. (In fact, there is some room for cheating even here: for instance, the physical environment can be specially simplified for the robot—and it can be very hard in some cases to identify such self-delusions.)

Without an ongoing participation in and perception of the world, there is no meaning for an agent—everything is empty symbols referring only to other symbols. Arguments might be made that, at some level of abstraction, even the human mind operates in this solipsist position. However, biological evidence suggests that the human mind's connection to the world is so strong, and so many-faceted, that these philosophical abstractions may not be correct.

The key idea from embodiment is: *The world grounds the regress of meaning-giving.*

23.8.3 Intelligence

Earlier, I argued that the sorts of activities we usually think of as demonstrating intelligence in humans have been taking place for only a very small fraction of our evolutionary lineage. I argued further that the "simple" things concerning perception and mobility in a dynamic environment took evolution much longer to perfect, and that all those capabilities are a necessary basis for "higher-level" intellect.

Therefore, I proposed looking at simpler animals as a bottom-up model for building intelligence. It is soon apparent, when "reasoning" is stripped away as the prime component of a robot's intellect, that the dynamics of the interaction of the robot and its environment are primary determinants of the structure of its intelligence.

Simon's (1969) discussion of the ant walking along a beach started off in a similar vein. He pointed out that the complexity of the behavior of the ant is more a reflection of the complexity of its environment than of its own internal complexity. He speculated that the same might be true of humans— but then, within two pages of text, reduced the study of human behavior to the domain of crypt-arithmetic problems.

It is hard to draw a line between what is intelligence and what is environmental interaction. In a sense, it doesn't really matter which is which, inasmuch as all intelligent systems must be situated in some world or other if they are to be successful or useful entities.

The key idea from intelligence is: *Intelligence is determined by the dynamics of interaction with the world.*

23.8.4 Emergence

In discussing where intelligence resides in an artificial intelligence program, Minsky (1961) points out that "there is never any 'heart' in a program," but rather that, if we look, "we find senseless loops and sequences of trivial operations." It is hard to point at a single component as the seat of intelligence. There is no homunculus. Rather, intelligence emerges from the interaction of the components of the system. The way in which it emerges, however, is quite different for traditional and for behavior-based artificial intelligence systems.

In traditional artificial intelligence, the modules that are defined are information-processing or functional modules. Typically, these might include a perception module, a planner, a world modeler, a learner, and the like. Such components directly participate in the functions of perceiving, planning, modeling, learning, and so on. Intelligent behavior of the system as a whole—such as avoiding obstacles, standing up, controlling gaze, et cetera—emerges from the interaction of the components.

In behavior-based artificial intelligence, by contrast, the modules that are defined are behavior-producing. Typically, these might include modules for obstacle avoidance, standing up, gaze control, and the like. Such components directly participate in producing the behaviors of avoiding obstacles, standing up, controlling gaze, and so on. Intelligent functionality of the system as a whole—such as perception, planning, modeling, learning, et cetera—emerges from the interaction of the components.

Although this dualism between traditional and behavior-based systems looks pretty, it is not entirely accurate. Traditional systems have hardly ever been really connected to the world, and so the emergence of intelligent behavior is, in most cases, more of an expectation than an established phenomenon. Conversely, because of the many behaviors present in a behavior-based system, and their individual dynamics of interaction with the world, it is often hard to say that a particular series of actions was produced by a particular behavior-module. Sometimes many behaviors are occurring simultaneously, or are switching rapidly.

It is not feasible to identify the seat of intelligence within any system, since intelligence is produced by the interactions of many components. Intelligence can only be determined by the total behavior of the system and how that behavior appears in relation to the environment.

The key idea from emergence is: *Intelligence is in the eye of the observer.*

23.9   Limits to growth

Since our approach is performance based, it is the performance of the systems we build which must be used to measure its usefulness and to point to its limitations.

We claim that our behavior-based robots, using the subsumption architecture to implement complete Creatures, are by now the most reactive real-time mobile robots in existence. Most other mobile robots are still at the stage of individual "experimental runs" in static environments, or at best in completely mapped static environments. Ours, on the other hand, operate completely autonomously in complex dynamic environments at the flick of their on-switches, and continue until their batteries are drained. We believe they operate at a level closer to simple insect-level intelligence than to bacteria-level intelligence. Evolution took 3 billion years to get from single cells to insects, and only another 500 million years from there to humans. This statement is not intended as a prediction of our future performance, but rather to indicate the nontrivial nature of insect-level intelligence.

Despite this good performance to date, there are a number of serious questions about our approach. We have beliefs and hopes about how these questions will be resolved, but under our criteria only performance truly counts. Experiments and building more complex systems take time. So, in the interim, the best we can do is indicate where the main questions lie, with the hope that there is at least a plausible path forward to more intelligent machines from our current situation.

Our belief is that the sorts of activity-producing layers of control we are developing (mobility, vision, and survival related tasks) are necessary prerequisites for higher-level intelligence in the style we attribute to human beings. The most natural and serious questions concerning limits of our approach are:

- How many behavior-based layers can be built in the subsumption architecture before the interactions between layers become too complex to continue?
- How complex can the behaviors be that are developed without the aid of central representations?
- Can higher-level functions such as learning occur in these fixed topology networks of simple finite state machines?

Only experiments with real Creatures in real worlds can answer the natural doubts about our approach. Time will tell.

Notes for Chapter 23

1 *Editor's note:* Newell and Simon presented the first working AI program, *The Logic Theorist*, at a famous workshop organized by John McCarthy at Dartmouth College in the summer of 1956.

What Does Biorobotics Offer Philosophy? A Tale of Two Navigation Systems

24

Barbara Webb
2023

24.1 Introduction

The biorobotic approach is an identifiable strand of artificial intelligence that has two distinctive features. First, it sets out to reproduce (or account for) animal intelligence, focusing on those aspects of mind that humans have in common with other species capable of complex, goal-directed and adaptive behaviour. Second, it uses robotic models—real, physical systems that interact with the real world—to test hypotheses about intelligent function.

Although never mainstream, some of the earliest approaches to AI were biorobotic, e.g., Walter (1961). Brooks's influential essay "Intelligence without Representation" (Brooks, 1991) is appropriately credited with reviving the approach for a generation of AI researchers. Brooks argued that what is normally considered intelligence in AI research (language, logical reasoning, playing chess) is a recent, largely cultural, development that depends on a deep foundation of successful world-interaction common to most animals. Moreover, the latter is the part of intelligence we have least understanding of, or ability to replicate. Perhaps, Brooks suggested, trying to reproduce the intelligence of insects would be a good way to approach some key problems in AI. Much of AI glosses over the problem of interaction with the world by not requiring the systems to act in the real world. It assumes an abstracted representation for reasoning and planning rather than requiring this representation to be derived from raw sensory data. Indeed, understanding what is needed for acting in the world often reveals that an abstracted representation is not actually needed for the task: getting across the room without running into objects may not require a veridical three-dimensional map of the room and explicit path planning.

In this chapter, I want to reflect on the outcome of taking the biorobotic approach to AI as a serious research agenda; and more specifically examine how building robot models of insect intelligence might provide novel insight into Mind Design. The essential motivation from an AI perspective remains the same: despite advances on many fronts, we are still largely unable to replicate the kind of animal intelligence that would allow a physical robot to achieve an interesting task under realistic and varying conditions. An example of the kind of task performed successfully by many animals but beyond the state of the art in robotics is central-place foraging as seen in ants and bees. Individual insects are able to traverse long distances over unknown terrain, identify scarce resource items from amongst a huge array of distractor objects, manipulate them for transport, and return to the origin of their journey despite having moved far beyond the range of any direct sensory contact with the hive or nest. This level of behavioural competence seems to strongly motivate the assumption that representational processes are taking place in the animal's brain—even if not in the form of a full "cognitive map" (Webb, 2019) then at least in the ability to track internally the distance and direction of the nest (Webb, 2006).

Although insect navigation has been previously debated as an exemplar of how intelligence requires representation (e.g. Gallistel, 2003), it has not been so widely discussed as the rodent navigation system (e.g. Bechtel, 2014). But it has a particular, recently developed advantage: we now have detailed and thoroughly grounded models of some of the key neural mechanisms of insect navigation. Despite many fascinating neuroscientific findings in rodents (and particularly interesting comparative insights from bats (Geva-Sagiv et al., 2015)), the actual, functional relevance for behaviour of the place-and-grid-cell systems in the mammalian brain are essentially unknown. Indeed, activity in these systems could even be epiphenomena of some more fundamental process. This leaves philosophers open to argue that rodent navigation operates with symbols, distributed representations, predictive models, or as a (non-representational) dynamical system (e.g. Segundo-Ortin and Hutto, 2019). By contrast, for the foraging insect we can describe, at the level of single identified neurons, the full pathway linking sensory input to motor commands that enable it to navigate back to its nest and demonstrate a circuit that supports this function when implemented on a robot. This would seem to provide a unique opportunity to resolve some of the fundamental questions around the representational nature of biological intelligence. When we look at the actual brain mechanisms underlying this task of significant cognitive complexity, do we see "Intelligence without Representation"?

24.2   Representation—what is at issue?

I should outline, at this point, the sense of "representation" that I take to be at issue when using robots as a comparison point for animal intelligence. It is clear that, in both robots and animals, an important contributor to the flexibility of behaviour of which they are capable is the fact that a wide array of physical signals are transformed into a common electronic currency that supports sophisticated internal processing (e.g., with arbitrary input output functions, delays, memory, gating, etc.). I do not take this in itself to constitute "representation" but will call it "computation" (inclusive of analog computation), in order to denote the difference from the type of processing (also necessary for a robot or an animal to behave in the world) that is inherently tied to one physical basis, such as sensory transduction, production of locomotor forces, or digestion/power consumption. In conventional robotics, such computational processing typically (but not necessarily) takes a representational form: reconstructing an internal model of relevant properties of the external world; and using operations on this model to determine suitable actions to be executed. Someone examining the robot's code (although possibly not its instantiation in silicon operations) could point to particular variables that stand in for, and are operated on in logical accordance with, relevant world properties. The empirical question at issue is whether this is the correct, or most productive, way to interpret at least some of the brain processing that occurs in animals.

Some might argue that in the robot case, the "standing-in" properties of its variables are dependent on the intentionality of the human programmer, and not inherently "representational" from the robot's point of view (Searle, 1980). I think this is a defensible position, which also undermines the interpretation of any neural process as "representing" the world to the animal. However, this by no means settles the empirical question just posed, which I take to be the question of more practical interest to cognitive neuroscience and AI. More specifically, the issue I want to examine is the validity of a methodological approach to understanding natural brains that takes "representation" to be a key concept in two complementary ways. One is from the top-down: that to understand an intelligent behaviour, we should consider what representational format and processes (if any) are required to derive appropriate actions from inputs, and then (if we care about implementation) look for these in brain processes. The other is bottom up: by measuring the response of neurons or brain areas to external cues, we will build up an understanding of what those responses represent and how they are processed to control behaviour. Both of these have been challenged by philosophers (e.g., Brette, 2019), but they remain the prevailing view.

Note here that the biorobotic approach per se is agnostic on this issue. Biorobotics seeks to discover and implement (as machines) the mechanisms of animal intelligence, whether or not these take a representational form. My aim in the following sections is to make the issue of "Intelligence without Representation" more concrete by explaining what we have learnt by taking a biorobotic approach to uncovering the neural circuits for insect navigation. I will first describe a specific navigational problem and an example of a human-designed (representational) tool used to solve it. I will then describe the neural circuit that appears to underlie the same performance in the insect, which has some striking correspondences. I will then reflect on the role of representational thinking in uncovering and understanding this circuit. I conclude that representational perspectives have an important explanatory role, but problems arise when that perspective is applied in neurocognitive contexts without appropriate consideration of the actual, embodied, behavioural task that the relevant circuit supports. In other words the behavioural and mechanistic embedding that is inherent in the biorobotic approach facilitates discovering what is represented.

24.3   Dead reckoning and the traverse board

Tracking your current location relative to a starting point and/or a goal destination has
been important throughout human civilization and is particularly difficult when undertaking journeys out of sight of landmarks. It became crucial in the age of ocean-crossing
exploration. Before the advent of satellite navigation, a key method used on ships was
so-called "dead reckoning," that is, keeping track of the direction and distance travelled
on each leg of the journey and combining them to estimate the current location relative
to the starting point. An aid to this process is a tool known as a "traverse board" (May
and Holder, 1973), designed as a simple way for sailors to collect the relevant information
on the ship's travel during the standard watch of four hours (figure 24.1). It consists of a
wooden board with peg holes arranged in radiating lines to represent each compass direction, and below, further holes in rows to represent speed. For each half-hour of the watch,
a linked pair of pegs would be placed to mark the compass bearing and speed of sailing
(measured in knots). Afterwards, a navigator could use the eight vectors thus represented
to calculate the new position on a chart, and the board could then be reset for the next
watch.

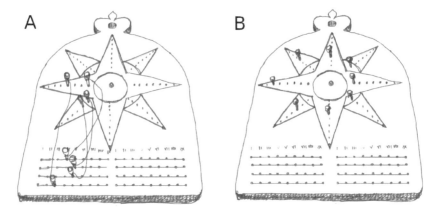

Figure 24.1
The principle of traverse board navigation. A: Actual usage: each connected pair of pegs records the compass
heading (above) and speed of travel (below) for one leg of the journey. This can be used to estimate the position
with respect to the starting point by summing the vectors. B: Alternative usage: each peg is moved outwards on
each leg proportionally to the speed travelled in that direction. The peg pattern is a distributed representation of
the vector sum.

It seems self-evident that the traverse board is a representational device. The positions of the pegs stand in for the actual journey made in the last four hours. This tracks a distal property of the world—the ship's location relative to its starting point—which is not recoverable from an immediate proximal signal. The board exists to perform this function, is designed to be robust with respect to this function, but can nevertheless misrepresent the true state of the world. It has a producer (the sailor) and a consumer (the navigator). It is an "information bearing structure" that can play a role in various navigational functions: for example, it can be projected into a map, predict landfall, or be used to set a course for home. And if one imagined a sailor with a good memory internalising the board—keeping mental track of the eight compass points and speeds during their watch, and maybe even doing a rough addition in their head to estimate their progress—it would seem a cardinal example of mental representations in the service of intelligent action.

To help provide insight into what follows, I am going to describe some simple variants on how the physical traverse board could have been used (although I have not discovered any actual account of it being used in the way I am about to describe). In conventional use, the speed and direction encoding are separated, but an obvious way to combine them would be to choose the radial line of pegs representing the current heading and count outwards from the centre to place the peg at a point representing the speed. If the same direction occurred during a later segment of the watch, the peg could just be moved farther out—effectively doing some online processing toward the final summation. One advantage would be that it would become relatively easy to see, from a glance at the board, what the approximate total progress of the ship has been.

In fact, it would be possible to convert the traverse board into a physical computer for the sum of the legs of travel, with the following augmentation. Instead of just moving one peg, representing the current compass heading, all the pegs could be moved proportionally to the projection of the current vector onto the directional axis they represent. Mathematically, the correct proportion is given by taking the cosine of the difference in the compass heading from the axis in question, but for the sailors' convenience, a simple guide showing the relative amounts (for each gradation in speed) by which each peg should be moved could be provided in advance. After the eight half-hour watches, the vector sum can be read directly from the board, as the direction will correspond to the outermost peg, and the distance to the difference between the innermost and outermost peg (which should fall opposite to one another). This calculation will only be approximate, due to the coarse encoding imposed by the pegholes, but it will be at least as accurate as the original method. It might seem obvious to the more geometrically astute that in fact, two axes would be sufficient and would constitute a cartesian encoding of the vectors, and the equivalent of algebraic summation to get the vector sum. If we were indeed to translate the method to an actual computer, this would be the efficient way to solve the problem. On the other hand, the use of redundant vectors makes the information more easily perceptible at a glance for the sailors.

Note also that if the sailors' aim in tracking their position was solely to be able to return to their point of origin (e.g., returning to port after a fishing excursion), they could potentially use the traverse board information directly, without explicitly extracting the vector sum. In the original version, a simple strategy would be to sail back along each of the eight legs that has been recorded—this would not need to be in order, as the sum would come out the same. But using the augmented version, this homeward journey would be more efficient— they should simply move in the direction opposite to the outermost peg, which should be the straight direction home. Indeed, even more simply, they should try and maintain this compass bearing, that is, adjust their course to the right or left if the compass indicates they are left or right of the direction indicated on the board. If they continue to update the board throughout the homeward journey, then gradually the difference between the pegs on each radii will be reduced, at each point indicating the remaining distance to travel. When all the pegs are level again, this signals that the origin should have been reached (all legs taken sum to zero). Note that this method (constantly updating the board to always represent the current vector sum relative to the origin) will also automatically correct the course if adverse conditions such as the prevailing wind force a deviation from the desired homeward direction.

The use of the traverse board, particularly as an immediate guide to control navigation back to the starting point, might be considered a nice example of "extended cognition" (Clark and Chalmers, 1998). By placing the burden of memory outside the head, and in- deed, by using external aids such as a compass to get global directional information, it significantly enhances the human's cognitive capacity to track their location in space. It might also be discussed as an example of a distributed representation (Gelder, 1992)— no single peg position "stands in for" the distance or the direction to the origin, but their collective positions encode this information in a manner that can be used effectively to get home, even without explicitly decoding the information. However, the reason I have discussed the traverse board at such length is not to illustrate extended or distributed cogni- tion, but because it provides a surprisingly close analogy to the mechanism in the insect's brain that supports the same behaviour.

24.4   Path integration and the central complex

It has been known for a long time that insects (and other animals) are able to perform the equivalent of navigational dead-reckoning, that is, to integrate motion on along the legs of an outbound path and take the direct path back to the starting location. The terminology most often used is "path integration" (Heinze et al., 2018), and it has been most strikingly demonstrated in desert ants (Müller and Wehner, 1988). Individual ants, after taking a convoluted outward foraging route that can be hundreds of meters in length (Huber and Knaden, 2015), will run on a bee-line home when they discover food. If displaced just after they collect the food, they will follow an exactly parallel path, and stop to search after traversing the appropriate distance. This demonstrates that no landmark or chemical cues are required to guide the homeward journey and that both the direction and length of the "home vector" guides correct action.

This behaviour has been popularly used to argue for internal representations in the insect brain (Gallistel, 1990) yet is also often cited as an alternative explanation to a "cognitive map" for the insect (Cruse and Wehner, 2011). Indeed, it seems possible that the ant might be able to keep an estimate of its location, at any moment, relative to home without necessarily forming any enduring representation of the overall layout of its environment, just as the sailors described above could potentially get home using their traverse board without ever plotting their position on a map. On the other hand, the ability to correctly and consistently update an internal estimate of how to return to a home location that has gone far out of sensory range requires, on the face of it, impressive geometrical operations. Certainly, this exceeds the simple sensorimotor reflexes, fixed action patterns, or stimulus-response associations that might be thought to exhaust the capabilities of a brain that has only ∼100,000 neurons. The desert ant has been shown to use celestial information (the sun and polarisation pattern in the sky) to detect its compass direction (Wehner, 2008) and both step-counting and optic flow to estimate distance travelled (Wolf et al., 2018). It can also use memory of the home vector taken from a food location to subsequently return to that location (Wehner et al., 2004). Bees appear able to do vector addition to find shortcuts between food locations (Menzel et al., 2012), and honeybees are famous for being able to communicate a food vector to a nestmate through the waggle dance (Riley et al., 2005). As such, this seems an astonishingly flexible system, yet consensus on whether it constitutes an example of internal representations in the service of cognition is lacking.

One reason for this impasse has been that, despite decades of research into the behaviour, and many algorithmic models, the actual mechanisms supporting path integration in the insect brain were unknown. However, we have recently gained unique insight into the neural circuitry that is almost certainly responsible for the vector operations that occur in the insect brain, both to maintain an accurate home vector estimate and to use it to steer home (Stone et al., 2017; Stankiewicz and Webb, 2020).

As has been anticipated, the essence of this circuit is an implementation of the "augmented traverse board" I have described above. The central complex of the insect brain has an eight-fold columnar structure that topologically forms a circle (figure 24.2). Identified "compass" neurons (inner ring) in the protocerebral bridge region have been shown to respond according to the heading direction of the animal, relative to visual cues including polarised light. Thus each column corresponds to a geocentric (more precisely, a celestial) compass direction. Transverse neurons (labelled as "speed") connecting to all columns

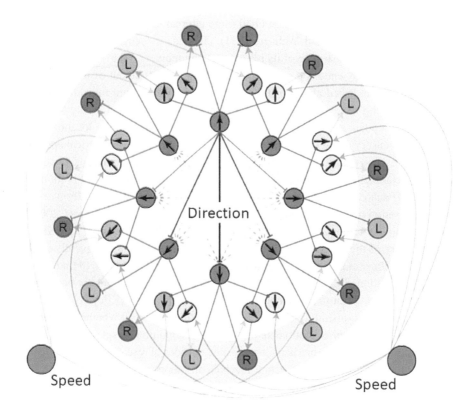

Figure 24.2
The neural circuit that underlies path integration in insects (Stone et al., 2017). Note that each element and connection of the illustrated circuit has a direct correspondence in known neuroanatomy. See text for details.

provide input from neurons that respond to optic flow, proportionally to the speed of the insect. A set of identified neurons in each column have precisely the right connections to be able to augment their activity based on these two inputs; that is, the speed signal can be accumulated differently in each neural column according to how closely the current heading direction matches that column's preferred compass tuning. Thus, following just the same principle as described for the traverse board, at any point in time, the distributed pattern of activity across this set of "home vector" neurons (middle ring) will be equivalent to the vector sum of all legs of an outbound path.

In principle, the downstream circuit could read off the home vector, by finding the column with highest activity (direction) and taking the difference between the highest and lowest activity across the columns (distance). In practice, however, the downstream connections appear to implement a steering circuit that can directly control the animal so that it moves back to the origin. In essence, this occurs through connections that shift the output of the "home vector" neurons by one column to the left and one column to the right, respectively. The "steering" neurons (outer ring) receiving these inputs also receive direct inhibition from the "compass" neurons encoding the current heading of the animal so that their activity reflects the difference of the current heading from a left- or right-shifted home vector. What this tells the insect is whether turning left or right would produce a better match, or in other words, at any moment, how to correct its course to go in the home vector direction. Indeed, these steering neurons connect directly to steering circuitry in the premotor area of the insect brain.

There are a number of additional subtleties that optimise this circuit for the function of accurate path integration. For example, inhibitory connections between the compass neurons appear to shape the response across them to closely approximate a cosine—the correct mathematical mapping of the vector heading onto the axis corresponding to each column (Lyu et al., 2020). The optic flow neurons are in fact responsive to translation of the animal in orthogonal directions, which allows the system as a whole to track the actual ground velocity even if the animal is not moving in the direction it is facing, for example, during side-slip in flight (Stone et al., 2017). The constant update of the circuit, including during the homeward journey, results in an emergent search behaviour centred on the home location when the origin of the journey has been reached. It has also been possible to show that very minimal additions (as yet to be confirmed neurophysiologically) to this circuit would support the ability to memorise and return to food locations and to do the vector addition needed to take shortcuts between them (Le Moël et al., 2019).

24.5 Representation and the insect brain

I have endeavoured in the above description to avoid as far as possible representational language, but this is a struggle, and certainly biologists have no hesitation in saying each column "represents" a compass direction, and the activity "encodes" the distance travelled, etc. There seems the most direct (and productive) correspondence possible between the function of the traverse board + ship's crew in controlling the ship and the central complex + insect sensory and motor neurons in controlling the insect's body. The understanding of the computation required—that a "home vector" representing the position must be calculated by accumulating velocity and that possession of such a vector can be used flexibly in alternative behaviours such as short cuts and communication of salient locations—would seem a vindication of adopting a top-down representational approach to the explanation of behaviour. Indeed, many of the salient neural mechanisms that have now been mapped in the insect brain were anticipated in a purely hypothetical model suggested some twenty years earlier (Wittmann and Schwegler, 1995), in which it was suggested that the best way to represent and process vectors in a neural system for path integration would be as a distributed sinusoidal activity across a neural array representing different directions.

The close connection that has now been discovered between this hypothetical network and the actual neural circuitry was highly dependent on neurophysiological results derived by the classic method: testing stimulus changes to which individual neurons were responsive, and hence characterising their functional role as representing a particular property required for a high-level computation. In this case, the clearest example is the discovery of the "compass" encoding of preferred polarisation direction responses across successive columns of the protocerebral bridge (Heinze and Homberg, 2007). Thus the bottom-up approach suggested by the representational viewpoint also seems to have been vindicated.

Moreover, this representational account seems more productive than considering the whole as a coupled dynamical system (Van Gelder, 1998). We might suggest an alternative metaphor to the traverse board, in which an agent is connected into an environment with a set of springs along different axes. Motion of the animal stores kinetic energy in the springs as the agent moves away from the (stable) home position, and when released, the agent should be pulled directly back to this attractor. So perhaps the whole neural system I have described can be thought of as a purely physical system with the requisite dynamics to create such an energy landscape. However, the transduction and transformation involved in going from multiple sensory inputs to neural firing patterns creates a significant discontinuity in this physical intepretation. A neural activation pattern is being set up (with some effort) to parallel an external state of affairs that is of relevance to the animal. Factually, there is separate processing in the brain of information about direction and speed, which are only subsequently combined. There are points in the system where the physiological mechanism seems arbitrary, as it could have been differently implemented as long as it preserved the informational structure. For example, it remains uncertain whether the incremental accumulation of activity in each direction in the "home vector" neurons is a property intrinsic to individual neurons or established through small recurrent networks. This discontinuity and arbitrariness seems characteristic of representational systems and can only be subsumed in a dynamical account if the latter remains at a very high level—one that seems more descriptive than explanatory.

The representational view is also clearly generative for improving our future understanding of this system. Taking again the example of the substrate for activity accumulation, some obvious "representational" issues are what accuracy and stability in the memory of the accumulated total is required to support the observed behaviour of the animal. This may make some neural substrates more plausible than others, depending on their resolution and tendency to drift. Similarly, the assumption that the neural activity pattern should represent the geocentric coordinates of the animal makes it relevant to look for a mechanism that allows time compensation of the celestial compass input (Pfeiffer and Homberg, 2007), given that sky cues change relative to the earth throughout the day.

24.6   Victory or lessons learned?

The forgoing discussion would seem strongly supportive for the representational point of view in cognitive neuroscience, but there are some crucial caveats. A major strength of the insect navigation field is that it has a strong grounding, over decades of study, in the actual behavioural capabilities of the animal in its natural habitat (Cheng and Freas, 2015). As a consequence, when constructing the top-down computational level description, it is less likely that we will assert the need for representational capabilities in the brain that are not actually necessary to account for the behaviour. This is also helped by the fact we are dealing with insects and hence have an a priori tendency towards simpler explanations of their navigational abilities, rather than anthropomorphically assuming the equivalent of an internal map.

Nevertheless, some of the "computational level" assumptions made about this system have led research astray. For example, it might seem obvious that a home vector, indicating the distance and direction to the nest, should be neurally encoded in ego-centric polar coordinates: how far the animal needs to turn and how far it needs to run to get home. Indeed, one of the first explicit neural models of ant path integration implemented separate circuits for distance and direction in a polar coordinate encoding (Hartmann and Wehner, 1995) (and this was the first model of path integration we attempted to test on a robot, with rather ineffective results (Chapman, 1998)). However, both some earlier insights (Mittelstaedt and Mittelstaedt, 1973) and more recent thorough analysis (Vickerstaff and Cheung, 2010) show that both ego-centric and polar representations of path integration have substantial limitations as a computational method for keeping track of the nest.

Similarly, although some key insights into the circuit came from the conventional neurophysiological methods of probing, in a non-behaving animal, the response of single neurons to well-controlled stimuli, some results from this approach were actively misleading. The use of an artificial linear polariser rather than the actual polarisation pattern of the sky meant that the "compass" was assumed to range from 0 to 180 across one half of the protocerebral bridge, with the eight columns encoding 22.5 degree increments (Homberg et al., 2011). Our breakthrough in modelling the circuit only came when this assumption was abandoned and a 360 degree encoding with 45 degree increments (seemingly in direct contradiction to the neurophysiological results (Heinze and Homberg, 2007)) was used. As it happened, in parallel, experiments using visual bars and light dots as the orientation stimulus started to support this alternative (Seelig and Jayaraman, 2015). Subsequently, we have shown how 360 degree encoding could indeed be obtained from the whole sky pattern of polarisation, in a model that can also reproduce the original 180 degree results when an impoverished experimental stimulus is presented (Gkanias et al., 2019).

The key message here is that understanding the neural circuit needed grounding in the actual behaviour of the animal (and in a robot imitation). This is fundamentally different from assuming that the function of the neural circuit is to reconstruct an internal analog of the external world—even if it is sometimes the case that this is just what the circuit needs to do to support the behaviour. A neural model of path integration should be a model that does the behaviour of path integration, not of producing a neural correlate of distance and direction. This point of view was fundamental to "cracking" the circuit. I would argue that for much of current cognitive neuroscience, the failure to think this way is a significant barrier to progress. Arguably, an example is the rodent "place cell" where the name has probably obscured its actual function (Eichenbaum et al., 1999; Dudchenko and Wood, 2015). Indeed the whole neuroscience research programme of "decoding," in which the aim is to show that the stimulus stream experienced by an animal can be reconstructed from the pattern of neural activity (e.g., Kay et al., 2008), makes little sense when pursued without understanding what is relevant in the stimulus for behaviour (Ritchie et al., 2019).

Further, this view of the brain as engaged in (behaviour-neutral) reconstruction of the external world is also sometimes a barrier to progress in AI. Indeed, there is a strange bifurcation in recent AI approaches. On the one hand, Deep Learning and related methods would appear to be extreme examples of paying attention only to the desired outcome (the behaviour), expressed as an objective function, and using a largely mechanism-neutral method to generate a working neural solution, unbiased by any representational assumptions. On the other hand, these methods are frequently put to use within larger architectures that still fully subscribe to the internal world model assumption. For example, in robotics, Deep Learning is often used to produce a highly veridical mapping of 3D space, as a precursor to taking the simplest action such as a step forward or a reach towards an object (Yan et al., 2018; Yeboah et al., 2018).

Bringing this back to our starting point in insect biorobotics as a research agenda for Mind Design, let me reflect on the lessons learned. Both the robotic point of view and the choice of a simpler animal to study have been important. We might still debate whether insects have minds (Klein and Barron, 2016; Birch, 2020), but there is no question that they have behavioural capacities such as navigation that are considered prime exemplars of cognition in other species. Establishing a complete explanation of how rodent navigation is neurally implemented would seem highly relevant to philosophical questions around the mechanisms of intelligence; but as we are approaching such an explanation more rapidly for the insects, it seems worth more attention. Our greater insight into the natural conditions of the behaviour and our relative preference for simple mechanistic explanations for insects have helped to maintain focus on how rich environmental interaction and embodied cognition reduce the complexity of the internal processing required. Having robot-building as a requirement for our models similarly pushes us towards thinking in mechanistic rather than representational terms and in making the most of physical as well as neural computation. Perhaps surprisingly, given the starting point, the emerging picture from this research seems to vindicate representational accounts of cognitive neuroscience. Nevertheless, many of the arguments made by Brooks thirty years ago remain relevant and can help us avoid pitfalls in making assumptions about the degree, nature, and role of representation in intelligent behaviour.

Acknowledgments

Seven of the twenty-four essays in this volume were retained from the second edition of *Mind Design* (Haugeland's introduction, Newell and Simon, Turing, Dennett, Searle, Rummelhart, and Brooks). Eleven more were originally printed elsewhere, and appear in this edition with varying degrees of editing and abridgment (Marr, Levesque, Russell, Fodor, Boden, Egan, Clark, Pearl, Churchland and Sejnowski, Cowie and Woodward, and Haugeland). The remaining six (Craver and Klein, Maley, Mitchell, Buckner, Haas, and Webb) were written for this edition.

This volume was partly supported by funding from an Australian National University Futures Grant (to C.K.).

1. CRAVER AND KLEIN

    "Introduction to Mind Design III" and the the introductions to the six parts appear for the first time in this edition.

2. HAUGELAND

    "What Is Mind Design?" was written as the introduction of *Mind Design II*. It is included with light abridgment to remove intertextual references to works no longer included in the present volume. It is reprinted here by permission of the MIT Press.

3. NEWELL AND SIMON

    "Computer Science as Empirical Inquiry: Symbols and Search" was first published as Newell and Simon (1976). It is reprinted here by permission of the ACM.

4. MARR

    The excepts from Marr's *Vision* are originally found in the introduction and chapters 1 and 6 of Marr (1982). It is reprinted here by permission of the MIT Press.

5. MALEY

"The Analog Alternative" appears here for the first time. It is printed with permission of the author.

6. TURING

"Computing Machinery and Intelligence" was first published as Turing (1950). It is reprinted here by permission of *Mind*.

7. LEVESQUE

"On Our Best Behaviour" was originally delivered at IJCAI-13. We include here the version that appeared as Levesque (2014). It is reprinted here by permission of *Artificial Intelligence*.

Author acknowledgments: This paper is a written version of the Research Excellence Lecture presented in Beijing at the IJCAI-13 conference. Thanks to Vaishak Belle and Ernie Davis for helpful comments.

8. RUSSELL

"Rationality and Intelligence" was originally printed as Russell (1997). It is reprinted here by permission of *Artificial Intelligence*.

9. FODOR

These excepts from *The Modularity of Mind* are originally found in part IV, "Central Systems" of Fodor (1983). It is reprinted here by permission of the MIT Press.

10. MITCHELL

"Why AI Is Harder than We Think" appears here for the first time. It is printed with permission of the author.

Author acknowledgments: This material is based upon work supported by the National Science Foundation under Grant No. 2020103. Any opinions, findings, and conclusions or recommendations expressed in this material are those of the author and do not necessarily reflect the views of the National Science Foundation. This work was also supported by the Santa Fe Institute. I am grateful to Philip Ball, Rodney Brooks, Daniel Dennett, Stephanie Forrest, Douglas Hofstadter, Tyler Millhouse, Melanie Moses, and Jacob Springer for comments on an earlier draft of this manuscript.

11. DENNETT

"True Believers: The Intentional Strategy and Why It Works" was originally presented as a Herbert Spencer Lecture at Oxford in November 1979, and was first published in Heath (1981); it is reprinted in Dennett (1987b), and is included here by permission of the author and the MIT Press.

12. SEARLE
"Minds Brains, and Programs" was first published as Searle (1980). It is reprinted here by permission of the publisher.
Author acknowledgments: The author acknowledges his debts to a rather large number of people for discussion of these matters and for their patient attempts to overcome his ignorance of artificial intelligence (AI)—with special thanks to Ned Block, Hubert Dreyfus, John Haugeland, Roger Schank, Robert Wilensky, and Terry Winograd.

13. BODEN
"Escaping from the Chinese Room" was originally published in Boden (1988, 238–251). It is reprinted here with permission of Cambridge University Press.

14. EGAN
"Computation and Content" was originally published as Egan (1995). It is reprinted here with permission of Duke University Press.
Author acknowledgments: Thanks to Kent Bach, Noam Chomsky, Patricia Pitcher, Robert Matthews, Colin McGinn, Rob Wilson, and the editors for helpful comments on earlier versions of this paper.

15. BUCKNER
"Transformational Abstraction in Deep Neural Networks" appears here for the first time. It is printed with permission of the author.

16. HAAS
"The Evaluative Mind" appears here for the first time. It is printed with permission of the author.

17. CLARK
"Whatever Next? Predictive Brains, Situated Agents, and the Future of Cognitive Science" is an abridgment of Clark (2013). It is printed here with permission of the publisher.

18. PEARL
"Theoretical Impediments to Machine Learning with Seven Sparks from the Causal Revolution" was originally presented as a keynote talk at WSDM'18: Proceedings of the Eleventh ACM International Conference. It is printed here with permission of the author.

Author acknowledgments: This research was supported in parts by grants from Defense Advanced Research Projects Agency [#W911NF-16-057], National Science Foundation [#IIS-1302448, #IIS-1527490, and #IIS-1704932], and Office of Naval Research [#N00014-17-S-B001].

19. RUMMELHART "The Architecture of Mind: A Connectionist Approach" first appeared in Posner (1989). It is reprinted here by permission of the MIT Press.

20. CHURCHLAND AND SEJNOWSKI
The excerpts from Churchland and Sejnowski's *The Computational Brain* originally appeared in Churchland and Sejnowski (1992). They are reprinted here by permission of the MIT Press.

21. COWIE AND WOODWARD
"The Mind Is Not (Just) a System of Modules Shaped (Just) by Natural Selection" originally appeared as Cowie and Woodward (2004). It is reprinted here with permission of the publisher.

22. HAUGELAND
"Mind Embodied and Embedded" originally appeared in *Acta Philosophica Fennica* and was reprinted in Haugeland (1997a). It appears here with permission of the Philosophical Society of Finland.

23. BROOKS
"Intelligence without Representation," in its original form, was first presented at the Workshop on Foundations of Artificial Intelligence at Endicott House in June 1987, and subsequently appeared in *Artificial Intelligence* 47: 139–159 (1991). The version in this volume differs from that earlier one in two main ways: about thirty paragraphs have been added, and ten deleted. The added paragraphs now make up subsection 6.3 and section 8; they are extracted from "Intelligence without Reason," by Rodney A. Brooks, MIT AI Memo #1293 (1991), later published in the proceedings of the 1991 International Joint Conference on Artificial Intelligence. The deleted paragraphs were all taken from the final section (8.1–8.3 in the earlier version). There have also been a few other changes, including new photos. This version, compiled by John Haugeland, is published by permission of the author.
Author acknowledgments: Phil Agre, David Chapman, Peter Cudhea, Anita Flynn, Ian Horswell, David Kirsh, Pattie Maes, Thomas Marill, Maja Mataric, and Lynn Parker were helpful in the preparation of one or both of the two essays that were combined to make this one. The research described here was done at the AI Laboratory at the

Massachusetts Institute of Technology (MIT). Support has been provided by an IBM Faculty Development Award, by grants from the Systems Development Foundation, the Hughes AI Center, Siemens Corporation, and Mazda Corporation, by the University Research Initative under ONR contract N00014-86-K-0685, and by ARPA under ONR contract N00014-85-K-0124.

24. WEBB

"What Does Biorobotics Offer Philosophy? A Tale of Two Navigation Systems" appears here for the first time. It is printed with permission of the author.

Bibliography

Abraham, T. H. 2002. (Physio)logical circuits: The intellectual origins of the McCulloch–Pitts neural networks. *Journal of the History of the Behavioral Sciences* 38 (1): 3–25.

Adams, F., and K. Aizawa. 2009. Why the mind is still in the head. In *The Cambridge Handbook of Situated Cognition*, eds. M. Aydede and P. Robbins, 78–95. Cambridge University Press.

Adams, T. 2015. Self-driving cars: From 2020 you will become a permanent backseat driver. *The Guardian*. https://tinyurl.com/zepc5spz.

Adrian, E. D. 1926. The impulses produced by sensory nerve endings: Part I. *The Journal of Physiology* 61 (1): 49–72.

Agre, P. E., and D. Chapman. 1987. Pengi: An implementation of a theory of activity. In *Proceedings AAAI-87*, 268–272. AAAI Press.

Alexander, S. 2019. GPT-2 As Step Toward General Intelligence. *Slate Star Codex*, URL = https://tinyurl.com/36rkhzrz.

Allman, J. 1990. The origin of the neocortex. *Seminars in the Neurosciences* 2: 257–262.

Allman, J. 1999. *Evolving Brains*. Scientific American Library/W. H. Freeman.

Altgassen, M., M. Kliegel, and M. Martin. 2009. Event-based prospective memory in depression: The impact of cue focality. *Cognition and Emotion* 23 (6): 1041–1055.

Altman, J. S., and J. Kien. 1989. New models for motor control. *Neural Computation* 1: 173–183.

Altman, S. 2021. Moore's law for everything. https://moores.samaltman.com.

Andersen, R. A., A. P. Batista, L. H. Snyder, C. A. Buneo, and Y. E. Cohen. 2000. Programming to look and reach in the posterior parietal cortex. In *The New Cognitive Neurosciences*, 2nd ed., ed. M. S. Gazzaniga, 515–524. MIT Press.

Anderson, B. A., and H. Kim. 2018. Mechanisms of value-learning in the guidance of spatial attention. *Cognition* 178: 26–36.

Anderson, K. C., C. P. Brown, and P. Tallal. 1993. Developmental language disorders: Evidence for a basic processing deficit. *Current Opinion in Neurology* 6 (1): 98–106.

Anderson, M. L. 2010. Neural reuse: A fundamental organizational principle of the brain. *Behavioral and Brain Sciences* 33 (4): 245–266.

Anderson, M. L. 2014. *After Phrenology*. MIT Press.

Andrews, M. 2021. The math is not the territory: Navigating the free energy principle. *Biology & Philosophy* 36 (3): 30.

Antonelli, G. A. 2010. Notions of invariance for abstraction principles. *Philosophia Mathematica* 18 (3): 276–292.

Arbib, M. 1989. *The Metaphorical Brain 2: Neural Networks and Beyond*. Wiley-Interscience.

Arias-Carrión, O., M. Stamelou, E. Murillo-Rodríguez, M. Menéndez-González, and E. Pöppel. 2010. Dopaminergic reward system: A short integrative review. *International Archives of Medicine* 3: 24. doi:10.1186/1755-7682-3-24..

Aron, J. 2016. AI landmark as Googlebot beats top human at ancient game of Go. *New Scientist*. https://tinyurl.com/2ztrk6hv.

Arpaly, N., and T. Schroeder. 2014. *In Praise of Desire*. Oxford University Press.

Arulkumaran, K., M. P. Deisenroth, M. Brundage, and A. A. Bharath. 2017. A brief survey of deep reinforcement learning. *IEEE Signal Processing Magazine* 34.

Ashworth, P. D. 2009. William James's "psychologist's fallacy" and contemporary human science research. *International Journal of Qualitative Studies on Health and Well-being* 4 (4): 195–206.

Bacchus, F., and A. J. Grove. 1995. Graphical models for preference and utility. In *Proceedings of the Eleventh Conference on Uncertainty in Artificial Intelligence*, 3–10. Kaufmann.

Balcetis, E., D. Dunning, and Y. Granot. 2012. Subjective value determines initial dominance in binocular rivalry. *Journal of Experimental Social Psychology* 48 (1): 122–129.

Baldwin, R. 2021. Tesla tells California DMV that FSD is not capable of autonomous driving. *Car and Driver*. https://tinyurl.com/p8aw9jke.

Balke, A., and J. Pearl. 2011. Probabilistic evaluation of counterfactual queries. In *Proceedings of the Twelfth National Conference on Artificial Intelligence*, 230–237.

Balleine, B. W., and A. Dickinson. 1998. Goal-directed instrumental action: Contingency and incentive learning and their cortical substrates. *Neuropharmacology* 37 (4-5): 407–419.

Bareinboim, E., and J. Pearl. 2016. Causal inference and the data-fusion problem. *Proceedings of the National Academy of Sciences* 113 (27): 7345–7352.

Barrett, L. F., and M. Bar. 2009. See it with feeling: Affective predictions during object perception. *Philosophical Transactions of the Royal Society of London B: Biological Sciences* 364 (1521): 1325–1334.

Barsalou, L. W. 1999. Perceptual symbol systems. *Behavioral and brain sciences* 22 (4): 577–660.

Barsalou, L. W., and K. Wiemer-Hastings. 2005. Situating abstract concepts. In *Grounding Cognition: The Role of Perception and Action in Memory, Language, and Thought*, eds. D. Pecher and R. A. Zwaan, 129–163. Cambridge University Press.

Batali, J. 1993. Trails as archetypes of intentionality. In *Proceedings of the 15th Annual Conference of the Cognitive Science Society, University of Colorado at Boulder*, 220–225. Lawrence Erlbaum Associates.

Bates, E., J. Elman, M. Johnson, A. Karmiloff-Smith, D. Parisi, and K. Plunkett. 1998. Innateness and emergentism. In *A Companion to Cognitive Science*, eds. W. Bechtel and G. Graham, 590–601. Blackwell.

Baxt, W. G. 1990. Use of an artificial neural network for data analysis in clinical decision-making: The diagnosis of acute coronary occlusion. *Neural Computation* 2: 480–489.

Bechtel, W. 1998. Representations and cognitive explanations: Assessing the dynamicist's challenge in cognitive science. *Cognitive Science* 22 (3): 295–317.

Bechtel, W. 2014. Investigating neural representations: The tale of place cells. *Synthese* 193: 1287–1321.

Bechtel, W., and O. Shagrir. 2015. The non-redundant contributions of Marr's three levels of analysis for explaining information-processing mechanisms. *Topics in Cognitive Science* 7 (2): 312–322.

Bengio, Y. 2009. Learning deep architectures for AI. *Foundations and Trends in Machine Learning* 2 (1): 1–127.

Berkeley, G. 1710. A treatise concerning the principles of human knowledge, 1982 ed., ed. Kenneth Winkler. Hackett Publishing.

Berliner, H. J. 1975. Chess as problem solving: The development of a tactics analyzer. PhD diss., Carnegie Mellon University, Pittsburgh.

Birch, J. 2020. The search for invertebrate consciousness. *Noûs*. https://doi.org/10.1111/nous.12351.

Blair, R. J. R. 2007. Empathic dysfunction in psychopathic individuals. *Empathy in Mental Illness* 1: 3–16.

Blair, R. J. R. 2018. Traits of empathy and anger: Implications for psychopathy and other disorders associated with aggression. *Philosophical Transactions of the Royal Society B: Biological Sciences* 373 (1744): 20170155.

Block, N. 1978. Troubles with functionalism. In *Perception and Cognition: Issues in the Foundations of Psychology*, ed. C. W. Savage, 261–325. University of Minnesota Press.

Block, N. 1986. Advertisement for a semantics for psychology. In *Midwest Studies in Philosophy*, eds. T. U. P. French and H. Wettstein, vol. 10. University of Minnesota Press.

Blundell, C., B. Uria, A. Pritzel, Y. Li, et al. 2016. Model-free episodic control. *arXiv preprint arXiv:1606.04460*.

Bobrow, D. G., C. Condoravdi, R. Crouch, et al. 2007. Precision-focused textual inference. In *Proceedings of the ACL-PASCAL Workshop on Textual Entailment and Paraphrasing*, 16–21. ACM Press.

Bobrow, R. J., and J. S. Brown. 1975. Systematic understanding: Synthesis, analysis, and contingent knowledge in specialized understanding systems. In *Representation and Understanding*, eds. R. J. Bobrow and A. M. Collins, 103–129. Academic Press.

Boden, M. A. 1970. Intentionality and physical systems. *Philosophy of Science* 37: 200–214.

Boden, M. A. 1988. *Computer models of mind: Computational Approaches in Theoretical Psychology*. Cambridge University Press.

Bostrom, N. 2014. *Superintelligence: Paths, Dangers, Strategies*. Oxford University Press.

Botvinick, M., D. G. T. Barrett, P. Battaglia, et al. 2017. Building machines that learn and think for themselves. *Behavioral and Brain Sciences* 40 E255.

Boyd, R. 1999. Kinds, complexity and multiple realization. *Philosophical Studies* 95 (1–2): 67–98.

Brandom, R. 1994. *Making it explicit: Reasoning, Representing, and Discursive Commitment*. Harvard University Press.

Breese, J. S., and M. R. Fehling. 1990. Control of problem solving: Principles and architecture. In *Machine Intelligence and Pattern Recognition*, eds. R. D. Shachter, T. S. Levitt, L. N. Kanal, and J. F. Lemmer, vol. 9, 59–68. Elsevier.

Brentano, F. 1874/1973. *Psychology From an Empirical Standpoint*. Duncker and Humblot. Translation, A. C. Rancurello, D. B. Terrell, and L. L. McAlister, 1973. London: Routledge.

Brette, R. 2019. Is coding a relevant metaphor for the brain? *Behavioral and Brain Sciences* 42 E215.

Briscoe, R., and R. Grush. 2020. Action-based theories of perception, Summer 2020 ed. In *Stanford Encyclopedia of Philosophy*, ed. E. N. Zalta. Available at. https://plato.stanford.edu/archives/sum2020/entries/action-perception.

Brook, M., and D. S. Kosson. 2013. Impaired cognitive empathy in criminal psychopathy: Evidence from a laboratory measure of empathic accuracy. *Journal of Abnormal Psychology* 122 (1): 156.

Brooks, R. A. 1986. A robust layered control system for a mobile robot. *IEEE Journal on Robotics and Automation* 2: 14–23.

Brooks, R. A. 1987. A hardware retargetable distributed layered architecture for mobile robot control. In *Proceedings of IEEE International Conference on Robotics and Automation*, vol. 4, 106–110.

Brooks, R. A. 1989. Engineering approach to building complete, intelligent beings. In *Intelligent Robots and Computer Vision VII*, vol. 1002, 618–625. SPIE.

Brooks, R. A. 1990. Elephants don't play chess. *Robotics and Autonomous Systems* 6 (1-2): 3–15.

Brooks, R. A. 1991. Intelligence without representation. *Artificial Intelligence* 47 (1-3): 139–159.

Brooks, R. A. 2019. The cul-de-sac of the computational metaphor. *Edge*. https://tinyurl.com/rjtumkca.

Brooks, R. A., and J. H. Connell. 1986. Asynchronous distributed control system for a mobile robot. In *Proceedings SPIE*, vol. 0727, 77–84.

Brown, H., K. Friston, and S. Bestamnn. 2011. Active inference, attention and motor preparation. *Frontiers in Psychology* 2 218.

Brown, T. B., B. Mann, N. Ryder, et al. 2020. Language models are few-shot learners. *arXiv:2005.14165 [cs.CL]*.

Büchel, C., C. Price, and K. Friston. 1998. A multimodal language region in the ventral visual pathway. *Nature* 394 (6690): 274–277.

Buckner, C. 2013. Morgan's canon, meet Hume's dictum: Avoiding anthropofabulation in cross-species comparisons. *Biology & Philosophy* 28 (5): 853–871.

Buckner, C. 2017. Understanding associative and cognitive explanations in comparative psychology, 409–418. Routledge.

Buckner, C. 2018. Empiricism without magic: Transformational abstraction in deep convolutional neural networks. *Synthese* 195 (12): 5339–5372. doi:10.1007/s11229-018-01949-1.

Buckner, C. 2019a. Deep learning: A philosophical introduction. *Philosophy Compass* 14: 12625. https://onlinelibrary.wiley.com/doi/full/10.1111/phc3.12625.

Buckner, C. 2019b. Rational inference: The lowest bounds. *Philosophy and Phenomenological Research* 98 (3): 697–724.

Buckner, C. 2020. Black boxes or unflattering mirrors? Comparative bias in the science of machine behavior. *The British Journal for the Philosophy of Science*. doi:10.1086/714960.

Burge, T. 1979. Individualism and the mental. *Midwest Studies in Philosophy* 4: 73–121.

Burge, T. 1986. Individualism and psychology. *The Philosophical Review* 95 (1): 3–45.

Bush, V. 1931. The differential analyzer: A new machine for solving differential equations. *Journal of the Franklin Institute* 212 (4): 447–488. doi:10.1016/S0016-0032(31)90616-9.

Business Insider Intelligence. 2016. 10 million self-driving cars will be on the road by 2020. *Business Insider*. https://tinyurl.com/9mr6x8zk.

Buss, D. M. 1995. Evolutionary psychology: A new paradigm for psychological science. *Psychological Inquiry* 6 (1): 1–30.

Bynum, W. F. 1976. Varieties of Cartesian experience in early nineteenth century neurophysiology. In *Philosophical Dimensions of the Neuro-medical Sciences*, eds. S. Spicker and H. Engelhardt, 15–35. Reidel.

Calcott, B. 2014. Engineering and evolvability. *Biology & Philosophy* 29 (3): 293–313.

Campbell-Kelly, M., W. Aspray, N. Ensmenger, and J. R. Yost. 2013. *Computer: A History of the Information Machine*. Routledge.

Caramazza, A. 1986. On drawing inferences about the structure of normal cognitive systems from the analysis of patterns of impaired performance: The case for single-patient studies. *Brain and Cognition* 5 (1): 41–66.

Carey, S., and E. Spelke. 1996. Science and core knowledge. *Philosophy of Science* 63 (4): 515–533.

Carlsmith, J. 2020. New report on how much computational power it takes to match the human brain. *Open Philanthropy*, URL = https://www.openphilanthropy.org/blog/new-report-brain-computation.

Carnap, R. 1950. *Logical Foundations of Probability*. University of Chicago Press.

Carruthers, P. 2004. The mind is a system of modules shaped by natural selection. In *Contemporary Debates in Philosophy of Science*, ed. C. Hitchcock, 293–311. Blackwell.

Carruthers, P. 2006. The architecture of the mind.

Cassandra, A. R., L. P. Kaelbling, and M. L. Littman. 1994. Acting optimally in partially observable stochastic domains. In *Proceedings of AAAI-94*, 1023–1028. AAAI Press.

Chalmers, D. 1990. Why Fodor and Pylyshyn were wrong: The simplest refutation. In *Proceedings of the Twelfth Annual Conference of the Cognitive Science Society*, 340–347.

Chalmers, D. J. 1994. On implementing a computation. *Minds and Machines* 4 (4): 391–402.

Chapman, T. 1998. Human models of navigation in ants: Testing the Hartmann-Wehner model. In *Gottingen Neurobiology Report*, eds. N. Elsner and R. Wehner, vol. 1, 28. Thieme Publishing Group.

Chater, N., and C. Manning. 2006. Probabilistic models of language processing and acquisition. *Trends in Cognitive Sciences* 10 (7): 335–344.

Chelazzi, L., J. Eštočinová, R. Calletti, et al. 2014. Altering spatial priority maps via reward-based learning. *Journal of Neuroscience* 34 (25): 8594–8604.

Chemero, A. 2000. Anti-representationalism and the dynamical stance. *Philosophy of Science* 67 (4): 625–647.

Chemero, A. 2009. *Radical Embodied Cognitive Science*. MIT Press.

Chemero, A. 2013. Radical embodied cognitive science. *Review of General Psychology* 17 (2): 145–150.

Chen, S., R. Zhou, H. Cui, and X. Chen. 2013. Deficits in cue detection underlie event-based prospective memory impairment in major depression: An eye tracking study. *Psychiatry Research* 209 (3): 453–458.

Cheng, K., and C. A. Freas. 2015. Path integration, views, search, and matched filters: The contributions of Rüdiger Wehner to the study of orientation and navigation. *Journal of Comparative Physiology. A, Neuroethology, Sensory, Neural, and Behavioral Physiology* 201: 517–532. doi:10.1007/s00359-015-0984-9.

Cherniak, C. 1986. *Minimal Rationality*. MIT Press.

Chiew, K. S., and T. S. Braver. 2014. Dissociable influences of reward motivation and positive emotion on cognitive control. *Cognitive, Affective, & Behavioral Neuroscience* 14 (2): 509–529.

Chisholm, R. M. 1967. Intentionality. In *The Encyclopedia of Philosophy*, ed. P. Edwards, 201–204. Macmillan.

Chollet, F. 2019. On the measure of intelligence. *arXiv:1911.01547.*

Chollet, F. 2020. Why abstraction is the key to intelligence, and what we're still missing. In *NeurIPS 2020 tutorial series https://nips.cc/Conferences/2020/Schedule?type=Tutorial.*

Chomsky, N. 1965. *Aspects of the Theory of Syntax*. MIT Press.

Chomsky, N., and H. Lasnik. 1977. Filters and control. *Linguistic Inquiry* 8: 425–504.

Chow, S. J. 2013. What's the problem with the frame problem? *Review of Philosophy and Psychology* 4 (2): 309–331.

Chrisomalis, S. 2020. *Reckonings: Numerals, Cognition, and History*. MIT Press.

Christian, B. 2011. *The Most Human Human*. Doubleday.

Church, A. 1936. An unsolvable problem of elementary number theory. *American Journal of Mathematics* 58 (2): 345–363.

Churchland, P. M. 1979. *Scientific Realism and the Plasticity of Mind*. Cambridge University Press.

Churchland, P. M. 1981. Eliminative materialism and propositional attitudes. *Journal of Philosophy* 78 (2): 67–90.

Churchland., P. M. 1989. *A Neurocomputational Perspective*. MIT Press.

Churchland, P. M. 1990. On the nature of theories: A neurocomputational perspective. *Minnesota Studies in the Philosophy of Science* 14: 59–101.

Churchland, P. S., and T. J. Sejnowski. 1992. *The Computational Brain*. MIT Press.

Churchland, P. S., and T. J. Sejnowski. 1988. Perspectives in cognitive neuroscience. *Science* 242: 741–745.

Clark, A. 1987. The kludge in the machine. *Mind and Language* 2 (4): 277–300.

Clark, A. 1989. *Microcognition: Philosophy, Cognitive Science and Parallel Distributed Processing*. MIT Press.

Clark, A. 1997. *Being There: Putting Brain, Body and World Together Again*. MIT Press.

Clark, A. 1998. Time and mind. *The Journal of Philosophy* 95 (7): 354–376.

Clark, A. 2008. *Supersizing the Mind: Embodiment, Action, and Cognitive Extension*. Oxford University Press.

Clark, A. 2013. Whatever next? Predictive brains, situated agents, and the future of cognitive science. *Behavioral and Brain Sciences* 36 (3): 181–204.

Clark, A. 2015a. Perceiving as predicting. In *Perception and Its Modalities*, eds. D. Stokes, M. Matthen, and S. Biggs, 23–43. Oxford University Press.

Clark, A. 2015b. *Surfing Uncertainty: Prediction, Action, and the Embodied Mind*. Oxford University Press.

Clark, A., and D. Chalmers. 1998. The extended mind. *Analysis* 58 (1): 7–19.

Clatterbuck, H. 2016. Darwin, Hume, Morgan, and the verae causae of psychology. *Studies in History and Philosophy of Science Part C: Studies in History and Philosophy of Biological and Biomedical Sciences* 60: 1–14.

Collins, A., E. H. Warnock, N. Aiello, and M. L. Miller. 1975. Reasoning from incomplete knowledge. In *Representation and Understanding: Studies in Cognitive Science*, eds. D. Bobrow and A. Collins, 383–415. Academic Press.

Colombo, M. 2014. Deep and beautiful. The reward prediction error hypothesis of dopamine. *Studies in History and Philosophy of Science Part C: Studies in History and Philosophy of Biological and Biomedical Sciences* 45: 57–67.

Coltheart, M. 2007. Cognitive neuropsychiatry and delusional belief (the 33rd Sir Frederick Bartlett Lecture). *The Quarterly Journal of Experimental Psychology* 60 (8): 1041–1062.

Conant, R. C., and R. W. Ashby. 1970. Every good regulator of a system must be a model of that system. *International Journal of Systems Science* 1 (2): 89–97.

Connell, J. 1989. Task-oriented spatial representations for distributed systems. PhD diss., Massachusetts Institute of Technology, Cambridge MA.

Cooper, L. A., and R. Shepard. 1973. *Mental Images and Their Transformations*. MIT Press.

Copeland, B. J. 1996. What is computation? *Synthese* 108 (3): 335–359.

Copeland, B. J. 1997. The broad conception of computation. *American Behavioral Scientist* 40 (6): 690–716.

Copeland, B. J. 2000. The Turing test. *Minds and Machines* 10 (4): 519–539.

Corlett, P. R., C. D. Frith, and P. C. Fletcher. 2009a. From drugs to deprivation: A Bayesian framework for understanding models of psychosis. *Psychopharmacology (Berlin)* 206 (4): 515–530.

Corlett, P. R., J. K. Krystal, J. R. Taylor, and P. C. Fletcher. 2009b. Why do delusions persist? *Frontiers in Human Neuroscience* 3.

Corlett, P. R., J. R. Taylor, X. J. Wang, P. C. Fletcher, and J. H. Krystal. 2010. Toward a neurobiology of delusions. *Progress in Neurobiology* 92 (3): 345–369.

Cosmides, L., and J. Tooby. 1987. From evolution to behavior: Evolutionary psychology as the missing link. In *The Latest on the Best: Essays on Optimality and Evolution*, ed. J. Dupre, 277–307. MIT Press.

Cosmides, L., and J. Tooby. 1992a. Cognitive adaptations for social exchange. In *The Adapted Mind: Evolutionary Psychology and the Generation of Culture*, eds. L. C. J. Barkow and J. Tooby, 163–243. Oxford University Press.

Cosmides, L., and J. Tooby. 1992b. From evolution to adaptations to behavior: Toward an integrated evolutionary psychology. In *Biological Perspectives on Motivated and Cognitive Activities*, ed. R. Wong. Ablex Publishing.

Cosmides, L., and J. Tooby. 1994. Origins of domain specificity: The evolution of functional organization. In *Mapping the Mind: Domain Specificity in Cognition and Culture*, eds. L. Hirschfeld and S. Gelman. Cambridge University Press.

Costenaro, D. 2018. New AI model exceeds human performance at question answering. From BecomingHuman.ai. https://tinyurl.com/ujwp6s95.

Cottrell, G., P. Munro, and D. Zipser. 1987. Learning internal representations from gray-scale images: An example of extensional programming. In *Proceedings of the 9th Annual Conference of the Cognitive Science Society*. Erlbaum.

Coundouris, S. P., G. Terrett, L. Laakso, et al. 2020. A meta-analytic review of prospection deficits in Parkinson's disease. *Neuroscience & Biobehavioral Reviews* 108: 34–47.

Cowie, F., and J. Woodward. 2004. The mind is not (just) a system of modules shaped (just) by natural selection. In *Contemporary debates in philosophy of science*, ed. C. Hitchcock, 312–334. Blackwell.

Crane, T. 1998. Intentionality as the mark of the mental. *Royal Institute of Philosophy Supplements* 43: 229–251.

Craver, C. F. 2007. *Explaining the Brain: Mechanisms and the Mosaic Unity of Neuroscience*. Oxford University Press.

Craver, C. F. 2021. Towards an epistemology of intervention: Optogenetics and maker's knowledge. In *The Tools of Neuroscience Experiment*, eds. J. Bickle, C. F. Craver, and A.-S. Barwich, 152–175. Routledge.

Crick, F. H. C. 1979. Thinking about the brain. *Scientific American* 241: 219–232.

Cruse, H., and R. Wehner. 2011. No need for a cognitive map: Decentralized memory for insect navigation. *PLoS Computational Biology* 7: 1002009.

Cubillo, A., A. B. Makwana, and T. A. Hare. 2019. Differential modulation of cognitive control networks by monetary reward and punishment. *Social Cognitive and Affective Neuroscience* 14 (3): 305–317.

Cummins, R. 1975. Functional analysis. *Journal of Philosophy* 72: 741–764.

Cummins, R. 1983. *The Nature of Psychological Explanation*. MIT Press.

Cummins, R. 1989. *Meaning and Mental Representation*. MIT Press.

Cummins, R., and G. Schwarz. 1991. Connectionism, computationalism, and cognition. In *Connectionism and the Philosophy of Mind*, eds. T. Horgan and J. Tienson, 60–73. Kluwer Academic Publishers.

Dagan, I., O. Glickman, and B. Magnini. 2005. The PASCAL recognising textual entailment challenge. In *Proceedings of the 1st International Conference on Machine Learning Challenges. MLCW'05*, 177–190. Springer.

Darwiche, A. 2018. Human-level intelligence or animal-like abilities? *Communications of the ACM* 61 (10): 56–67.

Davidson, D. 1995. Laws and cause. *Dialectica* 49 (2–4): 263–280.

Davidson, E. H. 2001. *Genomic Regulatory Systems: In Development and Evolution*. Academic Press.

Davies, M. 1991. Individualism and perceptual content. *Mind* 100 (4): 461–484.

Davis, E., and G. Marcus. 2015. Commonsense reasoning and commonsense knowledge in artificial intelligence. *Communications of the ACM* 58 (9): 92–103.

Davis, R. 1980. Meta-rules: Reasoning about control. *Artificial Intelligence* 15 (3): 179–222.

Daw, N. D., Y. Niv, and P. Dayan. 2005. Uncertainty-based competition between prefrontal and dorsolateral striatal systems for behavioral control. *Nature Neuroscience* 8 (12): 1704–1711.

Dayan, P. 1997. Recognition in hierarchical models. In *Foundations of Computational Mathematics*, eds. F. Cucker and M. Shub, 43–57. Springer.

Dayan, P. 2011. Interactions between model-free and model-based reinforcement learning. In *Seminar Series from the Machine Learning Research Group*. University of Sheffield. Lecture recording. http://ml.dcs.shef.ac.uk/.

Dayan, P., and L. F. Abbott. 2001. *Theoretical neuroscience: Computational and mathematical modeling of neural systems*. MIT Press.

Dayan, P., and G. E. Hinton. 1996. Varieties of Helmholtz machine. *Neural Networks* 9: 1385–1403.

Dayan, P., G. E. Hinton, and R. M. Neal. 1995. The Helmholtz machine. *Neural Computation* 7: 889–904.

Dayan, P., and Y. Niv. 2008. Reinforcement learning: The good, the bad and the ugly. *Current Opinion in Neurobiology* 18 (2): 185–196.

de-Wit, L., B. Machilsen, and T. Putzeys. 2010. Predictive coding and the neural response to predictable stimuli. *Journal of Neuroscience* 30: 8702–8703.

Dean, T., J. Allen, and Y. Aloimonos. 1995. *Artificial Intelligence: Theory and Practice*. Benjamin-Cummings.

Dean, T., and M. S. Boddy. 1988. An analysis of time-dependent planning. In *Proceedings of AAAI-88*, 49–54. AAAI Press.

Dean, T., and K. Kanazawa. 1989. A model for reasoning about persistence and causation. *Computational Intelligence* 5 (2): 142–150.

DeAngelis, G. C., B. G. Cumming, and W. T. Newsome. 2000. A new role for cortical area MT: The perception of stereoscopic depth. In *The New Cognitive Neurosciences,* 2nd edition, ed. M. S. Gazzaniga, 305–314. MIT Press.

Della Libera, C., and L. Chelazzi. 2009. Learning to attend and to ignore is a matter of gains and losses. *Psychological Science* 20 (6): 778–784.

Dempster, A. P., N. M. Laird, and D. B. Rubin. 1977. Maximum likelihood from incomplete data via the EM algorithm. *Journal of the Royal Statistical Society, Series B* 39: 1–38.

den Ouden, H. E. M., J. Daunizeau, J. Roiser, K. Friston, and K. E. Stephan. 2010. Striatal prediction error modulates cortical coupling. *Journal of Neuroscience* 30: 3210–3219.

Denker, J., D. Schwartz, B. Wittner, S. Solla, R. Howard, L. Jackel, and J. Hopfield. 1987. Automatic learning, rule extractionand generalization. *Complex Systems* 1: 887–922.

Dennett, D. C. 1969. *Content and Consciousness*. Routledge and Kegan Paul.

Dennett, D. C. 1971. Intentional systems. *Journal of Philosophy* 68: 87–106.

Dennett, D. C. 1976. Conditions of personhood. In *The Identities of Persons*, ed. A. O. Rorty. University of California Press.

Dennett, D. C. 1978a. *Brainstorms: Philosophical Essays on Mind and Psychology*. MIT Press.

Dennett, D. C. 1978b. How to change your mind. In *Dennett (1978a)*. MIT Press.

Dennett, D. C. 1981. Making sense of ourselves. *Philosophical Topics* 12 (1): 63–81.

Dennett, D. C. 1982. Beyond belief. In *Thought and Object: Essasys on Intentionality*, ed. A. Woodfield. Clarendon Press.

Dennett, D. C. 1986. *The moral first aid manual (the tanner lectures on human values)*. University of Michigan.

Dennett, D. C. 1987a. Evolution, error, and intentionality. In *Dennett (1987b)*, 287–322. MIT Press.

Dennett, D. C. 1987b. *The Intentional Stance*. MIT Press.

Dennett, D. C. 1991. *Consciousness Explained*. Little, Brown.

Desimone, R., and J. Duncan. 1995. Neural mechanisms of selective visual attention. *Annual Review of Neuroscience* 18: 193–222.

Despres, J. 2008. Scenario: Shane Legg. *Future*. https://tinyurl.com/hwzna364.

Devlin, J., M. W. Chang, K. Lee, and K. Toutanova. 2018. BERT: Pre-training of deep bidirectional transformers for language understanding. *arXiv:1810.04805*.

Dewdney, A. K. 1984. On the spaghetti computer and other analog gadgets for problem solving. *Scientific American* 250 (6): 19–26.

DiCarlo, J. J., and D. D. Cox. 2007. Untangling invariant object recognition. *Trends in Cognitive Sciences* 11 (8): 333–341. doi:10.1016/j.tics.2007.06.010.

DiCarlo, J. J., D. Zoccolan, and N. C. Rust. 2012. How does the brain solve visual object recognition? *Neuron* 73 (3): 415–434.

Ding, D., F. Hill, A. Santoro, and M. Botvinick. 2020. Object-based attention for spatio-temporal reasoning: Outperforming neuro-symbolic models with flexible distributed architectures. *arXiv:2012.08508 [cs]*. arXiv: 2012.08508. http://arxiv.org/abs/2012.08508.

D'Iorio, A., G. Maggi, C. Vitale, M. Amboni, D. Di Meglio, L. Trojano, and G. Santangelo. 2019. Prospective memory in Parkinson's disease: The role of the motor subtypes. *Journal of Neurology* 266 (10): 2505–2511.

Di Paolo, E. A. 2009. Extended life. *Topoi* 28 (1): 9–21.

Domes, G., P. Hollerbach, K. Vohs, A. Mokros, and E. Habermeyer. 2013. Emotional empathy and psychopathy in offenders: An experimental study. *Journal of Personality Disorders* 27 (1): 67–84.

Downes, S. M. 2011. Scientific models. *Philosophy Compass* 6 (11): 757–764.

Doyle, J., and R. S. Patil. 1991. Two theses of knowledge representation: Language restrictions, taxonomic classification, and the utility of representation services. *Artificial Intelligence* 48 (3): 261–297.

Drayson, Z. 2014. The personal/subpersonal distinction. *Philosophy Compass* 9 (5): 338–346.

Dretske, F. 1981. *Knowledge and the Flow of Information*. MIT Press.

Dreyfus, H. 1979. From micro-worlds to knowledge representation: AI at an impasse, 2nd ed. In *Mind Design II: Philosophy, Psychology, Artificial Intelligence*, ed. J. Haugeland, 143–182. MIT Press.

Dreyfus, H. L. 1972/92. *What Computers Can't Do: The Limits of Artificial Intelligence*. Harper & Row.

Dreyfus, H. L. 2012. A history of first step fallacies. *Minds and Machines* 22 (2): 87–99.

Dudchenko, P. A., and E. R. Wood. 2015. Place fields and the cognitive map. *Hippocampus* 25: 709–712.

Dumoulin, S. O., and R. F. Hess. 2006. Modulation of V1 activity by shape: Image-statistics or shape-based perception? *Journal of Neurophysiology* 95: 3654–3664.

Durkin, J. 1996. Expert systems: A view of the field. *IEEE Annals of the History of Computing* 11 (02): 56–63.

Eberhardt, F. 2009. Introduction to the epistemology of causation. *Philosophy Compass* 4 (6): 913–925.

Egan, F. 1991. Must psychology be individualistic? *The Philosophical Review* 100 (2): 179–203.

Egan, F. 1992. Individualism, computation, and perceptual content. *Mind* 101 (403): 443–459.

Egan, F. 1995. Computation and content. *The Philosophical Review* 104 (2): 181–203.

Egan, F. 1996. Intentionality and the theory of vision. In *Perception*, ed. K. Akins, 232–247. Oxford University Press.

Eggert, G. H. 1977. *Wernicke's Works on Aphasia: A Sourcebook and Review*. Mouton.

Egner, T., J. M. Monti, and C. Summerfield. 2010. Expectation and surprise determine neural population responses in the ventral visual stream. *Journal of Neuroscience* 30 (49): 16601–16608.

Eichenbaum, H., P. Dudchenko, E. Wood, M. Shapiro, and H. Tanila. 1999. The hippocampus, memory, and place cells: Is it spatial memory or a memory space? *Neuron* 23: 209–226.

Eliasmith, C. 2007. How to build a brain: From function to implementation. *Synthese* 159 (3): 373–388.

Elman, J. L. 1988. Finding structure in time, Technical Report CRL-88-01, Center for Research in Language, University of California, San Diego.

Elman, J. L., and D. Zipser. 1987. Learning the hidden structure of speech, Report 8701, Institute for Cognitive Science, University of California, San Diego.

Engelhardt, H. T. 1974. The disease of masturbation: Values and the concept of disease. *Bulletin of the History of Medicine* 48: 234–248.

Ephrati, E., and J. S. Rosenschein. 1991. The Clarke tax as a consensus mechanism among automated agents. In *Proceedings of AAAI-91*, 173–178. AAAI Press.

Epley, N., A. Waytz, and J. T. Cacioppo. 2007. On seeing human: A three-factor theory of anthropomorphism. *Psychological Review* 114 (4): 864.

Epstein, R. A., E. Z. Patai, J. B. Julian, and H. J. Spiers. 2017. The cognitive map in humans: Spatial navigation and beyond. *Nature Neuroscience* 20 (11): 1504.

Ergo, K., E. De Loof, and T. Verguts. 2020. Reward prediction error and declarative memory. *Trends in Cognitive Sciences* 24 (5): 388–397.

Eriksen, C. W., and J. D. St. James. 1986. Visual attention within and around the field of focal attention: A zoom lens model. *Perception and Psychophysics* 40: 225–240.

Feigenbaum, E. A., and J. Feldman, eds. 1963. *Computers and Thought*. McGraw-Hill.

Feldman, H., and K. Friston. 2010. Attention, uncertainty, and free-energy. *Frontiers in Human Neuroscience* 4.

Feldman, J. A. 1985. Connectionist models and their applications: Introduction. *Cognitive Science* 9: 1–2.

Feldman, J. A. 2010. Cognitive science should be unified: Comment on Griffiths et al. and McClelland et al. *Trends in Cognitive Sciences* 14 (8): 341.

Felleman, D. J., and D. C. van Essen. 1991. Distributed hierarchical processing in the primate cerebral cortex. *Cerebral Cortex* 1: 1–47.

Feyerabend, P. 1978. *Science in a Free Society*. New Left Bank.

Fiddick, L., L. Cosmides, and J. Tooby. 2000. No interpretation without representation: The role of domain-specific representations and inferences in the wason selection task. *Cognition* 77 (1): 1–79.

Field, H. H. 1978. Mental representation. *Erkenntnis* 13 (1): 9–61.

Field, H. H. 1986. The deflationary conception of truth. In *Fact, Science, and Morality: Essays on A.J Ayer's Language, Truth, and Logic*, eds. G. McDonald and C. Wright, 55–117. Basil Blackwell.

Fincher-Kiefer, R. 2019. *How the Body Shapes Knowledge: Empirical Support for Embodied Cognition*. American Psychological Association.

Fine, K. 2002. *The Limits of Abstraction*. Clarendon Press.

Finlay, B. L., and R. B. Darlington. 1995. Linked regularities in the development and evolution of mammalian brains. *Science* 268: 1578–1584.

Finn, C., P. Abbeel, and S. Levine. 2017. Model-agnostic meta-learning for fast adaptation of deep networks. In *Proceedings of the International Conference on Machine Learning (ICML)*, 1126–1135.

Fletcher, P., and C. Frith. 2009. Perceiving is believing: A Bayesian approach to explaining the positive symptoms of schizophrenia. *Nature Reviews: Neuroscience* 10: 48–58.

Fodor, J. A. 1980. Methodological solipsism considered as a research strategy in cognitive psychology. *Behavioral and Brain Sciences* 3 (1): 63–73.

Fodor, J. A. 1981. The mind-body problem. *Scientific American* 244 (1): 114–123. doi:10.2307/24964264.

Fodor, J. A. 1983. *The Modularity of Mind: An Essay on Faculty Psychology*. MIT Press.

Fodor, J. A. 1984. Observation reconsidered. *Philosophy of Science* 51 (1): 23–43.

Fodor, J. A. 1987. *Psychosemantics*. MIT Press.

Fodor, J. A. 1990. *A Theory of Content and Other Essays*. MIT Press.

Fodor, J. A., and Z. W. Pylyshyn. 1988. Connectionism and cognitive architecture: A critical analysis. *Cognition* 28 (1-2): 3–71.

Forbes, J., T. Huang, K. Kanazawa, and S. J. Russell. 1995. The BATmobile: Towards a Bayesian automated taxi. In *Proceedings of IJCAI-95*, 1878–1885. Morgan Kaufmann.

Friston, K. 2002. Beyond phrenology: What can neuroimaging tell us about distributed circuitry? *Annual Review of Neuroscience* 25: 221–250.

Friston, K. 2003. Learning and inference in the brain. *Neural Networks* 16 (9): 1325–1352.

Friston, K. 2005. A theory of cortical responses. *Philosophical Transactions of the Royal Society of London B: Biological Sciences* 360 (1456): 815–836.

Friston, K. 2009. The free-energy principle: A rough guide to the brain? *Trends in Cognitive Sciences* 13 (7): 293–301.

Friston, K. 2010. The free-energy principle: A unified brain theory? *Nature Reviews Neuroscience* 11 (2): 127–138.

Friston, K. 2011a. Embodied inference: Or I think therefore I am, if I am what I think. In *The Implications of Embodiment: Cognition and Communication*, eds. W. Tschacher and C. Bergomi, 89–125. Imprint Academic.

Friston, K. 2011b. What is optimal about motor control? *Neuron* 72: 488–498.

Friston, K., J. Daunizeau, and S. J. Kiebel. 2009. Reinforcement learning or active inference? *PLoS One* 4 (7).

Friston, K., J. Daunizeau, J. Kilner, and S. J. Kiebel. 2010. Action and behavior: A free-energy formulation. *Biological Cybernetics* 102 (3): 227–260.

Friston, K., and S. Kiebel. 2009. Cortical circuits for perceptual inference. *Neural Networks* 22: 1093–1104.

Friston, K., J. Mattout, and J. Kilner. 2011. Action understanding and active inference. *Biological Cybernetics* 104: 137–160.

Friston, K., and K. Stephan. 2007. Free energy and the brain. *Synthese* 159 (3): 417–458.

Fukushima, K. 1979. Neural network model for a mechanism of pattern recognition unaffected by shift in position-neocognitron. *IEICE Technical Report, A* 62 (10): 658–665.

Fukushima, K., and S. Miyake. 1982. Neocognitron: A self-organizing neural network model for a mechanism of visual pattern recognition. In *Competition and Cooperation in Neural Nets*, 267–285. Springer.

Gagne, C., and P. Dayan. 2022. Peril, prudence and planning as risk, avoidance and worry. *Journal of Mathematical Psychology* 107: 102617.

Gaines, B. R. 1984. Perspectives on fifth generation computing. *Oxford Surveys in Information Technology* 1: 1–53.

Gallagher, S., and K. Miyahara. 2012. Neo-pragmatism and enactive intentionality. In *Action, Perception and the Brain*, 117–146. Springer.

Gallistel, C. R. 1990. *The Organization of Learning*. MIT Press.

Gallistel, C. R. 2003. Animal cognition: The representation of space, time and number. *Annual Review of Psychology* 40: 155–189.

Gärdenfors, P. 2004. *Conceptual spaces: The geometry of thought*. MIT Press.

Gatys, L. A., A. S. Ecker, and M. Bethge. 2016. Image style transfer using convolutional neural networks. In *Proceedings of the IEEE Conference on Computer Vision and Pattern Recognition*, 2414–2423.

Gauker, C. 2011. *Words and images: An essay on the origin of ideas*. Oxford University Press.

Geirhos, R., J. H. Jacobsen, C. Michaelis, R. Zemel, W. Brendel, M. Bethge, and F. A. Wichmann. 2020. Shortcut learning in deep neural networks. *Nature Machine Intelligence* 2 (11): 665–673.

Gelder, T. v. 1992. Defining 'distributed representation'. *Connection Science* 4 (3-4): 175–191.

Gerrans, P. 2007. Mechanisms of madness. Evolutionary psychiatry without evolutionary psychology. *Biology and Philosophy* 22: 35–56.

Gershman, S. J. 2015. A unifying probabilistic view of associative learning. *PLoS Computational Biology* 11 (11): 1004567.

Gershman, S. J., and N. D. Daw. 2012. Perception, action and utility: The tangled skein. In *Principles of Brain Dynamics: Global State Interactions*, eds. M. I. Rabinovich, K. Friston, and P. Varona, 293–312. MIT Press.

Gershman, S. J., J. Zhou, and C. Kommers. 2017. Imaginative reinforcement learning: Computational principles and neural mechanisms. *Journal of Cognitive Neuroscience* 29 (12): 2103–2113.

Gęsiarz, F., and M. J. Crockett. 2015. Goal-directed, habitual and Pavlovian prosocial behavior. *Frontiers in Behavioral Neuroscience* 9: 135.

Geva-Sagiv, M., L. Las, Y. Yovel, and N. Ulanovsky. 2015. Spatial cognition in bats and rats: From sensory acquisition to multiscale maps and navigation. *Nature Reviews Neuroscience* 16: 94–108. doi:10.1038/nrn3888.

Gibson, J. J. 1979. *The Ecological Approach to Visual Perception.* Houghton Mifflin.

Gilbert, S. F. 2000. *Developmental Biology*, 6th ed. Sinauer Associates.

Ginsberg, M. L., and D. F. Geddis. 1991. Is there any need for domain-dependent control information? In *Proceedings of AAAI-91*, 452–457. AAAI Press.

Gkanias, E., B. Risse, M. Mangan, and B. Webb. 2019. From skylight input to behavioural output: A computational model of the insect polarised light compass. *PLoS Computational Biology* 15: 1007123.

Glimcher, P. W. 2011. *Foundations of Neuroeconomic Analysis.* Oxford University Press.

Glimcher, P. W., and E. Fehr, eds. 2013. *Neuroeconomics: Decision Making and the Brain.* Academic Press.

Gluck, M. A., and C. E. Myers. 2001. *Gateway to Memory: An Introduction to Neural Network Modeling of the Hippocampus and Learning.* MIT Press.

Glymour, C. 1980. *Theory and Evidence.* Princeton University Press.

Glymour, C. N. 2001. *The Mind's Arrows: Bayes' Nets and Graphical Causal Models in Psychology.* MIT Press.

Gödel, K. 1931. Über formal unentscheidbare Sätze der Principia Mathematica und verwandter Systeme I. *Monatshefte für Mathematik und Physik* 38 (1): 173–198.

Godfrey-Smith, P. 2006. The strategy of model-based science. *Biology and Philosophy* 21 (5): 725–740.

Godfrey-Smith, P. 2009. Triviality arguments against functionalism. *Philosophical Studies* 145 (2): 273–295.

Gold, J. I., and M. N. Shadlen. 2007. The neural basis of decision making. *Annual Review of Neuroscience* 30: 535–574.

Gold, J. N., and M. N. Shadlen. 2001. Neural computations that underlie decisions about sensory stimuli. *Trends in Cognitive Sciences* 5 (10): 238–255.

Good, I. J. 1971. Twenty-seven principles of rationality. In *Foundations of statistical inference*, 108–141. Holt, Rinehart and Winston.

Goodale, M. A., and A. D. Milner. 1992. Separate visual pathways for perception and action. *Trends in Neurosciences* 15 (1): 20–25.

Goodfellow, I. 2016. NIPS 2016 tutorial: Generative adversarial networks. *arXiv preprint arXiv:1701.00160.*

Goodfellow, I. J., J. Shlens, and C. Szegedy. 2014. Explaining and harnessing adversarial examples. *arXiv preprint arXiv:1412.6572.*

Goodman, N. 1954. *Fact, Fiction, and Forecast.* University of London, Athlone Press.

Goodman, N. 1968. *Languages of Art: An Approach to a Theory of Symbols.* Hackett Publishing.

Gopnik, A., C. Glymour, D. M. Sobel, L. E. Schulz, T. Kushnir, and D. Danks. 2004. A theory of causal learning in children: Causal maps and Bayes nets. *Psychological Review* 111 (1): 3.

Gould, S. J., and R. C. Lewontin. 1979. The spandrels of San Marco and the Panglossian paradigm: A critique of the adaptationist programme. *Proceedings of the Royal Society of London, Series B. Biological Sciences* 205: 581–598.

Grace, K., J. Salvatier, A. Dafoe, B. Zhang, and O. Evans. 2018. When will AI exceed human performance? Evidence from AI experts. *Journal of Artificial Intelligence Research* 62: 729–754.

Graves, C., J. J. Katz, Y. Nishiyama, S. Soames, R. Stecker, and P. Tovey. 1973. Tacit knowledge. *The Journal of Philosophy* 70 (11): 318–330.

Graziano, M. 2008. *The intelligent movement machine: An ethological perspective on the primate motor system.* Oxford University Press.

Gregory, R. L. 1980. Perceptions as hypotheses. *Philosophical Transactions of the Royal Society of London B* 290 (1038): 181–197.

Griffiths, P. E. 2001. Evolutionary psychology: History and current status. In *The Philosophy of Science: An Encyclopedia*, eds. S. Sarkar and J. Pfeifer, 263–268. Routledge.

Griffiths, T., N. Chater, C. Kemp, A. Perfors, and J. B. Tenenbaum. 2010. Probabilistic models of cognition: Exploring representations and inductive biases. *Trends in Cognitive Sciences* 14 (8): 357–364.

Grossberg, S. 1976. Adaptive pattern classification and universal recoding: Part I. parallel development and coding of neural feature detectors. *Biological cybernetics* 23 (3): 121–134.

Grush, R. 2004. The emulation theory of representation: Motor control, imagery, and perception. *Behavioral and Brain Sciences* 27: 377–442.

Gupta, A. S., M. A. van der Meer, D. S. Touretzky, and A. D. Redish. 2010. Hippocampal replay is not a simple function of experience. *Neuron* 65 (5): 695–705.

Gustin, S. 2011. IBM's Watson supercomputer wins practice Jeopardy round. *Wired.* https://www.wired.com/2011/01/ibm-watson-jeopardy/.

Haas, J. 2021. Can hierarchical predictive coding explain binocular rivalry? *Philosophical Psychology* 34 (3): 424–444.

Haas, J., and C. Klein. 2020. Holistic resource-rational analysis. *Behavioral and Brain Sciences* 43.

Haigh, T., and P. E. Ceruzzi. 2021. *A New History of Modern Computing.* MIT Press.

Halevy, A., P. Norvig, and F. Pereira. 2009. The unreasonable effectiveness of data. *IEEE Intelligent Systems* 24 (2): 8–12.

Halpern, J. Y., and J. Pearl. 2005. Causes and explanations: A structural-model approach. Part I: Causes. *The British Journal for the Philosophy of Science* 56 (4): 843–887.

Hannan, B. 1993. Don't stop believing: The case against eliminative materialism. *Mind & Language* 8: 165–179.

Hare, R. D. 1998. Psychopathy, affect and behavior. In *Psychopathy: Theory, Research and Implications for Society*, eds. D. J. Cooke, A. E. Forth, and R. D. Hare, 105–137. Springer.

Harman, G. 1983. *Change in View: Principles of Reasoning.* MIT Press.

Harnad, S. 1991. Other bodies, other minds: A machine incarnation of an old philosophical problem. *Minds and Machines* 1 (1): 43–54.

Hartmann, G., and R. Wehner. 1995. The ant's path integration system: A neural architecture. *Biological Cybernetics* 73: 483–497.

Hartree, D. R. 1949. *Calculating Instruments and Machines.* The University of Illinois Press.

Hassabis, D., D. Kumaran, C. Summerfield, and M. Botvinick. 2017. Neuroscience-inspired artificial intelligence. *Neuron* 95 (2): 245–258.

Haugeland, J. 1979. Understanding natural language. *The Journal of Philosophy* 76 (11): 619–632.

Haugeland, J. 1981. Analog and analog. *Philosophical Topics* 12 (1): 213–225.

Haugeland, J. 1997a. *Having Thought: Essays in the Metaphysics of Mind.* Harvard University Press.

Haugeland, J., ed. 1997b. *Mind Design II: Philosophy, Psychology, Artificial Intelligence*, 2nd ed. MIT Press.

Haugeland, J. 1998. *Having thought.* Harvard University Press.

Hawkins, A. J. 2019. Here are Elon Musk's wildest predictions about Tesla's self-driving cars. *The Verge.* https://tinyurl.com/4ap2rm2n.

Hawkins, J., and S. Blakeslee. 2004. *On Intelligence.* Owl Books/Times Books.

Haxby, J. V., M. I. Gobbini, M. L. Furey, A. Ishai, J. L. Schouten, and P. Pietrini. 2001. Distributed and overlapping representations of faces and objects in ventral temporal cortex. *Science* 293 (5539): 2425–2430.

Hayes, P. J. 1979. The naive physics manifesto. In *Expert Systems in the Microelectronic Age*, ed. D. Michie, 46–63. Edinburgh University Press.

Hayes, P. J., and K. Ford. 1995. Turing test considered harmful. In *Proceedings of the Fourteenth International Joint Conference on Artificial Intelligence*, 972–977. IJCAI.

Hayhoe, M., and D. Ballard. 2005. Eye movements in natural behavior. *Trends in Cognitive Sciences* 9 (4): 188–194.

Heath, A. F., ed. 1981. *Scientific Explanation: Papers Based on Herbert Spencer Lectures Given in the University of Oxford*. Clarendon Press.

Hebb, D. O. 1949. *The Organization of Behavior*. Wiley.

Heinze, S., and U. Homberg. 2007. Maplike representation of celestial e-vector orientations in the brain of an insect. *Science* 315: 995–997.

Heinze, S., A. Narendra, and A. Cheung. 2018. Principles of insect path integration. *Current Biology* 28 (17): 1043–1058.

Helmholtz, H. v. 1860/1962. *Handbuch der Physiologischen Optik*, vol. 3. Dover. (ed. and trans. J. P. C. Southall. Original work published in 1860; Dover English edition in 1962).

Hernández-Orallo, J. 2017. *The Measure of All Minds: Evaluating Natural and Artificial Intelligence*. Cambridge University Press.

Hesselmann, G., S. Sadaghiani, K. Friston, and A. Kleinschmidt. 2010. Predictive coding or evidence accumulation? False inference and neuronal fluctuations. *PloS One* 5 (3): 9926.

Hewitson, C. L., D. M. Kaplan, and J. Sutton. 2018. Yesterday the earwig, today man, tomorrow the earwig? *Comparative Cognition & Behavior Reviews* 13: 25–30.

Heyes, C. 2018. *Cognitive Gadgets*. Harvard University Press.

Hickey, C., L. Chelazzi, and J. Theeuwes. 2010. Reward guides vision when it's your thing: Trait reward-seeking in reward-mediated visual priming. *PloS One* 5 (11): 14087.

High, R. 2013. *The Era of Cognitive Systems: An Inside Look at IBM Watson and How it Works* IBM Redbooks. http://www.redbooks.ibm.com/abstracts/redp4955.html.

Hikosaka, O., K. Nakamura, and H. Nakahara. 2006. Basal ganglia orient eyes to reward. *Journal of Neurophysiology* 95 (2): 567–584.

Hinton, G. E. 2002. Training products of experts by minimizing contrastive divergence. *Neural Computation* 14 (8): 1711–1800.

Hinton, G. E. 2007a. Learning multiple layers of representation. *Trends in Cognitive Sciences* 11: 428–434.

Hinton, G. E. 2007b. To recognize shapes, first learn to generate images. In *Computational Neuroscience: Theoretical Insights into Brain Function*, eds. P. Cisek, T. Drew, and J. Kalaska, 535–547. Elsevier.

Hinton, G. E. 2010. Learning to represent visual input. *Philosophical Transactions of the Royal Society, B* 365: 177–184.

Hinton, G. E., P. Dayan, B. J. Frey, and R. M. Neal. 1995. The wake-sleep algorithm for unsupervised neural networks. *Science* 268: 1158–1160.

Hinton, G. E., and Z. Ghahramani. 1997. Generative models for discovering sparse distributed representations. *Philosophical Transactions of the Royal Society B* 352: 1177–1190.

Hinton, G. E., S. Osindero, and Y. Teh. 2006. A fast learning algorithm for deep belief nets. *Neural Computation* 18: 1527–1554.

Hinton, G. E., and R. R. Salakhutdinov. 2006. Reducing the dimensionality of data with neural networks. *Science* 313 (5786): 504–507.

Hinton, G. E., and T. J. Sejnowski. 1986. Learning and relearning in Boltzmann machines. In *Parallel Distributed Processing: Explorations in the Microstructure of Cognition. Volume 1: Foundations*, eds. D. E. Rumelhart, J. L. McClelland, and the PDP Research Group, 282–317. MIT Press.

Hinton, G. E., and R. S. Zemel. 1994. Autoencoders, minimum description length and Helmholtz free energy. In *Advances in Neural Information Processing Systems 6*, eds. J. Cowan, G. Tesauro, and J. Alspector, 3–10. Morgan Kaufmann.

Hitchcock, C. 2009. Causal modelling. In *The Oxford handbook of causation*, eds. H. Beebee, C. Hitchcock, and P. Menzies, 299–314. Oxford University Press.

Hochstein, E. 2016. Giving up on convergence and autonomy: Why the theories of psychology and neuroscience are codependent as well as irreconcilable. *Studies in History and Philosophy of Science Part A* 56: 135–144.

Hofstadter, D. R. 1979. *Gödel, Escher, Bach: An Eternal Golden Braid*. Basic Books.

Hofstadter, D. R. 1985. Waking up from the Boolean dream; or, subcognition as computation. In *Metamagical Themas: Questing for the Essence of Mind and Pattern*, ed. D. R. Hofstadter, 631–665. Viking.

Hohwy, J. 2007. Functional integration and the mind. *Synthese* 159 (3): 315–328.

Hohwy, J. 2013. *The Predictive Mind*. Oxford University Press.

Hohwy, J., A. Roepstorff, and K. J. Friston. 2008. Predictive coding explains binocular rivalry: An epistemological review. *Cognition* 108 (3): 687–701.

Holleman, J. R., and W. Schultz. 1998. Dopamine neurons report an error in the temporal prediction of reward during learning. *Nature Reviews: Neuroscience* 1: 304–309.

Homberg, U., S. Heinze, K. Pfeiffer, M. Kinoshita, and B. el Jundi. 2011. Central neural coding of sky polarization in insects. *Philosophical Transactions of the Royal Society of London. Series B, Biological sciences* 366: 680–687.

Hopfield, J. J. 1982. Neural networks and physical systems with emergent collective computational abilities. In *Proceedings of the National Academy of Sciences*, vol. 79, 2554–2558. National Academy of Sciences.

Horvitz, E. J. 1987a. Problem-solving design: Reasoning about computational value, tradeoffs, and resources. In *Proceedings of the 2nd Annual NASA Research Forum*, 26–43. NASA Ames Research Center.

Horvitz, E. J. 1987b. Reasoning about beliefs and actions under computational resource constraints. In *Proceedings of the 3rd Conference on Uncertainty in Artificial Intelligence. UAI'87*, 429–447. AUAI Press.

Horvitz, E. J., and J. S. Breese. 1990. *Ideal Partition of Resources for Metareasoning*. Knowledge Systems Laboratory, Medical Computer Science, Stanford University, Stanford CA..

Howard, R. A. 1966. Information value theory. *IEEE Transactions on Systems Science and Cybernetics* 2 (1): 22–26.

Huang, Y., and R. Rao. 2011. Predictive coding. *Wiley Interdisciplinary Reviews: Cognitive Science* 2: 580–593.

Hubel, D. H., and T. N. Wiesel. 1962. Receptive fields, binocular interaction and functional architecture in the cat's visual cortex. *Journal of Physiology (London)* 160: 106–154.

Hubel, D. H., and T. N. Wiesel. 1967. Cortical and callosal connections concerned with the vertical meridian of visual fields in the cat. *Journal of Neurophysiology* 30 (6): 1561–1573.

Huber, R., and M. Knaden. 2015. Egocentric and geocentric navigation during extremely long foraging paths of desert ants. *Journal of Comparative Physiology A* 201 (6): 609–616.

Hume, D. 1739. *A Treatise of Human Nature*, 2000 ed., eds. David F Norton and Mary J Norton. Oxford University Press.

Hunter, L. E., and N. D. Daw. 2021. Context-sensitive valuation and learning. *Current Opinion in Behavioral Sciences* 41: 122–127.

Hutter, M. 2012. One decade of universal artificial intelligence. In *Theoretical Foundations of Artificial General Intelligence*, eds. P. Wang and B. Goertzel, 67–88. Springer.

Hutto, D. D. 2006. Knowing what? Radical versus conservative enactivism. *Phenomenology and the Cognitive Sciences* 4 (4): 389–405. doi:10.1007/s11097-005-9001-z.

Huys, Q. J., N. D. Daw, and P. Dayan. 2015. Depression: A decision-theoretic analysis. *Annual Review of Neuroscience* 38: 1–23.

Huys, Q. J., D. A. Pizzagalli, R. Bogdan, and P. Dayan. 2013. Mapping anhedonia onto reinforcement learning: A behavioural meta-analysis. *Biology of Mood & Anxiety Disorders* 3 (1): 1–16.

Hyman, S. E. 2005. Addiction: A disease of learning and memory. *American Journal of Psychiatry* 162 (8): 1414–1422.

IEEE Information Theory Society. 2016. The Shannon Centennial: 1100100 Years of Bits. https://www.youtube.com/watch?v=pHSRHi17RKM.

Indefrey, P., and W. J. Levelt. 2000. The neural correlates of language production. In *The New Cognitive Neurosciences,* 2nd edition, ed. M. S. Gazzaniga, 845–865. MIT Press.

Isaac, A. 2018. Embodied cognition as analog computation. *Reti, Saperi, Linguaggi* 7 (14): 239–260. doi:10.12832/92298).

James, M. L., G. M. Smith, and J. C. Wolford. 1971. *Analog Computer Simulation of Engineering Systems*, 2nd ed. Intext Educational Publishers.

James, W. 1892. *Psychology: The Briefer Course*. Henry Holt.

Janssen, A., C. Klein, and M. Slors. 2017. What is a cognitive ontology, anyway? *Philosophical Explorations* 20 (2): 123–128.

Jawad, U. 2021. Microsoft's AI model has outperformed humans in natural language understanding. *Neowin*. https://tinyurl.com/2x4r54ad.

Jefferson, G. 1949. The mind of mechanical man. *British Medical Journal* 1 (4616): 1105. Lister Oration for 1949.

Jehee, J. F. M., and D. H. Ballard. 2009. Predictive feedback can account for biphasic responses in the lateral geniculate nucleus. *PLoS Computational Biology* 5 (5): 1000373.

Ji-hye, S. 2016. Mixed outlook for human-versus-AI match. *Korea Herald*. https://tinyurl.com/zb3ywabe.

Johnson, M. 1997. *Developmental Cognitive Neuroscience*. Blackwell.

Johnson, M. 2017. *Embodied Mind, Meaning, and Reason: How Our Bodies Give Rise to Understanding*. University of Chicago Press.

Jonas, E., and K. P. Kording. 2017. Could a neuroscientist understand a microprocessor? *PLoS Computational Biology* 13 (1): 1005268.

Jordan, M. I. 1986a. Attractor dynamics and parallelism in a connectionist sequential machine. In *Proceedings of the 8th Annual Meeting of the Cognitive Science Society*, 112–117. Erlbaum.

Jordan, M. I. 1986b. An introduction to linear algebra in parallel distributed processing. In *Parallel Distributed Processing*, eds. J. L. McClelland, D. Rumelhart, and T. P. R. Group, vol. 1, 365–422. MIT Press.

Jordan, M. I. 1988. Supervised learning and systems with excess degrees of freedom (COINS technical report 88-27), Technical report, University of Massachusetts.

Juechems, K., and C. Summerfield. 2019. Where does value come from? *Trends in Cognitive Sciences* 23 (10): 836–850.

Jumper, J., R. Evans, A. Pritzel, et al. 2020. High accuracy protein structure prediction using deep learning. *Fourteenth Critical Assessment of Techniques for Protein Structure Prediction (Abstract Book)* 22: 24.

Kageyama, Y. 2015. CEO: Nissan will be ready with autonomous driving by 2020. *Phys.Org*. https://phys.org/news/2015-05-ceo-nissan-ready-autonomous.html.

Kaiser, M. K., M. McCloskey, and D. R. Proffitt. 1986. Development of intuitive theories of motion: Curvilinear motion in the absence of external forces. *Developmental Psychology* 22 (1): 67.

Kalman, R. E. 1960. A new approach to linear filtering and prediction problems. *Journal of Basic Engineering* 82 (1): 35–45.

Kandel, E. R., and J. Schwartz, eds. 1985. *Principles of Neural Science*, 2nd ed. Elsevier.

Katai, S., T. Maruyama, T. Hashimoto, and S. Ikeda. 2003. Event based and time based prospective memory in Parkinson's disease. *Journal of Neurology, Neurosurgery & Psychiatry* 74 (6): 704–709.

Katz, M. 2016. Analog representations and their users. *Synthese* 193 (3): 851–871. doi:10.1007/s11229-015-0774-5.

Kawato, M., H. Hayakama, and T. Inui. 1993. A forward-inverse optics model of reciprocal connections between visual cortical areas. *Network* 4: 415–422.

Kay, K. N., T. Naselaris, R. J. Prenger, and J. L. Gallant. 2008. Identifying natural images from human brain activity. *Nature* 452 (7185): 352–355.

Kearns, M. J., R. E. Schapire, and L. M. Sellie. 1992. Toward efficient agnostic learning. In *Proceedings of the 5th Annual Workshop on Computational Learning Theory. COLT '92*, 341–352. ACM Press.

Keeney, R. L., R. R. Keeney, H. Raiffa, and R. F. Meyer. 1976. *Decisions with Multiple Objectives: Preferences and Value Tradeoffs*. Wiley.

Kelner, K., and D. E. Koshland, eds. 1989. *Molecules to Models: Advances in Neuroscience*. American Association for the Advancement of Science.

Khaligh-Razavi, S.-M., and N. Kriegeskorte. 2014. Deep supervised, but not unsupervised, models may explain it cortical representation. *PLoS Computational Biology* 10 (11). doi:10.1371/journal.pcbi.1003915.

Kinsella, G. J., K. E. Pike, M. G. Cavuoto, and S. D. Lee. 2018. Mild cognitive impairment and prospective memory: Translating the evidence into neuropsychological practice. *The Clinical Neuropsychologist* 32 (5): 960–980.

Kitcher, P. 1988. Marr's computational theory of vision. *Philosophy of Science* 55 (1): 1–24.

Kleene, S. C. 1936. General recursive functions of natural numbers. *Mathematische Annalen* 112 (1): 727–742.

Klein, C. 2008. Dispositional implementation solves the superfluous structure problem. *Synthese* 165 (1): 141–153.

Klein, C. 2018. What do predictive coders want? *Synthese* 195 (6): 2541–2557.

Klein, C., and A. Barron. 2016. Insects have the capacity for subjective experience. *Animal Sentience* 1: 1. doi:10.51291/2377-7478.1113.

Kliegel, M., M. Altgassen, A. Hering, and N. S. Rose. 2011. A process-model based approach to prospective memory impairment in Parkinson's disease. *Neuropsychologia* 49 (8): 2166–2177.

Kliegel, M., L. H. Phillips, U. Lemke, and U. A. Kopp. 2005. Planning and realisation of complex intentions in patients with Parkinson's disease. *Journal of Neurology, Neurosurgery & Psychiatry* 76 (11): 1501–1505.

Knight, W. 2018. The US military wants to teach AI some basic common sense. *Technology Review.* https://tinyurl.com/2xuvxefe.

Koch, C. 1999. *Biophysics of Computation: Information Processing in Single Neurons*. Oxford University Press.

Korb, K. B. 1998. The frame problem: An AI fairy tale. *Minds and Machines* 8 (3): 317–351.

Kosslyn, S. M., W. L. Thompson, I. J. Kim, and N. M. Alpert. 1995. Topographical representations of mental images in primary visual cortex. *Nature* 378: 496–498.

Krishnan, H. S., and S. Shapiro. 1999. Prospective and retrospective memory for intentions: A two-component approach. *Journal of Consumer Psychology* 8 (2): 141–166.

Kubricht, J. R., K. J. Holyoak, and H. Lu. 2017. Intuitive physics: Current research and controversies. *Trends in Cognitive Sciences* 21 (10): 749–759. doi:10.1016/j.tics.2017.06.002.

Kuhn, T. S. 1970. *The Structure of Scientific Revolutions*, 2nd ed. University of Chicago Press.

Kulvicki, J. 2015. Analog representation and the parts principle. *Review of Philosophy and Psychology* 6 (1): 165–180.

Kumar, P. R., and P. Varaiya. 1986. *Stochastic Systems: Estimation, Identification, and Adaptive Control*. Prentice-Hall.

Kurniawati, H. 2021. Partially observable Markov decision processes (POMDPs) and robotics. *arXiv:2107.07599*.

Lai, G., Q. Xie, H. Liu, Y. Yang, and E. Hovy. 2017. RACE: Large-scale reading comprehension dataset from examinations. *arXiv preprint arXiv:1704.04683*.

Laird, J. E., P. S. Rosenbloom, and A. Newell. 1986. Chunking in soar: The anatomy of a general learning mechanism. *Machine Learning* 1 (1): 11–46.

Lake, B. M., T. D. Ullman, J. B. Tenenbaum, and S. J. Gershman. 2017. Building machines that learn and think like people. *Behavioral and Brain Sciences* 40.

Lakoff, G. 1987. *Women, Fire, and Dangerous Things: What Categories Reveal about the Mind*. University of Chicago Press.

Lakoff, G., and M. Johnson. 2008. *Metaphors We Live By*. University of Chicago Press.

Landy, D., C. Allen, and C. Zednik. 2014. A perceptual account of symbolic reasoning. *Frontiers in Psychology* 5: 275.

Langdon, A. J., M. J. Sharpe, G. Schoenbaum, and Y. Niv. 2018. Model-based predictions for dopamine. *Current Opinion in Neurobiology* 49: 1–7.

Lapuschkin, S., S. Wäldchen, A. Binder, et al. 2019. Unmasking Clever Hans predictors and assessing what machines really learn. *Nature Communications* 10 (1): 1–8.

Lauritzen, S. L. 1995. The em algorithm for graphical association models with missing data. *Computational Statistics & Data Analysis* 19 (2): 191–201.

Lazebnik, Y. 2002. Can a biologist fix a radio?–Or, what I learned while studying apoptosis. *Cancer Cell* 2 (3): 179–182.

LeCun, Y., Y. Bengio, and G. E. Hinton. 2015. Deep learning. *Nature* 521: 436–444.

LeCun, Y., B. E. Boser, J. S. Denker, et al. 1990. Handwritten digit recognition with a back-propagation network. In *Advances in Neural Information Processing Systems*, 396–404.

LeDoux, J. 1996. *The Emotional Brain: The Mysterious Underpinnings of Emotional Life*. Simon and Schuster.

Lee, M. 2010. Emergent and structured cognition in Bayesian models: Comment on Griffiths et al. and McClelland et al. *Trends in Cognitive Sciences* 14 (8): 345–346.

Lee, T. S., and D. Mumford. 2003. Hierarchical Bayesian inference in the visual cortex. *Journal of Optical Society of America, A* 20 (7): 1434–1448.

Legg, S., and M. Hutter. 2007. A collection of definitions of intelligence. *Frontiers in Artificial Intelligence and Applications* 157: 17.

Lehnert, W. 2007. Cognition, computers, and car bombs: How Yale prepared me for the 90's. In *Beliefs, Reasoning, and Decision Making: Psycho-logic in Honor of Bob Abelson*, eds. R. Schank and E. Langer, 143–173. Erlbaum.

Le Moël, F., T. Stone, M. Lihoreau, A. Wystrach, and B. Webb. 2019. The central complex as a potential substrate for vector based navigation. *Frontiers in Psychology* 10: 690.

Lenat, D. B., R. V. Guha, K. Pittman, D. Pratt, and M. Shepherd. 1990. CYC: Toward programs with common sense. *Communications of the ACM* 33 (8): 30–49.

Levesque, H. J. 1986. Making believers out of computers. *Artificial Intelligence* 30 (1): 81–108.

Levesque, H. J. 1988. Logic and the complexity of reasoning. *The Journal of Philosophical Logic* 17: 355–389.

Levesque, H. J. 2009. Is it enough to get the behaviour right? In *Proceedings of the 21st International Joint Conference on Artificial Intelligence. IJCAI'09*.

Levesque, H. J. 2014. On our best behaviour. *Artificial Intelligence* 212: 27–35.

Levesque, H. J. 2017. *Common Sense, the Turing Test, and the Quest for Real AI*. MIT Press.

Levesque, H. J., and R. J. Brachman. 1987. Expressiveness and tractability in knowledge representation and reasoning 1. *Computational Intelligence* 3 (1): 78–93.

Levesque, H. J., E. Davis, and L. Morgenstern. 2012. The Winograd schema challenge. In *Proceedings of 13th International Conference on the Principles of Knowledge Representation and Reasoning. KR'12*, 552–561. AAAI Press.

Lewis, D. K. 1971. Analog and digital. *Noûs* 5 (3): 321–327.

Lewontin, R. C. 1990. The evolution of cognition: Questions we will never answer. In *An Invitation to Cognitive Science,* 2nd edition, eds. D. Scarborough and S. Sternberg, vol. 4, 107–132. MIT Press.

Li, Y. R., M. Weinborn, S. Loft, and M. Maybery. 2013. Patterns of prospective memory impairment among individuals with depression: The influence of cue type and delay interval. *Journal of the International Neuropsychological Society* 19 (6): 718–722.

Liao, M. R., and B. A. Anderson. 2020. Reward learning biases the direction of saccades. *Cognition* 196: 104145.

Lighthill, J. 1973. Artificial intelligence: A general survey. In *Artificial Intelligence: A Paper Symposium*. Science Research Council.

Lindsay, G. W. 2020. Attention in psychology, neuroscience, and machine learning. *Frontiers in Computational Neuroscience* 14: 29.

Linzen, T. 2020. How can we accelerate progress towards human-like linguistic generalization? In *Proceedings of the 58th Annual Meeting of the Association for Computational Linguistics (ACL)*, 5210–5217.

Loar, B. 1988. Two kinds of content. In *Contents of Thought*, eds. R. H. Grimm and D. D. Merrill, 121–139. University of Arizona Press.

Locke, J. 1690. An essay concerning human understanding, 1975 ed., ed. Peter H. Nidditch. Oxford University Press.

Lotter, W., G. Kreiman, and D. Cox. 2016. Deep predictive coding networks for video prediction and unsupervised learning. *arXiv preprint arXiv:1605.08104*.

Lovelace, A. C. 1842. Translator's notes to an article on Babbage's analytical engine. *Scientific Memoirs* 3: 691–731.

Luc, P., N. Neverova, C. Couprie, J. Verbeek, and Y. LeCun. 2017. Predicting deeper into the future of semantic segmentation. In *Proceedings of the IEEE International Conference on Computer Vision*, 648–657.

Luck, S. J., and S. A. Hillyard. 2000. The operation of selective attention at multiple stages of processing: Evidence from human and monkey electrophysiology. In *The New Cognitive Neurosciences,* 2nd edition, ed. M. S. Gazzaniga, 687–700. MIT Press.

Lyu, C., L. Abbott, and G. Maimon. 2020. A neuronal circuit for vector computation builds an allocentric traveling-direction signal in the Drosophila fan-shaped body. *bioRxiv*. https://doi.org/10.1101/2020.12.22.423967.

MacKay, D. M. 1956. The epistemological problem for automata. In *Automata Studies*, eds. C. E. Shannon and J. McCarthy, 235. Princeton University Press.

MacLennan, B. J. 2003. Transcending Turing computability. *Minds and Machines* 13 (1): 3–22.

Maher, B. 1988. Anomalous experience and delusional thinking: The logic of explanations. In *Delusional Beliefs*, eds. T. F. Oltmanns and B. A. Maher, 15–33. Wiley.

Mahmut, M. K., J. Homewood, and R. J. Stevenson. 2008. The characteristics of non-criminals with high psychopathy traits: Are they similar to criminal psychopaths? *Journal of Research in Personality* 42 (3): 679–692.

Mahoney, M. S. 2011. *Histories of Computing*. Harvard University Press.

Maley, C. J. 2011. Analog and digital, continuous and discrete. *Philosophical Studies* 155 (1): 117–131. doi:10.1007/s11098-010-9562-8.

Maley, C. J. 2018. Toward analog neural computation. *Minds and Machines* 28 (1): 77–91.

Maley, C. J. 2021. The physicality of representation. *Synthese* 199: 14725–14750.

Maley, C. J. forthcoming. Analog computation and representation. *The British Journal for the Philosophy of Science*. doi:10.1086/715031.

Malpeli, J. G. 1983. Activity of cells in area 17 of the cat in absence of input from layer A of lateral geniculate nucleus. *Journal of Neurophysiology* 49: 595–610.

Malpeli, J. G., C. Lee, H. D. Schwark, and T. G. Weyand. 1986. Cat area 17. I. Pattern of thalamic control of cortical layers. *Journal of Neurophysiology* 56: 1062–1073.

Marcus, G. 2008. *Kluge: The Haphazard Construction of the Human Mind*. Houghton-Mifflin.

Marcus, G. 2018a. Deep learning: A critical appraisal. *arXiv:1801.00631*.

Marcus, G. 2018b. Innateness, Alphazero, and artificial intelligence. *arXiv:1801.05667*.

Marcus, M. P. 1980. *A Theory of Syntactic Recognition for Natural Language*. MIT Press.

Marr, D. 1969. A theory of cerebellar cortex. *Journal of Physiology (London)* 202 (437-470): 11–46.

Marr, D. 1970. A theory for cerebral neocortex. *Proceedings of the Royal Society of London B* 176 (161-234): 129–203.

Marr, D. 1982. *Vision*. Freeman.

Marr, D., and E. Hildreth. 1980. Theory of edge detection. *Proceedings of the Royal Society of London. Series B. Biological Sciences* 207: 187–217.

Marr, D., and T. Poggio. 1976. Cooperative computation of stereo disparity. *Science* 294: 283–287.

Marr, D., and T. Poggio. 1977. From understanding computation to understanding neural circuitry. *Neuroscience Research Program Bulletin* 15: 470–488.

Marr, D., and T. Poggio. 1979. A computational theory of human stereo vision. *Proceedings of the Royal Society of London. Series B* 204: 301–328.

Marr, D., and H. K. Wishihara. 1978. Representation and recognition of the spatial organization of three-dimensional shapes. *Proceedings of the Royal Society of London. Series B* 200: 269–294.

Marx, S., and W. Einhäuser. 2015. Reward modulates perception in binocular rivalry. *Journal of Vision* 15 (1): 11–11.

Matheson, J. E. 1968. The economic value of analysis and computation. *IEEE Transactions on Systems Science and Cybernetics* 4 (3): 325–332.

Matthews, R. 1988. Authoritative self-knowledge and perceptual individualism. In *Contents of Thoughts*, eds. R. Grimm and D. Merrill, 208–220. University of Arizona Press.

Matthews, R. J. 1994. The measure of mind. *Mind* 103: 131–146.

Maudlin, T. 1989. Computation and consciousness. *The Journal of Philosophy* 86 (8): 407–432.

Maunsell, J. H. R., and D. van Essen. 1983. Connections of the middle temporal visual area (MT) and their relationship to a cortical hierarchy in the macaque monkey. *Journal of Neuroscience* 3: 2563–2586.

May, W. E., and L. Holder. 1973. *A History of Marine Navigation. With a Chapter on Modern Developments by Leonard Holder*. Foulis.

Maynard Smith, J., R. Burian, S. Kauffman, et al. 1985. Developmental constraints and evolution: A perspective from the mountain lake conference on development and evolution. *The Quarterly Review of Biology* 60 (3): 265 - 287.

McCarthy, G. 2000. Physiological studies of face processing in humans. In *The New Cognitive Neurosciences, 2nd ed.*, ed. M. S. Gazzaniga, 393–409. MIT Press.

McCarthy, J. 1960. Recursive functions of symbolic expressions and their computation by machine. *Communications of the ACM* 3 (4): 184–195.

McCarthy, J. 1968. The advice taker. In *Semantic Information Processing*. MIT Press.

McCarthy, J. 1979. Ascribing mental qualities to machines, Technical report, Stanford AI Lab Memo 326.

McCarthy, J. 1980. Circumscription—A form of non-monotonic reasoning. *Artificial Intelligence* 13: 27–39.

McCarthy, J. 1986. Programs with common sense. In *Readings in Knowledge Representation*, eds. H. Levesque and R. Brachman, 299–308. Morgan Kaufmann.

McCarthy, J., and P. Hayes. 1969. Some philosophical problems from the standpoint of artificial intelligence. In *Machine Intelligence 4*, eds. B. Meltzer and D. Mitchie, 463–502.

McClelland, J. L., M. Botvinick, D. Noelle, D. Plaut, T. Rogers, M. Seidenberg, and L. Smith. 2010. Letting structure emerge: Connectionist and dynamical systems approaches to cognition. *Trends in Cognitive Sciences* 14 (8): 348–356.

McClelland, J. L., and D. E. Rumelhart. 1981. An interactive activation model of context effects in letter perception: Part 1. an account of basic findings. *Psychological Review* 88: 375–407.

McClelland, J. L., D. E. Rumelhart, and the PDP Research Group. 1986a. *Parallel Distributed Processing: Explorations in the Microstructure of Cognition, Vol. 1: Foundations*. MIT Press.

McClelland, J. L., D. E. Rumelhart, and the PDP Research Group. 1986b. *Parallel Distributed Processing: Explorations in the Microstructure of Cognition, Vol. 2: Psychological and Biological Models*. MIT Press.

McCormick, R. 2017. NVIDIA is working with Audi to get you a self-driving car by 2020. *The Verge*. https://www.theverge.com/2017/1/5/14174740/nvidia-audi-zf-bosch-self-driving-cars-2020-parts.

McCoy, T., E. Pavlick, and T. Linzen. 2019. Right for the wrong reasons: Diagnosing syntactic heuristics in natural language inference. In *Proceedings of the 57th Annual Meeting of the Association for Computational Linguistics (ACL)*, 3428–3448.

McCracken, H. 2015. Inside Mark Zuckerberg's bold plan for the future of Facebook. *Fast Company*. www.fastcompany.com/3052885/mark-zuckerberg-facebook.

McCulloch, W. S. 1961. What is a number, that a man may know it, and a man, that he may know a number. *General Semantics Bulletin* 26 (27): 7–18.

McCulloch, W. S., and W. Pitts. 1943. A logical calculus of the ideas immanent in nervous activity. *Bulletin of Mathematical Biophysics* 5 (4): 115–133.

McDermott, D. 1976. Artificial intelligence meets natural stupidity. *ACM SIGART Bulletin* 57: 4–9.

McDermott, D., M. M. Waldrop, B. Chandrasekaran, J. J. McDermott, and R. Schank. 1985. The dark ages of AI: A panel discussion at AAAI-84. *AI Magazine* 6 (3): 122–134.

McFarland, C. P., and J. J. Vasterling. 2018. Prospective memory in depression: Review of an emerging field. *Archives of Clinical Neuropsychology* 33 (7): 912–930.

McGinn, C. 1989. *Mental Content*. Basil Blackwell.

McNamara, P., and R. Durso. 2018. The dopamine system, Parkinson's disease and language function. *Current Opinion in Behavioral Sciences* 21: 1–5.

Mead, C. 1989. *Analog VLSI and Neural Systems*. Addison-Wesley.

Megiddo, N., and A. Wigderson. 1986. On play by means of computing machines: Preliminary version. In *Theoretical Aspects of Reasoning about Knowledge*, ed. J. Y. Halpern, 259–274. Elsevier.

Melloni, L., C. M. Schwiedrzik, N. Muller, E. Rodriguez, and W. Singer. 2011. Expectations change the signatures and timing of electrophysiological correlates of perceptual awareness. *Journal of Neuroscience* 31 (4): 1386–1396.

Menzel, R., K. Lehmann, G. Manz, J. Fuchs, M. Koblofsky, and U. Greggers. 2012. Vector integration and novel shortcutting in honeybee navigation. *Apidologie* 43: 229–243. doi:10.1007/s13592-012-0127-z.

Merker, B. 2004. Cortex, countercurrent context, and dimensional integration of lifetime memory. *Cortex* 40: 559–576.

Merzenich, M. M., W. M. Jenkins, P. Johnston, C. Schreiner, S. L. Miller, and P. Tallal. 1996. Temporal processing deficits of language-learning impaired children ameliorated by training. *Science* 271: 77–81.

Metz, C. 2017. A new way for machines to see, taking shape in Toronto. *New York Times.* https://tinyurl.com/5bwd3u9n.

Mignard, M., and J. G. Malpeli. 1991. Paths of information flow through visual cortex. *Science* 251: 1249–1251.

Milkowski, M. 2013. *Explaining the Computational Mind.* MIT Press.

Millikan, R. G. 1984. *Language, Thought, and Other Biological Categories: New Foundations for Realism.* MIT Press.

Milner, D., and M. Goodale. 2006. *The Visual Brain in Action.* Oxford University Press.

Mindell, D. A. 2002. *Between Human and Machine.* Johns Hopkins University Press.

Minsky, M. 1961. Steps toward artificial intelligence. *Proceedings of the IRE* 49 (1): 8–30.

Minsky, M. 1967. *Computation: Finite and Infinite Machines.* Prentice-Hall.

Minsky, M., ed. 1968. *Semantic Information Processing.* MIT Press.

Minsky, M. 1975. A framework for representing knowledge. In *The Psychology of Computer Vision*, ed. P. Winston. McGraw Hill.

Minsky, M. 1980. Decentralized minds. *Behavioral and Brain Sciences* 3 (3): 439–440.

Minsky, M. 1986. *The Society of Mind.* Simon and Schuster.

Minsky, M., and S. A. Papert. 1969. *Perceptrons: An Introduction to Computational Geometry.* MIT Press.

Minton, S. 1996. Is there any need for domain-dependent control information? A reply. In *Proceedings of AAAI-96*, vol. 1, 855–862. AAAI Press.

Mitchell, M. 2019. *Artificial Intelligence: A Guide for Thinking Humans.* Penguin UK.

Mitchell, M. 2021. Abstraction and analogy-making in artificial intelligence. *arXiv:2102.10717.*

Mitchell, S. D. 1989. The causal background of functional explanation. *International Studies in the Philosophy of Science* 3: 213–229.

Mittelstaedt, H., and M. L. Mittelstaedt. 1973. Mechanismen der orientierung ohne richtende aussenreize. *Fortschr. Zool* 21: 46–58.

Miyata, Y. 1987. The learning and planning of actions. PhD diss., University of California, San Diego.

Moewes, C., and A. Nürnberger. 2013. *Computational Intelligence in Intelligent Data Analysis.* Springer.

Mohan, K., and J. Pearl. 2017. Graphical models for processing missing data, Technical Report r-473, http://ftp.cs.ucla.edu/pub/stat_ser/r473.pdf, Department of Computer Science, University of California, Los Angeles.

Montague, R. 2006. *Why Choose This Book? How We Make Decisions.* Dutton.

Montufar, G. F., R. Pascanu, K. Cho, and Y. Bengio. 2014. On the number of linear regions of deep neural networks. *Advances in neural information processing systems* 27.

Moosavi-Dezfooli, S. M., A. Fawzi, O. Fawzi, and P. Frossard. 2017. Universal adversarial perturbations. In *Proceedings of the IEEE Conference on Computer Vision and Pattern Recognition (CVPR)*, 1765–1773. IEEE.

Moravec, H. P. 1984. Locomotion, vision and intelligence. In *Robotics Research*, eds. M. Brady and R. Paul, 215–224. MIT Press.

Moravec, H. P. 1988. *Mind Children: The Future of Robot and Human Intelligence.* Harvard University Press.

Morgan, S. L., and C. Winship. 2015. *Counterfactuals and Causal Inference: Methods and Principles for Social Research (Analytical Methods for Social Research)*, 2nd ed. Cambridge University Press.

Morton, P. 1993. Supervenience and computational explanation in vision theory. *Philosophy of Science* 60 (1): 86–99.

Mozer, M. C. 1988. A focused back-propagation algorithm for temporal pattern recognition, Technical Report 88-3, Departments of Psychology and Computer Science, University of Toronto, Toronto.

Muckli, L. 2010. What are we missing here? Brain imaging evidence for higher cognitive functions in primary visual cortex V1. *International Journal of Imaging Systems Technology (IJIST)* 20: 131–139.

Müller, M., and R. Wehner. 1988. Path integration in desert ants, cataglyphis fortis. *Proceedings of the National Academy of Sciences* 85 (14): 5287–5290.

Müller, V. C., and N. Bostrom. 2016. Future progress in artificial intelligence: A survey of expert opinion. In *Fundamental Issues of Artificial Intelligence*, ed. V. C. Müller, 555–572. Springer.

Mumford, D. 1992. On the computational architecture of the neocortex. II. The role of cortico-cortical loops. *Biological Cybernetics* 66 (3): 241–251.

Mumford, D. 1994. Neuronal architectures for pattern-theoretic problems. In *Large-Scale Theories of the Cortex*, eds. C. Koch and J. Davis, 125. MIT Press.

Murray, S. O., D. Kersten, B. A. Olshausen, P. Schrater, and D. L. Woods. 2002. Shape perception reduces activity in human primary visual cortex. *Proceedings of the National Academy of Sciences USA* 99 (23): 15164–15169.

Murray, S. O., P. Schrater, and D. Kersten. 2004. Perceptual grouping and the interactions between visual cortical areas. *Neural Networks* 17 (5-6): 695–705.

Musmann, H. 1979. Predictive image coding. In *Image Transmission Techniques*, ed. W. K. Pratt, 73–112. Academic Press.

Musser, G. 2018. Job one for quantum computers: Boost artificial intelligence. *Quanta Magazine*. https://tinyurl.com/2k8fw628.

Musslick, S., A. Shenhav, M. M. Botvinick, and J. D. Cohen. 2015. A computational model of control allocation based on the expected value of control. In *The 2nd Multidisciplinary Conference on Reinforcement Learning and Decision Making*.

Neal, R. M., and G. E. Hinton. 1998. A view of the EM algorithm that justifies incremental, sparse, and other variants. In *Learning in Graphical Models*, ed. M. I. Jordan, 355. Kluwer.

Neander, K. 1995. Misrepresenting & malfunctioning. *Philosophical Studies* 79 (2): 109–141.

Neisser, U. 1967. *Cognitive Psychology*. Appleton-Century-Crofts.

Newell, A. 1980. Physical symbol systems. *Cognitive Science* 4 (2): 135–183.

Newell, A. 1982. The knowledge level. *Artificial Intelligence* 18 (1): 87–127.

Newell, A., and H. A. Simon. 1976. Computer science as empirical inquiry: Symbols and search. *Communications of the ACM* 19: 113–126.

Newen, A., L. De Bruin, and S. Gallagher. 2018. 4E cognition: Historical roots, key concepts, and central issues. In *The Oxford Handbook of 4E Cognition*, eds. A. Newen, L. De Bruin, and S. Gallagher, 2–16. Oxford University Press.

Newsome, W. T., K. H. Britten, and J. A. Movshon. 1989. Neuronal correlates of a perceptual decision. *Nature* 341: 52–54.

Ng, A. 2016. What artificial intelligence can and can't do right now. *Harvard Business Review*. https://tinyurl.com/udnzhuk.

Nilsson, N. J. 1971. *Problem Solving Methods in Artificial Intelligence*. McGraw-Hill.

Nilsson, N. J. 1983. Artificial intelligence prepares for 2001. *AI Magazine* 4 (4): 7–7.

Nilsson, N. J. 1984. Shakey the robot, Note 323, SRI AI Center, Menlo Park, CA.

Nilsson, N. J. 2005. Reconsiderations. *AI Magazine* 26 (4): 36–36.

Nisbett, R. E., and L. Ross. 1980. *Human Inference: Strategies and Shortcomings of Social Judgment*. Prentice-Hall.

Nishimura, H., K. Hashikawa, K. Doi, et al. 1999. Sign language "heard" in the auditory cortex. *Nature* 397: 116.

Niv, Y., and A. Langdon. 2016. Reinforcement learning with Marr. *Current Opinion in Behavioral Sciences* 11: 67–73.

Norvig, P. 2011. On Chomsky and the two cultures of statistical learning. Available at https://norvig.com/chomsky.html. https://norvig.com/chomsky.html.

Nyce, J. M. 1996. Guest editor's introduction. *IEEE Annals of the History of Computing* 18 (4): 3–4.

Oba, T., K. Katahira, and H. Ohira. 2021. A learning mechanism shaping risk preferences and a preliminary test of its relationship with psychopathic traits. *Scientific Reports* 11 (1): 1–11.

Odegard, D. 1965. Locke as an empiricist. *Philosophy* 40 (153): 185–196.

Olshausen, B. A., and D. J. Field. 1996. Emergence of simple-cell receptive field properties by learning a sparse code for natural images. *Nature* 381 (6583): 607–609.

Orhan, E., V. Gupta, and B. M. Lake. 2020. Self-supervised learning through the eyes of a child. *Advances in Neural Information Processing Systems* 33.

Ortony, A., ed. 1979. *Metaphor and Thought*. Cambridge University Press.

Oyama, S. 1985. *The Ontogeny of Information: Developmental Systems and Evolution*. Cambridge University Press.

Papadimitriou, C. H., and M. Yannakakis. 1994. On complexity as bounded rationality. In *Proceedings of the 26th Annual ACM Symposium on Theory of Computing*, 726–733.

Papayannopoulos, P. 2020. Computing and modelling: Analog vs. analogue. *Studies in History and Philosophy of Science* 83: 103–120. doi:10.1016/j.shpsa.2020.05.001.

Parr, R., and S. J. Russell. 1995. Approximating optimal policies for partially observable stochastic domains. In *Proceedings of the 14th International Joint Conference on Artificial Intelligence*. vol. 2 of *IJCAI'95*, 1088–1094. Morgan Kaufmann.

Patel, A. B., M. T. Nguyen, and R. Baraniuk. 2016. A probabilistic framework for deep learning. In *Advances in neural information processing systems*, eds. D. Lee, M. Sugiyama, U. Luxburg, I. Guyon, and R. Garnett, vol. 29. Curran Associates, Inc..

Patil, A., V. P. Murty, J. E. Dunsmoor, E. A. Phelps, and L. Davachi. 2017. Reward retroactively enhances memory consolidation for related items. *Learning & Memory* 24 (1): 65–69.

Patterson, J., and A. Gibson. 2017. *Deep Learning: A Practitioner's Approach*. O'Reilly Media.

Pearce, J. M. 2002. Evaluation and development of a connectionist theory of configural learning. *Animal Learning & Behavior* 30 (2): 73–95.

Pearce, J. M., and M. E. Bouton. 2001. Theories of associative learning in animals. *Annual Review of Psychology* 52 (1): 111–139.

Pearl, J. 1988. *Probabilistic Reasoning in Intelligent Systems: Networks of Plausible Inference*. Morgan Kaufmann.

Pearl, J. 1993. Comment: Graphical models, causality and intervention. *Statistical Science* 8 (3): 266–269.

Pearl, J. 1995. Causal diagrams for empirical research. *Biometrika* 82 (4): 669–688.

Pearl, J. 2000. *Models, Reasoning and Inference*. Cambridge University Press.

Pearl, J. 2001. Direct and indirect effects. In *Proceedings of the Seventeenth Conference on Uncertainty and Artificial Intelligence, 2001*, 411–420. Morgan Kaufman.

Pearl, J. 2015a. Causes of effects and effects of causes. *Sociological Methods & Research* 44 (1): 149–164.

Pearl, J. 2015b. Trygve Haavelmo and the emergence of causal calculus. *Econometric Theory* 31 (1): 152–179.

Pearl, J., and D. Mackenzie. 2018. *The Book of Why: The New Science of Cause and Effect*. Basic Books.

Penn, D. C., K. J. Holyoak, and D. J. Povinelli. 2008. Darwin's mistake: Explaining the discontinuity between human and nonhuman minds. *Behavioral and Brain Sciences* 31 (2): 109–130.

Penrose, R. 1989. *The Emperor's New Mind: On Computers, Minds, and the Laws of Physics*. Oxford University Press.

Peters, J., D. Janzing, and B. Schölkopf. 2017. *Elements of Causal Inference: Foundations and Learning Algorithms*. MIT Press.

Pfeiffer, K., and U. Homberg. 2007. Coding of azimuthal directions via time-compensated combination of celestial compass cues. *Current Biology* 17: 960–965.

Pham, S. 2018. Computers are getting better than humans at reading. *CNN Business*. https://tinyurl.com/k48xa8nj.

Piccinini, G. 2004. The first computational theory of mind and brain: A close look at McCulloch and Pitts's "Logical calculus of ideas immanent in nervous activity". *Synthese* 141 (2): 175–215.

Piccinini, G. 2015. *Physical Computation: A Mechanistic Account*. Oxford University Press.

Piccinini, G., and S. Bahar. 2013. Neural computation and the computational theory of cognition. *Cognitive Science* 37 (3): 453–488.

Piccinini, G., and C. J. Maley. 2021. Computation in physical systems, summer 2021 ed. In *The Stanford Encyclopedia of Philosophy*, ed. E. N. Zalta. Metaphysics Research Lab, Stanford University.

Pinker, S. 1994. *The Language Instinct: The New Science of Language and Mind*. Harper Collins.

Pinker, S. 1999. *How the Mind Works*. W. W. Norton & Company.

Pirogovsky, E., S. P. Woods, J. V. Filoteo, and P. E. Gilbert. 2012. Prospective memory deficits are associated with poorer everyday functioning in Parkinson's disease. *Journal of the International Neuropsychological Society* 18 (6): 986–995.

Plassmann, H., J. O'Doherty, and A. Rangel. 2007. Orbitofrontal cortex encodes willingness to pay in everyday economic transactions. *Journal of Neuroscience* 27 (37): 9984–9988.

Plaut, D. C. 1995. Double dissociation without modularity: Evidence from connectionist neuropsychology. *Journal of Clinical and Experimental Neuropsychology* 17 (2): 291–321.

Poole, D., A. Mackworth, and R. Goebel. 1998. *Computational Intelligence: A Logical Approach*. Oxford University Press.

Posner, M. I. 1978. *Chronometric Explorations of Mind*. Erlbaum.

Posner, M. I. 1989. *Foundations of cognitive science*. MIT Press.

Posner, M. I., and M. E. Raichle. 1994. *Images of Mind*. Scientific American Library/HPHLP.

Potts, R. 1996. *Humanity's Descent: The Consequences of Ecological Instability*. Avon.

Potts, R. 1998. Variability selection in hominid evolution. *Evolutionary Anthropology* 7 (3): 81–96.

Putnam, H. 1962. The analytic and synthetic. In *Minnesota Studies in the Philosophy of Science,* Vol. III, eds. H. Feigl and G. Maxwell. University of Minnesota Press.

Putnam, H. 1975. The meaning of "meaning". In *Language, Mind and Knowledge*, ed. K. Gunderson. University of Minnesota Press. Minnesota Studies in the Philosophy of Science VII.

Putnam, H. 1991. *Representation and Reality*. MIT Press.

Pylyshyn, Z. W. 1984. *Computation and Cognition*. MIT Press.

Quine, W. V. O. 1951. Two dogmas of empiricism. *Philosophical Review* 60: 20–43.

Quine, W. V. O. 1960. *Word and Object*. MIT Press.

Quine, W. V. O. 1971. Epistemology naturalized. *Akten des XIV. Internationalen Kongresses für Philosophie* 6: 87–103.

Rahwan, I., M. Cebrian, N. Obradovich, J. Bongard, J.-F. Bonnefon, C. Breazeal, J. W. Crandall, N. A. Christakis, I. D. Couzin, and M. O. Jackson. 2019. Machine behaviour. *Nature* 568 (7753): 477–486.

Rajpurkar, P., J. Zhang, K. Lopyrev, and P. Liang. 2016. Squad: 100,000+ questions for machine comprehension of text. *arXiv preprint arXiv:1606.05250.*

Ramanan, S., and D. Kumar. 2013. Prospective memory in Parkinson's disease: A meta-analysis. *Journal of the International Neuropsychological Society* 19 (10): 1109–1118.

Rangel, A., C. Camerer, and P. R. Montague. 2008. A framework for studying the neurobiology of value-based decision making. *Nature Reviews Neuroscience* 9 (7): 545–556.

Rao, R. P. N., and D. H. Ballard. 1999. Predictive coding in the visual cortex: A functional interpretation of some extra-classical receptive-field effects. *Nature Neuroscience* 2 (1): 79–87.

Raphael, B. 1971. The frame problem in problem-solving systems. In *Artificial Intelligence and Heuristic Programming*, eds. N. Findler and B. Metzler. Edinburgh University Press.

Rauss, K., S. Schwartz, and G. Pourtois. 2011. Top-down effects on early visual processing in humans: A predictive coding framework. *Neuroscience and Biobehavioral Reviews* 35 (5): 1237–1253.

Reali, F., and M. H. Christiansen. 2005. Uncovering the richness of the stimulus: Structure dependence and indirect statistical evidence. *Cognitive Science* 29 (6): 1007–1028.

Reddy, D. R., L. D. Erman, R. D. Fennell, and R. B. Neely. 1973. The hearsay speech understanding system: An example of the recognition process. In *Proceedings of the 3rd International Joint Conference on Artificial Intelligence. IJCAI'73*, 185–194. Morgan Kaufmann.

Reddy, L., N. Tsuchiya, and T. Serre. 2010. Reading the mind's eye: Decoding category information during mental imagery. *NeuroImage* 50 (2): 818–825.

Redish, A. D. 2004. Addiction as a computational process gone awry. *Science* 306 (5703): 1944–1947.

Redish, A. D. 2013. *The Mind within the Brain: How We Make Decisions and How Those Decisions Go Wrong.* Oxford University Press.

Redish, A. D., S. Jensen, and A. Johnson. 2008. A unified framework for addiction: Vulnerabilities in the decision process. *Behavioral and Brain Sciences* 31 (4): 415.

Reichardt, W., and T. Poggio. 1976. Visual control of orientation behavior in the fly. Part I. A quantitative analysis. *Quarterly Review of Biophysics* 9 (75): 311–375.

Reiter, R. 1978. On closed world databases. In *Logic and Databases*, eds. H. Gallaire and J. Minker. Plenum Press.

Requin, J., A. Riehle, and J. Seal. 1988. Neuronal activity and information processing in motor control: From stages to continuous flow. *Biological Psychology* 26: 179–198.

Rescorla, M. 2014. A theory of computational implementation. *Synthese* 191 (6): 1277–1307.

Riehle, A., and J. Requin. 1989. Monkey primary motor and premotor cortex: Single-cell activity related to prior information about direction and extent of an intended movement. *Journal of Neurophysiology* 61: 534–548.

Rieke, F. 1999. *Spikes: Exploring the Neural Code.* MIT Press.

Riesenhuber, M., and T. Poggio. 1999. Hierarchical models of object recognition in cortex. *Nature Neuroscience* 2 (11): 1019–1025.

Riley, J. R., U. Greggers, A. D. Smith, D. R. Reynolds, and R. Menzel. 2005. The flight paths of honeybees recruited by the waggle dance. *Nature* 435: 205–207. doi:10.1038/nature03526.

Ripollés, P., J. Marco-Pallarés, U. Hielscher, A. Mestres-Missé, C. Tempelmann, H. J. Heinze, and T. Noesselt. 2014. The role of reward in word learning and its implications for language acquisition. *Current Biology* 24 (21): 2606–2611.

Ritchie, J. B., D. M. Kaplan, and C. Klein. 2019. Decoding the brain: Neural representation and the limits of multivariate pattern analysis in cognitive neuroscience. *The British Journal for the Philosophy of Science* 70 (2): 581–607.

Robbins, H. 1956. An empirical Bayes approach to statistics. In *Proceedings of the Third Berkeley Symposium on Mathematical Statistics and Probability, Vol. 1: Contributions to the Theory of Statistics*, 157. University of California Press.

Robins, J. M., and S. Greenland. 1992. Identifiability and exchangeability for direct and indirect effects. *Epidemiology* 3 (2): 143–155.

Rockland, K. S., and D. N. Pandya. 1979. Laminar origins and terminations of cortical connections of the occipital lobe in the rhesus monkey. *Brain Research* 179: 3–20.

Rorty, R. 1979. *Philosophy and the Mirror of Nature*. Princeton University Press.

Rosch, E. 1978. Principles of categorization. In *Cognition and Categorization*, eds. E. Rosch and B. Lloyd, 27–48. Lawrence Erlbaum Associates.

Rosenbaum, D. A., V. Hindorff, and E. M. Munro. 1987. Scheduling and programming of rapid finger sequences: Tests and elaborations on the hierarchical editor model. *Journal of Experimental Psychology: Human Perception and Perfomance* 13: 193–203.

Rosenbaum, P. R., and D. B. Rubin. 1983. The central role of the propensity score in observational studies for causal effects. *Biometrika* 70 (1): 41–55.

Rosenberg, J. 1997. Connectionism and cognition. In *Mind Design II: Philosophy, Psychology, Artificial Intelligence*, ed. J. Haugeland, 293–308. MIT Press.

Rosenblatt, F. 1961. *Principles of Neurodynamics: Perceptrons and the Theory of Brain Mechanisms*. Spartan Books.

Rosenblatt, F. 1962. *Principles of Neurodynamics*. Spartan.

Rosser, B. 1936. Extensions of some theorems of Gödel and Church. *The Journal of Symbolic Logic* 1 (3): 87–91.

Rumelhart, D. E., G. E. Hinton, and R. J. Williams. 1986a. Learning internal representations by error propagation. In *Parallel Distributed Processing: Explorations in the Microstructure of Cognition. Volume 1: Foundations*, eds. D. E. Rumelhart, J. L. McClelland, and the PDP Research Group, 318–362. MIT Press.

Rumelhart, D. E., J. L. McClelland, and the PDP Research Group. 1986b. *Parallel Distributed Processing: Explorations in the Microstructure of Cognition. Volume 1: Foundations*. MIT Press.

Rupprechter, S., A. Stankevicius, Q. J. Huys, P. Seriès, and J. D. Steele. 2021. Abnormal reward valuation and event-related connectivity in unmedicated major depressive disorder. *Psychological Medicine* 51 (5): 795–803.

Rupprechter, S., A. Stankevicius, Q. J. Huys, J. D. Steele, and P. Seriès. 2018. Major depression impairs the use of reward values for decision-making. *Scientific Reports* 8 (1): 1–8.

Russek, E. M., I. Momennejad, M. M. Botvinick, S. J. Gershman, and N. D. Daw. 2021. Neural evidence for the successor representation in choice evaluation. *bioRxiv*. doi:doi.org/10.1101/2021.08.29.458114.

Russell, B. 1945. *A History of Western Philosophy*. Simon and Schuster.

Russell, S. J. 1997. Rationality and intelligence. *Artificial Intelligence* 94 (1-2): 57–77.

Russell, S. J. 2019a. How to stop superhuman A.I. before it stops us. *New York Times*. https://www.nytimes.com/2019/10/08/opinion/artificial-intelligence.html.

Russell, S. J. 2019b. *Human Compatible: Artificial Intelligence and the Problem of Control*. Penguin.

Russell, S. J., J. Binder, D. Koller, and K. Kanazawa. 1995. Local learning in probabilistic networks with hidden variables. In *Proceedings of the 14th International Joint Conference on Artificial Intelligence*. vol. 2 of *IJCAI'95*, 1146–1152. Morgan Kaufmann.

Russell, S. J., and P. Norvig. 1995. *Artificial Intelligence: A Modern Approach*. Prentice-Hall.

Russell, S. J., and D. Subramanian. 1995. Provably bounded-optimal agents. *Journal of Artificial Intelligence Research* 2 (1): 575–609.

Russell, S. J., and E. Wefald. 1989. On optimal game-tree search using rational meta-reasoning. In *Proceedings of the 11th International Joint Conference on Artificial Intelligence*. vol. 1 of *IJCAI'89*, 334–340. Morgan Kaufmann.

Russell, S. J., and E. Wefald. 1991a. *Do the Right Thing: Studies in Limited Rationality*. MIT Press.

Russell, S. J., and E. Wefald. 1991b. Principles of metareasoning. *Artificial Intelligence* 49 (1-3): 361–395.

Russell, S. J., and S. Zilberstein. 1991. Composing real-time systems. In *Proceedings of the 12th International Joint Conference on Artificial Intelligence*. vol. 1 of *IJCAI'91*, 212–217. Morgan Kaufmann.

Sakaguchi, K., R. Le Bras, C. Bhagavatula, and Y. Choi. 2019. Winogrande: An adversarial winograd schema challenge at scale. *arXiv:1907.10641v2*.

Samuels, R. 1998. Evolutionary psychology and the massive modularity hypothesis. *The British Journal for the Philosophy of Science* 49 (4): 575–602.

Samuels, R., S. Stich, and P. D. Tremoulet. 1999. Rethinking rationality: From bleak implications to darwinian modules. In *What is Cognitive Science?*, eds. E. Lepore and Z. Pylyshyn, 74–120. Blackwell.

Savine, A. C., and T. S. Braver. 2010. Motivated cognitive control: Reward incentives modulate preparatory neural activity during task-switching. *Journal of Neuroscience* 30 (31): 10294–10305.

Saygin, A. P., I. Cicekli, and V. Akman. 2003. Turing test: 50 years later. In *The Turing Test: The Elusive Standard of Artificial Intelligence*, ed. J. H. Moor, 23–78. Springer.

Scarantino, A., and R. Sousa. 2021. Emotion. In *The Stanford Encyclopedia of Philosophy*, ed. E. N. Zalta. Available at. https://plato.stanford.edu/archives/sum2021/entries/emotion.

Schank, R. C., and R. P. Abelson. 1975. Scripts, plans, and knowledge. In *Proceedings of the 4th International Joint Conference on Artificial Intelligence*, vol. 75, 151–157.

Schank, R. C., and R. P. Abelson. 1977a. *Scripts, Plans, Goals, and Understanding*. Lawrence Erlbaum Press.

Schank, R. C., and R. P. Abelson. 1977b. *Scripts, Plans, Goals, and Understanding*. Erlbaum.

Scheutz, M. 2001. Computational versus causal complexity. *Minds and Machines* 11 (4): 543–566.

Schmidhuber, J. 2015. Deep learning in neural networks: An overview. *Neural Networks* 61: 85–117.

Schonbein, W. 2014. Varieties of Analog and Digital Representation. *Minds and Machines* 24 (4): 415–438. doi:10.1007/s11023-014-9342-x.

Schroeder, T. 2004. *Three Faces of Desire*. Oxford University Press.

Schultz, W. 2015. Neuronal reward and decision signals: From theories to data. *Physiological Reviews* 95 (3): 853–951.

Schultz, W., P. Dayan, and P. R. Montague. 1997. A neural substrate of prediction and reward. *Science* 275 (5306): 1593–1599.

Searle, J. R. 1969. *Speech Acts: An Essay in the Philosophy of Language*. Cambridge University Press.

Searle, J. R. 1979. What is an intentional state? *Mind* 88 (349): 74–92.

Searle, J. R. 1980. Minds, brains, and programs. *Behavioral and Brain Sciences* 3 (3): 417–424.

Searle, J. R. 1983. *Intentionality: An Essay in the Philosophy of Mind*. Cambridge University Press.

Searle, J. R. 1992. *The Rediscovery of the Mind*. MIT Press.

Seelig, J. D., and V. Jayaraman. 2015. Neural dynamics for landmark orientation and angular path integration. *Nature* 521: 186–191.

Segal, G. 1989. Seeing what is not there. *The Philosophical Review* 98 (2): 189–214.

Segal, G. 1991. Defence of a reasonable individualism. *Mind* 100 (4): 485–494.

Segundo-Ortin, M., and D. D. Hutto. 2019. Similarity-based cognition: Radical enactivism meets cognitive neuroscience *Synthese 2019 198:1* 198: 5–23. doi:10.1007/S11229-019-02505-1.

Sejnowski, T. J., C. Koch, and P. S. Churchland. 1988. Computational neuroscience. *Science* 241: 1299–1306.

Sejnowski, T. J., and C. R. Rosenberg. 1987. Parallel networks that learn to pronounce English text. *Complex Systems* 1: 145–168.

Sellars, W. 1956. Empiricism and the philosophy of mind. *Minnesota Studies in the Philosophy of Science* 1: 253–329.

Seth, A. K. 2013. Interoceptive inference, emotion, and the embodied self. *Trends in Cognitive Sciences* 17 (11): 565–573.

Shagrir, O. 2006. Why we view the brain as a computer. *Synthese* 153 (3): 393–416.

Shallice, T. 1988. *From Neuropsychology to Mental Structure*. Cambridge University Press.

Shamma, S. 2000. Physiological basis of timbre perception. In *The new cognitive neurosciences,* 2nd ed., ed. M. S. Gazzaniga, 411–423. MIT Press.

Shapiro, L. A. 1993. Content, kinds, and individualism in Marr's theory of vision. *The Philosophical Review* 102 (4): 489–513.

Shapiro, S. 2004. The nature and limits of abstraction. *The Philosophical Quarterly* 54 (214): 166–174.

Shea, N. 2018. *Representation in Cognitive Science*. Oxford University Press.

Shead, S. 2017. Google DeepMind is edging towards a 3-0 victory against world Go champion Ke Jie. *Business Insider*. https://tinyurl.com/svb7x7e6.

Shepard, R. N. 1975. Form, formation and transformation of internal representations. In *Information Processing and Cognition: The Loyola Symposium*, ed. R. Solso, 87–122. Lawrence Erlbaum Associates.

Shepard, R. N. 1989. Internal representation of universal regularities: A challenge for connectionism. In *Neural Connections, Mental Computation*, eds. L. Nadel, L. A. Cooper, P. Calicover, and R. M. Harnish. MIT Press.

Shepherd, G. M. 1988. *Neurobiology*, 2nd ed. Oxford University Press.

Shi, Y. Q., and H. Sun. 1999. *Image and Video Compression for Multimedia Engineering: Fundamentals, Algorithms, and Standards*. CRC Press.

Shortliffe, E. H. 1976. *MYCIN: Computer-Based Medical Consultations*. Elsevier.

Shouse, B. 2002. Human gene count on the rise. *Science* 295: 1457–1457.

Shpitser, I., and J. Pearl. 2008. Complete identification methods for the causal hierarchy. *Journal of Machine Learning Research* 9: 1941–1979.

Silver, D. 2015. Reinforcement learning [Video]. YouTube. Available at:. https://www.youtube.com/watch?v=2pWv7GOvuf0.

Silver, D., J. Schrittwieser, K. Simonyan, I. Antonoglou, et al. 2017. Mastering the game of Go without human knowledge. *Nature* 550 (7676): 354–359.

Silver, D., S. Singh, D. Precup, and R. S. Sutton. 2021. Reward is enough. *Artificial Intelligence* 299: 103535.

Simon, H. A. 1955. A behavioral model of rational choice. *The Quarterly Journal of Economics* 69 (1): 99–118.

Simon, H. A. 1956. Rational choice and the structure of the environment. *Psychological Review* 63 (2): 129.

Simon, H. A. 1960. *The Ford Distinguished Lectures, Volume 3: The New Science of Management Decision*. Harper and Brothers.

Simon, H. A. 1969. *The Sciences of the Artificial*. MIT Press.

Simonyan, K., B. Horwitz, and E. D. Jarvis. 2012. Dopamine regulation of human speech and bird song: A critical review. *Brain and Language* 122 (3): 142–150.

Skinner, B. F. 1948. *Walden Two*. Hackett Publishing.

Sloman, A. 1986a. Reference without causal links. In *Seventh European Conference on Artificial Intelligence*, eds. B. du Boulay and L. J. Steels, 369–381. North-Holland.

Sloman, A. 1986b. What sorts of machines can understand the symbols they use? *Proceedings of the Aristotelian Society, Supplementary Volumes* 60: 61–80.

Sloman, A. 1990. Must intelligent systems be scruffy? In *Evolving Knowledge in Natural Science and Artificial Intelligence*, eds. J. E. Tiles, G. T. McKee, and G. C. Dean, 17–32. Pitman.

Smith, B. C. 1982. Reflection and semantics in a procedural language. PhD diss., Massachusetts Institute of Technology Ph.D. dissertation and Technical Report LCS/TR-272.

Smith, P. L., and R. Ratcliff. 2004. Psychology and neurobiology of simple decisions. *Trends in Neuroscience* 27: 161–168.

Smolensky, P. 1991. The constituent structure of connectionist mental states: A reply to Fodor and Pylyshyn. In *Connectionism and the Philosophy of Mind*, eds. T. Horgan and J. Tienson, 281–308. Springer.

Sober, E. 1994. The adaptive advantage of learning and a priori prejudice. In *From a Biological Point of View: Essays in Evolutionary Philosophy*, ed. E. Sober, 50–70. Cambridge University Press.

Soderstrom, H. 2003. Psychopathy as a disorder of empathy. *European Child & Adolescent Psychiatry* 12 (5): 249.

Sondik, E. J. 1971. The optimal control of partially observable Markov processes. PhD diss., Stanford University, Stanford, CA.

Spelke, E. S., and K. D. Kinzler. 2007. Core knowledge. *Developmental Science* 10 (1): 89–96.

Spirtes, P., C. N. Glymour, and R. Scheines. 2000. *Causation, Prediction, and Search*, 2nd ed. MIT Press.

Spratling, M. W. 2008. Predictive coding as a model of biased competition in visual attention. *Vision Research* 48 (12): 1391–1408.

Sprevak, M. 2007. Chinese rooms and program portability. *The British Journal for the Philosophy of Science* 58 (4): 755–776.

Sprevak, M. 2018. Triviality arguments about computational implementation. In *The Routledge Handbook of the Computational Mind*, eds. M. Sprevak and M. Colombo, 175–191. Routledge.

Squire, L. R. 2004. Memory systems of the brain: A brief history and current perspective. *Neurobiology of Learning and Memory* 82 (3): 171–177.

Stampe, D. W. 1977. Toward a causal theory of linguistic representation. In *Midwest Studies in Philosophy*, ed. H. W. P. French T. Uehling, vol. 2, 42–63. University of Minnesota Press.

Stankiewicz, J., and B. Webb. 2020. Using the neural circuit of the insect central complex for path integration on a micro aerial vehicle. *Lecture Notes in Computer Science (including subseries Lecture Notes in Artificial Intelligence and Lecture Notes in Bioinformatics)* 12413 LNAI: 325–337.

Stefik, M. 1985. Strategic computing at DARPA: Overview and assessment. *Communications of the ACM* 28 (7): 690–704.

Sterelny, K. 2003. *Thought in a Hostile World: The Evolution of Human Cognition*. Blackwell.

Sterelny, K. 2012. *The Evolved Apprentice*. MIT Press.

Sterelny, K., and P. E. Griffiths. 1999. *Sex and Death: An Introduction to Philosophy of Biology*. University of Chicago Press.

Stevens, K. A. 1979. Surface perception from local analysis of texture and contour. PhD diss., Massachusetts Institute of Technology. (Available as "The information content of texture gradients". *Biol. Cybernetics* 42 (1981), 95-105; also, "The visual interpretation of surface contours". *Artificial Intelligence* 17 (1981), 47-74.).

Stich, S. P. 1983. *From Folk Psychology to Cognitive Science: The Case Against Belief*. MIT Press.

Stich, S. P. 1996. *Deconstructing the mind*. Oxford University Press.

Stone, T., B. Webb, A. Adden, N. B. Weddig, A. Honkanen, R. Templin, W. Wcislo, L. Scimeca, E. Warrant, and S. Heinze. 2017. An anatomically constrained model for path integration in the bee brain. *Current Biology* 27: 3069–3085.

Stotz, K. C., and P. Griffiths. 2002. Dancing in the dark: Evolutionary psychology and the argument from design. In *Evolutionary Psychology: Alternative Approaches*, eds. S. Scher and M. Rauscher. Kluwer.

Sullivan, J., M. Mei, A. Perfors, E. H. Wojcik, and M. C. Frank. 2020. SAYCam: A large, longitudinal audiovisual dataset recorded from the infant's perspective. *PsyArXiv*. https://doi.org/10.31234/osf.io/fy8zx.

Sutton, R. S. 1988. Learning to predict by the methods of temporal differences. *Machine Learning* 3 (1): 9–44.

Sutton, R. S., and A. G. Barto. 2018a. *Reinforcement Learning: An Introduction*, 2nd ed. MIT Press.

Sutton, R. S., and A. G. Barto. 2018b. *Reinforcement Learning: An Introduction*. MIT Press.

Tadepalli, P. 1991. A formalization of explanation-based macro-operator learning. In *Proceedings of the 12th International Joint Conference on Artificial Intelligence*. vol. 2 of *IJCAI'91*, 616–622. Morgan Kaufmann.

Takahashi, T., H. Takagishi, H. Nishinaka, T. Makino, and H. Fukui. 2014. Neuroeconomics of psychopathy: Risk taking in probability discounting of gain and loss predicts psychopathy. *Neuroendocrinology Letters* 35 (6): 510–517.

Takamura, M., Y. Okamoto, G. Okada, et al. 2017. Patients with major depressive disorder exhibit reduced reward size coding in the striatum. *Progress in Neuro-Psychopharmacology and Biological Psychiatry* 79: 317–323.

Thagard, P. *Scientific Theories as Frame Systems*. Unpublished ms.

The New York Times. 1958. New Navy Device Learns by Doing. *New York Times*. https://tinyurl.com/yjh3eae8.

Thompson, E. 2007. *Mind in Life: Biology, Phenomenology, and the Sciences of Mind*. Harvard University Press.

Thornhill, R., and N. W. Thornhill. 1987. Human rape: The strengths of the evolutionary perspective. In *Sociobiology and Psychology*, eds. M. S. C. Crawford and D. Krebs, 269–292. Erlbaum Associates.

Thornhill, R., and N. W. Thornhill. 1992. The evolutionary psychology of men's coercive sexuality. *Behavioral and Brain Sciences* 15 (2): 363–375.

Tian, J., and J. Pearl. 2002. A general identification condition for causal effects. In *Proceedings of the Eighteenth National Conference on Artificial Intelligence*, 567–573. AAAI Press/The MIT Press.

Todd, P. 1989. A sequential network design for musical applications. In *Connectionist Models*, eds. D. Touretzky, G. E. Hinton, and T. Sejnowski. Morgan Kaufmann.

Todorov, E. 2009. Parallels between sensory and motor information processing. In *The Cognitive Neurosciences*, 4th edition, ed. M. Gazzaniga, 613. MIT Press.

Todorov, E., and M. I. Jordan. 2002. Optimal feedback control as a theory of motor coordination. *Nature Neuroscience* 5 (11): 1226–1235.

Tooby, J., and L. Cosmides. 1990. On the universality of human nature and the uniqueness of the individual: The role of genetics and adaptation. *Journal of Personality* 58 (1): 17–67.

Tooby, J., and L. Cosmides. 1992. The psychological foundations of culture. In *The Adapted Mind: Evolutionary Psychology and the Generation of Culture*, eds. L. C. J. Barkow and J. Tooby, 19–136. Oxford University Press.

Tooby, J., and L. Cosmides. 1997. Evolutionary psychology: A primer. Available at: https://www.cep.ucsb.edu/primer.html.

Toulmin, S. 1961. *Forecast and Understanding: An Enquiry Into the Aims of Science*. Indiana University Press.

Toussaint, M. 2009. Probabilistic inference as a model of planned behavior. *Künstliche Intelligenz* 3: 23–29.

Treisman, A. 1988. Features and objects: The Fourteenth Bartlett Memorial Lecture. *Quarterly Journal of Experimental Psychology* 40A: 201–237.

Tribus, M. 1961. *Thermodynamics and Thermostatics: An Introduction to Energy, Information and States of Matter, with Engineering Applications*. Van Nostrand.

Tsitsiklis, J. N., and B. Van Roy. 1997. Analysis of temporal-diffference learning with function approximation, Technical Report LIDS-P-2322, Laboratory for Information and Decision Systems, MIT, Cambridge, MA.

Tucker, D. M. 2007. *Mind from Body: Experience from Neural Structure*. Oxford University Press.

Turek, M. 2018. Machine common sense. https://www.darpa.mil/program/machine-common-sense.

Turing, A. M. 1937. On computable numbers, with an application to the entscheidungsproblem. *Proceedings of the London Mathematical Society* s2-42: 230–265.

Turing, A. M. 1948/2004. Intelligent machinery. In *The Essential Turing*, ed. B. J. Copeland, 410–432. Clarendon Press.

Turing, A. M. 1950. Computing machinery and intelligence. *Mind* 59: 433–460.

Vaina, L., ed. 1991. *From Retina to the Neocortex: Selected Papers of David Marr*. Birkhauser.

van Essen, D., and C. H. Anderson. 1990. Information processing strategies and pathways in the primate retina and visual cortex. In *An Introduction to Neural and Electronic Networks*, eds. S. F. Zometzer, J. L. Davis, and C. Lau, 43–72. Academic Press.

van Essen, D., D. Felleman, E. DeYoe, and J. Knierim. 1991. Probing the primate visual cortex: Pathways and perspectives. In *Advances in Understanding Visual Processes*, eds. A. Valberg and B. B. Lee, 227–237. Plenum.

van Essen, D., and J. H. R. Maunsell. 1980. Two-dimensional maps of the cerebral cortex. *Journal of Comparative Neurology* 191: 255–281.

Van Gelder, T. 1995. What might cognition be, if not computation? *The Journal of Philosophy* 92 (7): 345–381.

Van Gelder, T. 1998. The dynamical hypothesis in cognitive science. *Behavioral and Brain Sciences* 21 (5): 615–628.

VanderWeele, T. 2015. *Explanation in Causal Inference: Methods for Mediation and Interaction*. Oxford University Press.

Varela, F. J., E. Thompson, and E. Rosch. 1991. *The Embodied Mind*. MIT Press.

Vargha-Khadem, F., and R. E. Passingham. 1990. Speech and language defects. *Nature* 346: 226–226.

Velleman, J. D. 1989. *Practical Reflection*. Princeton University Press.

Venter, J. C., M. D. Adams, E. W. Myers, et al. 2001. The sequence of the human genome. *Science* 291: 1304–1351.

Vickerstaff, R. J., and A. Cheung. 2010. Which coordinate system for modelling path integration? *Journal of Theoretical Biology* 263: 242–261. doi:10.1016/j.jtbi.2009.11.021.

Von Ahn, L., M. Blum, N. J. Hopper, and J. Langford. 2003. CAPTCHA: Using hard AI problems for security. In *Proceedings of the 22nd International Conference on Theory and Applications of Cryptographic Techniques. EUROCRYPT'03*, 294–311. Springer.

von Neumann, J. 1951. The general and logical theory of automata. In *Cerebral Mechanisms in Behavior: The Hixon Symposium*, ed. L. A. Jeffress, 93–134. Wiley.

von Neumann, J. 1952. *Lectures on Probabilistic Logics and the Synthesis of Reliable Organisms from Unreliable Components*. California Institute of Technology.

von Neumann, J. 1982. First draft of a report on the EDVAC, 3rd ed. In *The Origins of Digital Computers: Selected Papers*, ed. B. Randell, 349–401.

von Uexküll, J. 1921. *Umwelt und Innenwelt der Tiere*. Springer.

Vong, W. K., and B. M. Lake. 2020. Learning word-referent mappings and concepts from raw inputs. *arXiv:2003.05573 [cs]*. http://arxiv.org/abs/2003.05573.

Waddell, S. 2013. Reinforcement signaling in Drosophila; dopamine does it all after all. *Current Opinion in Neurobiology* 23 (3): 324–329.

Waelti, P., A. Dickinson, and W. Schultz. 2001. Dopamine responses comply with basic assumptions of formal learning theory. *Nature* 412: 43–48.

Walter, S., and B. Meier. 2014. How important is importance for prospective memory? A review. *Frontiers in Psychology* 5: 657.

Walter, W. G. 1961. *The Living Brain*. Penguin Books.

Wandell, B. A. 2000. Computational neuroimaging: Color representations and processing. In *The new cognitive neurosciences,* 2nd edition, ed. M. S. Gazzaniga, 291–303. MIT Press.

Wang, A., A. Singh, J. Michael, F. Hill, O. Levy, and S. R. Bowman. 2019. GLUE: A multi-task benchmark and analysis platform for natural language understanding, 353–355. Association for Computational Linguistics. IProceedings of ICLR..

Warrington, E. K. 1975. The selective impairment of semantic memory. *Quarterly Journal of Experimental Psychology* 27: 635–657.

Webb, B. 2006. Transformation, encoding and representation. *Current Biology* 16: 184–185.

Webb, B. 2019. The internal maps of insects. *Journal of Experimental Biology* 222 (Suppl_1): 188094.

Wehner, R. 2008. The architecture of the desert ant's navigational toolkit (Hymenoptera: Formicidae). *Myrmecological News* 12: 85–96.

Wehner, R., C. Meier, and C. Zollikofer. 2004. The ontogeny of foraging behaviour in desert ants *Cataglyphis bicolor*. *Ecological Entomology* 29: 240–250.

Weigend, A. S., and D. E. Rumelhart. 1991. Generalization through minimal networks with application to forecasting, Technical Report ADP007170, Stanford University.

Weiskopf, D. A. 2011. Models and mechanisms in psychological explanation. *Synthese* 183 (3): 313.

Weizenbaum, J. 1966. ELIZA—A computer program for the study of natural language communication between man and machine. *Communications of the ACM* 9 (1): 36–45.

Weizenbaum, J. 1976. *Computer Power and Human Reason: From Judgment to Calculation*. W.H. Freeman.

Wellman, M. P. 1985. *Reasoning about Preference Models*. MIT Press.

Wellman, M. P. 1993. A market-oriented programming environment and its application to distributed multicommodity flow problems. *Journal of Artificial Intelligence Research* 1: 1–23.

Wheeler, M. 2008. Cognition in context: Phenomenology, situated robotics and the frame problem. *International Journal of Philosophical Studies* 16 (3): 323–349.

Whitley, D., and J. P. Watson. 2005. Complexity theory and the no free lunch theorem. In *Search Methodologies: Introductory Tutorials in Optimization and Decision Support Techniques*, eds. E. K. Burke and G. Kendall, 317–339. Springer.

Widrow, B., and M. E. Hoff. 1960. Adaptive switching circuits. In *Institute of Radio Engineers, Western Electronic Show and Convention, Convention Record, Part 4*, 96–104.

Wiener, N. 1948. *Cybernetics or Control and Communication in the Animal and the Machine*. Technology Press.

Wilbertz, G., J. Slooten, and P. Sterzer. 2014. Reinforcement of perceptual inference: Reward and punishment alter conscious visual perception during binocular rivalry. *Frontiers in Psychology* 5: 1377.

Wilson, R. A. 1994. Causal depth, theoretical appropriateness, and individualism in psychology. *Philosophy of Science* 61 (1): 55–75.

Winograd, T. 1972a. Understanding natural language. *Cognitive Psychology* 3 (1): 1–191.

Winograd, T. 1972b. *Undertanding Natural Language*. Academic Press.

Winograd, T. 1973. A procedural model of language understanding. In *Computer Models of Thought and Language*, eds. R. C. Schank and K. M. Colby. W. H. Freeman.

Winograd, T. 1977. On some contested suppositions of generative linguistics about the scientific study of language. *Cognition* 5 (2): 151–179.

Wittmann, T., and H. Schwegler. 1995. Path integration—A network model. *Biological Cybernetics* 73 (6): 569–575.

Wolf, H., M. Wittlinger, and S. E. Pfeffer. 2018. Two distance memories in desert ants–modes of interaction. *PLoS One* 13 (10): 0204664.

Woodward, J., and F. Cowie. 2005. *Naturalizing Human Nature*. Oxford University Press.

Woollaston, V. 2013. We'll be uploading our entire minds to computers by 2045 and our bodies will be replaced by machines within 90 years, Google expert claims. *Daily Mail*. https://tinyurl.com/ht44uxzv.

Wright, L. 1973. Functions. *Philosophical Review* 82 (2): 139–168.

Wright, R. 1994. *The Moral Animal: Evolutionary Psychology and Everyday Life*. Pantheon Books.

Yamins, D. L., and J. J. DiCarlo. 2016. Using goal-driven deep learning models to understand sensory cortex. *Nature Neuroscience* 19 (3): 356.

Yan, X., J. Hsu, M. Khansari, Y. Bai, A. Pathak, A. Gupta, J. Davidson, and H. Lee. 2018. Learning 6-DOF grasping interaction via deep geometry-aware 3D representations. In *2018 IEEE International Conference on Robotics and Automation (ICRA)*, 3766–3773. IEEE.

Yeboah, Y., C. Yanguang, W. Wu, and Z. Farisi. 2018. Semantic scene segmentation for indoor robot navigation via deep learning. In *Proceedings of the 3rd International Conference on Robotics, Control and Automation*, 112–118.

Yoshida, H., and L. B. Smith. 2008. What's in view for toddlers? Using a head camera to study visual experience. *Infancy* 13 (3): 229–248.

Yu, A. J. 2007. Adaptive behavior: Humans act as Bayesian learners. *Current Biology* 17: 977–980.

Yuille, A., and D. Kersten. 2006. Vision as Bayesian inference: Analysis by synthesis? *Trends in Cognitive Science* 10 (7): 301–308.

Zabberoni, S., G. A. Carlesimo, A. Peppe, C. Caltagirone, and A. Costa. 2017. Does dopamine depletion trigger a spreader lexical-semantic activation in Parkinson's disease? Evidence from a study based on word fluency tasks. *Parkinson's Disease*. doi:10.1155/2017/2837685.

Zador, A. M. 2019. A critique of pure learning and what artificial neural networks can learn from animal brains. *Nature Communications* 10 (1): 1–7. doi:10.1038/s41467-019-11786-6.

Zellers, R., Y. Bisk, A. Farhadi, and Y. Choi. 2019. From recognition to cognition: Visual commonsense reasoning. In *Proceedings of the IEEE Conference on Computer Vision and Pattern Recognition (CVPR)*, 6720–6731. IEEE.

Zilberstein, S., and S. J. Russell. 1996. Optimal composition of real-time systems. *Artificial Intelligence* 82 (1-2): 181–213.

Zipser, D., and R. A. Andersen. 1988. A back-propagation programmed network that simulates response patterns of a subset of posterior parietal neurons. *Nature* 331: 679–684.